Studia Fennica
Folkloristica 17

The Finnish Literature Society was founded in 1831 and has from the very beginning engaged in publishing. It nowadays publishes literature in the fields of ethnology and folkloristics, linguistics, literary research and cultural history.

The first volume of Studia Fennica series appeared in 1933.

Since 1992 the series has been divided into three thematic subseries: Ethnologica, Folkloristica and Linguistica. Two additional subseries were formed in 2002, Historica and Litteraria. Subseries Anthropologica was formed in 2007.

In addition to its publishing activities the Finnish Literature Society maintains a folklore archive, a literature archive and a library.

Mícheál Briody

The Irish Folklore Commission 1935–1970

History, ideology, methodology

Finnish Literature Society • Helsinki

Studia Fennica Folkloristica 17

The publication has undergone a peer review.

VERTAISARVIOITU
KOLLEGIALT GRANSKAD
PEER-REVIEWED
www.tsv.fi/tunnus

The open access publication of this volume has received part funding via
a Jane and Aatos Erkko Foundation grant.

A digital edition of a printed book first published in 2008 by the Finnish Literature Society.
Cover Design: Timo Numminen
EPUB: eLibris Media Oy

ISBN 978-951-746-947-0 (Print)
ISBN 978-952-222-810-9 (PDF)
ISBN 978-952-222-811-6 (EPUB)

ISSN 0085-6835 (Studia Fennica)
ISSN 1235-1946 (Studia Fennica Folkloristica)

DOI: http://dx.doi.org/10.21435/sff.17

BoD – Books on Demand, Norderstedt, Germany

Contents

'I wish to thank you again for the warm-hearted appreciation of my talk at the Finnish Literary [*recte* Literature] Society. I was myself deeply moved by the experience, and I shall never forget that night as long as I live. It will always be my proudest memory, and I value the great privilege accorded to me of speaking in the heart of Finland – your archive. When I got home I spoke in Irish about that visit to the room where the Irish Folklore Commission was born, 23 years ago.' Séamus Ó Duilearga to Martti Haavio, 7.IX.1951

To my father, Thomas (Tosty) Briody, and in memory of my mother, Nora O'Hickey

Preface

This is the last part of this long work to be undertaken, but in many ways the hardest part to write: so much to say, and so much that cannot be said. This present work grew out of another study, on the Irish Heroic Folktale, that I began in the late 1980's, which I had hoped to present as a doctoral thesis. When most of the basic archival work was complete around autumn 1990 certain difficulties arose that forced me in time to abandon this piece of research. A day or two after these difficulties first arose, by a strange coincidence, or perhaps a stroke of fate, I became aware of the existence of files on the Irish Folklore Commission in the National Archives of Ireland. However, it was not until the summer of 2000 that I officially applied to undertake a doctoral thesis on the subject of the Irish Folklore Commission, and later that year, while on a sabbatical in Ireland, began in earnest to research the subject.

Researching and writing up this work has not been an easy task as most of my sources lie at the other periphery of Europe. It could not have been brought to completion without the assistance of many individuals and institutions. First and foremost I have to thank Diarmuid Ó Giolláin of University College Cork. If it were not for his encouragement and inspiration, it is unlikely that I would have persisted with this work, and indeed with the study of folkloristics. He has also assisted this work in numerous other practical ways. I also owe a particular debt of gratitude to Jukka Saarinen of the Finnish Literature Society for coming to my aid on innumerable occasions with help and advice while I was engaged in this study, as well as for his friendship down through the years.

But for a chance conversation with the late Dr. Philomena Connelly one afternoon in August 1990 as I was about to leave the National Archives of Ireland I would not have become aware of the existence of Government files on the Irish Folklore Commission in the first place. Moreover, without the assistance of her colleague Eamonn Mullally, who during the early 1990's helped locate further material on the Commission in the National Archives for me, my interest in this subject might not have been sustained nor have developed beyond the initial fascination it stirred in me. To both I owe a great debt of gratitude.

The Irish proverb says 'Níor dhún Dia doras riamh nár oscail sé doras eile' ('God never closed one door but He opened another'). Philomena Connelly and Eamonn Mullally opened a door for me back in 1990, which might otherwise have remained closed, but many people in Ireland and abroad have subsequently opened other doors for me. In respect of Ireland, I must first thank Denis Tuomey of the Department of Education. But for his quick action in 1994 a great deal of the files on which this study is based might have been lost. Denis Tuomey's successor, Andrea Hudson, also assisted my research both by finding further Education files for me and by facilitating my access to them in the Department of Education. Without the files that both Denis and Andrea saved and made available to me I could never have attempted writing a comprehensive work on the Commission.

In respect of those who have helped me access archives outside Ireland, above all I must thank Marlene Hugoson of the Institute for Language and Folklore in Uppsala. From the first initial contact I made with her she has gone out of her way to help me in my research. Moreover, during my short visit to Uppsala in December 2004 she and her colleague, Bodil Nildin-Wall, did their utmost so that I could maximise the short time I had available to me to spend researching among the Åke Campbell papers, a source that was to prove crucial for aspects of my research.

In connection with the archive whose collections I have used most in this study, namely the National Archives of Ireland, in addition to the two members of staff mentioned above, I would like to thank all the rest of staff who have helped me down through the years. Moreover I would like to thank the Director of the National Archives of Ireland for permission to publish material in its possession. The papers of Stith Thompson and Richard M. Dorson are utilised courtesy of the Lilly Library, Indiana University, Bloomington, Indiana (my thanks to Saundra Taylor and Rebecca C. Cape), and various papers in the National Library of Ireland courtesy of its Trustees. I would also like to acknowledge the UCD Archives as well as the UCD-OFM Partnership for permission to quote from materials in their possession, and to express a special word of thanks to Seamus Helferty for all his help. In addition, I would like to thank the following institutions and individuals for help in accessing as well as permission to utilise and publish materials in their care: (in Ireland) 1) Coláiste Íde, an Daingean (Fionán Ó hÓgáin); 2) National Museum of Ireland/Museum of Country Life (Séamas Mac Philib); 3) Radio Telefís Éireann/Sound Archive (Malachy Moran and Ian Lee); 4) University College Cork, Folklore Archive (Diarmuid Ó Giolláin and Marie-Annick Desplanques); 5) University College Dublin, James Joyce Library, Special Collections (Catherine McSharry and Norma Jesop); 6) University College Dublin, Delargy Centre for Irish Folklore (Prof. Patricia Lysaght, then Acting Head of Department); 7) University College Galway, Hardiman Library Archives (Kieran Hoare); (Nordic/Baltic) 8) Eesti Kirjandusmuuseum, Tartu (Piret Noorhani, Ergo-Hart Västrik, Kristin Kuutman and Monika Tasa); 9) Institutet för Språk och Folkminnen, Uppsala (Bodil Nildin-Wall); 10) Suomalaisen Kirjallisuuden Seura (Anna Makkonen); and 11) Universitesbiblioteket, Lund (Birgitta Lindholm).

I would also like to thank the following people who have provided me with information and assistance: Jonathan Bell; Marie Boran; Diarmuid Breathnach, Neil Buttimer; Michael Coady; Niall de Barra; Kelly Fitzgerald;

Alan Gailey; Susanna Helander; Anne M. Kenna; Liisa Lehto; Séamus Mac Philib; Raija Majamaa; Dymphna Moore; the late Liam Mac Coisdeala; Andrew Newby; Gearóidín Ní Nia; Aoibheann Nic Dhonnchadha; Máirín Nic Eoin; Stiofán Ó Cadhla; Éamon Ó Ciosáin; Seán Ó Duinnshléibhe; Breandán Ó Madagáin; Máirtín Ó Murchú; Pádraig Ó Siochrú; Gearóid Ó Tuathaigh; Patrick C. Power; Päivi Raitio; Jan Eric Rekdahl; Pádraigín Riggs; Åsa Thorbech; Tony Varley; Emma Verling; Stuart von Wolf; Pat Wallace; and Kirsi Ylänne. In addition to the above, two individuals, Ríonach uí Ógáin (University College Dublin) and Anne O'Connor (Radio Telefís Éireann), have been of especial assistance to me, helping me in many small but crucial ways. I have had strong links with University College Cork for many years, both with the Department of Folklore and Ethnology and the Department of Modern Irish. I am particularly grateful for the support and encouragement down through the years of Professors Gearóid Ó Cruadhlaoich and Seán Ó Coileáin of these respective departments. The latter I also need to thank especially for allowing me access to the Tyers/Ó Dálaigh transcripts, and Pádraig Tyers himself for permission to utilise this source. I would also like to thank the staffs of the Ethnology Library of the Finnish Literature Society (particularly Terttu Kaivola), the National Library of Finland, and the Boole Library, University College Cork for all their help.

To my supervisor Prof. Satu Apo I owe a special debt of gratitude. The initial positive feedback and practical advice I received from her on my rather bulky text was a source of much solace and help to me. Anne O'Connor, already mentioned, in time became one of my two doctoral examiners and her reader's report was both a source of encouragement and practical assistance to me, as was that of my other doctoral examiner, Guy Beiner. I benefited much from many conversations I had with Guy over a period of some years after our first meeting in June 2001. While working on this research I have also greatly benefited from regular discussions I had with my colleague and friend Gaela Keryell, who is not only a gifted scholar, but a rarity enough among scholars, someone with many original ideas.

I also need to thank Prof. Anna Leena Siikala for accepting this work for publication in the Studia Fennica/Folkloristica series of the Finnish Literature Society. Some may wonder why a work on the history of the Irish Folklore Commission should be published in this Finnish series. The epigraph to this work, I hope, shows how the contrary is in fact the case. I would also like to thank Päivi Vallisaari and Kati Lampela of the Finnish Literature Society for seeing this long work through the press, and a special word of thanks to Paddy Sammon for all his help with proofreading.

Apart from the assistance I received from the people listed above, this work could not have been completed without the help of my large family in Ireland. I owe a special debt to my father, now in his ninety fourth year. He was my first reader, of a much longer earlier draft. Born the same year as a number of the staff of the Irish Folklore Commission (1913) and having worked as a Civil Servant (as a State Forester) for most of the period of the Commission's operations, the insights he has given me into the workings of the Civil Service and into the history of the early decades of the independent Irish state, as he lived and experienced them, have been of much assistance to me. He has also helped my research in another very substantive way, which I detail in the Introduction to this work. I dedicate this work to him and to my late mother, who died suddenly in November 2000 when this work was only in its embryonic stage. All my siblings and extended family, too numerous to name, have helped my research in various ways: by accommodating me while accessing the primary and secondary sources used in this work; by ensuring that I was not distracted too much or too many demands made on my time when I needed to write or rewrite parts of this work while staying with them on my trips to Ireland; and by helping me procure books, newspapers and journals that I needed. In this connection, I also wish to thank Martin Arthur and Janet Rooney, Séamas Mac Philib and Emer Crean as well as Geraldine Prunty and Derek Hanley for also accommodating me on my many trips to Ireland, and for the hospitality they have shown me.

My late cousin Máirtín Verling provided me with the photographs of Bólas Head and the ruined hamlet of Cill Rialaigh on the cover of this book, the district where Séamas Ó Duilearga was first inspired to save the folklore of Ireland. These pictures were taken in mid-August 1990. Máirtín died suddenly in March 2007 when I was in the final stages of preparing this work for publication, finishing his fifth anthology of material collected by the Irish Folklore Commission a short time before he died. Down through the years I benefited greatly from his intimate knowledge of the Commission's collections, as I have from his publications. Of all those who edited material derived from the Commission's Main Collection, Máirtín Verling was, without doubt, if not the most professional, certainly one of the two most professional and thorough. His books should stand as exemplars for those who in years to come will mine this great treasure house. Confined to his home for the past few years by illness, I had hoped my study of the Commission when published would help him pass the long hours of the day and night. Alas, that was not to be!

The University of Helsinki assisted this study on two occasions. Firstly by facilitating my going to Ireland for the academic year 2000–2001 and subsequently by allowing me three months' leave in early 2005. Otherwise this research was completed while holding down an ever-demanding teaching post. I could not have completed it without the understanding of my many students. To them I owe more than I can ever express.

My wife Tuula I need to thank on many counts. After the fate of my first attempt at a doctorate in the early 1990's, I might, in despair, have lost all hope of ever undertaking a doctorate again but for her constant support and encouragement. Throughout the process of researching and writing this study, which has often necessitated trips to Ireland and Sweden, she has accepted my absences with understanding, no matter how inconvenient such trips have sometimes been for her. She has also helped my work in many other ways, not least in being prepared to listen to me expound on aspects of my research, and in giving much solid advice on how best to present my ideas. For all this, and much else, especially for her companionship of almost three decades' duration I am eternally grateful. To my children Katariina and Tuomas I wish to express my gratitude for their forbearance during the years I have been researching this long work and for agreeing that the family go to Ireland for a year, which in contrast to the many summer holidays they had hitherto spent in Ireland was, in many respects, time out of their lives. Another family member also comes in for mention, our beloved dog Nasta (*ár maidrín beag bán*), who died in mid-December 2006. This beautiful little creature, who was a researcher in her own right, was my constant companion as I wrote up this research at home.

Finally, I must take leave of this long work, which has occupied so much of my time for the past six years, and often come between me and sleep. I will take a rest, but hopefully return to the subject.

Helsinki, Easter 2007
Mícheál Briody

Introduction

A national folklore collection

When the Folklore of Ireland Society was founded in 1927, the Irish Free State had no national collection or archive of folk traditions. This did not place it in an anomalous position when viewed from the perspective of Europe as a whole, as no such archive existed anywhere in Britain[1] or in Northern Ireland, and on the Continent archives of folk tradition were, for the most part, only to be found in northern Europe, particularly in Scandinavia and the Baltic States.[2] However, viewed from an Irish perspective, the situation appeared to certain people quite different. Ireland was believed to possess a folk tradition, particularly in the Irish language, incomparable in its richness to anywhere else in western Europe, with the exception of Gaelic Scotland, and relatively little Irish folklore had been collected up to that time. Furthermore, the fact that Irish was in rapid decline as a spoken language meant that unless something was done soon to initiate extensive collecting the bulk of these traditions would be lost for ever.

The Folklore of Ireland Society, established in 1927, endeavoured to make a last-minute effort to save as much of the riches of Irish folklore for posterity before they were irretrievably lost. The following year Séamus Ó Duilearga, the Society's young Librarian and Editor of its journal, *Béaloideas*, went on a study and fact-finding trip to northern Europe and returned convinced that Ireland needed to create a national collection of folk tradition of similar proportions, indeed of greater proportions, to the collections he encountered on his travels. Efforts by Ó Duilearga and fellow members of the Folklore of Ireland Society to get state support for the mammoth task of collecting systematically the folklore of Ireland within a few years bore fruit, and in less than twenty years the South of Ireland would be able to boast of possessing one

---

1   There were, however, substantial collections of folklore in the National Library of Scotland. See Mackechnie 1973.
2   In southern Europe, however, a folklore archive was established in Athens in 1918. Erixon 1955, p. 135. The reason for the establishment of this archive at such an early date is most likely due to the fact that folklore figured significantly in the development of Greek nationalism. For more on this matter, see Herzfeld 1982.

of the largest folklore collections in the world, assembled by the Irish Folklore Commission (established in 1935). However, it would take another twenty five years or so before the Commission would be put on a permanent footing and its archive made more accessible to scholars and the general public.

International and national reputation of the IFC

There is no doubt that the Irish Folklore Commission in its day enjoyed a very high international profile. Even before the Commission was set up in 1935, folklorists outside Ireland recognised the rich sources of Irish folklore that awaited discovery, and one eminent European folklorist, Carl William von Sydow, played an active part in the negotiations to set up the Irish Folklore Commission, while another Nordic folklorist, Reidar Th. Christiansen, was instrumental in establishing one of the precursors of the Commission, namely the Folklore of Ireland Society.

The extensive systematic collecting initiated by the Irish Folklore Commission from its inception quickly caught the attention of foreign scholars. By the mid 1940's the Commission had as a result of its extensive collecting, undertaken on an unprecedented scale, amassed a very large archive of folk tradition, reputedly one of the largest in the world.[3] Partly in recognition of this achievement, the Irish Folklore Commission was signalled out in 1946 by receiving a special invitation to attend a conference of Nordic folklorists held in Oslo. Also, in 1946, Stith Thompson in the first edition of *The Folktale* had this to say of the Commission: 'By far the most spectacular achievement in the field of the folktale in recent years has been that of the Irish Folklore Commission under the leadership of Seamus O'Duilearga [sic].'[4] With all this international attention, it was perhaps not so surprising that Séamus Ó Duilearga began to see a major international role for the Commission. In his memorandum to the Taoiseach (Irish Prime Minister) in 1947, he wrote: 'It has now become clear that, given facilities

---

3   In his annual reports to the Irish Government, Ó Duilearga ever since the late 1930's, was wont to claim that the collections of the Irish Folklore Commission were the largest in the world. However, in comparing the Commission's burgeoning collections with those folklore collections he had seen on his trip to northern Europe in 1928, he failed to consider that some of these collections might have grown substantially in the meantime. For example, the folklore archive of the Finnish Literature Society was greatly augmented as a result of the Kalevala centenary folklore competition of 1935, and the success of this competition both stimulated and widened the scope of collecting activity over the coming decades (for this competition, see Peltonen 2004). This archive is nowadays believed to constitute the largest folklore archive in the world, with the Irish National Folklore Collection in Dublin possibly the next biggest. The difficulty of comparing the size of these two archives (a rather futile exercise, it must be said) is compounded by the fact that the Helsinki archive enumerates its manuscript holdings in terms of shelf space (metres) as well as the number of individual items of tradition (see Laaksonen and Saarinen 2004) while the manuscript holdings of the Dublin archive are enumerated in terms of pages (see e.g. S. Ó Catháin 1991b).

4   Stith Thompson 1977 [1946], p. 399.

20

and power we can make Ireland the centre of West European scholarship in the field of oral tradition and European ethnology.'[5]

International recognition of the Commission continued throughout the 1950's, with many foreign scholars visiting its Head Office in Dublin or accompanying its collectors in the field. Other foreign scholars also came to do research in the Commission's archive and library. Moreover, one eminent foreign folklorist, Reidar Th. Christiansen, after retiring from his post in Oslo, joined the staff of the Commission on a temporary basis on two occasions in the late 1950's and early 1960's.[6] In a lecture Christiansen gave at the Commission's Head Office in 1960, speaking of various European folklore institutes, he had this to say:

> Among these institutes, Dublin has in recent years attained a place for itself. It is younger than most of the others and yet in these few years, it has become, perhaps, the most important of them all. There are several reasons: the main one is that nowhere else has old tradition been alive so long and so extensively as in Ireland and western Scotland. And nowhere else has such an effort been made to record what is still alive.
>
> In times to come these new collections will completely alter our vision of European folklore. They have shown that it is not only eastern Europe that has an oral tradition — just as much is to be found in the west and in this way the Irish institute has filled a gap, has made it possible for students to ascertain what we have inherited from the Middle Ages, what is indigenous, and, to a certain extent, by what strange routes interchange has taken place.[7]

However, Ó Duilearga's dream that Dublin one day would become an international centre for the study of folklore and ethnology was not to be realised. The Commission continued on for another ten years – non-permanent and insecure – with an aging staff and an aging Director. Moreover, with the passing of some of the old guard in other countries, its international profile naturally weakened somewhat.

If the Commission, on being established, rapidly gained an international reputation, on the home front it was also held in high regard. In his report to the Government for 1950–1951, looking back on the first fifteen years of the Commission, Ó Duilearga stresses the close associations between the Commission and the rural population: 'It should be mentioned here that the contact the Irish Folklore Commission has with the rural population is closer than is the case with any other cultural institute of its type in the country.'[8] By this time in many parts of Ireland, particularly the Irish-speaking districts, the full-time collectors of the Commission, would have been a familiar sight. Part-time collectors, both in Irish-speaking districts and elsewhere in the country, would also have made many ordinary people aware

5   D/T S 6916B: 'Irish Folklore Commission' dated June 1947, p. 4.
6   D/T S 16378B/62: 'Gearr-Thuar./1960–61', p. 5.
7   Quoted in S. Ó Catháin 1991a, p. 64.
8   D/T S 15548B: 'Gearr-Thuar./1950–51', p. [7].

of the Commission's work, as indeed would the hundreds of questionnaire correspondents who elicited information throughout the length and breadth of the country. Furthermore, the Commission's scheme to collect folklore from schoolchildren in the school year 1937–1938 made a whole generation of schoolchildren in rural areas aware, to varying degrees, of the existence of the Commission. Frequent newspaper articles, radio broadcasts, and public lectures by members of the Commission's staff also helped to raise the profile of the Commission with the general public.

It goes without saying that the Commission enjoyed a high profile within Irish academic circles as well, particularly within University College Dublin (UCD), where Ó Duilearga first held the post of statutory lecturer and later that of professor.[9] Not only did UCD help the Irish Folklore Commission in numerous ways, not least in agreeing to second Ó Duilearga to act as its Director, and in so doing relieve him of most of his university duties, the Commission, although formally an independent institution, was housed by the College, first in its main building at Earlsfort Terrace and later in a separate house fronting St. Stephen's Green.

Need for a reassessment of the IFC's work

The Irish Folklore Commission was probably a unique organisation in its time, devoted solely, or almost solely, to the collecting of folklore. It was certainly the first such organisation to be established for this purpose in any country. However, the high profile the Commission once enjoyed is a thing of the past. In Ireland today those who are interested in folklore know something about it and where its collections are now housed, but its successor, the Department of Irish Folklore, UCD, enjoys nothing like the same high profile.[10] Historians of modern Irish history and cultural commentators, with few exceptions, seem unaware, or only vaguely so, of the great achievements of the Commission. Moreover, among young or middle-aged folklorists outside Ireland, the situation would appear to be little different. It is within Ireland, however, that the fading of the Commission's star is most significant, and, it must be said, most worrying. In Donal McCartney's history of University College Dublin, the Irish Folklore Commission, and its close links to the College, is referred to only in passing, and although mention is made of the College's 'flourishing Department and Archive of Irish Folklore', no mention is made of the fact that thirty years after the transfer of the Commission's collections to UCD, a proper, secure, spacious, well-staffed archive has yet to be provided by the College to house this national treasure bequeathed by the state to its care.

It is more than seventy years since the Irish Folklore Commission was

9   Members of UCD's staff expressed admiration for the Commission's work in print. See, e.g. Shaw 1944, p. 35 and O'Meara 1947, p. 93.
10 The Department of Irish Folklore was renamed the Delargy Centre for Irish Folklore and the National Folklore Collection in autumn 2005. For convenience, I will refer to it in this study by its former name.

established. It is longer still since Séamus Ó Duilearga and the Folklore of Ireland Society first set about saving the folklore of Ireland for posterity. Ó Duilearga is dead more than twenty-five years. Also dead are almost all of his colleagues. Moreover, most of those, both at home and abroad, who held the Irish Folklore Commission in high esteem are also dead. Despite the great achievement of Séamus Ó Duilearga and his co-workers in assembling one of the finest and most extensive collections of folk tradition in the world, to date no in-depth study of the Irish Folklore Commission has been attempted. I hope this study will go some way towards setting the Irish Folklore Commission in greater perspective for the benefit of present and future generations alike, and, in time, that others will build on the strengths and weaknesses of my research, and hopefully also place some of its limitations in perspective.

International dimension

Foreign folklorists, particularly Nordic ones, were instrumental in setting up and nurturing the Irish Folklore Commission, and share some of the credit for its achievements. In this way the story of the Irish Folklore Commission is part of a wider story, namely the history of European folkloristics, as well as that of North America. In turn, the Irish Folklore Commission helped initiate or intensify the collecting of folklore in parts of Atlantic Europe, e.g. in Scotland, Wales, Iceland and the Faeroe Islands. This study has also a wider international dimension as well. There are many areas of the world today where traditional life is breaking down and ancestral languages are being abandoned, a situation not so dissimilar from Ireland in the 1920's and 1930's. Properly funded collecting programmes might well result in the creation of many fine collections of oral tradition in areas of the Third World, or indeed remote or marginalised parts of the developed world, some of them perhaps even dwarfing those of the Finnish Literature Society and the Irish Folklore Commission. Nevertheless, it is interesting to note, in this respect, that the 'Recommendations on the Safeguarding of Traditional Culture and Folklore' issued to member states at the UNESCO General Conference in October/November 1989 do not feature the type of intensive 'salvage' collecting practised by the Irish Folklore Commission, entailing the employment of collectors working individually, usually with no definite research purpose in mind.[11] This is not surprising, of course. After all, time had moved on since the heyday of the Commission, bringing new collecting methods with it and new insights to collecting. Nevertheless, the achievements of the Commission, often in the face of great adversity, should prove a source of inspiration to folklorists engaged in recording the rapidly disappearing oral traditions of many areas of the world as well as pinpointing some of the pitfalls to be avoided in such work.

11   See Honko 1990, pp. 3–7.

Aim and scope of work

The original working title for this study contained the word 'chronology'. When the work was at quite an advanced stage, however, I was advised to substitute 'history' for 'chronology' as it was felt the latter word did not adequately describe the nature of the work, dealing, as it does, to a large degree, with the history of the Irish Folklore Commission. Nevertheless, this study still betrays evidence of my original working title in its attention to detail and in the manner of the presentation of the activities and vicissitudes of the Commission. My reason for choosing this approach initially was my belief that those who would most benefit from this study, and who would consult it most often, would be those who work, or will work, in future, with the collections of the Irish Folklore Commission (be they the custodians or users of these collections). It is my hope that for such people this work will function as kind of reference work on the Commission and that its detailed exposition of the activities of the Commission, in particular, will assist them in their own research into these collections. Although I have trimmed this work a good deal in preparing it for publication, I have purposely kept a lot of the detail as I feel much of it will be of interest to that other target audience of mine, namely those interested in the history of European and North-American folkloristics and ethnology (an area of growing interest); workers in (other) tradition archives both in Ireland and abroad; and those engaged in the collecting of oral tradition, be it in the developed or developing world. This study is also aimed at a still wider audience: the Irish public, Irish academics, particularly historians, and, of course, international folklorists in general. Some of this wider reading audience may consider my attention to detail tedious and excessive at times, but I hope nevertheless this study will give them a greater appreciation of the achievement of the Irish Folklore Commission and, in the case of academic readers, be of assistance in their own research and acquisition of knowledge. Below I outline briefly what each of the seven chapters of the study deals with.

Chapter I: The cultural, political, and ideological background

This Chapter outlines the cultural/linguistic, political, and the ideological milieu that lead to the systematic collecting of the oral tradition of Ireland. The decline of Irish over a number of centuries from a position of dominance to near-extinction, as well as efforts to restore it as the main vernacular of the independent Irish state in the first half of the twentieth century, is crucial for an understanding of both the urgency felt in certain quarters to initiate a salvage operation to record for posterity the rich oral traditions of Gaelic Ireland, in particular, as well as the many vicissitudes experienced by the body established by the Irish Free State to accomplish this task, namely the Irish Folklore Commission. Section 1 of this Chapter will deal roughly with the period before the establishment of an independent Irish state, and Section 2 with the first two decades of native government. It should be stressed that this chapter does not aim at providing an in-depth analysis of Irish history or society during the period, rather it aims to give readers a framework to help them understand the rest of this work. If this study were solely directed at an Irish audience, treatment of certain matters in this chapter could be somewhat briefer than is the case.

Chapter II: Saving the folklore of Ireland

Section 1 of Chapter II deals with the foundations that were laid over a number of decades for the establishment of the Irish Folklore Commission. It briefly traces efforts to have the folklore of Ireland collected by various bodies and individuals from the Gaelic League in the late nineteenth century down until the setting up of the Folklore of Ireland Society in 1927 and the Irish Folklore Institute in 1930. Section 2 deals with the formative years of the main progenitor of the Commission, and its Director for the three and a half decades of its operation, Séamus Ó Duilearga. The treatment of bodies such as the Folklore of Ireland Society and the Irish Folklore Institute in this chapter, is meant to illustrate the chain of events that led to the setting up of the Commission. Both these bodies deserve full-length studies in themselves. I have not sought to outline the evolution of folklore collecting in Ireland further back than the Gaelic League. To have done so would have greatly enlarged this work.[12]

Chapter III: The Irish Folklore Commission: Founding and re-establishment

Chapter III deals in detail with the setting up and making permanent of the Irish Folklore Commission. Section 1 deals with the preliminary efforts to transform the Irish Folklore Institute into a more effective collecting body as well as the protracted negotiations that in time resulted in the setting up of a reconstituted body, the Irish Folklore Commission, in April 1935. Section 2 deals with such matters as the Commission's Terms of Reference, the membership of its Advisory Board and Finance Sub-Committee, and the inauguration of the Commission itself. Sections 3 to 7 treat of efforts from the early 1940's to the late 1960's to have the Commission made permanent. These efforts eventually resulted in the transfer of the Commission to UCD in 1971, where it was reconstituted as the Department of Irish Folklore. The problems and vicissitudes that delayed for more than a generation the finding of a permanent home for the temporary Irish Folklore Commission are also dealt with in detail. In section 8, I briefly assess the various other options proposed for the Commission apart from incorporation into UCD.

Chapter IV: The Commission's collectors and collections

Section 1 of Chapter IV deals with the full-time collectors: their selection and training, their collecting methods and equipment, their workload, and

---

12   For an account of some of the pioneer collectors of Irish oral tradition during the late 18th and 19th centuries, see Ó Giolláin 2000, pp. 94 ff.

their reception among the people. It also deals with the work of special and part-time collectors. Sections 2 to 7 deal with various collecting programmes of the Commission: for example, the Schools Scheme, collecting by means of questionnaires, and collecting in Gaelic Scotland. It has not been my intention to undertake a complete assessment of the collections of the Commission, nor of any individual collector. Even if such were possible, it would be a huge undertaking, and certainly not possible for somebody who does not live in Ireland, nor have ready access to all the relevant sources.

Chapter V: The work of Head Office

Chapter V deals with the work of the Head Office staff. Section 1 will deal with Séamus Ó Duilearga's direction of the Commission both in the field and at Head Office, as well as other aspects of his work such as public relations and lecturing at home and abroad. Section 2 will deal with the work of the actual Head Office staff: their recruitment and duties in the early years, the archiving and cataloguing of the material, as well as the indispensable work done by the secretarial and typing staff. This section will also deal in brief with the work of the Commission's ethnographer, Caoimhín Ó Danachair, who worked from Head Office. Space does not allow me to deal in greater detail with Ó Danachair's work in this section, but his work, both ethnographic and other, is dealt with in various parts of this study.[13] The folk-music collector Séamus Ennis also worked from Head Office, but he is treated of in Section 3 of Chapter IV. This Chapter also deals with the creation of a sound archive and a research library by the staff of Head Office and the Commission's Director.

Chapter VI: The seeds of discontent

This chapter deals with certain matters at once peripheral and central to an understanding of the Commission's work and achievement, and in some cases lack of achievement. Section 1 of this chapter deals with the salaries and conditions of work of the staff of the Commission. It is only by looking at such matters that we can understand fully the great personal sacrifice many of the Commission's employees made, and indeed the great achievement of the Commission as a whole, which managed to do so much on very slim resources. Section 2 deals with conflict at Head Office between Ó Duilearga and senior members of staff. The deterioration of relations between the Director of the Commission and certain members of his office staff greatly affected the work of the Commission, especially during its latter years, and had repercussions even after Ó Duilearga's retirement and the transfer of the Commission to UCD. Although this is a sensitive issue, it is necessary to deal with the matter in this study, for it also forms part of the history of the Irish Folklore Commission: a story of at times almost superhuman effort,

---

13 I hope in a separate publication to deal more comprehensively with Caoimhín Ó Danachair's work for the Commission.

but all too human effort nonetheless. It should be emphasised that all the participants in this dispute are now dead.

Chapter VII: Assessment of aspects of the work of the Commission

Section 1 of Chapter VII consists of an assessment of aspects of the work of the Commission's staff, both in the field and at Head Office. It treats of such matters as the coordination of the work in the field from Head Office; the processing of the material being collected; the working methods of the full-time collectors; and the work of part-time collectors vis-à-vis full-time collectors. It also looks at the suitability of collectors for the job and their possibilities to develop as folklorists. In Section 2 the pioneering role of the Irish Folklore Commission is examined, particularly in respect of the recording of contextual data. Section 3 deals with the claim that the Commission neglected more recent living tradition, and Section 4 with the failure of the Commission to collect urban tradition to any significant extent. Closely linked to issues dealt with in the above two sections is the relative neglect by the Commission of the English-speaking rural areas of the South of Ireland. The extent of this neglect is assessed in Section 5. Finally, the question of gender in respect of the Irish Folklore Commission is examined in Section 6.

Conclusion and aftermath

Given the length of this study, it would be tedious in a conclusion to attempt to summarise or comment on everything that has been said in the body of the text about the Irish Folklore Commission. Moreover, as Section 8 of Chapter III as well as Chapter VII are summative in themselves, this obviates such an approach, to quite an extent. My conclusion should therefore be read in conjunction with the above-mentioned Section and Chapter. However, at the risk of being repetitious, I will make some final comments on the main actors in the story of the Commission: the storytellers, the collectors, the Head Office staff, members of the Board of the Commission, as well as politicians, officials, and others who played a part in the long quest for a permanent home for the Commission. Last but not least I will take a retrospective look at the Commission's Honorary Director, Séamus Ó Duilearga. The Irish Folklore Commission came to an end in 1970, but that was not the end of the story. My work does not concern the history of its successor, the Department of Irish Folklore. However, a study dealing in detail with the establishment and making permanent of the Irish Folklore Commission would be incomplete if it did not at least comment on the aftermath, i.e. on the fate of the Commission's collections in their new home, University College Dublin.

Sources and source criticism

In researching the linguistic, cultural, political, and ideological background to the Irish Folklore Commission, I have utilised a wide range of published sources. To a very large extent, however, the bulk of this study is based on primary sources, most of which have not previously been utilised in research.[14] The fact that very little research has been done on the history and activities of the Commission has made the utilisation of primary sources all the more essential. In studying the setting up, financing, and future organisation of the Irish Folklore Commission, I have utilised the extensive files relating to the Commission of the Departments of Finance, Education, and the Taoiseach (i.e. Prime-Minister) now deposited in the National Archives of Ireland. An invaluable source for elucidating official attitudes towards the Commission, its Director, and its activities has been the inter- and intra-departmental correspondence found in these official files. Although I have not had access to the files of the Irish Folklore Commission as such, nor to most of Séamus Ó Duilearga's private papers, both in the safekeeping of the Department of Irish Folklore, University College Dublin, I feel justified in presenting the results of my research without having gained access to these sources for a number of reasons. Firstly, the bulk of the correspondence and other documentation found in the Commission's files concerning the genesis and contorted history of the Commission is certainly duplicated in official Government files, to which I have had ready access. Secondly, I have been able to access hundreds of letters written by Ó Duilearga, and other members of his staff, to a number of eminent Nordic and North-American folklorists/ethnologists, as well as, in many cases, copies of the replies written by these scholars to their Irish colleagues. This correspondence is highly revealing of the work of the Commission, and also of the mentality of its Director and his staff, and has enabled me to fill gaps in my knowledge. In researching this subject I have also consulted the papers of certain eminent politicians, academics and cultural figures who had dealings with the Commission. These are mainly to be found in the School of History and Archives (formerly the Archives Department), University College Dublin.

In assessing the methodology of the Commission, I have used a variety of sources both secondary and primary. I have examined the collectors' diaries on microfilm at University College Cork and St. Patrick's College Maynooth, and have used them in this work, to a limited extent, as well as other manuscripts of the Commission's Main Collection. In addition to this, I have also drawn on much published material derivative of the collectors' diaries and the Commission's Main Collection. It should be remembered, however, that the collectors' diaries were not personal diaries as such where the collector might freely write about conditions of work and such matters. The intended initial reader was Ó Duilearga himself, or some other member of the Head Office staff. A number of full-time collectors published descriptions of their collecting, and the Commission's Archivist, Seán Ó Súilleabháin, has left us an invaluable account of many aspects of the work of the Commission both in the field and at Head Office recorded from him at the Midcentury International Folklore Conference in Indiana in 1950. I

---

14   Gerard O'Brien in his recent short study of the Irish Folklore Commission has utilised a
      small number of the official files used in this work. See G. O'Brien 2004, pp. 109–120.

have also used a very extensive questionnaire completed at my request by the collector Liam Mac Coisdeala on the work of the Commission as well as a less complete questionnaire return by his colleague Liam Mac Meanman. Many of Séamus Ó Duilearga's published papers have also been utilised. Bríd Mahon's autobiography, *While Green Grass Grows*, deals, among other matters, with life at the Commission's Head Office over a thirty-year period. The only extensive study of a collector that has so far been undertaken is Eibhlín Nic Craith's unpublished MA thesis on Tadhg Ó Murchadha. I have made extensive use of the interviews recorded by Pádraig Tyers with full-time collector Seosamh Ó Dálaigh in the 1980's. These have proved an invaluable source of information about the collectors' working methods and conditions of work. Unlike certain other sources that I have utilised such as articles by various collectors in *Béaloideas* or the collectors' diaries, Ó Dálaigh had free rein in these interviews to express his opinions openly.[15] Also of great use to me has been the Sound Archive of Radio Telefís Éireann (the Irish national broadcasting station), where numerous recordings of Séamus Ó Duilearga and his staff on aspects of the work of the Commission are to be found.

I have conducted few interviews for the purpose of this research. When I began writing up this research in autumn 2000 all the surviving members of the Commission, with one or two exceptions, were at an advanced age. I thought it best not to disturb them. As a student in the Department of Irish Folklore I heard from time to time a good deal of lore about the days of the Commission, particularly about infighting between Ó Duilearga and his staff. Some of these anecdotes I remember, I believe, quite accurately, but others only vaguely. During my time as a student and later I met a number of the collectors of the Irish Folklore Commission. All of them made a deep impression on me. Seosamh Ó Dálaigh was the collector I got to know best. He spoke a lot of his days in the Commission and of Ó Duilearga, but unfortunately I did not record any of this at the time, nor make notes subsequently. Nonetheless, certain things both he and his wife, Peig, said about the Commission and its Director remain as vividly in my mind today as does Ó Dálaigh's wonderful expressive face and the roguish glint in his eyes, although it is more than twenty years since I last saw him. I also had the privilege of spending an afternoon, along with another student, visiting Séamus Ó Duilearga in his home, a year and a half or so before his death. He, who had listened to so many stories, had also a story to tell, and I was an eager listener and conscious that I was savouring a moment in time. Some of what he told us that cold wintry afternoon I recall quite vividly; much I do not, alas. Some of these personal memories I have used in this study, some I recollect too poorly to use, and some I reserve for another day.

It should be said that most, if indeed not all, the officials who compiled the extensive government files utilised in this work could never have imagined that the day would come when their opinions would be broadcast to the four winds. This must be taken into account when assessing what they wrote. If

---

15   These interviews have since been edited and published by Pádraig Tyers in book form. I have, for the most part, used the tape transcripts rather than the published text as they are more complete (see Tyers 1999).

they had known that such would come to pass, they might have been less free with their opinions. In contrast, Ó Duilearga was certainly aware of his own historical role and that his writings, be they published or unpublished, would be the subject of future study. Ó Duilearga in one of his reports to the Government said that the Commission no longer simply belonged to Ireland but to the whole of Europe and, by implication, to the whole world.[16] The same could be said of Ó Duilearga himself: i.e. he does not simply belong to his family and descendants, but to Ireland and to all of mankind. He was a great man, and great men and women are made up of parts great and small, of virtues as well as faults and failings. To understand the man, one must look at the various facets of his make-up and actions. The same could be said of a number of his colleagues, who, similar to him, were exceptionally talented individuals. However, despite Ó Duilearga's sense of being engaged in making history, much of what he wrote in private communications was not written with an eye on what historians might say of him, but in the heat of the moment. The letters are very revealing of the man. Although I have learned much about him from his personal correspondence, I have been sparing in my use of it. I have, for the most part, used his private letters to shed light on the focus of my subject of study, not to reveal Ó Duilearga's soul. That would be work for a biographer at some stage in the future.

Finally, I should say that indispensable to my research has been the, to date, eight-volume national biography of individuals and scholars associated with the Irish language compiled by Diarmuid Breathnach and Máire Ní Mhurchú.[17] I am under a debt to both authors, as indeed are all who are working with, or interested in, Irish language tradition and literature.

The author's experience of collecting

Although my own experience of fieldwork is minimal compared to the full-time collectors, and many of the part-time collectors, of the Irish Folklore Commission, in this work I dare to comment on and assess the collecting methodology of the Irish Folklore Commission. I feel justified in doing so for a number of reasons. Firstly, ever since my student days I have collected a certain amount of folklore and oral history which has given me an insight into some of the problems collectors can encounter. Secondly, in conjunction with writing up this work, from the summer of 2001, on my frequent trips to Ireland, I have made extensive recordings of my father (a native of Mullahoran, Co. Cavan, now in his ninety-fourth year) telling of traditional life as he experienced it, as well as eliciting biographical details from his long life. In recording from him, I consciously sought to use many of the methods employed by the Commission's collectors: for example, taking down notes from casual conversation for future reference; recording interviews with him on a mini disc recorder; having him dictate to me; reassembling things he had

16   D/T S 15548B: 'Gearr-Thuar./1945–46', p. 8.
17   Breathnach and Ní Mhurchú 1986–2003.

said in conversations or unrecorded interviews with the aid of rough notes; and transcribing recorded interviews. I have also kept an extensive diary of my conversations and interviews with my father. All this has given me an insight into the work of the Commission's collectors, although, naturally, their lot was much harder than mine, and my recording equipment more sophisticated and easier to use. My work with my father, as well as my research over the years into the collections assembled by the Commission, have taught me the importance of research-driven collecting. The salvage collecting initiated by the Commission was understandable in the context of the time, but it did leave gaps in the documentation of the tradition, and went on for too long. The pressures of having to salvage as much tradition as possible also prevented the full-time collectors of the Commission from developing in certain ways.

A note on nomenclature and translated passages

The names of many people who feature in this work occur in two forms in my sources, an Irish-language form and an English-language form. I have, in most cases, opted for the more usual form, but not invariably so. The result of this may be that certain people are referred to below by a form of their name they may not generally have used or been known by. The index to this work gives both forms of the names of these persons, so everybody named in this work should be identifiable. Most large placenames such as the names of counties, islands, towns, and cities are given in their anglicized form. A number of placenames of parishes and villages are given in their Irish forms (the anglicised form is also to be found in the index). This work also contains many passages translated from Irish into English taken mainly from primary sources. Space has not allowed me to give the original passages as well, desirable as that might be. I hope to publish these passages in the original Irish elsewhere so those interested in utilising or scrutinising them will have an opportunity to do so. Where a passage or word has been translated from Irish, this is indicated in the relevant footnote by '(trans.)'. Where a passage has been translated from a language other than Irish, the language in question is specified in the footnote. In translated passages I occasionally give the Irish word or wording in brackets in cases where my translation may be open to question.

I
The Political, Ideological and Cultural Background

1. Pre-independence period

The decline of the Irish Language

English, along with Norman French, gained a foothold in parts of Ireland from the late twelfth century when the Normans, the ruling dynasty of England and Wales, conquered large tracts of the country. Until the third decade or so of the sixteenth century the English crown held most of Ireland in name only, its rule not extending very far beyond the Pale (as the enclave around Dublin was known) and a few major towns, although its influence extended, to a lesser or greater extent, throughout Ireland.[1] Many of the early Norman/English settlers in time became either bilingual with Irish or were linguistically assimilated, even if not completely culturally assimilated.[2] However, the assimilating power of Gaelic Ireland was not to last. As a result of various policies pursued by Tudor monarchs from the 1530's onwards the political power of Gaelic Ireland was in effect destroyed by 1601 when the English defeated a combined force of Irish rebels and their Spanish allies at the battle of Kinsale. As a result of these events, the fortunes of the Irish language were reversed from a position where it posed a threat to the survival of English in Ireland to a position where its own survival was threatened.[3]

The destruction of the Gaelic polity also resulted in the decline of native learning along with the patronage of the Gaelic ruling dynasties that had been its mainstay. This decline, although a relatively slow process, was ultimately to bring about a situation where Irish was spoken only by the poorest classes.[4] Liam de Paor has said that: 'The Gaelic world died from the top down'.[5] Nevertheless, while the destruction of the native aristocratic Gaelic society can be seen as a landmark in the decline of Irish, the language remained

---

1   For more on the complexities of the initial Norman/English colonisation and the subsequent Gaelic resurgence, see Simms 2000 [1987]), pp. 10–20. See also Lydon 2003 [1972]), passim.
2   For more on this, see Cosgrove 1979.
3   On the subjugation of Gaelic Ireland, see Ellis 1998, p. 119 ff.
4   On the learned orders of medieval Ireland, see Carney 1987, pp. 688–707 and Ó Cuív 1976, pp. 509–545.
5   Quoted in Ó Riagáin 1997, p. 4.

strong on the ground for almost two centuries after the battle of Kinsale. Moreover, its decline as the common vernacular was not at all inevitable. If the new English rulers had not taken such an antagonistic stance towards Irish, the fortunes of the language, and indeed of Protestantism in Ireland, might have been quite different. Patricia Palmer says:

> The Elizabethan conquest of Ireland is the point in history where the fortunes of the two languages briefly intersect, then spectacularly diverge. For one, the conquest marks the inaugural episode of its imperialist expansion. For the other, it is the originary moment of a language shift that constitutes the great drama of Irish cultural history.[6]

Many factors contributed to the decline of Irish over the next two centuries apart from official antagonism and indifference. The introduction of large numbers of English-speaking settlers, particular in the province of Ulster, during the seventeenth century was to have a long-term effect on the linguistic make-up of the country. Sir William Petty, the English surveyor, estimated 'that just under one-third of the country's inhabitants in 1672 were immigrants or of immigrant origin.'[7] Moreover, the Catholic Church itself would eventually cease to foster Irish, but it would take more than a century and a half for this to become apparent. However, Irish remained the language of the majority of the population down until the last quarter of the eighteenth century, or thereabouts. By the beginning of the nineteenth century, although still spoken over extensive areas of the country, it had become more and more a badge of poverty, at least when combined with a lack of knowledge of English. Nevertheless, although Irish was in rapid decline in percentage terms, in absolute terms the number of Irish speakers rose dramatically from 1800 to the eve of the Great Famine of the mid to late 1840's. Of the eight million or so people in Ireland in 1841, it is estimated that at least two and a half million were Irish speakers, and possibly many more.

The Great Famine of 1845-1849, which resulted in the death of approximately one million people, and the emigration of another million and a half, was to render a death blow to Irish in many areas of the country where it was still extensively spoken. In the main, the Famine affected the west of the country more than it did the east. As Irish was strongest in western areas, death and emigration took a heavier toll on Irish speakers than on English speakers.[8] If aristocratic Gaelic Ireland died with the Battle of Kinsale, many would contend that 'vernacular' Gaelic Ireland died with the Great Famine. Even in the east of the country, the Famine hit those elements of the population hardest who were most likely to have remained Irish-speaking.

6   Palmer 2001, p. 1. For more on the politics of language contact in Ireland, see Crowley 2000.

7   Mac Laughlin 2001, p. 55. Some of the Scottish settlers who came to Ulster in the early 17th century would appear to have been speakers of Scottish Gaelic, while lesser numbers spoke Manx Gaelic. See Adams 1976, pp. 80–81. For more on the settling of Ulster by Scottish and English planters, see Robinson 2000 [1984], passim.

8   Ó Riagáin 1997, pp. 4–5.

The census of 1851, which was the first to seek information on a knowledge of Irish, recorded somewhat in excess of one and a half million speakers of Irish. This amounted to approximately 30% of the population. It is generally agreed that this census under-recorded the number who knew Irish due to various factors, including the unwillingness on the part of many Irish speakers to admit to a knowledge of the language, which for many had become a badge of poverty and shame.[9] Subsequent decennial censuses proved more accurate in respect of a knowledge of Irish, but nonetheless each continued to show that the language was declining at an alarming rate.

The rapid decline of Irish in the wake of the Great Famine made 'certain sections of the educated classes' acutely concerned about 'the long-term survival of Irish' unless something was done.[10] In time, albeit after almost forty years, this concern would give rise to a mass movement to staunch the decline of Irish and regain lost ground for the language, in a movement that became know as the 'Gaelic Revival'. However the origins of this revival are older, and can be traced back to the mid-eighteenth century. In fact there were a number of earlier 'Gaelic revivals'.

The Gaelic Revival and cultural nationalism

These early revival movements, although quite different in certain essentials from later revivalist efforts, are worth examining, for therein we find the genesis of certain ideas that were later to play a prominent role in Irish cultural nationalism. Unlike the later revivalist movement of the late nineteenth century, which was to develop into a separatist movement (i.e. seeking political separation from Britain), this early revivalism of the mid to late eighteenth century was not separatist in nature, nor was it concerned with reviving a dying language (as Irish was at the time still spoken extensively), but rather with elucidating the richness of the Gaelic heritage and Irish history, and in so doing refuting the commonly held view that the ancient Irish were a backward and barbarous people. This movement was also confined, as John Hutchinson notes, to 'small groups of enthusiastic amateurs – clergymen, Trinity College [Dublin] dons, lawyers and country gentlemen.' Speaking of the image of Ireland that emerged in the writings of Charles O'Connor, Sylvester O'Halloran and others, Hutchinson remarks:

> An image of Ireland began, therefore, to crystallize as a holy island – insula sacra – blest by nature with peculiar advantages of climate, soil and geography for commerce and arts in peace and defence in war, which nurtured a singular people. Isolated from intercourse with Greece and Rome, they had created an original integrated and self-governing culture,

---

9   The question eliciting information on knowledge of Irish was contained only in a footnote in the 1851 census, as well as in those of 1861 and 1871, and was often overlooked by census enumerators. See Murray 2000, p. 83.

10   Ó Riagáin 1997, p. 5.

one that had not only withstood conquest by the Ancient Romans and the Anglo-Normans, but which had also, through its early settlements in its sister island, made a major contribution to British civilization, including the English language.[11]

Thomas Davis

Despite the limited impact of these late-eighteenth century 'revivalists' some of their ideas were to prove very enduring. These ideals re-emerged in the 1840's in the writings of Thomas Davis, a young Protestant who tried to develop a cultural nationalism which he hoped would unite Irish people of different religious persuasions. Davis was influenced by German romanticism and believed that culture rather than religion should define a nation. D. George Boyce says that for Davis:

> A nation was defined by its culture, by which Davis meant its literature, its history, and above all, embodying these, its language. Language was the vehicle of a nation's historical memory, not merely an accidental set of speech patterns. A nation should therefore 'guard its language more than its territories', for a people without a language of its own was 'only half a nation'.

Boyce notes that Davis saw language as having a 'two-fold purpose': 1) it formed a 'barrier to Anglicization', and 2) 'it gave the national soul its vitality'. In his view, for a people to lose their native language 'and to learn that of the alien was the worst badge of conquest'. Consequently, Davis maintained that: '"Ireland must be unsaxonized before it can be pure and strong."'[12] This talk of 'unsaxonizing' Ireland was a cry that was to be taken up again by the Gaelic League half a century later. Nevertheless, Davis's exhortations on behalf of Irish amounted to little more than rhetoric.[13] He himself knew little Irish and consequently did not have the competence to effect any turn in the tide of the fortunes of the language. The time, the eve of the Great Famine, was also not opportune; nor was Davis allowed sufficient time to attempt to 'unsaxonize' Ireland, dying in 1845 at the age of thirty one. Despite Davis's failure to establish machinery that would have helped preserve the Irish language, his ideas were to have a lasting effect on Irish nationalism, among other things, as Oliver MacDonagh notes, 'rivetting', intentionally or not, 'nationalism to cultural separation, and cultural separation to the Gaelic "heritage" in general, and to the Gaelic language in particular.'[14]

---

11 Hutchinson 1987 pp. 55–56. For more on this revival movement, see O'Halloran 2004, passim, and Leerson 1996, pp. 294 ff.
12 Boyce 1991, pp. 155–156.
13 For more on Davis's ideas on nationality, see Molony 1995, pp. 137–162.
14 MacDonagh 1983, p. 111.

The rise of the Gaelic League

In November 1892, Douglas Hyde, Irish scholar and folklore collector, and son of a Protestant clergyman from the west of Ireland, delivered what proved to be an historic inaugural lecture to the National Literary Society in Dublin, entitled 'The De-Anglicisation of Ireland'.[15] Less than a year later, on July 31st, 1893 ten men came together in a house in Sackville Street, Dublin to found the Gaelic League. Douglas Hyde, one of the ten, was elected the League's first president, but another of those present, Eoin Mac Néill, a young civil servant and Irish language scholar, was probably the person most responsible for convening the meeting, and the driving force behind the movement that was to subsequently emerge.[16] While initially the League's stated aim was 'the maintenance of Irish as a spoken language in Ireland', by 1900 it had become more ambitious. It now sought 'the preservation of Irish as the National Language of Ireland', and to this end 'the extension of its use as a spoken tongue'. From the beginning, the League also sought to advance 'the study and publication of existing Irish literature [mainly preserved in manuscript] and the cultivation of a modern literature in Irish.'[17] Although from the early twentieth century the League had a revivalist, expansionist policy, it did not seek the displacement of English as such, envisaging instead some sort of bilingual future for the country.

The League grew from small beginnings and was slow to make headway outside Dublin. In time, however, it was to expand into the provinces, and within fifteen years of its foundation it had some 950 branches ('with an estimated membership of 100,000'), mainly in Ireland but with branches also in Britain and the United States.[18] Thus, the League by the early years of the twentieth century had become an influential mass movement that could not be ignored. In addition to holding Irish language classes for both native speakers and learners, organising cultural events of various types, publishing books, collecting folklore, as well as other activities, it concentrated much of its efforts from the closing years of the nineteenth century onwards on bettering the position of Irish in the educational system at all levels. Its crowning achievement in the educational area was its successful campaign from 1908-1910 to make Irish a compulsory subject for Matriculation to the newly established National University of Ireland.[19]

The League subsequent to this victory went into relative decline in any case. It had, by this time, as Tom Garvin says, been 'colonised by people with different purposes from those of the founders' and 'an organisation that had been started with inter-faith cultural intentions' was 'transformed into

---

15 Welch 1996, p. 255.
16 The Gaelic League did have a number of immediate precursors such as the Society for the Preservation of the Irish Language, founded in 1878, and the break-away Gaelic Union, founded in 1882 – both organisations being primarily concerned with getting recognition for Irish on school curricula in Irish-speaking areas. See Ó Murchú 2001. See also Welch 1996, pp. 529 and 209–210.
17 Ó Riagáin, 1997 p. 10.
18 Ibid., p. 8.
19 Garvin 1987, pp. 81 and 85.

a mass organisation dominated by Catholics and increasingly subservient to political forces that were republican, separatist, or clerical.'[20]

The 1916 Rising and Political Foment

The Easter Rising of 1916 and subsequent political developments breathed new life into the League and its ideals. The rebellion lasted less than a week, resulting in approximately 1,500 casualties, as well as in much physical destruction, particularly in central Dublin. While initially unpopular with the general populace of Dublin, and the country at large, or at least with the influential middle classes, the draconian measures resorted to by the British to punish those involved in or associated with the rebellion, including the execution of sixteen of the rebel leaders and the deportation of thousands of nationalist activists to prison camps in Britain, in time, had the effect of increasing public sympathy for the rebels and their ideals. Under pressure of international and national opinion, most of the prisoners were released in early 1917. The Rising, and the subsequent sanctification of its executed leaders, by much of nationalist Ireland, was to prove the death knell for the Irish Parliamentary Party and the moderate constitutional politics it espoused. The limited autonomy offered by the Irish Home Rule Bill passed by the British Parliament just before the outbreak of conflict in Europe in 1914, but postponed for the duration of the War, by the end of hostilities in November1918 was no longer acceptable to a substantial section of nationalist Ireland. A much more radical separation from Britain was now sought. In the General Election of November 1918, shortly after the end of the First World War, Sinn Féin won a majority of nationalist seats and totally eclipsed the constitutional Irish Parliamentary Party. In fulfilment of its election promise, its elected MP's refused to attend the British Parliament. Instead, on January 21st, 1919, Sinn Féin elected representatives, in defiance of Britain, set up a Parliament or *Dáil* of their own in the Mansion House, Dublin, declaring an Irish Republic. On the same day the opening shots, of what was to become known as the War of Independence, were fired at Solaheadbeg, Co. Tipperary.

Political independence

The War of Independence eventually resulted in a Truce in July 1921 and in the signing of the Anglo-Irish Treaty with Britain on December 6th of the same year. This Treaty, which was signed by four Sinn Féin plenipotentiaries delegated by the Dáil, without consulting their colleagues in Dublin, fell far short of the sovereign republic for which many had fought and died. The new state, henceforth to be known as 'Saorstát Éireann/The Irish Free State', was given a substantial measure of autonomy, including control over taxation and

20   Ibid., pp. 81 and 85.

defence, but elected representatives would have to take an oath of allegiance to the British Sovereign.[21] Moreover, the six north-eastern counties of Ireland, where there was a Protestant/Unionist majority, were allowed to secede from this agreement, which they promptly did, leaving the new state comprising only twenty six counties.

Many both inside and outside the Dáil believed that to accept such a treaty was to betray the ideals for which the leaders of the Easter Rising had died. Ominously, the President of the Irish Republic, Éamon de Valera, one of the few 1916 leaders not to have been executed, possibly on account of his American birth, opposed the settlement. When the Dáil eventually voted on the Treaty in early January 1922, it was passed by a slight majority. Those who opposed the Treaty withdrew some time later from the Dáil, along with their leader, de Valera.

The Irish Civil War

Not only was the Dáil and the Sinn Féin party split on this question, so too was its military wing, the Irish Republican Army (IRA). As a majority of the IRA opposed the settlement, in order to establish control, the Provisional Government was forced to recruit soldiers for a Free State Army, among them many Irish veterans of the First World War. Civil war was not inevitable even at this stage, but with emotions running high on both sides, it was an acute possibility. Efforts to avoid open conflict failed and matters came to a head in late June 1922 when the Free State Army decided to attack the irregular forces opposed to the Treaty, who had been in occupation of the Four Courts (housing the four highest courts of the country) in central Dublin since mid April. They proceeded to bombard this complex of buildings with artillery acquired from the British. The rebel forces eventually surrendered but not before fighting spread to other parts of the centre of the city and large stretches of the countryside. Over the next nine months or so, killings by the anti-Treaty irregulars were followed by government reprisals, many prisoners being shot by the Free State Army without due process. However people felt about the rights and wrongs of the settlement with Britain, the vast majority of the populace wanted peace, and lacking extensive popular support the anti-Treatyites were not able to sustain an effective campaign. Gradually they were hunted down and rounded up. Finally, in May 1923 the irregular Republican forces ceased their operations, hiding rather than surrendering their weapons.

---

21   Despite the restrictions imposed on the new state, it was, to quite a degree, independent. The Treaty also contained enough loopholes to allow for development towards full independence. In 1949 the Irish Free State declared itself an independent republic. In practice, it had long been that.

Bitterness, disillusionment and political polarisation

Although the Civil War did not, relatively speaking, result in a great deal of loss of life, it did leave a legacy of bitterness and recrimination that was to last for more than a generation, and even to this day has left its mark on Irish politics.[22] Part of the reason for this may have been that although the opposing sides, to some extent, split along class lines among the population at large, the Civil War actually involved comrades falling out. For this reason it is often known in Irish as 'Cogadh na gCarad' ('The War of the Friends'). In some cases members of the same family found themselves on opposite sides. As we will see below, not only did the Civil War embitter Irish political life for more than a generation, but this bitterness was also to affect the fortunes of the Irish Folklore Commission.

In late 1922, during the Civil War, pro-Treaty Sinn Féin members of the Dáil and party activists formed a new party, Cumann na nGaedheal ('Association of the Gael').[23] This was to be the party of government for the next ten years or so. As things turned out, Cumann na nGaedheal in government proved quite reactionary. This was partly a consequence of the violence and mayhem of the Civil War and its aftermath, and the need to maintain public order, indeed to preserve the state itself. Nonetheless, the Cumann na nGaedheal party as it emerged from the Civil War contained some very conservative elements. Theirs, however, was an unenviable position. There was much reconstruction work to be carried out as a result of the destruction of the Civil War, and indeed the War of Independence. To make matters worse, the state had few natural resources apart from agriculture and there was little native industry. The Civil War would appear to have blunted the ideals of many who had fought for or supported a culturally and economically independent Ireland. The reality that faced the country at the close of the Civil War was very different from the dream that had inspired people some years earlier. The meagre resources available to the government had to meet the cost of reconstructing buildings and infrastructure damaged or destroyed in the conflict, as well as finance the Civil Service and education, and provide various services to the community.

Prior to and subsequent to the cessation of hostilities hundreds of Republicans (i.e. anti-Treatyists) were imprisoned. De Valera himself was taken prisoner in August 1923 while campaigning in the general election of that year. On release from prison, almost a year later, he set about reorganising his anti-Treaty Sinn Féin party. Although his party had contested the 1923 general election, they abstained from taking their seats in the Dáil, objecting to the oath of allegiance to the British monarch. In 1926, however, de Valera and his supporters split from Sinn Féin on the question of the oath of allegiance and formed a new party known as Fianna Fáil ('Soldiers of Destiny'), and the following year he brought his new party into the Dáil, after contesting the 1927 general election and winning a substantial number of seats.

22 For more on this influence, see Fitzgerald 2003b, passim.
23 For the birth of this new party, see Regan 2001, pp. 129.

2. Culture, language and ideology in the new state

Cultural destruction

As mentioned already, apart from the wholesale destruction of property in the country at large, many buildings in or near the centre of Dublin had been destroyed in the fighting during the Civil War, among them the Four Courts. Not only did the Four Courts house the highest courts in the land; also situated in this complex of buildings was Ireland's Public Records Office, containing much of the documentation of the English administration since medieval times. In the latter stages of the battle for the Four Courts most of the records housed in this repository were destroyed. The Public Records Office (PRO) had survived intact the fighting in 1916, when the Four Courts were also occupied by rebel forces. The sequence of events that led up to the destruction of the PRO is not entirely clear. David Edwards says: 'It is now beyond doubt that the destruction of these documents was a deliberate act' on the part of the rebel leader of the Four Courts, Rory O'Connor, who he says 'was determined to make an ideological statement—to strike a blow for Ireland's freedom by blowing up the records of its shameful colonial past.'[24] Gerard O'Brien, however, in a more recent study suggests that it was much less a deliberate act, than a casualty of the fighting when a shell fired by Government forces ignited munitions stored in the building.[25] This is not to exonerate Rory O'Connor and other rebel leaders, since the decision by the rebels to use the Treasury building, where most of the PRO's records were kept, as a munitions' store and bomb-making workshop, showed contempt for the safety of these records to begin with.

Some of the records that were destroyed were duplicated elsewhere, some survived because they were not in the Treasury building at the time of its destruction, a few had already had transcripts made of them, but the vast bulk of records were irretrievably lost. It has been said that the Irish Public Records Office constituted one of the finest medieval state archives in

---

24 D. Edwards 2001, p. 117. For more on the nature of some of the documents that were destroyed, and what survived or can be replicated from other sources, see Connolly 2002, pp. 14 ff.
25 O'Brien 2004, pp. 21–22.

Europe.[26] Its destruction has cast a shadow over Irish historical scholarship ever since. David Edwards says that the destruction of the PRO 'has proved, in retrospect, to be one of the Civil War's most lasting legacies, namely the handicapping of Ireland's history.' He also notes that the documents that perished comprised not just 'the history of English colonial rule in Ireland', they also contained much 'documentary evidence pertaining to Ireland's Gaelic past.'[27]

Brian C. Donovan and David Edwards decry both the destruction of the Public Records Office and the 'burning of many Anglo-Irish Protestant houses during the War of Independence and the Civil War and the loss of the private records they contained'.[28] In all, seventy six 'big houses' (mansions) were burned during the War of Independence, fifty five percent of these in the province of Munster. Many more big houses were burned during the Civil War, one hundred and ninety nine in all, with a much wider geographical spread than in the War of Independence.[29] These houses were seen to be bastions of colonial rule, but the history of the occupants of many such houses was inextricably bound up with that of their tenants. Material for the social history of many estates was also destroyed with some of these houses.[30] However, the loss of documents was wider than that. The destruction of the homes of prominent nationalists sometimes also resulted in the loss of documents of historical and cultural value. In other cases collections of documents were destroyed by their owners for fear certain materials might incriminate them if their homes were raided by Forces of the Crown. Collections of folklore also appear to have been destroyed in the tumult of war. For instance, during the War of Independence manuscripts belonging to the nineteenth-century Irish scribe and recorder of Meath literary and oral tradition, Peadar Ó Geallacháin, were burned by a descendent of his as they were attracting the suspicion of Black and Tans who raided the house.[31] Moreover, sometimes collections of folklore and other manuscript material in Irish were confiscated and subsequently lost without trace, because being in Irish they were considered suspicious.[32] In terms of the quantity of the material involved, these private collections of manuscripts and papers lost in this way may not have been all that great when compared to the contents of the Public Records Office and great country houses, nevertheless their destruction or disappearance was without doubt a significant loss.[33]

26 See Otway-Ruthven 1971, p. 17.
27 D. Edwards 2001, p. 117.
28 Donovan and Edwards 1997, p. xi.
29 See Dooley 2001, pp. 171–207.
30 See, e.g. *Analecta Hibernica* 12 (1943), pp. 131 ff.
31 Ó Buachalla 1969 [1968], p. 278, n. 2.
32 See Ó Ríordáin 2000, p. 166.
33 In this regard, it should also be noted that the 19th century witnessed the wholesale destruction of Irish language manuscripts in the transition from Irish to English. See, e.g. Ó Buachalla 1979, p. 344.

State ideology in respect of native Irish culture

Tom Garvin says that although 'Irish political radicals often had a fascination with the past,' combining a 'nostalgia for the rural society' with a reverence for a 'remote Gaelic medieval and pre-medieval past', they, along with many Gaelic Leaguers, were not very informed about the Gaelic past they so often expounded on.[34] However, not all Gaelic Leaguers and cultural nationalists were ill-informed about the Gaelic Past. For example, Eoin Mac Néill, Minister for Education in the first Irish Free State government, was Professor of Early Irish History at University College Dublin, as well as being one of the foremost architects of Irish cultural nationalism. Although a scholar, whose scholarship has, to a large extent, stood the test of time, he was motivated by ideals that few modern historians would aspire to, believing that in loving one's country and fostering its culture one was 'only doing the will of God'. He also held the view that 'Ireland's destiny was to be a teaching nation, setting an example to the rest of the world with "our ancient ideals, faith, learning, generous enthusiasm, self-sacrifice – the things best calculated to purge out the meanness of the modern world."' Mac Néill believed that 'the true basis of the Irish nation was to be found in the remote Gaelic Past and that the language was the lifeline of nationality'. He considered 'the period when Ireland was "the island of saints and scholars" as the proudest hour in Irish history.'[35]

Mac Néill was first and foremost a cultural nationalist, a scholar sucked into politics by events. The majority of the first Dáil (1919–1922) and the first Free State government differed from him in putting politics before culture. Nonetheless, cultural ideals were not lost sight of, and many of his colleagues shared, to a lesser or greater extent, his vision of a glorious Past, 'a golden age', as did many among the populace at large. That they should have done so is not all that surprising. Síghle Bhreathnach-Lynch notes:

> In keeping with other nations emerging from colonial rule, not surprisingly, the new Irish state was anxious to establish as soon as possible a distinctive national character, one as different as possible from that of its erstwhile ruler. Great Britain was perceived as urban, English-speaking and Protestant. Ireland would go to endless lengths to prove itself to be the opposite: rural, Irish-speaking and Catholic. A significant aspect of this construct of identity was the belief that Ireland's national identity was rooted in a Golden Age, that is the ancient Celtic past.

She adds: 'Reconnecting with and restoring that past would provide the ground upon which a sense of national self could take root and flourish.'[36]

We have seen above how ideas about Ireland's glorious past had engaged Irish minds since the eighteenth century, and perhaps even earlier, but now for the first time there was a native government in power which included

---

34   Garvin 1987, p. 108.
35   McCartney 1973, pp. 87–88, and 92.
36   Bhreathnach-Lynch 1999, p. 148.

people who, to a lesser or greater degree, held to the belief that the Irish were somehow 'elect' and that the Irish as a people had a mission. Within a few years of the setting up of the state, the relics of Ireland's Golden Age would also be given prominence in the restructured National Museum of Science and Art, which was renamed the National Museum of Ireland. This restructuring was the result of a report of inquiry headed by Professor Nils Lithberg, Director of the Northern Museum in Stockholm. As recommended in this report, the collections were rearranged so that the ground floor, earlier occupied by the Museum's industrial collections, would contain the antiquities section, 'which in several respects is preeminent among the collections of the world', and consequently 'should receive the most prominent position in the Museum, so that the visitor at his first entrance should at once recognise its national character.'[37]

However, the state's interest in the National Museum remained, for the most part, superficial and only three of Lithberg's more than thirty practical recommendations were implemented. Elizabeth Crooke contrasts the extent to which 'the importance of the collections exhibited in the Dublin museum dominated the writing of cultural nationalists' in the pre-independence period with the relatively low priority given the Museum in the Irish Free State. She says:

> In the case of the Dublin museum, it was important only to have it reorganised into a useful national symbol and certain artefacts prominently displayed. With that achieved, not as much political support was given for the provision of less appealing museum services.

Crooke implies that this state of affairs was not unique to Ireland, but it must surely contrast with the priority given (folk)museums in many Nordic and Baltic nations.[38] In this connection, it has to be noted that although the National Museum of Ireland began systematically collecting artifacts of folk culture already in the late 1920's, despite many governmental promises to establish a national folk museum, it is only in relatively recent years that such a museum has been set up.[39]

In certain respects the treatment of the National Museum of Ireland is illustrative of the treatment of many other cultural and academic institutions by the new state. There was much rhetoric about fostering native culture and learning, but very often not enough practical efforts to develop such institutions, and more importantly not enough financial support. Nonetheless, there were a small number of officials and politicians who had a genuine concern for such matters, for whom Ireland's 'Golden Age', and native

---

37   Crooke 2000, p. 144.
38   See ibid., pp. 141–147.
39   Indeed, the National Museum of Ireland could be said to have fallen victim to the independent Irish state. The Museum initially lost valuable office space when Leinster House was taken over in 1922 to accommodate the Dáil (Parliament) of the Irish Free State, and in the ensuing decades the state further encroached on its remaining space. Hayes-McCoy 1971, p. 132.

culture generally, amounted to more than simply putting it on display for public consumption. Two such persons were Eoin Mac Néill and Éamon de Valera. Mac Néill retired from active politics in 1925; Éamon de Valera, although still in the political wilderness in 1925, was in less than ten years to come to power and to dominate Irish politics for almost three decades. Both Mac Néill and de Valera, directly and indirectly, were to play a part in the setting up of the Irish Folklore Commission, the focus of this study. Like Mac Néill, de Valera was a scholar sucked into politics by events, but unlike Mac Néill he was destined not to return to the academic life.

The fledgling state's Irish-language policy

The struggle for independence from Britain had been dominated by men and women who had come via the Gaelic League to politics and armed struggle. Tom Garvin says:

> The Gaelic League was in many ways the central institution in the development of the Irish revolutionary élite. Most of the 1916 leaders and most of the leading figures in the Free State, whether pro-Treaty or anti-Treaty, had been members of the League in their youth and had imbibed versions of its ideology of cultural revitalization.[40]

In particular, it is often claimed that the Civil War lessened the enthusiasm for learning Irish among the general population.[41] Be that as it may, the pre-Treaty Sinn Féin policy of restoring Irish was not to become a victim of the Civil War, as both victors and vanquished still held to this ideal. The reason why politicians did not baulk at implementing a revival policy may partly be explained by the fact that many of them may have felt that they had no other choice, if Ireland was to survive as a nation. As P. S. O'Hegarty, a supporter of the Free State Government, put it, if Irish were not revived, Ireland, a small country with large English-speaking countries on either side, would be 'assimilated by one of these two communities, or by the combined power which they must eventually form, and in that case our name and tradition and history will vanish out of human ken, and our national individuality will be lost.'[42]

Of course, not all the ministers in the first Free State Government were enthusiastic supporters of reviving Irish. Nevertheless, despite the misgivings or indifference of some ministers, the new state set about consciously implementing the policies of the Gaelic League. The Irish Free State Constitution, adopted by the Dáil in 1922, defined the Irish language as 'the national language', but English was 'equally recognised as an official language'. Despite this parity between Irish and English, the Constitution nevertheless stated that Irish, as the national language, was therefore the

---

40 Garvin 1987, p. 78.
41 For some of the effects it had on language activists, see Ó Huallacháin 1994, p. 86.
42 O'Hegarty 1924, pp. 175–176.

'first official language of the state'. It could only be such, of course, in a very notional sense; in practice to achieve such a position would take years of endeavour. How long few seem to have pondered, or wished to ponder. Instead, belief in the ideal itself was in many cases substituted for systematic language planning. Despite misgivings in certain quarters, the state's revival policies initially met with quite a degree of acceptance across the political spectrum and among the general public. Referring to the new state's language policies, Oliver MacDonagh remarks: 'There could be no clearer evidence that a new orthodoxy, identifying political independence and national self-regard with the restoration of the Irish language, had been established'.[43]

There were four elements to the state's language strategy: 1) 'maintenance of Irish as a spoken language' in the Gaeltacht; 2) reviving Irish in the rest of the country; 3) gaelicising the public service; and 4) standardising and modernising the language.[44] However, the main efforts of the state to regaelicise the country from the beginning was concentrated on imparting a knowledge of Irish through the educational system, and involved a strong element of compulsion. The 'ultimate objective' of this language policy 'was to gradually replace English with Irish as a medium of instruction,' in primary schools. The policy of teaching infants through the medium of Irish was fraught with difficulties, initially not least by the lack of sufficient teachers with a good knowledge of the language. In time, some of the problems facing primary schools in respect of Irish-medium instruction, in particular, were solved through better teacher training. By the early 1940's, around 12% of the state's primary schools 'were teaching entirely through the medium of Irish', while in excess of 43% of primary schools 'were teaching varying proportions of children through Irish'.[45] While initially many English-speaking parents may have acquiesced to their children being taught through Irish, when it was realised that most children were leaving primary school without being fluent in Irish or to any real extent conversant with the language, opposition to Irish-medium instruction for infants grew, although it went unheeded for almost two decades. The late 1940's marked a watershed in the gaelicisation of primary education. The failure of the policy was tacitly acknowledged at an official level, if not always openly. From the early 1950's onward the number of primary schools teaching wholly or partly through Irish declined rapidly. The 1960's saw the wholesale abandonment of instruction through Irish, outside the Gaeltacht.

The new state not only set about teaching Irish extensively through the schools, it also sought to inform pupils on Gaelic culture and Irish history. As early as 1922, Pádraig Ó Brollcháin informed the National School Commissioners that 'the intention of the new regime was to Gaelicise all aspects of the curriculum so as to create a truly Irish outlook, in particular one which would highlight the struggle against oppression down through the centuries.'[46] The Programme of Primary Instruction, published that same year, stated:

43 Ó Riagáin 1997 and MacDonagh 1983, p. 117.
44 Ó Riagáin 1997, p. 15.
45 Ibid., pp. 15–16.
46 Farren 1995, p. 147.

> One of the chief aims of the teaching of history should be to develop the best traits of the national character and to inculcate national pride and self-respect. This will not be attained by the cramming of dates and details but rather by showing that the Irish race has fulfilled a great mission in the advancement of civilisation and that, on the whole, the Irish nation has amply justified its existence.[47]

Moreover, while 'Irish achievements were to be elevated' in the new curriculum, 'those of the English were to be minimised.'[48] Mindful of the pervasive influence of England on Irish culture, this was most likely an effort to minimise British influence in future.

Although these proposals were formulated literally at the birth of the new state, they were to continue to affect state policy for decades to come. In 1933 the Dept. of Education circulated notes for history teachers stating that 'among the specific objects for that subject "...is the study of the Gaelic race and Gaelic civilization and the resistence of that race and civilisation for a thousand years to foreign domination, whether Norse, Norman or English"'.[49]

The Gaelic League and the new state

We will see below how the state-supported, systematic collecting of folklore, initiated in 1930, was to be closely linked with the state's revival policies in respect of Irish. However, attitudes in the Irish language movement itself were also to affect the fate of the organisation of folklore collecting in Ireland. After the Irish Free State adopted many of the Gaelic League's policies, some thought that the League's work was done, but others felt that the League needed to be vigilant, to act as a watchdog for the language. From the mid 1920's onwards, the Gaelic League veered towards conservatism, espousing many puritanical attitudes. This was, partly, in line with certain trends in society at the time, such as the growth of religious devotion, support for the censorship of literature, and views concerning the role of women in the public sphere. However, if the League was becoming more conservative, it was also becoming more extreme, or, at least, elements of it were. This was, to some extent, in response to the slow progress of the state's efforts to revive Irish, and to the belief of many in the Irish language movement that the state's revival policies were only half-hearted.

One matter that particularly annoyed the League was the fact that the constituent colleges of the National University of Ireland, with the exception of University College Galway, were not promoting Irish as a medium of teaching, or else were doing so only in a very limited way. The state had since the mid 1920's been endeavouring to spread the use of Irish in university

---

47 Quoted in Titley 1983, p. 81.
48 Ibid., p. 81.
49 Quoted in Farren 1995, p 147.

education with grant incentives. The University College Galway Act of 1929 sought to develop Irish-medium teaching in that college, with a certain measure of success.[50] Of all the colleges of the National University of Ireland, University College Dublin was viewed by the Irish-language movement, and various governmental departments, as the one most reluctant to initiate teaching through the medium of Irish. As we will see later in this study, its reluctance to do so was to have a major impact on efforts to re-establish the Irish Folklore Commission in that college.

The Gaelic League was not only preoccupied with the need for measures that would help Irish take root at all levels of society, they were also extremely worried about the fate of Irish in the Gaeltacht. In 1925, under pressure from the Gaelic League, the Government set up the Gaeltacht Commission:

> To enquire and report to the Executive Council as to the percentage of Irish speakers in a district which would warrant it being regarded as (a) an Irish speaking district or (b) a partly Irish speaking district, and the present extent and location of such districts. To inquire and make recommendations as to the use of Irish in the administration of such districts, the educational facilities therein, and any steps that should be taken to improve the economic conditions of the inhabitants.[51]

The Commission commenced its work on 4th March 1925 and presented its report in July 1926. When published in August of that year the President of the Executive Council, W.T. Cosgrave, expressed his regret that 'the economic scheme advocated could not be implemented for want of money.' Only a few of the Gaeltacht Commission's eighty or so proposals were immediately implemented.[52] The Gaeltacht was not rescued by any economic package and continued to decline, but part of its rich store of traditions was in time to be saved for posterity, with state assistance, by the Folklore of Ireland Society, the Irish Folklore Institute, and especially the Irish Folklore Commission.

The Gaeltacht Commission estimated the number of native Irish speakers to be 257,000, of which 100,000 'were in Breac-Ghaeltacht areas, that is in areas where from 25% to 79% of the people spoke Irish.' Brian Ó Cuív says there are good reasons to think that the figure of 257,000 speakers to be an overestimation. One reason for this is that in enumerating native speakers no effort was made to ascertain 'whether those described as Irish Speakers did in fact use the Irish language as their normal medium of expression'.[53] In different circumstances a figure of 257,000 native speakers, if cross-generational transmission of the language was ensured, might have meant that Irish would hold its own, but few at the time who knew the facts on the

---

50 For efforts to promote Irish-medium teaching in the universities, see Kelly 2002, pp. 74 ff.
51 Quoted in Ó Muimhneacháin 1975, pp. 50–51.
52 Ó Huallacháin 1994, p. 90.
53 Ó Cuív 1971 [1951], p. 29. The fact, as Ó Cuív notes (ibid., p. 29), that there were more native Irish speakers in Co. Cork alone in 1851 than in the whole of the Gaeltacht in 1925, illustrates very graphically the rapid retreat of Irish on a national scale.

ground could have had any such illusions. Very many elderly people who knew Irish represented the last generation of Irish speakers in their locality. Moreover, in many parts of the Gaeltacht proper, Irish was not being passed on to children.

The failure to implement most of the recommendations of the Gaeltacht Commission had the effect of further alienating many Gaelic League activists from the Government, and the further weakening of Irish as a spoken vernacular in the Gaeltacht over the next decade or so resulted in some elements of the Irish-language movement becoming desperate and more extreme.

Nostalgia for rural life and the Gaelic past

Speaking of the focus of the Irish Folklore Commission on 'non-elite and non-urban tradition' as well as 'the cultural ideology' that lay behind it, Gearóid Ó Crualaoich notes that it privileged 'the memory of traditional cultural forms that were expressive of the world-view and lifestyle of former rural, relatively unsophisticated, largely under-educated and perhaps only partly-literate segments of the Irish population.' He comments also on the essentialist nature of this orientation:

> The sense of an essential heritage of cultural riches in danger of being lost forever in the displacement and destruction of tradition by the forces of modernity was well caught in the motto of the Folklore of Ireland Society's Journal, *Béaloideas*, every number of which since 1927 has carried the Gospel quotation: *Colligite quae superaverunt fragmenta ne pereant*, a sacred injunction to preserve precious survivals now in danger of discard.[54]

With respect to the rural orientation of the Irish Folklore Commission, at any rate, it must be remembered that the young Irish Free State was primarily a rural country, with only a small industrial base. According to the census of 1926, '61 per cent of the population lived outside towns or villages.'[55] Given the demographic dominance of the countryside, it is not surprising that the ideal of rural life, often a harsh reality for those who had to endure it, was idealised by members of the up-and-coming professional, political, and academic urban élites, who when not engaged in bettering their lot, as members of the bourgeoisie are wont to do everywhere, could afford to engage in such fantasies. For some of those who had left the countryside to achieve success, or a measure of it, in cities and big towns, or for people a generation or two removed from their rural roots, the countryside, and in particular the West of Ireland, came to symbolise the 'real Ireland', for it was in the West, where Irish was still spoken in parts, that genuine Irish culture persisted:

54   Ó Crualaoich 2003, p. 158.
55   Brown 1985, p. 18.

> The West came to stand for Ireland in general, to be representative of true Irishness. It could be seen as a way of access into the Irish past through its language, folklore, antiquities, and way of life, yet also be conceived of as outside time, separated from normal temporal development...[56]

Brian Fallon argues that there was a certain unreality about the nostalgia of the middle classes 'for the old ways and the simple, frugal country life'.[57] Nevertheless, this hankering after an ideal rural life, i.e. the perception that the real Ireland was in the countryside, meant that little value was placed on urban culture, especially urban working-class culture, and indeed on much of rural culture as well, for the real Ireland was much further west, where Irish was spoken. However, it must be said that nostalgia for rural life was not a peculiarly Irish phenomenon. It was widespread in most western countries that had experienced industrialisation and urbanisation, being a reaction against the perceived ugliness and materialism of much of modern life.[58] Moreover, international folklore scholarship at this time was also oriented towards rural life. Neither was Ireland unique in that a particular part of the countryside more than others was thought to embody the soul of the nation. In Finland in the nineteenth century, Karelia, which lay in the east of the then Grand-Duchy of Finland as well as across the border in Russia, became a Mecca for 'nationalistically orientated artists, scholars and intellectuals, members of the Finnish upper and educated elite' who 'travelled there from Helsinki in search of the '"origins of Finnishness", "original Kalevala life", and "former Finnish 'Golden Age'"'.[59]

Given the independent Irish state's official policy of regaelicising the country, it is not surprising that the Gaeltacht should have been seen as a place to learn Irish and from where Irish might spread to the rest of the country. However, anglicisation was not seen simply as the abandonment of a distinctive language for another, it was also believed to have resulted in cultural and spiritual impoverishment.[60] The Gaeltacht was thus seen not simply as a linguistic source, but as a place of national and spiritual regeneration. In 1926, Cormac Breathnach, a teacher and Gaelic League activist, wrote:

> There are in the Gaeltacht –and there alone– special things, such as the culture and civilisation and folklore and true genius of the Gaelic race. These are things that are interwoven with the language; indeed, they are the life of the language, and the person who does not absorb them with the language is felt to be lacking something; for although he has Irish, he does not have the Gaelic character. That character can only be engendered and nourished in the Gaeltacht. [61]

---

56   Nash 1993, pp. 86–87. See also Belanger 2000, pp. 95–107.
57   Fallon 1998, p. 1.
58   See, e.g. Peer 1998.
59   Anttonen 2005, p. 139.
60   On this matter, see the opinions of Aodh de Blácam quoted and translated in O'Leary 2004, p. 91.
61   Quoted and translated in O'Leary 2004, p. 91.

Although there is no denying that the inhabitants of the Gaeltacht of the 1920's were heirs to an exceptionally rich oral culture, many of them had to eke out a mere existence, and emigration was endemic in their communities. The contrast between the richness of the oral tradition of these areas and the poverty of many of the bearers of tradition is striking. Speaking of the social discrepancy between folklorists and informants, Diarmuid Ó Giolláin says:

> The social distance is obvious in the literature, yet is rarely commented upon except in the most superficial way. In fact poverty and isolation were necessary to the specificity of folklore since prosperity and integration of necessity involved the assimilation of modern values inimical to it. The key observers, that is those such as Yeats and Ó Duilearga who helped to shape the folkloric discourse in Ireland, took a strong position against the materialism of a modern urban, industrial world and a fatalistic view, coloured by a nostalgic Romanticism, of the inevitable decline of folklore communities. How could they come to grips with the poverty of the storyteller if it seemed to be the precondition of his or her art?[62]

Séamus Ó Duilearga was not blind to the poverty of communities in the west of Ireland where he himself collected, and had others collect, but the richness of the oral tradition in those areas, perhaps, blinded him to the implications of that poverty. He had no solution to the poverty of his informants, apart from wishing to see them honoured, as they were heirs to an age-old, venerable tradition. For him the death of these old bearers of tradition meant 'the end of the Middle Ages in Western Europe', and with their passing 'the chain that is still a link between this generation and the first people who took possession of Ireland will be broken.'[63] There is no doubt that 'nostalgia for the old ways and the simple, frugal country life', among other things, motivated Ó Duilearga in his efforts to save Irish folklore for posterity, and that he was, at the same time, content with the benefits his position as an aspiring member of the up-and-coming Catholic bourgeoisie gave him in greater and greater abundance. The same could be said of many other members of the Folklore of Ireland Society. Of course, in the case of Ó Duilearga, nostalgia for the past was only part of the complex mix that made up the man. Mere nostalgia would not have made him persevere, often against insurmountable odds, to achieve his dream.[64] Given the state's gaelicisation policies and the precarious position of the Irish language, when the extensive collecting of folklore did take place in the 1930's, it is not surprising that the vast bulk of

---

62   Ó Giolláin 2000, p. 142.
63   Quoted and translated in ibid., p. 140.
64   At the same time, it should be remembered, almost all the full-time collectors of the Irish Folklore Commission, who amassed some 53% of its Main Collection, as well as many of the part-time collectors, came from the communities in which they first began collecting, and lived among their own people. While the meagre salaries of the full-time collectors gave them a higher standard of living than most of those they worked with and amongst, by any standards theirs was a harsh lot, especially in the early years, and one wonders what place some of them found in it for nostalgia.

the material collected was in the Irish language – at least that collected by full-time collectors. It should be stressed, however, that bodies such as the Folklore of Ireland Society, the Irish Folklore Institute, and the Irish Folklore Commission never discouraged the collecting of material in English as such, although they saw as their priority the collecting of material in Irish. Neither did any official directive specifically discourage the collecting of folklore in English, although as we will see in this study at least one official of the Dept. of Education did question the need to extend collecting by full-time collectors to English-speaking areas. It is doubtful, however, if the state in the 1920's and 1930's would have agreed to the collecting of material in English on a similar scale to that which it sanctioned for collecting mainly in Irish-speaking districts, and almost certain that any extensive project to collect urban folklore would have got scant official support.

The fact that English was believed not to have very deep roots in most parts of the country also tipped the balance in favour of collecting in Irish-speaking districts, or areas with residual Irish. It was at the time commonly believed that the Great Famine of the 1840's had been the deciding factor in the demise of Irish over much of the country. We now know, however, that Irish was in retreat in many areas long before the Great Famine and was preceded by a period where bilingualism, extending in some cases over a number of generations, if not longer, was a feature of large tracts of the country.[65] However, it was not only the fact that Irish had deeper roots in the country than English that tipped the balance in favour of collecting in Irish, nor the precarious position of the Irish language itself, but also the richness of the tradition in Irish-speaking districts, peripheral and poverty-stricken for the most part.

While the approach of the Irish Folklore Commission towards Irish tradition was essentialist in nature, as Gearóid Ó Crualaoich notes above, and resulted in a somewhat narrow and unrepresentative image of traditions being recorded, given the prevailing ideology of the time it is understandable that its approach should have been so. However, in concentrating initially on what it saw as the richest veins of Irish tradition, namely traditions in the Irish language, it was not simply motivated by narrow linguistic nationalism. Scholars like Reidar Th. Christiansen and Carl Wilhelm von Sydow believed, rightly or wrongly, that in the rich body of folklore still extant in the Gaeltacht lay a key to understanding much of the lost oral tradition of medieval Europe. Thus, viewed from an international perspective, rather than a purely national one, the focus of the Irish Folklore Commission was far less essentialist – at any rate, certainly far less narrow.

The growing power of the Catholic Church

If the newly independent Irish state was trying to reinvent itself by endeavouring to revive the Irish language as the main vernacular, on another

---

65   For more on the retreat of Irish, see Fitzgerald 1984 and Fitzgerald 2003.

front it was forging a strong identity, of a different sort, for itself. The new state was to pursue policies that would give expression to the Catholic faith of the majority of the population. In doing so, and in allowing the Catholic Church an undue say in certain matters of social policy, it militated against its own stated aspirations of achieving Irish unity, and against one of the basic tenets of Irish Republicanism since the late eighteenth century, namely 'to unite Catholic, Protestant, and Dissenter [Presbyterian] under the common name of Irishmen'. On the one hand, the state was now proclaiming, or at least implying, that Irishness was on the secular level to be equated with the Gaelic tradition, and on the religious level with Catholicism.

There was the feeling that Ireland, if not the most, was one of the most Catholic countries in the world, and many with power and influence, as well as much of the populace in general, were proud that such was the case. Whether consciously or not Catholicism became a surrogate for national identity. Unlike efforts to regaelicise the country, the entrenchment of religious faith and the growth of the influence of the Catholic Church was far more easily achieved. This growing influence of the Catholic Church permeated most aspects of Irish life and affected in subtle ways the work of the Irish Folklore Commission, as indeed it did the lives of many of the staff of the Commission. For example, along with an increase in religious devotion and deference towards the Catholic Church, puritanism, which had been gaining ground with the decline of the Irish language, became further entrenched in Irish society, as exemplified in the Censorship of Publications Act of 1929. As a result of this growing puritanism, certain types of folklore were under-collected and certain aspects of folk life under-investigated, not due to any directive from above as such, but simply because many collectors (and some informants), for whatever reason, steered clear of such matters.[66] The reticence of Seán Ó Súilleabháin's A Handbook of Irish Folklore on sexual matters may also, in part, be attributed to this puritanism (see Chapter VII/6 below). It should be remembered, however, that puritanism was not simply an Irish phenomenon at this time. Other countries were also experiencing similar trends.

There is no doubt that the efforts to collect folklore in the South of Ireland had the blessing of Catholic bishops and priests. Many priests were members of the Folklore of Ireland Society and active in the Irish language movement. The Irish Folklore Commission, when initially set up, had three priests on its Board. Many priests would have viewed the Gaeltacht not only as a place for rejuvenating native culture but also native spirituality.[67] However, although gaelicisation and Catholicism often seemed to go hand in hand, this was not always the case. Michael Tierney, Professor of Greek in University College Dublin, member of the Irish Folklore Commission, and friend of Séamus Ó Duilearga, by the mid 1930's had lost his belief in the Gaelic Revival. When he became President of UCD in the late 1940's he set about making his college one of the foremost Catholic universities in the English-speaking world. He

---

66 For the scruples of one full-time collector, Seán Ó Flannagáin, see C. Breatnach 2003, pp. 21–22.

67 On this matter, see the views of Irish Jesuit Edward Cahill, quoted in O'Leary 2004, p. 92.

was vehemently opposed to allowing even a modicum of teaching through Irish in UCD, partly, perhaps, because he wanted his university to serve the English-speaking world. Tierney's plans for UCD were directly opposed to those of the Irish language movement, and more than any other figure in that college he became the *bête noire* of many activists in the movement. The question of Irish-medium instruction at UCD, as we will see below, was to impinge greatly on the fate of the Irish Folklore Commission. Tierney's ambition to place his college on the international stage conflicted with certain national interests and, ironically, that most national of institutions, the Irish Folklore Commission, was caught in the middle.

If the restoration of the Irish language was seen by many Catholic priests and bishops as a possible bulwark against foreign influence, of more immediate concern for the Church was the demise of traditional life all over rural Ireland, and the threat this posed to public morality. In an oft-quoted passage, Bishop Thomas Gilmartan of Tuam contrasted the 'low sensuality' of foreign dances and '[c]ompany keeping under the stars of night' with the virtues of the 'old Irish custom of visiting, chatting and story-telling from one house to another, with the Rosary to bring them all home in due time.'[68] Despite Bishop Gilmartin's praise for the virtues of the old Irish dances and the innocent pastime of storytelling, within ten years the Church would be involved in having a piece of legislation enacted that would put an end to the practice of these old dances in their traditional setting (the farmhouse), and in so doing do great damage to the fabric of rural life, namely the Public Dance Halls Act (1935). Farmhouse dances, apart from dancing and socialising as such, also involved the exchange of local and national news as well as the telling of traditional lore and stories. [69]

There is surely more than irony in the fact that in the same year that the Irish Folklore Commission was set up to collect Irish folk tradition, the Irish Government passed this Act, which was to affect living rural Irish culture profoundly. The countryside, so idealised by sections of the political élite, administrators, academics, the middle classes, and the Catholic Church, also needed to be controlled, it would appear. One might have expected bodies such as the Folklore of Ireland Society, the Irish Folklore Institute, and the Irish Folklore Commission to have warned of the possible effects of this Act on the culture of rural Ireland, or to have appealed for it to be amended when the negative consequences of the Act should have been clear to all. As far as I am aware, none of these bodies appealed to the authorities on behalf of 'the country people'. For the most part an older world was what they were interested in.

Gender and the new state

Irish women had taken an active part in numerous cultural and political organisations since the beginning of the twentieth century, and many

---

68 Quoted in Keogh 1994, pp. 28–29.
69 For more on this Act, its background, and its consequences, see Austin 1993. See also Brennan 1999, pp. 125 ff.

women had been to the fore in the struggle for independence. There had, however, been tension between women and men engaged in the struggle for independence and working to promote a separate Irish national identity.[70] The post-independence period, however, saw a narrowing of attitudes towards women in respect of their role in society. Such attitudes were eventually to be enshrined in de Valera's new Constitution of 1937, which in recognising 'the Family as the natural primary and fundamental unit group of Society', sought to restrict women to the home:

> In particular, the State recognises that by her life within the home, woman gives to the State a support without which the common good cannot be achieved.
> The State shall, therefore, endeavour to ensure that mothers shall not be obliged by economic necessity to engage in labour to the neglect of their duties in the home.[71]

However, long before de Valera's new Constitution, negative attitudes towards women participating in public life and white-collar employment were growing. Because all the women members of the Dáil had opposed the Treaty with Britain, many in the Cumann na nGaedheal party felt they were, due to their violent, outspoken opposition, partly responsible for the Civil War. P. S. O'Hegarty, a supporter of the Treaty, in his book *The Victory of Sinn Féin* (1924) described women as 'unlovely, destructive-minded, arid begetters of violence, both physical and mental'. O'Hegarty believed that 'with women in political power there would be no more peace.' Maryann Gialanella Valiulis, speaking of O'Hegarty's attitude, says:

> Women's hostility to the treaty rebounded against them. Some, like O'Hegarty, blamed women for the divisiveness and violence which plagued the country, a position clearly not supported by the events of the period. However, the civil war was such a devastating experience that the need to scapegoat, to blame was enormous. Women were an easy and obvious target. Thus, the civil war had a very clear, albeit negative effect, on male perception of women's right to participate in the political life of the country. This negative effect translated into legislation, into an effort on the part of successive Free State governments to define women out of politics. In fact, simply put, the Cosgrave and then the de Valera government sought to eliminate women from public life.

The Jury Acts of 1924 and 1937 effectively 'barred women from serving on juries'. The Civil Service Act of 1925 'restricted women's right to employment in the upper echelons of the [Civil] Service.' This was followed in 1932 by a 'ban on employing married women teachers', later extended to the Civil Service as a whole.[72] Finally, the Conditions of Employment Act

---

70 See Ward 1983, pp. 248 ff.
71 *Bunreacht na hÉireann. Constitution of Ireland*, Articles 41 and 41.2.
72 Valiulis 1994, p. 86.

of 1936 further constrained women, allowing the Minister for Industry and Commerce to restrict the employment of women in certain types of work.[73] Thus, the foundations for the Constitution of 1937 in respect of women were well laid by legislators over a period of more than ten years. It should be noted, however, that Caitriona Clear in a recent study argues that not all the restrictions placed on women's employment in this period were specifically aimed at preventing married women from working outside the home, but rather at restricting the formation of two-income families, a phenomenon which in the economic circumstances of the time was thought by many to be socially undesirable.[74]

The fact that the Irish Folklore Commission did not employ any women full-time collectors can, in part, be explained by the restrictions placed on female employment at the time and the official attitude towards women working outside the home. However, it was not simply a question of the Commission complying with official restrictions in respect of employment. Women were not only not employed as full-time collectors, they were significantly under-represented among the Commission's informants. Moreover, no woman ever sat on the Irish Folklore Commission. Ó Duilearga and his male colleagues on the Commission were products of their time and appear to have felt no need of a female perspective in supervising the running of the Commission.

If antipathy towards women in Irish society, particularly in rural society, affected the number of women the Commission collected from as well as the amount and the nature of the material collected from them, certain influences extraneous to Ireland were to affect what in general was collected as well as the quantity of material amassed by the Commission.

Comparative folklore studies and northern Europe

The collections of the Irish Folklore Commission were amassed at a time when comparative studies were in vogue in folkloristics. In order to understand what fuelled the collecting drive of the Commission, it is necessary to keep this in mind. Folklore was not just national, it was also international. In a lecture Séamus Ó Duilearga delivered in 1942 at the Irish Book Fair, he said:

> The student of Irish folklore, whether his interests be primarily literary or historical, must approach his studies from a comparative or an international standpoint. If he be a medievalist he is quite at home and needs no guide through the golden land. For in Irish folklore we have the last echo of medieval romance. The fireside tales of Ireland have their origin—many of them, at any rate—in a world as far removed from the medieval period as that loosely defined period of time is from us. They

---

73 Daly 1992, pp. 122–123.
74 Clear 2003, p. 107. See ibid. for a reappraisal of the complexities of the position of women in Ireland in the 1930's and 1940's.

were told when Homer was a lad, when the Odyssey was unwritten. They are the very stuff of the oldest literature of the West and of the Orient, and to this remote island of ours they have come—not all of them, but a good number—by various ways at various times—in them one hears 'the murmurings of a thousand years and yet a thousand years.'

Not only, in Ó Duilearga's estimation, was much of Irish folklore derived ultimately from Europe and the Orient, and consequently of intrinsic interest to other nations, he stressed that its study also demanded international contacts, 'far beyond our borders', with northern Europe in particular, for it was there that the science of folklore was most developed.[75]

In the above passage Ó Duilearga places emphasis on the folktale (*märchen*), and although the Irish Folklore Commission collected a wide range of folklore genres, there is no doubt that right from the start it paid special attention to the systematic collecting of folktales as it was believed that Ireland had a special contribution to make to the advancement of the international study of the folktale in particular (see below). The method of studying folktales in vogue in northern Europe at the time, namely the historic-geographic or Finnish method, developed by Kaarle Krohn and Antti Aarne, required that as many variants of a particular tale be collected as possible in order to determine the 'proto-tale' (or ur-form) and place of origin.[76] By the time the Irish Folklore Commission began its work, there were scholars who doubted if it was really possible to determine such 'proto-tales' with any certainty; nevertheless Ó Duilearga was probably correct when he stated in a lecture he gave in UCD in November 1941 that the historic-geographic method was 'with certain modifications ... used by most students of storyology.'[77] However, it should be stressed that the Irish Folklore Commission did take some of the criticisms of the historic-geographic/Finnish method on board. This is not surprising as one of the foremost critics of aspects of this method at the time was the Swedish folklorist Carl Wilhelm von Sydow, who, as we will see below, had a strong input into the Irish Folklore Commission.[78]

The historic-geographic method also fuelled the collecting of genres other than the folktale by the Commission, for it was also applied to the study of fixed genres such as anecdotes, songs, riddles, proverbs, and such like. As was the case with folktales, for the purpose of comparison, and to determine proto-types, as many variants as possible should be collected. This endless search for variants was something which many government officials who dealt with the Irish Folklore Commission did not always appreciate or understand. In the main, as we will see below (Chapter III), Irish officials saw the Commission's collections as a source for linguistic and cultural regeneration, not as a resource for international scholarship. Nevertheless,

---

75 Ó Duilearga 1942a, pp. 25–26.
76 See Krohn 1926.
77 Ó Duilearga 1942b, p.35.
78 For some of these criticisms, see Honko 1986, Chestnut 1993, and Holbek 1987, pp. 242 ff.

but for the requirements of international scholarship the collections amassed by the Commission would probably have been on a much smaller scale.

Writing in 1971 in an obituary of Reidar Th. Christiansen, Ó Duilearga, speaking of the help various Nordic folklorists gave him and the Irish Folklore Commission, quotes the Irish phrase: "Ón áird tuaidh tig an chabhair! 'from the North help comes'!".[79] And that is how it was: he did not seek help, not initially at any rate, rather Nordic folklorists interested in saving the riches of Irish folklore offered their help. If this help had not been offered, there is no telling what direction the collecting of Irish folklore would have taken, but it is unlikely that there would have been the same emphasis on the folktale or comparative research based on the historical-geographic method.

The Irish Folklore Commission achieved international status by bypassing England and going to, what it considered, the fountainhead of folklore scholarship. In his report to the Government for 1950–1951, speaking of the Irish Folklore Commission's high international status and of its links with, and resemblance, in respect of methods and organisation, to similar institutions in Europe, Ó Duilearga wrote: 'We had to leave England out of the equation ('as an áireamh') as there was nobody there who could help or advise us.'[80] There is no doubt that the Irish Folklore Commission trod a very different path to that of the Folk-Lore Society of London. As Richard Dorson notes, many of the Folk-Lore Society's leading folklorists engaged in 'ingenious speculation conceived at the writing desk and in the library' rather than in field work. Nevertheless, he further points out that 'the London group perfectly understood the prime importance of systematic field collecting and encouraged collectors in the countryside, who in turn looked for guiding principles and scholarly direction to the leaders of The Folk-Lore Society.' Despite this understanding for the need to collect folklore systematically, Dorson admits, '[t]he bright promise of folklore collecting in England was never fulfilled' and '[t]he English would perform their greatest feats of collecting in faraway lands.' It has also to be noted that the Folk-Lore Society never established a folklore archive as such, nor did it achieve recognition for folklore as a university subject, and went into rapid decline after the First World War.[81] In these circumstances, it is hardly surprising that Ó Duilearga, who became a committed folklorist in the 1920's, would not have sought to emulate the Folk-Lore Society.

It is, perhaps, not surprising that links would in time have been forged between Ireland and northern Europe in respect of folklore collecting and scholarship. The decline of the Folk-Lore Society of London after the First World War in itself might have forced Irish folklorists to look towards Europe for inspiration and help, but Ireland's historical development also played a part. In much of Continental Europe the interest in folklore grew out of romantic nationalism during the course of the nineteenth century, while in England, to a large extent, it grew out of antiquarianism. Folklorists had an important role to play in nation-building in many emerging European nation

---

79   Ó Duilearga 1969–70, p. 347.
80   D/T S 15548B: 'Gearr-Thuar./1950–51', p. [8] (trans.).
81   Dorson 1968, pp. 316, 331, and 440–441.

states, but where the nation was long-established, as in England and France, folklorists did not 'share the sense of national mission that allowed folklore to find a privileged intellectual niche' elsewhere. Ireland, politically linked to England/Britain, may have been in somewhat of an anomalous position in this regard. Gearóid Ó Crualaoich notes 'in the years preceding the Great War ... the collecting and study of folklore was then, still, in these islands, regarded as an aspect of antiquarian and anthropological study as much as it was regarded as the work of nationalist, cultural reclamation by scholars sympathetic to the ideals of the Anglo-Irish Literary Revival and the Gaelic League.'[82]

While folklore in Ireland, in the pre-independence period, played less of a role in the growth of nationalism than in some European countries, there is no doubt that it was seen in the early decades of the independent Irish state, in certain circles at least, to have an important role to play in building up the nation, or rather 'a nation' moulded to a particular image.

Conflicting ideologies at home and abroad

Contrasting Ireland and Germany, Gearóid Ó Crualaoich notes that in Germany 'a similar later nineteenth and early twentieth century preoccupation in national cultural ideology, with the symbolic recovery and repossession of the past, had a more directly political and sinister outcome than was the case in Ireland.' He also notes that in both Ireland and Germany 'cultural nationalism took on radically political and militaristic form' in the twentieth century, but in respect of 'folklore studies in the newly established Irish Free State and in the later Republic' while it was 'accorded symbolic importance' he stresses '[i]ts influence on social and political affairs, however, was largely confined to its diverting of official and scholarly attention away from the lived popular culture of Irish people in the 1930s and 1940s in favour of a concern for the preservation of the record of past cultural forms.'[83] One reason why folklore studies was not put to more sinister uses in the South of Ireland is linked to the state's political development since independence. Of those European states that came into being in the wake of the First World War, the Irish Free State was one of the few to remain democratic during the inter-war period. Nevertheless it was not able to remain aloof from the struggle of conflicting ideologies in Europe, and for a time it was not at all certain that the young state would preserve its democratic ethos. The early 1930's saw the rise of a 'para-fascist' movement in Ireland that in time came to be known as the Blueshirts. Although its origins were not entirely undemocratic, many of the trappings of the Blueshirt movement, as well as much of its official ideology, in time came to resemble that of contemporary Continental fascist organizations, particularly after July 1933 when it was led by Eoin O'Duffy. In late 1933 the movement merged with the Cumann

---

82   Ó Giollain 2000, p. 49 and Ó Crualaoich 2000, p. i.
83   Ó Crualaoich 2003, pp. 158–160.

na nGaedheal Party and the Centre Party to form a new party called Fine Gael, with O'Duffy as leader. In little over a year O'Duffy was forced to resign his leadership of Fine Gael, and with him went most of the fascist ideology he espoused.[84]

The Blueshirt movement was nipped in the bud before it managed to destabilise the young state irretrievably, and before it could give rise to civil unrest on a large scale. The main significance of the Blueshirts for this study is that the rise of the Blueshirt movement, and Fianna Fáil's perception of it as being ostensibly a movement seeking to wrest power from the democratically elected government of the day, had the effect of adding fuel to the bitter legacy of the Civil War, and the fact that prominent members on the staff of UCD were closely associated with the movement, most likely, increased antagonism within Fianna Fáil towards that college. We will see later in this study how this antagonism affected the fortunes of the Irish Folklore Commission from its inception.

While the threat to stability in the state posed by the Blueshirts was thwarted, the rise of fascism in Europe impinged on the Irish Folklore Commission in a number of ways. Two members of the Board of the Commission itself, (Adolf Mahr, an Austrian by birth, and Daniel Binchy) had diametrically opposed views on Nazism, and this affected the attendance of the latter, in particular, at meetings of the Board.[85] Ó Duilearga, like many others of his compatriots, was, perhaps, initially complacent or naive about the usurpation of power by the Nazis in Germany. One could say that Ó Duilearga's, and later the Irish Folklore Commission's, approach to Nazi Germany in the 1930's in many ways reflected that of the Irish state, whose stance, as Mervyn O'Driscoll argues, was characterised by 'ambiguity'.[86] In June 1935, although aware that Adolf Mahr was the head of the *Auslandsorganisation*, and thus the most prominent Nazi in Ireland, Ó Duilearga appears to have trusted him, on a personal level, completely.[87] Ó Duilearga's friendship with Mahr was to result in him compromising his principles somewhat and undertaking an ill-advised lecture tour of Germany in January/February1937. With the benefit of hindsight, we can say that Ó Duilearga's decision to accept this invitation was the wrong thing to do.[88] However, it should be remembered that in going to Germany he had the approval, indirectly at least, of the Irish Government as the invitation was extended to him through the Irish Dept. of Education. It was also approved, at the request of the Dept. of Education, by the Finance Sub-Committee of the Commission.[89]

---

84 For more on this movement, see Cronin 1997.
85 Binchy, an expert on the Old Irish Law Tracts, had acted as Irish Minister in Germany from 1929 to 1932 and witnessed the rise of the Nazis and their seizure of power. In the early 1930's he wrote a number of articles very critical of Hitler and the Nazis in the Irish journal *Studies*. See Binchy 1932 and 1933. Adolf Mahr left Ireland in August 1939, shortly before the outbreak of the Second World War. O'Donoghue 1998, p. 29. For a biography of Mahr, see Mullins 2007.
86 O'Driscoll 2004, pp. 277 ff.
87 See LUB Saml. von Sydow: Ó Duilearga to von Sydow, letter dated 25.6.1935.
88 For more on Ó Duilearga's trip to Germany, see Ó Dochartaigh 2004, pp. 111–112.
89 ED [FL 9]: 'IFC. Fin. Sub-Com./ Min. 7th Meeting, 10.9 1936', par. 67.

As a result of Ó Duilearga's lecture tour of Germany, in the late 1930's a number of German scholars, some of them with Nazi associations, visited the Commission. Given the attention the work of the Commission was attracting internationally at the time, it was natural enough that German folklorists and Celtic scholars coming to Ireland would make contact with it. Moreover, the Commission could hardly have shunned those whom its Director had possibly played a part in encouraging to come to Ireland in the first place. Nevertheless, the association of these German Nazi scholars with the Commission naturally enough came to the attention of the Irish intelligence service, and but for the fact that the South of Ireland remained neutral throughout the War might have resulted in official censure.[90]

Neutrality and the Second World War

The Irish Folklore Commission managed to stay in operation throughout the Second World War. Nevertheless the outbreak of the War, and its prolonged nature, in time would impinge on the work of the Commission in many ways, some of them of long-lasting consequence. In particular, it prevented it expanding its collecting activities at a crucial stage. Moreover, as the War progressed, the Commission had to cut back on its work due to its reduced grant. Isolation from the conflict in Europe, however, did allow it to pursue its collecting, albeit at a reduced rate. If the South of Ireland had been drawn into the War, either by being invaded by one of the belligerents or by allying itself with Britain, the work of the Commission would either have been further disrupted or have had to be suspended for the duration of the hostilities. The Commission's collections were packed off to the suburbs of Dublin and the west of Ireland for safekeeping, but it continued operating from its Head Office at University College Dublin. An occasional stray bomb did fall in the sea off Dublin or along the east coast, but, apart from one major incident, the city was not bombed.[91] Participation in the war effort on Britain's side would have changed all that. At any rate, recruitment or conscription would probably have depleted the ranks of the Commission's full-time collectors as most of them were young men.

In Southern Ireland most people supported the policy of neutrality, either out of principle or expediency, and the Government, although secretly pro-Allied, felt that any other policy would be too divisive, as a sizable section of the population espoused German sympathies. The majority of the population were content to live in isolation and relative tranquillity, while strict press censorship kept the public, to quite an extent, ignorant about much of what was happening in Europe and elsewhere in the world. Moreover, a certain sense of moral superiority also prevailed in many circles: i.e. that the Irish were above all this slaughter and destruction. This was, no doubt, partly induced by the idea, prevalent at the time, that Southern Ireland was a paragon among Catholic (Christian) nations.

---

90 For an incident in which the Commission's Nazi 'links' led to one of its collectors being interrogated by Irish detectives, see O'Donoghue 1998, pp. 35–36.
91 See Allen 1996, pp. 63–64 and 181.

It is consequently not surprising to find that Ó Duilearga was also relieved that Ireland was far removed from all this destruction. In his report to the Government in early summer 1940, noting with satisfaction that the war and strife going on elsewhere had not yet impinged very much on the work of the Commission, he went on to say

> It is a source of great joy to us all that the situation is so, and that the Commission succeeded in advancing its work and making available another large collection of the lore of Ireland. When the wars and struggle and dissatisfaction of this time will be over and a new life (world) flourishes in Europe that is the time when the national importance of the work that is being done by the Irish Folklore Commission under the auspices of the National Government will be understood.[92]

What sort of Europe he envisaged emerging from the conflagration that was engulfing Britain and the Continent at the time is not at all clear, and his optimism is also hard to fathom. Many in Ireland would have given Britain little chance of holding out against Germany in the summer of 1940. While some might like to give a sinister interpretation to the above, I think it best viewed as an expression of a view quite common in certain circles in Ireland at the time, namely that Ireland had a role to play 'in the rejuvenation and re-Christianisation of a post-war Europe'.[93]

Despite the cut-backs due to the War, Ó Duilearga in his report to the Government for 1942–1943 notes the haven-like nature of the country: 'It is a great source of joy to us in the island of Ireland that we can, despite the war so destructive of life that is being waged without pity or compassion all around us, continue to collect our ancestral oral tradition.' While this attitude may appear rather smug and superior, given what was happening elsewhere, it should be noted that he adds that 'the folklore now being collected and preserved by us belonged to the whole of Europe once', and he expressed the hope that making available the results of the collecting in Ireland when the War would be over would be Ireland's way of contributing to the cultural rehabilitation of Europe.[94] If Irish folklorists had been blessed by being spared the destruction that had engulfed Europe, they now had obligations towards Europe. In another memorandum he sent to the Dept. of Education he had this to say:

> I hold obstinately to the belief that we in Ireland, as a result of the war and our immunity hitherto from invasion and disruption of national life, have a duty to Europe. The world we once knew has been uprooted and disrupted as it was during the *Völkerwanderung* when the ancient ways of life and the traditions inherited from the older world were broken up

---

92 D/T S 15548A: 'Gearr-Thuar./1939–40', p. 8 (trans.). For Ó Duilearga's expression of support for the Allies, albeit in the wake of the War, see Mullins 2007, p. 190.

93 Riordan 2000, p. 103. For more on attitudes in the South of Ireland during the War, see Wills 2007.

94 D/T S 15548B: 'Gearr-Thuar./1942–43', p. 2 (trans.).

and scattered to the four winds. Here we have been left alone. We owe it to Europe to preserve by whatever means we can the traditions of Ireland, a large part of which were once the traditions of the Atlantic Kulturgebiet. Upon this pious task our Commission has been quietly engaged since 1935. For a small annual expenditure the nation (and the world of European culture) has reaped a bountiful harvest.

In the post-War period, Irish folklorists were never in a position to make 'the results of the collecting in Ireland' available to a wider European audience and in so doing attempt to contribute 'to the cultural rehabilitation of Europe.' Although Ó Duilearga was sincere in expressing such sentiments, he was given to rhetoric. How was all this to be achieved by a Commission that was hard-pressed even to keep afloat? However, as we will see below, in the post-War period, Ó Duilearga did try to encourage other countries to microfilm their folklore collections as a precautionary measure, and helped establish the international Folktale Institute in Copenhagen, which, unfortunately, did not live up to its founders' expectations, nor survive very long.

Although the Commission survived the War, restrictions and cutbacks during the War were to leave a lasting mark on it. By the end of the War, the Commission had no full-time collector in Connaught, the province with the most native Irish-speakers. It was not to have a full-time collector again in Connaught until 1951. This weighed heavily on Ó Duilearga's mind and accounts for his concentrating an undue amount of the Commission's resources in this province in the 1950's and 1960's, at the expense of other areas of the country. In the late 1940's and early 1950's two Eastern European nationals were to find a refuge in the Irish Folklore Commission, the Latvian Janis Mezs and the Hungarian Joseph Szövérffy. While initially there may have been good reasons for employing both these men, Ó Duilearga's decision to take them on was as much motivated by ideology as by practicality. In doing so he could show his solidarity with the people behind the Iron Curtain, as well as acquire the services of two individuals with a wide knowledge of languages. Szövérffy was to stay only some years with the Commission, Metz to the very end of its operations and beyond.

Partition and Northern Ireland

At the inaugural meeting of the Irish Folklore Commission in early April 1935, the Minister for Education, Tomás Ó Deirg, told those present that the work of the Commission would not be confined to the twenty six counties of the state, but to the whole island, 'in order that a complete picture of Ireland may be formed with materials gathered from the whole country.' In stating this the Minister was venturing into a very sensitive area. Although, from a scientific point of view there was nothing wrong with the Commission seeking to collect the folklore of the whole island, especially as no body in Northern Ireland at that time was engaged in similar work, given the sensitivities of Ulster Unionists, it was perhaps unwise to state it so explicitly.

Under the terms of the Anglo-Irish Treaty, the six north-eastern counties of the island were given one month to opt out from coming under the jurisdiction of the Free State Government. This they promptly did. Many nationalists in the South held out hope that the 'Boundary Commission', to be set up under the terms of the Treaty, would result in the transfer of large areas of Northern Ireland to the South, and possibly result in unification as what would be left of the northern state might prove unviable. However, these hopes came to nought. The few adjustments the Boundary Commission recommended actually favoured the North, and when this was leaked to the press in November 1925, it led to the resignation of the Irish Free State's representative on the Commission, Eoin Mac Néill, and to the Commission being disbanded.[95]

Although the Boundary Commission was disbanded, the border and partition were to remain a political issue in the South. Nationalists still hoped for unification and felt aggrieved that this division of the island had been forced on them by Britain. Moreover, Nationalists in the North of Ireland particularly felt betrayed, and many of them refused to recognise the Northern Ireland Government. Most of their elected representatives for a time even abstained from taking their seats in the Northern Ireland Parliament. However, there was little that the South could do to effect unification, except hope that time would solve the problem for it. De Valera's new Constitution of 1937 sought to give voice to Nationalist aspirations in respect of the North. Article 2 of that Constitution read: 'The national territory consists of the whole island of Ireland, its islands and territorial seas.'[96] Although Article 3 qualified the above claim to Northern Ireland somewhat, both articles caused great offence to many Northern Unionists and remained a bone of contention between North and South for more than sixty years until finally deleted from the Irish Constitution in the late 1990's.

A few days before the Southern electorate voted on de Valera's new Constitution, a scheme for collecting folklore through the agency of National School children in the Irish Free State was initiated. The Ministry of Education in Northern Ireland was asked in due course by the Dept. of Education in Dublin to initiate a similar scheme in the North's National Schools but declined to do so; perhaps not surprisingly given the South's recently declared constitutional claim over the territory of Northern Ireland. However, even if de Valera's Constitution had not contained these provocative articles, it is unlikely that official support for cooperation with the South on a cultural venture of this sort would have been forthcoming at this time. De Valera's Constitution was only putting into words what very many Irish Nationalists, North and South, believed in their hearts, and Northern Unionists were well aware of such sentiments. Many Unionists in the North since the partition of the country, and even before, had sought to distance themselves from the rest of the island, and protect themselves from the 'enemy within', namely the Catholic minority that, for the most part,

95   Garvin 1996, pp. 183–184. See also Lee 1995, pp. 140–150.
96   See Barrington 1988, p. 62.

sought unity with the South. Speaking of the cultural politics of Northern Protestants, Joseph Ruane and Jennifer Todd say:

> Protestants in Northern Ireland after partition were divided about what their culture was and what, if anything, they wanted it to become. Some saw it as a distinctive strand within the wider Irish weave. Others stressed its English or Scottish origins. Still others emphasised Ulster's regional distinctiveness and its blend of British and Irish cultures. Some took questions of cultural distinctiveness seriously; others saw such concerns as an expression of the nationalism they had been struggling against. The unionist cultural project reflected this diversity. It had three aspects – to separate Northern Ireland from the rest of the island and strengthen its relationship to Britain, to allow the different strands of Protestant culture and identity to coexist in harmony, and to contain northern Catholic cultural self-expression. The new official public culture was pluralist and inclusive in respect of Protestant differences and exclusionary with respect to the Catholic minority.

Ruane and Todd go on to say that: 'From the foundation of the state unionists defined the two parts of Ireland as different places, separate from and alien to each other. Politicians and journalists were careful to avoid statements that implied that North and South were part of a single larger entity and the unionist public was quick to criticise any such implications.'[97]

We will see below (Chapter IV/5) how in time the Irish Folklore Commission extended its activities across the border, after initially supporting the efforts of certain people in the North to get state assistance from the authorities there to collect folklore. The outbreak of the Second World War delayed official support for such collecting, but it has to be noted that when in the post-War period efforts again began to establish some sort of body that would oversee folklore collecting in the North, the Irish Folklore Commission played only a very minor role in these efforts, in sharp contrast to the role it played in the establishment of the School of Scottish Studies. The politics of partition would appear to have got in the way of cooperation, to quite an extent. But at issue was more than politics: personalities and wider ideology also played a part.

The pivotal figure in the development of folklore collecting and folklife studies in the North of Ireland was the ethnologist Emyr Estyn Evans (1905–1989). Born in Shropshire close to the border with Wales, to Welsh-speaking parents, Evans joined the staff of the Queen's University, Belfast in 1928 as a young man of twenty three. A social geographer by training, he was to devote most of his long career at Queen's to archaeology and ethnology, particularly the latter discipline.

Evans arrived in Northern Ireland in the same year Ó Duilearga set out on his tour of northern Europe (see below). In different circumstances they might have cooperated professionally and become close associates. It would appear, however, that they never were close, and in time an antipathy developed between them. The fact that Evans displayed no great interest in Irish and in Gaelic tradition in general would have been sufficient to drive a wedge between himself and Ó Duilearga. Moreover, Evans's perceived promoting of Ulster, and implicitly, of Northern Ireland, as some sort of natural age-old entity may also have cut close to the bone. As a native of the Glens of Antrim, partition had effectively cut Ó Duilearga off from his place of birth and childhood memories, and much of Evans's work and writings appeared to solidify and justify the political division of Ireland. Nevertheless, despite their differences, both men shared much in common, in particular, their belief that Ireland constituted a veritable storehouse of ancient survivals. Of course, there was a basic difference in their attitude towards survivals. For Evans there was a continuum: each new wave of settlers brought change with them but in time adapted to local ways and conditions. The result was an interesting mosaic, evidenced particularly in the landscape and material culture. Something essentially Irish survived all the change and tumult of centuries and millennia. For Ó Duilearga, on the other hand, while the presence of survivals added to the intrinsic importance of Ireland as an object of study, this was overshadowed by the tremendous sense of loss he felt at the decline of the Irish language and the rich traditions enshrined in it. If Evans felt such loss, he chose not to express it.[98] We will see below how the politics of partition and less than cordial relations between Ó Duilearga and Evans restricted cooperation between North and South in organising the collecting of folklore.

---

98   The neutrality of the South of Ireland during the War would also appear to have soured Evans' relations with the independent Irish state and its institutions. See Stout 1996, pp. 118–119.

3. Conclusion to Chapter I

If the Irish language had not been in such a precarious position in the late 1920's, it is highly unlikely that the systematic collecting of folklore would have been initiated to the extent that it was. For it was the very fact that Irish was so threatened that inspired Séamus Ó Duilearga and others to appeal for state support to save for posterity the lore of Gaelic Ireland, and for some officials to heed their appeals. In supporting the collecting of folklore the Irish state was also supporting the putting on record of far more than the oral traditions enshrined in Irish, they were also putting on record vernacular Irish itself, to be utilised in re-gaelicising the country, as well as for scholarly purposes. Ó Duilearga, although he would seem to have lost heart in the revival of Irish early on in his career, was no doubt also endeavouring to save as much of modern vernacular Irish as possible. It is impossible to understand Ó Duilearga and what motivated him without understanding the great sense of loss he felt not just at the demise of the old way of life with all its traditions, but also at the decline of the Irish language itself.

Without the Gaelic League and the cultural and political movements it unleashed, the systematic collecting of folklore might never have got under way in Ireland, and, moreover, the South of Ireland might never have gained full political independence from Britain. Not only were many of those who founded the state and who governed it for the first few decades 'children of the Gaelic League', so also were those who set about founding a society to collect Irish folklore in the mid-1920s. Tom Garvin, speaking of the Gaelic League, says:

> It could be argued that in the long run the true loser was general Irish culture and intellectual life, whether expressed in English or the Irish language; the politicization of culture effected by the League in the early years of the century was to create an official cultural ideology which was arguably hostile to much of the real culture of the community; 'Gaelic Unrealism' might be a just term for it. This official ideology was to dominate much of Irish cultural life for a generation after independence.[99]

99   Tom Garvin 1987, p. 78.

While I would agree with Garvin, to quite an extent, on the ill effects of the politicisation of the Gaelic League and some of the language policies it pursued, I think his is too narrow a view. Apart from anything else, it is unlikely that Ireland today would possess one of the great folklore archives of the world but for this 'Gaelic Unrealism'. Moreover, without the existence of the Gaelic League in the first place, would Séamus Ó Duilearga have developed an interest in the Irish language at school, and subsequently in the oral traditions enshrined in that language? It is quite likely that he would not. Moreover, although the politicisation of the Gaelic League damaged both the League and the Irish language in the long term, it is perhaps unrealistic to imagine that the League could have remained aloof from a revolution which it had a large part in inspiring. Neither did the League itself have the resources to initiate the large-scale collecting of folklore. If Southern Ireland had not achieved independence in 1922, or if instead of the Irish Free State a less Irish-Ireland-minded Home Rule government had been established by the British to administer a measure of autonomy, would the extensive collecting of folklore have begun in the 1930's? In Scotland state-funded collecting did not begin until the 1950's, and even then on a much more limited scale than that undertaken by the Irish Folklore Commission already in the 1930's and 1940's.

Nevertheless, although the official ideology Garvin is so critical of had a large part to play in the setting up of the Irish Folklore Institute and later the Irish Folklore Commission, there is no doubt that this ideology also restricted the workings of both these bodies, as we will see later in this study.

II
Saving the Folklore of Ireland

1. Laying the foundations

The Gaelic League's Oireachtas competitions

The origin of the Irish Folklore Commission is often traced to the Folklore of Ireland Society, established in January1927. However, the setting up of this Society was the culmination of numerous abortive attempts by various bodies and individuals to save the folklore of Ireland over more than a quarter of a century. The first such body was the Gaelic League. The League's annual Irish-language cultural festival, *An tOireachtas*, initiated in 1897, almost from the beginning promoted the collecting of folklore, offering prizes for the best efforts. It is probably true to say that many in the League saw folklore simply as reading matter, of little intrinsic importance in itself; an easy way of providing texts in good vernacular Irish for learners of the language pending the day when a modern literature in Irish would service that need. Others valued folklore as a source for linguistic analysis. Nonetheless, there were some in the League who placed a high value on folklore, a few for its scientific interest, but many more as an expression of Irish identity, believing that literature in Irish should be based on folklore.

Through its *Oireachtas* competitions the Gaelic League succeeded in gathering quite an amount of folklore. In late 1900 the League's Publication Committee announced:

> It is the intention of the committee to include in these annual volumes of folklore all the unpublished folklore of value that comes into its hands over the years, as it believes that the only adequate means of preserving the vast mass of oral literature still extant is to get it into print as soon as possible. In six or seven years there will be in print what will probably be the most extensive published collection of National folklore of which any country can boast. The successful carrying out of this project will mean the saving for all time of the existing body of Irish folklore, which is now threatened with extinction. Secretaries of Feiseanna and others who

have folklore in their hands are invited to forward them to the committee for publication purposes.[1]

The Gaelic League sought not only to collect and preserve oral tradition, but Irish native tradition in general. Many Irish language manuscripts, containing literary as well as oral tradition, in private possession, from the eighteenth and nineteenth centuries, and earlier, were in danger of perishing. Some had already been procured by academic bodies, but many had not, and in the wholesale abandonment of Irish after the Great Famine many manuscripts had been wilfully destroyed. Given this state of affairs, the Executive Committee (Coiste Gnótha) of the Gaelic League, on the recommendation of the bibliophile E. R McKlintock Dix, it would appear, decided at the turn of the twentieth century to establish a National Collection of Irish Manuscripts.[2] This project, which does not seem to have really got off the ground, appears not to have envisaged promoting collecting oral traditions as such, but it had the potential to become a national depository of oral as well as literary tradition.[3]

Some ten years later, certain people attached to the Folklore Society of London, established the Irish Folklore Association with a view to collecting the folklore of Ireland. One of the people involved, the versatile scholar and folklorist Eleanor Hull, wrote to a number of learned journals to advertise the project: 'There is at the moment an urgent necessity for bestirring ourselves to preserve from complete extinction what still remains of the folk-lore of Ireland, the last lingering tradition of an ancient form of thought, much of which is already lost beyond recovery, and of which every year is lessening the amount that still remains to us.' It was proposed 'during the next three or four years, to make a simultaneous effort over the whole country, by an organised body of collectors, to collect and record whatever may be of interest in the beliefs and old customs, stories, and legends, proverbs and charms, &c., in their own part of the country.' It was envisaged that the association would avail of the free services of collectors, although in was hoped to finance sending 'special Irish-speaking collectors into some of these isolated places, which are likely to contain the richest deposits of folk-material', to be financed by subscriptions and donations of collectors and others. Eleanor Hull informed her readers that already 'about forty collectors' in various parts of the country had 'promised to assist' them.[4]

---

1   O'Leary 1994, pp. 94–95. Shortly after the founding of the Folklore of Ireland Society, its Committee requested the Gaelic League to donate the folklore material derived from the *Oireachtas* competitions to the Society. However, the League instead decided to donate these manuscripts to the National Library of Ireland. See NLI Ms. 9774. Minutes of Coiste Gnótha (Executive Committee), meetings held on 8.2.1927 and 17.5.1927. Copies of the material accumulated by means of these competitions were later deposited in the Irish Folklore Commission and bound with the Main Collection.

2   See NLI: MacNeill Papers, 10, 880: two letters from Dix to Mac Néill, one undated, the other dated December 1900.

3   For more on this proposal, see UCDA Eoin MacNeill Papers LAI/F/3: 'A National Manuscript Collection'. See also Briody 2006, pp. 1–2.

4   Hull 1911b, pp. 188–190.

Despite such promises of assistance, this association was short-lived and produced few results. The fact that no one person could be found to devote all their time and energy to this project probably played a part in its demise. Indeed it is arguable whether the Irish Folklore Association ever really got off the ground, nor existed in anything but name. At any rate, during its first year or so of operation, its committee never convened.[5] Georges Denis Zimmerman also suggests that the time was not propitious for such an association, as Ireland from 1913 onwards 'entered a period of turmoil' involving revived Home-Rule agitation, Ulster Protestant reaction, the growth of rival paramilitary formations...' Not only, he suggests, would it soon be difficult to 'ramble and ask questions in out-of-the way places' he notes that 'at a certain stage it might become dangerous' to do so.[6] However, the Irish Folklore Association may well have been effectively moribund by 1913. The fate of the Society of Irish Tradition is further evidence that preoccupation with political events distracted people's attention from cultural pursuits. Established in 1917, this Society, whose aim was not the collection of folklore as such but rather 'to make national tradition a source of fellowship for all the people of Ireland and a base for the regeneration of Irish society', ceased to function after less than two years as a result, it would appear, of the disturbed state of the country from 1919 onwards.[7]

The establishment of a native Government in 1922, committed to the restoration of the Irish language and to fostering Ireland's Gaelic inheritance, was eventually to lead to state-supported efforts to collect folklore. For a number of reasons, however, this was not to happen in the short term. The rebuilding of much of the infrastructure of the state after the destruction of the Civil War meant that money was in short supply for cultural pursuits in the first decade or so of independence. While the new native Government sought to foster Ireland's cultural inheritance, particularly its Gaelic inheritance, folklore had to compete with Irish literary tradition, and may have been seen in some circles as somewhat of a poor relation. It is significant that the remit of a Committee of Seanad Éireann set up in April 1923 'to submit to the Government a scheme for the editing, indexing, and publishing of manuscripts in the Irish language, now lying in the Royal Irish Academy, Trinity College, and elsewhere; for the scientific investigation of the living dialects; for the compiling and publishing of an adequate dictionary of the older language' did not include folklore as such, although the Committee's report, published the following year, does give some recognition to the richness of Ireland's oral tradition.[8]

---

5   Ó Catháin 1991, p. 61, quoting from Ó Duilearga's papers, has the latter give the credit for this initiative to the Norwegian Celtic scholar Carl Marstrander. However, Marstrander himself recalls that the suggestion originally came from Eleanor Hull (Marstrander 1912, p. 373.) Pádraigín Riggs suggests that there may have existed a degree of apathy between Ó Duilearga and Hull (Riggs 2005, pp. 17–18 and 37, n. 44). This might explain Ó Duilearga's failure to give credit to Hull for her role in this abortive venture.

6   Zimmerman 2001, p. 385.

7   It has to be noted that in 1919 the radical priest Fr. Michael O'Flannagan, proposed 'a nationwide competition for the collection of local folklore', but this would also appear to have produced few results. Carroll 1993, p. 107.

8   *Seanad Éireann. Tuarasgabháil Dheiridh.*, pp. 1–2.

Around the same time as this Committee of Seanad Éireann began its work, the Schools Inspector and folklore collector Énrí Ó Muirgheasa recommended to that Dept. of Education 'that a special blank manuscript book be furnished to each [primary] school in the Saor Stát [Irish Free State], so that each teacher might collect and record therein the traditions and folk-lore of the neighbourhood'. He also prepared a short memorandum to be pasted 'as a printed preface in the book, for the teacher's help and guidance.' Ó Muirgheasa proposed that the scheme should be voluntary: '... the presence of the book in the school would be a reminder to the teacher of the great national work in which he could assist and partake; that the facility afforded by the blank book and the helpful suggestions might tempt him to do what he could in his own area.' Although this project could have been implemented without a great deal of expense, the Dept. of Education 'busied at the time with its many other new projects, took no action on the matter'. Ó Muirgheasa's memorandum containing instructions to teachers was, however, considered by the National Programme Conference of the Irish National Teachers Organisation in 1926 and was 'referred to approvingly' in its Report.[9]

By 1924 the two members of Government who had most interest in the rich folklore inheritance of Ireland, Richard Mulcahy and Eoin Mac Néill, had resigned from the cabinet. Mulcahy had to resign as Minister for Defence in 1924 due to the Army Mutiny crisis and the following year saw the departure of Eoin Mac Néill, Minister for Education, from the Government due to the Boundary Commission fiasco (see above). Mulcahy remained on in the Cabinet but without portfolio, Mac Néill returned to his post in UCD. Mac Néill's successor in Education, John Marcus O'Sullivan had little interest in folklore, and was lukewarm on the question of restoring Irish. With their departure, there was little hope of getting state support for folklore collecting in the short term. As Government support for the collecting of folklore was unlikely to be forthcoming, those with an active interest in preserving the folklore of Ireland had no option but to seek to gain public support for such a venture.

The Founding of the Folklore of Ireland Society

In 1925, Séamus Ó Duilearga, then a young assistant in University College Dublin, along with the Gaelic League veteran Fionán Mac Coluim tried to set up a society for Irish Folklore but with no success. Not losing hope, in January 1926, Ó Duilearga wrote to Reidar Th. Christiansen, whom he had met some years earlier, seeking advice about founding such a society. Towards the end of that year a meeting took place in Dublin, attended by sixteen people, at which it was decided to set up a society for the collecting, investigation, and publication of Irish folklore. On January 11th, 1927 this society was formally launched, to be known as An Cumann le Béaloideas

---

9   UCD Lib. Spec. Col. Morris 10.6.3: 'National Tradition'. On Ó Muirgheasa's scheme , see also Briody 2006, pp. 2 ff.

Éireann/The Folklore of Ireland Society. The meeting was chaired by Douglas Hyde and those present represented a wide spectrum of political opinion. The purpose of this society was 'to collect, to examine, to publish, and make available the folklore of Ireland.' It was also decided to publish a journal at least twice a year, which members would receive free of charge. The meeting elected officers and a committee. Among the officers elected were Pádraig Ó Siochfhradha (better-known under his pseudonym, 'An Seabhac', meaning 'The Hawk') as President of the society; Douglas Hyde as Treasurer; Fionán Mac Coluim as Assistant Treasurer; and a young man of 28, Séamus Ó Duilearga, as Editor and Librarian.[10]

Many of the founding members of the Society were active in the movement to revive the Irish language, as indeed were most of the officers and members of its committee. Given the bitter legacy of the Civil War, and the fact that many of those who founded and supported this new society had taken opposite sides during that conflict, the setting up of this society was a great achievement in itself. In time, however, a conflict of interest would arise between those whose main interest in collecting folklore was the belief that such collections could help in the efforts to revive the Irish language, and those whose primary interest in collecting folklore was scholarly. However, although it would be some time before such differences would become apparent, the seeds of contention were there from the beginning. Various people at the first annual general meeting of the Society expressed high hopes for the work it was undertaking, and indicated how they believed folklore could help in the revival of Irish. It would appear this was to be achieved, for the most part, by means of education and publication. Fionán Mac Coluim is reported as saying that:

> ...education was based on national folklore in every country where matters were as they should be. That keeps people safe and virtuous so that they will be faithful to their own country and race ('cine'). For Irish culture to grow naturally, the folklore of the Gael should prevail in this country.

Séamus Ó Fiannachta, who was a Schools Inspector with many years experience, expressed a very similar view to Fionán Mac Coluim, stating that educational experts are agreed that 'the ancestral knowledge in the possession of the ordinary people' should be utilised in teaching. He also felt that folklore could apart from its intrinsic value as 'ancestral knowledge' give further incentive to pupils to learn Irish, as the Irish then being taught in the schools was 'dry and without life'. The schools, he said, 'were trying to light a fire without using the live embers'. Pádraig Ó Siochfhradha said that 'if people are serious about the regaelicisation of Ireland' they should 'collect everything characteristic of the Irish (Gaelic) mind – and our old

---

10   Ó Muimhneacháin 1977–79, pp. 1–2 (trans.) and *Irish Independent* 12.1.1927, p. 8 (trans.). The day after the public launching of the Folklore of Ireland Society, an article by Reidar Christiansen entitled 'A Plea for Popular Tradition' appeared in *The Irish Statesman*, January 8, 1927, pp. 433–434. A follow-up article by the same author, entitled 'Irish Popular Tradition', appeared in *The Irish Statesman*, April 23, 1927, pp. 162–164.

folklore is part of that'. The folklore of Ireland should not only be collected, but also disseminated: 'We will not be Irish [i.e. Gaelic] again until the best of that is in common possession among the people – as a foundation for culture and as colouring and an echo in our literature and in those matters that demonstrate and make one person a Spaniard and another a Russian.' However, although he saw nationality as the main reason why people in Ireland should be interested in folklore, he also recognised its importance 'for the purpose of making scientific comparison with the folklore of other peoples, to demonstrate the historical growth of humanity, to measure the development and decline of old religions, etc.'[11]

The Folklore of Ireland Society depended on members' subscriptions to finance collecting and publish its journal, *Béaloideas*, twice annually. Much of its collecting, however, was undertaken on a voluntary basis. Its economic situation was somewhat alleviated by Pádraig Mac Mághnuis, an Irishman living in Argentina, who offered to clear any debts incurred in the Society's first year of operation. When no such debts were incurred, he donated £150 to the Society and got others of the Irish community in Argentina to contribute also.[12] Despite Mac Mághnuis's generosity, however, the Society needed all the financial help it could get. Pádraig Ó Siochfhradha at its first annual general meeting in January 1928 informed those present that hundreds of collectors were needed and that to defray the cost of publishing the material collected would require access to substantial funds. In order to publish six hundred pages of folklore annually they would need the subscriptions of between 800 and 1,000 members.[13]

The fate of the short-lived Irish Folklore Association or Society of Irish Tradition was not to be that of the Folklore of Ireland Society. Almost eighty years on it is still in existence. Established in the wake of Civil War, the circumstances of its birth were only slightly more favourable than those of the other two above-mentioned bodies, but unlike them it numbered among its members and on its executive committee a talented, dynamic young man, Séamus Ó Duilearga (the Society's Editor and Librarian), who was determined that the Folklore of Ireland Society would not be another ephemeral organisation. This is not to downplay the importance of other active members of the Society such as Fionán Mac Coluim and Pádraig Ó Siochfradha. Both these men, and others, might have kept the Society going for many years, but it is unlikely that the Society would have spawned offshoots such as the Irish Folklore Institute and the Irish Folklore Commission without the drive, determination, and vision of Séamus Ó Duilearga, nor would it have assembled on its own such an extensive archive of folk tradition. Before looking at the circumstances in which these two bodies were created it is first necessary to look at the early career of this remarkable man.

11   *Irish Independent* 13.1. 1928, p. 5 (trans.).
12   See Mac Mághnuis's obituary in *Béaloideas* 2 (1929), p 112. It would also appear that he supplied the Society with notebooks for its collectors. See *Irish Independent* 12.1.1927, p. 8.
13   *Irish Independent* 13.1.1928, p. 5.

2. Séamus Ó Duilearga's vision and mission

The Road from the Glens

From the mid 1920's to his retirement in the early 1970's, Séamus Ó Duilearga was by any estimation the central figure in Irish folkloristics, exercising an indirect influence on the way folkloristics developed even in his retirement, and one could argue from beyond the grave, after his death in 1980. Whatever about his posthumous influence, Ó Duilearga's contribution while he lived is crucial to any study of Irish folklore collecting and the development of Irish folkloristics in the twentieth century.

Ó Duilearga was born on May 26th, 1899 in Cushendall, Co. Antrim, on the northeast coast of Ireland. He was christened James Hamilton Delargy, Hamilton being his paternal grandmother's surname. As a child he was known in family circles as Hamilton in preference to James, but as an adult he seems to have preferred to be called Séamus, the Irish form of James. Throughout his long career he signed himself both Séamus Ó Duilearga and James Hamilton Delargy. As he would appear to have used the former far more frequently than the latter, I have chosen to use (Séamus) Ó Duilearga throughout in this study. However, it should be remembered that for thousands of people throughout Ireland, be they Irish or English speakers, he was simply 'Delargy', the only bearer of that name most of them ever met or heard of, as it is a rare surname in Ireland.

Ó Duilearga's mother was Mary McQuillan, his father James Delargy. The Delargys had a long tradition of going to sea, but James Delargy had given up the sea by the time his first son was born and was the owner of a small hotel in Cushendall on the Antrim coast.[14] He died when Séamus Ó Duilearga was only two, leaving his wife a widow with two young sons, James and his infant brother Jack. Mary Delargy tried to run the family hotel 'but it did not prosper'. For a time she went to live with her two sons a few miles down the coast at Glenariffe. It was in Glenariffe that the young James was to hear his first folktale, from a part-time barber who came to cut his hair. In order to stop the terrified child from howling, the barber promised to

---

14   Breathnach and Ní Mhurchú 1997 (*Beathaisnéis a Cúig*), p. 163.

tell him a story while cutting his hair. On each subsequent visit, the barber would tell a story to the child.[15]

In 1907, Mrs Delargy left Co. Antrim with her two boys. She herself went to work in England, where she had been brought up, as a hotel manageress, while her two sons were sent south to a convent boarding school in Kilcool, Co. Wicklow. This uprooting must have been quite traumatic for Ó Duilearga and his brother, especially as Máire MacNeill says '[f]rom that time until he and his brother were able to earn they had no home of their own.' However, both brothers managed to retain links with the Glens of Antrim, as they would spend every summer with their widowed aunt, their father's sister, in Cushendall. She lived for the rest of the year in Belfast, and they used also stay with her there while on vacation.[16] Ó Duilearga's brother Jack was in time to go to sea, keeping up the Delargy's sea-faring tradition. It would appear that the older boy took after his maternal grandmother's family, the Hamiltons. Later in life Ó Duilearga used to maintain that it was from the Hamiltons, who were agents on the Turnley Estate, that he 'got his urge to save documents' as 'they never destroyed a letter or a piece of paper.'[17] Of course, there was nothing inevitable about all this. Instead of becoming a great folklore collector, he might have made a name for himself in some other profession, or even lived out his life in obscurity.

Interest kindled in the Irish language

Ó Duilearga's paternal grandfather, a sea captain, was a native speaker of Irish, as was his paternal grandmother. Irish had been the dominant language in the parish of Layd, Ó Duilearga's native parish, in the 1830's when the Ordnance Survey workers were mapping and investigating the area, but within two generations it had almost disappeared.[18] By the time Ó Duilearga began showing an interest in Irish only vestiges of it remained. On his trips back to the Glens he was in the habit of fishing with an old man named James MacAuley, a native speaker of Irish. It was from him that he heard his first folktales in Irish and at the age of fifteen or so he wrote them down.[19]

After primary school in Kilcool, Ó Duilearga was sent to Castleknock College, Co. Dublin, also a boarding school, where he remained from September 1911 to June 1916, matriculating in the National University of Ireland in 1916. At Castleknock his teacher of Irish was Proinnsias Ó Fathaigh, who was a member of the Irish Volunteers, was to be imprisoned for his part in the 1916 Rising, and was later to be active in nationalist

---

15 Whitaker 1981–82, pp. 101–102.
16 Whitaker 1981–82, pp.101–102, and RTÉSA BB2453, 'Lest They Perish' (1985). For a slightly fuller version of Whitaker's above article, see Whitaker 1982, pp. 23–30.
17 Whitaker 1981–82, p.102 and RTÉSA BB2453 (1985).
18 See J. McCann 1981, p. 62.
19 RTÉSA A5382, 'Here and Now' (1971). However, the copybook containing this story bears the date '1920', leaving Ó Duilearga 20/21 at the time. See Whitaker 1981–82.

politics.[20] Ó Fathaigh encouraged the young Ó Duilearga's interest in Irish and may well have instilled in him a love of the language as well. He also made available to him a large press full of Irish books in the College, so that Ó Duilearga had read most of modern Irish printed literature by the time he left secondary school.[21]

Ó Duilearga's first visit to an Irish-speaking district as such was also at the age of sixteen, when he attended an Irish language summer school on Rathlin Island, off the north coast of Co. Antrim. He returned to Rathlin again the following year, and on a number of subsequent occasions between 1916 and 1920. Already as a young student on Rathlin, Ó Duilearga was noting down 'differences of pronunciation, grammar and idiom'. The Irish spoken on Rathlin was more like a dialect of Scottish Gaelic than mainstream Irish dialects, and it is no surprise that Ó Duilearga while still a young man of twenty paid his first visit to the Hebrides (1919). He again returned to the Hebrides in 1922.[22]

While Proinnsias Ó Fathaigh played an important role in directing Ó Duilearga towards Irish, it was Eoin Mac Néill, one of the leading cultural figures in the country at the time, who put him on the path of scholarship. An aunt of Ó Duilearga's was a distant relative of Mac Néill's. As a young boy she brought him to visit the Mac Néill family in Dublin. He became a frequent visitor to the household, himself and his brother staying with them 'on their way from school ... back home to Belfast or the North'. Ó Duilearga, who had a 'studious disposition', even as a young boy would go into Mac Néill's study and chat with him.[23] Mac Néill, no doubt, recognised Ó Duilearga's scholarly inclinations. Not only at a very young age did Ó Duilearga rub shoulders with scholarly Ireland, he also encountered 'revolutionary' Ireland, for Mac Néill the scholar was also Chief of Staff of the Irish Volunteers, a nationalist militia opposed to Irish participation in the First World War and pledged to defend Ireland's right to Home Rule, by force of arms if necessary. In 1915, when Ó Duilearga was around sixteen years of age, Mac Néill got permission for him to read in the library of the Royal Irish Academy.[24] That was the last occasion for quite some time to come that Mac Néill could have interceded with the Academy authorities on his behalf, for the following year he was disgraced in their eyes by his association with the 1916 rebellion and expelled from the Academy.[25]

---

20 See Breathnach and Ní Mhurchú (*Beathaisnéis a Ceathair*), pp. 115–116.
21 RTÉSA BB2453 (1985), T.K. Whitaker on Ó Duilearga. Although Ó Duilearga told Whitaker that Ó Fathaigh initiated him to Irish, elsewhere Ó Duilearga implies that but for Eoin Mac Néill's encouragement he might not have developed this interest. Ó Duilearga 1959, p. 16.
22 Whitaker 1981–82, pp. 102.103.
23 RTÉSA BB2453 (1985), Máire MacNeill on Ó Duilearga.
24 Ó Duilearga 1959, p. 16.
25 Although unaware that a rebellion was being planned, Mac Néill as head of the Irish Volunteers was sentenced, in the wake of the 1916 Rising, to penal servitude for life, and temporarily lost his chair in UCD. He was, however, released in June of the following year and was officially reinstated to his university post in May 1918. For more on the fate of Mac Néill's Chair of Early Irish History while he was in captivity and subsequent to his release, see Martin and Byrne (eds) 1973, pp. 387–390.

In the reading room of the Royal Irish Academy, Ó Duilearga met Mac Néill's old teacher of literary Irish, the scholar Edmond Hogan, who had himself been taught the literary language by none other than Eugene O'Curry, one of the greatest authorities on Irish in the nineteenth century, and one of the last native links with Medieval Irish scholarship and scribal tradition. Later in life Ó Duilearga would be proud of this scholarly pedigree: O'Curry, Hogan, Mac Néill, Ó Duilearga.[26]

University: studies and tribulations

Ó Duilearga began his university studies at University College Dublin (UCD) in 1917 as a novice with the Vincentian Fathers, Blackrock, Co. Dublin, studying Latin and Irish in his first year. However, he soon realised that he did not have a vocation for the priesthood and left the Vincentians, but continued his studies at UCD. In his second year at university his health broke down. For a time, for financial as well as health reasons, he considered abandoning his university studies, but due to 'the discreet intervention of the formidable but shy Professor of Old Irish, Osborn Bergin, he was enabled to stay on.' He eventually resumed his studies and would appear to have put this disruption to good use. He spent '[t]he greater part of 1918-1919 ... in various parts of the Gaelic-speaking districts of Ireland and Scotland, where [he] studied Irish and Scottish Gaelic.' On his return to UCD in October 1919 he enrolled for 'a course of study in the Faculty of Celtic Studies', and received his BA degree in 1921,'obtaining first place in [his] group and First Class Honours, together with a Post-Graduate Scholarship.' He continued studying for an MA degree, which he was awarded, with First Class Honours, in 1923.[27]

There is no doubt that the major influence on Ó Duilearga at university was Osborn Bergin, the giant of Irish language scholarship, who although Professor of Early Irish, had a deep knowledge of all periods of the language.[28] Bergin, although a formative influence on Ó Duilearga, may also have had a negative effect on him, as it seems he also had on other pupils of his: namely that he instilled in them an abhorrence of ever putting in print anything that might possibly be proved wrong. Some, at any rate, have attributed Ó Duilearga's somewhat meagre scholarly production to Bergin's negative influence.

While studying for his MA in Celtic Studies, Ó Duilearga applied for one of the travelling studentships offered by the National University of Ireland

---

26 Ó Duilearga 1959, p. 16.
27 Information from following sources: *Óráidí ar Oscailt.* p. 5; Whitaker 1981–82, pp. 103–104; and UCDA Tierney Papers LA30/98 (2): 'Lectureship in Irish Folklore. Application, and Testimonials of James Hamilton Delargy'. Ó Duilearga told Breandán Ó Madagáin in the early 1970's that Bergin actually paid his university fees so he could continue his studies. Conversation with Breandán Ó Madagáin, November 2004.
28 See McCartney 1999, pp. 68–69. For more on Bergin's life and work, see Binchy 1970. See also Ua Súilleabháin 1997.

and was greatly disappointed when he failed to obtain one. His expectations were probably high as he had come first in his class for the BA Degree. The fact that a fellow student and friend of his, Myles Dillon was awarded a travelling studentship would appear to have greatly agitated him. Myles Dillon left for the Continent in October 1922 to spend three years in Germany (at Berlin, Bonn, and Heidelberg) and another two at the Sorbonne in Paris. He did not return to Ireland until 1927. Dillon's sojourn abroad afforded him an opportunity to deepen his knowledge of Celtic Studies and linguistics, and laid the foundation for a distinguished academic career.[29]

The academic fate of the young Ó Duilearga featured in a rather bizarre incident at the height of the Irish Civil War. It would appear that Myles Dillon felt sorry at his friend's disappointment at not being awarded a travelling scholarship, and through the agency of his father tried to get him awarded what was to be known in time as the Mansion House Scholarship. This scholarship took its name from the Mansion House Conference against conscription to the British Army in 1918. A number of trustees were appointed to decide what should be done with a sum in excess of two thousand pounds left over after the successful conclusion of the campaign against conscription. The trustees were John Dillon, Myles's father and the former leader of the Irish Parliamentary Party at Westminister, Éamon de Valera, and the Lord Mayor of Dublin. By late 1922 it was still undecided what to do with the money, but one proposal was to fund a scholarship. John Dillon seems to have been very much in favour of the scholarship idea, and for granting the first scholarship to Séamus Ó Duilearga, but by late October 1922 de Valera had not yet agreed to the disposal of the money in this manner.[30] He had, of course, other matters on his mind, and was strictly speaking on the run from the Free State army.

Assistantship to Douglas Hyde

While de Valera vacillated about what to do with these funds, Ó Duilearga was offered temporary employment in his own College, which he accepted. If he had been awarded the first Mansion House Scholarship at this juncture he might well have gone to study Celtic Studies in Germany. However, de Valera's and Ó Duilearga's paths were to cross again, as we will see below, and this was not the last time the former would hold the latter's fate in his hands. It would appear that on the initiative of Douglas Hyde, Professor of Modern Irish, Ó Duilearga was employed as a temporary assistant in the Dept. of Modern Irish, commencing in January 1923.[31] In November of that year the Academic Council of UCD recommended that his temporary assistantship

---

29 Ó Duilearga, it would appear, believed he was unjustly treated in not being awarded a travelling studentship. When I visited him in the winter of 1978/79 he suggested that Myles Dillon was awarded a travelling studentship on the strength of his father's connections. John Dillon was also on the Governing Body of UCD at the time.

30 Fischer and Dillon 1999, p. 24.

31 Fischer & Dillon 1999, p. 57.

become a regular assistantship, but the College's finances were not sufficient to implement this proposal at this juncture. It was to be spring 1925 before his assistantship was regularised and his salary raised from £150 to £300 per annum.[32] Although not a permanent appointment, being regularised did give him greater security as well as a substantially higher salary. It also allowed him to concentrate more on what, in time, was to become his life's mission, namely the collecting of Irish folklore. He was to remain an assistant in the Department of Modern Irish until 1934.[33]

In order to supplement his university salary during the late 1920's, Ó Duilearga assisted Kathleen Mulchrone in cataloguing Irish-language manuscripts in the possession of the Royal Irish Academy.[34] Then, in 1928 an edition by Ó Duilearga of an early modern adaptation of a middle Irish tale, 'Tóruigheacht Duibhe Lacha Láimh-ghile' ('The Pursuit of Bright-Handed Dubh Lacha'), from a manuscript in the possession of Douglas Hyde, was published. As well as editing the tale, Hyde tells us in an introductory note that Ó Duilearga assembled a great deal of background information from Irish literary sources about the characters in the tale, and that he intended later writing an article based on his researches.[35] He was never to do so, at least he was never to publish anything of this nature, nor was he to edit any other early modern Irish romance. As this edition of 'Tóruigheacht Duibhe Lacha Láimh-ghile' appeared in one of the most prestigious journals devoted to Celtic Studies, a volume moreover dedicated to the most eminent scholar of Old Irish, Rudolf Thurneysen, on his seventieth birthday, the young Séamus Ó Duilearga was afforded a chance to present his work alongside many of the great Celtic scholars of his day. However well trained he was by Bergin, and to a lesser extent by Hyde, for work of this kind, his scholarly pursuits were to lead him in another direction, away from dusty manuscripts to the open field. To what extent Hyde influenced him in his decision to specialise in folklore is difficult to say. Hyde was not only Professor of Modern Irish, he was also a collector of folklore. But he was more of a fatherly figure than an inspiring teacher. Nevertheless, as a folklorist, he would have had a lot of solid advice to offer the young Ó Duilearga.

Apprenticeship as collector/Seán Ó Conaill

During visits to the Glens of Antrim between 1920 and 1926 Ó Duilearga noted down a great deal of folklore as well as much linguistic data from the last native speakers in the area. Already in these notebooks he was developing

---

32 UCDA: Min. of Gov. Body Vol. 7, meeting of 6.11.1923 and Vol. 8, meeting of 31.3.1925.
33 In 1927, Myles Dillon, after his return from the Continent, joined him as a second assistant on the staff of UCD's Department of Modern Irish. UCDA: Min. of Acad. Coun. Book II, meeting of 9. 5. 1927.
34 Published as 'Fasciculus V' of the Academy's *Catalogue of Irish Manuscripts* (Royal Irish Academy; Dublin 1930).
35 *Zeitschrift für celtische Philologie* 17 (1928), pp. 347–370.

an orthography that would allow him to render dialect as faithfully as possible without resorting to phonetic script.[36] Although Ó Duilearga had collected a certain amount of folklore material from his mid-teens, and this interest had persisted into his early manhood, there was no certainty that he would develop an academic interest in folklore, or devote his life to collecting folklore. In fact, if he had been awarded the travelling scholarship he sought, he might, like Myles Dillon, have become a scholar of Old Irish, or of some earlier period of the language and literature. In this respect, it is interesting to note that in late 1919 or early 1920, Ó Duilearga, along with J.J. O'Neill (possibly a fellow-student), proposed establishing a society to be known as 'The Manuscript and Record Society of Ireland'. The aims of this society were (a) to 'promote the study and, where necessary, assist in the preservation of MSS, and Records chiefly of the Eighteenth Century', (b) to 'register collections of MSS. of Literary, Linguistic and Historical importance, which are in private possession', and (c) to 'edit and publish, as occasion arises, the researches of the members.'[37] Both Ó Duilearga and O'Neill were to be the joint honorary secretaries of this proposed society. It appears nothing came of this proposal, but given Ó Duilearga's later career, the absence of any mention of folklore records is remarkable.

In 1923, however, Ó Duilearga decided to emulate his mentor, Osborn Bergin, and visit southwest Munster to perfect his knowledge of vernacular Irish. Bergin, a generation earlier, had learned modern Irish on the Beara Peninsula in southwest Cork. Irish had weakened in Beara in the intervening years, and possibly for this reason, he directed his young protégé to the Ballinskelligs area of southwest Kerry, lying to the north of the Beara Peninsula. It was here that Ó Duilearga was to meet the storyteller who would change the direction of his life and inspire him to collect the folklore of Ireland.

Close to Ballinskelligs, where Ó Duilearga found lodgings, was the small mountain hamlet of Cill Rialaigh. He had heard from an acquaintance before leaving Dublin of a certain Seán Ó Conaill who lived in this hamlet, a monoglot Irish-speaker, and gifted storyteller. The tradition of telling long folktales had died out in the region some twenty years before Ó Duilearga's first visit, but Ó Conaill could still recall many of his stories. Initially Ó Duilearga did not write down these stories. He listened and made notes, and moreover concentrated on getting to know Ó Conaill and learning his rich dialect. While staying in Ballinskelligs he would visit this old storyteller a few nights a week, returning to the area to work with Ó Conaill as often as his university duties allowed him. In this way a deep friendship developed over time between collector and storyteller. It was not until August 1925 that he began systematically writing down Ó Conaill's repertoire of stories. As he did not have access to any sort of recording apparatus at this time, he was forced to take these tales down from dictation. The narrator, however, was very patient, and this was a help in the painstaking job of transcription.[38]

36 Watson 1984, pp. 74, and 78–80.
37 *The Irish Book Lover* 11 (1920), p 81.
38 In 1948, Ó Duilearga published the entire corpus of tales, as well as miscellaneous lore

Ó Duilearga's making the acquaintance of Seán Ó Conaill was crucial for his later career, and for the history of Irish folklore collecting. Ó Duilearga was wont to quote the Irish proverb: 'B'fhearr seachtain sa Phriaireacht ná bliain ar scoil' ('A week in the parish of Prior [the parish of Ballinskelligs] is better than a year at school'). For him Ballinskelligs was more than a school, it was a university. In his farewell speech at the opening of the Department of Irish Folklore in autumn 1971, some half a year or so before his retirement, he thanks his teachers in the Faculty of Celtic Studies at UCD, Osborn Bergin, J Lloyd Jones, Eoin Mac Néill and R.A.S. Macalister, and says that he went from there 'to another university–a thatched house on the edge of the world in Kerry where I did post-graduate work with an unlettered but inspiring Professor of Irish, Seán Ó Conaill'. It was in Seán Ó Conaill's house in Cill Rialaigh he says that he 'found the inspiration to help in some measure to save from oblivion the tradition of my people.'[39] Of course, he would not have been able to realise his vision without the help of many at home and abroad. Moreover, if he had not met with as skilled a storyteller as Seán Ó Conaill in Ballinskelligs in 1923, he might never have set out on the road he chose to follow, nor have set for himself such a daunting task. The meeting of these two men was crucial, for it inspired Ó Duilearga to seek to save not just the lore of one individual, but that of 'a whole people'. His meeting with Carl Wilhelm von Sydow in 1927 and his trip to northern Europe the following year were to shape his vision of how best to realise this goal.

Meeting with Carl Wilhelm von Sydow

On June 28th and July 1st, 1927, to coincide with the launching of the Folklore of Ireland Society's journal, *Béaloideas*, Reidar Th. Christiansen gave two public lectures in University College Dublin on 'The Value of Folklore' and 'Irish Folklore', in which he highlighted the importance of the work undertaken by the Society.[40] Christiansen had first met Ó Duilearga in spring 1921 by chance in a Dublin bookshop, and, as we have seen above, had advised the latter about how best to go about establishing a folklore society.[41] At one of Christiansen's lectures, Ó Duilearga was introduced to somebody who was to be instrumental in helping him later to arrange for the extensive collecting of folklore in Ireland, and who was to encourage and aid his study of the science of folklore, namely Carl Wilhelm von Sydow of the University of Lund. It was a chance meeting. More than forty years later Ó Duilearga describes meeting von Sydow for the first time, and how 'Wilhelm von Sydow walked across the path of [his] life'. He had returned from Kerry

and songs, that he collected from Ó Conaill, amounting to almost 400 pages of text, Ó Duilearga 1977 [1948]. In 1981, subsequent to his death, Máire Mac Neill's translation of this work appeared, Ó Duilearga 1981b.

39   *Óráidí ag Oscailt.*, pp. 5-6.
40   *Béaloideas* 1(2) (1927), p. 206. Copies of Christiansen's two lectures are to be found in UCDNFC 1122, pp. 5–77.
41   *Béaloideas* 37–38 (1969–1970), pp. 345–346.

to hear the second of Christiansen's lectures on 'Irish oral tradition', which was attended by 'at least four hundred people'. He says that coming out of the lecture theatre Pádraig Ó Siochfhradha, President of the Folklore of Ireland Society:

> Introduced me to this enormous man, who found difficulty in getting out of the door of ... the Physics Theatre, and his name was Wilhelm von Sydow. He had come here on his honeymoon. And he introduced me to him and I asked him and his wife, as I've asked so many more people like him all over the world over the years to come to visit me at my home. My mother was alive at the time, and we entertained them to tea.[42]

Von Sydow had studied Irish under Carl Marstrander in Oslo and had visited Ireland in 1920 and again in 1924 in order to perfect his knowledge of Irish.[43] In February 1927, Pádraig Ó Siochfhradha, who had met von Sydow some seven years earlier in Ireland, wrote to him about recent folklore developments in Ireland, namely the re-issuing of the monthly newspaper *An Lóchrann*, devoted to publishing folklore, a year or so earlier, as well as the founding of the Folklore of Ireland Society the previous month.[44] It is not clear if Ó Siochfhradha's letter as such influenced von Sydow's decision to come to Ireland, as it was probably only a question of time before he would again visit Ireland, but he at least helped finance his trip and perhaps lengthened its duration. Ostensibly, von Sydow came to Ireland in the summer of 1927 on his honeymoon (he had recently remarried after being widowed in middle-age). It was, however, to be a working honeymoon, as Ó Siochfhradha arranged for him to lecture to various groups of teachers attending Irish language courses during the month of August on the importance of folklore for such matters as 'nationality' and 'history'.[45]

Von Sydow's chance meeting with Ó Duilearga, which might not have happened at this juncture at any rate, was to change the course of Ó Duilearga's life, and indeed von Sydow's life. If Ó Duilearga 'was a helper looking for a master', as Irish folktales phrase it, von Sydow was 'a master looking for a helper'. Both men were to assist each other in many ways and became lifelong friends. Forty years later Ó Duilearga recalls that von Sydow explained to him why he considered a knowledge of Irish 'necessary in connection with his work as a lecturer in the University of Lund':

> Because in the Irish language and in the oral literature associated with it, in the old sagas as well as in the folktales of today, there lay he thought a

---

42 RTÉSA 233/69: Séamus Ó Duilearga on Wilhelm von Sydow, 23.12.1968.
43 Bo Almqvist 2002, pp. 8 ff.
44 LUB Saml. von Sydow: Ó Siochfhradha to von Sydow, 4.2.1927.
45 LUB Saml. von Sydow: Ó Siochfhradha to von Sydow, 24.5.1927. Von Sydow also visited the Dept. the Education, where Ó Siochfhradha was employed, in an effort to encourage officials to support the collecting of folklore. *Béaloideas* 1(2) (1927), p. 206.

forgotten key which could, if used properly, open up to him a possibility of the explanation of many things in early Norse/Icelandic literature.[46]

In his lectures to schoolteachers he also stressed the international importance of Irish folklore. On August 5th at a lecture von Sydow gave to National Teachers in Dublin he was quoted as saying: 'If the folk-stories of other European countries are precious, the folk-stories of Ireland are seven times more precious, because they are older and better. Some of these go back hundreds of years before the birth of Christ.'[47]

While in Ireland von Sydow sought an interview with Éamon de Valera, the leader of the defeated side in the Civil War and of the newly-founded Fianna Fáil party, who after being released from prison in 1924 had spent the subsequent three years in the political wilderness. This meeting was to prove advantageous in years to come, when von Sydow interceded on Ó Duilearga's behalf with de Valera, who was then President (i.e. Prime Minister) of the Executive Council of the Irish Free State, to get increased state financial support for the collecting of folklore.[48] However, of more immediate benefit to Ó Duilearga was an interview von Sydow had with the President of University College Dublin, Dr Denis Coffey, in order to seek a stipend from the College for Ó Duilearga to travel to Scandinavia to study folkloristics in Sweden.[49] This took some time to arrange, but on March 20th, 1928 the Governing Body of UCD agreed to a recommendation of the Academic Council, namely 'That Mr. J. H. Delargy, MA, be awarded a Research Scholarship [to the value of a £100] for the study of Folklore in a Swedish University centre at which arrangements can be made for him.'[50] The following day, Ó Duilearga wrote to von Sydow informing him that he had been given six months' leave of absence.[51]

Study trip to northern Europe

Ó Duilearga's trip to northern Europe in 1928 was crucial for his development as a folklorist, and for the initiation of the systematic collecting of folklore in Ireland. He was away from early April 1928 to early October of the same

---

46   RTÉSA 233/69, 23.12.1968.
47   As quoted in Hanly 1931, p. 141.
48   It is most likely that it was as Chancellor of the National University of Ireland that von Sydow sought an interview with de Valera at this time, rather than as leader of a still somewhat constitutionally suspect, and officially disapproved of, political party. However, it should be noted that despite de Valera's temporary fall from grace in the wake of the Civil War, for von Sydow he always remained a hero, so it is quite possible that von Sydow had personal as well as professional reasons to seek an interview with de Valera. See Almqvist 2002, p. 20.
49   See Almqvist 2002, p. 43.
50   UCDA: Min. of Gov. Body Vol. 10, meeting of 20.3. 1928.
51   LUB Saml. von Sydow: letter dated 21.3.1928. Before setting out for Sweden he busied himself learning Swedish with the aid of books von Sydow sent him and assisted by a Swedish woman resident in Dublin. LUB Saml. von Sydow: Ó Duilearga to von Sydow, letters dated 22.9.1927, 25.10.1927, 26.11.1927, and 10.2.1928.

year. During these six months, among other things, he widened his knowledge of folkloristics, became aware of the importance of material culture, learned how folklore collecting and research were organised in other countries, and met many folklorists and ethnologists, thus extending his network of international contacts.

The first two and a half months of Ó Duilearga's trip were spent in Lund with von Sydow, learning from him and deepening their friendship. In early June he spent ten days or so at a Folk Highschool (Folkhögskolan) in Fristad. Waiting for him at the railway station in Fristad was one of the teachers at the School, the ethnologist Åke Campbell, with whom he was to have a great deal of contact over a period of almost thirty years, and who was to greatly assist the work of the Irish Folklore Commission.[52] Some days into the course, Ó Duilearga wrote to von Sydow saying that his eyes had been opened to the importance of material folk culture, and said that on his return to Ireland he must set about getting support for the establishment of a folk museum, like those he had seen in Fristad and elsewhere in Sweden.[53] Two days later in another letter to von Sydow he speaks further about his newly discovered understanding of the importance of the study of material culture:

> I see now what a great work lies to be done in Ireland and how necessary it is for us to get our people interested in their own country-life. But many workers will be required & it will be necessary for others to study at Nordiska Museet [Nordic Museum] and elsewhere. I myself can look after the folklore but it will not be possible for me to take up the study of material culture in any very intensive and thorough way so we must look out for someone else.[54]

From the middle of June to late July 1928 he spent six weeks travelling in Sweden, Denmark, Finland and Estonia. Everywhere Ó Duilearga went he made contacts, often prearranged by von Sydow[55] and others, and everywhere he went he was impressed by what he saw and the hospitality shown him. He had been given a hundred pounds travelling expenses by UCD, but very often he was put up free of charge in the homes of folklorists and ethnologists. In Tallinn, Estonia, he stayed with a niece of Kaarle Krohn and her husband, Laine (née Kallas) and Jaan Poska. Krohn himself met him off the Turku train at Helsinki railway station, and on his return to Finland from Estonia he visited the Krohns in Jyväskylä in the centre of Finland.[56] Ó Duilearga was never to forget the hospitality shown him on his travels and throughout his life he would assiduously maintain contact with many of those whom he met on this trip.

---

52 ULMA Saml. Åke Campbell subnr. 165: Ó Duilearga to Campbell, letter dated 29.1.1955.
53 LUB Saml. von Sydow: Ó Duilearga to von Sydow, letter dated 11. 6.1928.
54 LUB Saml. von Sydow: Ó Duilearga to von Sydow, letter dated 'Wednesday' = 13.6.1928.
55 e.g. ibid., Ó Duilearga to von Sydow, letter dated 'Wednesday' = 13.6.1928.
56 For a description of this encounter, see Tynni 1954, pp. 119–110.

The tradition archives and folk museums he saw on his travels also greatly impressed him. Recalling more than twenty years later the impression his visit to the Finnish Literature Society made on him, in a letter to Martti Haavio, he said:

> Now, I would consider it a very great honour & privilege if, as you so kindly suggested, I could speak at the Finnish Literary [recte Literature] Society, which for me is holy ground. I was there long ago (in 1928) with Kaarle Krohn, & and it was there that I determined to do what I could in Ireland to emulate – a longe intervallo – the work of Elias Lönnrot.[57]

Moreover, everywhere he went those he met showed an interest in Ireland, and they expressed regret that Ireland was 'still, in spite of political changes, a terra incognita', in respect of Irish folklore and ethnography. In Tartu (Dorpat), Estonia, he met Oskar Loorits, who was aware how little had been done to collect Irish folklore. Loorits expressed the view that 'most Irishmen did not understand what nationality really meant', despite their struggle for political freedom. In his opinion, cultural independence was 'of far greater importance than political freedom when the soul of a nation is enslaved'. Commenting on the interest in Ireland he encountered on his travels, Ó Duilearga wrote to his teacher and mentor, Eoin Mac Néill:

> So it comes to this then that scholars everywhere expect us to preserve our folklore, to collect it systematically and thoroughly and to make it known to the outside world. I wonder if this will be done and I also wonder if our Government will ever realize that they owe a duty to Ireland and to the civilized world to make the literature, history and folklore of our people known and respected everywhere.[58]

Some days earlier he had written to Kaarle Krohn in much more hopeful mood: 'I grudge the time I spend abroad when I think of what remains to be done at home and how few there are who care. But, please God, it won't be always so and in a few years we may have something and a national collection to be proud of.' He thanked Krohn for encouraging him: 'In my work in Ireland I have not received much encouragement so you can understand that I value it highly when coming from a person such as you.'[59]

Ó Duilearga would appear to have vacillated between hope and despair on his trip to northern Europe. The previous March, just before he set out on his travels, he had written to von Sydow in very hopeful mood and expressed confidence that UCD would in future help save the extant remnants of Irish folklore for posterity.[60] Now he had reason to be less hopeful of getting

---

57 SKS M. Haavio Papers 12:58:19: dated 25.3.1951, p. 1.
58 UCDA MacNeill Papers LAI/H/155 (1) and (2).
59 SKS Kaarle Krohn Papers: letter dated 25.7.1928. In the same letter he suggests that at some future date he might have to call on Krohn 'to write to our Government and tell them what to do'.
60 LUB Saml. von Sydow: Ó Duilearga to von Sydow, letter dated 21.3.1928.

further assistance from his college. He had been given permission by the UCD authorities to purchase books on his travels to the value of £20, but this proved an inadequate sum. As well as receiving free of charge 'as a special favour ... scores of important works' on folkloristics from various institutes, he had been offered 'at less than half-price several hundred volumes in German, French & Scandinavian languages dealing with the subject.' He estimated that £40 would have been sufficient to cover the costs involved, but although he had written a number of letters to the UCD authorities urging them 'to take advantage of this offer' he had received no reply. Expressing his frustration at the situation to Eoin Mac Néill, he says of UCD's indifference to this offer: 'Oh the College is a joke and it is no wonder that no one takes it or its work seriously.'[61] In time, as we will see below (Chapter III), he would change his opinion about his college.

On his return from Finland to Sweden towards the end of July he went to stay on a farm in Mistelås in Skåne in order to perfect his Swedish. Then towards mid-August he travelled to Oslo, where his sojourn was prolonged somewhat by a bout of illness. Nevertheless he was very pleased with his visit to Norway and the hospitality shown him there.[62] Before leaving for Ireland in late September, he attended a conference in Leipzig, along with von Sydow. Thus, Ó Duilearga's trip in all took in six countries: Sweden, Norway, Denmark, Finland, Estonia, and Germany.[63]

Ó Duilearga's historic journey to northern Europe ended on Thursday morning, October 4th when the mail boat drew into Dún Laoghaire harbour to the south of Dublin. Many years later he recorded on tape for T. K. Whitaker his feelings on the final leg of that eventful journey of 1928 as the mail boat came within sight of land:

> I went right out to the bow and I saw the Irish hills. That is a long time ago −1928− and I said 'the tradition of Ireland is behind those hills and we've got to rescue it before it's trampled into the dirt' ... because it was a jewel of great price and one had to see that it was given a refuge and an appreciation by the Irish people.[64]

Return from northern Europe

Ó Duilearga on his return to Ireland could have had few illusions about the uphill struggle facing the Folklore of Ireland Society. Although membership of the Society had increased, not enough members were interested in 'collecting and research'. The Society still had only a handful of collectors. Two years after the setting up of the Society, there was still nobody, to their

---

61   UCDA MacNeill Papers LAI/H/155 (3).
62   LUB Saml. von Sydow: Ó Duilearga to von Sydow, postcard (15.8.1928) and letter (2.9.1928.)
63   UCDA MacNeill Papers, LAI/H/155 (3): Ó Duilearga to Mac Néill, dated 29.7.1928.
64   Whitaker 1981–82, p. 101.

knowledge, collecting folklore in the province of Ulster. It was obvious to Ó Duilearga that the Folklore of Ireland Society as then constituted could not on its own save the oral tradition of Ireland.

Given the fact that the UCD authorities had financially supported his trip to northern Europe, Ó Duilearga was justified in expecting that they should wish to hear some account of his travels. However, almost four months after his return he bitterly complained to von Sydow that President Coffey had never spoken to him about his foreign trip, had not answered any of his letters, and gave 'the impression that he does not want to be bothered either with me or with the question of folklore.'[65] Whatever about Coffey's behaviour towards him, his initial hope that UCD would help him establish some sort of folklore institute within the College was too optimistic. Given the scant resources of the College at the time, without state aid it could not establish such an institute. Ó Duilearga does not appear to have realised this at first. Coffey may well have been avoiding him because there was little he or the College could do, in the short term, to help this young man realise his dream. Ó Duilearga had left Ireland full of enthusiasm, he had come back full of ambition and plans, and with a mission. Patience was not a word in this young man's vocabulary. Exactly three weeks after he arrived back in Ireland, he wrote to von Sydow expressing his frustration with the College, who were too 'stupid', in his opinion, to see the advantage, in terms of publicity, that would accrue to it by having such an institute within its walls. He was 'chastened' but 'not disheartened' and was not going to 'bother' with the College authorities any further. Instead he intended writing a memorandum to be submitted to the Minister for Finance, Ernest Blythe.[66]

State support sought for collecting

Although he informed von Sydow in his letter of October 25th that the Minister for Finance, Ernest Blythe, was 'interested' it would appear he had few illusions about Blythe. Less than a week later in another letter to von Sydow he says of Blythe: 'I hear he is prepared to spend £50,000 on publication of Irish books but I am afraid that folklore means as much to him as it does to English people.' Nevertheless, he hoped that Blythe could be convinced and stated that '[i]t is my job to convince him that it is worth while spending money on [collecting folklore].' He proposed asking for the following:

> (a) Establishment of an Irish Folklore Institute with money for collection of folklore & for publication. System of stipends for workers. Material to be collected to include personal and place-names, linguistic study.
> (b) Establishment of a Committee appointed by Government to enquire into Allmogekultur and folklore giving the widest interpretation to both.

65   LUB Saml. von Sydow: Ó Duilearga to von Sydow, letter dated 20.2.1929.
66   LUB Saml. von Sydow: Ó Duilearga to von Sydow, letter dated 25.10.1928.

(c) Suggestion that I should be placed in charge of (a) and devote most of my time to the work.[67]

His reason, most likely, for approaching the Minister for Finance directly rather than via the Minister for Education was because Blythe was the most enthusiastic supporter of the Irish language within the Free State Government, while the Minister for Education, John Marcus O'Sullivan, was not particularly interested in Irish. Moreover, in the above letter he says: the 'educational authorities only smile when some enthusiast like myself tells them of the work to be done!'[68]

Michael Tierney, Prof. of Classics at UCD, an influential member of *Dáil Éireann*, interceded on Ó Duilearga's behalf to arrange an interview with Ernest Blythe. On November 23rd, Ó Duilearga and Tierney met the Minister. In a letter to Carl von Sydow, written a few days after this meeting, Ó Duilearga describes what happened:

> I write you this letter with a light heart. We are to have an Irish Folklore Institute and I am to be in charge of it! On Nov. 23rd after a certain amount of negotiation had been done, I, in company with Prof. Tierney a member of Dáil Éireann waited on Mr. Blythe, the Minister for Finance and put the matter before him. He received us very kindly and asked me what I proposed to do. Well Wilhelm, I was nervous before the interview took place but when I was asked this question I forgot all about Blythe and saw only a long procession of old Irish speakers tottering towards their graves with their lore unrecorded, and I made an appeal which surprised myself and Blythe also for he surrendered at once! He is a man like myself from the Black North and I think he appreciated the fact that I, a Northerner, was prepared to tackle a big job and get the work of collecting Irish Folklore done at once in a businesslike way.

To what extent Blythe capitulated at this meeting is difficult to ascertain. Both Tierney and Ó Duilearga may have felt beforehand that little, or far less than they desired, would result from the interview, as they were most likely both aware of the Minister's scant regard for folklore as such. His agreeing to set up an institute to advance the collecting of folklore, may consequently have appeared to Ó Duilearga as 'surrendering', but this may not have been what actually happened. In any case, considering subsequent events, Blythe does not appear to have been won over to the cause of folklore as such. Nevertheless, he would appear to have committed himself to supporting Ó Duilearga's proposed institute. In the same letter Ó Duilearga tells von Sydow:

> This is what it all comes to. I am to have a large office well-equipped with office-furniture, a library, filing cabinets, a typist, cameras, a Dictaphone

67   LUB Saml. von Sydow: Ó Duilearga to von Sydow, letter dated 30.10.1928
68   LUB Saml. von Sydow: Ó Duilearga to von Sydow, letter dated 30.10.1928.

etc., and my job will be to make available to native & foreign scholars the remains of Irish folklore in both Irish & English. I shall have to collect myself a great deal but now I shall have five months per annum instead of five weeks in An Ghaeltacht. We are to get £1000 for the first year and, at least, £600 for each subsequent year. All my time outside my duties at the University is to be given up to this work and we expect to get started after Christmas. I shall let you have the details later.

He added to the above: 'Well, Wilhelm, I assure you that if you had not brought me to Lund this Institute would never have been. So you can say to yourself that you have done something big and something good and, if our efforts are successful and we save our country's folklore, to you a great deal of the credit must be given.'[69]

Whatever was decided at the above meeting, the Institute was not up and running after Christmas, as Ó Duilearga hoped, nor indeed after Christmas 1929. Neither was the figure of £1,000 for the first year ever realised. It would be well over a year before the Institute began operating.

In late February 1929, Ó Duilearga wrote to von Sydow of a changed situation. His hope of the Institute being up and running early in the New Year had not been realised:

The Gov[ernmen]t too were interested & promised £1000 towards the establishment of an Irish Folklore Institute on one condition 'that University College had nothing to do with it.' We had everything ready when, at the last moment, the grant was withheld on the plea of economy. I do not intend to get discouraged & I have taken all the necessary steps to get the work started before Easter.[70]

In April he again wrote to von Sydow from Ballinskelligs, clarifying the situation: although the Institute would not be provided with funds in the current financial year, funds would be made available the following year. Defiantly, he adds: 'Meanwhile I shall go on and show both friends and foes that I can do something. So we shall go ahead as if nothing had happened.' He ended his letter with two Irish proverbs: 'Meanwhile remember: 'Is giorra cabhair Dé ná an dorus!' and 'Tá Dia láidir agus tá máthair mhaith aige!' ('God's help is closer than the door! and 'God is strong and he has a good mother!').[71]

In late November 1929, Ó Duilearga again wrote in despondent mood to von Sydow. He was overburdened with work, with only Pádraig Ó

69 LUB Saml. von Sydow: Ó Duilearga to von Sydow, dated 26.11.1928. Reproduced in *Comóradh Céad Bliain*, unpaginated.
70 LUB Saml. von Sydow: Ó Duilearga to von Sydow, letter dated 20.2.1929. In this letter, he also informed him: 'In order that a connection should be made between the [Royal] Irish Academy and the F[olklore] Institute I have been elected a member (nem. con.) of the Academy and also of its Board of Irish Studies.' He added: 'Bergin was my proposer, unasked by me, and, I hear, was good enough to pay me some very nice compliments.'
71 LUB Saml. von Sydow: Ó Duilearga to von Sydow, dated 9.4.1929.

Siochfhradha to help him. There was 'indifference, ignorance, and mis-understanding on all sides.' Those 'who should help, who should understand' he complained were 'the obstacles to our success':

> Gaeldom is slowly disappearing, our folk-culture will soon be but a memory, the old seanachaidhes [storytellers] are fast dying out while all the time the fools in high places squabble over trivialities, occupy themselves with things which can be very well attended to in fifty years time — and slowly but steadily the only sources of supply for the study of our people are dying in the remote places, among the hills & in the valleys of the barren lands of Munster, & of Connacht & the North.

The worry of all this was affecting his health and it grieved him that he had to 'fritter away priceless years in Dublin at a job which others can do as well as I while opportunities, which will never come again, are being lost all over Ireland.' In his despondency he hit out at members of the executive committee of the Folklore of Ireland Society and blamed them for the delay in getting the Institute up and running. Referring to the initial offer to found a Folklore Institute in November 1928, he says: 'Our Committee lost this offer last year because they couldn't realise what it all meant and talked and talked until I thought I should have to come along some night and toss a few bombs among them to liven them up. Well we lost that last year!' The same offer came again this year, he informed von Sydow, and 'I had only one week in which to get everything done.' Nevertheless, on a more hopeful note he said that they hoped to be in possession of the rooms they had been given at a house in the vicinity of Merrion Square after Christmas 'and to have the nucleus of our library there and all in good order.'[72]

Ernest Blythe's attitude to folklore

Since Ernest Blythe was the strongest supporter of the Irish language in the Free State Government in the late 1920's, one might consequently have expected from him a sympathetic attitude towards the collecting of folklore in Irish. However, Blythe was apathetic, to say the least, to folklore, or at least to folktales,[73] and had a very poor opinion of many of the members of the Folklore of Ireland Society. It must also be remembered that Blythe, whatever his personal views on the value of folklore, was not a free agent. Money was in short supply and he had to take the views of his Departmental Secretary, the formidable J. J. McElligott, into account.

While the initiative to seek state support for folklore collecting came initially from Ó Duilearga, and although he was the unanimous choice for

---

72 LUB. Saml. von Sydow: Ó Duilearga to von Sydow, letter dated 11.11.1929, pp. 1–2. Ó Duilearga may have felt that if the Society had been quicker to grasp Blythe's offer, the Institute might have been established before the above-mentioned financial cutbacks came into effect.

73 Ó Broin n.d. p. 94.

the post of Director, much of the subsequent negotiations, with the Dept. of Finance at any rate, from January 1929 onwards would appear to have been conducted by Pádraig Ó Siochfhradha. Almost twenty years Ó Duilearga's senior, President of the Folklore of Ireland Society, and a well-respected figure in Irish language circles, he would at the time have had much more influence and standing than Ó Duilearga, who was still relatively unknown outside Irish folklore circles at this time. Ó Siochfhradha's neutral stance during the Civil War also meant that he could more easily do business with ministers such as Blythe, who were by this time apathetic towards many in the official Irish language movement, considering it somewhat a thorn in the Government's side.

Initially the Minister for Finance proposed that the governing body of the Institute should have three members appointed by the Folklore of Ireland Society, three by the Board of Irish Studies of the Royal Irish Academy, and one representative nominated by the Dept. of Finance.[74] The Folklore of Ireland Society objected to this arrangement, as it, unlike the Academy, would be contributing funds to the Institute. It proposed that four representatives be nominated by the Society, two by the Academy, and one by the Government.[75] A compromise was reached by allowing the Society to nominate four and the Academy three, with one Government representative. In a letter to Anthony Farrington of the Royal Irish Academy in late 1929, Blythe explains: 'My desire to have a number of members nominated by the Academy is to prevent sudden and undesirable changes of policy that might affect the Institute if its governing body were simply a Committee elected annually by members of the Folklore Society whose only qualification was that they had been interested enough to pay an annual subscription of 7/6.'[76] Whatever about the membership of the Folklore of Ireland Society generally, its Committee, as well as the hard core of its active members, was composed of dedicated and knowledgeable people. There was no question of them electing people to sit on the Board of the Institute whose only qualification was that they had the wherewithal to pay the annual subscription. It is difficult to understand Blythe's cynicism. Does it derive from bitterness against certain members of the Society as a result of the Civil War and tension between the Gaelic League and the Free State Government or does it betray a fundamental difference of opinion with the aims of the Society? It should be noted that Blythe did not want to save the Gaelic past, he wanted to create a Gaelic future. He wanted to save and modernise the Gaeltacht in order that Irish could be spread from there throughout the state.

Whatever the reason for his cynicism, it did not bode well for relations between him and the new Institute. In a letter he wrote to Pádraig Ó Siochfhradha in May 1929, Blythe says:

---

74   D/F F 006/0002/29: Blythe to Ó Siochfhradha (An Seabhac), 8.5.1929.
75   See UCDA Blythe Papers P24/369: Ó Siochfhradha to Blythe, 4.6.1929.
76   See UCDA Blythe Papers P24/369: Blythe to Ó Siochfhradha, dated 8.5.1929; Ó Siochfhradha to Blythe, dated 4.6.1929; and Blythe to Farrington, dated November, 1929. It would appear, however, that it was Ó Siochfhradha who originally suggested this composition for the Institute and not Blythe. See D/F F 0006/0002/29: 'Proposed Scheme for Irish Folklore Institute', p. [1].

> It will be understood that the interest of the Government in the matter arises from the fact that the work to be done by the proposed Institute is likely to help in the steps which are being taken to preserve and revive the Irish language and it will be expected therefore that a great part of the grant from public funds will be expended in the publication of suitable matter in Irish.[77]

This stipulation was to hamper the work of the Institute and to make it far less effective than it might otherwise have been. Moreover, from Ó Duilearga's point of view at least, it was a stipulation that needed to be amended sooner rather than later.

The Irish Folklore Institute

Ó Duilearga hoped that the Institute would be in operation after Christmas 1929 but it was not until early April 1930, the beginning of the financial year, that it was officially established. The three representatives nominated to the Board of the Institute by the Royal Irish Academy were Prof. Douglas Hyde, Prof. Micheal Tierney, and Séamus Ó Duilearga; the Folklore of Ireland Society's four representatives were Prof. Éamonn Ó Tuathail, Fionán Mac Coluim, Seán Mac Giollarnáth, and Pádraig Ó Siochfhradha; and the Government's appointee was Énrí Ó Muirgheasa, Schools Inspector, folklore collector, and antiquarian.[78] It was to be the autumn of 1930, however, before the Board of the Institute, at a meeting on October 11th, delegated responsibilities to its various members. Douglas Hyde was chosen as President, Pádraig Ó Siochfhradha as Treasurer, and Séamus Ó Duilearga as Director and 'Chief Editor' of the Institute's future publications.[79]

The Irish Folklore Institute was beset with problems from the start – in fact, as mentioned above, even before it was set up. Ó Duilearga had hoped for a grant of £1,000 for the Institute during its first year of operation. In May 1929, Blythe suggested a grant of £400 or £500 per annum, but this was not accepted by his Department without some deliberation. In October 1929 an internal departmental memo stated in connection with the Institute's grant:

> A grant of £300 a year would bring the new service into line with the Hibernian Academy and the Academy of Music, but presumably this amount would be insufficient as premises have to be taken. £500 a year suggests itself, or £600 would bring up the amount spent on cognate services to £4000 (Royal Irish Academy £3,400 for 1929-30).

Rounding off figures and parity with similar institutions were some of the yardsticks Finance used to assess proposals for state funding, and also in order

---

77   UCDA Blythe Papers P24/369: letter dated 8.5.1929.
78   UCDA Blythe Papers P24/369: letter from Secretary of Academy to Blythe (5.11.1929) and two letters from Ó Siochfhradha to Blythe, both dated 7.11.1929.
79   Lysaght 1993, p. 57.

to keep state expenditure to a minimum. In those days Irish governments balanced their budgets: consequently the Dept. of Finance had to be extra vigilant. However, a price had to be paid for such vigilance. Very little consideration seems to have been given to the actual costs of running such an institute as the one proposed. In fairness to Finance officials, however, it should be said that the fact that the Folklore of Ireland Society was to contribute a substantial part of its funds to the new institute would also have figured in its calculations. An annual grant of £500 was eventually decided upon for the Institute. However, no provision was made for remunerating the Director (described initially as Editor/Archivist) of the new institute, on whose shoulders the bulk of the organising work would fall. Realising that the Institute would not be able to compensate the Director for expenses he would incur travelling about the country organising collecting, Ó Siochfhradha wrote to Blythe in November, 1929 on the matter. This lack of provision, Ó Siochfhradha felt, was a defect that would have 'to be remedied in some way.'[80] His appeal to remunerate Ó Duilearga for his services to the Institute fell on deaf ears, and was to hamper its work greatly.

From the outset the Institute was hindered by lack of resources on all fronts, but more particularly by not being able to spend all its resources on collecting. The Institute possessed no written constitution, which was probably an oversight as the Dept. of Finance believed that a draft constitution was prepared in 1929.[81] This oversight was to have serious consequences, for the Institute and the Dept. of Finance were at variance from the outset as to what the priorities of the Institute should be. For many of those on the Board its task was perfectly clear, namely the collecting and preservation of the rapidly diminishing traditional lore of rural Ireland and of the Gaeltacht areas in particular. The Dept. of Finance saw the duty of the Institute as being somewhat different. We have already seen how Blythe from the start linked the grant-in-aid to the proposed Institute to publishing material in Irish. In a letter to Pádraig Ó Siochfhradha in December 1929 (when most of the details regarding the new institute had been finalized) he was more specific. In this letter he stipulated that the continuance of the grant-in-aid would 'be conditional upon the Institute expending a very substantial proportion of all the funds at its disposal in printing folklore material in Irish with a view to making it available for students and the general public.'[82] Over the five years of the Institute's operations a good deal of Ó Duilearga's time was to be taken up trying to convince Finance that the Institute was spending 'a very substantial proportion of all the funds at its disposal' on publishing material in Irish, in order to secure its annual grant. This was a most unsatisfactory situation, but it was one that was not so easily rectified as the various parties involved in saving the folklore of Ireland did not represent a unified front (see below).

80   UCDA Blythe Papers P24/369: letter dated 7.11.1929.
81   D/F F 75/2/30: internal memo, Ó Broin to Redmond, dated 5.12.32, p [3]. This draft constitution probably refers to Pádraig Ó Siocfhradha's document entitled 'Proposed Scheme for Irish Folklore Institute', dated 30.1.1929. D/F F 006/0002/29.
82   UCDA Blythe Papers P24/369: letter dated 13.12.1929.

The setting up of the Irish Folklore Institute did not mean the demise of the Folklore of Ireland Society. Indeed, the report of the annual general meeting of the Society, held in early 1931, published in *An Claidheamh Soluis* does not mention the Irish Folklore Institute at all.[83] It is as if for some in the Society the Institute did not exist or was but an appendage of the Society. It would also appear that for some of the time Ó Duilearga behaved as if the Institute had subsumed the Society. However, it had not been subsumed, but continued to function and increase its membership. At the annual general meeting of the Society the following year, Pádraig Ó Siochfhradha informed those present that the Society's membership was now at 600. This enabled them to increase the size of *Béaloideas*, but in respect of collecting 'the situation was not so satisfactory'. Public interest was increasing in folklore, but although people expressed regret at its decline, the same few were collecting material and forwarding it to them.[84]

Most members of the Folklore of Ireland Society probably agreed with Ó Duilearga that for the time being priority should be given to collecting over publication. At any rate, when the Institute's grant was cut by the Dept. of Finance in 1933 for failure to satisfy the Department on the question of publication, at a meeting of the Society a motion was passed complaining at the decision of Finance to reduce the Institute's grant, and a letter of protest was forwarded to the Government.[85] Nevertheless, there is evidence that there existed from early on a degree of tension within the Folklore of Ireland Society and the Irish Folklore Institute. In a Dept. of Finance memorandum of August 1933 it is stated that

> ...for practical purposes the Institute and the Society are one body while maintaining separate accounts. The Institute has derived considerable advantage from its association with the Society and has been able to draw freely upon the materials collected by the Society out of its own resources. It has also behind it whatever element of popular enthusiasm there may be in the country for the preservation of Irish folklore, and it may be said in passing that this Department's experience has been that the non-professorial element in both the Society and the Institute has been the more active in the fulfilment of the conditions attaching to the Government grant.[86]

Another Finance memorandum is more specific about divisions between members of the Society and Institute, stating that the Society was set up 'by persons who were interested in the collection and preservation of folklore as a means of strengthening the language revival.' Although such people 'were in a general way aware of the efforts that had been made, particularly in Germany and the Scandinavian countries, to evolve a comparative science out of the scattered remnants of ancient and mediaeval tales, philosophies and customs',

83   *An Claidheamh Soluis* Feabhra 14, 1931, p. [1].
84   *An Claidheamh Soluis* Feabhra 6, 1932, p. 2.
85   D/F F 75/2/30: Fionán Mac Coluim to the Sec. Executive Council, dated 15.5.1933.
86   D/T S 9244: untitled Finance memo, dated August 1933, p [2].

and 'while they realised that Ireland had something to contribute to that science and that the more folklore which they collected and published the greater the advantage the comparative folklorists would derive from it', nonetheless 'they, themselves, were mainly interested in perpetuating in the spoken and written Irish of to-day the richness of phrase, the expressiveness and the imagery which are such extraordinary features of what is loosely called folklore.'[87] These underlying tensions between the Folklore of Ireland Society and the Irish Folklore Institute, and indeed within both bodies, were to play a major role in the fortunes of the Irish Folklore Commission, as was Ó Duilearga's own commitment, and that of his College, to the revival of Irish.

Ingenuity in the face of adversity

On a grant of only £500 per annum, and with little or no money to compensate the Director or others in the field for any collecting or supervisory work done, Ó Duilearga was forced to seek extra funding to further collecting. He turned to the Rockefeller Foundation of America. His appeal for funds fell on receptive ears and in July 1930 the Foundation granted the Irish Folklore Institute £300. In his report to the Foundation for the year July 1930 to July 1931 he informed them that £200 of this grant had been 'expended in small grants to collectors (living, principally, in remote rural areas)', and for the 'purchase of recording equipment ... stationery, etc'; the remaining £100, he says was 'awarded to me to compensate me for (a) loss of income; (b) to enable me to encourage[,] by personal contact, the collectors and to control and supervise their work, and (c) to permit me to carry out certain research work and the collection of folkloristic material.'[88]

It would appear that initially, at any rate, Ó Duilearga saw himself as shouldering the burden of the collecting.[89] Nevertheless, he realised that the services of many individuals, both voluntary and remunerated would be needed if the folklore of Ireland was to be saved. He proposed interesting students in the various university colleges, teacher training colleges, and such like 'in the work of collecting', and 'to train and assist' interested candidates. He felt that 'it should be possible during the next year to get at least six persons trained as collectors.' It is most likely that he envisaged these working as part-time collectors, as he did not ask for the funds to pay them full-time salaries. The idea of using students probably came from the Scandinavian and Baltic countries, but for whatever reason university students were not destined to play a major part in the collecting of Irish folklore. Nevertheless, some university students did collect for the Institute. His pinpointing of schoolteachers and pupils, however, was in the long term to prove more productive. In the above memorandum to Blythe in 1929, he wrote:

87 D/F F 75/2/30: León Ó Broin to Mr. Redmond, memo dated 5.12.1932, p. [1].
88 D/T S 9244: 'Memorandum. The Grant-In-Aid to the Irish Folklore Institute, Dublin, 1930–31', p. [1].
89 D/F 006/0002/29: untitled memo of Ó Duilearga's to Blythe (cov. letter dated 17.1.1929) passim.

It is highly desirable to get into touch through the Dept. of Education, with the National Schools all over the country. Through the teachers and the pupils a vast amount of important material may be obtained all of which can later be verified and properly recorded, if necessary by the Director or by persons deputed by him.[90]

During the five years of the Institute's operations an assortment of people contributed material to it, often via the Folklore of Ireland Society. These included university students, trainee teachers, schoolteachers and pupils (primary, vocational and secondary). Quite a few of those who were later to collect for the Commission in a full-time or part-time capacity also collected for the Institute, among them Seán Ó Dubhda, Tadhg Ó Murchadha, Seán Mac Mathghamhna and Liam Mac Coisdeala.

Due to insufficient funding and restrictions placed on it by the Dept. of Finance, the high hopes Ó Duilearga and others had for the Irish Folklore Institute could not be realised. Although in his correspondence with von Sydow, he liked to lay stress on what was being collected, he realised better than anybody that what was being collected was far less than what could be collected in different circumstances. When the Irish Folklore Commission was transferred to UCD in 1971 its Main Collection alone comprised in excess of 1,750 manuscript volumes (c. 720,300 pages), of which 102 volumes (c. 50,000 pages) were inherited from the Folklore of Ireland Society and the Irish Folklore Institute. In other words, on average from 1927 to 1935 approximately eleven manuscript volumes (c. 5,400 pages) were being added to the collection each year, but from 1935 to 1970 the collection grew on average by forty seven volumes (c. 19,100 pages) per year. This was a quantum leap. If the Irish Folklore Institute had continued operations, its folklore collections would, no doubt, have continued to grow, but nothing like the same quantity of folklore would have been amassed, nor it should be said the same variety of material.[91]

We will see below how, soon after the establishment of the Irish Folklore Institute, Ó Duilearga began to seek ways of taking the Institute out of the clutches of the Dept. of Finance and, in time, to seek a new organisation for collecting Irish folklore. As a result of his efforts the Irish Government in 1935 set up a commission to save for posterity the folklore of Ireland, with Ó Duilearga as full-time Honorary Director. This commission, to be known as the Irish Folklore Commission, within less than fifteen years was to assemble one of the great folklore archives of the world. 'Great', it should be said not just in terms of quantity, but in terms of quality as well. The rest of this study will be concerned with the setting up and making permanent of this Commission, with its staff, with its programmes of work (both in the field and at Head Office), with its collecting methods, and with an assessment of aspects of its work.

---

90   Ibid., sections (6) &(7).
91   For a general description of the work of the Irish Folklore Institute, see S. Ó Catháin 2005 (this article contains a lengthy summary in English.). See also Briody 2005b.

III
The Irish Folklore Commission:
Founding and Re-establishment

1. Negotiations and interventions

Genesis of a new organisation for collecting folklore

The advent of a new Minister for Finance, Seán MacEntee, in March 1932 resulted in a worsening of relations between the Institute and the Dept. of Finance; making a bad situation worse, as far as Ó Duilearga was concerned. However, apart from the question of inadequate funding and interference from Finance, Ó Duilearga was under tremendous pressure having to serve two masters at once. In July 1931 he wrote to von Sydow saying that the strain was affecting his health. In effect he had to organise the collection of the folklore of Ireland in the time he managed to spare from his College duties and he feared that he would break under the strain.[1] Given these circumstances, it is not surprising that he began to look for ways to strengthen the position of the Irish Folklore Institute and lessen direct interference from the Dept. of Finance.

In an effort to alleviate pressure on the Institute from the Dept. of Finance, in late 1931 he approached the Royal Irish Academy to see if it would be possible to bring the Institute more within its fold. However, the results of these negotiations with the Academy proved unsatisfactory.[2] If a satisfactory agreement had been reached with the Academy, it was hoped that the Institute's collections could be housed in the National Museum of Ireland, and to this end Ó Duilearga also had discussions with Adolf Mahr, at the time the Museum's Curator of Irish Antiquities.[3] Although the above proposal came to nought, within a few months of Fianna Fáil assuming power in March 1932, Ó Duilearga approached the new Minister for Education, Tomás Ó Deirg, with a view to improving the position of the Institute and, more particularly, the collection of Irish folklore. Unlike the previous Minister, John Marcus O'Sullivan, Ó Deirg was an enthusiastic supporter

---

1 LUB Saml. von Sydow: Ó Duilearga to von Sydow, letter dated 6.7.1931.
2 O'Brien 2004, p. 111. The unsuitability of their accommodation as well as the high rent also influenced Ó Duilearga's decision, approved by the Board of the Institute, to approach the Royal Irish Academy. S. Ó Catháin 2005, p. 94.
3 S. Ó Catháin 2005, p. 94, and LUB Saml. von Sydow: Ó Duilearga to von Sydow, letter dated 20.12.1931.

of the revival of the Irish language. In June 1932, Ó Duilearga wrote to von Sydow informing him that he had had an interview with the new Minister for Education, and reported: 'He is very interested in our work and I think I can get him to do something for us soon.'[4] Ó Duilearga's first impressions of Ó Deirg proved correct.[5] Here was a Government Minister with a genuine interest in saving the traditions of Ireland.

By this time negotiations were in progress between the UCD authorities and the Government to effect the expansion of its Department of Modern Irish with a view to increasing the general competence in Irish of students taking degrees in the College. One of the posts involved in this expansion, a full-time Statutory Lectureship in Irish Folklore, was earmarked for Ó Duilearga, who since 1931 had been a part-time lecturer in Irish Folklore in addition to being Assistant to the Professor of Modern Irish.[6] These negotiations, which were delayed by the advent of Fianna Fáil to power [7], were eventually to result in the passing of the University College Dublin Act in 1934. Pending his appointment as Lecturer, and to alleviate the pressure on him, in the spring of 1933, Ó Duilearga approached the President of UCD, Denis Coffey, with the view to getting the services of someone to help with transcribing Ediphone cylinders. As a result of this meeting, Coffey, on Ó Duilearga's recommendation, proposed to the Dept. of Education that the young Celtic scholar Gerard Murphy be appointed Assistant to the Lecturer in Folklore. However, something more than an assistant to Ó Duilearga was being contemplated. Referring to the desire in Government and other quarters to expedite the publication of folklore material in Irish, Coffey says:

> As to the publication of the Folk-lore matter I am in favour of the transference of this work to the Lectureship in Irish Folk-lore. A room would be provided in the College for the collections and for [a] Library. How far the Grant made for the Institute under subhead C. (Miscellaneous Expenses) in the Estimates would cover the expenses of the Assistant and of publications, collections, etc., I do not know. But my view is that Mr. Delargy would regard the Assistantship as his first necessity from the point of view of making his collection ready for publication and for effective working.[8]

For an assistant to be appointed and to cover the costs of publishing folklore material in Irish on a more extensive scale than hitherto possible, extra money

4   LUB Saml. von Sydow: Ó Duilearga to von Sydow, letter dated 10.6.1932, p. [4].
5   Despite Ó Deirg's belief in the desirability of expediting the collecting of folklore, his first loyalty was to Irish. He was very dissatisfied with the position of Irish within UCD, and was instrumental in having the passing of the University College Dublin Act postponed until 1934. Failure to pass this act in 1932 in effect delayed Ó Duilearga's appointment as statutory lecturer in Irish Folklore for some two years. See D/T S 6240, passim.
6   UCDA Blythe Papers P24/449(1): Denis J. Coffey to Ernest Blythe, dated 4.3.1932.
7   See D/T S 6240: Máire Ní Gríobhtha to Sec. Dept. of the President, dated 3.5.1932 and file generally.
8   D/T S 9244: Coffey to Joseph O'Neill, dated 21.3.1933, pp. 2-3.

would be needed as this expansion of its activities could not be met out of the Institute's grant. In effect, Ó Duilearga would appear to have been trying to get the Irish Folklore Institute transferred to UCD and to set up an embryo folklore department in the College, initially, at least, within the Department of Modern Irish.

The Dept. of Education submitted this proposal to the Dept. of Finance, and also forwarded copies of its correspondence with the President of UCD on the matter to the Dept. of the President. If it had been left to the Dept. of Finance to make a decision on the proposal, it would have died there and then, as it would have been interpreted as an attempt to get the Institute into UCD through the back door and free it from the direct supervision of Finance. However, it was not to die in this way, but to be magnified and transformed in a way that Ó Duilearga could only in his wildest dreams have imagined possible. Whether as a result of interest this proposal aroused in the Dept. of the President or not, on April 3rd, Ó Duilearga had an interview with an official in that department (John O'Donovan). At this meeting Ó Duilearga outlined the priorities as he saw them in respect of folklore: '(a) Collection, (b) Publication, (c) Provision for employee'. He stressed that '(a) was vital'. The possibility of employing Gerard Murphy was broached, 'the only person who could systematise the information available.' The question of providing 'small honoraria to rural collectors at a rate of two to three guineas per volume' was also discussed.[9]

Ó Duilearga meets de Valera/Folklore survey agreed

Although the seeds of a future Department of Folklore at University College Dublin were contained in Ó Duilearga's proposal for an Assistant to the Lecturer in Irish Folklore, his discussions with John O'Donovan of the Dept. of the President appear to have concerned quite modest proposals. Subsequent to this meeting, the Dept. of the President, on April 19th, decided to arrange for Ó Duilearga to meet Éamon de Valera, President of the Executive Council.[10] In a radio interview many years later Ó Duilearga said that it was Fianna Fáil Senator Joseph Connelly, a friend of his, whose people also came from the Glens of Antrim, who was instrumental in arranging for him to meet de Valera.

Ó Duilearga and de Valera met on May 10th, 1933. Ó Duilearga describes the scene:

> It was the night of the Budget, and officials were coming in to him, into his room, and he was pushing them aside. And he talked about something... he talked about his youth: when he was a boy that he had heard folktales, told in English of course, in Co. Limerick. And he went on talking, and then I couldn't ... it was a tense moment for me, and I said: 'Excuse me! Sir! I

---

9   D/T S 9244: 'Interview with Mr. J. Delargy - Monday 3rd April, 1933'.
10   Ibid.

don't speak the language of diplomacy. I have just one thing to say to you. The material is there, it's dying and you know it. You are interested in the Irish language as I am, and I think it is about time that something was done to put on paper or to record in some way the oral tradition of a silent people' (who as I said a moment ago had so much to say). 'So please, take that pen in your hand and write "Let it be done!" and I'll do it and get all the people to help me.' And that's how the Folklore Commission started.[11]

Ó Duilearga's above account may be somewhat dramatised, but there is no doubt that he came away from his interview with de Valera very satisfied. Despite the difficulties with the Dept. of Finance, he realized that he had a sympathetic ear in the President of the Executive Council, and that at last his ambitions for Irish folklore were within his grasp. The covering letter he sent de Valera a week or so later, along with a memorandum the latter had requested, exudes hope and confidence. He begins his letter thus:

> May I be allowed to express my gratification for your courtesy and for the interest you have in getting recorded speedily, efficiently and once and for all the fast-perishing oral traditions of our country.
>
> I feel certain that in your hands the entire matter treated of in the memorandum rests secure.[12]

De Valera was to leave for Rome shortly after his meeting with Ó Duilearga on May 10th and wished to have a detailed memorandum from him outlining his proposals for the reorganization of folklore collecting before he left.[13] This meant that Ó Duilearga had only about a week to compile this memorandum. In his memorandum to de Valera, Ó Duilearga refers to the problems that arose from the condition attached to the grant-in-aid for the Irish Folklore Institute and admits that this 'condition was interpreted in a very liberal fashion' by the Board of the Institute. He goes on to say:

> Apart altogether from its vast linguistic importance, the uncollected oral literature of our people is unequalled in variety, extent and intrinsic merit in Western Europe. Students of the Irish language have long since recognised that the only literary material of value in the everyday spoken Irish language is the oral literature, in particular the more formal type of prose and poetical composition comprised in the popular tale and song. These tales and songs are in greater danger of immediate and irrevocable destruction than the other forms of folk composition (Volksdichtung), and to ensure their preservation immediate steps must be taken to collect them accurately and scientifically.[14]

11 RTÉSA L46/74: 'Unwritten Ireland' (1974). In this programme Ó Duilearga incorrectly recalls 1934 as being the year of this incident.
12 D/T S 9244: letter dated 18.5.1933.
13 See D/T S 9244: internal memo dated 12.5.1933, signed 'JO'D'. On de Valera's reasons for going to Rome at this juncture, see. Whyte 1980, p. 47 and Keogh 1995, pp. 103–106.
14 D/T S 9244: 'Collection of Oral Tradition of Ireland', p. 4.

Much of what Ó Duilearga had to say to de Valera would thus have fallen on fertile soil. In many respects both men shared the same vision, although the former, being politically opposed to de Valera, may not have cared to dwell too much on what they had in common. Their views of rural life were very similar and were rooted in nineteenth-century Romanticism, involving an idealisation of a 'changeless' peasantry. For both men, as indeed was the case for many of their contemporaries, the real Ireland was situated in the countryside.[15] Ó Duilearga in approaching de Valera would have been aware of the essence of de Valera's nationalistic philosophy, and that before him was someone with scholarly interests, if albeit a shrewd politician too, and that scholarly proposals to foster Ireland's native culture and enhance its international role on the world stage might be well received. Even though de Valera sought to develop and preserve Ireland's native Gaelic culture as 'the surest defence against the nation's absorption into an English world', as Michelle Dowling notes, he did not seek to isolate Ireland from the world, rather he saw Ireland as having a civilising role to play on the world stage: 'Antique Ireland civilised Europe, modern Ireland can replicate this achievement.'[16] Moreover, de Valera was also one of the few Irish politicians who believed that Ireland should actively foster close relations with other Celtic lands. He was, in a certain sense, a Pan-Celtic nationalist, and had an intense pride in Ireland's Celtic inheritance. Not surprisingly, Ó Duilearga stresses the Celtic dimension of Irish folklore. He proposed that 'a folklore survey' be undertaken along the following lines:

> (a) Systematic co-ordination and arrangement of the existing literary material [i.e. printed oral tradition].
> (b) Systematic collection of the unrecorded oral traditions with a view to
> (c) The eventual co-ordination and treatment of the whole material thus obtained and its linking up with the culture of the other Celtic nations, in order to clarify its position in the shaping of a distinct Irish nationality and its inter-relations with European civilization in general.[17]

Ó Duilearga also had many practical suggestions as regards the staff required for such a project, and in respect of collecting proposed that the 'main work of the survey' be 'carried out by a selected body of full time field workers'. In the first year he suggested these 'may be confined to ten to fifteen in number, to be increased in subsequent years to thirty or more.'[18] Although he proposed that the survey to be justified, 'either from the standpoint of economy or scholarship', should 'continue for at least five years', he envisaged more than a five-year rescue plan. Under 'Other Recommendations' he has this to say:

15   For more on de Valera's views on this matter, see Ó Crualaoich 1986, pp. 50 ff.
16   Dowling 1997, pp. 37–38.
17   D/T S 9244: 'Collection of Oral Tradition of Ireland', p. 6.
18   Ibid., p. 7.

> In view of the inadequacy of funds, equipment and staff, and the unsuitability of location of the Irish Folklore Institute as at present constituted, it is clear that the ultimate aims of the Institute are impossible of fulfilment, and it would appear to be absolutely essential that the existing Governing Body of the Institute be dissolved, and the Institute re-constituted as the Department of Irish Folk Culture in University College, Dublin.

Ó Duilearga further proposed that the collection of oral tradition would be the main concern of this university department and asked that the conditions hitherto pertaining to the giving of the grant-in-aid to the Irish Folklore Institute be revoked.[19]

Divergent views and delays

Even if de Valera had accepted everything Ó Duilearga proposed in this memorandum, it would still have had to pass the hurdle of the Dept. of Finance. From the outset Finance was unhappy with these proposals, but it was late August before it outlined its objections to the Dept. of the President. Apart from other reservations, Ó Duilearga's lack of provision for publication of collected material was the main reason why the Dept. of Finance opposed the new scheme. Finance's letter to the Dept. of the President says:

> It is thought that Mr. Delargy's proposals should be turned down if the Government seriously wish to make Irish Folklore in the early future a vitalising factor in the thought and speech of Irish speakers and of those who are becoming Irish speakers.

While the ideology of reviving Irish played a part in Finance's initial rejection of these proposals, they also opposed it on other grounds, reflecting ideology of a different type. It was 'elaborate, directed towards new ends' and also because it would 'cost much more money, and ultimately if not immediately, will be free from the control of the Government which is asked to supply the money.'[20]

Ó Duilearga's proposals received a more sympathetic reception from Education officials. On October 16th, 1933 a meeting took place at the Dept. of Education to discuss these proposals. In addition to the Minister and senior Departmental officials, this meeting was also attended by John O'Donovan of the Dept. of the President, as well as Séamus Ó Duilearga, Énrí Ó Muirgheasa and Pádraig Ó Siochfhradha (representing the Irish Folklore Institute/Folklore of Ireland Society). As Ó Duilearga's memorandum to the President had not touched on the cost involved at all, the meeting, in discussing his proposals, also made an effort to cost them. It was agreed to request the Minister for

---

19   Ibid., pp. 7 and 24.
20   D/T S 9244: J.A. Carrell to Sec. Dept. of the Pres., dated 24.8.1933.

Finance to sanction a scheme costing £4,900 per annum with an initial capital cost of £600 for ten recording machines. Ominously for Ó Duilearga, Pádraig Ó Siochfhradha 'pointed out that neither the Folk-lore Institute nor the Folk-lore [of Ireland] Society had been consulted about this scheme and the transfer to University College, and [he] considered it desirable and necessary that the goodwill of all people interested should be procured.' The meeting consequently 'decided that a conference between members of the Folk-lore Institute, the Folk-lore Society, Mr. Delargy and Dr. Coffey [President of UCD] be arranged as soon as possible.'[21] Ó Duilearga had moreover informed the meeting that 'he understood from Dr. Coffey that ... [t]hree suitable rooms at 86 Stephen's Green [Newman House]' would be made available to accommodate the survey, as well as another room in the main building of the College at Earlsfort Terrace.[22] There were no objections to this proposal as such. Accommodating a reorganised Institute in UCD was never an issue; placing it under the control of that college was. The proposed 'conference' with Dr Coffey to be attended by representatives of the Folklore of Ireland Society and the Irish Folklore Institute does not appear to have taken place. However, the following month, November 1933, Ó Duilearga and Eoin Mac Néill had a successful interview with Dr Coffey on the question of 'finding suitable accommodation in the University buildings' at Earlsfort Terrace 'for the offices of the Commission.'[23]

The Dept. of Education's acceptance of Ó Duilearga's scheme (or a slightly watered-down version of it) most likely put pressure on the Dept. of Finance to defend its position. From now on the Minister for Finance, Seán MacEntee, corresponds personally with the President of the Executive Council on the matter. The Minister probably sensed that he would have to agree to some sort of scheme that would allow for the more extensive collecting of folklore, but he was adamant that the Government should keep control of such a large sum of public money. On November 16th he forwarded a memorandum and covering letter to the President in which he recommended that the new scheme be placed under the Irish Folklore Institute rather than University College Dublin. This letter contains personal observations and criticisms of Séamus Ó Duilearga:

> In addition to the objections expressed in a general way in the Memorandum, to entrusting the responsibility for Folklore collection to University College, I think that the fundamental difference between Mr. Delargy's attitude and that of what I may call the Language Revivalists in the Institute cannot be overstated. Mr. Delargy looks upon Folklore mainly, if not solely, as a comparative science, whereas the interest of

21 ED CO3/15/9 (495/I): 'Béal Oideas Conference, 16th October, 1933', p. 4. John O'Donovan of the Dept. of the Pres. also records Ó Siochfhradha as stating: 'Many are not easy in their minds about the handing over of control to U.C.D. and feared that the transfer might result later in the annihilation of the movement.' D/T S 9244: 'Meeting in Room of Minister of Education at 11. a.m. on 16/X/1933'.

22 ED CO 3/15/9 (495/I): 'Béal Oideas Conference, 16th October, 1933', p. 5.

23 ED CO 3/15/9(495/II): 'Irish Folklore Commission', dated 10.1.1934, p. [2].

the Revivalists, which coincides with our own, lies entirely in the ability of Folklore to act as an auxiliary in improving the quality of the Irish taught in the Schools.

Ó Duilearga's reluctance to lecture (and possibly to speak) in Irish to students also comes in for comment: 'Mr. Delargy's attitude to Irish may be gauged from the fact that in his capacity as lecturer in University College, Dublin, he at present rarely, if ever, addresses his students in Irish and if University College, Dublin is given control of the enlarged Folklore Scheme I fear that English will continue to be the language of instruction in his classes and the language for direction in the Folklore department which his scheme envisages.'[24]

For Seán MacEntee promoting the Irish language was not the priority it was for his predecessor as Minister for Finance, Ernest Blythe. Indeed, as a younger man he appears to have had some misgivings that the state's gaelicisation policies might become a divisive issue between North and South.[25] His daughter, Máire Cruise O'Brien, says of her father that he 'was a theoretical revivalist only' and that: 'He learnt Irish as an adult as he had learnt German, but never spoke any language other than English with any ease.' Nevertheless, despite being 'a theoretical revivalist only', MacEntee, whose wife, Margaret, was an Irish scholar, ensured that through her agency and with the help of his brother-in-law, the mathematician and linguist Pádraig de Brún, that all his children grew up Irish speakers.[26] It is quite possible that some of MacEntee's negative views on Ó Duilearga were influenced by his wife, who was also a member of staff of UCD's Department of Modern Irish.[27]

Finance had other objections also. MacEntee had been informed 'that Mr. Delargy's direction of the Irish Folklore Institution in the past [had] lacked drive and enthusiasm'. This was a rather strange accusation, and he adduced no evidence to back it up. Certainly, Ó Duilearga had proved a difficult person for Finance to deal with, but that was another matter. This seems to have been the root cause of misgivings about Ó Duilearga's directing of the Institute, for MacEntee adds:

> ...my Department's very strong view is that if the supervision which they have found it possible to exercise over him and the Institute generally, so long as the accounting for the Grant-in-Aid remained in their hands, is withdrawn, it will lead to carelessness and laxity which the kind of audit possible under the Universities Act, 1908, will not be able to correct.

24   D/T S 9244: MacEntee to de Valera, dated 16.11.1933.
25   See what he had to say on the proposed gaelicisation of the South of Ireland when the Anglo-Irish Treaty was being debated in the Dáil in December 1921. Quoted in Hepburn 1980, p. 125.
26   M. Cruise O'Brien 2003, pp. 79–81.
27   Margaret MacEntee was appointed Assistant in the Dept. of Modern Irish, UCD, in October 1932. See UCDA: Min. of Acad Coun. Book III, p. 38.

Both MacEntee and Finance were unable to suggest 'anybody else who would be competent and willing to direct the collection of a Folklore scheme', and could not deny Ó Duilearga's 'admitted knowledge of his subject'. Somewhat reluctantly they saw no option but to retain him as Director of the new scheme, but MacEntee strongly urged de Valera 'that the incentive which derives from Departmental supervision should not be removed.'[28]

In the memorandum accompanying the Minister's above letter, the attitude of University College Dublin to the Irish language and to the revival policies of the Government was criticised. Finance, given 'the history of University College, Dublin, in relation to the Irish language movement generally' was reluctant to place a large scheme such as that envisaged by the Director under a body not subject to Government supervision. Nonetheless they were willing to sanction a scheme to collect folklore for a period of five years (only) at £2,750 per annum. In addition to five or six collectors, the scheme would allow for an office staff of two (as well as the Director, whose salary would come from the University). Moreover, it was proposed that £300 - £400 per annum should be set aside for publications.[29]

Ironically, while the Dept. of Finance raised objections to the scheme being placed under the care of UCD, in part because of that college's seeming lack of enthusiasm for restoring Irish, the government department most associated with restoring Irish, the Dept. of Education, raised no such objections. On November 30th, Seosamh Ó Néill of that Department wrote to his counterpart in the Dept. of Finance, informing him that the Minister for Education, taking everything into consideration, felt that it would be best to transfer the collecting of folklore from the Institute to UCD. In support of this position, Ó Néill had this to say:

> It is felt that by associating the Folklore scheme directly with the work of the College, the Lecturer in Folklore will be in a position to train students in the work and to secure material assistance from them. In the matter of accommodation, especially for the library [i.e. archive], University College is in a position to afford better accommodation than is available at present for the work of the Folklore Institute.

As regards the Dept. of Finance's worry that the Government would not be able to maintain 'an adequate measure of check and supervision' over state funds if the scheme were to be placed under UCD, Ó Néill said that the Minister felt that 'on the contrary, control could be exercised more readily, and perhaps more effectively, over the work if it were done by University College instead of by the Folklore Institute as at present.'[30]

---

28   D/T S 9244: Sean MacEntee to de Valera, dated 16.11.1933. It is possible, however, that overburdened by work, and worry, Ó Duilearga's direction of the Institute was at times wanting. See Col. Íde Ó Siochfhradha Papers: Gearóid Ó Murchadha to Ó Siochfhradha, dated 27.2.1931.
29   D/T S 9244: untitled memorandum accompanying above letter, pp. [3-4].
30   D/T S 9244: Ó Néill to Sec. Dept. of Fin., dated 30.11.1933, pp. [1–2].

There was little substance to Education's contention in respect of financial supervision, but when Ó Néill broached the question of what should take priority, collecting or publication, he was on firmer ground. The Minister for Education felt that collecting was by far the more important task at the time, and that it was 'very desirable that as large and representative a collection as possible should be made of the oral literature in Irish still available mainly in the Irish-speaking districts.' He also touched on the obligations binding on the Institute to produce reading material in Irish:

> I am to point out, however, that modern young people, for whom it is most urgent to supply suitable Irish reading, are not interested to any considerable extent in Folklore, and it is a mistake to assume that the interests of these young people can be forced in such a matter. While the Minister agrees that it would be desirable to have a few volumes of carefully selected and well-told tales from each of the three provinces, he considers that from the point of view of catering for readers of Irish there is greater urgency for a supply of modern literature than for Folklore publications.[31]

However, an earlier draft of this letter is revealing of a somewhat different attitude in the Dept. of Education, which was to affect the fate of the Irish Folklore Commission when set up.

> The Minster has given careful consideration to the question of the relative importance of collecting and of publishing folklore. The matter is a debatable one, and is complicated by the fact that the protagonists of collection and of publication are both inclined to hold exaggerated views on the question. No doubt the amount of folklore available for collection is being reduced daily by the death of old people, especially in the Gaeltacht, and collection is for this reason a matter of urgency. Nevertheless, provided a fairly representative collection of our remaining Folklore can be made, the Minister for Education is not disposed to attach undue value and importance to the collection of all material of this kind. He has difficulty in seeing how the making of an exhaustive collection could give much help to our actual development, however valuable it might be from a scientific and international point of view. The making of an exhaustive collection might put this country in the unique position of having collected more folklore than any other country of the same size, and a certain amount of prestige would undoubtedly attach to the position, but the Minister for Education has no reason to assume that the Government would consider the attainment of this record worth the expenditure involved.[32]

Most likely, either the Minister of his own accord, or on the advice of his senior officials, decided that it would be best not to express the above views

---

31 D/T S 9244: Ó Néill to Sec. Dept. of Fin., dated 30.11.1933, p. [2].
32 ED CO 3/15/9(495/I): Sec. Dept. of Educ. to Sec. Dept. of Fin., 25.11.1933, pp. [2–3].

at this juncture, lest they might give the Dept. of Finance an excuse to curtail the folklore survey in some manner or other.

As agreed at the conference on October 16th, 1933, the Minister for Education was now proposing that a scheme costing annually £3,000 be sanctioned, employing eight full-time collectors. Finally, Ó Néill reminds the Dept. of Finance that placing the scheme under UCD would involve a saving of between £150 - £200 annually as it was understood the College were willing to provide rooms free of charge with heating and lighting.[33] This may have been meant to impress the Dept. of Finance, who were always eager to learn of ways to cut public spending, but on this occasion it was not impressed. Finance asked the Dept. of Education to justify its claim that 'there would be no diminution in Government check and supervision of expenditure from state funds' if the scheme were placed under UCD.[34] It seems that the Dept. of Education was unable, or unwilling, to put forward arguments to contradict the view of Finance on this matter. Opposition from elements in the Folklore of Ireland Society and the Irish Folklore Institute to placing the survey under the care of UCD also emerged and influenced Education's volte-face on this issue.[35] By June 1934, Arthur Codling of the Dept. of Finance was able to inform the Dept. of the President that the Dept. of Education 'no longer desires to press its view that the scheme should be worked by University College, Dublin.' The Dept. of Finance, according to Codling's letter, took it for granted that the new scheme would be placed in charge of the Irish Folklore Institute and 'that the Department of Finance, as hitherto, will exercise supervision over the expenditure of the Grant-in-Aid.' The Minister for Finance proposed (the letter went on to say) to inform the University authorities and the Irish Folklore Institute of their proposal 'and to seek from the former Body the necessary formalities for Mr. Delargy to act as Director of the scheme'.[36]

Éamon de Valera's views

Not only did the Dept. of Finance and the President of the Folklore of Ireland Society, Pádraig Ó Siochfhradha, have reservations about the wisdom of placing the new scheme under the control of UCD, the President of the Executive Council, Éamon de Valera, was also opposed to the idea. Whether he was so from the beginning, and whether for a time he led Ó Duilearga to believe otherwise, is not clear. The extant government files give no indication that de Valera, or his Department, argued the case for reconstituting the Irish Folklore Institute in UCD. De Valera's private papers are also silent on this

---

33 D/T S 9244: Ó Néill to Sec. Dept. of Fin., dated 30.11.1933, p. [3–4].

34 D/T S 9244: Seán MacEntee to the de Valera, dated 16.1.1934.

35 ED CO 3/15/9(495 I): Ó Dubhthaigh to Sec. Dept. of Fin., dated 11.6.1934 and internal Educ. memo, Ó D[ubhthaigh] to Sec. dated 27.2.1934. Ó Dubhthaigh, who had negotiated with Dr Coffey on the possibility of transferring the work of folklore collecting to UCD, felt that Coffey was less than enthusiastic about the proposal: '...it is very probable that Dr. Coffey did not want the additional trouble of administering the scheme, and he will not be sorry to hear it has not been approved.' Ibid.

36 D/T S 9244: Codling to Sec. Dept. of Pres., dated 9.6.1934.

matter, as they are on the question of why he preferred a non-university setting for Ó Duilearga's folklore survey. Given his subsequent unflinching opposition to transferring the Irish Folklore Commission to UCD, it is quite probable that he never seriously contemplated reconstituting the Irish Folklore Institute in that college. I will examine this question further below.

In June 1934 the Dept. of the President informed the Dept. of Finance that the President agreed that the scheme should be placed in charge of the Irish Folklore Institute, but wished to put a number of suggestions before the Dept. of Finance. These were:

> (1) That the Institute should be reorganised and that it should consist henceforth of a small Executive Committee and Council, the function of the latter to be mainly advisory;
> (2) That the Executive Committee should include Mr. Delargy, as Director, one representative of the Department of Education, one representative of the Department of Finance, and, say, two other persons;
> (3) That the representative of the Department of Finance should be charged with the supervision of expenditure from the Grant-in-Aid, so as to avoid the delays consequent on detailed supervision in the Department;
> (4) That adequate accommodation, including a strong room for the keeping of records, should be provided for the Institute;
> (5) That the records of the Institute should be Government property and that the officer in charge of them should be a Government official.[37]

While de Valera wished to see the state keep a measure of control over the new scheme for collecting folklore, it would appear, he did not wish this control to be excessive.

Carl von Sydow's and Eoin Mac Néill's intervention

To what extent Ó Duilearga was kept informed of developments concerning the stance of various government departments vis-à-vis placing the new folklore scheme under UCD is not clear. When he eventually became aware that this was not the preferred option, he seems to have thought that behind-the-scenes activity by associates of his in the Folklore of Ireland Society and the Irish Folklore Institute was chiefly responsible for dashing his hopes in this area. In late May 1934 he wrote a frantic letter to von Sydow seeking his help. In his dramatic fashion he said that the whole scheme was in danger of being wrecked by the actions of associates of his.[38] While it is easy to understand the anger he felt towards certain of his fellow workers in the Folklore of Ireland Society for going behind his back in this way (although he told von Sydow in the above letter that he had suspected that something was going on), one might also ask to what extent his own tendency to keep certain matters to

---

37 D/T S 9244: Dept. of Pres. to Sec. Dept. of Educ., dated June 1934.
38 LUB Saml. von Sydow: Ó Duilearga to von Sydow, dated 22.5.1934.

himself contributed to associates of his acting surreptitiously in this way.[39] Moreover, while the Dept. of Finance definitely noted opinions opposed to including this scheme in UCD, from whatever source they came, opposition of this sort was not the deciding factor in Finance's resolute stance against incorporating a reconstituted Institute into UCD.

Ó Duilearga quickly recovered his composure and summoned other forces to his aid. In the above letter to von Sydow (22nd May, 1934) he had requested that he come to Ireland that summer as his help would be needed, and had told him that Eoin Mac Néill was interceding with de Valera in order to try to rectify the situation.[40] Von Sydow agreed to this request. In June, Ó Duilearga wrote to him with further details of what he wanted him to do for the new scheme. He realised that he was imposing on von Sydow, but it was essential that the latter meet with de Valera and impress on him the importance of folklore.[41]

In early July, Eoin Mac Néill wrote to de Valera requesting that he grant von Sydow, who had already arrived in Ireland, an interview. Mac Néill, as we have seen above, had retired from politics in 1925 and had resumed his academic career as Professor of Early Irish History in UCD. Although no longer active in politics, nor indeed in Irish language circles, he still commanded respect across the political spectrum. Mac Néill requested de Valera to grant von Sydow an interview. In his letter to the President he did not simply request an interview for von Sydow, but argued the case for putting the proposed folklore scheme under UCD. Mac Néill emphasised that he was not only addressing the President as the head of Government, but also as Chancellor of the National University of Ireland. He also reminded de Valera that von Sydow had been a staunch supporter of Irish independence: 'In the crisis of 1920-21, he held meetings all over Sweden in support of the Irish cause.' Mac Néill based his case for placing the folklore scheme under UCD and Ó Duilearga on two grounds:

> The first is that the endowment will be most effectively administered in that way. The alternative, I suppose, would be that it would be administered under the supervision of the Department of Finance. This, I venture to say with all respect, would be a reversion, and an extreme case of reversion, to the old method of Dublin Castle.

Mention of Dublin Castle (i.e. the former nerve-centre of the British administration) was meant, no doubt, to strike a chord with de Valera. Von Sydow, he informed de Valera was in agreement with him as regards the above. But he had another reason for placing the scheme under UCD, an 'even more important' reason, which again sought to appeal to de Valera's patriotism:

---

39 A meeting of the Institute was convened on May 22nd, 1935 to discuss these tensions. LUB Saml. von Sydow: Ó Duilearga to von Sydow, dated 22.5.1934, and ULMA Saml. Åke Campbell, subnr. 203: Ó Duilearga to Campbell, letter dated 28.5.1934.
40 LUB Saml. von Sydow: Ó Duilearga to von Sydow, dated 22.5.1934.
41 LUB Saml. von Sydow: Ó Duilearga to von Sydow, dated 12.6.1934.

It is a matter of national policy and of national reconstruction. Dr. von Sydow will tell you that Ireland is regarded in point of her folk traditions as one of the most important, perhaps quite the most important, country in Europe. At the same time it is plain truth to say that our national folk traditions are regarded with nothing less than contempt by the public at large and especially by those who claim to be educated. Such persons may pride themselves on an acquaintance with scraps of ancient folklore gathered from the Classics of Ancient Greece and Rome but they have not learned to appreciate the existence of similar treasures in the traditions of their own country. Their attitude towards Irish folk tradition governs in no small way their attitude towards the national language. A kind of duty towards the language to be more or less mechanically performed is admitted by some and denied by others. We are told that it is a peasant language. It should be the function of the National University to bring about a complete change in the mental attitude on these matters. One means of doing so will be to place the whole body of our folk traditions on the highest possible plain in University education. No specialised body or society can have any such effect.[42]

It is obvious from the above that Mac Néill was disillusioned at the way cultural nationalism in the struggle for independence had fallen victim, to a very large extent, to political nationalism. In addressing de Valera he knew that although political opponents, they both shared a strong belief in the importance of Ireland's ancient Celtic/Gaelic/Christian inheritance, and the belief that Ireland, as of old, could once again be a beacon of learning, and a fountain of moral values, and set an example for the world.

Not surprisingly, von Sydow was granted an interview. He met de Valera on July 14th, but it seems he did not have sufficient time to discuss everything he wanted to discuss with the President. He therefore promised to furnish de Valera with a memorandum on the way the collecting of folklore was organised in Sweden. At the meeting itself he presented the President with a memorandum containing some of the matters that he wished to discuss, and which may have been discussed. Writing about the Gustavus Adolphus Academy for folklife research he had this to say:

> We regard Ireland as the key country, the only country where it is possible to study certain problems of international importance in the field of folklore and comparative literature. If a folklore survey be attempted in Ireland I respectfully suggest that the authorities of the National University be asked to place at its disposal the services of their staff and students, and organisation. Speaking from experience stretching over many years, I am convinced that the only centre for a survey of this kind should be the university.[43]

42   D/T S 9244: Mac Néill to de Valera; dated 6.7.1934. Mac Néill had experience, as chairman
       of the Irish Manuscripts Commission, of the negative effects of Civil Service interference
       in a state-funded academic body. See R. D. Edwards 1973, pp. 293–294.
43   D/T S 9244: 'To Éamon de Valera, President of the Executive Council of the Irish Free

Whether de Valera was swayed to any considerable extent by Mac Néill's and von Sydow's arguments is a matter for conjecture, but the fact that he asked him for a second memorandum would seem to indicate that he, at least, wished to consider the question further before coming to a definite decision. He would, however, have been all too well aware of the failure of the National University of Ireland, of which UCD was the largest constituent college, to develop Irish studies to any appreciable extent.

It may be of significance that de Valera also forwarded von Sydow's two memoranda to the Dept. of Finance. Von Sydow's arguments made little impression on Finance officials. In late July 1934, Seán MacEntee wrote a letter to the President in which he stated that von Sydow's description of folklore collecting in Sweden was very interesting, but was hardly relevant in the Irish situation. He goes on to undermine von Sydow's arguments:

> In Sweden there is no language problem and the collection of Folklore is carried out in the interest of Science. Hence Professor von Sydow stresses the dangers of placing amateurs in control of the collection of Folklore. Folklore in this country has a scientific value, too, but its primary usefulness is as an adjunct to the language revival.

He reminded the President that the three people responsible for most of the folklore collected in Ireland hitherto had a great deal of experience in this area, and that it was not his Department's intention to remove these people from decision making and hand the scheme over to amateurs. He went on to make a case once again for publishing folklore:

> Experience has proved the folktale, irrespective of its scientific value, a better means of acquiring a knowledge of the living language than either text books or works of modern literature in Irish. There is everything then, I think, to be said in favour of releasing to the public as much colloquial Irish as can be collected. Furthermore, in the evolution of a literary language the availability in print of large volumes of colloquial Irish is important.[44]

In the above passage 'folktale' probably refers to folk narratives in a general sense, rather than to *Märchen* as such.

Pádraig Ó Siochfhradha's intervention

If Mac Néill and von Sydow were interceding in the hope of having the new scheme placed under UCD, others, as we have seen above, were working to

---

State', p. [3].

44   D/T S 9244: MacEntee to de Valera, July 1934 (stamped 26.7.1934). It is not exactly clear which three collectors of folklore MacEntee is referring to above. The list might include the following members of the Board of the Irish Folklore Institute: Douglas Hyde, Pádraig Ó Siochfhradha, Fionán Mac Coluim, Énrí Ó Muirgheasa, and Éamonn Ó Tuathail.

exclude it from UCD, or at least to insist on safeguards if it was placed in the care of that college. Pádraig Ó Siochfhradha, who was a friend of von Sydow's, may have heard from the latter that at his meeting with de Valera on July 14th he had been asked to furnish the President with a further memorandum on the organisation of folklore collecting in Sweden.[45] Ó Siochfhradha may therefore have feared that de Valera was veering more towards placing the new scheme under UCD. At any rate, on July 22nd, Ó Siochfhradha wrote a letter to P. Ó Cochláin, Private Secretary to the Minister for Education, in which he seems to take it for granted that the new scheme would be placed under UCD. Instead of arguing the case against doing so, however, he contents himself with ensuring that the rights of members of the Folklore of Ireland Society and the general public would be protected. Addressing Ó Cochláin, he says: 'If you [i.e. the Dept. of Education] have an opportunity to give advice on the Government's scheme to collect folklore, perhaps you would take into consideration the points in the enclosed memo. Certain people would be satisfied with you if they would be put as conditions.' Some of Ó Siochfhradha's recommendations are of a very general nature and need not be detailed here. However, he made a number of specific recommendations that reveal the apprehensions of those who opposed handing over the work of folklore collecting to UCD.

He proposed that a small board be appointed to examine and report to the Government on the work of the survey, and that it should be chosen in the following manner: '(a) the Government to elect four (non-university) knowledgeable persons from the public, or (b) one person from the University, two from the Folklore of Ireland Society, and one person from the Dept. of Finance, or the Dept. of Education.' He further proposed that the Irish Folklore Institute and the Folklore of Ireland Society 'should give on loan, (and temporarily) all their manuscripts, books and other folklore material' to the new 'folklore library' (to be housed by UCD in Newman House, St. Stephen's Green), and that all the material collected under the survey should be made 'available for consultation under reasonable conditions without restriction by the public at times suitable to that element of the public who will be interested in it', and that the state have '[copy]right and ownership' of this material 'in perpetuity on behalf of and for the use of the public.' In respect of the Folklore of Ireland Society in particular, he asked that the Society 'always have the right to consult folklore writings and to make copies of them for the purposes of publishing them or disseminating them in other fashion', and have an office and accommodation in the same building as the Institute under the new scheme.'[46]

It is clear from the above that Ó Siochfhradha at this juncture supported the placing of this folklore survey under the care of UCD as a temporary measure only. He did not wish that College to be the permanent home of

---

45 D/T S 9244. This memorandum, entitled 'Swedish Universities and the Collection of National Tradition', was sent to de Valera some days after their interview. Covering letter dated 16.7.1934.

46 D/T S 9244: Ó Siochfhradha to P. Ó Cochláin, dated 22.7.1934 and accompanying untitled memo in Irish.

the collections amassed under the survey. As we will see below, he would in time be adamantly opposed to transferring the Irish Folklore Commission permanently to UCD. It should be said that people like Ó Siochfhradha, although, for the most part, ideologically opposed to UCD because of its failure to initiate Irish-medium teaching, had genuine concerns about the wisdom of placing the work of folklore collecting within a university milieu.

Dept. of Finance proposes limited role for UCD

We have seen above that both Mac Néill and von Sydow argued for a strong role, indeed a central role, for the university in any folklore scheme. However, while the Dept. of Finance was opposed to including the new scheme under UCD from the beginning, even prior to the intercession of Mac Néill and von Sydow, they were beginning to see a role, albeit a limited one, for UCD in the new scheme. The College might be asked to provide accommodation for the new folklore scheme, but would not be allowed to exercise control over it. In early July 1934 the Dept. of Finance prepared two draft letters, one addressed to the Director of the Irish Folklore Institute and the other to the President of University College Dublin. Copies of these draft letters were sent to the Dept. of the President. The letter to be sent to Ó Duilearga states that 'the Minister feels [that such a scheme] can best be operated by the Irish Folklore Institute in co-operation with University College, Dublin.' The draft letter to the President of University College Dublin is more specific as to what this co-operation should entail. Interestingly, however, the word 'co-operation' as such is not used in this draft letter. The letter states: 'The Minister understands that you have already promised that suitable accommodation for Mr Delargy and the headquarters staff, and for the housing of records, will be made available in the University College buildings.' The draft letter to Ó Duilearga also contains an interesting proposal in respect of training students. The Dept. of Finance envisaged six collectors being employed for the first two years, to be financed out of a total annual grant of £2,750. However, during the first two years of operation it promised to provide £250 per annum extra 'to enable Post Graduate courses in Folklore to be given to selected students in University College, Dublin, who will form a body of trained outdoor workers, to be drawn on, if required, as the scheme develops.' After two years, the Minister, 'provided he is fully satisfied that the Scheme had thus far developed successfully ... would be disposed favourably to consider increasing the grant' to £3000 per annum 'in each of the remaining three years'.[47] It is not clear if either of these letters, or revised versions of them, were ever sent, but it appears that MacEntee discussed the content of both letters with de Valera (see quotation below).

In any event, by early August, the Dept. of Finance had changed its position somewhat in respect of linking the new folklore scheme in some way with

47   D/T S 9244: Both these draft letters are dated July 1934.

UCD. It now felt that the scheme should not be associated solely with UCD, 'which, of all the branches of the National University, is the one least in touch with the Gaeltacht.' The Minister for Finance now proposed that 'the Government should establish an Irish Folklore Commission with members drawn from the constituent colleges of the National University [Dublin, Cork, and Galway], as well as from Trinity College [Dublin], the Irish Folklore Society and representatives of the Department of Education and Finance.' He also proposed the retention of Ó Duilearga as Director, adding, 'the presence of the Government representatives on the Commission would help to ensure that the work of collection and publication was systematically carried out.' Not only did MacEntee propose that all university colleges in the state should be represented on the board of the new body, '[i]n order to stimulate the interest of the University Institutions in the work of the Commission', he proposed funding the creation of lectureships in folklore (to run for five years) in the other university colleges, and that the holders of these posts 'superintend the actual collection in their respective areas.'[48]

Idea of folklore commission takes shape

By early August 1934 the outline of new scheme, as sanctioned by Finance, in particular, was beginning to take shape. Although Ó Duilearga's desire for this scheme to be placed under the care of UCD was rejected, his proposal that the Institute be abolished was agreed to. A new name was therefore needed. The Dept. of Finance got the idea of calling the scheme the Irish Folklore Commission from the Irish Manuscripts Commission, set up in 1928.[49] But the new commission was to get more than its name from the Irish Manuscripts Commission, its terms of reference, for better or for worse, were also to be modelled on those of the latter as well.

Finance initially proposed a board of fifteen members for the Irish Folklore Commission, consisting of six 'Gaelic scholars of high reputation' to be nominated by the Government as well as representatives of the Royal Irish Academy, the Folklore of Ireland Society, and the Departments of Finance and Education.[50] It still proposed that Séamus Ó Duilearga be Honorary Director of the new Commission, which would 'act largely in a supervisory and advisory capacity and the presence on it of representatives of the Departments of Education and Finance would tend to ensure that work was done systematically and with due expedition.' Finance at this stage was willing to fund the Commission to the extent of £2,600 per annum for five years (a somewhat lower sum than it had proposed some months earlier,

---

48 D/T S 9244: MacEntee to de Valera, dated July 1934 (stamped 26.7.1934). The creation of these university lectureships would 'on precedent' have required legislation, and this may be the reason why nothing came of this proposal. See D/T S 9244: MacEntee to de Valera, dated 3.11.1934, p. [3].

49 D/T S 9244: letter from Seán MacEntee to the President, dated 2.8.1934.

50 D/T S 9244: memorandum entitled 'Proposal for the Establishment of an Irish Folklore Commission', pp.[3–5].

see above). In addition, an extra £400 would be given for publications. It is obvious from the way the above memo closes that the Minister was swayed somewhat by the arguments of von Sydow, not to mention by Ó Duilearga himself:

> It is considered that an organisation constituted with the representation and terms of reference and workers already suggested and operating under the aegis of the Government would enhance the country's prestige and considerably advance the scientific study of the folklore, manners and customs of the Irish people. Through its work and its members it would maintain contact with and secure the services of the Universities while ensuring that they do not attain such a position of autonomy that through indolence or otherwise the scheme might fail to achieve its object.[51]

Ó Duilearga's reluctant acceptance of a government commission

Ó Duilearga when informed of the plan to set up a folklore commission reluctantly had to accept it as a fait accompli. He had a meeting with de Valera on August 16th at which the latter may have suggested that he could propose alterations to the scheme put forward by Finance. On August 18th he wrote a long letter to the President, in which, although stressing that he did not 'distrust in any way any branch or officer of the Civil Service with whom our institution will in future have to cope', he does not hide his disappointment at the scheme:

> I feel it my unshirkable duty to emphasise with all the power of conviction I can command that the State cannot create a spiritual movement, and that there is inevitably the danger of an intolerable interference from the purely routine viewpoint, which, as in many cases, can lead to the fossilization of a line of work which is highly individualistic, and in which the spiritual impetus is the indispensable factor. This impetus must be most carefully preserved and fostered.

He goes on to plead that if he has to abandon his 'long-coveted scheme to make Folklore and Irish National Tradition an outstanding activity of [his] University' that 'the following scheme as the minimum requirement for a sound scientific working of the new Commission' be conceded.[52]

He had many suggestions to make as regards the functioning of the new Commission. Most significantly, he proposed that the Commission be purely advisory, and he proposed a list of powers for the Director which left those of the Commission very restricted.[53] In effect, Ó Duilearga was proposing

---

51   Ibid., pp. [4–6].
52   D/T S 9244: Ó Duilearga to de Valera; dated 18.8.1934, pp. 2–3.
53   Ibid., pp. 3–5.

that he should have a free hand in most matters concerning the day-to-day running of the Commission. Not an unreasonable desire, it must be said, but given the Dept. of Finance's rather caustic view of him, perhaps unwise.

Not only was Ó Duilearga forced to accept less than he had hoped for, all the strain involved in negotiating with officials was having an adverse effect on his health and in late August his wife insisted that he take a holiday in the west of Ireland. After his return to Dublin, refreshed from his rest, he felt more optimistic about what was being offered. In a letter he wrote to von Sydow in mid-September, he stated that although the latter's interview with de Valera had not achieved its main purpose, it had not been in vain. He claimed that the proposal to establish a government commission of 15 persons to oversee the work had come out of that interview, and that was an advance.[54] Although he does not explain why he saw this as a development, the fact that the Irish Folklore Institute was to be disbanded meant that he could start with a clean slate. Disbanding the Institute had long been his aim, and now finally he was to have his wish

Finance's reaction to Ó Duilearga's proposed emendations

Not surprisingly, the Minister for Finance was not too pleased with many of Ó Duilearga's suggested amendments to his Department's proposals for the new commission. A somewhat irate Minister for Finance wrote to the President on October 18th:

> I have read Mr Delargy's letter of the 18th August on the subject of the proposed Irish Folklore Commission. At the outset, I may say that the letter does not disclose the extent to which Mr Delargy has been made acquainted with the details of the scheme adumbrated in my communications of the 26th July and the 2nd August last, for the letter gives the impression either that he has not seen the details in full or has failed to understand the main essential in them, namely, that the Commission when established will function in a supervisory and advisory capacity, under the Minister for Education, with a Director generally responsible for the day to day work, working in collaboration with it. Mr. Delargy, it appears, has reluctantly accepted the Commission idea, but the suggestions which he has put forward for consideration by you, flow from the notion that the Commission should act merely as an advisory body to the Director. This is the very antithesis of our scheme. That it is Mr. Delargy's view that the Commission should definitely play second fiddle to the Director is especially evident from the functions he assigns to the Director in Suggestion 5 and to the Commission in Suggestion 6. There is not a word in these paragraphs that could be relied on to guarantee a check on the activities of the Director or his staff...'.[55]

54   LUB saml. von Sydow: Ó Duilearga to von Sydow, dated 14.9.1934.
55   D/T S 9244: Seán MacEntee to de Valera, dated 18.10.1934, p. [1].

While adamant that the Commission should have a supervisory as well as an advisory function, MacEntee was not, ostensibly at least, proposing to put a very tight rein on the Commission, nor on its Director, or, at least, he did not wish to appear to be doing so:

> It is not, of course, contemplated that the Commission should submit to the Minister for Education for his approval anything more than the general outlines of the programme of work it proposes to undertake from year to year nor that the Commission should exercise more than a general supervision over the activities of the Director. But it must be obvious that upon work so highly technical and upon which so large a sum of public money will be spent we must interpose between ourselves and the Director an organisation of competent persons who will ensure that the Director works with efficiency, expedition and economy in accordance with a well considered plan.

Finance, on the other hand, did not quibble with many of Ó Duilearga's emendations, and felt that certain practical details could be worked out later when the Commission was established.[56] On the question of accommodation, however, the Dept. of Finance had objections. Ó Duilearga had in his above letter to de Valera requested that the state provide suitable accommodation for the Commission: a fireproof building with a 'caretaker in residence, preferably in a building belonging to the Government', and that the Commission only have to pay 'a nominal rent' for this accommodation, and that it be partly furnished from 'redundant stock' in the possession of the Office of Public Works.[57] MacEntee rejected this proposal outright: '...the proposal that the State should provide furnished accommodation with a resident caretaker at a nominal rent is tantamount to suggesting that the grant be increased by a further £250 a year or more.' The state had difficulty enough providing accommodation for its own personnel without aggravating the situation further. The Minister for Finance finished, however, on a somewhat more conciliatory note:

> What I have written relates largely to matters of detail, many of them premature, on which no difficulty need be anticipated in reaching agreement once the Commission itself gets down to business. The sole principle at issue is one of control: if our extended scheme is to go on Mr. Delargy must accept the position that, subject to the Minister for Education, the Commission will have the ultimate responsibility and that he, as Director, must work in harmony with them. It is easy to exaggerate, as Mr. Delargy does, the possible drawbacks of such an arrangement, but experience shows they are more theoretical than real. Given a reasonable measure of goodwill, I am perfectly satisfied our scheme can be relied on to give the best all-round results.[58]

56 Ibid., pp. [1–2].
57 D/T S 9244: Ó Duilearga to de Valera, dated 18.8.1934, pp. [5–6].
58 D/T S 9244: MacEntee to de Valera, dated 18.10.1934, pp. [2-4].

Finance's rather negative attitude to Ó Duilearga at this time needs, however, to be placed in context. While these negotiations were going on, the Irish Folklore Institute was still at loggerheads with the Dept. of Finance over publications, and was still seeking to have its grant for 1933-1934 paid. In late March 1934, Finance agreed to pay the Institute's grant for the previous year, the payment of which had been delayed because of the Institute's failure to fulfil its duties in respect of publication in Irish. It did so, however, only on certain conditions. As the Institute was unable to fulfil these conditions to the satisfaction of the Dept. of Finance, the state grant for its final year of operations (1934-1935) was never paid. This unresolved dispute between the Institute and the Dept. of Finance was to have long-lasting consequences for its successor, and to leave a legacy of suspicion in respect of Ó Duilearga in this most influential of government departments. However, the long-term effects of this dispute could not have been predicted at the time, and Ó Duilearga may have felt that with the disbanding of the Irish Folklore Institute imminent, he could leave that dispute behind him.[59]

Further Dept. of Finance emendations

By the start of the winter of 1934, Ó Duilearga had already had some months to accommodate himself to the fact that his dream of incorporating a restructured Irish Folklore Institute into UCD was no longer achievable (in the short term at any rate), but he was still not sure what form the Irish Folklore Commission when eventually constituted would take, as the authorities had not yet finalised their plans. In early November 1934, Seán MacEntee wrote to the President with regard to a draft scheme for the Commission that had been drawn up by the latter's department. He suggested quite a few emendations which were accepted, and one of these in particular was to facilitate, to a certain extent, the future working of the Commission. While the President's scheme made the Commission responsible to the Minister for Finance as well as to the Minister for Education, MacEntee proposed that 'there is no point ... in making two executive Ministers responsible for the work of the Commission.' Instead, he suggested that the Commission be directly responsible to the Minister for Education.[60] The reasons for MacEntee's decision are not entirely clear. As Finance was to have its own representative on the Commission, they would in any case be kept reasonably well abreast of developments, and in any event, little of crucial importance would escape their notice. To some extent, Finance officials may also have been endeavouring to extricate themselves from the particular quagmire they had got themselves into. They had demanded their pound of flesh from the Institute over publication in Irish, but nonetheless had grudgingly been forced to accept the argument for giving priority to collecting over publication. Being responsible to the Minister for Education, did not, of course, mean complete freedom from

59 For more on the Institute's difficulties with the Dept. of Fin. over the question of publications, see Briody 2005b.
60 D/T S 9244: MacEntee to de Valera, dated 3.11.1934, p. 1.

Finance interference, not to mention Finance control, but this decision was crucial nevertheless for it did allow the Commission a measure of freedom to organise its own affairs, and it is unlikely that it would have been able to carry out its work with such effect if it were directly accountable to the Dept. of Finance (or jointly accountable to both Finance and Education). Whatever the reason for this partial disengagement, the Dept. of Finance, as we will see below, was to keep quite a tight rein on the Irish Folklore Commission, in respect of salaries in particular, for the first twelve years of its operations. The Commission might have been treated more sympathetically by the Dept. of Finance and Finance control over salaries eased sooner but for a certain lack of trust (see above) in that department in respect of the Director of the Commission, Séamus Ó Duilearga.

MacEntee was to have another long-term effect on the future Commission. At a meeting between Ó Duilearga and John O'Donovan of the Dept. of the President on October 10th, 1934, the former expressed the wish 'that offices would be available in the Vice-Regal lodge for the proposed Commission.'[61] For some time plans had been afoot to find a new use for the Vice-Regal Lodge, vacated by the Governor General after Fianna Fáil had come to power in 1932, as part of its plan to dismantle the Anglo-Irish Treaty and any remaining symbols of British power in the South of Ireland.[62] Various uses had been suggested for this complex of buildings including utilising it for a museum or art gallery.[63] It is not clear whether Ó Duilearga's suggestion that the Commission be housed in the Vice-Regal Lodge was his original idea or whether it was in response to being informed by John O'Donovan, or some other official, that it might be possible to house the Commission in that location. Be that as it may, for a time in late 1934 and early 1935 it appears that in certain official quarters the creation of 'a museum of Irish Folklore and antiquities' was being contemplated, and that this complex would 'contain provision for the housing of [a] Folklore Library, of discs, cylinders and transcripts and printed works.'[64] The Minister for Finance from the outset opposed plans to house the Commission in the Vice-Regal Lodge, arguing that the Commission, with 'the assistance of the Office of Public Works', should 'make its own arrangements as regards accommodation', and insisted that '[i]n the event of accommodation eventually being made available in the Vice Regal Lodge or in other Government premises,' that it should be required to pay 'a fair rent.'[65]

At some stage in the spring of 1935 the idea of locating the Irish Folklore Commission in the Vice-Regal Lodge was abandoned. Accommodating it there, especially as part of a larger museum complex, may also have been

61   D/T S 9244: handwritten record of telephone conversation, dated 10.10.1934.
62   D/F S 002/0015/32: internal Fin. memo to Mr Dagg, dated 11.7.1933.
63   D/F S 002/0015/32: 'Vice Regal Lodge. Memorandum from the Commissioners of Public Works', dated January 1933.
64   UCDA de Valera Papers P150/2535: 'Notes on the Collection of Irish Folklore' This document would appear to derive from the Dept. of Educ. Parts of it are almost identical to the speech Tomás Ó Deirg gave at the opening of the Irish Folklore Commission. See below.
65   D/T S 9244; MacEntee to President, dated 3.11.1934, p. [2].

found to have been difficult to realise in the short term as the Commission needed to be in operation as soon as possible, and the Vice Regal Lodge was in a state of disrepair. Ó Duilearga may also have had second thoughts about the Vice-Regal Lodge, situated as it was in the Phoenix Part on the outskirts of the city and far from his alma mater and employer, UCD. In any event, UCD's offer of late 1933 still stood and three small, adjacent rooms were made available to the Commission free of charge in Earlsfort Terrace, the main building of the College.[66] As this location was more central and ready to be occupied, it was an offer Ó Duilearga could hardly refuse, even if the space provided was quite limited.

---

66   Michael Tierney says of these rooms that they had by 'a fortunate chance' become available around this time as they 'were not much needed by their nominal occupiers'. Tierney 1975, p. xi.

2. The Board of the Commission

'Terms of Reference' and duties

Once the Dept. of Finance decided to delegate responsibility for it to the Dept. of Education, the latter automatically became midwife to the Commission. In little over a month from the sending of MacEntee's above letter, in early December 1934, the Dept. of Education submitted a draft proposal to the Executive Council for the establishment of an Irish Folklore Commission.[67] By this time, the Terms of Reference of the Commission, which since early autumn 1934 were negotiated between various government departments, had been finalised (see Appendix 1). On New Year's Eve 1934, Ó Duilearga wrote to von Sydow in very hopeful mood. Despite all the trials and tribulations of the previous year he described 1934 as an *'annus mirabilis'*. The Dáil had approved an annual grant of £3,250 for the Commission, to extend for five years. He now felt that it was within his grasp to place Ireland on the folkloristic map. Although a Government commission was not his preferred choice, he knew it offered him an opportunity to achieve what had long been his dream.[68]

Early in the New Year, the Dept. of Education proposed that the Government nominate fifteen members to the Commission from a list provided. However, the Executive Council when they met on February 8th, 1935 chose to invite more than the fifteen members, possibly because they had difficulty eliminating certain names from the list. In all, twenty one persons (see Appendix 2(c)) were asked by the Government to sit on the Commission.[69] Of these all but two agreed to do so: Douglas Hyde and

---

67 D/T S 6916A: 'An Roinn Oideachais. Proposed Irish Folklore Scheme', covering letter dated 4.12.1934.
68 LUB Saml. von Sydow: Ó Duilearga to von Sydow, dated 31.12.1934.
69 The range of expertise of many of the members was quite narrow even for the time. Of the twenty one people invited to sit on the Commission, fourteen were Irish-language scholars or active in the Irish-language movement. Three were Catholic priests, two could be described as antiquarians, two were professors of Classics, and one was an educationalist. There were no historians, no geographers, and no experts on Hiberno-English, and there were no women. No woman was ever to sit on the Commission.

Pádraig Ó Siochfhradha. Hyde declined, citing health reasons.[70] Pádraig Ó Siochfhradha initially turned down a place on the Commission in order to allow the names of the other three representatives of the Folklore of Ireland Society on the board of the Irish Folklore Institute to be nominated. The Society had four representatives on this body, and was hoping to have at least the same number on the Commission, and was not pleased with the reduction in its representation.[71] In the event, the Government invited Ó Siochfhradha to sit on the Commission, but he nonetheless declined the invitation. In a letter to the Dept. of Education he simply says that he regrets not being able to accept the invitation and adds that 'there will be plenty of people in [his] absence to see the work to be done brought to a successful completion', now that the Government had made available a large sum of money for the purpose.[72] If Ó Siochfhradha had accepted a place on the Commission, he would very likely have been a formidable opponent of Ó Duilearga's on issues such as where the Commission's collections should ultimately be housed, as well as on the question of the desirability of publishing the collections without too much delay. His eminent reputation might also have necessitated his presence on the Finance Sub-Committee (see below), which would have created even further problems for Ó Duilearga.

The Government had hoped that Douglas Hyde would act as chairman, but on his declining to accept a place on the Commission it was decided on February 22nd, 1935 to invite Peadar Mac Fhionnlaoich (President of the Gaelic League) to fill the post.[73] The decision to offer Mac Fhionnlaoich (better known under his pseudonym Cú Uladh, 'Hound of Ulster') the post of Chairman at this juncture was most likely made to placate the League, as somebody like Osborn Bergin would have had much greater prestige. The previous month the Executive Committee (Coiste Gnótha) of the League had written to the Minister for Finance, Seán MacEntee, informing him that they had 'no confidence in the persons mentioned for the Folklore Commission because of the professions they practise'. In its view, 'the scheme should be best operated for the benefit of the Irish language among the public instead of for the benefit of professors'. They wanted three representatives on the Commission and stated that 'it is our belief that nobody should be appointed to the Commission except people who know modern Irish, who have the right attitude in respect of the Irish language and who have already collected folklore, prose, poetry and music.'[74]

Many of those initially appointed to the Commission were elderly (see Appendix 2(c)), or their health was failing. By the mid-1940's four members were dead, Peadar Mac Fhionnlaoich, Séamus Ó Casaide, Énrí Ó Muirgheasa,

---

70 ED CO 3/15/9(495/II): Hyde to Seosamh Ó Néill, dated 17.2.1935.
71 ED CO 3/15/9(495/II): internal memo, [Ó Dubhthaigh] to Sec. Dept. of Educ., dated 22.12.1934.
72 ED CO 3/15/9(495/II): letter dated 4.3.1935.
73 D/T S 6916A: Cabinet Minutes, dated 22.2.35.
74 D/F S 101/0011/34: cov. letter dated 29.1.1935 (trans.). On Mac Fhionnlaoich's death, Osborn Bergin was offered the Chairmanship of the Commission, but declined. See D/T S 6916C: 'IFC. Summary of Government Decisions, 1935-1953'.

and Lorcán Ó Muireadhaigh. Initially, vacancies on the Commission were filled, and departmental representatives were replaced from time to time, especially those of the Dept. of Education. However, as the years passed, vacancies on the Commission were not filled and death and resignations took their toll, so that by 1970 when it was eventually disbanded its ranks were greatly depleted (See Appendix 2(a)).

The Finance Sub-Committee

As we have seen already, in June 1934, de Valera informed the Dept. of Finance that, in his opinion, the restructured Institute 'should consist henceforth of a small Executive Committee and a Council, the functions of the latter to be mainly advisory.' He also suggested that the 'Executive Committee should include Mr. Delargy, as Director, one representative of the Department of Education, one representative of the Department of Finance, and, say, two other persons.'[75] An internal Education memorandum dealing with de Valera's above proposals questions the wisdom of appointing a Council in addition to an 'Executive Body', believing 'it would merely complicate matters, lead to difficulties and cause delay.'[76] In the event, as we have seen above, a Council (i.e. the Commission proper) was to be appointed, but for whatever reason the Terms of Reference of the Commission contain no reference to the establishment of an executive committee. The reason for this is not clear, nor is the relation of the Finance Sub-Committee vis-à-vis the Commission clear. For example, did the former have powers in respect of non-financial matters over and above the Commission proper? Whether it had or not, it certainly acted much of the time as if it had, and though it usually sought sanction for its decisions from the Commission, it did not invariably do so. Even if the powers of this sub-committee were not formally specified, the presence of a representative on it of both the Dept. of Education and the Dept. of Finance would have lent more weight to its decisions than they might otherwise have had.

The second meeting of the Irish Folklore Commission appointed this sub-committee from among its members. Those appointed were Liam Price (as Chairman), Séamus Ó Duilearga, Séamus Ó Casaide, and the representatives of the Departments of Education and Finance, Lughaidh Maguidhir and León Ó Broin.[77] It has to be noted that the Finance Sub-Committee was free of certain ideological tensions that from time to time characterised meetings of the Commission. Whether this was by design or otherwise is difficult to say. However, given the responsibility of this committee in respect of the spending of Government grants, it is unlikely that its membership was left completely to chance.[78]

75   D/T S 9244: S[eán] Ó M[uimhneacháin] to Sec. Dept. of Finance, dated June 1934.
76   ED CO 3/15/9(495/I): [Ó Dubhthaigh] to Sec. Dept.of Educ., dated 27.6.1934.
77   ED [FL 9]: 'CBÉ. Miont. 2ú Cruinniú, 31.5.1935', par. 17.
78   e.g. shortly before the Commission was inaugurated the Minister for Education requested an urgent meeting with Séamus Ó Casaide, possibly to ascertain if the latter would

The Inauguration of Coimisiún Béaloideasa Éireann

On the March 29th, 1935 the members of the Board of the Irish Folklore Institute convened for the last time. A letter was read out from the Dept. of Finance explaining that in Finance's opinion it would not be necessary to pay the Institute's grant for the year 1934-1935, which, as we have seen above, had been delayed due to the ongoing dispute over publications in Irish. The letter assumed that the Institute had sufficient funds to clear any outstanding debts before closing down. Finance also proposed that the Institute donate its 'papers, mss., library, etc' to the Irish Folklore Commission. The meeting decided to offer the Institute's office equipment to the Commission, and whatever the Commission did not need to the Folklore of Ireland Society. More importantly the board of the Institute decided to donate:

> ...the Institute's manuscripts and library to the State, and to request the State to allow the Folklore Commission use of the manuscripts and books for as long as it would have need of them, and for them to eventually be preserved under the State's protection in some public Library or archive where they will be available for consultation and the use of the public.[79]

Four days later, on April 2nd, 1935, the first meeting of Coimisiún Béaloideasa Éireann (Irish Folklore Commission) took place in the Council Chamber of University College, Dublin. None of those present could have had any idea that what was being initiated that day would run not only for the proposed five years of its term of office, but for thirty five years, and that none but a handful of those present would still be alive when the Commission would be finally disbanded. Among those who would be alive, but not present on that day, was Éamon de Valera. Although Ó Duilearga did not get all he hoped for from him, as we have seen, without de Valera's goodwill it is unlikely there would have been an Irish Folklore Commission.

The meeting was opened by the Minister for Education, Tomás Ó Deirg, 'in the unavoidable absence of Mr. de Valera'. Although the public were not admitted, 'a report was issued at the conclusion' for the benefit of the press. The Minister for Education spoke in Irish, saying 'that the establishment of this Commission marked a very important moment in the cultural history of Ireland'. He is reported to have said of the setting up of the Commission:

> It was a public act of homage to our own people, the fulfilment of a filial duty towards the unknown Irish dead. It was a mighty monument to the poor nameless country people who have preserved the stories of the joys

---

be willing to act as a member of the Finance Sub-Committee. NLI Ó Casaide Papers 10,688(5): P. Ó Cochláin to Ó Casaide, dated 25.3.1935.

79 D/T S 7537: 'Copy of minutes of board of the Irish Folklore Institute - 29th March, 1935.' (trans). It would appear that the £234/10/8 in the Institute's two bank accounts was sufficient to clear all debts, and it was decided to transfer this balance to the Irish Folklore Commission. Ibid.

and sorrows of Ireland, who had passed on to us the whisperings of the centuries during which our country lay under the blanket of the dark.

The account of the proceedings in the *Irish Press* carries the heading 'Work Abandoned 100 Years Ago Resumed', echoing the Minister's speech where he referred to the work of the Ordnance Survey of the 1830's and 1840's:

> A hundred years ago work was begun by the Ordnance Survey established by the British Government. O'Curry and O'Donovan set themselves to amass a wealth of folklore under the headings topography and local history. But the work did not survive the publication of the first report —the Londonderry Survey—because it was calculated in the eyes of the authorities to make the Irish restive, to arouse race-consciousness, to awaken nationalism.
>
> Now a hundred years later, the Commission had the honour of resuming the interrupted labours of the Ordnance Survey under a native Government; and for the very reason for which it was then abandoned—to make the Irish people realise who they are—to establish a linguistic, social and cultural history of our own people; not of the wealthy and influential among them, but of the poor and forgotten ones who have preserved the lore and spirit and faith of our forefathers for us.[80]

The Minister spoke of 'three stages in the process of folklore collection.' The first of these was 'the propaganda stage, the arousing of enthusiasm for the work.' The second stage involved 'the actual collecting', and the third and final stage, ' the exploitation of the materials collected.' The Minister reminded those present that the 'establishment of this Commission marked the beginning of the second stage', adding that collecting was not being confined to the Irish language, nor to the twenty six counties of the state, but to the whole island, 'in order that a complete picture of Ireland may be formed with materials gathered from the whole country.' He expressed the hope that '[t]his is a work in which all Irishmen will be united', and that it would 'link together all men of good-will, of every political and religious persuasion, in a truly national cause.'[81]

The Chairman, Peadar Mac Fhionnlaoich, thanked the Minister on behalf of the Commission, and asked him 'to convey to the President of the Executive Council [Éamon de Valera] their appreciation of the state's action in establishing the Commission', adding 'that every effort would be made to justify the confidence reposed in them.' He further added: 'Steps would be taken to record every aspect of the oral tradition of the past generations,

---

80 *Irish Press* 3.4.1935 (trans.). The reasons why the preparation of these reports (memoirs) was abandoned by the Ordnance Survey are now known to have been more complex than suggested by Ó Deirg. For more on the fate of these memoirs and the Ordnance Survey project in general, see Andrews 2001 [1975], Doherty 2004, and ÓCadhla 2007.

81 *Irish Times* April 3rd, 1935, p. 6. Much of what Ó Deirg had to say at this meeting echoes various writings of Ó Duilearga's and it is more than likely that the latter had some input, direct or indirect, into the Minister's speech.

so that it might be handed on to the Ireland of to-day, and to the still greater Ireland of tomorrow.' The *Irish Times* concluded its report of the opening of the Commission by informing readers: 'The administrative offices of the Commission will be in University College, Earlsfort Terrace, where ample accommodation has been generously provided by the authorities of University College.'[82]

It would appear that the press were given an edited account of all that happened at this meeting, for tensions appear to have surfaced at the opening meeting of the Commission that were to linger for as long as the Commission itself. Fr. Eric Mac Fhinn, who was to be chairman of the Commission from 1942 until its disbandment in 1970, has left us an eye-witness account of the first meeting:

> Cú Uladh [i.e. Peadar mac Fhionnlaoich] was in the Chair. Tomás Ó Deirg, the Minister for Education, was there to get us started. He explained to us that Séamus [Ó Duilearga] was to be director. (Cú Uladh spoke entirely in Irish – Tomás Ó Deirg also spoke in Irish). Cú Uladh spoke very eloquently about the importance of folklore. Séamus then spoke. He made a long, verbose speech in English, that really was not very good as a piece of English – he was too serious. When he had finished, I rose and said that I would like to hear what he had said in Irish. Bergin looked down at the table and said in a kind of whisper: 'I don't see the necessity.' Fr. Lorcán Ó Muireadhaigh's eyes lit up and he emitted a hearty chuckle, and he was rubbing his hands together. Cú Uladh looked at Séamus [Ó Duilearga] with a glint of glee in his eye. 'Are you satisfied?' he asked him. 'Yes' he replied. In my estimation, his talk in Irish was better that the one in English... On our way out, Cú Uladh said to me: 'You taught them a lesson Father.'[83]

Fr. Eric Mac Fhinn, later Monsignor, was a very staunch supporter of the revival of Irish. Obviously, everybody at the meeting understood what Ó Duilearga had said in English, so Osborn Bergin in a sense was right in not seeing the 'necessity' of repeating in Irish what had already been said in English. But for many members of the Gaelic League, and the Irish -language movement in general, it was important that Irish become the language of as many of the state's institutions as possible. The fact that the Commission's work was to be so bound up with the Irish language made it all the more imperative for them that Irish should become the language of the Commission's meetings and administration. Ó Duilearga's tendency to use English on the Commission to facilitate those who did not know Irish (or were not at ease conversing in Irish) would have continued to irritate some members, especially if they felt he was trying to use it excessively, or exclusively.[84] However, not all the tension that existed in the Commission

---

82   *Irish Times* April 3rd, 1935, p. 6.

83   Ní Nia (MA thesis), p. 82 (trans.). Quoted from letter Mac Fhinn wrote to Prof. Breandán Ó Madagáin, dated 15.9.1981.

84   Gearóidín Ní Nia, who has had access to the extensive diaries Eric Mac Fhinn kept

down through the years involved the use of Irish at meetings or indeed attitudes towards the restoration of the Irish language, although much of it did. Ó Duilearga's style of leadership also played a part. León Ó Broin, who served on the Commission for many years as the Dept. of Finance's representative, speaks of 'a certain tension at the first meetings' and says 'Delargy was short-tempered, and usually raised his voice unpleasantly till he got his way.'[85] The Commission had a daunting task ahead of it, namely to collect the folklore of Ireland. It was only natural that among such a large body of people a variety of opinions would exist as to what should take priority. For example, it is certain that the collecting of folksongs was less of a priority for Ó Duilearga than it was for others on the Commission, while his predilection for collecting folktales was not shared by some of his colleagues. In many cases where a difference of opinion on policy emerged, Ó Duilearga managed to get his way, by a variety of strategies, including that which Ó Broin refers to above. Getting one's way too often, and being seen to get one's way, does not necessarily win over hearts and runs the risk of concerted opposition at some stage. The Board of the Commission was there not only to advise the Honorary Director, it was also authorised to consider his proposals, and could, if it so desired, reject them. As we will see below, on one crucial proposal of Ó Duilearga's, he failed to get the support he needed from his colleagues on the Commission.

throughout most of his long life, says that Mac Fhinn continuously finds fault in his diaries with Ó Duilearga because 'he used too much English at the meetings to facilitate people on the Commission who had no Irish.' Ní Nia (MA thesis), pp. 82-83 (trans.).

85 Ó Broin n.d., pp.100-101. On Ó Duilearga's behaviour at meetings of the Commission, see also Ní Nia (MA thesis), p. 196.

3. Making the Commission permanent

End of five-year term of office

The Irish Folklore Commission was initially intended to last for five years, during which time it was hoped that the bulk of the folklore that needed to be collected, or, at least, that urgently needed to be collected, would be collected. However, as the first fruits of the collecting began to come in, it became evident that the amount of folklore that was there to be collected had been underestimated. In a letter Ó Duilearga wrote to von Sydow in December 1935 he spoke of the quantity and quality of the material coming in and of its importance not just for Ireland but for Europe as a whole.[86] With so much folklore coming in, the fact that the Commission was only to run for five years could not but have been uppermost in Ó Duilearga's mind. Two years later he wrote to von Sydow stating that he was constantly trying to have the Commission made permanent, as 'we *may* be dissolved in 1940 at the end of our five years.'[87] This worry did not just apply to the fate of the collecting itself, but also to the Commission's staff, particularly his office staff. Writing to von Sydow in May 1938 he spoke of the 'irreparable blow' to 'Irish culture and scholarship' if Seán Ó Súilleabháin and Máire MacNeill would have to return to other employment in the event of the Commission being disbanded. The Commission, he complained, was being expected to do in five years what other countries took a number of generations to accomplish.[88] If he had known that the Commission was to run not for five years but for thirty five years in all, and that it would be kept in a sort of semi-permanent limbo for decades, he might have been even more worried at this juncture, but there was no knowing that.

When the Commissions's five years was almost up, Séamus Ó Duilearga officially requested the Government that its term of office be extended in order for it to continue collecting in the Gaeltacht and later on in the rest of the country where much historical lore, in particular, was to be had. Mindful

---

86 LUB Saml. von Sydow: Ó Duilearga to von Sydow, letter dated 19.12.1935.
87 LUB Saml. von Sydow: Ó Duilearga to von Sydow, letter dated 20.12.1937, italics underlined in original.
88 LUB Saml. von Sydow: Ó Duilearga to von Sydow, letter dated 31.5.1938.

of the need to consider a more permanent organisation for the Commission in the not too distant future, in closing his letter to the Secretary to the Government he made this appeal:

> The establishment of the Commission in 1935 was hailed by the learned bodies of Europe and the United States with enthusiasm and approval, and the interest of the Irish Government in preserving the native traditions and folklore was appreciated in many quarters where interest in Irish affairs had up till then not been in evidence. The new institution became at once international in its character, and from the very beginning began to exercise considerable influence in the fields of research in pre-history, comparative literature and medieval studies. At present the archive of the Commission is recognised as being the most extensive and most important in existence, while it is still conceded by European research that the Commission's work is of necessity in its initial stages only. My personal opinion is that the national folklore archives should become a permanent institution and take its place with Government folklore archives of a similar character in many other countries.[89]

It would be the following spring before the Government officially sanctioned the extension of the Commission's term of office for another four years 'in order to further the completion of the work originally assigned to it'.[90] However, long before the Cabinet gave its seal of approval to this extension, the Commission were given informal assurances that its term of office would be extended.[91] In the meantime war had broken out in Europe and this fact, most likely, delayed a formal decision being made by the Government on this matter. The state needed to cut back on its expenditure and the Commission like every other state-funded body came in for scrutiny. The Dept. of Finance sanctioned a further term of office for the Commission somewhat reluctantly. One Finance official wrote: 'While we may not agree as to the utility of the work being done or as to its value the fact remains that many people regard the work of the Commission as of first class importance and consider that the work of collection should be pushed ahead as rapidly as possible.' Another Finance official in a note appended to this internal memo termed the work of the Commission 'an inessential service which could very well be suspended during the emergency [i.e. Second World War].' As 'a question of [Government] policy' was involved, he nonetheless felt it would 'be necessary to have a Ministerial direction.'[92] However inessential this 'service' appeared in the eyes of the above official, this project had the blessing of the Head of Government. De Valera might agree to a cutback in the Commission's grant, but he would not have countenanced its suspension.

89 D/T S 6916A: letter dated 15.06.1939, pp. 4-6.
90 D/T S 6916A: copy of 'Cabinet Minutes', dated 16/4/40, and ibid., Educ. memo to Gov., dated 8.4.1940.
91 ULMA Saml. Åke Campbell, subnr. 203: Seán Ó Súilleabháin to Campbell, 17.12.39.
92 D/F S 101/0011/34; K[ealy] to Almond dated , 28.11.1939, pp. [3-4].

In his letter to the Government, Ó Duilearga does not specify what type of permanent organisation he envisaged for the Commission, and interestingly no mention is made of incorporating a restructured Commission into UCD. In a letter he wrote to Seosamh Ó Néill of the Dept. of Education more than a month later he says more about this matter:

> I would like to particularly emphasise the following point. Viz. that at some future date the folklore collection has to be made permanent in some way, for instance, under different direction compared to the Commission's present arrangement. When that time comes in three or four years time, let's suppose, that will be the most suitable time, less wrought with difficulty to decide how best to publish or make available to the public in other ways the fruits of the collection.

He proposed that during the second term of office of the Commission a decision should be made to found a 'special permanent department to house for posterity our books, Mss, etc in a State archive and that this institution should be open to the public as the RIA [Royal Irish Academy] is.'[93]

If the work of the Commission had been completed at the end of its first five years, the collectors could have been let go and a decision made as to where to house the accumulated collections. However, the work was not complete by 1940, and in a sense it could never be complete, something which the officials dealing with Ó Duilearga did not fully appreciate. When the Commission had been set up neither Ó Duilearga nor anybody else involved had suggested that the amount of folklore available was infinite, but as time went on Ó Duilearga seemed to be suggesting it was. Some officials probably felt they had been misled to some extent. But apart from the question of how much folklore there was to be collected and how much should be collected, there was the problem posed by these burgeoning collections, temporarily crammed into a few small rooms in UCD. These rooms would soon burst at the seams. Later, as we shall see, UCD was to provide better, though not ideal accommodation for the Commission and its collections, but even that was considered a temporary solution.

Most people agreed that the Irish Folklore Commission should be placed on some sort of permanent footing and its collections safeguarded for posterity. The basic questions were where it should be located and what sort of organisation was needed in future to care for and utilise these collections. Should the final home of the Commission's collections be in a university milieu, in an institution of higher learning such as the National Library or the Dublin Institute for Advanced Studies, or should it be re-established as a permanent independent body, possibly within the Civil Service? We have already seen that in 1933/1934 when proposals to reorganise the state-aided collecting of Irish folklore were being drawn up, opposition from a number of quarters prevented Ó Duilearga from realising his declared dream of having the new scheme placed under the care of UCD, his alma mater

---

93   D/F S 101/0011/34, letter dated 17.7.1939 (trans.).

and employer. UCD had, however, in the meantime accommodated the Commission rent-free since 1935 and provided it with various services free of charge, as well as seconding Ó Duilearga to act as Director. As a result, some felt that the College had, by so doing, a claim to the Commission and that the best solution would be to integrate it fully into UCD. There were others, however, who felt that irrespective of the debt the state owed UCD for helping the Commission there were other factors that had to be weighed in the balance. Indeed by the time Ó Duilearga again proposed that the Irish Folklore Commission be placed in UCD, from the mid-1940's, that college was in the eyes of some even less acceptable as a permanent home for a national folklore collection.

Time would, however, eventually secure a home for the Commission in UCD, but by then Ó Duilearga would be an old and frail man, and the intervening years, and long wait, would take a heavy toll on him, and on the staff of the Commission, it must be said. For the most part, the same factors that initially prevented this work of national importance being placed in the care of UCD in 1933/1934 continued to frustrate efforts to have the fruits of this work placed in the lasting care of this institution. Before examining in detail the efforts to re-establish the Irish Folklore Commission from the early 1940's to the late 1960's, and in order to help readers focus on events as they unfold, I will a) outline some of the issues and problems of the period that had a bearing on this protracted and, in many respects, tragic saga, and b) present the main agents (i.e. the protagonists) along with the attitudes they held, and the arguments they advanced, or, as was sometimes the case, did not advance, openly at least.

Issues and problems of the period

In Dublin middle-class parlance, UCD was known as 'National' (from the National University of Ireland, of which it was the biggest constituent college), but in the estimation of some elements of Fianna Fáil, as well as sections of the Irish-language movement, 'national' was an appellation it did not deserve, and by implication neither did it deserve to be given the care of a national institution such as the Irish Folklore Commission. This was in many ways was the crux of the matter.

Although rejected by a majority of the electorate in 1922 and defeated in the Civil War, Fianna Fáil, as a party, believed that it was the true heir of the revolutionary movement that had forced the British to initiate peace negotiations in the summer of 1921. Its political opponents, Cumann na nGaedheal (later reconstituted as Fine Gael), were at worst national apostates; at best their national credentials were suspect. University College Dublin was considered by many in Fianna Fáil to be a bastion of Cumann na nGaedheal/ Fine Gael support and while UCD as the largest constituent college of the National University of Ireland could not be ignored, there was an antipathy towards that college in certain echelons of Fianna Fáil. While this antipathy, fuelled by Civil War animosities (and possibly by the rise of the Blueshirts), was a factor that frustrated efforts to incorporate the Commission into UCD, on its own it might not have been potent enough to prevent such a transfer for such a long time. It would appear that it was a combination of Fianna Fáil antipathy towards UCD and resentment in Irish-language circles in general over the failure of UCD to advance the state's policies of gaelicisation – resentment shared by elements in Fianna Fáil – that dashed Ó Duilearga's hopes of finding a permanent home for the Commission in UCD.

Fianna Fáil antipathy towards UCD might not figure so much in this story but for the fact that this party dominated the political scene for the lifespan of the Commission, being in power for almost twenty nine of the thirty five years of the Commission's operations. Moreover, de Valera, who, as we shall see below, was strongly opposed to incorporating the Commission into UCD, was head of government for more than eighteen of those years. Even after de Valera's retirement from active politics in June 1959, quite a few of the old guard of Fianna Fáil remained in Government until the mid-1960's or thereabouts. [94]

Although the first Cumann na nGaedheal Government initiated the policy of gaelicisation in the early 1920's, Fianna Fáil on coming to power in 1932 intensified these efforts, and as time went on, gaelicisation, mainly through the schools, became more associated with that party than with Fine Gael, Cumann na nGaedheal's successor. Perhaps also the fact that the restoration of Irish was the first of Fianna Fáil's two stated national aims – the second being the reunification of the country – made it more difficult for the party to begin to reassess the state's language policies, when doubts began to be expressed in many quarters as to their effectiveness. It should be noted that elements in Fine Gael began much sooner to seek a revision of the state's gaelicisation policies than did members of Fianna Fáil.

Right throughout the 1930's and into the early 1940's the Gaelic League was dissatisfied with the failure of UCD to initiate teaching through the medium of Irish. Then in 1943 a report by a sub-committee of UCD's Academic Council came out strongly against initiating teaching through Irish. While not expressing opposition to the state's revival policies as such, this report did not see a central role for the universities in realising these policies, although it did see a limited role. This report made many valuable recommendations for improving the knowledge of Irish among the student body, but on the substantive issue of teaching through the medium of Irish it held firm:

> It must be clearly understood, therefore, that the task of assisting the national policy on Irish among the student body can only be undertaken without prejudice to the maintenance of the existing standards of university education in all subjects. In practice this reservation leads us (a) to exclude Irish under present conditions as a normal teaching medium

94 Fianna Fáil came to power in March 1932 and remained in power until February 1948, crucial years for the Commission. Between February 1948 and March 1957 they spent two periods in opposition, and on resuming power in 1957 remained in office until March 1973. The Commission was established by a Fianna Fáil Government, and it was a Fianna Fáil Government that eventually oversaw its transfer to UCD in 1971.

in courses for a University degree; (b) to draw a distinction between the teaching of Modern Irish as a degree subject and the teaching of Irish in the pursuance of national policy.[95]

The report itself was meant to be confidential, but it was leaked to people in the Irish-language movement and to the press. In the July issue of the Irish-language monthly *Comhar*, the Chairman of the Irish Folklore Commission, Fr. Eric Mac Fhinn, commented adversely on this report, and in its August issue, *Comhar* printed the main findings of the report, as well as a good deal of adverse commentary. After a certain amount of revision, in January 1944, UCD's Academic Council decided to forward the report to de Valera, as Chancellor of the National University of Ireland, as well as to the Minister for Education.[96] A year earlier, at a meeting of representatives of the constituent colleges of the National University of Ireland, de Valera, in his capacity as Chancellor of the University, had asked 'what is being done, or could be done, in the University to continue the education of students who had been taught wholly or partly through the medium of Irish in the Secondary Schools.'[97] This was UCD's reply to his query, which had probably been more in the nature of a request that something should be done, rather than a simple query. Nothing was being done in UCD in this area, and nothing was going to be done, it appeared. The report, in effect, postponed teaching through the medium of Irish in UCD into the distant future when Irish, it was hoped, somehow would have put down roots in the community at large. De Valera must have been displeased with UCD both as Chancellor and as Taoiseach, and this report would have done nothing to raise the College's national credentials in his eyes.

Whether this report was an honest attempt or not to investigate how best UCD could further the state's revival policies, it has to be noted that the initial report was compiled in little more than a week, and no interested parties would appear to have been consulted, such as students, other UCD staff, and the authorities and staff of University College Galway, which had a good deal of experience of teaching through Irish.[98] Moreover, although all the members of the sub-committee were members of UCD's Faculty of Celtic Studies, with the exception of Michael Tierney, none of them could be described as an Irish-language revivalist. Irish revivalists in the Faculty, such as Cormac Ó Cadhlaigh, Professor of Modern Irish, and his colleague Prof. Úna Ní Fhaircheallaigh, were not included on the sub-committee. It is hard not to escape the impression that this sub-committee was somewhat

---

95 UCDA Blythe Papers P/24/998: The Revival of Irish as a National Language and the Study of Irish as a University Subject', par. 5 and par. 6.

96 UCDA: Min. of Acad. Coun. Book IV p. 310.

97 UCDA Blythe Papers P/24/998: 'University College, Dublin', p. [2]. This document appears to be a copy of the minutes of a meeting of the Governing Body of the National University of Ireland.

98 Tierney admitted to the Commission on Higher Education many years later that those who compiled this 1943 report did not consult 'with U.C.G [University College Galway] or other institutions teaching through Irish.' *Commission on Higher Education 1960-67 II. Report Volume 2*, p. 696.

of a packed jury and that a verdict had been reached on the feasibility of initiating teaching through Irish even before the sub-committee convened to examine this and other related matters that it had been asked to report on. Be that as it may, while from a modern perspective, a good deal of what the report had to say on the feasibility of teaching through Irish was reasonable, in the emotionally charged atmosphere of the time in Irish-language, and some government, circles these arguments were not seen as reasonable objections, but as an evasion of national duty.

With this report UCD had nailed its flag to the mast as far as the Irish-language movement was concerned. It was unfortunate for Ó Duilearga that he had been asked to convene and sit on this sub-committee, and that he signed his name to the report, for this fact did not go unnoticed in Irish-language circles, nor in Irish-folklore circles, in should be said. Indeed his association with this report would some years later be flung in his face by the writer Máirtín Ó Cadhain at a public lecture the latter gave on folklore in 1950.[99]

Opposition to transferring the Irish Folklore Commission to UCD was not simply motivated by prejudice: for some there was also a question of principle involved. It was intended by those who drew up the Terms of Reference of the Commission that the collections amassed by the Irish Folklore Commission should remain the property of the state. Paragraph 'II, 6' of the Terms of Reference specifically state that the materials that would be collected by the Commission 'be deemed always to be the property of the State'[100] Moreover, as we have seen above, some six months or more before these Terms of Reference were finalised, de Valera had stipulated that the records accumulated by the reorganised Irish Folklore Institute 'should be Government property and the officer in charge of them should be a Government official.' However, when a final resting place was found for the collections of the Folklore of Ireland Society and those of the Irish Folklore Institute, along with the far greater collections amassed by the Irish Folklore Commission during its thirty five years of operation, it would not be in a 'public library or archive' but in a private institution, namely University College Dublin. In effect, collections created, for the most part, with taxpayers' money were to pass out of the control of the state, despite stipulations that were given during negotiations to set up the Commission that such would never happen.

Despite the intentions of those who formulated these Terms of Reference in respect of the future ownership of the collections to be amassed by the Commission, these Terms of Reference, not having been sanctioned by an Act of Dáil Éireann, were not statutorily binding, and, as we will see below, did not tie the hands of officials later in seeking a permanent home for the Commission. What the state owned, it could disown; what it drew up, it could, in time, tear up. This may explain why some officials of the Dept. of Education in the 1940's saw the transfer of the Commission to UCD in purely pragmatic

99   See Ó Laighin 1990, p. 134.
100 D/F S 101/0011/34: 'Irish Folklore Commission [Terms of Reference]'.

terms, and do not seem to have pondered too much the national implications of such a move. However, there is no doubt that the rights and wrongs of transferring state property to public ownership did exercise the minds of some officials, although such matters were rarely verbalised as such.

Another issue of the period, and one that had a crucial effect on efforts to re-establish the Irish Folklore Commission, was the question of finance. It was always going to cost much more money to make the Commission permanent than to keep it going from year to year. Moreover, making it an integral part of UCD, because of higher salaries in universities vis-à-vis the Civil Service, would be more expensive than making it permanent under the Civil Service. Some officials of the Dept. of Finance may have felt UCD could have done more to help the revival of Irish, and some indeed, with Republican leanings, may have been against UCD for political reasons. But apart from such prejudices, and overriding them, Finance officials had a way of looking at requests for extra funding which disposed them to resist such requests as much as possible. Ministers might come and go but attitudes in the Dept. of Finance did not change greatly.[101]

Tom Garvin suggests that the methods and attitudes of the Dept. of Finance derived from the immediate aftermath of the Civil War. The hiring of 50,000 soldiers by the Free State Government to defeat the rebels as well as 'the systematic wrecking of the country's infrastructure by the IRA' was estimated at the time to have cost the young independent state £50,000,000 ('close on three billion euro' in today's money). Garvin comments: 'This crippling blow to the infant state was to make the penny-pinching traditions of the new Department of Finance institutionalised at the moment of birth.'[102] We will see many examples of penny-pinching below in this work, but it should be remembered that pennies were also often scarce, particularly during the War years and during the 1950's, which was a decade of severe economic depression.

Agents: attitudes and arguments

Above I have looked at some of the general issues of the period that for more than a generation hampered efforts to place the Commission on a permanent foundation. Issues cannot, of course, exist without human agents. Agents, in turn, hold attitudes on numerous matters, and advance arguments to further their points of view, beliefs, and prejudices. The two main agents in this saga are Séamus Ó Duilearga and Éamon de Valera. Without the cooperation of both these men, and their common understanding on the importance of gathering for posterity the rich treasures of Irish folklore, the Commission would perhaps never have been established in the first place. But while de Valera can, in a sense, be considered the 'giver-of-life' of the Commission and a caring father, in the early years at least, he was in time to

---

101 See what Michael Hayes had to say on the parsimonious ways of Ministers for Finance in a Senate debate in the late 1940's: *Seanad Éireann*. Vol. 34, p. 9.
102 Garvin 2003, p. 77.

become something of an autocratic parent in respect of the Commission, and Irish society in general, it should be said. Certainly, Ó Duilearga, a man of autocratic tendencies himself, met his match in de Valera. It was, of course, an unequal match, as de Valera had the machinery of state behind him; Ó Duilearga little more than his wits at times.

De Valera's opposition to making the Commission permanent within UCD may partly have been motivated by prejudice against that College for the stance many prominent members of its staff took in the Civil War against opponents of the Anglo-Irish Treaty (and continued to take against him personally), and also by the failure of UCD to develop Irish as a medium of teaching. However, his opposition to transferring the Commission to UCD is more complex than that. Whatever he thought personally about UCD, as Chancellor of the National University of Ireland, a post he had held since 1921, and which military defeat, imprisonment, and years in the political wilderness, had not deprived him of, he had to be seen to deal evenhandedly with all its constituent colleges.[103] Thus, favouring one constituent college of the National University of Ireland over the others might have made his job as Chancellor more difficult. Donal McCartney says of de Valera's work as Chancellor: 'Next to his homelife, it provided a haven of relaxation for him, away from the hurly-burly of the political arena.' Here he could meet academics, some of them former colleagues and acquaintances: 'Through the Chancellorship he had managed to hold on, vicariously, to that scholarly career he loved so much, but from which revolutionary politics had snatched him.'[104] As a result of his experience as Chancellor, more than most of his political colleagues, he had an intimate knowledge of universities, of their potential, as well as their limitations. Of course, a cynic might say that he himself, by underfunding the state's universities, was partly responsible for some of these limitations. Be that as it may, there is no doubt that there is a place for institutes of research and learning outside of universities. De Valera's decision to establish the Dublin Institute of Advanced Studies in 1940, against the opposition of many in his own party, bears witness to his belief that there were certain types of programmatic scholarly work that could best be undertaken independent of universities. Speaking in Seanad Éireann in May 1940 on the Dublin Institute for Advanced Studies Bill, he spoke of the need for 'independent autonomous' institutes to undertake programmatic research: 'In modern times, on account of the great specialisation of knowledge, the need for institutes of this sort has been felt more and more.' In the case of Celtic Studies, he said: 'there was very good reason for establishing some independent autonomous body which would be charged' a) 'with the task of editing, publishing and making available for scholars the large mass of material which has accumulated,' and b) 'with the task of training future scholars and giving to advanced students who would be interested lectures on this subject.'[105] In his speech, he also referred to the setting up of both the

103 For more on de Valera's role as Chancellor of the National University of Ireland, see McCartney 1983.
104 Ibid., pp.45–46.
105 Moynihan 1980, p. 438.

144

Irish Manuscripts Commission and the Irish Folklore Commission. Speaking of the work of these two bodies, he said:

> All that had to be undertaken outside the universities. It may be said that it could have been done in the universities. It could, of course, if you wished to expand a university and give it a special branch; but, if you want to have freedom of operation, to have the work carried out without any inconvenience, to have immediate control of that sort, it was necessary to have it carried out by an independent body.[106]

In the mid 1940's, de Valera proposed creating a separate School of Folklore within the Dublin Institute for Advanced Studies. In doing so, I believe, he was not motivated simply by political prejudice against UCD, but had the interests of the Commission at heart. Locating the Commission in an autonomous and prestigious institute of learning offered possibilities for its development not offered by any of the constituent colleges of the National University of Ireland (nor indeed Trinity College Dublin), none of which at the time had a strong research tradition, particularly in the Humanities. That is not to say that prejudice did not also play a part in his aversion to re-establishing the Commission in UCD, especially in the 1950's when he himself had become disillusioned with the Dublin Institute for Advanced Studies, particularly its School of Celtic Studies.

If Ó Duilearga had totally abandoned his desire that the organisation of folklore collecting and research be made an integral part of the work of UCD, a solution to the non-permanent status of the Commission would probably have been found sooner. Although he reluctantly agreed to the idea of an independent Commission in 1934, and although for a time in the early 1940's he seems to have been reconciled to the Commission being made permanent outside of that College, as the decade advanced, he once again reverted to his original position. Moreover, while the Dept. of Education was of all the government departments Ó Duilearga had dealings with, the one most in sympathy with the proposal to incorporate the Commission into UCD, Education officials often had difficulty determining exactly what Ó Duilearga really wanted. Requests for the clarification of certain points sometimes resulted in more elaborate, and more expensive, proposals being made by the Director. This not only caused great frustration among these officials but greatly exacerbated their efforts to help him. It was as if he had some sort of death wish, for whatever chance some of Ó Duilearga's proposals had with de Valera, they would have had little or no chance with the Dept. of Finance. This erratic behaviour, during the latter part of the 1940's in particular, can partly be explained by the pressures involved in trying to keep operations going from month to month, worry about the future of the Commission, as well as a weak constitution that made him susceptible to illness and prone to breakdown.[107] However, more was involved. As the Commission's collections

---

106 Ibid., p, 438.
107 Worry about the fate of the Commission and its staff was eventually to lead to a serious breakdown in his health in the late 1940's, from which, in many respects, he was never

grew along with his own realisation of the vast amount of oral tradition that still remained to be collected, he became more ambitious and perhaps unrealistic. It has to be noted that despite all the various detailed memoranda he drew up on the future of the Commission in the 1940's, he never succeeded in convincing even the Dept. of Education that anything more than a skeletal staff was needed in the future to take care of these collections.

In the 1950's, it appears, Ó Duilearga no longer had any heart for writing memoranda on the future of the Commission, nor for negotiating with officials on making it permanent. The fact that the Commission was now housed in more spacious accommodation and had, as a result of an increase in its grant, been able to expand its activity, may, in the short term at least, have allowed Ó Duilearga to postpone making further official representations to secure its future. The state authorities also allowed matters to drift in respect of the status of the Commission. Perhaps opportunities were lost during this decade, but as we will see below the 1950's was not a very propitious time for proposals for restructuring the Commission that would have involved significant extra spending on the part of the state, as the money simply was not available. Ó Duilearga still held to his dream of one day incorporating the Commission into UCD, but even if the economic climate had been more favourable, the forces opposed to transferring this national institute to UCD were still to be reckoned with. Although ideological factors continued to affect the fortunes of the Commission into the 1950's, as they had done in the 1940's and earlier, what was eventually, towards the end of that decade, to force the authorities to take action in respect of the Commission was not any weakening of this ideology as such, but the fact that the fate of the staff of the Commission in time became a humanitarian issue that could no longer be ignored. The staff of the Commission despite years of devoted service had no security, poor salaries, and no prospect of a pension, and as the 1950's advanced were all getting nearer to retirement age. This, rather than any ideological shift, eventually forced both the Commission and the state to take action.

The 1960's saw a weakening of the ideological opposition to incorporating the Irish Folklore Commission into UCD, but it was by no means certain that this would work in favour of Ó Duilearga and the Commission. The decision by the state in the late 1960's to transfer the Commission to UCD was influenced by a number of factors, as we will see, but it would appear that neither the Dept. of Education nor the UCD authorities who negotiated the terms of this transfer devoted much time to pondering the future needs of a reconstituted Commission within UCD. A safe home was found for the collections amassed by the Commission, and satisfactory terms of employment and pensions were ensured for its staff, but it was left to future negotiations to decide how extensive the new institute should be in respect of staffing and the scale of its operations.

Despite Ó Duilearga's desire to have the Commission reconstituted in UCD, his resolve might not have been strong enough against de Valera's opposition but for the support of Michael Tierney. It is quite likely that but

to fully recover.

for Tierney's encouragement and resolve Ó Duilearga might have opted for making the Commission permanent outside of UCD. Tierney had been on the Commission since 1935 and on the Finance Sub-Committee since 1943. Ó Duilearga had known him since the 1920's as a colleague in UCD and had worked with him on the Board of the Irish Folklore Institute from 1930 to 1935. Tierney had been a mainstay of the Commission within the College from the beginning, and after he became President of UCD in autumn 1947 he was in an even better position to help Ó Duilearga and the Commission. Tierney was a good friend to Ó Duilearga and the Commission, but there were dangers in being too closely associated with him. Moreover, while he had a genuine interest in Irish folklore and in the welfare of the Commission and its staff, he was also highly ambitious for his college. Tierney was well aware that for UCD to gain possession of the Commission would increase both its national and international standing.

In Irish-language circles Tierney was somewhat suspect, to say the least, ever since early 1936 when in a series of newspaper articles he addressed various aspects of the revival of Irish and, in particular, questioned the wisdom of using Irish as a medium of teaching for English-speaking children as well as for second- and third-level instruction.[108] Given the hopes many in the Irish-language movement had of gaelicising the entire education system, not surprisingly, Tierney's series of articles drew the ire of many in that movement. Tierney's election as President of UCD in 1947 may have placed him in a better position to help Ó Duilearga, but it also probably damaged the latter in the eyes of the Irish-language movement, as he was henceforth seen to be in Tierney's camp, so to speak. In autumn 1949, on Tierney's orders, the sale of the Irish-language monthly *Comhar*, long critical of UCD (and indeed other constituent colleges of the National University of Ireland) for its failure to provide entrance examination papers in Irish as well as further Irish-medium teaching, was banned by Tierney from being sold on the College premises. The banning of *Comhar* (an inter-university student magazine) got a lot of publicity, as did various efforts by students to elicit from Tierney his reasons for the banning of the magazine. Tierney had chaired the sub-committee of the Academic Council in 1943 that had come out against initiating teaching through the medium of Irish. His views on the subject were well known, but now they were to get a fresh airing. Unfortunately for Ó Duilearga, Tierney when confronted by a delegation from *Comhar*, as support for his stance against teaching through Irish, said that they should heed the opinions of experts such as Séamus Ó Duilearga, Gerard Murphy, Osborn Bergin, and others.[109] Ó Duilearga could well have done without this adverse publicity.

However reasonable and principled Tierney believed his stance was in opposing any attempt at whole-scale gaelicisation of the constituent colleges of the National University of Ireland, the state authorities and the Irish-language movement had a certain case for partial gaelicisation. A degree of Irish-language-medium teaching, if well taught, might have helped to reinforce Irish

---

108 Published in *The Irish Independent* on January 6th, 8th, 11th, 13th, and 25th, 1936.
109 See 'Comhar fé Chosc i gColáiste Ollscoile', *Comhar* Nollaig, 1949, pp. 3–4 & 15.

in those students who had received their secondary education through Irish. Moreover, even if the state had embarked on a much more gradual approach at gaelicising the country, a certain degree of third-level Irish-medium teaching would have been essential, as it would have been impossible to keep the Gaeltacht Irish-speaking as some sort of reservation in which Irish would continue to thrive without Irish taking root to a significant extent outside the Gaeltacht as well. Tierney's total opposition to Irish-medium university education may also have been influenced by his desire to make UCD a major Catholic university of the English-speaking world. He sought a role for his college on a world stage, and this, as I have already suggested above, became a surrogate for his earlier dream of restoring Irish.

Tierney's support for the candidature of Michael Hayes for the Chair of Modern Irish further angered the Irish-language movement, and calls into question his own advocacy of high academic standards. In 1951, Michael Hayes was appointed to the chair of Modern Irish Language and Literature in UCD, defeating a number of more academically qualified candidates for the post – his closest rival being Dr Tomás de Bhaldraithe. Although Hayes had an excellent knowledge of spoken Irish, he had no academic publications to his name, despite being on the staff of UCD's Department of Modern Irish for many years.[110] He was really more of a politician (being a Senator in Seanad Éireann and an active member of Fine Gael) than an academic, and was also a practising barrister. Michael Tierney was a member of all the various UCD bodies that dealt with the filling of this Chair, and played a crucial role in promoting Hayes's candidature both on these bodies and within the College generally.[111] Although outsiders were not privy to the voting of these bodies, the role UCD's Faculty of Celtic Studies and Michael Tierney played in Hayes's selection, and in the sidelining of better-qualified candidates, would have been known in Irish-language and folklore circles as a number of prominent Irish revivalists were on UCD's Governing Body. One such person was Pádraig Ó Siochfhradha, President of the Folklore of Ireland Society. At a meeting of the Governing Body of UCD in June 1951 there was an altercation between Tierney and Ó Siochfhradha when the latter questioned the basis on which the Faculty of Celtic Studies (which had rated Hayes highest) ranked the candidates for this post. At this meeting Ó Siochfhradha also voted for Tomás de Bhaldraithe.[112]

As mentioned above, Pádraig Ó Siochfhradha had taken a neutral stand in the Civil War, which later stood him in good stead with Cumann na nGaedheal Ministers like Ernest Blythe, but as the years went by he became more associated with Fianna Fáil and in 1946 he was nominated by de Valera to Seanad Éireann. This meant that he had access to de Valera when needed, and we will see below how he used this to good effect. Although not a member of the Irish Folklore Commission, as President of the Folklore of Ireland

---

110 See UCDA Michael Hayes Papers P53/490(34): 'Professorship of Modern Irish Language at University College, Dublin. Application and Testimonials of Michael Hayes, M.A., H.Dip. in Ed., Barrister at Law'.
111 See UCDA Michael Tierney Papers LA30/158(10): Hayes to Tierney, dated 13.7.1951.
112 UCDA: Min. of Gov. Body (19.12.1950–20.10.1953), meeting of June 26th, 1951.

Society, as a Senator in Seanad Éireann, and because of widespread respect for him in various circles, he was someone whose opinion held weight. In the late 1940's, Ó Siochfhradha stood for election to UCD's Governing Body in order to effect changes in the College's attitude towards Irish. Although he achieved very little in the years he spent on the Governing Body, his experience not only gave him an insight into the way the College was run, but would also have reinforced his animosity towards UCD. He was to remain until his death in 1964 an inveterate opponent of UCD.

There is little doubt that Michael Hayes's promotion to the Chair of Modern Irish was, was to a large extent, political. It was well known that Hayes, like Tierney, no longer believed it was possible to restore Irish. His predecessor, Cormac Ó Cadhla, was an recognised Irish revivalist, and certain influential elements within the College did not want another Irish revivalist to fill this Chair at this juncture. Moreover, the fact that Hayes was active in Fine Gael politics may also have played a role in his election to the post, given the strong identification of UCD with this party at that time.[113] In fairness to Michael Hayes, however, it has to be said that although his nomination as Professor of Modern Irish did not result in him devoting any of his time to scholarly pursuits as such, the Department of Modern Irish actually developed during his time as Head of Department. How crucial a role he played in these developments is, of course, a matter for further research, but it would appear, at any rate, that he was not an obstacle to development. On Hayes's retirement in 1960, Tomás de Bhaldraithe was appointed to the Chair of Modern Irish. His high profile as an Irish-language revivalist, and the further expansion of UCD's Dept. of Modern Irish under his charge during the 1960's, in my view, played a part in muffling opposition in Irish-language circles to the transfer of the Irish Folklore Commission to UCD some ten years later.

Another agent in this thirty-year-long saga of the Commission's fate who cannot be overlooked is J.J. McElligott, Secretary of the Dept. of Finance from 1927 to 1953, and Governor of the Central Bank from 1953 to 1960, where he continued to exercise influence over state finance. His career in these two posts spans the life of the Irish Folklore Institute and the first twenty five years of the Irish Folklore Commission. Cormac Ó Gráda speaks of the 'relentless anti-spending negativism of Dept. of Finance Secretary J. J. McElligott, the "Dr. No" of Irish economic policy'.[114] We will see below that even during the two short periods when Fianna Fáil was not in power, February 1948 to June 1951 and June 1954 to June 1957, the Dept. of Finance was never very sympathetic towards the Irish Folklore Commission. The economic recession of the 1950's, of course, meant that the money was not there to be spent, even if there had been a will to grant it. But there was no will, it seems, in certain quarters of the Dept. of Finance. The 1960's, in contrast, were a decade of rising economic fortunes generally in Ireland and this may also have played a part in softening the Dept. of Finance's opposition to the transfer of the Commission to UCD.

113 His appointment also smacks of favouritism: someone long on the staff was being rewarded by colleagues for years of service.
114 Ó Gráda 1997, p. 227.

4. The nineteen forties/ebb and flow

A permanent, independent foundation

In July 1943, with less than a year left of the Commission's second term of office, Ó Duilearga sent a short memorandum to the Dept. of Education in which he stated that after consulting various people he was of the opinion that the Commission should be made 'a permanent, independent foundation' (i.e. on the same level as similar institutions in countries such as Norway, Sweden, and Denmark) in order to fulfil the objects mentioned in its terms of reference, namely:

> (1) the collection, the assessment and the classification of oral and literary tradition, and
> (2) the editing of these materials for publication when considered appropriate.

He reminded the Department of the high esteem in which the Commission was held abroad and of efforts to establish similar institutions in various countries inspired by its work. He could think of no other activity pertaining to Ireland that was of such interest to the world of learning, and 'it was imperative to continue this work not only for the benefit of Ireland but for the benefit of the Europe that would emerge after the war.' Moreover, despite the large amount of folklore that had been collected up until that time, it was evident that this was only a fraction of the 'ancestral oral heritage' that needed to be saved. Ó Duilearga also reminded the Dept. of Education of the Trojan work being done by the staff of the Commission despite their poor conditions of employment, and implicit in this memorandum is his desire that they be treated fairly.[115]

The Dept. of Education although appreciative of the great work being done by the Commission, felt that the Government needed more detailed information before it could consider such a proposal as that made by the Honorary Director, as his proposal would involve the state in permanent

---

115 ED CO 495(8): 'CBÉ. Memorandum Gairid' dated 12.7.1943 (trans.).

expenditure.[116] In particular, they wished to know more about the situation regarding the organisation of folklore-collecting in other countries. At this stage Education was not certain that an independent institute was the best way to organise folklore in Ireland. When the Commission furnished them with all the information they needed, they could then consult UCD and the Dublin Institute for Advanced Studies to see if it could not be reconstituted as a department in the Faculty of Celtic Studies of the University or as a school of the Institute. Whatever the final decision, all this, it was felt, would take at least a year to arrange.

Education's view on the future work of the Commission

The type of work to be undertaken by such a reconstituted Commission as envisaged by some officials of the Dept. of Education differed somewhat from what Ó Duilearga had in mind. Ó Duilearga had touched on the question of publishing in his above short memorandum of July 12th, 1943, and had proposed publishing at least three hundred volumes over a period of time. In 1939 he had also told the Dept. of Education, when asked by officials, that some three to five years would be needed to complete the collecting. Based on this, Rita Ní Mhaolchatha of that Department in an internal memo concluded that:

> It appears that the vast bulk of the knowledge that is worth collecting in the Gaeltacht and Breac-Ghaeltacht [partly Irish-speaking districts] will have been stored away for safe keeping by the Commission by the end of March 1944 [i.e. by the end of the Commission's second term of office]. If the Commission were to continue under its present terms of reference, it would be possible, I think, to commence editing the material collected in the Gaeltacht, while the whole matter of the Commission would be under discussion. To that end, I propose, in the meantime that the Director be asked to inform the Department what changes would be necessary in respect of the amount of grant, the number of staff, etc., to initiate a publishing scheme from the beginning of April, 1944, under the terms of reference that already pertain.[117]

One of her superiors, Proinnsias Ó Dubhthaigh, Assistant Secretary of the Department, was worried that the Dept. of Finance would adopt a negative stance to Ó Duilearga's proposals. Ó Dubhthaigh noted that '[t]he arguments mentioned in support of the proposal are not very convincing, and are not likely to be of much help to us if we try to get Finance approval for it.' He went on to say :

> As already mentioned Mr. De Largy [sic] thought in 1939 (when he had 5 years experience of the work) that from 3 to 5 years should be enough

---

116 ED C 495(8): Ó Dubhthaigh to Ó Duilearga, dated 27.9.1943.
117 ED CO 495(8): 'CBÉ. Téarma Oifige an Choimisiúin', dated 23.8.1943 (trans.).

to complete the collecting; he now appears to propose a permanent whole-time staff of collectors. I doubt if we could justify or defend this proposal. The amount of folklore (in the usual meaning of the term) available for collection must be limited. A *permanent* staff of collectors could be justified only if it is assumed that new folklore is being formed according as the existing supply is being collected.

Ó Dubhthaigh also wondered if it was 'necessary or worthwhile to collect every scrap of material that comes within the term folklore, or if a good representative amount of such material should not suffice.' The fact that during the previous year, two of the Commission's collectors had been reported as spending 'much time compiling biographies of two persons from whom they had previously recorded collections of folklore' worried him, as he feared Finance might question 'if such work comes fully or properly within the Commission's terms of reference.' Ó Duilearga, it appeared to him, was extending the boundaries of what would hitherto have generally been considered folklore.[118]

In Ó Dubhthaigh's view, only a skeletal permanent organisation would be needed in the future. Once a decision had been made on winding up the collecting, two matters, he felt, needed consideration: 1) 'the safe custody and preservation of the collections', and 2) 'the publication of works based thereon.' Although he realised that the publication of the collections would 'take many years', he nonetheless was not aware of the magnitude of such a task; concluding 'it would be gradually reduced in amount according as the collections are studied and dealt with.' Consequently, in his estimation: 'The only permanent provision therefore that would appear to be necessary, in addition to the proper safeguarding of the collections and making them accessible to persons who wish to consult them, would be the appointment of one or at the most two competent persons (who might be part-time) to deal with inquiries and any problems raised.' In respect of severing the links between the Commission and UCD, Ó Dubhthaigh also drew attention to 'the complication that Mr. Delargy is a lecturer on the staff of U.C.D. with permanent pensionable status, and it is not easy to see what his position would be in relation to the new independent body or Commission if it was established.'[119] Moreover, even if agreement could be reached on re-establishing the Commission as an independent body, legislation would most likely be required, and as this could not be completed by December 1st, when the 'Estimates for the following financial year had to be settled', Ó Dubhthaigh proposed giving the Commission one or two more years to 'complete the collection'. This would allow time 'for the future work of the Commission' to 'be fully considered and the necessary arrangements made.'[120]

---

118 ED CO 495(8): 'Folklore Commission. Proposed Permanent Appointment etc.' signed FO'D[uffy], 1.9.43 (italics underlined in original).

119 Ó Dubhthaigh also mentions the possibility of depositing the Commission's collections in the 'Manuscripts Section' of the projected new National Library. For more on plans to build such a library , see file D/T S 13795A.

120 ED CO 495(8): 'Folklore Commission. Proposed Permanent Appointment etc.' signed

Dept. of Education seeks clarification from Ó Duilearga

Mindful of the objections that the Dept. of Finance might raise to any proposal to reconstitute the Commission as a permanent body, the Dept. of Education sent a list of questions and comments to Ó Duilearga on September 27th, 1943. These pertained to the following matters: the position and organisation of folklore institutes in other countries; the powers he envisaged for the independent foundation he was proposing; the annual cost of maintaining such a foundation; and whether a permanent staff of collectors would be needed. He was also informed that if he wished to extend collecting beyond what he had proposed in 1939, it was necessary to produce 'well-founded arguments' and it was suggested to him that there must be a limit to the amount of folklore that there was to be collected, and whether the material collected to date, and what would be collected in the coming year, might not suffice, as it was not necessary to collect everything.[121]

Subsequently, a meeting was arranged in the Dept. of Education for October 8th between Ó Duilearga and Ó Dubhthaigh to discuss the above matters. At this meeting it was explained to Ó Duilearga that while the Department '...agreed that arrangements should be made for completing the Commission's work and especially for the preservation and proper use (publication etc.) of the material collected', the 'difficulty was to decide what was the most economical and efficient way of getting this done.' Ó Duilearga was also made aware that there might be objections from certain quarters to his proposal to replace the Commission with an 'independent autonomous body'. In this connection, his opinion was sought on 'the possibility of attaching the Folklore work to some existing institution such as the National Library, the Museum or University College.'

Ó Duilearga promised to furnish details of the situation in other countries. Ó Dubhthaigh understood from their conversation 'that in most cases folklore was dealt with by a section of some institution such as a National Library, a Museum, etc., with a separate board or authority in charge of that section.' Ó Duilearga had 'no objection to a similar arrangement being made with the National Library provided the necessary accommodation could be found in the Library, and the Folklore Section was kept distinct'. He felt, however, that 'separate control of some kind' was needed, but 'that a body so large as the present Commission would not be necessary and that a Board or Commission of about five persons would be sufficient.'[122] The 'National Library' Ó Duilearga spoke of was presumably not the National Library of Ireland as then constituted, which certainly could not have accommodated the Commission's collections, but the new National Library being planned at the time (see above p. 152, n. 119).

FO'D[ufffy], 1.9.43.

121 ED CO 495(8): 'CBÉ. Fundúireacht Neamh-Spleadhach a dhéanamh do'n gCoimisiún', cov. letter dated 27.9.1943 (trans.).

122 ED CO 495(8): 'Future Organisation of Folklore Commission. Note of Interview with Mr. Delargy'.

Delay in furnishing Education with relevant information

Ó Duilearga was slow in providing the information the Dept. of Education needed to precede with his request. By June 1944 Education officials had not yet heard from him and decided to remind him of the information they required. In a letter to the Director, Proinnsias Ó Dubhthaigh stressed that the Department urgently needed the information they had requested of him the previous October:

> As you know a good deal of time is needed to make this sort of arrangement, and especially if legislation will be required, and consequently the Dept. would like to finalise their proposals soon. In order that it will be possible to do this, however, we would like that you would send us all possible information about the matters mentioned in the letter we sent to you last September.

He was again asked to furnish particulars on the following matters: (1) the organisation of folklore in other European countries; (2) his own organisational preference for the new body and whether he would like to see it attached to any existing institution (mention again being made of University College, Dublin); (3) the estimated amount of work the new body would have to do in respect of collecting, publication, and the staff they would need; and (4) an estimate of the annual cost.[123]

A reply did not come from Ó Duilearga until August 31st, 1944, when he forwarded to the Dept. of Education what he described as a 'short interim memorandum' relating to the queries of the Department. In this memorandum Ó Duilearga furnished details about the organisation of folklore in Denmark, Norway, Sweden, Finland, Estonia, Germany, and France, but because of the War he says he could only provide general information about folklore institutes in those countries, but promised to procure more information on them in the future if required. Significantly, in regard to the location of the National Folklore Archive, he now proposed that it be accommodated in UCD, and that provision could be made for it when the proposed extension to the College was being planned. If it were not possible to locate it in U.C.D, the new National Library would be a suitable venue, or 'in a separate building'. It would appear from Ó Duilearga's memorandum that he was proposing close association with (or physical location in) UCD or the new National Library, rather than it being an integral part of either of these two institutions, as he says that 'an independent archive should be established, with its own board of directors', similar to the Commission that had operated till then, with representatives from of the Departments of Education and Finance.[124]

---

123 ED CO 495(8): Ó Dubhthaigh to Ó Duilearga, dated 16.6.1944 (trans.).
124 ED CO 495(8): Ó Duilearga to Sec. Dept. of Educ., dated 31.8.1944 (trans.). A Dept. of Fin. internal memo (D/F S 101/ 0011/34: M[áire] B[hreathnach] to Mr. Hanna, dated 12.6.1944) tells us that this memorandum was amended by León Ó Broin and Michael Tierney before being submitted to the Minister for Educ. This may be of significance, considering Tierney's desire to get the Commission for UCD (see below).

Ó Duilearga proposes a more elaborate organisation

In his interview with Proinnsias Ó Dubhthaigh in October 1943, Ó Duilearga had proposed retaining Seán Ó Súilleabháin and Máire MacNeill on the office staff, and in the region of three collectors, 'who would also be competent to assist in editing and preparing for publication some of the material collected by them.'[125] Now he proposed a staff of six to seven full-time collectors in addition to some part-time collectors to be employed when the need arose. At least one more cataloguer would be needed to catalogue the archives, as well as more typists.

Ó Duilearga made many other proposals in this memorandum such as the need to make gramophone recordings of existing dialects, both in Irish and English, as well as motion films of storytellers and aspects of rural life. He ended his memorandum with an appeal for the staff of the Commission:

> I would like, with your permission, to place before you in an outspoken fashion my opinion on this matter. This is it: this Commission has now assembled, with the help of a small grant, the finest body of folklore in the world. That was done quietly, without any fuss. The staff of the Commission, both indoor and outdoor, did their utmost (and it was no easy task, especially in the case of the collectors in the countryside) to save from oblivion all the native lore they saw disappearing before their eyes. I considered their pay small from the beginning. In the future this should be rectified, and a satisfactory salary as well as pension rights should be provided for the Commission's workers that would enable us to employ the best people...[126]

This memorandum, as well as the delay in furnishing it, caused some annoyance in the Dept. of Education. Rita Ní Mhaolchatha noted that although Ó Duilearga proposed that the Commission be reconstituted as an independent body within University College Dublin or the National Library, the exact status it would enjoy under the new arrangement was not specified. She had more to say on the staffing of such an institute. She believed, from the information available to her Department, in respect of the work of the full-time collectors, that 'the work of collecting was drawing to a close already in the Gaeltacht and in the Breac-Ghaeltacht.' As evidence of this, she noted the fact that during the year 1943-1944 the full-time collectors had spent much of their time collecting from one or two informants, not realising that this situation was necessitated by wartime cutbacks and, in particular, by the unavailability of petrol that would have allowed the collectors travel further afield. Moreover, Ó Duilearga's proposal to employ five to six full-time collectors, as well as part-time collectors, could only mean, in her estimation, that he was intent on initiating extensive collecting in English-speaking districts, although his memorandum does not specify so. She continues:

---

125 ED CO 495(8): 'Future Organisation of Folklore Commission. Note of Interview with Mr. Delargy'.

126 ED CO 495(8): Ó Duilearga to Sec. Dept. of Educ., dated 31.8.1944 (trans.).

With regard to producing basic material for study involving the national language, it would appear that whatever material worth collecting has been assembled as a result of the collecting in the Gaeltacht and Breac-Ghaeltacht. In my opinion, the most important folklore material would be available in the Gaeltacht, i.e. in respect of the language, historical matters, etc. As the folklore collection already in the possession of the Commission is one of the largest in the world (like that of Finland and Estonia) it would appear that all the worthwhile material in the Gaeltacht (or at any rate most of it) has been placed in safekeeping by the Commission at present. From the amount of information that has been placed before us so far, we would not be able to present the Dept. of Finance with any good reasons in support of the large collecting scheme now contemplated. From the facts available to this Department, it would appear that the new Commission should be able to organise any collecting that will take place by means of part-time collectors trained for the purpose, and by means of questionnaires.[127]

Her superior Proinnsias Ó Dubhthaigh, Assistant Secretary of the Dept. of Education, was also dissatisfied with some of Ó Duilearga's proposals, particular with regard to the costing of the scheme (£6,000, rising to £8,500 per annum). However, in respect of Ó Duilearga's proposal that the Commission be reconstituted in University College Dublin, he felt that 'there are good reasons in favour of this suggestion, including the fact that Professor Delargy is a lecturer on the staff of the College.' Nonetheless, although he supported this proposal, he admitted 'that it would not be popular for obvious reasons' and might require legislation.

With regard to Ó Duilearga's costing of the new scheme, he had this to say:

As regards the permanent financial provision required, I think Mr. Delargy's estimate is rather high, viz. from £6,000 to £8,300 per annum, without taking into account the cost of accommodation. The present annual grant is £3,650; it was reduced to that figure from £4,250 at the beginning of the present Emergency [i.e. the Second World War]. When the amount of the grant was originally fixed, it was represented that the work of collection was very urgent, and it was not expected that as large a grant would be necessary when this work was completed. It appears that the work of collecting has been slowed up in recent years, and the suggested staff of permanent collectors is rather excessive. In any event it will be very difficult to get sanction for a permanent grant of the amount suggested by Mr. Delargy.

Similar to his colleague Rita Ní Mhaolchathaigh, Ó Dubhthaigh does not appear to have realised that the collecting had 'been slowed up' not for want of

---

127 ED CO 495(8): 'CBÉ., Téarma Saoghail an Choimisiúin', pp. 6-8, dated 2.10.1944 (trans.).

material to collect, but because of wartime restrictions and the Commission's reduced grant-in-aid.

Mícheál Breathnach, Secretary of the Dept. of Education, concurred with most of Ó Dubhthaigh's opinions on Ó Duilearga's memorandum. However, in respect of reconstituting the Commission in University College Dublin or in the National Library, he noted the lack of space in either of these institutions to house a reconstituted Commission. Moreover, before any decision would be made on providing these institutions with more space, the fate of the Commission needed to be decided. In his opinion, Ó Duilearga's scheme, 'as outlined in this memorandum', was too 'nebulous' ('san aer'). On November 17th, 1944 he suggested that the Ó Duilearga be asked to drop into the Department before Christmas to clarify certain matters, among others how folklore archives in other countries were financed. On December 13th, 1944, Ó Duilearga had a meeting with Mícheál Breathnach at which he promised to furnish the Department with a much more detailed 'application'.[128] This he did not do until July 1945.

A still more elaborate scheme proposed by Ó Duilearga

The previous December, Ó Duilearga had promised to provide the Dept. of Education with a much more detailed application, but the detail this new memorandum contained was not the type of detail Education officials were expecting, or needed. To their great surprise, Ó Duilearga now proposed a more extensive plan costing between £13,050 - £16,250. Under 'Accommodation and Administration of Folklore Archive', Ó Duilearga proposed the construction of a 'detached fireproof building' in which the Commission's growing collections 'could be displayed and consulted by students.' He proposed that such 'a building could be most fittingly provided in close association with University College, Dublin'. Association with the College had over the years 'been of the greatest assistance to the Commission, enabling it to carry out its duties in the most pleasing conditions and obviating many possible occasions of difficulty and friction.' The memorandum says:

> The Director, after examining all aspects of the problem and considering all possible solutions, is convinced that it would be of inestimable value to the conduct of the work still awaiting to be done if these arrangements could be as nearly as possible perpetuated in the future.[129]

The title of this document, 'Memorandum on the Irish Folklore Commission with Recommendations for its Development and Extension', is strange

---

128 ED CO 495(8): internal memo of Ó Dubhthaigh's entitled 'Folklore Commission. Permanent Organisation, Etc.', dated 15.11.1944; as well as Mícheál Breathnach's appended marginal comments.

129 D/T S 6916B: 'Memorandum on the IFC with Recommendations for its Development and Extension', pp. 29–30.

when one recalls that all the Dept. of Education had asked Ó Duilearga to furnish was more precise details on a certain administrative problem, namely that a body having its own board of directors could not so easily be incorporated into UCD. Instead, he proposed a new plan for restructuring the Commission costing twice as much as the previous one. This is a long memorandum, running to more than thirty pages. While reasons are given for attaching the Commission to UCD, the difficulties involved are not dealt with, difficulties which the Dept. of Education had specifically asked him to consider. However, the memorandum does state that legislation would be required for these proposals to be realised, presumably to allow for an outside body ('Committee') to act in an advisory capacity to the Director and ensure the financial endowment of the new institute. This, of course, was something the Dept. of Education already knew, and was the main reason why it had asked him to clarify the matter in the first place. Education's frustration with this latest memorandum is understandable, but Ó Duilearga may partly have been encouraged to expand his plans for the Commission by an interview he had with de Valera in March 1945. Nothing definite seems to have been decided at this interview, but the Taoiseach asked him to send his proposals to the Dept. of Education.[130]

In a covering letter to the above memorandum Ó Duilearga explains the reason for the long delay. It had been necessary to seek advice and to examine the matter thoroughly. He says: 'I have done my best, and I think I have dealt herein with all the matters that you suggested I should mention.'[131] If Ó Duilearga imagined he had done his best, his efforts did not satisfy the Dept. of Education, who were in a hurry and growing more impatient with the Director, it would appear, as the Commission's term of office was to end on March 31st, 1946. Proinnsias Ó Dubhthaigh in a memorandum to his superiors, Mícheál Breathnach, Secretary of the Department, and Tomás Ó Deirg, Minister for Education, says that it had been expected that a permanent scheme would be ready before the end of March 1946, but because the 'progress made in the preparation of this scheme has been very slow ... it cannot now be completed within the time mentioned.' Although he does not say so directly, he seems to place much of the blame for the delay on Ó Duilearga: because 'Professor Delargy was the person most intimately concerned we relied on his advice and assistance for the preparation of a permanent scheme, but the proposals made by him present some difficulty.' The previous December the Director had been asked to try and reconcile how the Commission could be incorporated into UCD and at the same time 'be independent with its own board of management.' The Director's most recent memorandum did not tackle this matter. Ó Dubhthaigh says:

> It would appear from this document that he did not understand what was needed. It deals chiefly with the magnitude and importance of Irish

130 Ibid., p. 30 and D/T S 6916B: Ó Duilearga to de Valera, 7.3.1945.
131 ED CO 495(8): Ó Duilearga to Sec. Dept. of Educ., dated 19.7.1945 (trans.).

folklore; it proposes a scheme whose estimated cost (£13,000/£16,000) is just twice that previously proposed; but it contains no useful or practical proposals for overcoming the difficulty already mentioned in connection with the form of control.

He noted, however: 'It is clear from this that Delargy wishes that the Folklore Archive should be an independent body with statutory authority, but that it should remain in University College, Dublin.'

Ó Dubhthaigh felt that 'it would not be possible to devise a satisfactory arrangement on the lines mentioned.' In the first place, it would be resisted by the authorities of UCD. Secondly, it was his opinion that even if the Dept. of Finance and the Government could be convinced 'that it was desirable to establish by legislation an independent Folklore Archive, such a proposal would be opposed in the Dáil and the Seanad by the University representatives on the grounds that the work could be more satisfactorily and economically done in the universities.' He was certain 'that the assistance which University College has already given would be quoted as an argument to which there is no satisfactory reply.'

Although the Dept. of Education had difficulty determining why exactly Ó Duilearga wanted the reconstituted Commission to be 'independent' in nature, wherever its location, it was Ó Dubhthaigh's understanding at this stage that 'one of the main purposes in insisting on the independence of the proposed Folklore Archive' was ' to get complete control in the employment and payment of staff, and to provide pensions for the present officers, some of whom have been employed for over ten years.' It is not clear whether 'complete control' in this case meant freedom from College interference in addition to freedom from governmental interference. In any event, Ó Dubhthaigh commented that 'whatever form of scheme is established it must be assumed that the Department of Finance will insist on a certain amount of control in such matters'.[132]

Ó Duilearga and Tierney meet with Education officials

In late October or early November 1945 the Secretary and Assistant Secretary of the Department of Education had an interview with Ó Duilearga. This interview dealt, for the most part, with 'the importance of the work remaining to be done.' However, when Ó Duilearga was asked:

> to explain more fully the form of organisation that he had suggested in his memorandum, it became evident that he had not adverted to or considered the difficulties connected with his proposals for establishing an independent folklore archive, and having this situated in University College Dublin. It was pointed out that the establishment of such a Body

132 ED CO 495(8): 'Folklore Commission. Proposed Permanent Organisation', dated 22.10.1945.

by legislation must automatically involve the removal from University College authorities of all control and responsibility for the work.

As he was unable to inform Education officials 'how the Authorities of the College would regard such a proposal, or what its effect might be on his own position, or the possibility of continuing the present association of the work with the College', a second meeting was arranged for November 7th, which was also attended by Prof. Michael Tierney, an influential member of the staff of UCD as well as a member of the Commission. Both the Secretary and Assistant Secretary of the Dept. of Education (Breathnach and Ó Dubhthaigh) were present at this meeting. On this occasion Ó Duilearga 'explained that he was opposed to having the work of the Commission transferred to the Institute for Advanced Studies, or to a body working under the same restrictions as the Schools of the Institute.' This meeting came up with two alternatives: 'a) to appoint an independent body to take charge of folklore or b) to entrust the control of the work to University College Dublin.'

The first of these alternatives would necessitate enacting legislation, and in the opinion of these two Dept. of Education officials 'would be subject to certain criticism in the Dáil which would be difficult to answer' – presumably from Deputies sympathetic to the Universities, and UCD in particular. Moreover, in their estimation, it 'was unlikely that any [independent] Body that might be established would be given the degree of independence (i.e. without the Dept. of Finance's interference) which Mr. Delargy considered necessary.' At this meeting, Prof. Tierney is reported to have stated that the College would strenuously oppose 'any proposal which would involve the removal from the College of the Folklore Department.' He said that even members of staff he had spoken to 'who were not very interested in folklore' were strongly opposed to separating folklore from the College. He stressed that 'much of the credit for the work already done' was 'due mainly to its [UCD's] action in appointing Mr. Delargy as a Lecturer (his salary for many years having been paid by the College)', and reminded those present that accommodation 'for the material already collected had been provided free of charge by the College'. Tierney also informed the meeting that Ó Duilearga was to be promoted to the rank of professor. This piece of information may have added further weight to UCD's claim to the Commission with Education officials.

In any event, the meeting decided that the only 'satisfactory' arrangement for reorganising folklore was 'the transfer of the control and supervision' of the work hitherto done by the Commission to University College Dublin, 'subject to satisfactory arrangements for the purpose being made with the authorities of the College.' However, certain difficulties stood in the way of transferring the Commission to the care of the University, even if Finance were to concur. The meeting discussed 'the arrangements for the control and supervision of any additional grant that might be provided by the Government for Folklore, if that suggestion was adopted.' Prof. Tierney suggested two ways such a grant might be administered: '(i) by attaching conditions to the grant itself, or (ii) by providing the grant only after the College had made the necessary statutes to regulate its expenditure.' The meeting decided on the second option, as the former would have required that an outside body such as the Dept. of Education would 'see that the conditions were fulfilled'. The advantage of the second option was that 'the Professor in charge of the Folklore Department would be mainly responsible for the expenditure subject to the provisions of the governing statutes.'[133]

Reception of Dept. of Education's proposal

The two Dept. of Education officials, in agreeing to the above, would seem to have been motivated by the desire not to do anything that would weaken Ó Duilearga's status within UCD. In a letter written on November 28th, 1945 to the Dept. of the Taoiseach, one of these officials, Mícheál Breathnach, had this to say:

> In respect of the permanent arrangements that have to be made to organise the folklore work in the future, care must be taken of the position of the Director, as the work is greatly beholden to him. He spent more than ten years as a permanent lecturer on the staff of University College and it is understood that he has been promoted to professorial rank. Considering his achievement to date, and the recognition he has received as an authority on folklore, it is our opinion that whatever permanent arrangement will be made to further the work should be under his charge; and we think that the scheme here proposed is the best way of ensuring that this object is fulfilled.[134]

In making this proposal, the Dept. of Education may also have been influenced by other factors. For example, by the sympathies of certain senior Department officials in respect of the importance of the universities, and a reluctance to see anything done that might diminish their status. Moreover, they may have wished to advance the fortunes and national status of University College Dublin, the largest constituent college of the National University of Ireland.

It should be noted that since July 1943, almost two and a half years before, Ó Duilearga had continuously emphasised that a reconstituted Commission, wherever it was situated, should be an independent body. Now he was accepting less, under pressure from the Dept. of Education and Michael Tierney, it would appear. One wonders whether the Dept. of Education and Tierney did him a great disservice, for while an independent foundation within UCD did appear to be in conflict with the Statutes of UCD, surely legislation as well as a leap of the imagination might have produced a solution acceptable to all parties. If Ó Duilearga thought he could live with this solution, he was soon to find out it was not something de Valera could

---

133 ED CO 495(8): 'Folklore Commission and Proposed Permanent Scheme of Organisation. Note of Discussions with Mr. Delargy and Professor Tierney'.
134 D/T S 6916B: M. Breathnach to the Dept. of the Taois., dated 28.11.1945 (trans.).

live with, and there lay the crux of the problem. A month after Breathnach wrote the above letter, an official in the Dept. of the Taoiseach appended a note in pencil to his letter: 'I spoke with the Taoiseach. He does not agree with the proposal of the Dept of Education. He decided to leave this matter aside "for the time being."'[135]

Procrastination and frustration

It would be many months before the fate of the Commission would again be considered by the Dept. of the Taoiseach. The reasons for this are not clear, but it would appear that de Valera, dissatisfied with the Education's proposals, was trying to wear down the opposition. By mid May 1946 the Dept. of Education had received no reply from the Dept. of the Taoiseach. Proinnsias Ó Dubhthaigh felt something needed to be done soon about the staff of the Commission, and as proposals were in the offing to extend UCD's accommodation he felt 'suitable provision' needed to be made for the Commission in these plans if Education's proposal on the Commission was accepted. His own Minister, however, proposed no further action other than reminding the Dept. of the Taoiseach that as yet no reply had been received from it in respect of the future of the Commission.[136] Around this time Ó Duilearga came to see an official in the Dept. of the Taoiseach, urging 'strongly and at length the importance, from the point of view of (a) the preservation of the national culture, and (b) our cultural relations with other countries, of early action being taken to re-establish the Folklore Commission, place it on a more permanent basis and ensure its financial position.' The Taoiseach was informed of the 'substance' of Ó Duilearga's 'representations', but is reported as not being 'disposed to take any action at present.'[137] Ó Duilearga at this meeting (or soon afterwards) also requested a meeting with de Valera.

On May 22nd, 1946 the Dept. of Education was informed (by word of mouth) that the Dept. of the Taoiseach was not satisfied with Education's proposal and that it intended to discuss the matter with the Director of the Commission.[138] It would seem, however, that the Dept. of the Taoiseach was in no hurry to discuss matters with the Director. Ó Duilearga ends his annual report to the Government for 1945-1946 with a plea for help, and reminds the authorities that the Commission 'was now one of the important institutions of Europe: it does not only belong to Ireland'. Unless something were done, he felt they would not be able to continue their operations.[139] This document is dated June 1946, and Ó Duilearga's plea fell on deaf ears, or at least was not considered to be so urgent.

135 Ibid., appended note dated 28.12.1945. There is a possibility that Ó Duilearga's elevation to the rank of professor in 1946 played a part in his abandoning the idea of an independent folklore institute at this juncture.

136 ED CO 495(8): 'IFC. New Organisation, etc', dated 16.5.1946.

137 D/T S 6916B: internal untitled Dept. of Taois. memo, dated 15.5.1946.

138 D/T S 6916D: Educ. memo entitled 'Coimisiún Béaloideasa Éireann' [1959], p. 3.

139 D/T S 15548B: 'Gearr-Thuar./1945-46', pp. 7-8 (trans.).

It would appear Ó Duilearga made a number of efforts to get an interview with de Valera over the next number of months, but while his request was not turned down, no such interview materialised.[140] Then in December 1946, Ó Duilearga sent a (long, detailed) memorandum to the Taoiseach, via the Minister for Posts & Telegraphs, P. J. Little, towards the end of which, under 'Future Policy', he lists the desiderata needed. Among other matters, he mentions adequate accommodation, and permanent establishment, but does not elaborate on these matters. He concludes his memorandum by saying that his estimate of £13,050 to £16,250 of July 1945 was a minimum estimate and that given changed circumstances, an annual grant of £20,000 would be needed.[141] Whatever about convincing de Valera to grant him an interview, this increased sum of £20,000 per annum was not a figure that would have gone down well with the Dept. of Finance, if it had got to hear of it. It is to be noted, however, that the above memorandum does not mention UCD. P. J. Little's covering letter to this memorandum also contains a request that the Taoiseach receive a deputation consisting of the Director, Prof. Michael Tierney, and Liam Price, i.e. the non-departmental members of the Finance Sub-Committee of the Commission. In late January 1947, Muiris Ó Muimhneacháin, de Valera's Secretary, discussed Little's letter with the Taoiseach, but nothing further seems to have happened.[142]

Earlier that month Ó Duilearga had written to von Sydow on the matter. Although careful not to criticise de Valera, he informs him that no word had yet been received from the Government regarding the fate of the Commission and that their situation was desperate. The staff were 'scandalously underpaid' and, he hints, there was discontent among them; the work of the Commission was being hindered or rendered null. He speaks of what they could achieve if properly funded and established and of his dreams of utilising modern technology such as sound film and field gramophones, of depositing microfilm copies of both the Commission's manuscripts and sound recordings in foreign institutions, of sending Caoimhín Ó Danachair and other members of staff abroad for training to Lund, Copenhagen, Stockholm and other centres, and of employing more collectors both in Ireland and western Scotland.

Obviously, discontent among the staff over the unsatisfactory conditions of their employment must greatly have increased Ó Duilearga's anxiety about the fate of the Commission. In the same letter to von Sydow he asks him to intercede with de Valera, feeling that the latter if he fully realised how important foreign scholars, and particularly von Sydow, believed the Commission's collections to be in respect of international scholarship, would take positive action to remedy the situation. Ó Duilearga admitted he was in despair and asked von Sydow to come to Ireland the following summer as his 'advice' and 'wise council' were again needed.[143]

---

140 ED CO 495(8): internal memo, Ó Muircheartaigh to Ó Dubhthaigh, dated 18.10.1946.
141 D/T S 6916B: 'Irish Folklore Commission', no date , p. [26].
142 D/T S 6916B: Little to de Valera, dated 11.11.1946, as well as Ó Muimhneacháin's appended note.
143 LUB Saml. von Sydow: Ó Duilearga to von Sydow, dated 5.1.1947.

In early June 1947, Ó Duilearga wrote a rather frantic letter to the Taoiseach, which is worth quoting in full:

> The Irish Folklore Commission which you established in 1935 has now reached a critical stage in its work and development which demands immediate attention; otherwise the whole intricate fabric, so carefully built up from a tiny nucleus, with many associations of the most intimate kind with many lands and people is in danger of falling to pieces to the dismay of the learned world of Europe and elsewhere, and of the many thousands of Irish stock at home and abroad who are in sympathy with our ideals and appreciating of the achievements attained in a brief span of years by our Commission.
>
> I have prepared a short and factual memorandum on our position which I should be glad to discuss with you personally. I know – and the world now knows also – of your deep and sincere interest in our work, and of your desire to further our ideals. In 1935 you told me that should just occasion offer you would always be most willing to see me at all times and to help me. I need your help and active guidance now. I have refrained hitherto from troubling you, as I realise fully the extent of your commitments in many directions. But I cannot struggle further without your help, and therefore wish to see you.[144]

The position of the Commission was quite desperate by this time, hampered by lack of funds and space. Ó Duilearga seems to have been willing to settle for less than he had hitherto requested. In the accompanying memorandum, he deals with many of the problems besetting the Commission but does not mention his earlier proposal to associate the Commission with UCD. All he says, under 'Permanency', is that in order to 'consolidate' the achievements of the Commission and expand its work, 'it is necessary to establish a foundation on a permanent basis'. On the question of the 'Location' of such a permanent foundation he had an open mind. All he wished was that it be housed in a manner that would accord with its high national and international reputation.[145] This time the Taoiseach saw him promptly. One wonders whether the reason for this, after so much delay, was that he sensed that Ó Duilearga would now be more amenable to his own plans for the Commission.

Ó Duilearga accepts de Valera's offer

Ó Duilearga met with de Valera on June 7th, 1947. Some two weeks later he wrote in jubilation to von Sydow of his success in getting de Valera to agree to making the Commission permanent, and that the possibility of housing the staff and collections in a house in Merrion Square, one of Dublin's

---

144 D/T S 6916B: Ó Duilearga to de Valera, dated 5.6.1947. Along with this letter Ó Duilearga sent the Taoiseach a recent number of *Béaloideas* as well as a copy of his booklet, *The Gaelic Story-Teller*.
145 D/T S 6916B: 'Irish Folklore Commission', p. [3].

finest Georgian squares, was mentioned.[146] Later that month Ó Duilearga told a meeting of the Commission that at his interview with de Valera, the Taoiseach had praised the work of the Commission and assured him that henceforth there was no need to worry. He was willing to concede what Ó Duilearga had asked: namely a 'permanent foundation', a large house of their own, and freedom from official interference. De Valera said that the Commission could itself decide whether to have 'a house of their own or a house under the Institute for Advanced Studies.' Peadar Ó Muircheartaigh, Education's representative on the Commission, explained what being a sub-department of the Institute would involve. In his view, 'the greatest single advantage pertaining to this' arrangement would be permanence. The Director further explained that the Taoiseach planned to house all the historical records in one single depository, namely in the new, projected National Library that was being planned, and that perhaps that would be the best place for the folklore collection later on. The members were of the opinion that permanence and independence were 'essential for the new foundation'. They felt that a house of their own would be preferable 'where anybody interested in Irish and in its related culture' could utilise the Commission's collections.[147] At a further meeting of the Finance Sub-Committee on August 9th, Ó Duilearga reported that his interview with the Taoiseach in June:

> ...had been entirely satisfactory. The Taoiseach had assured him of the Government's favour and had promised that a permanent foundation with satisfactory conditions for the staff would be established as soon as possible and that a suitable house would be provided for it. The members expressed their satisfaction at this news. The Director added that he expected no developments until after his return from Iceland in the autumn. Should a suitable house come on the market during his absence he felt the matter could safely be left in the hands of the other members of the Sub-Committee.[148]

De Valera had already in June asked the Board of Works to look out for a suitable house for the Commission. However, neither of the two buildings initially suggested to Ó Duilearga were ideal for the Commission's purposes, namely 85 Merrion Square and 69 Lower Leeson St.[149] As things turned out, however, even if suitable accommodation had become available, it might have placed Ó Duilearga in a very awkward position, for shortly he was once again about to change his mind.

146 LUB Saml. von Sydow: Ó Duilearga to von Sydow, letter dated 20.5.1947.
147 ED FL 6: 'CBÉ. Miont. 49ú Cruinniú, 27.6.1947', par. 382 (trans.).
148 ED FL 6: 'IFC. Fin. Sub-Com./ Min. 62nd Meeting, 9.8.1947', par. 505.
149 See D/T S 6916B: J. Connolly to de Valera, dated 12.7.1947, and accompanying memorandum.

Ó Duilearga changes his mind

Ó Duilearga was away in Iceland from August 13th to October 24th. A month after his return in a telephone conversation with Proinnsias Ó Dubhthaigh he expressed dissatisfaction with de Valera's proposals. Ó Dubhthaigh says: 'Prof. Delargy told me that he would prefer the arrangement suggested by us [i.e. a Folklore Dept. in U.C.D.] as he felt he could not fill the dual roles of a Professor in U.C.D. and Director of an independent Commission.' Ó Dubhthaigh recorded: 'Though he did not definitely say so, I gathered from my talk with him that he anticipated stormy opposition by the President of U.C.D to such a proposal.'[150]

While Ó Duilearga was away in Iceland the campaign to elect the new President of University College Dublin was in full swing. His friend and close associate on the Commission, Michael Tierney was one of the contenders. Against the odds, Tierney was elected in the final round of voting on October 30th.[151] The election of Tierney may indeed have affected Ó Duilearga's change of attitude. As already mentioned, Tierney had been a mainstay of support for the Irish Folklore Institute and later the Irish Folklore Commission within the College since the late 1920's. He was also a member of the Commission and its Finance Sub-Committee. We have seen above that some years earlier, in the mid 1940s, he may have caused Ó Duilearga to change his mind about the best location for a reconstituted Commission. Then, he did not have the same power or influence that he now had. He had always been highly ambitious for his College and was now in a position to fight any plan to remove the Folklore Commission from the orbit of UCD. Donal McCartney has said of Tierney that no other president of the College 'had so deep a sense of UCD's history and of its role in the development of Irish society' nor 'so deep a scholarly involvement in areas outside his own specialism'.[152] One such area of scholarly interest for Tierney was folklore, another the Irish language. In getting possession of the world-famous collections of the Commission, Tierney could raise UCD's profile both nationally and internationally. It is interesting to note, however, that at the August meeting of the Finance Sub-Committee, Tierney did not voice any opposition to de Valera's proposals. Had he also at that stage succumbed to the Taoiseach's determination to separate the Commission from UCD, or was he just biding his time? In any event, he was now in a position to resist de Valera's proposals more effectively.

In early December 1947, Ó Duilearga told a meeting of the Finance Sub-Committee that although the Taoiseach had asked him 'to submit a scheme deciding between various alternatives for the new establishment' of the Commission, he 'had not yet done so, partly because of his absence in Iceland and partly because of certain difficulties affecting himself.'

---

150 ED CO 495(8): '[I]FC. New Scheme of Organisation etc. Note on Phone Message', dated 25.11.1947.
151 For the intricacies of Tierney's election, see McCartney 1999, pp. 127 ff.
152 Ibid., p. 134. It should also be noted that perhaps his own elevation to the rank of professor in 1946 played a part in this volte-face.

These difficulties pertained to his position in the College. He said that at 'his interview with the Taoiseach, he had not stressed the personal element of his own position as Professor of Folklore in University College, Dublin', adding '[i]f the new establishment were to sever connection with the College, the question of the directorship would become a problem. The Department of Education, he knew, favoured the handing over of the Commission to the College, and, in his view, this would be the most satisfactory outcome.'

Michael Tierney now proposed a compromise of sorts to the conflicting proposals of incorporation within UCD or being established as an independent body. He said: 'It was possible that an arrangement, similar to that whereby the Albert College [UCD's Faculty of Agriculture] was run by a small committee representative partly of the Government and partly of the College with a special grant, would be more suitable than handing it over entirely to the College with an increase in the College grant.' He said 'he would like to discuss the matter both with members of the College, and with the Secretary of the Department of Finance, and then go to the Taoiseach with a definite proposal.' He further hoped that it 'would be possible to provide suitable temporary accommodation for the Commission on the College premises and to include it in the plans for building which were being drawn up at present.' He added: ' It was unthinkable that Professor Ó Duilearga should be separated from the direction of folklore activities.' Not only did the Sub-Committee agree with Ó Duilearga and Tierney's assessment that 'the best solution' for 'the future of the Commission seemed to be incorporation in the College', they, moreover, thanked Tierney for offering to undertake 'the representation of the [Commission's] case to Government, and expressed satisfaction that, as a result of his election to the Presidency of the College, the future of the Commission seemed more hopeful and assured.'[153]

Ó Duilearga was not as forthcoming about this matter at the next meeting of the Commission itself in February 1948. When asked if there had been any progress with regard to making the Commission permanent, he simply informed members that there had been no change: 'that it was a matter for the Government', and that he 'had already sent two memoranda to the Government.' The minutes record that the members present felt that he should continue to pressurise the Government on the matter.[154] At this meeting he did not, however, mention the change in his own attitude. It is hard not to believe that he was leaving those members of the Commission not on the Finance Sub-Committee somewhat in the dark on a very substantive issue. As further evidence that he was keeping the Commission, excluding those on the Finance Sub-Committee, in the dark on this question, it has to be noted that at the previous meeting of the Commission on November 28th, 1947, just a few days after his above conversation with Proinnsias Ó Dubhthaigh, he does not seem to have informed members of his 'new' position, although the Finance Sub-Committee, as we have seen above, was informed of his

153 ED FL 6: 'IFC. Fin. Sub-Com./Min. 63rd Meeting, 2.12.1947', par 312 [recte 512].
154 ED FL 6: 'CBÉ. Miont. 51ú Cruinniú, 20.2.1948', par. 400 (trans.).

change of heart some days later.[155] Some other members of the Finance Sub-Committee may have colluded with Ó Duilearga in this subterfuge, if indeed that is what it was.

A New Taoiseach and new opportunities

The determination of Michael Tierney and Ó Duilearga to resist the plans of de Valera were, however, not to be tested at this juncture. On December 21st, 1947, de Valera decided to call a surprise general election, fifteen months before he needed to. In doing so he was to a large degree motivated by the desire to stem the growth of the new radical Republican party, Clann na Poblachta, lest it eat too much into Fianna Fáil's support. Despite the threat posed by this new party, given the ostensible weakness of the opposition parties, de Valera could, initially at least, have had little idea that he was about to lose power. Nonetheless, there was evidence that Fianna Fáil's position was not so unassailable. They had been in power since 1932, and though the opposition were ideologically divided and weak, it was united by a dislike of Fianna Fáil and particularly of its leader, Éamon de Valera. On New Year's Eve 1947/48 Ó Duilearga wrote to von Sydow:

> Mr. de Valera last June promised me a large house to ourselves, and increased grant, & more liberty of action. But the General Election which begins 4 Feb. is important for us. Nobody can even guess at the outcome. A new party – or rather, the old left wing of the old Fianna Fáil adherents, called Clann na Poblachta, may make all the difference, & most people think that de Valera will never have a majority in the Dáil again. I am no politician, but I trust that whatever party comes to power our claims to attention will not be overlooked.[156]

In the subsequent General Election in the New Year, Fianna Fáil lost eight seats but still hoped to form a government. However, the opposition parties succeeded in putting a coalition government together by mid-February. When the Commission met on February 20th, 1948 the new Inter-Party Government, as it was called, headed by John A. Costello, had been in office only a few days. Few, given the ideological differences of the parties now in government together, would have predicted that this Government would hold together for very long, but it was to survive for three and a half years. For the first time since the Commission was set up the successors of the victors of the Civil War (and those Ó Duilearga felt most political allegiance to), Fine Gael, were in government, albeit in a coalition with a number of smaller parties. This may have raised his hopes of seeing the Commission re-established in UCD, as that College was closely associated with Fine Gael, but memories of his

---

155 See ED FL 6: 'Miont. 50ú Cruinniú, 28.11.1947', passim.
156 LUB Saml. von Sydow: Ó Duilearga to von Sydow, dated 'New Year's Night 1948 [1947]'. It is interesting to note that he fails to mention in this letter that by this time he himself was opposed to what de Valera had offered him the previous June.

treatment at the hands of Ernest Blythe, also of his own political persuasion, may have induced in him a degree of caution.

By the time the next meeting of the Finance Sub-Committee of the Commission took place in March 1948 the new Government had been in power less than a month. At this meeting Lughaidh Maguidhir, the representative of the Dept. of Education, proposed that the whole matter 'be re-opened with the Minister for Education by the Director'. As Proinnsias Ó Dubhthaigh, the Assistant Secretary of the Dept. of Education, would soon be retiring, and as he 'had been familiar with the affairs of the Commission from the beginning', Maguidhir felt 'it would be helpful to have negotiations under weigh [*recte* way] before his retirement which was soon due.' The Director informed the meeting that he 'had been waiting to hear the result of certain conversations which the President of University College, Dublin [Michael Tierney] was to have with the Minister for Education before re-opening the matter himself.'[157]

It would be October 1948 before Ó Duilearga could report to the Finance Sub-Committee on progress on this matter. The Minister for Education had agreed to meet him soon and he had suggested in a memorandum to the Minister that as UCD had offered 82 St. Stephen's Green for the use of the Commission, 'the State should defray the expenses of putting the house in order and furnishing it.' The estimated cost was £2,500. Ominously, Seán Ó Maonaigh, the representative of the Dept. of Finance, reminded the meeting that they bear in mind that the Minister for Finance wished 'to keep down expenditure'. The Sub-Committee, therefore decided that the Director should see the Minister for finance 'before the preparation of the Estimates' for the following year[158]

The new Minister for Education, General Richard Mulcahy, was the leader of Fine Gael, but because he had been Commander-in-Chief of the Free State Army during the Civil War and was seen to have too much Republican blood on his hands, Clann na Poblachta was unwilling to serve under him as Taoiseach. He appears for a time to have been considered for the post of Minister for Finance but eventually opted for Education.[159] Ironically, as things turned out, if he had taken the Finance portfolio, he might have been able to do more for the Irish Folklore Commission than he was ultimately able to do in Education. Moreover, if his role in the Civil War had not robbed him of the chance to be Taoiseach, he would have been in a far better position to see that justice, as he saw it, was done for this great national institution. Once again the animosities begotten by the Civil War were to affect the fate of the Commission at a crucial stage in its history.

Richard Mulcahy shared more than political allegiance with Ó Duilearga, he shared with him a deep interest in the Irish language. Although he was not the only politician of his generation to have a genuine affection for Irish, he was one of the few to have learned it well. His biographer says of him: 'For Mulcahy, the Irish language, Irish music – all of Irish culture – remained an

157 ED FL 6: 'IFC. Fin. Sub-Com./Min. 64th Meeting, 23.3.1948', par. 517.
158 ED FL 6: 'IFC. Fin. Sub-Com./ Min. 66th Meeting, 23.10.1948', par. 528.
159 McCullagh 1998, pp. 30 and 35.

integral part of his nationalist vision.'[160] On November 1st,1948, Ó Duilearga and Prof. Tierney had a meeting with Mulcahy. The Minister 'viewed favourably' their proposal 'that the needs of the organisation responsible for the collection, care, and utilisation of Irish oral traditional records could best be met by transferring it into a new department of Irish Oral Tradition in U.C.D., and by giving an appropriate grant to the College for the purpose.' On the Minister's request, Ó Duilearga promptly furnished Mulcahy with an estimate of £16,000 for the coming financial year, which included £3,600 'for the decorating and refurbishing' of 82 St. Stephen's Green. Mulcahy in turn forwarded a copy of Ó Duilearga's letter to the Minister for Finance, Patrick McGilligan, who asked his Department to look into the matter.[161]

Dept. of Finance assesses the Commission's position

McGilligan was a colleague of Ó Duilearga's in UCD, but may not have been a master in his own house, where he had the formidable Departmental Secretary, J. J. McElligott, to contend with. McElligott, the 'Dr. No' of Irish economic policy' (see above), looked at the pros and cons of Ó Duilearga's proposal. It is worth giving his assessment in full as it crystalizes attitudes in the Dept. of Finance that the Commission had to contend with:

> (1) Duration: The Folklore Commission in its present form was, as far as can be gathered from a quick reading of the papers, intended to come to an end within a definite time when the work of collection and classification had been completed. It was apparently intended that future scholars would work on the material in the manner in which normal historical, etc., research is carried out.
>
> The setting up of a Department of Oral Tradition in U.C.D. will give the work a permanence and the ultimate financial *cost* to the state will be greater in my view. Its value may of course be greater too.
>
> (2) Use made of Materials Collected: The setting up of a specialized University Department for dealing with Folklore will bring the work of collection and classification into direct contact with the potential researchers. The enthusiasm of the Folklore workers will be able to infect the advanced students of the language and so stimulate research, etc.
>
> (3) University Standards of Remuneration: The organisation of Folklore work on a University basis will mean that the higher standards of remuneration applicable to Universities will have to be paid. This will inevitably involve increased expense.
>
> (4) Financial Control: At present the Grant-in-Aid is reviewed annually and we have adequate control. If the proposed transfer were proceeded with the grants would probably be amalgamated with the general grant to U.C.D. or perhaps the 1934 Act grant and so would not be subject

---

160 Valiulis 1992, p. 239.
161 D/F S 101/0011/34: Ó Duilearga to Mulcahy, dated 5.11.1948, and Mulcahy to McGilligan, dated 11.11.1948.

to the same control. In addition, contact [i.e. by various government departments] with the Commission enables them to avoid duplication of work as for instance where the Gúm [Government Irish-language publishing house] might consider publishing works which would cover the same ground as those which might be published by U.C.D. If the transfer is approved the Commission will presumably disappear and this Department will not have as direct a voice as it has now, through its representative, in the work.

(5) Repercussions: The transfer in question could have repercussions in two directions and involve further State expenditure, viz.

(a) The other two Colleges of the National University – especially the one in Galway which has hitherto been regarded as *the* Gaelic College – may claim grants to establish Departments of Oral Tradition. Both could provide themselves with "materials" by having the U.C.D. records microfilmed.

(b) If U.C.D. succeed in getting control of the Folklore Commission it may encourage them to make designs on perhaps the Place Names Commission, the Manuscripts Commission, etc.

(6) A proposal to extend the activities of the Folklore Commission appears to be contrary to the trend indicated by the Government's suspension of the Place Names Commission.[162]

McElligott's fear that University College Galway (UCG) might wish to establish a Department of Oral Tradition might appear somewhat far-fetched, but it was not entirely so. In the early 1950's, and possibly even earlier, the President of UCG, Mons. Pádraig de Brún, contemplated establishing a Professorship of Folklore in his College but had to abandon the idea due to lack of funding.[163] McElligott would, of course, have had uppermost in his mind the expense to the state if UCG tried to emulate UCD and establish its own folklore archive.[164] But apart from this consideration, he may have been worried that the Cork and the Galway colleges of the National University of Ireland might consider a decision to transfer the Commission to UCD (providing the College with extra funds to effect this) as another example of preferential treatment by the state for the NUI's largest constituent college.

---

162 D/F S 010/0011/34: internal memo, McElligott to Bhreathnach, dated 23.11.1948, italics underlined in original.

163 de Brún 1950.

164 It is interesting to note, in this connection, that in 1953, UCG sought a grant to establish an Archive of Living Irish Speech ('Clárlann na Gaeilge Beo'), in association with a Professorship of Irish Dialects, which would have had its own field workers. In proposing the establishment of such an archive, the UCG authorities were hoping to make their College 'the headquarters for research on Modern Irish'. If such an archive had been established, UCG might well at a later stage have been able to make a strong claim for the Collections of the Irish Folklore Commission. As it was, however, their proposal received no official support. For more on UCG's proposal to establish an Archive of Living Irish Speech, see D/T S 10856A.

One of the main worries of Finance was the extra expenditure involved in transferring the Commission to UCD in the manner proposed. The Commission was at the time operating on a grant of £6,250; Ó Duilearga's most recent proposal would cost £12,400 per annum with an additional £3,600 to renovate 82 St Stephen's Green where the Commission was to be rehoused by UCD. Finance was also worried that extra expenditure might be sought on top of this as no provision was made, for example, for publications in this estimate. Máire Bhreathnach of the Dept. of Finance did not think a newly constituted Commission within UCD would be willing to carry on with a grant of £6,250. She, like McElligott, felt that such a move would mean that Finance would no longer be able to watch over 'administration and expenditure'. But she saw other objections:

> Apart from the financial aspect, however, I feel that U.C.D. is already large and unwieldy enough without taking on another Department. If we were commencing de novo under University auspices, I would prefer to see the Folklore work attached to Galway, which has a more Irish bent than Dublin. But as U.C.D. has assisted the Commission by the provision of accommodation and the services of Professor Delargy, it would be difficult to take such a step now.

For Máire Bhreathnach folklore involved 1) collecting folklore, and 2) making use of it. In her view, the work depended on 'two enthusiasts', Séamus Ó Duilearga and Séan Ó Súilleabháin, and 'the only difference which a transfer to the University would make would be that more money would be spent on collecting'; adding '[o]nly enthusiasts would keep on at the relatively small salaries paid to the collectors.' Moreover, in what turned out to be a quite astute observation, she further remarked: 'It is highly unlikely that the Governing Body of U.C.D. have any great interest in folklore – the Departments of Education and Finance are likely to have just as much.' She also noted that collecting would not continue for ever: 'it must finish sometime when the last seanachie [storyteller] dies. If the Folklore Commission is left under a Government Department there is a better chance of winding up the collection in due time.'

While recognising the value of the Commission's records, as it compensated for the lack of extensive 'written historical and semi-historical sources such as letters, memoirs, etc.', Máire Bhreathnach was not sure what to do with its collections. She noted that the 'change in language and the impact of modern conditions have made the break with the past a very definite one.' However, she went on to say:

> [T]he past which it [the Commission's collection] enshrines is a dead thing for most of the living. The average Irish reader is not interested in the ways of the countryside 50 or 100 years ago and is already bored by autobiographies of country people published by the Gúm. We may, I think, accept the contention that the collection will be of interest to enthusiasts, historians and musicians, who will quarry from it and present the results in a form acceptable to the moderns of their time. I

am not convinced that it is necessary that the custody of the collection should be in the hands of one University College rather than, say, the Public Record Office or the National Library. While Professor Delargy is in U.C.D he will be interested in the work, but at present, I have not come across many folklore enthusiasts in the College or any signs of a wide-spread interest in it among the students. When Professor Delargy goes, the raison d'etre of the connection with U.C.D. will go unless they produce another enthusiast. The next enthusiast may show up in Cork or Galway or Trinity.

UCD were proposing to house the Commission in 82 St. Stephen's Green, and Bhreathnach suggested that it 'might be possible to do a deal with the College to give this house to the Commission in return for the large grants we are giving them [i.e. UCD].' This, in her opinion, would have the advantage of retaining 'the collection in the University ambit', but 'would leave the position open for transfer to the Public Records Office, if this became desirable at a later stage.' She felt that keeping the Commission 'on a quasi-independent basis' was the best option, and even if they had to 'allow some extra expenditure for housing and publication', it would still be a cheaper solution than transferring it to UCD. She felt that the Public Records Office had a better claim to the Commission's collections than UCD, and also suggested that handing it over to UCD might 'provoke jealousy in Cork and Galway who might ask that the collection be split up on a regional basis.'[165] She concluded by saying:

> Also, and this is an important point, we could not have the same reliance as a custodian on a University College as on, say, the P.R.O. [Public Records Office]. If enthusiasm died down in U.C.D. the valuable collection might well be neglected or lost. There would be no obligation on them to keep it in 82, St. Stephen's Green. I would be altogether happier to see it in the P.R.O. [166]

Her superior, J. E. Hanna, agreed with much of what Máire Bhreathnach had to say, but did not think the Public Records Office was the best place for the Commission's collections. However, he did think 'that they should be

---

165 D/F S 101/0011/34: internal memo Bhreathnach to Hanna, dated 27.11.1948. Her fear that the Galway and Cork Colleges of the NUI might call for the collection to be split up while probably far-fetched was based not just on inter-university rivalry, but also on the provincialism still evident at the time in the Irish-language movement. As early as November 1929 a proposal for the establishment of an archive of Connaught folklore had been made to the then Minister for Finance. See UCDA P24/369: Tomás Ó Colmáin to Ernest Blythe, dated 6.11.1929.

166 D/F S 101/0011/34: internal memo Bhreathnach to Hanna, dated 27.11.1948. A note by a Finance official appended to the margin referring to Bhreathnach's proposal to do a deal with UCD says: 'It would I am afraid be highly injudicious in present circumstances to urge U.C.D. to hand over any of their university premises.' Given UCD's shortage of space, the Government would, most likely, have had to compensate the College for this loss of property.

in national custody and not in the custody of one constituent College of the National University.' He also felt that there could be 'little question that the other constituent colleges - Galway in particular - would have views on the subject seeing that the intention would be to create a fair number of posts.' Noting Máire Bhreathnach's comments on enthusiasm waning, he said:

> I feel that even if Professor Delargy passed from the scene and enthusiasm should wane the posts would continue to be filled - the proposal as to staff pensions will be noted. In plain truth, it seems to me hard to avoid the conclusion that the proposal is based in large measure on the desire to create jobs which, on the face of it, would be relatively well paid for the work to be assigned them - the suggested scales for typists as compared with Civil Service rates will be noted. It may be taken, therefore, that our views are that the proposal should be strongly resisted.[167]

On January 6th, 1949, Tarlach Ó Raifeartaigh[168], new Assistant Secretary of the Dept. of Education, wrote to the Secretary of the Dept. of Finance proposing that the Commission be transferred to the care of UCD and re-established as a 'Folklore Department' there, and that a grant of £16,000 for the first year be made available to the College for this purpose.[169] Máire Bhreathnach replied on January 18th, 1949 saying that the proposal was being examined, but that in the mean time her Department could not sanction a grant of more than £6,230 for the financial year 1949–1950.[170]

Ó Duilearga's health breaks down

Despite the presence of new political masters, the stance the Dept. of Finance was taking did not bode well for the future of the Commission. Moreover, by this time the deterioration in Ó Duilearga's health was also beginning to cast a shadow over his own future. The work of directing the Commission and his endless dealings with officials had worn him down, and he was forced to spend the period from mid-November 1948 until late April 1949 on leave, much of it recuperating abroad.[171] In mid-December 1948 he wrote to von Sydow on the occasion of the latter's seventieth birthday. Apologising for his long delay in writing, he explained that he had 'been very ill with a minor nervous breakdown, the result of some years of overstrain and worry.' He

---

167 D/F S 101/0011/34: internal memos, Bhreathnach to Hanna, and Hanna(?) to 'Finance Division', dated 27.11.1948 and 30.11.1948 respectively.

168 Ó Duilearga may have known Ó Raifeartaigh from his student days in UCD. Ó Raifeartaigh got his MA in Celtic Studies three years after Ó Duilearga. See McCartney 1999, p. 70.

169 D/F S 101/0011/34: Ó Raifeartaigh to Sec. of Dept. of Fin., dated 6.1.1949. Along with this letter, Ó Duilearga's letter of 5.11.1948 to Dept. of Educ was forwarded to Finance as well as estimates of the costs of his plan for the Commission.

170 D/F S 101/0011/34: letters dated 18.1.1949 and 28.1.1949 respectively.

171 D/T S 15548B: 'Gearr-Thuar./1948-49', p. 5. Ó Duilearga's letters to Prof. Martti Haavio preserved in the Finnish Literature Society give further evidence of his failing health and weakening energies.

had been advised by the doctor that he needed 'a complete change', and intended to go away with his wife 'for a while.' He writes:

> There is nothing very much wrong, but I cannot work at all, and am mentally & physically tired. I have fought for 20 years to have a permanent institute of Irish Folklore, & now that success is just around the corner, I get a relapse – much the same as when a watch-spring breaks when it is too tightly wound!'[172]

Ó Duilearga was unduly optimistic about the future of the Commission, but others, better able to access the situation, may have realised that a solution to the problems of the Commission was still a long way off. Just before Ó Duilearga went abroad, on February 2nd, 1949, Senator Michael Hayes, a colleague of his in UCD and prominent in Fine Gael, appealed to the Taoiseach, John A. Costello, on Ó Duilearga's behalf. He praised the work of the Commission, saying that of all the state grants that were being expended on the Irish language and 'allied purposes', that spent on the Irish Folklore Commission was 'the most fruitful and the most practical'. Hayes added: 'Whatever may happen to the Irish language itself everybody is in agreement that what remains of it and what remains of Irish oral tradition ought to be collected.' The success of the Commission was, in his opinion, 'mainly due to the genius, zeal and industry of the Director'. Of Ó Duilearga's abilities, he had this to say: he 'combines two rare qualities of being a good organiser and also a scholar.' Speaking of Ó Duilearga's talks with de Valera, he says that the latter 'was desirous that the Commission should be moved to the Dublin Institute for Advanced Studies', and implies that the reason that the Commission's grant was not increased was because Ó Duilearga 'desired to stay in the College'. It should be said that this is a simplification of what actually happened. A veteran of the Civil War, Hayes may have allowed party-political animosities to influence his assessment of the situation. Hayes also appealed to Costello's sense of national pride:

> Delargy is a recognised scholar of international repute, one of the very few whom we now have in Arts or indeed in any branch of learning. His work has attracted visitors here from Great Britain, the United States, Scandinavian countries and elsewhere. He has for a long time been doing work which belongs to the Department of External Affairs. He has lectured in Germany, in the United States and in Britain and is the kind of occasional Ambassador from whom we obtain most credit abroad.

But despite all this good work, Hayes explained, the situation was now desperate, both for the Commission and for Ó Duilearga: 'The Director's energies for some time have gone to lobbying and imploring until recently his health has broken down. He is leaving the country this week for two or three months after which it is hoped he will be all right.' Finally, he stipulated

172 LUB Saml. von Sydow: Ó Duilearga to von Sydow, letter dated 14.12.1948.

that the Commission could no longer survive on £6,250: 'If the grant is not substantially increased then the Commission should be dissolved and the work of collection stopped. If that has to be done, it will be too late to resume the work at any future date.' He said that he had brought up this matter on numerous occasions in Seanad Éireann, 'but nobody in the last Government had any appreciation of the realities in connection with the Irish language and Irish History.' In his opinion, the staff of the Irish Folklore Commission were 'doing admirable work to show us the history and life and thoughts of the ordinary Irish countryman,' and in conclusion he urged the Taoiseach 'with all the earnestness at my command that these highly competent people doing a good job should be given sufficient money to do it right.'[173]

Hayes' appeal seems to have been heeded. At any rate, a meeting took place in the Dept. of the Taoiseach in February 1949, while Ó Duilearga was away in France, to discuss the question of the Commission's grant. The meeting decided to provide a grant of £12,000 for the Commission for the coming financial year (i.e. 1949-1950). So by the time Ó Duilearga returned from France, the prospects for the Commission were much brighter, to say the least. Their grant had been doubled, and they were soon to be accommodated in a new, relatively spacious house of their own, 82 St. Stephen's Green, provided free of charge by UCD, and renovated at state expense. However, nothing had been decided in respect of making the Commission permanent, and nothing was to be decided for many years to come.

Nevertheless, the improved circumstances of the Commission gave him, if not all his staff, a breathing space. Not surprisingly, one senses a new vigour and optimism in a letter of Ó Duilearga's written in December 1949 to the Dept. of Education in connection with employing some new collectors:

> For years, due to lack of money and staff, we have had to make do with a small number of full-time and part-time collectors. Now that we have an adequate residence of our own and been provided with a proper grant, which is a source of great encouragement to us, we would like to endeavour to recover the remnants of folklore and national tradition in the Irish-speaking parts of Connacht and the English-speaking parts of Leinster and Ulster.[174]

173 D/T S 6916C: Hayes to Costello, dated 2.2.1949.
174 See D/F S 101/0011/34: Ó Duilearga to Sec. Dept. of Educ., dated 2.12.1949 (trans.).

5. The Nineteen Fifties/Commission adrift

New vigour but problems with Dept. of Finance

This new spurt of vigour was in time to be replaced by a degree of inertia, which gathered its own momentum as the years went by (see below). Moreover, although the Commission now had a bigger grant and more suitable premises, apart from the question of the future status of the Commission, there were continuing headaches for the Director. These were mainly caused by the Dept. of Finance. In 1947, Finance relaxed its control of the Commission, amongst other things, allowing it to decide salary scales for its staff (see Chapter VI/1 below). However, within a few years the Dept. of Finance came to regret this decision and tried to exercise as much control over the Commission as it could. Although the Government had agreed to double the Commission's grant in early 1949, in October of that year, the Dept. of Education had to ask the Dept. of Finance to pay the portion of the grant-in-aid for 1949-1950 that was still due the Commission. Finance acquiesced, but requested that when the grant for 1950-1951 would be sought, accounts for the three-year period up and including 1948-1949 should be submitted.[175] Finance's desire to keep stricter control of the Commission's expenditure once again did not augur well for the future.

Neither, in time, did Ó Duilearga resume his efforts to have the Commission reconstituted in UCD nor elsewhere as a permanent body.[176] Given the economic climate of the early 1950's and friction with the Dept. of Finance, he may have been loath to again broach the question of making the Commission permanent. But he would also have been mindful that his

---

175 D/F S 101/0011/34: Ó Raifeartaigh to Sec. Dept. of Fin., and Bhreathnach to Sec. Dept. of Educ; letters dated 27.10.1949 and 15.11.1949 respectively.

176 The material in the files of the Dept. of the Taois. on the Commission for the period commencing with the first Inter-Party Government up until the end of the second Inter-Party Government is very scant, but the records of the same Dept. for the late 1950's (many of them deriving from the Dept. of Education) indicate that the Director for most of this period made no formal approach to either the Dept. of the Taois. or the Dept. of Educ. about establishing the Commission on a more permanent footing. This is not to say that the matter was not brought up on a more informal basis from time to time, both between Ó Duilearga and officials, and among officials themselves.

earlier efforts to put the Commission on a more permanent footing had contributed greatly to the breakdown of his health in the late 1940's. So often in the past his hopes had been raised only to be dashed. In the covering letter he submitted along with the Estimates for 1953–1954 he does not mention making the Commission permanent, but speaks of the need for further collecting and about the international reputation of the Commission. The reason for continuing collecting was simple: 'The Commission has to push ahead without stop or stay with the collecting. The narrator who is alive this year, may well be dead by next year, and the knowledge he has will go with him to the grave.' He stressed that there was material to be had in Ireland that was not to be had anywhere else in western Europe, and gives Reidar Christiansen's opinion on the value of this material: 'henceforth what has already been written about European folklore will have to be reconsidered because the Mss of the Commission contain a vast amount of knowledge that was not available to scholars hitherto.' Ó Duilearga concludes from this that in future: 'folklore researchers will be heading for Ireland instead of going to Eastern Europe', and he adds that this fact 'is worth pondering.' His intention, no doubt, was to set the authorities thinking on the implications of Ireland's newly established importance in folklore research. It may have impressed Education officials, as a copy of the above letter was sent from the Dept. of Education to the Dept. of Finance. However, it has to be noted that in the latter department some official has added a number of sarcastic comments to Ó Duilearga's letter.[177]

General Mulcahy, to little avail, sought increased grants for the Commission, believing that it had 'been "starved" of money for years', and needed a grant of sufficient size to enable it to 'recruit and retain qualified staff and to make their plans well in advance.' Finance, while not thinking the salaries of the Commission's staff excessive, took the rather cynical view: 'that no matter how much money is made available [the Commission] will be able to spend it profitably. The idea of an "estimate" as we understand it is completely foreign to them.' Finance wished to know about the Commission's real needs and would have liked more detail about expenditure than was forthcoming. The Dept. of Finance also resented the fact that grants which it had given the Commission 'in recent years for a number of items had apparently been applied, not to these items, but to increasing salaries'.[178] In the early 1950's, and later, the Dept. of Education had an uphill battle to argue the Commission's case with Finance. Arguments that were meant to impress did not have the desired effect. For instance, when Tarlach Ó Raifeartaigh, Secretary of the Dept. of Education, informed Máire Bhreathnach that the 'Scottish people had been so impressed with [the Commission's] work that a Folklore Institute had been established by Edinburgh University' and that 'developments in this direction were also taking place in the Isle of Man, Wales, and London,' Bhreathnach somewhat sarcastically notes:

---

177 D/F S 101/0011/34: Ó Duilearga to Sec. Dept of Educ., dated 15.11.1952.

178 D/F S 101/0011/34: internal memo McElligott to Bhreathnach, dated 10.1.1950, and 'Extract from Miss Bhreathnach's submission (F 102/43/52) of the 3rd February, 1953) to Mr Almond on the Science and Arts Estimates 1953/54'.

With all this glory it is not easy to attack the provision for the Folklore Commission, albeit they might seem, so far, to have been embalmers rather than nurses of the oral tradition. They have collected tons of records, but none of the material has gone out again to the people, except for what is published in Bealoideas, a journal which is not in a very popular format.[179]

Political instability

The return of Fianna Fáil to power in June 1951, again under Éamon de Valera, meant that an opportunity to transfer the Commission to UCD had been lost. Seán Moylan, the new Minister for Education, unlike his predecessor, Richard Mulcahy, was not sympathetic to UCD's claims on the Commission. Neither did Moylan propose any alternative solution for placing the Commission on a permanent footing, preferring that 'it should continue under the then terms of reference.'[180] Given the opposition of the Minister for Education, there was little those Education officials most in sympathy with the plight of the Commission could do apart from, as the need arose, request the Government that it extend the Commission's term of office for a further period, usually of five years.

By June 1954, Mulcahy was back in office as Minister of Education, as Fianna Fáil was replaced by the second Inter-Party Government. Mulcahy would be Minister for almost three years, until March 1957. But despite his sympathy with the Commission, there is no evidence to show that he advanced the idea of transferring the Commission to UCD or succeeded in improving its status. The question to be asked is why did he not succeed in doing so in either of his two periods of office as Minister for Education. Part of the explanation lies in the economic policies pursued by the Dept. of Finance, and possible in the ideological opposition to UCD of certain officials of that Department. But it may also be the case that Mulcahy, despite his sympathy for the Commission, was not the best person to advance its interest at the Cabinet table. Noël Browne, a colleague of his in the first Inter-Party Government, says that Mulcahy was 'treated with a mixture of levity and contempt by his party colleagues.' Although very verbal, Browne says that Mulcahy 'appearedy unable to articulate his simplest ideas' and that '[d]eeply and impenetrably buried in the centre of all this tormented English was whatever happened to be the simple needs of his department.' Of Mulcahy's contributions to Cabinet discussions, Browne says:

> The invariable effect of the intervention by Mulcahy was to transform the Cabinet into a collection of openly chattering individuals, or small private cabals, completely ignoring him. They joined one another in noisy

179 Ibid.
180 ED CO 495(8): memo dated 8.5.1953.

discussions, sometimes even across the cabinet table. The more polite would appear to recall some problem for which their personal attention was urgently needed in their department.

Browne also says: 'I felt so ashamed by the ill-mannered behaviour of [my] colleagues and their obvious disinclination to try to decipher what Mulcahy was trying to say that, out of embarrassed pity, I recall attempting hopelessly to hold an interested conversation with him.'[181] While Noël Browne cannot be considered an impartial commentator, and even if the picture he draws of Mulcahy's discourse is somewhat dramatised, it may, to some extent, explain why ultimately this champion of the Irish Folklore Commission in Government achieved no real improvement in its status. Moreover, Browne's testimony receives support from less partial sources. Mulcahy in his recorded memoirs complains 'on several occasions that the then Minister for Finance, Paddy McGilligan, was not only parsimonious to a great degree in giving money to his department but was almost impossible to contact.' Moreover, Paddy Lynch, on the staff of UCD and 'a confidante' of John A. Costello, Taoiseach during both Inter-Party Governments, told Mulcahy's son, Risteárd, that 'the department of education was treated with little more than contempt by other ministers and departments' at that time. Risteárd Mulcahy, who edited his father's memoirs, suggests that this may explain his father's 'financial problems as Minister.[182]

It should be said that although Ó Duilearga made no official petition to the Government during this period (i.e. the early 1950's) to establish the Commission on a more permanent basis, his annual reports usually end on a plaintive note, a veiled hint, most likely, that something needed to be done in this respect. His annual report to the Government covering the financial year 1955–1956 ends with a longer and more poignant note than hitherto. Here is a quotation from it:

> At some future date when all of us now are dead, it is then that it will be understood how indebted the civilized world is to this small Irish nation for its effort to save from destruction Ireland's oral heritage. That is already understood abroad, and there are quite a few people at home who also understand.[183]

Pensions for staff of Commission

Whatever about making the Commission permanent, the question of pension rights could not be postponed indefinitely. As these two questions were inextricably interlinked, it is not surprising that when the issue of establishing the Commission was next raised it should be done in the context of pensions.

181 Browne 1986, pp. 125–126.
182 Mulcahy 1999, p. 229.
183 D/T S 15548B: 'Gearr-Thuar./1955-56', pp. 7–8 (trans.).

The question of pensions for the staff of the Commission began to be discussed at meetings of the Commission and the Finance Sub-Committee from mid-1956 onwards.[184] By this stage some of the staff had been more than twenty years in the employment of the Commission, and it was felt it was time the question of pensions was tackled. The Commission itself did not have the resources to invest in its own pension scheme for staff so it was decided to appeal to the state authorities to provide its staff with pensions. Various factors delayed anything of substance been done in the short term to solve this problem, chief of which was the decision to transfer the Commission out of the care of the Dept. of Education and under the care of the newly created Dept. of the Gaeltacht. This transfer came into effect in April 1957 and although the same Minister dealt with the Commission under this new arrangement, it was, in many respects, a retrograde step, and fortunately within less than six months this decision was rescinded.

The details of these early efforts to get pensions for members of the Commission's staff need not concern us here, as they had little impact on future developments. However, of crucial importance was a meeting in autumn 1957 between Pádraig Ó Siochfhradha, President of the Folklore of Ireland Society, and Éamon de Valera, who was again Taoiseach. At this meeting the question of pensions, amongst other matters, was raised. Ó Siochfhradha may have gone to see de Valera on the request of the Director of the Commission, but it is just as likely that he went of his own accord. Ó Siochfhradha was his own man when it came to matters concerning folklore and, as we will learn later on, there were certain matters he wished to discuss with the Taoiseach that were not for Ó Duilearga's ears.[185] This intervention by Ó Siochfhradha seems to have had some impact on the situation, for at a cabinet meeting in late January 1958 the Taoiseach enquired of the Minister for Education whether anything was being done about the status of the Commission and was told that proposals were being prepared to give 'established status [as Civil Servants] to the Commission's staff.' Moreover, the Minister for Finance, at this meeting, 'undertook to give sympathetic consideration to such proposals.'[186] By this stage the decision had been made to transfer the Commission back to the care of the Dept. of Education, to be effective from April 1st, 1958. The next development occurred on April 16th, 1958 when Ó Duilearga met with Tarlach Ó Raifeartaigh of the Dept. of Education. Ó Rafartaigh had requested this meeting to discuss matters concerning staffing in the Commission as well as the publication of material in its collections; the latter matter being something the Dept. of Education was also anxious to expedite. At the end of this meeting Ó Duilearga suggested that he himself and the President of UCD, Dr Michael Tierney, might discuss these matters with the Minister.[187]

---

184 ED FL 2: 'IFC. Fin. Sub-Com/ 101th Meeting, 21.9.1956', par 752 and : 'CBÉ. Miont. 86ú Cruinniú, 5.10.1956', par. 641.

185 D/T S 6916D: M. Ó Muimhneacháin to T. Ó Raifeartaigh, dated 15.9.1958.

186 D/T S 6916D: copy of 'Cabinet Minutes' ('Cruinniú Rialtais'), 28.1.58.

187 ED CO 495 (1): 'An Coimisiún Béaloideasa. Agallamh (16/4/58) leis an Ollamh Ó Duilearga', signed T. Ó Raifeartaigh, 16.4.1958.

Finance Sub-Committee meets with Education officials

As a result of this suggestion, a second meeting took place on April 24th, 1958, although not with the Minister for Education present. As well as Tierney and Ó Duilearga, Liam Price, of the Finance Sub-Committee, attended. The problem of pensions for the staff was again raised, and Ó Raifeartaigh explained some of the difficulties involved. However, the three above members of the Commission were not interested in the intricacies of making Civil Servants of the staff of a temporary state body such as the Commission. In their opinion, the solution to the pension dilemma was to attach the Commission to UCD. Not only was this the only way of ensuring pensions for staff, they believed it was 'the only proper solution' for the Commission. After some discussion, the meeting was postponed to a later date as it was felt that the Chairman of the Commission, Eric Mac Fhinn should be present, and Ó Duilearga was asked to inform him that 'informal discussions' had taken place, but that they had been postponed until he could be present.[188]

In his letter to Mac Fhinn, Ó Duilearga stated that it was explained to them at the outset that the meeting Michael Tierney, Liam Price, and he had with Education officials 'was only an informal discussion and that the question should not be examined without' the Chairman of the Commission. This would not appear to have been the case, however, from the Dept. of Education's report of the meeting. It is not clear from this account who decided that the meeting could not proceed without the Chairman, but it would appear to have been something that arose out of the turn the discussions took, rather than something that was stated at the beginning of the meeting. Be that as it may, a further meeting was arranged for May 10th. Mac Fhinn would appear to have been somewhat reluctant to accept this invitation without the rest of the Commission being present. However, he thought it would appear 'churlish' ('doichealach') to refuse, especially as the Secretary of the Dept. of Education would be present. His reluctance stemmed from the fact that the Commission as a body had not been consulted and when accepting the invitation he reminded the Director that the discussion would have to be informal, that they would have no authority to speak for the Commission.[189]

Mac Fhinn contacted both Fionán Mac Coluim and Pádraig Ó Siochfhradha before this meeting and forwarded copies of his correspondence with Ó Duilearga to both. In his letter to Mac Coluim, Mac Fhinn says that no 'major change' in respect of the status of the Commission should take place without every aspect of the matter being discussed 'in its entirety'. He was

---

188 ED CO 495 (1): 'An Coimisiún Béaloideasa. Agallamh leis an Dr. M. Ó Tighearnaigh, Séamus Ó Duilearga (An Stiúrthóir) agus Liam Price ar an 24.4.58', (trans.). At this meeting, Michael Tierney, resurrecting an idea he first mooted in 1947 (see above), proposed that in the event of the collections and staff of the Commission being transferred to UCD, the Commission itself might be reconstituted as a governing council similar to that of Albert College, (UCD's Faculty of Agriculture), whose membership consisted of both UCD and outside representatives. Ibid.

189 The correspondence between Mac Fhinn and Ó Duilearga in respect of this meeting is reproduced in D/T S 6916D: 'CBÉ. Miont. Cruinniú Speisialta, 27.6.1958, pp. 1–4.

aware that it was within the Minister's powers to do whatever he wished with the Commission, but it appeared that he wished to 'seek advice', as his Department had been reluctant to discuss the matter, 'even informally, without the Chairman of the Commission being present.'[190] Mac Coluim did not feel as assured as Mac Fhinn. In a letter Mac Coluim wrote to Pádraig Ó Siochfhradha subsequently on the matter, although he would appear to have been aware that the Taoiseach was contemplating resolving the issue of pensions for the staff of the Commission without incorporating it into UCD, he reminded him that the Secretary of the Dept. of Education, Tarlach Ó Raifeartaigh, had a close affinity with Michael Tierney and Ó Duilearga and would strongly support a proposal from them to transfer the Commission to the College. He told Ó Siochfhradha that he had advised Mac Fhinn to decline the invitation to the proposed meeting, unless he had already agreed to attend, lest anything he might say be construed as giving 'authority' to opinions that might be expressed by Ó Duilearga and others present.

As mentioned already, the three members of the Commission who had met Ó Raifeartaigh on April 24th were all on the Finance Sub-Committee. Even before he received the above letter from Eric Mac Fhinn, Mac Coluim was worried about the composition of this Committee and informed Ó Siochfhradha that prior to being contacted by Mac Fhinn, he had written to Donnchadh Ó Briain, Parliamentary Secretary to the Taoiseach, requesting that an additional two Civil Servants, Liam Ó Buachalla and Séamas Mac Úgo be appointed to the Finance Sub-Committee and that Caoimhín Ó Danachair be appointed 'Vice-Director or Co-Director' to the Commission.[191] It would appear ranks were being drawn up to do battle. If Ó Duilearga had his staunch supporters on the Finance Sub-Committee, some of those opposed to transferring the Commission to UCD were leaving nothing to chance. The most formidable, non-governmental figure among the opposition was, of course, Pádraig Ó Siochfhradha. The previous autumn, as we have seen above, Ó Siochfhradha had spoken to de Valera on the question of pensions for the staff of the Commission. On that occasion he also stressed to de Valera the undesirability of transferring the Commission to the care of UCD.[192]

Given Mac Fhinn's belief that all the members of the Commission needed to be consulted on its future, it was unlikely that the meeting arranged for May 10th would come to any definite decisions. It did, however, discuss the various ways of making the Commission permanent. In connection with the proposal to incorporate the Commission into UCD, Ó Duilearga said that 'he had often earlier proposed the same solution'. He also said that he had prepared 'a draft memorandum' on the matter which he circulated to members of the Commission 'around the year 1948', but 'that his health failed shortly afterwards and the matter had not been pursued.' Eric Mac Fhinn stated, in answer to this, that he remembered no such memorandum being

190 Col. Íde Ó Siochfhradha Papers: Mac Fhinn to Mac Coluim, dated 7.5.1958 (trans.).

191 Col. Íde Ó Siochfhradha Papers: Mac Coluim to Ó Siochfhradha, dated 9.5.1958 (trans.).

192 D/T S 6916D: M. Ó Muimhneacháin to T. Ó Raifeartaigh, dated 15.9.1958.

circulated in the Commission. Dr. Tierney, on the other hand, said that he recalled seeing such a document, but neither he nor anyone else present had any clear recollection of it. Given this difference of opinion about what had or had not been discussed at meetings of the Commission in respect of the future of its collections and staff, it was obvious to Ó Raifeartaigh that there was nothing like unanimity on the Commission in respect of these matters. To get around this impasse, on the request of those present, he outlined the alternative solutions to the problem in hand:

(1) To incorporate the Commission into University College, providing the College with an annual grant. Under this agreement the College could, 'where necessary', arrange pensions for the staff.

(2) To make the Commission a permanent division of the Civil Service. In this way, the staff would become Civil Servants and would consequently have pension rights. Under this arrangement the Minister for Education 'would appoint the staff'.

(3) To leave the Commission as then constituted but to appoint some of the staff Civil Servants 'in the public interest', and loan them to the Commission.

(4) To leave the Commission carry on as it was.

In response to the above alternatives outlined by Ó Raifeartaigh, Tierney reiterated his belief that the best solution was to incorporate the Commission into UCD and for the Government to foot the costs of pensions, as well as continuing their annual grant to the Commission. Mac Fhinn said that he had an 'open mind on the matter', but he reiterated his belief that the proposal had never been put before the Commission, and that it should be done. Ever given to the dramatic note, Ó Duilearga expressed the opinion that if the Commission were re-established in such a way that would separate it from UCD, 'he would have to sever his connections with the Commission – that he was a professor in the University and that is the place he intended to stay.'[193] Given this impasse, it was decided that a special meeting of the Commission should be convened to discuss the question of pensions and status.

Special meeting of Commission, June 27th, 1958

The Commission first met on June 26th for its normal June meeting, and convened the following day for a special meeting. Ó Duilearga was obviously apprehensive beforehand. What he had been trying to avoid for a long time was about to take place, namely the airing of the views of all the members of the Commission on the best future organisation for its collections and

---

193 ED FL 4: internal memo entitled 'An Coimisiún Béaloideasa', addressed to Assist. Sec., dated 10.5.1958 (trans.). It would appear that Mac Fhinn expressed his fear at this meeting that to incorporate the Commission into UCD would drive a wedge between folklorists in that college and those outside it. See ED CO 495(1): 'Coimisiún Béaloideasa Éireann', T. Ó R[aifeartaigh] to Min. For Educ., dated 9.8.1958, p. 2.

staff. On the morning of the special meeting he wrote to his friend, full-time collector Ciarán Bairéad, of his apprehensions about the meeting and of his fear that Fionán Mac Coluim, who he said had been obstreperous at the meeting the day before, would along with others 'ultimately destroy what they helped to create.'[194]

Ó Duilearga had reason to be worried. He should have allowed an open debate on the future organisation of the Commission long before he was forced to do so by the Dept. of Education and Eric Mac Fhinn. Ó Duilearga preferred, as we have seen above, to keep the Commission in the dark on this issue, and work surreptitiously without consulting it. In doing so, he had shown little respect for the Commission, who were after all appointed to consider his proposals, not just to rubber-stamp them. A more open discussion of his own plans for the Commission at meetings of the Board of the Commission might have resulted in winning over some of those who were not in favour of transferring the Commission to UCD. As for certain people destroying 'what they helped to create', it is not at all certain that Ó Duilearga's solution for making the Commission permanent was, in the long run, the best option.

Present at the special meeting of the Commission on June 27th, 1958 were: Eric Mac Fhinn (Chairman), Liam Price, Cormac Ó Cuilleanáin, Fionán Mac Coluim, Pádraig Mac Con Midhe, Seán Mac Giollarnáth, Seán Ó Maonaigh, Pádraig Ó Maoláin, and Séamus Ó Duilearga. Michael Tierney was not present. The discussion involved two matters: pension rights for staff and setting the Commission on a more permanent footing. The Chairman, Eric Mac Fhinn, started the proceedings by explaining at length, and somewhat contentiously, how this special meeting had come about in the first place. He reiterated his assertion that the question of the future organisation of the Commission had never been discussed by the Commission as a body and stated that for this reason they were now being asked by the Dept. of Education to do so. In order to defuse the situation, Ó Duilearga's requested Mac Fhinn to read out their correspondence on the matter (the Director's letter of April 24th and the Chairman's reply of April 27th) for the information of those present. This he did, and the actual discussion then commenced.

Ó Duilearga proposed that the Commission be made permanent a) to ensure the safety of the Commission's collections and library and its accessibility for future researchers in 'folk-literature' and ethnology, both native and foreign, and b) to secure pensions for the full-time staff of the Commission, some of whom had been with the Commission since the beginning. Bending the truth somewhat (see above), he claimed that he had often broached this subject at meetings of the Finance Sub-Committee as well as at meetings of the Commission itself, and also from time to time in his annual reports to the Government. Although he had often tried to approach the matter from different angles, he said, the result was always the same. From the beginning he was convinced that the Commission should be incorporated into UCD.

194 UCG Hard. Lib. Arch. Bairéad Papers: G3/557.

He added that although 'lacunae' in the Commission's large collection of *seanchas* ('lore') needed to be filled, 'all in all, it could be said that the first part of the task given to the Commission', namely 'the collecting of folklore in Irish, especially folk-tales (Märchen)' had been completed. In his estimation, the next task awaiting to be done 'was to devise a scheme to publish the best of the Irish-language collection' and that this could not be 'done properly outside of University College, Dublin, which was surrounded by the biggest libraries in the country.' He also reminded the meeting of the debt both the Folklore of Ireland Society and the Commission owed the UCD authorities since 1927.

Liam Price said that it was not necessary for the meeting to come to a 'combined opinion' but that members should express their views and that these should be minuted. For him there was an urgency about the matter. Prof. Ó Duilearga was 'in his 60th year' and consequently it was 'imperative for him to consider what the future of the Irish Folklore Commission is to be – for the creation of which he is in effect almost entirely responsible.' It was important that there should be continuity, and considering the help UCD had given the Commission over the years by providing accommodation, etc., and seconding Prof. Ó Duilearga to direct the work of the Commission, the 'most effective way to ensure' continuity would be to attach it to UCD. This, he stressed, would also be the cheapest way of making the Commission permanent, as it would reduce 'to a minimum the expenditure on the acquisition of new premises, their equipment, maintenance and staffing.' Price also said that '[a]ccording to Dr. Reidar Christiansen of Oslo ... all other bodies of this type in Scotland, in America and on the continent of Europe, come under the aegis of a University.' He consequently proposed that the Commission 'should be put – as a permanent and semi-independent body – into University College, Dublin', adding that it was 'difficult to see any alternative'. [195] Liam Price's arguments were cogent, but he does not seem to have realised that in the case of northern Europe, being 'under the aegis of a University' in some cases did not mean being part and parcel of a particular university, but rather working in close association with it. In fact, the Commission could be said to have been already under the aegis of UCD; the problem was how to make it permanent and secure pension rights for its staff.[196]

Liam Price was the only member present that day to come out strongly in support of Ó Duilearga's proposal to incorporate the Commission into UCD. A number of others gave him a degree of support by not taking any definite stance on his proposal. For example, Pádraig Mac Con Midhe, of

---

195 D/T S 6916D: 'CBÉ. Miont. Cruinniú Speisialta, 27.6.1958', pp. 1-5. All the members present at this meeting appear to have spoken in Irish, with the exception of Liam Price.

196 Answering a question from the Chair, Ó Duilearga informed the meeting that although 'there was an age limit to his appointment as professor of Folklore in University College, Dublin', as the Commission was not a permanent body, there was no age limit to him acting as Honorary Director (trans.). At the time, seventy was the age of retirement for professors and lecturers at the constituent colleges of the National University of Ireland. As Ó Duilearga was fifty nine years of age at the time, he had eleven years to go before retirement.

the Gaelic Athletic Association, proposed that the Commission should be made permanent, either within the University or 'as a separate institute'. In his opinion, it would not be proper to ask the Government to devise a pension scheme for a non-permanent body such as the Commission. Seán Mac Giollarnáth's position was quite similar to that of Mac Con Midhe's. For him the prevailing situation whereby the Commission was living from year to year was most unsatisfactory. It was essential to achieve permanent status for the Commission for the sake of the staff, but it was not important whether this was achieved within or without UCD. He believed that for the Commission to be disbanded altogether would be a severe blow to efforts being made to spread the use of Irish. Mac Giollarnáth, unlike Ó Duilearga, was still an Irish revivalist. His neutral stance in respect of UCD may reflect personal loyalty to Ó Duilearga, although he may well have actually preferred a non-UCD location for the Commission. Being a circuit judge his relationship with Ó Duilearga may always have been one of equals, and a certain camaraderie may have existed between them, something which does not seem to have existed between Ó Duilearga and Fionán Mac Coluim.

While Ó Duilearga might have taken some solace from the opinions expressed by Mac Con Midhe and Mac Giollarnáth, those of two other members of the Commission were far less supportive of UCD's claim to the Commission, although they did leave the option open of transferring the Commission at some future date to the College. Prof. Cormac Ó Cuileanáin, of University College Cork, like Mac Giollarnáth, believed that there existed, and would always exist a 'close link ... between the cultivation of folklore and the national work for the language.' In respect of the future of the Commission, he stated that it was best to leave the matter of pensions for staff to the Dept. of Education, and that they should not be too hasty to 'discuss attaching' the Commission 'to University College Dublin.' In other words, he was proposing that the staff of the Commission be provided with pensions without changing the status of the Commission. The stance taken by Seán Ó Maonaigh, the Dept. of Finance's representative, was somewhat similar. He did not see any urgent need to make the Commission permanent, stating 'there was permanency and permanency'. The Commission would be around long enough to set up a pension scheme for it. If that were achieved, and it was 'decided at some future date to disband the Commission', he thought it would not be difficult to find alterative employment for the staff. He reminded the meeting that the Dept of the Gaeltacht, when briefly in charge of the Commission, had not in principle opposed the idea of a pension scheme for its staff; there was therefore no reason why they could not proceed from 'where they were already' and devise a pension scheme for some of the staff 'without deciding beforehand that the Commission would be there forever.' As regards attaching the Commission to UCD, he said he neither supported nor opposed the idea, but it would appear that he did not see any urgency in deciding on this matter.

Two members of the Commission present that day directly opposed the idea of transferring the Commission to UCD, namely Fionán Mac Coluim and Eric Mac Fhinn. Mac Coluim, a Gaelic League veteran, stated 'there was no chance whatsoever that the Commission would be disbanded.' Moreover, 'although beholden to University College' he felt there 'was no reason to bestow the Commission on the College.' He reminded the other members that 82 St. Stephen's Green had been renovated and furnished at state expense, to the sum of £3,000. Neither did he think they should feel indebted to UCD for seconding Séamus Ó Duilearga down through the years, stating that it was nothing unusual for a university, as in the case of a 'research scholarship', to free a professor from his professorial duties to engage in work on some project or other. If the Commission was to be 'moved', he felt that the National Museum or the Institute for Advanced Studies might be the best place for it. He proposed that the Dept. of Education should be asked 'to make Civil Servants of the staff of the Commission'.

The Chairman of the Commission, Eric Mac Fhinn was also strongly opposed to transferring the Commission to UCD. He is recorded as saying:

> that he well understood, and respected, the loyalty of people to their own College. But he would be loath to take personal factors into account, especially as what they were proposing was to recommend a permanent settlement that would be there when we will be gone. It should be remembered that there is more than one University College in the country. If the Commission were to be under the care of any University College, in his opinion, University College Cork or University College Galway would be more suitable, since they were more associated with the Gaeltacht. But since the Commission was not directly involved with teaching, he would not be in favour of attaching it to any College. It should be a separate institute, like the National Museum or the National Library.

Although he felt that the 'main members of staff' should be given pension rights, he reminded members that however this was achieved, the money would come from the same source, the 'public purse'.[197] This was a sobering thought. Economics had always played an important role in the Commission's fate and would continue to do so to the very end, and beyond. UCD was never in a position to take the Commission out of the state's hands without additional state funding. Moreover, Mac Fhinn's comment on teaching was also very pertinent. Teaching was the weak link in Ó Duilearga's argument. He himself had neglected teaching for years, and his proposals did not seem to allow for the initiation of teaching in folkloristics. In this respect, his above threat to sever his links with the Commission if it was separated from UCD was probably only bluff, i.e. a bargaining chip. It is hardly likely that at sixty years of age he would have gone back to teaching and regular university duties.

There is one important observation of Mac Fhinn's in respect of pensions and UCD that he does not appear to have made at this meeting, or at least it was not minuted. In a letter he wrote to Pádraig Ó Siochfhradha the previous month he observed that it was his understanding that many of

197 D/T S 6916D: 'CBÉ. Miont. Cruinniú speisialta, 27.6.1958' (trans.) pp. 6-7.

the staff of UCD (among others, assistant lecturers) did not have pension rights.[198] Indeed, it would be the late 1960's before the grievances of the College's junior staff would be addressed and tenure extended to them.[199] Transferring the Commission to UCD at this juncture, especially if this agreement also involved providing its staff with pensions, could well have led to disenchantment among UCD's junior staff, many of whom, like the staff of the Commission, had been working for years with little or no security. Thus, apart from ideological opposition to transferring the Commission to UCD, it would appear that neither Tierney nor Ó Duilearga had fully considered some of the practical obstacles to such a transfer.

Officials assess the opinions of the members of the Commission

Very different views had been expressed at this special meeting and it concluded without reaching any agreement. Initially provisional minutes were written up and distributed to members for comment. More complete minutes with additions were then compiled.[200] This partly explains the delay in sending a copy of the minutes to the Dept. of Education before the Commission's office closed as usual for the month of August. However, both Mac Fhinn and Mac Coluim were late in furnishing their emendations, so that it was early September before the final version of the minutes could be drawn up.[201] Meanwhile de Valera was anxious to see movement on the question of pensions for the staff of the Commission and contacted the Dept. of Education on the matter. In response to de Valera's call, Tarlach Ó Raifeartaigh, Secretary of the Dept. of Education, drew up a memo for his Minister (Jack Lynch), outlining where matters stood before the June meeting of the Commission.

As well as noting Mac Fhinn's opposition to attaching the Commission to University College Dublin, Ó Raifeartaigh says that he understands that Pádraig Ó Siochfhradha is strongly opposed to the idea. He adds that although Ó Siochfhradha is not a member of the Commission, 'he is an important person in matters concerning folklore'. Ó Siochfhradha, as already mentioned, was also an important figure in Irish language circles, and as a member of Seanad Éireann had many political contacts. His opinion counted for a lot in official circles, and it is not surprising that Ó Raifeartaigh drew his Minister's attention to Ó Siochfhradha's views on this matter. Nevertheless, Ó Raifeartaigh himself thought the best way to provide pensions for the Commission's staff was to attach it to UCD. He notes:

198 Col. Íde Ó Siochfhradha Papers: Mac Fhinn to Ó Siochfhradha, dated 7.5.1058.
199 McCartney 1999, pp. 346 and 380–381.
200 A copy of these provisional minutes is to be found in ED FL 4. Although it is very revealing to contrast these two sets of minutes, for simplicity's sake, I have based my above description of what was said at the special meeting of June 27th, 1958 on the more complete version of the minutes (D/T S 6916D: 'CBÉ Miont. Cruinniú Speisialta, 27.6.1958), even though certain things this version relates as having been said on that day may actually have been added or modified by members later.
201 ED CO 495 (1): Ó Duilearga to Ó Raifeartaigh, dated 4.9.1958.

> Folklore is primarily a scholarly matter, in my opinion, and without this scholarly aspect it would be difficult to keep it together. It is also international, and it is being dealt with in a scholarly fashion in other countries, for the most part, as far as I understand.

Moreover, while he admits the danger of folklore becoming 'something completely "dead"', if incorporated into the University, he adds that this danger would also exist if it were to be made 'a branch of the Civil Service.' Nevertheless, he did not think it a good idea to put a body such as the Commission under the control of the Civil Service. In response to this memo, his Minister informed him that a proposal to attach the Commission to UCD stood little chance of being accepted.[202]

It was not until mid-September or thereabouts that the Commission forwarded the minutes of this special meeting to the Dept. of Education.[203] In forwarding these inconclusive minutes Ó Duilearga must have sensed that he was presenting 'a bad hand'. Even if he knew that he had the sympathy of Tarlach Ó Raifeartaigh, and possibly other officials in the Dept. of Education, the fact that the Commission was split on the question of attaching the Commission to UCD made it all the more difficult for Education to support such a proposal. However, even if the special meeting of June 27th had come out strongly in favour of incorporating the Commission into UCD, it is unlikely that the Dept. of Education would have been able to act on such a proposal as the political will was not there. Ominously, about the time Ó Duilearga forwarded these minutes to the Dept. of Education, Muiris Ó Muimhneacháin, Secretary of the Dept. of the Taoiseach, enquired of his counterpart in Education, Tarlach Ó Raifeartaigh, how matters then stood in respect of the staff of the Commission, and reminded him of Pádraig Ó Siochfhradha's discussion with the Taoiseach in late 1957 in which the undesirability of attaching the Commission to UCD was, among other matters, discussed.[204]

Later that month, Fionán Mac Coluim could write confidently to Pádraig Ó Maoláin of the Dept. of Education, who was also a member of the Commission, predicting that '82 [St. Stephen's Green] will henceforth be the address [of the Commission] as it is certain the Government will not accept UCD'. In other words, there would be no change in the Commission's status. Mac Coluim added: '"We consider it a joke"("Cúis gháire dhúinn é!") a member of the Government is reported as saying.'[205] Here 'It' refers either to UCD or the proposal to re-establish the Commission within UCD, most likely the latter. In another, undated, letter he wrote about this time Mac Coluim says that he has had a note from Donnchadh Ó Briain, Parliamentary Secretary to the Taoiseach, in which the latter stated:

202 ED CO 495(1): 'Coimisiún Béaloideasa Éireann', written by T. Ó Raifeartaigh, dated 9.8.1958, (trans.).
203 D/T S 6916D: Ó Raifeartaigh to Ó Muimhneacháin, 27.9.1958.
204 D/T S 6916D: Ó Muimhneacháin to Ó Raifeartaigh, 15.9.1958.
205 ED FL 4: letter dated 24.9.1958 (trans.).

I have learned that no proposal will be accepted that will place the Commission under the protection ('sciatháin') of the University ... I was speaking to the Minister himself and I have authoritative confirmation as to the attitude of the Long Fellow ('Fear Mór'[de Valera]) about the whole matter and I think neither flattery nor beguilement ('bladar ná mealla') will budge either of them.[206]

Ó Briain was a strong supporter of the revival of Irish, and was opposed to transferring the Commission to UCD.[207] Whatever de Valera's reasons were for opposing such a transfer at this juncture, Ó Briain was probably motivated by a mixture of political prejudice and Irish-language allegiance. In wider Irish-language circles opposition to UCD was still strong. The influential monthly magazine *Comhar* had an editorial opposing the incorporating of the Commission into UCD in its November 1958 number, mentioning, among other matters, the fact that there was no teaching of folklore in any of the state's university colleges.[208]

Meanwhile, the Dept. of Education, given the lack of unanimity on the Commission itself as well as certain political realities, assessed how best to solve the question of pensions for the Commission's staff, which their political masters wished to see expedited as soon as possible. All this took some time. De Valera was, however, anxious that a solution to the problem of pensions for the Commission be found as soon as possible and again raised the matter at a meeting of the Cabinet in January 1959. A month later, the Minister for Education informed the Cabinet that he expected to submit a proposal 'to make the Commission permanent and to provide for pensions for members of the staff' within five weeks or so. At this meeting de Valera also spoke about 'the desirability of arrangements to expedite the publication of material collected by the Commission.'[209]

Dept. of Education considers options for future of Commission

De Valera may have been impatient to see a solution to this problem before leaving office, as he was coming under strong pressure from within his own party to step down. He was then in his late seventies. However, finding a solution to this problem was not so easy. The Dept. of Education considered three options: 1) to put the Commission under the care of UCD, 2) to

206 Col. Íde Ó Siochfhradha Papers: Mac Coluim to Ó Siochfhradha, dated 'Dé Sathairn' ('Saturday') (trans.).
207 Ó Briain's papers show, however tenuously, that he was actively working behind the scenes to prevent the transfer of the Commission to UCD. See UCDA P 83/374 (3) and P 83/374 (15).
208 Moreover, *Feasta*, another Irish-language monthly, in an editorial a year earlier had proposed that the Government should not give any building grants to UCD, listing, amongst other shortcomings, its failure to promote Irish-medium teaching. *Feasta* Nollaig 1957, pp. 16, 23.
209 D/T S 6916D: Ó Muimhneacháin to Ó Raifeartaigh, 10.1.1959 and 'Cruinniú Rialtais', 6.2.1959.

incorporate it in the National Library, and 3) 'to allow the Commission to continue as it is was without placing any special limitation to its term of office and without altering the terms of reference laid down for the Commission at its inception', but at the same time 'to arrange pensions for some of the staff of the Commission'. They eventually decided on the third option.[210]

Although option number 1, i.e. to place the Commission under the care of UCD, might have been the easiest way to provide pensions for the staff of the Commission, the Dept. of Education saw certain objections. Máirtín ó Flathartaigh of Education in a memorandum outlined his Department's objections to Muiris Ó Muimhneacháin of the Dept. of the Taoiseach:

a) the views of quite a few members of the Commission itself;

b) the folklore collections belonged to the state;

c) that the day would come when the collecting work of the Commission would be complete, and that henceforth it would simply be a question of protecting it [the collection] and making it available to the public (scholars, etc), and that this was not necessarily the responsibility of the University;

d) the collections should be available at a centre to everyone for purposes of research and publication;

e) it would be difficult to decide which university college should be chosen [to house these collections]

f) there was, and is, hardly any student of folklore in the University, and it is not evident that there will be a chair or lectureship of folklore in University College Dublin always.

In particular, ó Flathartaigh noted the Chairman of the Commission's opposition to incorporating the Commission into UCD. While enumerating these objections, the Department was, however, mindful of all the help UCD had given the Commission over the years.

The second option, i.e. incorporating the Commission into the National Library, had, in the Dept. of Education's estimation, certain advantages. The collections would be kept in safekeeping for easy access by scholars and the general public. Moreover, the fact that the Commission's collections constituted state property, would made the National Library a possible suitable location for them. They also rejected the proposal of some of the Commission's staff that the Commission should be reconstituted as a permanent, separate institute. Ultimately, the collection would constitute an 'archive', and this fact 'would support' its inclusion in the National Library. The problem, however, of setting up a folklore archive as part of the National Library was 'that it would necessitate the passing of a special Act to give the workers of the Commission full recognition as officers of that Archive', because the Civil Service Superannuation Act would have to be amended to compensate them fully for their years of service in the Commission. If this Act

210 D/T S 6916D: Máirtín ó Flathartaigh to Ó Muimhneacháin, dated 11.5.1959, pp. 2-3 (trans.).

were amended, however, it would give other non-permanent Civil Servants a 'loophole' to seek similar pension rights. Nevertheless, the Department of Education felt that it would not be appropriate to transfer the Commission to the National Library as long as its then Director was a professor in the University, as it was he who had directed the collecting until now, and who was most responsible for the existence of this valuable collection.'[211] They forgot to say, or were unaware, that transfer to UCD would also cause problems in respect of superannuation (see below).

Civil Service status for staff of Commission

De Valera eventually agreed to stand as a candidate in the election for the largely symbolic office of President of Ireland to be held on June 17th, 1959, resigning as Taoiseach the day before the election. It was a close-run contest, his main opponent being War of Independence and Civil War veteran General Seán MacEoin, a member of Fine Gael and bitterly opposed to de Valera. Two days before he was elected President of Ireland, the Dept. of the Taoiseach informed the Dept. of Education that the Taoiseach agreed to Education's proposals to allow the Commission to continue indefinitely and to provide pensions for its staff.[212] Neither did the election of a new Taoiseach, Seán Lemass, change the situation. At a Cabinet Meeting on November 6th, 1959, Lemass requested the Ministers for Finance and Education to 'expedite the settlement of outstanding matters concerning the staff of the Irish Folklore Commission.' The new Taoiseach also expressed an opinion 'as to the undesirability' of transferring the Commission to UCD.[213] The Department of Education and Finance acted on Lemass's request and finalised their proposals for giving the staff of the Commission Civil Servant status.

On March 25th, 1960, Lemass saw Ó Duilearga and informed him about the decision to provide pensions for the staff of the Commission by establishing them as Civil Servants. A Dept. of Education official recorded: 'Professor Delargy said that he was very satisfied with the arrangement of which the Taoiseach had informed him.'[214] The Commission was not re-established as such, but allowed to continue under its original terms of reference for another five years. This decision by the Government was a decision 'in principle' that could not be put into effect immediately. It would take another five years before plans to give Civil Service status to the staff of the Commission would be put into effect. The Commission was also to continue to be housed by UCD, as no other provision was proposed for it. This, in effect, meant that Ó Duilearga did not have to act on his threat to resign as Honorary Director if the Commission were separated from UCD. That in itself was reason enough for him to be pleased with the arrangement agreed on. More importantly, however, although the Commission had not been incorporated into UCD, as

211 Ibid., pp. 2–3 (trans.).
212 D/T S 6916D: Sec. Dept. of the Taois. to Sec. Dept. of Educ., dated 15.6.1959.
213 D/T S 6916D: copy of Cabinet Minute, 6.11.1959.
214 ED FL 4: 'Pinsean Coim. Béal. Oid.', section 9.

he had so earnestly desired, the fact that his staff were finally to be provided with pensions, prospects of better salaries, and security in their jobs was definitely a great source of relief to him.[215] At last, something was being done to alleviate the plight of his colleagues. The solution arrived at was by no means an ideal solution for him, but it was one he could live with for the moment. Sooner or later, he would have known, the re-establishment of the Commission in some more permanent form would have to considered. He could not be certain, of course, that he would live to see that day.

The solution arrived at in 1959/1960 was seen in the Dept. of Education as no more than a stopgap solution. Opposition from various quarters prevented the transfer of the Commission to UCD, and deference to Ó Duilearga's position in that college made it reluctant to attach the Commission to some other institution or establish it as an independent body under the Civil Service. Although some officials in the Department were in sympathy with Ó Duilearga's proposal for incorporation into UCD, there was little they could do because of the stance taken by their political masters.[216] However, it must be said that there was scant understanding of the real needs of the Commission among officials of the Dept. of Education. We have seen how in the 1940's, Dept. of Education officials had also been in favour of transferring the Commission to the care of UCD, but failed to understand the type of permanent folklore institution that needed to be established and funded. In the meantime, officials of this Department had not gained any greater understanding of the needs of a reconstituted Commission. The lengthy report on the situation of the Commission forwarded by the Dept. of Education to the Dept. of the Taoiseach in May 1959 is revealing in its lack of understanding of the present and future needs of the Commission:

> More needs to be done on both these fronts [collation and cataloguing], however, and in regard to collecting also, and, of course, much would need to be done in regard to editing and publishing. It is not evident, nonetheless, that a large organization is needed to bring to completion what remains to be done. Neither is it evident that one could suggest that it would be completed within a certain period. Ultimately, some sort of system for the storage and safekeeping would be needed, and it would not be proper to keep it as moribund material.[217]

This lack of understanding continued to affect Education's dealings with the Commission down until its disbandment in 1970.

---

215 It is not certain, however, if it was intended to give all the staff of the Commission Civil Service status. For example, the Dept. of Finance initially may not have been contemplating making Civil Servants of the Commission's collectors. ED CO 495 (1): M. Breathnach to Sec. Dept. of Educ., dated March 1960.

216 Not all officials of the Dept. of Educ., however, were in favour of transferring the Commission to UCD: e.g. Máirtín ó Flathartaigh, who was also influential in Irish language circles, was against such a transfer. ED CO 495 (1): 'Coimisiún Béaloideasa Éireann' written by T. Ó Raifeartaigh, dated 9.8.1958, p. 3.

217 D/T S 6916D: 'Coimisiún Béaloideasa Éireann', p. 13, cov. letter dated 11.5.1959 (trans.).

6. The Nineteen Sixties/on a rising tide

*Passing of the 'old guard' and the reassessment
of nationalist ideals*

A new decade came, a new Taoiseach was in power. It was to be a decade
of great change, economically, socially, and culturally. Not only had de
Valera retired from politics, many of the old political guard were also
nearing retirement age. By the end of the 1960's all but one, Frank Aiken,
would have departed the political scene. Already there was new blood in the
Government: men who had not been through the Civil War, and some who
looked forward to a new, prosperous and, possibly, more culturally diverse
Ireland than the previous generation. The 1960's would see a weakening
of the old nationalistic principles on which the state had been nurtured:
political unification of the country, and the restoration of the Irish language.
Significantly, perhaps, the new Taoiseach, Seán Lemass, had scant knowledge
of Irish. Moreover, Lemass, although a veteran of the 1916 Rising, the War
of Independence, and the Civil War, and formerly a proponent of Sinn Féin's
doctrine of economic self-sufficiency, had, along with T.K. Whitaker, the
progressive Secretary of the Dept. of Finance, initiated a new outward-looking
economic programme.

General Richard Mulcahy had also retired as Leader of Fine Gael; its new
leader James Dillon, brother of the renowned Celtic scholar Myles Dillon,
Ó Duilearga's contemporary in UCD, was opposed to compulsory Irish,
cornerstone of the state's revivalist policies. Mulcahy, although he had for
many years misgivings about the efforts adopted to revive Irish, had possibly
too great a love for the language itself to have been able to tamper with those
policies.[218] With Mulcahy's departure from the leadership of Fine Gael,
the party had a freer hand to initiate a new language policy. The General
Election of 1961 saw the question of compulsory Irish become an issue for
the first time. Fine Gael proposed abolishing compulsory Irish. Nevertheless,
however dissatisfied many electors were with the methods adopted to revive
Irish, other issues proved of greater importance and Fianna Fáil remained

---

218 See Mulcahy 1999, pp. 229 ff.

in power. Despite Fianna Fáil's victory, Fine Gael's new language policy probably reflected the views of many politicians right across the spectrum of political allegiance. However, for Fianna Fáil jettisoning compulsory Irish was more difficult, as the restoration of the 'national language', along with the unification of the country, constituted the two main national aims of the party. Nevertheless, even within Fianna Fáil there was the realisation that the state's language policies needed to be reassessed. De Valera had come to realise this before his retirement as Taoiseach. In 1958 his Government had established a commission (Coimisiún um Athbheochan na Gaeilge) to investigate the success of the state's efforts to revive Irish and how best to realise this aim.[219] The report of this commission (published in 1963) was a very comprehensive study of many aspects relating to the restoration of Irish.[220] While neither this report itself, nor the Government's White Paper, based on it, issued the following year, backtracked as such from the ideal of language restoration, there is no doubt that replacing English with Irish as the dominant vernacular was no longer an aim. Henceforth some sort of bilingualism would be the state's official policy. While some might claim that this new policy was more practical and realistic,[221] much of the hypocrisy and ineptitude associated with the state's efforts to revive Irish was to remain in respect of its new bilingual policy.[222]

Death and old age depletes the Commission

On the Commission itself the passing of the old guard, particularly those opposed to a transfer to UCD, was also in evidence as the decade advanced. Cormac Ó Cuilleanáin had for many years, due to failing health, been an infrequent attender at meetings of the Commission. He does not seem to have attended meetings after June 1963. On March 2nd, 1964, Seán Mac Giollarnáth wrote to Ó Duilearga to inform him that he was retiring from the Commission for health reasons.[223] In November of that year Pádraig Ó Siochfhradha died. His death meant that one of the foremost opponents of the transfer of the Commission to UCD had departed the scene. No other single person opposed to that transfer, active in folklore circles, commanded the same respect as he did. His death, therefore, was of great significance. The following May, Liam Price, who had been chairman of the Finance Sub-Committee since 1935, resigned due to failing health; he was aged seventy four.[224] In contrast to Ó Siochfhradha, Price had been a strong supporter of transferring the Commission to UCD. By the time of Pádraig Ó Siochfhradha's death, Fionán Mac Coluim was eighty nine years of age. He does not appear

219 Ó Riain 1994, pp. 12–13.
220 *See An Coimisiún um Athbheochan na Gaeilge. An Tuarascáil Dheiridh* 1963.
221 e.g., Kelly 2002., p. 140.
222 See Comerford 2003, pp. 147–148.
223 ED FL 8: 'CBÉ. Miont. 119ú Cruinniú, 5.3.1964', par. 875.
224 ED FL 1: 'CBÉ. Miont. 124ú Cruinniú, 13.5.1965', par. 921. He was replaced by Michael Tierney as Chairman of the Finance Sub-Committee.

to have attended meetings of the Commission for the last few years of his life. He died in December 1966; a month or so later, in January 1967, Liam Price died. The ranks of the Commission were becoming very thin.

On March 31st, 1965, the Dept. of Education informed the Commission that its term of office was being extended for another five years from April 1st, 1965 under the same terms of reference that it had been operating under for the previous thirty years. All the members of the Commission were reappointed by the Government, with the exception of Pádraig Ó Maoláin, the Education representative, who was replaced by Liam Ó Laidhin.[225] The Government lost an opportunity to appoint new members to the Commission, perhaps with new and more modern ideas. Apart from occasional changes of departmental representatives, no new member had been appointed to the Commission since Cormac Ó Cuilleanáin in 1953. The Commission that had started out with nineteen members was by spring 1967 depleted to seven, one of whom no longer attended meetings (see Appendix 2(a)).

Six months before Mac Coluim's death, at a meeting of the Commission in June 1966, Seán Ó Maonaigh spoke of the necessity of having new members appointed, as 'many of the members had resigned due to ill health and it was difficult to get a quorum for meetings.' He proposed that the Dept. of Education should be informed of the situation and was seconded by the Chairman, Eric Mac Fhinn.[226] It is interesting to note that the minutes of this meeting do not record Ó Duilearga expressing an opinion on this matter. In any event, nothing came of Ó Maonaigh's suggestion. This probably suited Ó Duilearga. It is unlikely that he had forgotten what had occurred on the Commission at its special meeting of June 1958, when members were divided on the question of transferring the Commission to UCD. As the 1960's advanced, some of those members who had opposed such a transfer in 1958 either died or retired, leaving him in a somewhat more secure position. This is not to suggest that the death or departure of opponents of such a transfer gave him any satisfaction. Apart from anything else, Ó Duilearga was a sentimental (and loyal) man and would have been moved by the death and retirement of friends and acquaintances, however much they may have disagreed with him on certain issues.

Commission on Higher Education

As it happened, the Irish Folklore Commission as a body would never again be asked to discuss its own future. Two years previously, on June 27th, 1964, both Ó Duilearga and the Commission's chairman, Eric Mac Fhinn, had, on invitation, presented evidence before the Commission on Higher Education (CHE).[227] The CHE had been established by the Government in 1960 because there was a general understanding that the university colleges in the state were grossly underfunded and consequently not able to provide the type of

225 Ibid., par. 919.
226 ED FL 8: 'CBÉ. Miont. 128ú Cruinniú, 27.6.1966', par. 952.
227 ED FL 8: 'CBÉ. Miont. Miont. 120ú Cruinniú, 3.7.1964', p. 5.

higher education required by a modern society. Although the Irish Folklore Commission was not involved in teaching, as an institute of learning it came within the CHE's remit. On the appointed day, both Ó Duilearga and Mac Fhinn made written and oral submissions to the CHE. Seán Ó Maonaigh felt that the entire Commission should have been consulted. Ó Maonaigh had been neutral as to the question of transfer to UCD in 1958, but was opposed to Ó Duilearga on a number of substantive issues. It was unfortunate for those arguing against transferring the Commission to UCD that Eric Mac Fhinn was, along with Ó Duilearga, the only member of the Commission invited to report to the Commission on Higher Education. Mac Finn was not the best person to argue the case against transferring the Commission to UCD, nor would he appear to have made a very strong case.

The strongest case to be made against incorporating the Commission into UCD, would have been to have shown that in northern Europe it was not so unusual to keep folklore archives separate from university teaching departments, and that while folklore archives might work in close cooperation with universities, they were not invariably incorporated within them. Mac Fhinn most likely had no great knowledge of the organisation of folklore elsewhere. In his submission to the CHE he is reported as stating that there was no need to change the status of the Commission. It was a national organisation, like the National Library and the National Museum. It was his opinion that it should be separate from the universities and that 'its collections should be kept intact.' Nevertheless, he felt that if it should be associated with any one university college, it would be best to establish it in University College Galway (UCG). Although Mac Fhinn was on the staff of UCG, given his strong support for the revival of Irish, his reasons for proposing his own college as a possible home for the Commission were, for the most part, influenced by UCG's high profile in respect of the Irish language, and, moreover, by its proximity to the Gaeltacht.[228]

The CHE's Report gives much more space to Ó Duilearga's views than to those of Mac Fhinn, and it would appear his submission was longer and more comprehensive. Although Ó Duilearga also saw the national importance of the Commission, he was able to put it in a wider, international context, more in keeping with the spirit of the times. Ó Duilearga in his memorandum stressed 'the importance of the Commission's archives, both in the field of European ethnology, literature and social history and in the study of the Irish language and its associated traditions.' He listed 'the principal tasks facing the Commission as follows:'

> a) to ensure the permanency and the security of the Commission's collection as a unit;
> b) to continue field-work as heretofore with special reference to English-speaking districts;
> c) in view of the completion of the major work in regard to the collection of folk literature, to concentrate on the collection of social and historical material;

228 *Commission on Higher Education 1960-67. II Report Volume 1*, p. 364.

d) to continue and to complete the cataloguing and indexing of the collection;

e) the academic and comparative study of the material collected;

f) the publication of the material collected, particularly its publication in Irish;

g) the incorporation of folklore tradition into all levels—primary, secondary and higher—of formal education and into popular education.[229]

Ó Duilearga 'emphasised the importance of the collections and their value to both national and international scholarship.' While a certain amount of collecting still remained to be done, especially in English-speaking districts, 'the most important single task before the Commission was the publication of its material.' Ó Duilearga 'estimated that publication of the material would necessitate at least 500 volumes, and, possibly, 1,000 [volumes].' Preparing material for publication, he argued, 'would involve a high level of scholarship, for which training could only be given in the universities.' He added: 'The life of the collection ... would depend on its treatment inside an academic milieu.'[230]

Not surprisingly, the Honorary Director 'proposed that the Commission should be re-established and made permanent as an institute within University College, Dublin, and housed in a separate building. Reminiscent of his 1943 proposal, he suggested 'the institute might have a separate board of governors, which would include the President of the College, members of the College's Irish and history departments, and the directors of the National Library and Museum.' It should also have a special grant and maintain 'close associations with other institutions of higher education'.

One argument that seems to have especially swayed members of the CHE was the need to secure the safety of the Commission's collections, as 82 St. Stephen's Green, 'largely' retained 'its original character as a residence', and was considered 'scarcely suitable for housing the Commission's collections.' On this matter both Mac Fhinn and Ó Duilearga were in agreement:

> The Chairman and the Honorary Director emphasised that the present building was both unsuitable and unsafe, and those of us who have visited the Commission's premises know this to be true. While the manuscript collections have been microfilmed and the material on records has been transferred to tapes, the loss of the library, original documents, records and other material would be irretrievable. We strongly recommend, therefore, that early steps should be taken to ensure the safety of the Commission's library and collections.[231]

---

229 *Commission on Higher Education 1960–67. II Report Volume 1*, pp. 364–365.

230 *Commission on Higher Education 1960–67. II Report Volume 1*, p. 365.

231 Ibid., p. 365. Of course, the CHE could have suggested a solution to the question of the safety of the Commission's collections without recommending its incorporation into UCD, but it would appear to have been swayed by Ó Duilearga's other arguments. The fact that UCD was willing to take the Commission under its wing may also have affected

The Commission on Higher Education reaches a verdict

In any event, the CHE accepted Ó Duilearga's argument that an academic milieu was the place most appropriate for the future work of the Commission. The CHE considered it 'desirable that the study of our folk traditions should be a lively part of our higher system of education' and that from the universities would 'percolate', in time, 'through the whole education system and through the community at large, a growing interest in the country's wealth of folk traditions.' For a while they contemplated attaching the Commission to the Dublin Institute for Advanced Studies, but decided not to do so. For one thing, to establish the Commission in the Institute would have required amending the terms of the Establishment Order of the Institute. While they considered transferring the Irish Folklore Commission to the Institute, they do not seem to have contemplated establishing it as a separate School but rather as part of the School of Celtic Studies, and did not wish to burden that School any further. They also noted that the School of Celtic Studies lacked 'the wider ambience of historical and social studies that are relevant to the study of folklore.'[232]

In respect of Mac Fhinn's suggestion that the Commission be transferred to University College Galway, they felt that despite that college's 'propinquity to a Gaeltacht area and its special obligations in developing the use of Irish in higher studies', such arguments 'do not seem to supercede the link already established between the work of the Commission and University College, Dublin, or to justify a departure from what might be considered a natural development of this association.' However, in accepting UCD's claim to the Folklore Commission, the CHE was not oblivious to the fact that UCD's national credentials were somewhat suspect in certain quarters, as it expressed the hope that the 'direct association of folklore studies with University College, Dublin, would strengthen the development of Irish Studies in this, the largest of the colleges.'[233]

While mindful of the Commission's debt to UCD, the Report also recognised that transferring such an institute as the Irish Folklore Commission out of state control and ownership had certain national implications. It recommended that the reconstituted Commission would have a special status within the College and should preserve its characteristic of being a national institution:

> The institute should be given a special standing within the College. The institute would inherit, and should maintain, the characteristic, which has belonged to the Folklore Commission, of a national institution. Access to the institute and it collections should be available to all students and scholars from all institutions.

Apart from the usual functions and duties with respect to undergraduates and postgraduates, pertaining to any university department, the new institute should be responsible for :

its decision.
232 *Commission on Higher Education 1960–67. II Report Volume 1*, p. 366.
233 Ibid., p. 367.

'collecting folklore material'
'publishing the results of research'
'promoting folklore studies in other institutes of higher education'
'popularising these studies in the schools and throughout the community generally, and perhaps for founding and maintaining national or local folk museums.'

This was a burden to saddle any university institute with, but the CHE seems to have realized that the type of institute they were recommending might be difficult to fit into the structures of a university department. The Report says: 'Such functions and duties would not be appropriate to a department organised on the usual university lines.' It envisaged that there would be representatives of other universities on the new institute's board of directors and hoped this might encourage the development of folkloristics in these institutions.

Universities in Ireland value their independence and the CHE knew it was treading on very sensitive ground here. Thus, while recommending a different type of organisation for the reconstituted Commission within UCD, it still stipulated that though 'the institute should enjoy a necessary degree of independence, it should be administered within the general framework of University College, Dublin.' Moreover, it refrained 'from recommending what specific form should be given to the government of the institute', suggesting, however, 'that it should primarily be academic in character, with some representation from all the university colleges and from other suitable bodies.' It also recommended that the staff of the new institute 'be appointed on the usual academic basis and terms,' and that it be funded by 'grants from public funds', which although they 'might pass through the general accounts of U.C.D. ...would be specifically allocated for the work of the institute.'[234]

Ó Duilearga was obviously pleased with the decision of the CHE in respect of the Commission, although he knew, all too well, that there was no guarantee that its recommendations would be accepted by the Government. In March 1967 he sent Cearbhall Ó Dálaigh, Chairman of the CHE, and future President of Ireland, a short letter thanking him for a copy of the summary of the Report and expressing satisfaction that there had been unanimity in respect of the Irish Folklore Commission.[235]

Dept. of Education acts on CHE's report

Many, if indeed not most, of the numerous recommendations of the CHE in respect of the various institutions it examined were not acted upon, but its main recommendations in respect of the Irish Folklore Commission were, and, initially at any rate, without too much delay. In late December 1967 the Minister for Education, Donagh O'Malley, informed the Taoiseach, Jack Lynch, that '[c]ertain proposals with regard to the question of bringing the

234 Ibid., pp. 367–368.
235 UCDA Cearbhall Ó Dálaigh Papers P51/263: letter dated 25.3.1967.

[Irish Folklore] Commission under the aegis of University College Dublin are ... at present under consideration'.[236] By late February 1968, O'Malley had a memorandum ready for the Government in respect of the Commission. He felt that the Government should act on the recommendation of the CHE 'at an early date' for a number of reasons:

> (i) Ó Duilearga was due to retire in May 1969. This would mean the severance of the connection with the University, 'in the absence of an alternative suitable arrangement'.
> (ii) as UCD's Faculty of Arts was expected to be transferred to the new campus at Belfield, if the Commission were to remain in 82 St. Stephen's Green, its 'collection of manuscripts, etc. would become isolated and not readily available to students.'
> (iii) due to the risk of fire in 82 St. Stephen's Green 'a great part of the manuscript collection is already stored in the Science Building at Belfield, as a temporary measure.'
> (vi) if the Government were to agree to the transfer of the Commission to UCD, 'it will be necessary to make suitable provision for them in connection with the new Arts Building now in course of erection.'

Although the Minister does not appear to have pondered on the problems which finding a successor for Ó Duilearga posed, he was not unmindful of the welfare of the staff of the Commission, and also of the sensitivities of members of the Board of the Commission itself. He was also aware of the need to initiate instruction in folkloristics at an academic level. He further proposed:

> '(a) the staff of the Commission should be transferred to University College Dublin;
> (b) some members of the staff of the Commission would be appointed Lecturers on the staff of the College and would be required to lecture to students;
> (c) the manuscripts, etc., would be transferred to University College, Dublin, at Belfield on condition that they would be available to all scholars and other qualified persons who wished to study them;
> (d) the Commission would continue to exist and additional members would be appointed to it...;
> (e) an appropriate grant would be paid directly from the State to University College in connection with the activities of the Commission.
> (f) suitable accommodation should be provided for the collection of manuscripts etc. of the Commission in the Arts Building of University College, Dublin, by an addition to the proposed new building. The estimated cost of this new addition is £50,000...

For once the Dept. of Finance was in agreement with Education as regards plans for the Irish Folklore Commission. The Minister for Education

---

236 D/T 98/6/47 S 6916E: O'Malley to Lynch, dated 29.12.1967.

informed the Government that the Minister for Finance had been consulted and 'has no objection to the terms of the Memorandum being submitted to the Government.'[237]

Government approves transfer to UCD

The Government in early March 1968 sanctioned the Minister for Education's above proposal to transfer the Commission to UCD.[238] It would be March 1969, however, before most of the Commission, including its Chairman, Eric Mac Fhinn, would hear of the Government's decision. Ó Duilearga himself would seem not to have been informed officially until autumn 1968.[239] However, the sudden death of Donagh O'Malley in March 1968 may have delayed action being taken on the Irish Folklore Commission by his Department. Some six months later the Dept. of Education did as it had done some ten years before: on September 20th, 1968 they invited Ó Duilearga and Michael Tierney, of the Finance Sub-Committee, and former President of UCD, to come to an interview with officials of the Department. Unlike 1958, this time there seems to have been no question of eliciting the Commission's opinion on the transfer to UCD: the Chairman and other members of the Commission being ignored on this occasion. In doing so the Dept. of Education showed gross disregard for the Commission as a body. The Commission had after all been appointed by the Government to advise the Director. If it had invited J. J. Hogan, the then President of UCD, instead of Michael Tierney, UCD's former President, there might have been some justification for acting in this manner. Although the Government had already made the decision to transfer the Commission to UCD, as was their prerogative, members of the Commission were not to be asked at any stage how best this could be realised. However disrespectful of the Irish Folklore Commission this was, if the recommendations of the CHE had been implemented in full, the Dept. of Education would at least have had the excuse that it was acting on expert advice, but as we will see below one of the CHE's most crucial recommendations in respect of the Irish Folklore Commission was not implemented.

Insult to injury

During the course of this interview Ó Duilearga and Tierney were informed that the Government had decided to accept the recommendation of the CHE

---

237 D/T 99/1/62 S 6916E; ' Integration of IFC with University College, Dublin.', dated 26.2.1968.

238 D/T 99/1/62 S 6916E. 'Cabinet Minutes', dated 5.3.1968. The proposal, then in the offing, to merge UCD and Trinity College Dublin may have helped to stifle any residual animosity towards UCD among Fianna Fáil ranks.

239 E.g. in July 1968 he wrote to Ciarán Bairéad informing him that he had as yet heard nothing about what was being planned for the Commission. UCG Hard. Lib. Arch. Bairéad Collection G/599, letter dated 16.7.1968.

in respect of the Irish Folklore Commission. Ó Duilearga asked Education officials on that occasion, and on a number of occasions over the next six months, to inform the Chairman of the Irish Folklore Commission, Eric Mac Fhinn, about their decision. He most likely recalled Mac Fhinn's pique at not being invited to the initial meeting in the Dept. of Education in April 1958 (see above). The fact that the CHE had opted for Ó Duilearga's proposal instead of Mac Fhinn's may have been a further reason why Ó Duilearga wished the Dept. of Education to inform him of the Government's decision on this occasion.[240] This probably explains why at neither the meeting of the Commission in late October 1968, which Ó Duilearga could not attend, nor the following meeting of the Commission in January 1969, was the substance of his interview with Education officials in September 1968 communicated to members or even referred to. Members of the Finance Sub-Committee, apart from Tierney of course, were also, it would appear, kept in the dark about this meeting until March 1969.

The first the other members of the Commission heard about the Government's decision was when each of them received a letter from Seán Mac Gearailt, Secretary of the Dept. of Education, dated March 7th, 1969, informing them that the Government 'had accepted in principle the recommendation' of the CHE to transfer the Commission to UCD, 'subject to the proper preparations being made.' Mac Gearailt's letter recommended that the Commission 'examine the matter together with the authorities of University College, Dublin, and inform the Minister for Education about the arrangements that would have to be made in respect of staff, etc.' This was also the first Eric Mac Fhinn, Chairman of the Commission, had heard of the Government's decision to transfer the Commission to UCD. Obviously, he was very annoyed. He immediately wrote a letter to the Dept. of Education, asking what arrangements had been made, and what 'etc.' in the phrase 'the arrangements that would have to be made in respect of staff, etc' meant. He had received no reply by the time the next meeting of the Commission convened a week later.

Ó Duilearga informed this meeting that the Dept. of Education and the University authorities had agreed to make lecturers of Seán Ó Súilleabháin and Caoimhín Ó Danachair, and he hoped that the other members of the staff of the Commission would be accommodated satisfactorily. Mac Fhinn was not the only member present who was angry with the way the Commission had been treated, and with the decision to transfer the Commission to UCD. Seán Ó Maonaigh said that he was not 'satisfied with what the Commission on Higher Education had recommended' and he intended 'writing a memorandum to the Government on the entire matter.' He also proposed that the opinion of the members of the staff should be elicited 'to the extent that it concerned them'. In reply to this, the Director said that the staff had not yet been given such an opportunity. Pádraig Mac Con Midhe, who at the special meeting of the Commission in 1958 had been neutral on the question of transferring the Commission to UCD, was obviously now quite piqued at

---

240 ED FL 7: 'CBÉ. Miont. 139ú Cruinniú, 14.3.1969', p. 4.

not having been consulted. He asserted that the evidence presented before the CHE by the Chairman and the Honorary Director was simply their own opinions, and not those of the other members. Feardorcha Ó Dúill, who as an officer of the Dept. of Education may have had some prior knowledge of the decision, possibly in an effort to quieten passions, said that to the best of his knowledge, the Dept. of Education 'would like to hear the opinions of other members of the Commission, and the opinions of members of the staff about this matter.'[241]

Obviously, Ó Duilearga must have felt uncomfortable at this meeting. He repeated for those present some of the arguments he had placed before the Commission on Higher Education: '(a) fear of fire in the building occupied by the Commission till then; (b) the protection of the Mss and proper facilities for their utilization; and (c) [the need] to prepare for publication the most suitable Mss.' He further added: 'In Belfield a fireproof building would be provided for the Mss, and the public would have a chance to examine them.' Interestingly, he is not reported as mentioning specifically the need to initiate teaching.

The Chairman felt that the matter should be discussed further, and 'that the secretary should write to the Dept. of Education to elicit more information on certain points.' After further discussion the Commission decided to ask the Department to clarify the following points:

> (1) 'Did the Department of Education wish that every member of the Commission should give their views' on the transfer to UCD?
> (2) 'Did the Department wish to discuss the future status of the staff with the Commission or was that a matter for the Department itself as the staff were Civil Servants?'
> (3) Could the Department inform the Commission of any arrangements that had been made to date regarding the transfer of the Commission? and
> (4) What did 'etc' signify in the passage 'the arrangements that should be made in respect of staff, etc.'?

The letter sent to the Dept. of Education also stated that: '...in the interests of courtesy ('ar scáth láíochta') at any rate, the opinions of the Commission should be sought before any recommendation would be made to the Government or before the Government would consider it or make a competent ('forásach') decision on it.'[242]

The next meeting of the Commission, held on June 13th, 1969, did not discuss the transfer to UCD for whatever reason, but at a meeting of the Finance Sub-Committee held two days earlier the question of the future of the Commission was raised. Feardorcha Ó Dúill spoke of the 'importance of preparing a report on the work of the Irish Folklore Commission.' He said that Séan Ó Maonaigh 'had already raised the matter several times at

---

241 ED FL 7: 'CBÉ. Miont. 139ú Cruinniú, 14.3.1969', par. 1021 (trans.).
242 Ibid., par. 1021 (trans.).

previous meetings, and a rough draft had been prepared by Mr. Kevin Danaher [Caoimhín Ó Danachair].' He further said:

> ...that such a report, as well as setting out what had been accomplished by the Commission to date, should outline what was needed by way of additional staff, and future grants. It should also set out in broad outline a statement of general policy ... whether or not the Irish Folklore Commission was transferred to University College, it was highly desirable that such a report should be prepared ... the members of the Commission had [a] moral obligation to examine the whole question in the light of what remained to be done, and the best way of doing it.[243]

Despite the fact that what Ó Dúill had to say above was very relevant to the future of the reconstituted Commission, the minutes of the meeting do not record any discussion on his suggestion. However, the question of preparing a report on the work of the Commission was not to go away. This matter was again raised at the next meeting of the Finance Sub-Committee on October 15th, 1969, when it caused tempers to be raised. It would appear that Feardorcha Ó Dúill took issue on 'the manner in which the Director treated requests for information relating to what had been accomplished by the Commission and suggestions by members of the Commission as to making available to the public the folklore collected.' Moreover, he 'took serious exception to the manner in which [Ó Duilearga] spoke to Seán Ó Maonaigh' at this meeting.[244]

It would appear that the Dept. of Education was negotiating behind the Commission's back and did not reply to the Commission's letter of March 14th until mid-October when a letter (dated 16.10.1969) from the Department was sent to members of the Commission, who were to meet the following day. Despite what Feardorcha Ó Dúill had suggested at the March meeting of the Commission, it is clear that the Dept. of Education did not feel they needed to consult the Commission or its Chairman any further. Thus, the Dept. of Education had ignored completely one of the questions put to it in the Commission's letter of March 14th, namely whether they wished members of the Commission to express their views in respect of the transfer to UCD. Although this was couched as a question, it would appear to have been more in the nature of a request or, perhaps, a demand. The fact that no reference was made to this passage of the Commission's March letter in the Department's reply must have added insult to injury for some of those present. Education did, however, answer some of the Commission's requests for clarification and information. It informed the Commission that negotiations would begin shortly with the staff of the Commission with regard to their conditions of employment in the reconstituted Commission. The Dept. of Education understood that the UCD authorities were willing to ensure that the staff of the Commission would be as well off with regard to pension rights and increments

---

243 ED FL7: 'IFC. Fin. Sub-Com./Min. 145th Meeting, 11.6.1969', p. 3.
244 ED FL7: hand-written, unsigned page.

as members of the staff of the College as they would be as Civil Servants. The letter also informed members of the Commission that it was hoped the transfer would be completed by Christmas and that the functioning of the Commission as then constituted would cease. Moreover, the letter informed them that the UCD authorities were considering establishing an Advisory Committee and would request the current members of the Commission to sit on it.[245] However, when such an 'advisory' council was eventually set up, only two members of the Commission, to the best of my knowledge, were invited to participate, Séamus Ó Duilearga and Michael Tierney.[246]

One of the terms of reference of the Irish Folklore Commission was: 'The Commission to be responsible for the safe custody of its collected materials, such materials to be deemed always to be the property of the state.'[247] As the state was now bent on transferring the Commission's collections to private ownership, in not consulting the Board of the Irish Folklore Commission, as a body, on this matter it was guilty of sleight of hand to say the least. After all, the Commission was the body entrusted with the safekeeping of the Commission's collections. The fact that state property was also to be handed over to a private institution, without the Commission as a body being consulted, would appear to indicate that the authorities were either indifferent to, or not sufficiently aware of, the national implications of such a move.

The Commission's last meeting

We have seen how tempers flared up at the last meeting of the Finance Sub-Committee on October 15th in respect of the need for a comprehensive report on the work of the Commission (concerning what was already done and what remained to be done). However, the matter did not rest there. Two days later it came up at the last meeting of the Commission. At this meeting Seán Ó Maonaigh said that Caoimhín Ó Danachair had prepared quite a comprehensive document of this sort and had shown it to him, but 'nothing had happened since.' Ó Duilearga said that if such a document were to be compiled, the staff, which was very small, would have to abandon their other work. Feardorcha Ó Dúill agreed, at least partly, with Ó Maonaigh, stating that there was 'a great need for a report on the work hitherto done, as the Commission was to be placed under the aegis of University College

---

245 UCDA LA30/436 (17)-(18).

246 In April 1972, An Chomhairle Bhéaloideas Éireann/The Folklore of Ireland Council was established. In composition it was very different from the Commission in that of its initial ten members seven were either on the staff of UCD or retired members of staff. Its functions were as follows: '(1) to arrange for the cataloguing, editing and publication of material from the collections of books, manuscripts, other documents and recordings relating to folklore deposited, or to be deposited, in the Department of Folklore, University College, Dublin. (2) to arrange for appropriate access to and use of this material. (3) to administer the fund which the Department of Education has made, and will make, available towards the cost of cataloguing, editing, and publishing Irish folklore and studies relating thereto.' UCDA Michael Tierney Papers LA30/437(4).

247 D/T S 6916D: 'IFC. Terms of Reference', 2(vi).

Dublin.' Pádraig Mac Con Midhe agreed with Ó Dúill that a report on the work already done by the Commission should be compiled, but he felt that future work should be left to the authorities of University College Dublin, and the 'Advisory Board' that would be appointed. No decision was made on this matter, it would appear.[248]

Michael Tierney, rarely present at Commission meetings (although he regularly attended meetings of the Finance Sub-Committee), was again present at this meeting. However, the Chairman of the Commission, Eric Mac Fhinn, who had rarely missed a meeting, was absent. Given the importance of the meeting, Seán Ó Maonaigh and Feardorcha Ó Dúill were of the opinion that it should be postponed until the Chairman could attend, but Michael Tierney and Pádraig Mac Con Midhe felt the meeting should go ahead. The meeting passed the motion 'that it should be possible for the Chairman or the Director to convene another meeting, if necessary, before the Commission is transferred to Belfield. If that could not be done, it was thought that the members could come together informally in Belfield some time in January to see the new building.'[249]

The Commission was never to meet again. On October 22nd, 1969, Mac Fhinn replied to a letter Ó Duilearga sent him informing him of the possibility of meeting for one final time. He expressed dissatisfaction with the behaviour of the Dept. of Education for not sending him its letter of October 16th (see above) in time so that he could have put it on the agenda for the meeting, or so that he might send his opinions on the letter to the meeting (it appears he did not intend to attend). To make matters worse, this letter was posted to him the day of the Commission's meeting. So in effect he did not receive it until the day after the meeting. It would also appear from this letter that he took issue with the fact that the Dept. of Education's letter was not specifically addressed to him, as he understood each other member of the Commission had received an identical letter. Mac Fhinn's reply (October 18th) to the Secretary of the Dept. of Education was brief and pointed: 'I received your letter dated October 16th, 1969, which was posted in Dublin yesterday, October 17th.' Although he must have been disappointed at the decision to transfer the Commission to UCD, he had known since March 1969 what that decision was. While he had his misgivings about the wisdom of the transfer to UCD, he took this occasion to express his hope: 'that the staff would succeed in getting conditions to their satisfaction. The better they [the conditions] will be, the more pleased I will be.' He suggested a meeting before Christmas, but felt it would be best 'to wait until the status of the staff would be settled'.[250]

---

248 UCDA Michael Tierney Papers LA30/436: 'CBÉ. Miont. 141ú Cruinniú, 17.10.1969', par. 1035 (trans). Caoimhín Ó Danachair went ahead with completing his report, with or without Ó Duilearga's permission, and finished it in the year following the disbanding of the Commission in April 1970. It is not clear, however, if any use was made of a draft of this report in negotiations on the transfer of the Commission to UCD.

249 UCDA Michael Tierney Papers LA30/436(18): 'CBÉ. Miont. 141ú Cruinniú, 17.10.1969', par. 1038 (trans.).

250 UCDA Michael Tierney Papers LA30/436(12)–(13) (trans).

On October 21st, 1969 the President of UCD, J.J Hogan, informed the Governing Body of the College that he along with the Secretary of the College and Professor Ó Duilearga 'had an interview with the Secretary of the Department of Education the previous week during which it was made clear to him that the transfer of Folklore, i.e. of the staff and property, to the College would be made.' He further added: 'the College would take on all the charges of the Commission in regard to salaries and pension of staff, and the State would provide the finance for this by way of an addition to the annual grant.' However, significantly, it had been decided that: 'Provision for the Folklore Department would not be earmarked.' [251] As we have seen above, the CHE had recommended that although the state grant to fund the reconstituted Commission 'might pass through the general accounts of U.C.D.' it should 'be specifically allocated [i.e. earmarked] for the work of the institute.' [252] The decision that the state's 'provision' for the new folklore department should not be earmarked in time may have worked to the disadvantage of the Commission's successor.

Apprehension among staff of Commission

While some members of the Commission were justified in feeling that they had been ignored and slighted, members of the staff were in a worse position. Left in the dark, to a large extent, it appears many of the staff feared for their future. However, it seems that towards the end of the previous year the staff did learn something of what was discussed at the meeting Ó Duilearga and Michael Tierney had in the Dept. of Education in September 1968 regarding the transfer of the Commission to UCD, for the following December, Seán Ó Súilleabháin wrote to Richard Dorson:

> Next Summer this Commission will be handed over by the Government to University College (hitherto it has been under the Department of Education). We will probably move from here to the new buildings at Belfield, at the edge of Dublin, in the autumn. We don't know yet how it will be administered. Delargy is due to retire at 70 next May, but may stay on as 'Acting Professor' for a year or two. Kevin Danaher and I will become lecturers, and hope to give the first lectures in Folklore (for the past 28 years) then. [253]

However, the Commission was not ensconced in the new Belfied campus by the following autumn, nor had discussions been started with the staff regarding their future status. Naturally, they were worried. Moreover, the UCD authorities, it seems, were in no great hurry to begin discussions with the Commission's staff. At the above meeting of the College's Governing Body, the President informed members 'that it was not yet proposed to advertise

251 UCDA: Min. of Gov. Body Vol. 29, meeting 21.10.1969, item 4.
252 *Commission on Higher Education 1960-67. II Report Volume 1*, pp. 367–368.
253 Lilly Lib. Dorson Papers: Ó Súilleabháin to Dorson, dated 20.12.1968.

the two Lectureships in Folklore established by ... [UCD] Statute (LXVI)'. He also informed them 'that accommodation at Belfield was almost ready for the Folklore [Commission]', i.e. 'the collection and a teaching department'. He added: 'as soon as the transfer of the institute and its property to the College was made, the move to Belfield and the advertising of the posts would be brought up.'[254] Obviously, UCD were taking no chances: no folklore posts were going to be announced before it had gained possession, lest the Government change its mind, or some other obstacle occurred.

Not only were the staff of the Commission apprehensive about what the fate of each individual employee of the Commission would be, they were also worried about who would be in charge of them in UCD. A year or so earlier, Seán Ó Súilleabháin in mentioning to Dorson, in the above-quoted letter, that Ó Duilearga might be allowed to stay on for a year or two as 'Acting Professor' after reaching the age of seventy in May 1969, did not express opposition to the idea as such. A year later, however, Ó Súilleabháin did not relish the prospect of Ó Duilearga staying on, not simply as 'Acting Professor' of Irish Folklore in the College, but as effective head of the reconstituted Commission in UCD. Ó Súilleabháin felt impelled to take precipitate action.

On October 10th, 1969, Seán Ó Suilleabháin went to see the scholar Br. Liam P. Ó Caithnia (a member of the Christian Brothers teaching order), who had been researching in the Commission's archive for some years, and requested him to intercede with the authorities on behalf of the staff of the Commission. Ó Súilleabháin informed Ó Caithnia that he had heard that President Hogan had some days earlier promised Ó Duilearga, who since May had been Acting Professor, that 'he could stay on as Director' in UCD after the transfer. Ó Caithnia wrote to the Taoiseach, Jack Lynch, on the matter: 'The staff of the Commission are in disarray because of this [news] - indeed they have been very dissatisfied for a long time'. He then lists the reasons for this dissatisfaction, as outlined to him by Ó Súilleabháin:

(i) No lectures have been given in the University for many years;

(ii) No students have been working with the Commission for years, nor are they welcomed;

(iii) There are no young trained staff, nor intention to acquire them, to maintain the work and aims of the Commission;

(iv) ...if the Director remains on, the Commission will be dead and suffocated and be of no use to anybody. Seán Ó Súilleabháin himself was trained in Sweden and he, in turn, trained young scholars for other Governments – but no young scholars of our own country are being trained, although they come requesting it. They are turned away on some pretext or other....

(v) For a long time scholars have been refused permission to publish anything – be it prose, music, or anything else – so that people do not know of the existence of the Commission.

254 UCDA: Min. of Gov. Body Vol. 29, meeting 21.10.1969, item 4.

Although these accusations were filtered through Liam Ó Caithnia, it would appear, from the detailed nature of his letter to Lynch, that either Ó Caithnia took notes on what Ó Súilleabháin told him, or else the latter presented him with a written statement of some sort. Be that as it may, these were very serious accusations. Although some of them are self-evidently true, others are somewhat exaggerated and distorted. It should, however, be remembered that Seán Ó Súilleabháin may well have been greatly agitated when he made these accusations. I will examine some of these accusations in Chapter VI/2 below. Suffice it to say here that they betray a deep dissatisfaction among at least some of the staff of the Commission towards the Director and with the direction of the Commission.

Ó Caithnia also informed the Taoiseach that the staff wished to see appointed 'a fresh, young, active man as Director', and that this should be done as soon as possible. If the Government were to do this before the transfer to Belfield the Commission could be 'saved', but once the Commission became the charge of the University the Government would no longer have any say in the matter. In this way the former Director 'could be in charge ... for the next ten years and nothing happening there.' He added that the Government had 'another hold on the place', as the Commission could not transfer its collections to its new home in Belfield without financial assistance from the state. Ó Caithnia closed his letter by stressing the good character of Seán Ó Súilleabháin, whom he says he has known for years. He says of him that he is 'a noble, Christian, Irish-minded ('Gaelach') to the marrow of his bones, a first rate man who did excellent work quietly, without any recognition.' Moreover, as Ó Súilleabháin was over 65, Ó Caithnia was certain that he had approached him not on his own account. After all, 'if his intention was to cause a rumpus, he would have begun years ago.'

Ó Caithnia advised the Taoiseach, if he needed more information, to speak directly to Seán Ó Súilleabháin. He says: 'He will be willing to tell the bitter truth now – he has been hiding it too long.' What Ó Súilleabháin had told him had come as no surprise to him. He was aware of the situation in the Commission, but previously felt 'it was not his business to intervene'. He was himself 'fond of Séamus Ó Duilearga and indebted to him for a long time'. Before closing he said: 'all the staff are worried about going to Belfield, and as for myself, I would prefer greatly that the Commission should be in the charge of the Government than of UCD. But my letter is not about that.'[255]

Ó Caithnia was opposed to the transfer of the Commission to UCD, but the staff do not appear to have been opposed to the move in principle, but were worried about the practical arrangements in respect of their own positions and who would be in charge. In the event, Seán Ó Súilleabháin's worries about Ó Duilearga staying on indefinitely proved unfounded. It also appears that the staff of the Commission were not only being kept in the dark about their own future, it would seem that they had no idea what shape the reconstructed Commission would take in UCD. On October 22nd, 1969 the

255 D/T 2000/6/76 S 6916E: Ó Caithnia to Ó Loinsigh [Lynch], dated 13.10.1969 (trans.).

Minister for Education, Pádraig Faulkner, whom Lynch had contacted on the matter, informed the Taoiseach:

> There would appear to be some misapprehension in regard to the matter. The position is that on its transfer to U.C.D. An Coimisiún ['The Commission'] as it is at present constituted will cease to function and so the post of Director will disappear. Seán Ó Súilleabháin and Caoimhín Ó Danachair who are immediately under S. Ó Duilearga will be appointed Lecturers in the University. Their function will be to lecture to students in relation to various aspects of Folklore and to involve students and others in the carrying out of research into the material contained in the collections.

He also assured Ó Caithnia that although 'it is understood that S. Ó Duilearga will be retained in the College for some time further it has been verified that there could be no question of his being in a position to prevent research into or publication of the folklore material.' He added for Lynch's information that the 'existing members of the Folklore Commission will be invited to serve on a Consultative Committee in connection with folklore which it is proposed to constitute on a broadened basis in U.C.D.'[256]

Lynch forwarded this information to Ó Caithnia, who then communicated it to Ó Súilleabháin. In his reply to Lynch, Ó Caithnia thanked the Taoiseach for all the trouble he had gone to and says: 'I hope the Commission will prosper henceforth although the staff there are still despondent.' He closes his reply by again speaking highly of Seán Ó Súilleabháin: 'I would not have got involved at all except that a decent man was worried and because I am proud of the Commission.'[257]

Arrangements between Dept. of Education and UCD finalised

The Dept. of Education had hoped that the staff of the Commission would be transferred by Christmas 1969. This did not happen, however. The final five-year term of the Irish Folklore Commission came to an end on March 31th, 1970 and the Commission was disbanded. Eric Mac Fhinn in his above letter to Ó Duilearga (22.10.1969) had suggested that they postpone meeting for one last time 'until the status of the staff would be settled'. The reason, it would appear, that the Commission never met again was because by the end of March 1970 the position of the staff had not yet been clarified. Not only was there a delay in finalising conditions for the staff, but the Arts-Commerce-Law Building on the new Belfield campus, which was to accommodate the Commission's collections and staff, was still under construction, and was not officially opened until September 1970 by Éamon de Valera, still President of Ireland and in his late eighties. Further delay in

---

256 D/T 2000/6/76 S 6916E: Ó Fachtna to Ó Loinsigh, dated 22.10.1969.
257 D/T 2000/6/76 S 6916E: Ó Caithnia to Ó Loinsigh, dated 11.11.1969 (trans.).

transferring the Commission's collections to Belfield may have been caused by negotiations between the Faculties of Arts, Commerce and Law regarding the space they would be allotted in the new building. These three faculties wanted 160,000 square feet, but the initial plans allowed for only 120,000. Donal McCartney says: 'A compromise of 140,000 [square feet] was agreed, but only after the Government's insistence that the staff and collections of the Folklore Commission be accommodated in the building.'[258] If the competing faculties had to settle for less space than they required or would have liked, so too had the Commission. A room, not a purpose-built archive, with very little extra space to store new acquisitions, was provided for the Commission's manuscripts, but the room designated to serve as a library was most inadequate, and apart from other drawbacks, could not house all the Commission's book collections. This meant that much of the overflow had to be stored in the rooms of individual members of staff.

In early June 1970, approximately two months after the Commission had officially come to an end, the President of UCD contacted the Dept. of Education to enquire when the transfer to Belfield would be effected. Some two weeks later Seán Mac Gearailt, Secretary of the Department, replied to him and explained that the delay had been caused by the necessity of arranging for the superannuation of the Commission's staff:

> We understand from the Department [of Finance] that U.C.D. has recently been recognised under the 1963 Superannuation Act for the purpose of transferring pensionable service as between the College and the Civil Service and that therefore special superannuation provision, such as had been discussed previously and agreed to generally, in relation to the staff of the Commission may not now be required. The Department of Finance are to discuss this question with Mr MacHale, Secretary of the College.

When the situation with regard to superannuation would be clarified, Mac Gearailt informed President Hogan, his Department 'would hope to be in a position to have final discussions with representatives of the Commission's staff on the conditions of their transfer and to arrange for the transfer to be effected within a short time.'[259]

More than six months were to elapse before final arrangements for the transfer were completed. In early February 1971 the President of UCD informed the Governing Body 'that final arrangement had been reached with the Department of Education for the transfer to' the College 'of the Irish Folklore Commission as from 1 April 1971.' He also informed the meeting that the 'teaching of the subject and the supervision of the archives and other materials would be under the control of the Professor.' He added, in this connection, that 'Professor Delargy, as they all knew, was anxious to retire, and soon after the transfer, a new appointment to the chair would be sought.' With respect to the staff of the Commission, he said that they 'would

---

258 McCartney 1999, p. 390.
259 UCDA: Min. of Gov. Body Vol. 30, meeting 30.6.1970, item iv.

be transferred to the College under conditions which had been worked out by the Secretary [of UCD] and accepted by all those concerned, and by the Department of Education.'

At this meeting of the Governing Body a press release was read out 'which it was proposed to issue after the meeting, if the Governing Body Approved.' It read as follows, and I quote it in full because of its importance.

> At a meeting today (9 February 1971), the Governing Body accepted the offer of the Department of Education to have transferred to University College Dublin the work of the Irish Folklore Commission and noted that the official date of the transfer would be 1 April 1971. The staff of the Irish Folklore Commission, who are civil servants, have been invited to join the staff of University College Dublin. The Head of the Department of Irish Folklore is Professor J. H. Delargy, who is already a Professor of University College Dublin, and who, since 1935, has been seconded by the President and Governing Body of the College to act as Honorary Director of the Commission. A Section of the new Arts Building at Belfield has been specifically designed, with adequate precautions against fire, as a headquarters; and the transfer of staff, books, furniture, material and manuscripts will be effected as soon as possible after April 1.
>
> The transfer represents one of the most important acquisitions to University College Dublin since its foundation. In addition to a very valuable library, tapes, gramophone recordings and manuscripts, comprising many thousands, will now come into the possession of the College. It is intended to continue the work of Irish Folklore, as a unit, while extending the responsibilities of staff to include the teaching of students.
>
> A special publications fund is being made available to the College by the Department of Education and will be used for publications based on the material. A small Advisory Committee will be established, and they will assist in the arrangements for such publications.

The Governing Body 'expressed its satisfaction with this arrangement, and agreed that the press release should be issued.'[260] This was indeed a most important acquisition for the College, to say the least, and a most historic and perhaps fateful day. More than forty years had passed since Ó Duilearga had first made tentative steps to establish a department of folklore within his alma mater. Much had changed since then, and greater changes were in store.

Although the Commission on Higher Education had recommended a quite separate type of institute for the reconstituted Commission in UCD, there appear to have been objections to this idea. The Secretary of the Dept. of Finance, T.K. Whitaker, who was involved in official negotiations with UCD, says that objections were raised to this proposal, although he does not specify from what source.[261] Objections probably came from both the College and the

---

260 UCDA: Min. of Gov. Body Vol. 30, meeting of 9.2.1971, item 13.
261 RTÉSA BB2453 'Lest they Perish' (1985).

Dept. of Education. When Ó Duilearga proposed in the mid-1940's that the Commission should be reconstituted as a semi-independent institute within UCD, it was, as we have seen above, the opinion of the Dept. of Education that such a proposal would demand legislation and might be opposed by UCD. Drawing up legislation to give the reconstituted Commission a measure of independence within UCD, if it were possible, might have further delayed its transfer, and might have run the risk of raising old ideological animosities in Dáil and Seanad Éireann. Moreover, given the independence of Irish universities, it is unlikely that UCD at that time would have very willingly acquiesced in taking a semi-independent body into its fold, which might, in time, turn out to be a sort of Trojan Horse.[262]

It would also appear that the Faculty of Celtic Studies had a major say in the shape the reconstituted Commission took. In an undated document, dealing with the future development of Celtic Studies within the College it made a number of recommendations and observations in respect of folklore in the College. Among these were a) 'that steps be taken to introduce the subject Folklore as a full examination subject for the BA degree', and b) 'the importance of the archive of the Irish Folklore Commission for the academic study of Folklore as well as for research in Irish (both literary and dialect studies), Irish social history, Anglo-Irish studies, and possible future developments in anthropology and kindred subjects.' It consequently recommended that: 'It is therefore vital that the collections should continue to be located in University College Dublin within a fully-staffed Department of Folklore as an integral part of the Faculty [of Celtic Studies].'[263]

Thus, despite the recommendations of the CHE, as things turned out the newly reconstituted Commission hardly differed from other UCD departments in its structure and administration, except for the fact that it housed a world-famous folklore archive, and possessed certain trappings that went with it, such as a number of collectors in the field. Not only did the authorities reject the idea of 'a different type of organisation for the reconstituted Commission within UCD', as recommended by the CHE, they also chose to place the Irish Folklore Archive and the new fledgling teaching department under the one roof, not only physically, but more importantly, administratively. It would have been wiser, in the long run, to have kept them separate as we shall see.

262 On this occasion, it appears, the possibility of having the reconstituted Commission run by a governing council such as that which ran UCD's Albert College (Faculty of Agriculture) was either not considered or rejected. See above, p. 182, n. 188.

263 UCDA: Robin Dudley Edwards Papers LA 22/194(25). 'Memorandum from the Faculty of Celtic Studies on the Future Development of Celtic Studies'. Although this document is undated, it obviously predates the February 1971 meeting of UCD's Governing Body (see above).

7. Transfer to UCD

Choosing a successor to Ó Duilearga

When Ó Duilearga reached the age of seventy in May 1969, the form the reconstituted Irish Folklore Commission would take within UCD was still not clear. Indeed, it may well have been the case that the College authorities harboured doubts as to whether the transfer of the Commission to its charge and ownership would ever be realised. Such doubts may partly explain the delay in filling Ó Duilearga's Chair of Irish Folklore. It was not until the end of May 1971, almost two months after the official transfer of the Irish Folklore Commission to the College, that UCD's Governing Body dealt with the question of appointing a successor to Ó Duilearga, who was seventy two years of age by this time and still 'Acting Professor'.

Although various factors may have contributed to the delay in choosing a successor to Ó Duilearga, it is hard to avoid the conclusion that he was being kept on in order that he would still be around to take charge of the reconstituted Commission, and that after a symbolic period as head of the new university department he would hand over control to his successor, whoever that would be. One would not begrudge Séamus Ó Duilearga the chance of overseeing the handing over of the Commission to UCD, other circumstances being equal; but other circumstances were not exactly equal.

Seán Ó Súilleabháin was sixty six years of age when Ó Duilearga reached retirement age in May 1969, and consequently past the age when he could have reasonably aspired to succeed Ó Duilearga. Caoimhín Ó Danachair, on the other hand, was only fifty five years of age in May 1969. However, by the time Ó Duilearga's Chair was advertised Ó Danachair was going on fifty nine. On March 13th, 1971, some months after the state had finally reached an agreement with the College on the transfer of the Commission, the Academic Council recommended the appointment of Ó Danachair as Lecturer in Folklore ('with special regard for Material Culture').[264] Seán Ó Súilleabháin's age appears to have caused delay in his appointment to an

---

264 UCDA: Min. of Gov. Body Vol. 30, meeting of 24.3.1971. For this post, it should be noted, Ó Danachair had to compete with other candidates.

academic position within the College. On April 20th the President informed the Governing Body that he had appointed Ó Súilleabháin 'as acting Lecturer in Irish Folklore (with special regard to Archives) for one year from 1 April, 1971, the date on which the transfer had taken effect.'[265] Then in late June 1971 a meeting of the Governing Body decided that the vacancy in the Chair of Irish Folklore should 'be advertised as soon as possible, and August 21st, 1971 was fixed as the latest date for receipt of applications.'[266]

There were four applicants, Caoimhín Ó Danachair, Tomás Ó hAilín of UCD's Department of Modern Irish, John MacInnes of the School of Scottish Studies, and Bo Almqvist of the University of Uppsala. Looking at the list of candidates, one would have thought that the competition would have been between Almqvist and Ó Danachair. Bo Almqvist with a doctorate in folkloristics, teaching experience in the subject, administrative experience at running a folklore department, a good knowledge of Irish, and experience of collecting folklore in Ireland was beyond doubt a strong candidate. Ó Danachair's academic qualifications were not as strong as Almqvist's, as he did not have a doctorate. We will see below how the outbreak of the Second World War prevented Ó Danachair from completing his doctorate in Germany, and how Åke Campbell's death in 1957 robbed him of another chance of getting a doctorate from the University of Uppsala. Nevertheless, given the fact that possessing a doctorate was not a prerequisite for applying for a professorship in UCD at the time, and given the then system of filling chairs in the National University of Ireland, not having a doctorate, if he was otherwise deemed a worthy candidate for the post, should not have ruled Ó Danachair out of contention.

As things turned out, however, the contention was between Almqvist and Ó hAilín, although the latter had a very meagre publishing record and had published little, if indeed anything, that could be classified as having a bearing on folklore or ethnology. It should also be noted that Ó hAilín, like Ó Danachair, did not have a doctorate. The election of a professor in the National University of Ireland is a complicated process, and different bodies have to vote on the suitability of the various candidates. Although Almqvist was the choice of the Board of Assessors and scored highest, with Ó hAilín coming second, in the Faculty of Celtic Studies, the Faculty of Arts as well as the Academic Council, nonetheless Ó hAilín was ranked above him by the Governing Body. Whatever small amount of support Ó Danachair had in the Faculty of Arts and in the Academic Council, his qualifications and suitability for the post counted for nil with the Governing Body.[267] As things turned out, however, the decision of the Governing Body was reversed in the Senate of the National University of Ireland and Almqvist was appointed.

---

265 UCDA: Min. of Gov. Body Vol. 30, meeting of 20.4.1971. Both Ó Súilleabháin and Ó Danachair were engaged by the College as fee-paid lecturers from the previous autumn (1970) to lecture on folklore topics in UCD's Department of English (Anglo-Irish Literature and Drama). UCDA: Min. of Gov. Body Vol. 30, meeting of 18.12.1970.
266 UCDA: Min. of Gov. Body Vol. 31, meeting of 29.6.1971.
267 UCDA: Min. of Gov. Body Vol. 31, meeting of 17.12.1971.

If circumstances had been different and Ó Danachair had been appointed in preference to Almqvist, the latter would have had good grounds for grievance given his qualifications, but there is no doubt that an eminently eligible person would have been chosen for the post. Apart from his credentials in folkloristics, Almqvist's grounding in philology, and his reputation as an Icelandic scholar, would certainly have made him a strong candidate with the Faculty of Celtic Studies. Neither is it surprising that the academic assessors should have chosen him, given his doctorate and publications. Age was an added factor also, and favoured Almqvist, who was forty years of age or thereabouts. In selecting him, some were, no doubt, thinking of the long haul required to establish a university teaching department from scratch. However, the scant support for Ó Danachair in contrast to Ó hAilín in the Faculty of Arts and in the Academic Council is remarkable, and definitely finished any chances he had of winning in the Senate, or even in the Governing Body. Obviously, Ó hAilín, as a long-standing member of the staff of UCD would, in any event, have secured a certain number of votes on that account. Ó Danachair would have been seen as an outsider, but given the fact that the Irish Folklore Commission where he had worked since the 1940's had close associations with UCD, and that the Commission had now been taken into the bosom of the College, so to speak, the fact that his qualifications, experience, and overall suitability for the post counted for so little was perhaps ominous for future relations between the College and the new Department.

Of course, it may be that Ó Danachair did not lobby sufficiently for the position, believing that his academic qualifications and work experience were sufficient to see him appointed to the Chair of Irish Folklore. If that was the case, given the convoluted way professors were chosen in the National University of Ireland, it was a grave error on his part, as lobbying was important. While Ó Danachair may not have lobbied sufficiently for the post, it is quite probable that people lobbied against him. This does not necessarily mean that there was a concerted effort against him, but there is no doubt that Ó Duilearga did not want him to get the Chair of Folklore, a fact which close associates of Ó Duilearga's on various UCD bodies would have known, and some of them may have acted accordingly. However, at this distance from the events, it is difficult to say for certain whether animosities between himself and Ó Duilearga played a crucial role in weakening his chances of getting the Chair. He himself may have felt they did, but, without substantive evidence to support such a supposition, all that can be said more than thirty years on is that a combination of circumstances appears to have weighted the dice against Caoimhín Ó Danachair. A major factor was that while UCD showed great deference to the interests of Ó Duilearga after he reached retirement age at seventy, it did not show the same deference to the interests of the Commission's staff, particular those of Ó Danachair, who was the one member of staff in a position to aspire to succeed Ó Duilearga. Moreover, the fact that some six months before he applied for the Chair of Irish Folklore he was appointed Lecturer in Folklore ('with special regard for Material Culture') may have further weakened his chances of succeeding Ó Duilearga. Members of the various selection bodies in the College may have felt that he had been taken care of. This may, in part, explain his poor showing in these bodies. Caoimhín Ó Danachair bore his disappointment well – if not initially, certainly in time. Circumstances may have deprived him of leading the reconstituted Commission in UCD, but in the first ten years or so of the Department of Irish Folklore, for many students he was a guiding light and father-figure, and the life and soul of the Department.

If Caoimhín Ó Danachair was badly treated, the same cannot be said for the rest of the staff. All members of staff were retained, even the Latvian exile Janis Mezs, then in his nineties. The collectors, librarian, sound technician, and office manager all became pensionable members of staff and were designated folklorists. However, although promises seem to have been made that vacancies occasioned by retirements would be filled, the possibility of creating new posts in the future to augment the Commission's inadequate staff numbers was left for future negotiations to determine. Moreover, it would appear nothing very substantive was put on paper during negotiations to transfer the Commission to UCD.[268] Consequently a huge act of faith was involved. In many respects, it seems that the agreement reached between the state and UCD on the transfer of the Irish Folklore Commission and its collections was somewhat of a gentleman's agreement, and while gentlemen may give their word, what happens when those gentlemen depart the scene? I will touch on this question in my conclusion.

Opening of the Department of Irish Folklore

When the Department of Irish Folklore was finally opened on September 28th, 1971, Ó Duilearga had still not retired from his Professorship at UCD and was Head of the new Department as the *Irish Times* in its account of the ceremonies reported. It also published his photograph standing alongside Michael Tierney and the President of the College, J.J. Hogan'[269] Michael Tierney, the former President of the College, officially opened the new Department of Irish Folklore, after a few introductory words by President Hogan. Tierney in his speech spoke of his first encounter with Séamus Ó Duilearga, of the Trojan work achieved by him and his colleagues, of the value of the collection, and of the close connections between UCD and the Commission:

> I have always believed that the right place ultimately for the staff and archives of the Commission is within a university, where continuity and independence can be more readily assured than anywhere else. Difficulties of time and circumstance have made such an arrangement impossible until now, when the work of collection has come fairly near completion, and what is needed most is rather scientific arrangement, comparative study and the exploration of the many possibilities which this great collection

---

268 The files of the Dept. of Educ. on the IFC are not complete for the 1960's, and the College Archives of UCD contain almost nothing about these negotiations.
269 'Irish folklore finds an academic setting', *Irish Times* Wed., September 29, 1971, p. 13.

provides for the Irish scholar, and, indeed, for scholars of all nationalities who are interested in the history and character of the Irish people.'[270]

For Séamus Ó Duilearga September 28th, 1971 was a day he had long been waiting for, and had striven for over many decades, as was the case with Michael Tierney. It was a day to celebrate, but also a sad day. He recalled nostalgically his teachers and mentors, former Presidents of the College, and above all the numerous tradition bearers he had met. He was finally letting go the reins. Some of those who had worked with him over the years would stay on in the new department, but for him it was time to go. If he felt any pang of bitterness about this, he did not show it. Despite the many differences with members of staff over the years, he was magnanimous in his praise of colleagues on the staff of the Commission, and did not fail to mention his old adversary, Éamon de Valera, whose initial support had been so crucial. Nor did he forget to mention his great debt to UCD, and to his colleagues there. He concluded his speech, with a quotation from a book thus:

> I bring this inadequate record to a close with this quotation from a book on the barren lands of northern Canada, not inappropriate, I suggest—*mutatis mutandis*—in the present context of my thoughts:
> 'My journey was over, but I was still tied to the Barrens, not by the simple web of memories alone, but by something more powerful. There was, and is, an abiding affection in my heart for the men and women ... who lent me their eyes so that I was privileged to look backward through the dark void of dead years, and to see not only the relics of forgotten times, but also into the minds and thought of the men of those times. It was a great gift I had from the people and one that deserved a repayment.'
> This College has helped in large measure to repay.[271]

The end of a long road: Séamus Ó Duilearga retires

As with many people who have led an active life at the helm, retirement, most likely, did not come easy to Séamus Ó Duilearga. No longer being in the thick of things must have been hard for him. Unfortunately, he was not to be blessed with good health, which meant that many of the projects he had hoped to work on during his retirement were not seen to fruition. In April 1972 he was appointed a member of Comhairle Bhéaloideas Éireann/The Folklore of Ireland Council (see above). This might have been a possible outlet for him, but as things turned out, he was not to be a frequent attender at its meetings. However, he continued to edit *Béaloideas* for a year or so after retiring.

270 *Óráidí ag Oscailt.*, pp. 1–3.
271 *Óráidí ag Oscailt.*, pp. 4–8. Ó Duilearga quotes from Farley Mowat's *People of the Deer* (London 1954), p. 256.

A letter he wrote to Liam Mac Coisdeala in February 1973, a year after his retirement from UCD, reveals something of his isolation: 'Yes, both of us are now retired and the care of our affairs in the care of others. We have both earned a rest and tranquillity, if we will be granted it!' Mac Coisdeala had asked him to see if the new Department of Irish Folklore could use the services of an acquaintance of his. Ó Duilearga says that he has sent this request to his successor, Bo Almqvist; adding: ' I can do nothing else, unlike the time when I was Director of the old Commission. I do not go to Belfield, but I have enough to keep me busy here at home. I have given up editing the journal [*Béaloideas*] (1927–1973) apart from editing the double issue which I am finishing.' He ends his letter thus:

> I pray from the bottom of my heart that you should have the very best, both good health and peace of mind! And I will not [forget], as long as I live, the Trojan work you did, not only in Erris but especially in Carna and in Aill na Brón. If it weren't for your zeal many a gem of lore would have been lost with its narrators. That will be understood in time.
> With a thousand blessings to you all
> With respect and esteem
> Your old comrade
> Séamus Ó Duilearga[272]

272 Original lent to me by the late Liam Mac Coisdeala (copy in UCCFA) (trans.). For a moving tribute to Ó Duilearga on his retirement, see Anne-Berit Østereng Borchgrevink 1974.

8. A Postscript to transfer to UCD

If the Government of the Irish Free State had agreed to set up a well-funded, permanent institute to collect, preserve, and research Irish folklore in the late 1920's, it is quite possible that Séamus Ó Duilearga would never have sought to incorporate it into UCD. However, the inadequate funding of the Irish Folklore Institute, as well as the conditions pertaining to its grant-in-aid, forced him to reconsider the reorganisation of folklore collecting. There is no doubt that his rising star within UCD also played a part in his decision to have the systematic collecting of folklore placed under the care of his alma mater and employer. However, in seeking to have the Irish Folklore Institute reconstituted in this university college, he was not simply motivated by his own personal interests, but by a belief that an academic milieu, free from excessive outside interference, was the best location for such a body.

Ó Duilearga's trip to northern Europe in 1928 gave him a chance to acquaint himself with the situation regarding the organisation of folklore collecting in that region. In all of the countries he visited he encountered folklore archives/collections, some of them with long roots. He also saw that folklore as a subject was being catered for at university level. Moreover, many of the folklore institutes he visited were 'connected with universities', but being connected with a particular university did not in all cases imply being an integral part of it. This was the case with the two largest collections of folklore that he encountered, namely those of the Finnish Literature Society and the Estonian Literature Museum. Although it would appear that it was these two collections that made the greatest impression on him, it was the model of folklore organisation in Sweden that he especially sought to replicate in Ireland. This is not at all surprising. Of all the countries Ó Duilearga visited in 1928, and subsequently, Sweden was the country he was most familiar with, and of all the folklorists he met on that eventful journey it was Carl Wilhelm von Sydow of the University of Lund he was most beholden to and influenced by. In a memorandum von Sydow presented to de Valera in July 1934, he argued strongly the case that the best way to arrange for the systematic and scientific collecting of folklore was to place it under university control. In support of his case he says:

In the past before the Universities were placed in control by the State of the collection work, we have in Sweden had enthusiastic collectors who made large collections, but from the beginning failed to realise that the aim was not to amass huge and undigested piles of manuscripts. Many of these collectors neglected through ignorance to compile data relating to the provenance of their collections, the result being that when the collections were taken over by the State a vast quantity were found to have no scientific value.[273]

Von Sydow's memorandum does not tell the whole truth about what placing universities 'in control' of folklore collecting amounted to in Sweden. Although the folklore institute in Lund belonged to the University of Lund,[274] the Dialect and Folklore Archive in Uppsala (Landsmålsarkivet) while it rented space from the University of Uppsala and was housed in its Library, belonged to the state and its workers were civil servants.[275] On the other hand, the Norwegian Folklore Archive (Norske Folkminnesamling) was located in the Library of the University of Oslo and belonged to the University. However, in Denmark the Danish Folklore Archive (Dansk Folkemindesamling) was an independent institute situated in the Royal Library, Copenhagen. [276] Moreover, as stated above, in Finland and Estonia, through the agency of private learned bodies, large and valuable collections of folklore had been assembled in close association with universities, but nonetheless independent of them.[277] There was therefore an alternative model for organising folklore collection and research, yet on numerous occasions, as we have seen above, Ó Duilearga insisted that the only model was incorporation in a university, or rather a particular university. Indeed, the Irish Folklore Commission itself is living proof that a non-university body, in close association with a university, could collect folklore systematically and scientifically. The problem with the Commission was not that it was not an integral part of UCD, but that it was a non-permanent body, allowed to exist in a sort of limbo for decades.

However, with regard to the rights and wrongs of transferring the Irish Folklore Commission to UCD, it has to be said that the College's claim on the Commission was very strong. Long before the setting up of the Irish Folklore Commission in 1935, the UCD authorities had displayed an interest

---

273 D/T S 9244: 'Swedish Universities and the Collection of National Traditions'.
274 For more on the Lund Folklore Archive, see Bringéus 1988 and Salomonsson 2000.
275 For more on the Uppsala archive, see Strömbäck 1976 and Hedblom 1989. Somewhat ironically, the same year (1967) the Commission on Higher Education recommended that the Irish Folklore Commission be incorporated into UCD, the Landsmålsarkivet was physically separated from the University of Uppsala. Information supplied by Marlene Hugoson.
276 Herranen and Saressalo 1978, pp. 12 and 94. Interestingly, in the mid-1940's, Ó Duilearga thought that the Norske Folkminnesamling was located in the National Library of Norway and that it was an independent institution. ED CO 495(8): Ó Duilearga to Sec. Dept. of Educ., 31.8.1944, p. 1.
277 For more on the history of the Finnish and Estonian Folklore Archives, see Hautala 1957, pp. 2–36, and Korb et al 1990, pp. 1–6 respectively.

in efforts to promote the collecting and study of folklore. In the late 1920's they provided the Folklore of Ireland Society with a room for its library, and financed Ó Duilearga's trip in 1928 to northern Europe in order to broaden his knowledge of folkloristics. Moreover, in 1931, in recognition of the importance of folklore as an academic discipline and of Ó Duilearga's growing reputation in this field, a part-time lectureship in Irish Folklore was established for him within the College, and some three years later he was appointed Statutory Lecturer in Irish Folklore. In providing the Irish Folklore Commission with free accommodation, heating and light, as well as other services, UCD also, in effect, facilitated the Commission in the early years in employing at least one extra full-time collector from its slim resources. Moreover, in agreeing to second Ó Duilearga to the Commission and allowing him to act as Honorary Director at full salary, the College saved the Commission even greater expense, i.e. of having to pay a Director out of its grant-in-aid. Finally, in the post-War period UCD, although badly in need of additional space, on the instigation of its President, Michael Tierney, housed the Commission in 82 St. Stephen's Green, which although not ideal in many respects was a vast improvement on the cramped quarters they had previously occupied in the College. Of course, in providing the Commission with more spacious quarters at this juncture, UCD, or rather its President, may have been deliberately attempting to make the separation of the Commission from the College more difficult at a later date. Nevertheless, there is no doubt the Commission and the state were indebted to the College.

The fact that Ó Duilearga did not yield in the late 1940's to pressure being exerted by the Dept. of the Taoiseach to accept re-establishment outside the University, is probably in large part due to Michael Tierney. Tierney had sat on the board of the Irish Folklore Institute for the five years of its operation and subsequently on the board of the Irish Folklore Commission. He witnessed one of the great folklore archives of the world literally take shape before his eyes. In these burgeoning collections, he believed, were to be found a key to much of the country's Gaelic past. He wanted these collections for his College, not only in order to add to its status, but also, I have no doubt, because he believed a university milieu was the natural home for the Commission's archive. Although with the passage of the years, Tierney would appear to have lost all hope of saving the Gaeltacht, not to mention spreading Irish outside it, he never ceased to believe in the correctness of the ideals that the early Gaelic League set itself.[278]

Of the various alternatives to incorporating the Commission into UCD suggested over the years, de Valera's proposal of the late 1940's to re-establish the Commission in the Dublin Institute for Advanced Studies as a separate School was the one which would have most enhanced the status of the Commission, provided an academic milieu for the care and handling of its collections, as well as security and prospects of promotion for its staff. When in the 1960's the CHE came to consider the Dublin Institute for Advanced Studies as a possible home for the Irish Folklore Commission, unlike de

278 See Michael Tierney 1963.

Valera's earlier proposal, as noted above, it seemed only to contemplate incorporating the Commission within the School of Celtic Studies, not as a separate School. Not surprisingly, the CHE opted for not transferring the Commission to the Institute, not wishing to add 'a further substantial burden' to that school, which 'within its own field [had] a vast undertaking, both as regards research and publication'.[279]

Given the changed ideological climate of the late 1960's, and the Commission's debt to UCD, incorporating the Commission into that college must have appeared to many as the logical solution to a problem that had gone on all too long. Nevertheless, it is justifiable to pose the question: was the right decision made? To answer this question would need a study in itself. However, in considering whether there were better, or other plausible, alternatives to reorganising the Irish Folklore Commission other than by re-establishing it in UCD, it is necessary to keep in mind that whatever home had been found for the Commission, no learned institution in the state could have taken on the care of the Irish Folklore Commission without continuous state support. In 1969/1970, and earlier, UCD wanted the Commission, but it could not afford it. If a different home had been chosen for these world-famous collections in the late 1960's, would they have fared any better in respect of state funding than they have fared in UCD?

---

279 *Commission on Higher Education. II Report Volume 1*, p. 366.

IV
The Commission's Collectors and Collections

1. In the Field/the Collectors at work

Recruiting full-time collectors

As noted above, in the memorandum he sent de Valera in May 1933 concerning the reorganisation of folklore collecting, Ó Duilearga suggested employing ten to fifteen full-time collectors in the first year, 'to be increased in subsequent years to thirty or more.'[1] This was somewhat ambitious as well as unrealistic, given the funding that was being proposed. The Commission was never to have more than nine full-time collectors at any one time, and most of the time had to make do with far fewer. At a meeting held in the Dept. of Education on October 16th, 1933 (see Chapter III/1 above), ostensibly to discuss Ó Duilearga's above-mentioned memorandum, his proposals were brought down to earth somewhat. It was proposed to ask the Dept. of Finance to provide money for the employment of ten full-time collectors at £300 per annum.[2] The Dept. of Finance when informed of this proposal objected to the figure of ten full-time collectors. In November 1933, Finance in a memorandum to the Dept. of the President referred to the problem of recruiting collectors in sufficient numbers: 'It is questionable whether as many as even six qualified collectors can be put to work at the commencement of the scheme.'[3] They do not state their reasons for arriving at six full-time collectors at most, but another departmental memo on the above meeting is revealing on this matter:

> As there is clearly disagreement between the experts as to the number of persons who would be competent, after a short course of instruction, to undertake the collection of folklore, it seems essential that the scheme should be operated at the beginning only by such workers whose competence is beyond doubt. It is felt in the Department of Finance that the number of qualified persons does not at present exceed five or six.[4]

1   D/T S 9244: 'Collection of Oral Tradition of Ireland', p. 7.
2   D/T S 9244: Educ. memo entitled 'Meeting in Room of Minister for Education', dated 16.10.1933.
3   D/T S 9244: untitled memorandum, p. [3]; covering letter (MacEntee to President) dated 16.11.33.
4   D/T S 9244: 'Observations of the Dept. of Fin. on the Report of the Folklore Conference

In his above memorandum to de Valera, Ó Duilearga had proposed recruiting full-time collectors from 1) 'Postgraduate students of Universities', 2) 'Young men of sufficient education who have shown an aptitude for this work', 3) 'Irish teachers employed by the Branch of Technical Instruction under the Department of Education', and 4) 'Primary and Secondary teachers.'[5] For whatever reason university graduates did not figure very prominently among the collectors employed by the Commission, although a number of graduates had collected material for the Irish Folklore Institute. Speaking some fifteen years after the setting up of the Commission about the initial recruitment of collectors, Seán Ó Súilleabháin says:

> We didn't look around among the university students to act as collectors, for we have found that any attempt we have made in Ireland to have university students do collecting has been largely a failure. We looked among the fishermen along the coast, and to young primary teachers who had not yet got positions in schools, and from them we picked our collectors. Because they were of the people they had not been spoiled, as we say in Ireland, by university education and by city ways. Because anyone who does go among the people must go among them as one of themselves and have no high-faluting nonsense about them. He must become as they are and talk to them in their own language.[6]

Seán Ó Súilleabháin on this occasion would appear to have been speaking *ex tempore* at a conference, so we should not hold him to every single word he said; nonetheless it is interesting to note his dismissal of university graduates. As a matter of fact, the Commission did employ one university graduate initially, Liam Mac Meanman, and in the course of time a number of other university graduates became full-time collectors.[7]

Although the Dept. of Finance underestimated the number of potential collectors available initially to the Commission, there is no doubt that the pool of potential collectors was limited by a number of factors. What then were the qualifications required of collectors? Obviously, as no university college in the country offered courses in folklore, no professional qualifications in folkloristics could be expected from potential applicants. The most that could be expected was that people sufficiently enthusiastic for the work could be found, preferably with some experience of collecting folklore. As the Commission was initially concentrating on Irish-speaking districts, a good knowledge of Irish was essential for the work intended. With the exception of Liam Mac Coisdeala, Caoimhín Ó Danachair, and Séamus Ennis, all the full-

held on the 16th October, 1933', p. 1.

5   D/T S 9244: 'Collection of Oral Tradition of Ireland', p. 23. Part-time collectors were to be recruited from 'Teachers and others who will undertake work in their home districts following a definite plan. Remuneration to be at the discretion of the Director of the Research Institute.' Ibid., p. 23.

6   Stith Thompson 1976 [1953], p. 4.

7   Liam Mac Meanman had a BA in Celtic Studies from UCD. He had been a student of Ó Duilearga's, and already in 1933 had been recruited by him to collect folklore in his native Donegal. See S. Ó Catháin 1992–1993.

time collectors employed by the Commission in its first ten years were native Irish speakers.[8] Choosing native speakers of Irish had the added advantage, at least when they worked in their own areas or within reasonable distance of their home area, that they knew the community and were known. This made it easier for them to be accepted, and for less suspicion to adhere to them. Not only was there the danger that country people might suspect that collectors were some sort of officials working for government departments and agencies, but in the wake of the Civil War, strangers were suspect in certain areas of the country lest they be spying for state security forces. The reason why only one university graduate was initially employed as a full-time collector was most likely a result of the decision by the Commission to employ native speakers of Irish to work in their own areas. Few native speakers of Irish at the time would have had the benefit of a university education. It has also to be stated, however, that the salaries and conditions of work on offer with the Commission were, perhaps, not such as to entice young graduates in search of remunerative employment.

However, to be a native speaker of Irish was not enough, one had also to be literate in Irish, and of course interested in oral tradition. Given the fact that many native speakers of Irish, even those who had been through the school system since the setting up of the Irish Free State, were not proficient at writing their mother tongue, the choice of schoolteachers was obvious. Although Irish had been taught in most Gaeltacht schools for more than a decade, few native speakers of Irish had by then received a secondary education. However, since the setting up of the Preparatory Colleges (see Chapter I/2 above) in 1926, a small élite of native speakers were receiving secondary education and going on to become National School teachers. It is therefore not surprising that a number of the Commission's early recruits were National School teachers. However, one of the earliest full-time collectors to be employed, and the longest serving, was a fisherman, Seán Ó hEochaidh, but it should be said he was a very untypical fisherman.

The Commission does not seem to have advertised as such for collectors. Of course, the initial publicity that surrounded the setting up of the Commission would have made the general public aware of the type of work the Commission intended to do. For example, shortly after the setting up of the Commission, Seán Ó hEochaidh wrote to them advertising his services.[9] For other collectors, such as Seosamh Ó Dálaigh, it was a chance meeting with Séamus Ó Duilearga in Dún Chaoin in 1936 that resulted in his recruitment as a full-time collector for the Commission.[10] Some of the collectors were known by reputation to Séamus Ó Duilearga and contacted by him. Nioclás Breatnach was such a person. Ó Duilearga knew that Breatnach was interested in folklore and that he had published items of folklore he had collected in *An Lóchrann* (an Irish-language newspaper). He wrote to Breatnach some

8   Seán Ó Flannagáin learned Irish as a child from his grandmother, rather than from his parents. Ó Baoill/Ó Béarra 2005, p. xiii.
9   S. Ó Catháin 1989, p. 49.
10 UCCRNG Tyers/Ó Dálaigh, tapescript 1, p. 1.

months before the Commission was set up offering him a job as a full-time collector. However, it would be autumn 1935, more than six months after the Commission was established, before Breatnach's recruitment could be realised.[11] Michael J. Murphy, who joined the full-time staff of the Commission in the late 1940's, is another example of someone known to Ó Duilearga by reputation, in his case due to his book *At Slieve Gullion's Foot*. He was first employed as a part-time collector, before being given a full-time post. Michael J. Murphy was the only collector employed full-time by the Commission who did not have a knowledge of Irish.[12]

Two of the collectors appointed shortly after the setting up of the Commission, Liam Mac Coisdeala and Tadhg Ó Murchadha, had been collecting in a part-time capacity for the Folklore of Ireland Society and the Irish Folklore Institute. They were both Irish language teachers employed by the Vocational Education Committees in their respective areas. Part-time collecting for the Commission itself in a number of cases became a backdoor route to becoming a full-time collector. Seán Ó Cróinín had been working for two years as a part-time collector for the Commission before his appointment as full-time collector in April 1938.[13]

Collectors were usually taken on for a three-month probationary period.[14] Six collectors were employed during the first year of the Commission. These were: Liam Mac Coisdeala (1.8.1935, Galway); Tadhg Ó Murchadha (1.9.1935, Kerry); Seán Ó hEochaidh (1.9.1935, Donegal); Proinnsias de Búrca (1.9.1935, Galway); Liam Mac Meanman (9.9.1935, Donegal); and Nioclás Breatnach (1.11.1935, Waterford). In the Commission's second year of operation, three further collectors were appointed: Seosamh Ó Dálaigh (1.8.1936, Kerry); Brian Mac Lochlainn (1.8.1936, Galway); and Proinnsias Ó Ceallaigh (c. 1.9.1936, Cork).[15] For a short time in late 1936 the Commission had nine full-time collectors in the field. However, Ó Ceallaigh, who like Mac Coisdeala and Ó Murchadha had been seconded by his local Vocational Education Committee, was not destined to stay long with the Commission. Soon his health began to fail and he resigned his post after three months or so in late November 1936. The following autumn Nioclás Breatnach left the service of the Commission to return to teaching, after his two-year contract was up. Liam Mac Meanman also left the Commission after having spent just two years collecting. The departure of these three left the Commission again with six full-time collectors, but in October 1937

---

11 N. Breatnach 1998a, p. 40 and N. Breatnach 1998b, p. 71. It would appear that the cause of the delay in employing Breatnach was the fact that he would not have completed two years service for his teaching Diploma until autumn 1935. ED 42178: internal memo entitled 'Irish Folklore Commission', 6.5.1935, p. [1].

12 It is of interest to note, however, that Michael J. Murphy's maternal grandfather, William Jordan (Liam Ó Sriodáin) was an Irish-language scribe and collector of oral and literary tradition. Although some of his manuscripts have survived, many were destroyed by his son around the beginning of the 20th century. See *The Irish Book Lover* 17 (January–December 1929), p.125.

13 D/T S 15548A: 'Gearr-Thuar./1938–39', pp. [1].

14 See D/F S 101/0011/34: Ó Dubhthaigh to Sec. Dept. of Fin., dated 9.4.1938.

15 In brackets the date they officially commenced work and county of operation are given.

a new full-time collector, Seán Ó Flanagáin, was taken on to work in the Galway/Clare border region.[16]

Three of the six collectors employed in the first year, Seán Ó hEochaidh, Tadhg Ó Murchadha, and Proinnsias de Búrca, as well as Seosamh Ó Dálaigh recruited during the second year, were to spend many years with the Commission. However, only Ó hEochaidh was to remain on the payroll without interruption from beginning to end. In all, he was to spend almost thirty five years with the Commission and an additional thirteen years with its successor, the Department of Irish Folklore. Proinnsias de Búrca was also to see the changeover from Commission to Department in 1971, but his employment with the Commission was not to be continuous. Seosamh Ó Dálaigh was to spend fifteen years with the Commission before returning to teaching in 1951. Tadhg Ó Murchadha was to stay with the Commission for almost twenty three years before ill health finally forced him to retire in 1958.

From the late 1940's the Commission, due to an increased grant-in-aid, was able to employ more collectors than they had been able to for much of the War and early post-War period. Some of these were to spent long years with the Commission. Michael J Murphy, Ciarán Bairéad, and Jim Delaney spent approximately twenty two, twenty, and sixteen years with the Commission respectively, and all remained on to see the transition from Commission to university department. However, many collectors employed full-time by the Commission spent only a few years with it. Liam Mac Coisdeala, who did some of the most valuable collecting work done by the Commission, was employed full-time by them for only four years, returning to his job with the Galway Vocational Education Committee when his leave of absence expired, although he continued to collect part-time. Seán Ó Cróinín initially spent six years with the Commission before being let go during the Second World War due to cutbacks. He later resumed employment with the Commission and spent another five years or more with them from the late 1950's to his sudden death in 1965. He was the only collector to die 'in harness'.

Training of full-time collectors

In May 1933, Ó Duilearga informed de Valera that full-time collectors:

> ...must be given a thorough course of instruction in Dublin by the Director. This course will cover the nature and extent of the oral material to be collected, and will stress its importance culturally, nationally and linguistically, and will include instruction on the *modus operandi* based on the Director's practical experience of over ten years as a field worker in many parts of Ireland, and his knowledge of the methods employed in Scandinavia and in Germany by institutions directly financed by the State. The course should last at least three weeks.[17]

16   D/T S 15548A: 'Gearr-Thuar./1936–37', p. 1 and 'Gearr-Thuar./1937–38', p. 1.
17   D/T S 9244: 'Collection of Oral Tradition of Ireland', pp. 7–8 (italics underlined in original).

None of the collectors seem to have received such an extensive training at Head Office as that outlined above. Seán Ó Súilleabháin says that collectors were brought 'in turn to our office in Dublin, where we trained them for a week.'[18] Bringing collectors to Head Office may have been the original plan, but in many cases collectors were trained in the field long before they ever caught sight of the Head Office in Dublin. The fact that the Commission wished to get collecting going as soon as possible may also have meant that certain corners were cut in respect of training. However, in time, some collectors, at least, were brought to Dublin for further training. In February and March 1936, Liam Mac Coisdeala, Liam Mac Meanman, and Tadhg Ó Murchadha were in turn called to Head Office for several days where they received instruction from Ó Duilearga and Seán Ó Súilleabháin, and were accommodated in Ó Duilearga's home.[19] It was subsequently contemplated bringing the collectors *en bloc* to Dublin for training. In late spring 1936, Ó Duilearga told the Finance Sub-Committee that 'a short course of instruction for the collectors in Dublin would be desirable', at which they, among other things, might be given instruction in map reading by an official from the Ordnance Survey.[20] It would appear that this never materialised. Bringing the collectors all together to Dublin might have proved too expensive as they obviously could not all have stayed in Ó Duilearga's home and would have had to be accommodated in paid lodgings.

It must be said that the need for extensive training at Head Office was, perhaps, not all that necessary, given the circumstances. At any rate, the type of training envisaged above by Ó Duilearga, which was quite limited, did not require such a long sojourn in Head Office. Even if it had been possible to bring collectors to Dublin for three weeks, as Ó Duilearga initially suggested, that would have allowed time for the teaching of little more than the rudiments of folklore scholarship, for example, initiating them into the mysteries of the Aarne-Thompson classification system. Neither was it ever the intention to make the collectors into professional folklorists. Certain practical skills had to be imparted to them, and this sort of instruction was best given in the field. Moreover, it should be remembered that the initial training full-time collectors received, be it in the field or at Head Office, was only part of their overall training. Collectors not only learned from experience, they were also monitored from Head Office and learned in this way to correct their mistakes.

It would appear that the amount of training different collectors got varied from individual to individual, as indeed did their need for training. In fact, some of the collectors received a minimum of training. A number of them had already done some collecting and were as a result, to varying degrees, well acquainted with certain of the skills Ó Duilearga wished his collectors to have. Moreover, the background of the collectors, to some extent, made it less necessary to lecture them on the nature of folklore, as they all either

18   Stith Thompson 1976, p. 4.
19   ED [FL 9]: 'CBÉ. Miont. 5ú Cruinniú, 17.4.1936', par. 38(c).
20   ED [FL 9]: 'IFC. Fin. Sub-Com./ Min. 4th Meeting, 9.4.1936', par. 38.

came from traditional communities rich in folk tradition, or had experienced such communities at first hand. Nioclás Breatnach, one of the first full-time collectors, notes: 'In order to collect folklore, it was necessary for the collector to know a large amount of folk literature, and to have experience of being in the company of old people as well as respect for them and their culture, for I do not think they would willingly bestow their knowledge on someone else.'[21]

Liam Mac Coisdeala says that he received no training before starting work for the Commission, but he adds: 'That does not imply that I was not familiar with the work that was involved.' Mac Coisdeala had done a great deal of collecting on a part-time basis for the Irish Folklore Institute.' Liam Mac Meanman had also done some collecting for the Irish Folklore Institute, although not to the same extent as Mac Coisdeala. As an old man he recalled that 'Séamus Ó Duilearga spent a few days with me before I began. That is all I got by way of training.'[22] However, Ó Duilearga in a letter to the Dept. of Education says of Mac Meanman, 'that the business of collecting was explained to him in an interview, and he was instructed and advised in both Dublin and Donegal.'[23] As mentioned above, Ó Duilearga already knew Mac Meanman and had recruited him to do some collecting for the Irish Folklore Institute, so some of what Ó Duilearga says of his training may refer to his contact with him prior to the setting up of the Commission. Mac Meanman's recollection may also be defective in respect of the extent of the training he received, but it may also reflect a belief that his training was not sufficient.[24]

Although full-time collectors did not have to be instructed on the nature of folklore, and while some of them had already experience of collecting, as Séamas Ó Catháin notes, in the case of Seán Ó hEochaidh, Ó Duilearga had to teach him the skills necessary for him to be able to carry out 'his duties effectively'. This was the case with all the full-time collectors, even those with some experience of collecting. One of the first skills he needed to impart to the collectors was that they should record *verbatim* the words of the storytellers, and subsequently go over any obscure words or passages with the narrator. In addition, he wished them to record all the dialectical nuances, by adapting the traditional orthography of Irish to this purpose.[25] Nioclás Breatnach says that Ó Duilearga put him through a rigorous test to ascertain if his ear was sharp enough to detect subtleties of pronunciation.[26] Other full-time collectors may have been tested in a similar fashion.

Ó Duilearga spent some weeks initiating Seán Ó hEochaidh. This was longer than he spent with most full-time collectors. The reason for this

---

21 N. Breatnach 1998a, p. 41 (trans.).
22 UCCFA Mac Coisdeala and Mac Meanman questionnaire replies (1990), q. 3 (trans.).
23 D/S S 101/0011/34: letter dated 22.8.1935.
24 Mac Meanman met Ó Duilearga in August 1935 while Ó Duilearga was in Teileann, southwest Donegal, initiating Seán Ó hEochaidh, and it was there that he agreed to become a full-time collector for the Commission for a year at the lower salary of £150. S. Ó Catháin 1992–1993, p. 292.
25 S. Ó Catháin 1989, pp. 54 ff.
26 Recording made by Niall de Barra of talk N. Breatnach gave to the Dept. of Folklore and Ethnology, UCC (in private possession).

may have had more to do with the rapport that seems to have developed immediately between the two men, and Ó Duilearga's desire to familiarise himself with southwest Donegal, an area rich in tradition, than with any real need to give more instruction to Ó hEochaidh than, say, to other collectors.[27] Ó Duilearga and Ó hEochaidh visited tradition bearers together, quizzed them, collected their lore, and transcribed some of the material together. After spending some weeks in the area, Ó Duilearga left him with fifty four Ediphone cylinders to transcribe (sufficient for a month's transcribing), two dozen empty Ediphone cylinders, and a one-inch Ordnance Survey map of Donegal.[28] Ó hEochaidh's apprenticeship would appear from the above to have gone smoothly enough, but that was not always the case.

Séamus Ó Duilearga did not spend the same amount of time initiating Tadhg Ó Murchadha into the work of collecting. Both men were acquainted with each other, the former having encouraged the latter to begin collecting for the Folklore of Ireland Society since shortly after its founding in 1927.[29] However, Ó Murchadha had hitherto only collected with pen and paper, and therefore needed to be shown how to use the Ediphone. Ó Murchadha describes how he was instructed in the collecting methods required of the Commission's collectors. Ó Duilearga arrived one evening with an Ediphone and a box of cylinders. After tea they retired from the rest of the household and Ó Murchadha was given instructions as to what was required of him. This he described as 'a very long lecture as if he were lecturing his university students.' He was told to be particularly careful with the Ediphone: to keep it well oiled, and when removing a cylinder not to damage the needle. He would have 'to collect and transcribe two dozen cylinders at least per week to begin with'. More would be expected of him as he 'got used to the Ediphone.' In addition to a diary, he would be expected to keep a book of unusual words and sayings, and another book where he would record information regarding the personalities and narrative styles of informants. Ó Murchadha says: 'Upon my word it was no job for idling, and I suppose only for the interest I had in the work and how zealous I was to take it up, I would have turned it down there and then and stuck to the job I had.'

On the second day of Ó Duilearga's visit, a Sunday, they went to a storyteller who filled ten cylinders with a heroic tale. The next day Ó Murchadha began transcribing the tale, which proved very difficult. What he found most difficult was transcribing with one hand while holding the horn of the Ediphone in the other in order to listen. He also had to make sure he did not inadvertently jolt the 'lever that regulated the two needles' lest they be damaged. At the end of a sentence he would apply the break, and go back to check he had not missed any word. This initial transcription, he says, was made easier by the fact that the narrator was a clear speaker, who spoke slowly.

---

27 Ó Duilearga's stay in Donegal may also have been extended by the fact that he had gone there not just to meet Ó hEochaidh, but to convalesce from 'a severe attack of illness'. ULMA Saml. Åke Campbell, subnr. 203: Seán Ó Súilleabháin to Campbell, dated 6.8.1935.

28 S. Ó Catháin 1989, pp. 51–54.

29 Ó Murchadha 1941, pp. 13–14.

By evening he had transcribed three cylinders. He says Ó Duilearga was very satisfied with him, but he himself was 'tired and agitated', and had '[a] pain in [his] limbs from the erratic ('mí-chomhthromúil') transcription' and 'the bellowing of the horn in [his] ears'. He says he did not sleep a wink that night. The following day Ó Duilearga requested him to collect stories on his own with the Ediphone. That 'would complete the instruction he needed'. From then on he would be on his own, and he would have to get accustomed to the work 'without further guidance'. The choice of narrator was, however, unfortunate: a rapid speaker who would often go astray due to deteriorating faculties. To make matters worse, the narrator 'would forget to keep the horn close his mouth' so that Ó Murchadha used have to lay a steadying hand on it. The narrator filled a dozen cylinders on this occasion. Ó Murchadha says that he 'paid dearly for those dozen cylinders' when transcribing them later: as a result of his inexperience, this task 'tortured' and gave him 'grey hairs'.

After three days, Ó Duilearga returned to Dublin, leaving him, as Ó Murchadha says: 'ploughing away and struggling with the Ediphone and the cylinders.' For Tadhg Ó Murchadha transcription was the most difficult part of the work, especially when the speaker spoke unclearly. He says that it was 'a heroic feat' to transcribe three cylinders of the above material in a day. He was often up until two o'clock in the morning 'with the horn to my ear' endeavouring 'to make sense of the screeching of the cylinders', and he lost many a night's sleep as a result of being over-stressed by the work. This almost broke his resolve, and he says that he often thought of resigning, but his great respect for the Director kept him going.[30]

In Tadhg Ó Murchadha's case, as was to prove the case with other collectors, the more experience of collecting and transcribing he got as time went on, the easier the work became. Nonetheless, the work of the collector was never an easy one, and getting used to certain aspects of the work could be a slow process. In a diary entry of Ó Murchadha's for November 30th, 1935, almost three months after taking up employment with the Commission, he says:

> I am becoming fed up with this work [transcription]. It is drudgery ('obair chapaill') and the slightest excuse now would make me pack it in entirely for I fear it will break my health before I am done with it.[31]

Liam Mac Coisdeala had been collecting in the Carna region for six or seven years prior to his appointment as full-time collector for the Commission. Nevertheless, using the Ediphone machine was a new experience for him, as it had been for Tadhg Ó Murchadha, and it took time to get used to it.[32] Unlike Tadhg Ó Murchadha, he seems to have been left to his own devices, with unfortunate, unforeseen consequences. The machine he was given was defective with the result that it was next to impossible to make out what

30 Ibid., pp. 18–20 (trans.).
31 Eibhlín Nic Craith (MA thesis) p. 25 (trans).
32 UCDNFC 385: pp. 3–5.

the narrator was saying. Not being familiar with this apparatus, he did not realise what was the matter and tried to persevere. In the end his 'faith in this wonderful machine had vanished', and he wrote to Ó Duilearga, who, mesmerised, came down to Carna to investigate the matter. Soon a new machine was sent to him.[33]

Seosamh Ó Dálaigh did not have any experience collecting folklore. His father, Seán Ó Dálaigh, had, however, been collecting the folklore and traditions of his native Dún Chaoin in a private capacity since the late nineteenth century, so he was familiar with the idea of collecting folklore.[34] Moreover, his native parish was rich in traditions, and he had heard a great deal of lore from his mother. He met Ó Duilearga by chance. It was not his interest in folklore as such that was instrumental in setting him on the road to becoming a collector, but rather another interest of his, namely machines. Ó Dálaigh had a fascination for all sorts of machines, and when in May 1936 he heard that a stranger had come to his native parish and was recording people with an unusual machine his interest was aroused. He had been asked by people in Com Dhineoil, the townland where Ó Duilearga was recording, to look at a malfunctioning sewing machine, so he had 'an excuse' to go over and observe what the stranger was doing. The stranger was Séamus Ó Duilearga, who was even then, though a young man, Ó Dálaigh notes, grey-haired. As it happened, Ó Duilearga was staying with relatives of Ó Dálaigh's and he enquired of his hosts if there would be anyone in the area who could transcribe what he had been collecting in Com Dhineoil. Ó Dálaigh, on being informed of this, contacted Ó Duilearga and was instructed by him how to operate the Ediphone. He agreed to transcribe the tales, and on his return to Dublin, Ó Duilearga forwarded him writing materials. Ó Dálaigh spent five weeks transcribing this material, and did so sufficiently well for Ó Duilearga to offer him a job in July. Ó Dálaigh had till then had very erratic employment as a National School teacher and was unemployed at the time. However, at the same time as this offer came from Séamus Ó Duilearga, he got the offer of a teaching post in Dublin. He says:

> I was in between two minds, but I liked the machine, I liked the work and I said I'd take the collecting, at any rate, and that I would not be tied down with a school or anything. But I chose collecting. I don't know whether it was my making or my unmaking...[35]

It would appear Ó Duilearga was not able to spend much time tutoring Seosamh Ó Dálaigh in the skills required of a folklore collector. However, Ó Dálaigh's skill with machines may have made his task somewhat easier. Initially, as we have seen, he put Ó Dálaigh to transcribing tales he himself had collected. However, when the time came for Ó Dálaigh to begin collecting,

---

33 Mac Coisdeala 1982, p. 31.
34 Ó Dúbhshláine 2000, passim.
35 UCCRNG Tyers/Ó Dálaigh, tapescript 1, pp. 1–2 (trans.). See also D/F S 101/0011/34: 'Particulars of Persons Recommended for the Posts as Whole-Time Collectors on the Staff of the IFC', date-stamped 9.7.1936.

he had the benefit of a number of lists of tales that Ó Duilearga had made from informants in the area. Fortunately, for Ó Dálaigh, the first narrator he remembers recording from was a very clear speaker and transcribing from his speech posed no problem.[36]

Ó Duilearga or Seán Ó Súilleabháin might help start off a collector by quizzing an informant in their presence to elicit, in particular, the extent of the informant's repertoire of folktales. Ó Súilleabháin tells us how in the presence of Proinnsias de Búrca he visited an old storyteller after Mass:

> We took him to the taproom of a pub and there I took out Stith Thompson's *The Types of the Folktale* and started with Aarne-Thompson No. 1. I started questioning the old man and his replies were of three kinds. He would say, "I never heard that story," or he would say, "I heard that story but can't tell it," or, number three, he would say, "I have heard that story." And we had a break for lunch at about one o'clock for an hour, and by six o'clock that evening I had listed 250 tales which the man was able to tell. Then we had to stop. [37]

Once a collector became familiar with this procedure of assessing an informant's repertoire, he did this himself as a matter of course.

There is no doubt that full-time collectors, especially those who stayed many years with the Commission, were a very dedicated lot. The pay was poor and the work was arduous. Not only had they to endure hardship, for instance, in travelling to and from their informants or potential informants, their journeys could sometimes be in vain as the informant 'might not be at home, or sick, or perhaps reluctant to narrate anything on that particular day' At other times, the collector 'might be without a bed to sleep in' far away from home. On a number of occasions, in isolated places, Tadhg Ó Murchadha had to share a bed with an informant (male it goes without saying) as there was only one bed in the house.[38] Although the collectors' lot, in certain respects, improved with the passage of time, as they gained in experience and as conditions of employment improved, the pay was always inadequate, and the work never easy.

Collectors were given a trial period, and if their work was found to be satisfactory at the end of that time, they were appointed as full-time collectors. Judging how satisfactory a collector was seems to have depended a good deal on his transcriptions of material, and, of course, the amount of material he was able to collect and transcribe. According as a 'trainee' collector sent in his transcriptions (copybooks) to Head Office, they were compared with the Ediphone cylinders either by the Director or the Registrar/Archivist, or sometimes the Office Manager. This was time-consuming but necessary, as only in this way was it possible to see, among other things, if the transcriptions were faithful and the orthography illustrative of the dialect. Head Office corresponded with collectors to effect any changes in their transcription or

---

36 UCCRNG Tyers/ÓDálaigh, tapescript 2, pp. 5–6.
37 Stith Thompson 1976, p. 4.
38 Eibhlín Nic Craith (MA thesis), p. 34.

collecting methods they thought necessary. In some cases it took collectors some time to learn how to transcribe material exactly as Head Office wanted it transcribed. For collectors, already under a great deal of pressure, a letter of admonishment from Head Office might push them very near the brink. In early December 1935, Tadhg Ó Murchadha got such a letter. He records in his diary:

> Its contents did not agree with me very much. It seems they do not appreciate what I am doing. My plight is not dissimilar to the workman of old whose work was never praised and despite him doing his best nobody appreciated him.[39]

The exact nature of Head Office's complaint is not clear, but given Ó Murchadha's frustration with the transcription of material it may have involved the amount of material he was producing or the quality of the transcription.[40] Ó Murchadha replied the following day. Of his reply he says, it was 'rather bitter'('searbh'), adding 'as truth usually is.'[41] However his reply was received at Head Office, it was late March 1936 before anything was done about it. He says in a diary entry:

> I got a telegraph from the office of the Commission on Monday morning to go up to Dublin this week, that the Director wished to see me ... Both the Director and the Archivist were in the office when I arrived and made me very welcome. They showed me my own work and the work of my fellow collectors and indeed I was exceptionally proud when I saw the fine volumes of folklore bound in leather, and I thought to myself that if I got a little hardship from the collecting and transcribing that went with the work, it was all worth it.'

Ó Murchadha came to Dublin with his wife Máire. Not only was he well received at Head Office, but he and his wife were invited to the Director's home where they were entertained by Ó Duilearga, his wife, Maud, and his mother, Mary. Both were very impressed by the hospitality extended to them on this occasion, and by the further kind gesture of being driven to the railway station by Ó Duilearga and his wife at the end of the week in order to get the train back to Kerry.[42]

39 Ibid., p. 25 (trans.) Tadhg Ó Murchadha was not the only full-time collector to receive a warning of this sort. Moreover, a number of full-time collectors were dismissed when their work was considered not to be satisfactory – others for a time lived under the threat of dismissal.
40 See D/T 15548A: 'Gearr-Thuar./1936–37', p. 2.
41 Eibhlín Nic Craith (MA thesis), p. 26.
42 Quoted in ibid., p. 26.

Special and Part-time Collectors

In addition to employing full-time collectors, the Commission for most of the 1950's and into the early 1960's also employed a number of 'special collectors'. Unlike part-time collectors, who were paid according to the amount they collected, special collectors were given a fixed salary. Three of them were retired schoolteachers, Pádraig Ó Móghráin, Seán Ó Dubhda, and Micheál Mac Énrí. Proinnsias de Búrca, who had earlier been a full-time collector, was also taken on as a special collector. Special collectors were on what amounted to approximately a half salary. They were not expected, it would appear, to do the same amount of work as full-time collectors, but their duties were similar to those of the latter. In the case of retired schoolteachers, their pension would have supplemented their Commission salary. Proinnsias de Búrca was in a somewhat different position. He was holding down a part-time job with the Land Commission in addition to being a special collector for the Irish Folklore Commission. In 1964 he was reappointed full-time collector, although not a young man any longer. The distinction between special collector and full-time collector is not so clear, and it would appear they were often regarded as full-time collectors. Indeed Pádraig Ó Móghráin, who was the first such collector to be appointed in July 1951, is initially described in Ó Duilearga's reports to the Government as a full-time collector.[43] Only when he was joined by two other such collectors in 1953–1954 is the designation 'special collector' used in these reports.

From the very beginning the Commission employed, in addition to its team of full-time collectors, numerous part-time collectors.[44] Some of these had already collected part-time for the Irish Folklore Institute, but many were new and were recruited by means of various channels. In the early years of the Commission, up until the outbreak of the Second World War, the material sent in by part-time collectors exceeded that amassed by the full-time collectors. During the War years, however, the services of most part-time collectors had to be dispensed with as an economy measure.

Speaking in 1950 about the Commission's part-time collectors, Seán Ó Súilleabháin had this to say:

> In addition to the full-time collectors we have about fifty part-time collectors. These are people who are occupied daily at their ordinary jobs. They may be teachers, workers for our farmers in the country, clerks in shops, young secondary students in school, or anything of that kind. We have these people collect in both English-speaking and Irish-speaking districts in their spare time. Again we supply them with standard

---

43   See, e.g. D/T S 15548B: 'Gearr-Thuar./1951–52', p. 2. It has also to be noted that when Ó Duilearga proposed the appointment of Proinnsias de Búrca as special collector, he suggested that, given his less than arduous duties as paymaster for the Land Commission, he might be able to devote as much as 99% of his time to collecting folklore. ED [FL 10]: 'IFC. Fin. Sub-Com./Min. 85th Meeting, 9.12.1952', par. 648. For Land Commission, see Sammon 1997.

44   Appendix 4 contains a list of some significant part-time collectors.

notebooks and with the slips [see below] I spoke of and pay them at the rate of about five pounds for a notebook of ninety-six pages. This depends of course upon the value of the material and the manner, good or bad, in which it is done. We do not have the same control over these part-time collectors, who work very much as they please, as we have over the full-time people. But in general I may say that these part-time collectors have been excellent, because we do our best to pick them carefully.[45]

Part-time collectors at most received a minimum of training. When a person interested in doing part-time collecting contacted the Commission, they were supplied with a 'mimeographed list' known as 'items for the collector' – to supply them with copies of Ó Súilleabháin's *A Handbook of Irish Folklore* (see below) would have been too expensive. This list covered 'the main heads and subheads of the whole field of folklore.' They were also supplied with copybooks, 'some gummed slips' for recording personal data on informants, and a letter containing instructions. On receipt of a collection of folklore from such a collector for the first time, its value was assessed at Head Office, as well as the potential of the collector. If such a collector looked 'very promising', Seán Ó Súilleabháin informed the Midcentury Folklore Conference in Indiana: 'we bring him to Dublin to the archives and pay his expenses for a few days', and '[i]f he is willing and able to go on with part-time collecting we instruct him in the details of field work, and if he is especially good we give him an Ediphone machine and arrange for him to work for the next six months at a regular salary.[46] It is unlikely that very many of the Commission's part-time collectors were ever brought to Head Office for extra training of this sort. Ó Súilleabháin is, most likely, talking about the ideal rather than the reality. Apart from anything else, the Commission did not have the resources nor the manpower to bring part-time collectors to Head Office on a regular basis, nor to supply more than a few of them with Ediphone machines.

Ó Súilleabháin's mention of a 'regular salary' being paid to part-time collectors for a limited period probably refers to 'payment for special short-time surveys carried out by competent collectors, who can devote periods of varying length to the work.' In a memorandum written in 1945, Ó Duilearga lists under this type of work the collecting done by Tomás de Bhaldraithe in east Galway and Michael J. Murphy in the Mourne Mountains and the Glens of Antrim in the early 1940's; the ethnological surveys done by the Swedes Åke Campbell and Albert Nilsson in the 1930's; as well a house-type survey done by architectural students of UCD some ten years later.[47] The employment of the artist Simon Coleman for two periods in the 1950's[48] to accompany collectors in the field and make illustrations of objects pertaining

---

45 Thompson 1976 [1953], p. 9.
46 Ibid., pp. 69–70.
47 D/T S 6916B: 'Memorandum on the IFC with Recommendations for its Development and Extension', p. 35.
48 D/T S 16378A: 'Gearr-Thuar./ 1958-59', p. 5. Coleman kept a diary of his work for the Commission.

to material culture, would also appear to come under the above category of 'special short-time survey'.

There were some part-time collectors who collected a great deal, and contributed material regularly over a long period of time, but many collected very little or only sporadically. Some such collectors may have been discouraged from collecting further as the Commission may not have been satisfied with their work. In the case of some secondary school pupils, mentioned above, part-time collecting was only a stopgap activity. As Ó Súilleabháin explains:

> Then we get a number of second-rate school students who are at loose ends and who are finishing their secondary school education. They have nothing else to do and they may not be able to go to the university. They may not yet have a job in a shop or in an office and they may not yet have reservations for the United States. So we take them in, and I must say they do work out very well. Their chief value to us is that a great many of them come from the Gaelic-speaking districts of Ireland which are crucial places for us, and some of them from English-speaking parts of Ireland where we can never send a full-time collector.[49]

Despite what Ó Súilleabháin implies, it is unlikely that very many young people from Irish-speaking districts had the benefit of a secondary education at this time. There is no doubt, however, that many young people in their mid to late teens, be they from Irish- or English-speaking districts, were at a loose end, with few prospects of employment in Ireland.[50] Thus, there were limitations on how long the Commission could keep certain part-time collectors, even when they were found to be satisfactory, but there were other limitations as well. Ó Súilleabháin himself notes a particular limitation of 'amateur collectors'. Speaking of the Commission's questionnaire correspondents, many of whom would also have collected part-time, he says:

> We bring them to the archives for three or four days and take them in detail through the catalogue. We get them to read the works of other collectors and in that way try to broaden their interests. We usually find that is the difficulty because amateur collectors are ordinarily interested in just four or five different types of things. They may be interested in the storyteller, the song, the proverb, and the riddle, but not at all in social history.[51]

The Commission, by this time at any rate, was very interested in social history as the traditional way of life was changing 'almost overnight' and Ó Súilleabháin says they were doing their utmost 'to encourage our amateur

49 Thompson 1976 [1953], p. 70.
50 It should be noted that most young people in the post-War period emigrated to Britain rather than to America.
51 Thompson 1976 [1953], p. 70.

collectors to get all they can about the social history and cultural background of the whole district.'[52]

There is no doubt that part-time collectors contributed a great deal of valuable material to the Commission. It would appear, however, that Ó Duilearga saw them as somewhat of a 'second-best' option. If resources had allowed, he would probably have employed mainly full-time collectors. In a letter to the Dept. of Education a year after the end of the Second World War, he wrote:

> Part-time collection is now almost nonexistent because there are not sufficient funds to pay for it. This valuable means of recording folklore could be made to compensate in some degree for the absence of full-time collectors in certain districts (including the whole of Connacht) and to secure the recordings of traditions in districts where we can never hope to send a full-time collector.[53]

Equipment of collectors

By far the most important piece of equipment supplied to the full-time collectors was the Ediphone, which came to be seen as the characteristic tool of their trade. Although it had not been designed for field work as such, it was, in some respects, ideal for use in the field, as it worked on a spring mechanism and required no power source. A wax cylinder (c.15–18 cm in length and 5–7.5 cm in circumference) was attached to a revolving shaft. Above the cylinder was a needle which moved from left to right as the shaft and cylinder revolved. The speaker would speak into a horn-shaped tube and to listen to the recording one had to put this tube to one's ear. Nevertheless, the Ediphone had many disadvantages as a recording apparatus. It was cumbersome to transport, different models weighing anything from 20 to 25 kilos. Moreover, cylinders had to be changed frequently, especially when recording long tales as only something in the region of 800 to 900 words would fit on a cylinder, depending on how fast or slow the speaker spoke. Having to change cylinders in this way was not just bothersome for the collector, it also interrupted the flow of speech. Seosamh Ó Dálaigh says that it interfered greatly with the 'continuity of the tale', and forced the collector to remember where the narrator stopped, as he or she, depending on his or her age or alertness, might not necessarily remember.[54] Moreover, Ediphone recordings were often of poor sound quality. Apart from any indistinctness in the speech of informants, the quality of the recording itself often gave rise to further difficulties in clarifying at times what exactly was said. For this reason, collectors were encouraged to leave a space blank when transcribing material if they did not understand a particular word, and to consult the informant again.[55]

---

52   Ibid., p. 70.
53   D/F S 101/0011/34: Ó Duilearga to Sec. Dept. of Educ., dated 30.5.1946.
54   UCCRNG Tyers/Ó Dálaigh, tapescript 1, pp. 2, 3, and 7 (trans.).
55   S. Ó Catháin 1989, p. 59.

Every collector was also given a regular supply of Ediphone cylinders. To cut down on costs most cylinders were pared and rewaxed after they had been transcribed and returned to Dublin. A representative number were, however, kept to be transferred later to gramophone discs when the opportunity would arise. It is interesting to note that Seosamh Ó Dálaigh says that many informants in the early days, at least, did not realise that their recordings were not being preserved in acoustic format for posterity.[56] But although there were many disadvantages in using the Ediphone, there were many more advantages, not least the interest shown in these machines by informants, their families and neighbours. Tadhg Ó Murchadha says that the Ediphone was an enticement in itself to get narrators to divulge their lore. They loved to hear their own voice and they were particularly pleased when being recorded from in this manner if an audience was present, which often was the case.[57]

The collectors, as mentioned above, were also supplied from Head Office with 'standard notebooks' (approx. 30 cm by 23 cm) as well as smaller notebooks to record diary entries, and other kinds of data. In addition, they were supplied with pens and ink. Material from the Ediphone cylinders was transcribed into the large notebooks, as was lore collected by means of dictation, or by some other method. Full-time collectors were also provided with gummed slips to record certain contextual and biographical information. At the 'head of each tale' or other item of lore the collector would paste one of these slips with the appropriate data. The printed text on these slips is in Irish, but they would be completed in Irish or English depending on which language the material was in. In addition to the name and address of the collector, the name, age and address of the informant, date of recording, and place of birth were noted, as well as from whom a particular item of tradition was originally heard.[58]

Collectors were also supplied with six-inch Ordnance Survey maps to help them chart the progress of their work. As Seán Ó Súilleabháin puts it: 'for each district they will put down a dot or a cross pointing out the glens, the valleys, and so on, which they have covered.' In this way it was possible in the course of time to see 'what areas are still to be tapped' in a particular district.[59]

On his trip to Germany in 1936, Ó Duilearga bought a Rolleiflex camera for the Commission at a bargain price.[60] However, it was not possible for the Commission to equip all its collectors with cameras in the early years. In a report Ó Duilearga sent to de Valera in late 1946, it is stated: 'the Commission has at present only one small general-purpose camera, somewhat out of date,

---

56 UCCRNG Tyers/Ó Dálaigh, tapescript 2, p. 3. Ó Dálaigh also says that narrators did not always recognise their own voices. Some people would say, on hearing what they had recorded played back to them: 'He is absolutely right!' – imagining somebody else was talking. Ibid, tapescript 4, pp. 7–8 (trans.).
57 Ó Murchadha 1941, p. 26.
58 Stith Thompson 1976 [1953], p. 6.
59 Ibid., p. 7.
60 ED [FL 9]: 'IFC. Fin. Sub-Com./Min. 10th Meeting, 18.3.1937', par. 93.

and one 16-mm camera.' Speaking of the lack of photographic equipment, as well as the lack of any modern sound-recording apparatus, the report says: 'This lack of essential equipment has often been politely commented on by visitors from abroad, unfamiliar with the conditions under which we are endeavouring to work, with some credit to the Staff.'[61]

Modes of transport

Even when working in their own areas, or from a local base, collectors often needed some sort of motorised transport in order to move their heavy recording apparatus from place to place. Without motorised transport of their own, collectors had to make do with the help of friends and neighbours in their own areas to transport them and their heavy equipment.[62] There was, however, a limit to the extent collectors could avail of such services, be they gratis or for hire. Once collectors moved outside their own localities in search of informants, transport became more of a problem. Some collectors initially had to use bicycles to get from place to place. However, transporting the cumbersome and heavy Ediphone by bicycle was difficult. In time, Tadhg Ó Murchadha solved this problem by developing a special carrier for his bicycle to transport the Ediphone (see below). Ó Murchadha would appear to have used a bicycle for most of his long career as a collector for the Commission.

The salary of most of the full-time collectors initially employed by the Commission was not sufficient for them to purchase and maintain a car, and this greatly affected their mobility. By May 1937 only two of the collectors had cars, Liam Mac Coisdeala and Nioclás Breatnach. Both these men were in receipt of a higher salary than their colleagues, apart from Tadhg Ó Murchadha, who also was on a higher salary. Of course, this problem could have been solved by letting some of the collectors go and employing others for the new localities to be worked, but Ó Duilearga naturally enough was loath to resort to such a measure.[63] After much rankling with the Dept. of Finance, the salaries of three collectors were increased to enable them to purchase cars: these were Seosamh Ó Dálaigh, Proinnsias de Búrca, and Seán Ó hEochaidh.[64] During the War, however, collectors were grounded due to lack of petrol and again had to resort to bicycles. This very much restricted the movement of collectors. To facilitate collecting during the latter part of the War, Seosamh Ó Dálaigh had the use of two Ediphone machines: one he left at home for transcription work, and the other he would leave in the home of his informant.[65] The cessation of hostilities in May 1945 did not mean that every collector could once again afford to run a car. The cost of running a

---

61 D/T S 6916B: 'The Irish Folklore Commission', unpaginated, section 4 (4), cov. letter. dated 11.11.1946, .
62 D/T S 15548A: 'Gearr-Thuar./1936-37', p. [3].
63 D/F S 101/0011/34: Ó Duilearga to Sec. Dept. of Educ., dated 24.6.1937.
64 D/T S 15548A: 'Gearr-Thuar./1937-38', p. [1].
65 UCCRNG Tyers/Ó Dálaigh, tapescript 1, pp. 7–8.

car had increased, while the collectors' salaries were still at prewar levels. The granting of travelling expenses to collectors in March 1947, on top of a weekly 'Emergency bonus' conceded the previous April (see below), made it possible for collectors to again contemplate maintaining a car. It should be noted that Tadhg Ó Murchadha, although, as stated above, one of the three initial full-time collectors on a higher salary, was content with a bicycle until late 1951.[66] In contrast, in the early 1950's, Michael J. Murphy had to made do with a bicycle to travel around the glens in north Antrim, out of necessity rather than choice. As he had only been in the employment of the Commission a number of years, and had a young family, his salary, and the demands made on it, most likely meant that the purchase of a car was beyond his means. In order to come to his aid, the Finance Sub-Committee proposed purchasing a secondhand car to be lent him. In the event, however, difficulties arose with the custom officials of Northern Ireland and when it became apparent that Murphy would only be allowed to use this car in the Republic, it was given instead to Ciarán Bairéad, appointed full-time collector some two years earlier, to enable him to move further afield from his home base.[67] Michael J. Murphy had to continue to make do with a bicycle for many years, but in 1957 the Commission purchased an autocycle for his use.[68]

Collecting and working methods

To be a full-time collector for the Irish Folklore Commission was to be on call all the time. For the Commission's collectors, like priests, there was no such thing as a five-, or rather a five-and-half-day week, as was the norm in many jobs at the time. Collectors had to fill in a weekly schedule of work (i.e. a set form/sheet) and send it to Head Office - Sunday being 'marked as well as the six other days.' This does not mean, of course, that they were working around the clock without a break, but of necessity they had to work long and very unsocial hours, both when collecting and transcribing. When a collector actually collected was more often than not dictated by his informants. Seosamh Ó Dálaigh preferred to do his collecting in the evening or at nighttime. The morning, he says, was not a good time to collect, as many old people, in particular, might not get up until midday or so. Moreover, for the collector to go too early to a house 'would disturb the household'. Ó Dálaigh also says that Sunday evening was a good evening for collecting, as were 'wet days or holidays' if an informant was old.[69]

The decision to have collectors work in their own areas to begin with avoided lots of problems which might have compounded the work of

66 Dorson 1953, p. 20.
67 ED [FL 10]: 'IFC. Fin. Sub-Com./Min. 84th Meeting, 29.10.1952', par. 638 and 'IFC. Fin. Sub-Com./Min. 87th Meeting, 11.6.1953', par. 660. Proinnsias de Búrca when appointed a special collector in 1953 was also provided with a second-hand car by the Commission. ED [FL 10]: 'IFC. Fin. Sub-Com./Min. 55th Meeting, 9.12.1952', par. 648.
68 ED FL 2: 'IFC. Fin. Sub-Com./Min. 103rd Meeting, 13.6.1957', par. 765.
69 UCCRNG Tyers/Ó Dálaigh, tapescript 1, p. 4 (trans).

apprentice collectors. Not only was it an advantage for a collector starting off to be from the area to be covered, insofar as they would know certain bearers of tradition or could elicit others without too much bother, but being steeped in local tradition, as many of them were, was an added advantage. However, when they moved outside their own areas, they were at more of a disadvantage. Seosamh Ó Dálaigh, speaking many years later, said that although he perhaps rarely was wont to give Séamus Ó Duilearga credit, he must give him credit for having collectors work in areas where they knew the dialect. When he began collecting at first, although a native speaker of Irish and from the area, he soon realised that there was much he did not know about his own dialect. Ó Dálaigh also felt that it was very important that the same person who collected the material transcribe it.[70] This, of course, was set procedure for the Commission's collectors, until the early nineteen sixties at any rate (see Chapter V/3 below).

Although collecting was usually done indoors and in the evening, this was not always the case. Collecting was sometimes done in the open air during daytime. Tadhg Ó Murchadha says that he would set up the Ediphone wherever was most convenient, 'depending on where the storyteller was' when he came upon them, and depending on the weather. He would often put it up 'on the ditch [i.e. in Ireland an earthen bank or stone wall], by the roadside or inside in the middle of a meadow if the old man or woman happened to be saving hay.' Ó Murchadha adopted the same procedure when collecting without the Ediphone: 'Wherever I would meet the storyteller, by the roadside or beside a ditch, I only had to take out my book, to rest my back against the ditch and concentrate on transcribing from the old man.'[71]

Initially Head Office would send collectors lists of questions ('questionnaires') to aid them in their work, but in 1937, Seán Ó Súilleabháin produced his *Láimhleabhar Béaloideasa*, a 130-page guide to Irish folklore. This was followed in 1942 by *A Handbook of Irish Folklore* (699 pages) by the same author. Both these works were based on the Uppsala system of archiving folk material. The idea was that collectors should work through it chapter by chapter.[72] Copies of the *Handbook* for use by the Commission's collectors were divided and bound into several volumes in order to be able to fit into the collector's pocket while in the field. With some exceptional narrators, such as Niall Ó Dubhthaigh (Gort an Choirce, Co. Donegal), the collector went through the entire (or almost the entire) *Handbook*.[73] Obviously, it was not possible to do this with every narrator. Not all narrators would have had such an encyclopedic knowledge, nor would pressures of work always have allowed collectors to exhaust the repertoire and lore of a particular narrator. Moreover, not all informants would have had the time to devote to working in such an intensive way with a collector. Although great emphasis was placed from the beginning on collecting folktales, it would be wrong to conclude

---

70 UCCRNG Tyers/Ó Dálaigh, tapescript 8, p. 7 and tapescript 4, pp. 6–7.
71 Ó Murchadha 1941, pp. 25–26.
72 Stith Thompson 1976 [1953], p. 5.
73 See Ó hEochaidh 1960. For a published corpus of a narrator (Mícheál Turraoin) who was questioned at length on the basis of Ó Súilleabháin's *Handbook*, see Verling 2007.

that folktales were collected at the expense of other genres. In 1950, Seán Ó Súilleabháin could say:

> We have concentrated our collecting in the Gaelic-speaking parts and in the partly Gaelic-speaking parts, because, as I said, it is there that the folk tales are found in the greatest measure. But we have not actually concentrated on folk tales; we are equally interested and perhaps more interested in the social history.[74]

Nevertheless, there is no doubt that the Commission tried to collect as many folktales as possible, particularly in the Gaeltacht districts, in order to further international folktale scholarship. Moreover, pressures of work may have induced some collectors to concentrate on collecting long folktales because of the ease involved, rather than eliciting shorter genres and more varied material.

The Ediphone was used to record longer items of lore such as folktales, but pen and paper were used for shorter items such as historical lore. This would seem to have been an economy measure, but was also dictated by the nature of the material. However, some informants did not like the Ediphone, and in such cases even longer items of tradition had to be dictated. The accomplished narrator Peig Sayers was one such person: the Ediphone used to frighten her. When collecting certain types of lore, it was necessary for the collector to ask a lot of questions. For this sort of work, pen and paper was much better than the Ediphone.[75] Nevertheless, collecting lore 'sentence by sentence' with pen and paper caused problems. One often had to stop the narrator and this could put them astray. Seosamh Ó Dálaigh says that sometimes the narrator might even correct the collector, changing their mind about what was already recorded or noted down, perhaps even censoring it.[76] This method of collecting demanded a great deal from both collector and narrator.

Initially the transcripts sent in by the full-time collectors, as already explained, were checked for accuracy against the forwarded Ediphone cylinders, but once Head Office felt that a particular collector had acquired the necessary skills he was given a freer rein. However, Séamus Ó Duilearga, and sometimes Seán Ó Súilleabháin, in the early years particularly, would regularly visit the collectors in the field. Such visits may partly have been intended to supervise the collectors, but more often than not their purpose was probably less supervisory and more advisory.

Keeping of diaries by collectors

Each of the Commission's full-time and special collectors was expected to keep a diary, but part-time collectors were not usually requested to do so. One of the few part-time collectors to keep a diary was Seán Mac

---

74 Stith Thompson 1976 [1953], p. 5.
75 UCCRNG Tyers/Ó Dálaigh, tapescript 1, p. 8 and tapescript 2, p. 2.
76 UCCRNG Tyers/Ó Dálaigh, tapescript 1, p. 8, and tapescript 2, p. 2.

Mathghamhna. Mac Mathghamhna had already done some collecting for the Folklore of Ireland Society/Irish Folklore Institute and on the setting up of the Commission was asked by Ó Duilearga to become a full-time collector. He declined the offer due to family commitments, and perhaps because of his age – he was 59. However, he did consent to become a part-time collector. Possibly because of the copious and informative correspondence he maintained with Head Office, in 1937, Ó Duilearga asked him to keep a diary, as he believed it would be of great value.[77]

Collectors were asked to record in their diaries certain kinds of contextual information about recording sessions and visits to narrators, but they were also expected to give an account of themselves when transcribing, and even it would appear during their free time. Seán Ó Súilleabháin says:

> Owing to the nature of the work, as you can see, the diaries would fall into two types. The days when he was writing at home he would just mention that in a couple of lines. But on the nights he went out to visit an old storyteller for the first time or do recordings, he might devote perhaps twenty or thirty pages of his diary to a description of the whole atmosphere of the house, how he went there, who gathered around, who were in the house, how he questioned the old man, what kind of person he was physically and otherwise, and tell how he got the tales recorded.[78]

The reality was often quite different. Collectors vary a great deal in how they filled in their diary. Some were better at writing descriptions than others, some were more verbose, some more terse. Some wrote as little as possible, while others were only restricted, it would appear, by the constraints of time. One reason for the sparseness of some accounts is probably that collectors often fell behind in their diary writing, although entries may not always indicate that such was the case. Moreover, the fact that collectors were expected to be on call seven days a week means that many matters incidental to their lives can be found in the diaries, although not necessarily directly connected with their work. Indeed, for some collectors their diaries were both personal and professional records. Seán Ó hEochaidh took his diary with him on a holiday to Scotland in the late 1940's and Ciarán Bairéad on a trip to Rome in the 1960's, both recording incidents of their journeys.[79]

Other notebooks

Seosamh Ó Dálaigh remembers having three or four kinds of notebooks in his pocket going around: one listing the numbers of the Ediphone cylinders and the name(s) of the speaker(s); another to note 'phrases and unusual words' in the dialect; and another in which the names of tales, etc., were recorded for future reference. The first of these was to facilitate transcription and the

---

77 See Ó Héalaí 2000, p. 100, and uí Ógáin 2000a, pp. 142.ff.
78 Stith Thompson 1976 [1953], p. 7.
79 UCDNFC: 1289 (Ó hEochaidh), 1723 and 1742 (Bairéad).

checking of transcriptions at Head Office: i.e. to be able to trace a particular cylinder or group of 'filled' cylinders to a particular narrator. The notebook containing the names of tales along with informants was not just for future reference, but also for referring back. As these notebooks were not sent on to Head Office as a matter of course, but remained in the possession of the collector, they served also as a useful guide for the collector regarding what he had already collected from a particular individual. It is not clear how consistently collectors noted unusual words in the dialect into special notebooks designated for this purpose, as these notebooks are difficult to trace in the Archive. It should be noted that their workload was heavy enough without burdening them with this additional and time-consuming duty. Seosamh Ó Dálaigh says that he lost his notebook containing dialect data. Seán Ó hEochaidh, on the other hand, published two collections of dialect words and phrases, based on his collections, although it is not clear if they are based on notebooks of the above sort.[80]

The workload of the collectors

Although collectors got used to transcribing from the Ediphone, it remained an arduous task. Over a year after his appointment we find Nioclás Breatnach complaining about the job of transcription. On January 13th, 1937 he wrote in his diary:

> Today was a terribly wet day, and I run off my feet ('ar mo cheithre chrobh') from transcribing. I will get no proper sleep until I have again this damn Ediphone within a house [i.e. working with an informant] rather than this transcribing.'[81]

For those who were highly motivated, it was of course a stimulating job, but it was nonetheless very exacting. Collectors were expected to collect a certain amount of material each month and to send it on to Head Office. As well as transcribing what they collected and keeping a diary of contextual information and of their movements, as mentioned already, they were also expected to fill in a weekly work sheet, giving a day-by-day account of their work. Being a full-time folklore collector was a full-time job in more than one sense. Seosamh Ó Dálaigh, complaining about the lack of instruction given him, says:

> I got little other advice but to collect as much as I could. But indeed they would find fault with you unless you had collected that amount in the month. You would be informed that no copybook had been received for a while from you, and perhaps that was the hardest month of all you had been working. And we had a paper [a worksheet] that had Sunday,

---

80   Tyers 1999, p. 30 and Ó hEochaidh 1955 and 1962–64, pp. 1–90.
81   UCDNFC 382, p. 2 (trans.).

Monday, Tuesday, Wednesday, Thursday, Friday, Saturday on it, and you had to write down the work you were doing on each of those days on it. There was no break, there was no rest, but the seven days of the week, and I would say twenty four hours of the day. It was full-time work , and you can be certain it was full-time because when we would not be out collecting we would be inside writing, and we only had around eighteen days' holiday in the year. We used get nothing extra for Saturdays or Sundays, and we never did get anything.[82]

Obviously, Ó Dálaigh is overstating the case somewhat. Although collectors had a very heavy workload and were, as noted above, in many cases restricted in how they organised their time (e.g. the evenings often had to be reserved for visiting and collecting), it would be wrong to imagine that there was no respite in their work. They had a good deal of freedom to organise their daylight hours. Seosamh Ó Dálaigh, always an early riser, used to start writing early, but would break from it when he would be 'cramped from all the writing' and take his hound and spent a few hours in the middle of the day hunting in the hills.[83] Nevertheless, there is no doubt that in the early years of the Commission, at least, collectors were overworked, and while Ó Dálaigh's above description may contain a degree of exaggeration, it is revealing of the harsh conditions collectors often had to work under. Not least among these harsh conditions was the fact that collectors were expected to work in all weathers: often having to head out into howling winds and pelting rain. In the winter of 1943/1944 Tomás de Búrca contracted tuberculosis after receiving a severe wetting while out collecting in Achill. This forced his retirement from the Commission the following May.[84]

The severe pressures the Commission's collectors worked under no doubt contributed to the huge mass of material eventually assembled, but there was a downside to this. For example, Seosamh Ó Dálaigh says that even though he might like to follow up a particular topic until he had collected all there was to know about it, pressures of work often meant that he had to leave it aside:

> But we were restrained in the way that we had to fill the books quickly and when only a residue would remain, I would be kept busy ('ag bailiú liom'), because you never worked harder than when you collected least, and the time you collected most [i.e. when collecting folktales] was when collecting proved easiest.[85]

---

82 Tyers 1999, pp. 21–22 (trans.).
83 UCCRNG Tyers/Ó Dálaigh, tapescript 1, p. 4 (trans.)
84 D/T S 15548B: 'Gearr-Thuar./1944–45', p. 1. De Búrca never fully recovered and was to die from tuberculosis in 1957 (information supplied me by Ríonach uí Ógáin). Moreover, he was by no means the only collector whose health was adversely affected as a result of the harsh conditions collectors had to endure.
85 UCCRNG Tyers/Ó Dálaigh, tapescript 4, p. 3 (trans.).

The sheer weight of the Ediphone was an enormous problem for Tadhg Ó Murchadha, as it was for other collectors before they got cars. Initially he used to tie the heavy machine to the crossbar of his bicycle and attach the cylinders to the rear carrier, while he pushed the bicycle to his destination. This was all right for short journeys, but he often had to go to remote homesteads and hamlets, difficult to access. Sometimes, homes were not even accessible by bicycle. On one occasion, for instance, Ó Murchadha had to be transported by boat across a lake with his equipment. Once on the other side he had to put the Ediphone on his back while carrying the box of cylinders in his hands and plod across a bog and stretches of shallow water to his destination. He left his equipment there for a few days, and when he went to retrieve it, taking an in-law with him this time, they had to carry this heavy equipment between them over very rugged terrain in the pitch darkness, with just a torch to guide them. On another occasion Ó Murchadha had to carry the Ediphone tied to his back over three miles of mountain terrain, while also carrying the box of cylinders in his hands.[86]

As time went on, however, he says, instead of the Ediphone being his 'master', he was becoming its 'master'. Eventually, tormented by the hardship involved in transporting this heavy equipment by bicycle while walking alongside, Ó Murchadha devised a special case and carrier for the Ediphone on the rear of his bicycle, and a smaller carrier attached to the front for cylinders. Riding a bicycle bearing such a weight took some getting used to and on his first attempt, he fell off two or three times. It was particularly difficult to mount because not only had he to throw his leg over the box containing the Ediphone, he had also to keep the bicycle, with its heavy load, upright at the same time. Although it took time to get accustomed to, this 'invention' greatly eased travel for him, but where the terrain was rough he had to dismount and shove his bicycle as before, sometimes having to take the Ediphone out of the carrier-box to transport it and the bicycle across ditches. Ó Murchadha says: 'there are few glens or mountain recesses in south Kerry, in west Beara and in west Clare' that he had not travelled with 'that oppressive weight.' Many of these journeys were long and arduous, amounting to twenty or thirty miles.[87]

There were other problems also encountered by collectors. Houses were cold and draughty. Eibhlín Nic Craith in her study of Tadhg Ó Murchadha draws attention to the cold conditions the work of transcription often took place in. Tadhg's feet were often like 'two blocks of ice' while he was transcribing cylinders.[88] Moreover, during the War years, when commodities such as oil for lamps and candles had to be rationed, the collector had often to transcribe his texts in badly-lit rooms.[89]

Even if in time the pressure on collectors to collect and transcribe a certain amount per month eased off, other pressures remained. Suitable accommodation in new areas, especially if a collector was accompanied

86   Ó Murchadha 1941, pp. 21–24.
87   Ibid., pp. 21 and 24 (trans.).
88   Eibhlín Nic Craith (MA thesis), p. 24.
89   See uí Ógáin 2000a, p. 150.

by his wife and family, could be difficult to find. In December 1949, Michael J. Murphy moved with his wife, Alice, and young family to the Sperrin Mountains in Co. Tyrone to begin collecting for the Irish Folklore Commission. He describes the scene that awaited them when they reached their rented accommodation, a house that had formerly contained a shop, but that had been uninhabited for years:

> We looked around the place. Though the shutters were still in place slits let in a fair light. The ravages of damp were everywhere. No one spoke. Two flakings as big as table-tops bulged on either side of the chimney. Others here and there had dropped off walls originally white-washed.
>
> The fireside was simple and familiar: a large smithy-made grate set in two hobs, with swinging iron crane and crooks. Twigs, debris and sheep's wool in the grate reminded me at once of a chimney blocked with heaven knows how many Jackdaws' nests.[90]

Seosamh Ó Dálaigh and his young wife Peig also had difficulty finding suitable accommodation in An Rinn, Co. Waterford, but they were lucky in being able to find temporary accommodation in the local Irish College while searching for a more permanent place to live. Eventually they managed to rent an old barracks, but having no transport they encountered difficulty getting it heated as they had no means of transporting turf and coal out from Dungarvan, the adjacent town.[91]

The wives of full-time collectors

I have not been able to ascertain how many of the Commission's full-time collectors were married. In the early years of the Commission some of them were not. This is not surprising considering that many of them were still young men at the time. Seán Ó hEochaidh married in 1943 at the age of thirty; Seán Ó Cróinín also in 1943, aged around twenty eight. Seosamh Ó Dálaigh was almost thirty six years of age when he married in 1944.[92] Liam Mac Meanman and Nioclás Breatnach would appear to have been unmarried while working for the Commission (1935–1937), as was Proinnsias Ó Ceallaigh, who spent three months with the Commission in 1936 before resigning for health reasons, as already mentioned. Michael J. Murphy, and it would appear Tadhg Ó Murchadha, were already married when taking up work with the Commission. Whether low salaries and unsocial hours played a part in any of the collectors' delaying marriage is difficult to determine.[93] However, it

90 Murphy 1974, p. 14.
91 Verling 1999, p. 14.
92 Breathnach and Ní Mhurchú (*Beathaisnéis 1983–2002*), p. 182; D. Ó Cróinín 1964 [1966], p. 10; and Verling 1999, p. 13.
93 Although Liam Mac Coisdeala's leave of absence from the Galway Vocational Education Committee had in any case come to an end by September 1939, he might have considered seeking an extension of his leave but for his desire to marry. ED FL 9: 'CBÉ. Miont. 18ú

should be noted that unsocial hours and working away from home at least in the case of one collector resulted in marriage. Seán Ó hEochaidh met the informant Micí Mac Gabhann in 1941 in Gort an Choirce, Co. Donegal; two and a half years later he married his daughter, Anna.[94]

I have mentioned above the difficulties experienced by collectors and their wives in acquiring suitable accommodation in a new locality. Of course, wives did not always accompany their husbands' when they worked away from home. They would have had to become accustomed to their husbands being away from home for relatively long periods, but even when working locally the nature of their husbands' work meant that they could be out many nights of the week recording and getting to know informants. It has to be said, however, that to be left alone in the evenings, often with children to look after, was not their lot alone. Many wives, both in rural and urban Ireland, would have been used to their husbands absenting themselves several nights of the week to go to 'rambling houses' (i.e. where people gathered to exchange news and lore) or to visit the local pub. Nevertheless, while numerous other women might suffer being left alone, possibly with young children, because of their husbands' lifestyle, in the case of the wives of the Commission's collectors, it was not lifestyle as such that kept them away from home during the evenings but the nature of their work. However, it would be wrong to presume that all the wives of folklore collectors were lonely and miserable as a result of their husbands' nighttime visiting. As none of them, most likely, kept a diary, or have left an account of their lives, we can only surmise how they spent their time while their husbands were away, but it is certain that often neighbours dropped in for a chat as was the custom in rural Ireland at the time.

In addition to unsocial hours, low salaries would have been a source of grievance for the wives of full-time collectors. Not least of these women's worries was the lack of any pension arrangement for their husbands, and, worse still, what their own fate would be if their husbands should die while still in the Commission's employment? However, little is known about how these women viewed their husbands' work and working conditions. I recall Seosamh Ó Dálaigh's wife, Peig Ní Chonchúir, being very critical of Séamus Ó Duilearga, and her negative views of the man may partly derive from the working conditions pertaining to her husband's job as well as her own experience of being left alone with a young family while her husband worked unsocial hours.[95]

However, while some of the full-time collectors' wives may have resented their husbands' being absent from home so much, some took an active part in their husband's work. Tadhg Ó Murchadha's wife, Máire Ní Ghearailt, used often accompany her husband when he went collecting.[96] Moreover, Michael J. Murphy's wife, Alice, actively cooperated with her husband in gathering information, particularly relating to sexual matters, from women

Cruinniú, 27.10.1939', par. 150.

94   Breathnach and Ní Mhurchú (*Beathaisnéis 1983-2002*), p. 182.
95   From many conversations I had with her.
96   Ó Loingsigh 1999, p. 224.

informants.[97] Jim Delaney's wife, Mary (May), also actively assisted her husband in his collecting work.[98] The wives of other collectors may also have helped their menfolk in their work in less obtrusive ways, for instance, suggesting possible (women) informants to them. This is a matter that would need further investigation.

Reception of collectors by the people

Jim Delaney, one of the Commission's full-time collectors, speaking about active bearers of tradition, has written:

> As soon as he begins work in the field, the collector of folklore realises how few are these active bearers, but he also becomes aware at the same time, that the sympathy and good will of the community towards them is also extended most generously to him and his work of perpetuating their traditions and stories. It is this active and generous sympathy for the collector that makes his work, not a task, but a joy and a delight.[99]

Delaney's experience is echoed in the writings of other collectors. It should be noted that he was working in English-speaking areas where Irish was for the most part a dim memory. In areas where Irish was still spoken, but receding, the presence of a collector seeking out material in Irish might possibly be a source of tension if negative attitudes towards Irish pertained in the community or in the households of certain narrators. In the main, from the evidence I have seen, it would appear that the general attitude to collectors was positive. However, initially a certain degree of suspicion may have pertained to the work of folklore collectors, especially in areas where they were not known. Collectors might be suspected of being officials of some kind or other, engaged in covert activity. The very nature of their work might also be difficult for some people to comprehend. This was probably less of a problem in some Irish-speaking areas that would have experienced a certain amount of folklore collecting by Gaelic Leaguers and others from the early twentieth century onwards, but in English-speaking areas the arrival of someone interested in old traditions might be a completely new experience, and cause a degree of bewilderment.[100]

In time, in many places, collectors became almost part of the fabric of society. Richard Dorson, writing of Tadhg Ó Murchadha, with whom he spent a few days in late 1951, says:

> The observer notices curiously how the rural families now take for granted the visits of the field collector. He has become an institution, like the

---

97 Murphy 1974, pp. 38–39.
98 See Ní Fhloinn 2001b and Almqvist 2001, p. 184.
99 Delaney 1982, p. 44.
100 e.g. Michael J. Murphy says that in the Mourne Mountains he became known as 'The Man Who Was Following the Fairies'. Murphy 1974, p. 16.

priest and postman, and receives a friendly welcome and often a high tea when he arrives. The old men respond eagerly to his coming, both from social pleasure and from a vague appreciation of the significance of the work.[101]

Narrators not only very often looked forward to visits from the collector, they could also be jealous of one another. Seosamh Ó Dálaigh tells how one day an informant came to him complaining that he had not come to collect from him for some time and 'that he supposed that he had finished with him because he had heard that a couple of stories narrated by Cáit Ruiséal, an old woman living next door to him in Dún Chaoin, had surpassed all other stories in excellence.' Ó Dálaigh had to go to him immediately although he had only ten Ediphone cylinders left, lest he take offence and refuse him in future.[102] Not only did many narrators look forward to the visits of collectors, such feelings were reciprocated. Collectors in many cases became very attached to their informants. Seosamh Ó Dálaigh in June 1945 was transferred out of his home area for a time to Co. Waterford. Before his departure he records in his diary his feelings about leaving all the informants he had worked with over the previous three years, when as a result of the scarcity of petrol during the War he had to travel the roads of west Kerry by bicycle. He speaks of narrators as being his 'lasting friends', and although he wishes them all a long life, he knows some of them will not be alive on his return.[103]

Mention has already been made of the fascination of people with the Ediphone, and that it helped collectors gain acceptance with narrators and communities. There were few radios or gramophones in rural Ireland at the time, especially in the Gaeltacht. But as Seosamh Ó Dálaigh reminds us, the Ediphone was 'more amazing still' than the radio or gramophone as 'it would record their own speech and they loved to listen to their own speech again, or their father's speech or whoever would be listening [*recte* talking].'[104]

However, the reception of collectors and their work can best be measured by the hospitality afforded them by informants and their families, and by the interest shown in the work of collection. Seosamh Ó Dálaigh says that not everyone was aware that he was collecting for the Irish Folklore Commission, that some thought he was doing it on his own account. However, most were pleased that their lore was being collected and were proud of what they knew of the tradition. Nonetheless, as we have seen above, storytellers could be very envious of each other, and Ó Dálaigh remarks that it was important never to let a storyteller know 'who was the best narrator you had yet encountered'.[105]

However, while *Märchen* and certain other narrative genres might be given willingly to the collector, the sharing of certain types of traditional

---

101 Dorson 1953, p. 21.
102 UCDNFC 362, pp. 10–11.
103 Quoted in Verling 1999, p. 6 (trans.). See also UCDNFC 1045, pp.163–164.
104 UCCRNG Tyers/Ó Dálaigh, tapescript 1, p. 6.
105 UCCRNG Tyers/Ó Dálaigh, tapescript 2, pp. 2–3. The fact that Ó Dálaigh's father, Seán, had collected folklore on his own initiative may have caused some to think that the son was also collecting of his own accord.

knowledge could be a more sensitive issue, requiring a greater degree of trust between informant and collector. Michael J. Murphy says of the task of the collector:

> He has to win the confidence of the people adroitly, and patiently be able to ask them to confess to a knowledge which, if breathed abroad, can bring down the wrath of friend and neighbour, of priest or parson – even policeman. He wants not just the *tales* people can remember and narrate but just as important the *details* of their lives and living as well, their very thoughts and attitudes to all kinds of human, social and religious concepts – and the same of their people's people as far back as human memory can reach.[106]

Not surprisingly, sometimes people refused to share their traditional knowledge and stories with collectors. On one occasion a woman informant, whom Seosamh Ó Dálaigh had already collected from the previous day, refused to cooperate any further. Word had come that her son had not got a place in the Preparatory Training College for teachers, although others in the locality had been successful. In a pique of anger she decided 'she would do nothing more for the country'.[107] Other times, people might refuse because they felt the collector was intruding on areas that did not concern them or because of some trait or other of their personality. Donncha Ó Cróinín, writing about his brother Seán Ó Cróinín, says that although he encountered his 'share of odd people over the years' in all but one case he was able to entice them to narrate their lore. The one person who refused him was generally considered in the locality to be churlish.[108] The fact that more people did not refuse to cooperate with the collectors is probably, to a large degree, to the great credit of the collectors themselves, many, if not all, of whom had, like Seán Ó Croinín, a way of handling people gently, and of coaxing them to give up their lore.

Seosamh Ó Dálaigh says that 'if anyone or anything deserves to be praised, in respect of the collecting, it is the people themselves, the narrators.' In addition to the informants themselves, he mentions the sacrifice of their families, 'who often had their work disturbed by the collector's visit, sacrificing the evening for his benefit.' Such visits were not a once-off occasion, but repeated again and again. Moreover, he says in this connection that not only did he give small presents to informants, he often received presents as well.[109]

Although the sources tell of the general acceptance of collectors, it stands to reason that the presence of the Commission's collector might at times have been considered intrusive. Carmel Quinlan notes it is difficult to ascertain what 'the informants thought of the collectors'. She quotes from an interview she had with the granddaughter of one of the Irish Folklore Commission's informants, Taidhgín Ó hUrdail, of west Cork:

106 Murphy 1974 p. 16.
107 UCCRNG Tyers/Ó Dálaigh, tapescript 3, pp. 4–5.
108 D. Ó Cróinín 1964, p. 4, (trans.).
109 UCCRNG Tyers/Ó Dalaigh, tapescript 4, pp. 8–9.

My grandfather would see them [IFC collector sometimes accompanied by Delargy himself] coming along the long winding road west of the house and sometimes wouldn't have time for them. He liked nothing more than to go fishing off the rocky shoreline nearby - he was an old man at this time - and on a day when he had this lined up for himself collectors would not be met with the usual fáilte ['welcome']. 'A Íosa Chríost táid ag teacht arís' [Jesus Christ they're coming again] he'd say to himself and he'd race for the shore or the hill. 'Tis hard to be telling stories when you haven't the time or the humour.[110]

Like Séamus Ó Duilearga, Taidhgín Ó hUrdail had a passion for fishing. His behaviour, as described above, should not, of course, be taken as evidence that he would have disapproved altogether of the collector's visits, but simply that at times such visits were inconvenient for him, as no doubt they were for many other informants as well. We too easily assume that because very many narrators and their families extended a warm welcome to the collectors that this was always the case. There is no doubt that the presence of the collector, particularly if his visits were frequent and sometimes at inconvenient times, might on occasion give rise to a certain amount of disgruntlement, particularly among family members of informants who had unfinished work to do. Negative feelings of this sort, however, may not always have been expressed, as the rules of rural hospitality would have demanded that they be suppressed. Nevertheless, there is little doubt that the welcome extended to collectors was, for the most part, genuine. In the rather dull world of rural Ireland in the 1930's and later, visits from one of the Commission's collectors, however inconvenient such visits might at times have been, would have been a source of news, and have helped relieve some of the drabness of everyday life.

110 Quinlan 1996, pp. 71–72.

2. The Schools Scheme 1937–1938

Origins of scheme

In the school year 1937–1938 a scheme to collect folklore by the agency of senior primary schoolchildren was implemented in the National Schools of the South of Ireland. The origins of this scheme are complex, involving both native and, possibly, foreign influences. It is not my intention to trace these origins below. It should be said, however, that although Finnish, Estonian, and Swedish models may have played a role, however tenuous, in the conception and execution of this scheme[111], its roots can be traced more directly to the proposal Énrí Ó Muirgheasa made to the Dept. of Education in 1923, namely 'that a special blank manuscript book be furnished to each [primary] school in the Saor Stát [Irish Free State], so that each teacher might collect and record therein the traditions and folk-lore of the neighbourhood' (see Chapter II/1 above). Although there were those in the Dept. of Education at the time who saw the potential of Ó Muirgheasa's proposal for using the National Schools under its control to collect folklore, the Dept. of Education would not act on this proposal until late 1933. The following spring a blank memorandum book, along with a pamphlet containing guidelines on what to collect were sent to all primary schools, (i.e. National Schools) in the Irish Free State. However, not enough planning went into this scheme. In particular, the goodwill of the teachers was not solicited sufficiently beforehand, and this, to a large extent, was the reason that the 1934 Schools Folklore Scheme produced very little by way of results. The Irish Folklore Commission inherited this scheme and tried to work it, but the results were not promising from its point of view. By October 1937 only sixty six completed memorandum copybooks had been returned.[112] This amounted, at most, to some 16,500 pages – not a huge amount of material in terms of what the Commission was collecting at the time, e.g. by means of its full-time collectors, nor was its geographical spread all that extensive.

The 1934 Schools Folklore Scheme belongs, in a sense, more to the history of the Irish Folklore Institute, or rather the Folklore of Ireland Society,

---

111 For possible foreign influences, see Briody forthcoming in *Béascna* 4.
112 ED [FL 9]: 'CBÉ. Miont. 10ú Cruinniú, 15.10.1937', par. 86(e).

260

and need not be dealt with further here.[113] Suffice it to say that when the Commission came to devise its own scheme for collecting folklore via the National Schools of the Irish Free State, Ó Duilearga did not repeat the mistakes of those who planned the earlier scheme by failing to prepare the ground well in advance. Not only would the 1937–38 Schools Scheme differ from that of 1934 in terms of the amount of forethought and preparation that went into it, it also differed radically from the earlier scheme in that it directly involved the schoolchildren in collecting as a matter of course, rather than primarily the teachers.

Preparing the ground

Séamus Ó Catháin and Caitlín Ní Sheighin attribute the success of the 1937–1938 Schools Scheme to 'the enthusiasm of two far-seeing, able men', Seán Ó Súilleabháin and Séamus Ó Duilearga, the scheme's instigators. They go on to say:

> It was they who convinced the authorities to accept the idea in the first place, and it was they who conducted the extensive publicity for the scheme, explaining it and re-explaining to the teachers of the country what was meant by folklore — and how to collect folklore — on Radio Éireann, in the newspapers, and in countless meetings of teachers and trade-unionists throughout the length and breadth of the country. The skills of both were not insignificant in putting their case to busy teachers, shrewd, hard-baked trade-unionists, or distrusting Civil Servants.[114]

Speaking about this scheme at the Midcentury International Folklore Conference in Indiana in 1950, Seán Ó Súilleabháin gives no indication that they encountered 'distrusting Civil Servants' when they initially sought support for this scheme: 'We interviewed the educational authorities in Dublin and found them very amenable to our suggestions.'[115] That they should have been reasonably amenable is not all that surprising. After all, the scheme being proposed to them was but an extension of the scheme they themselves had initiated in spring 1934. Moreover, the foreward to the booklet of instructions that was sent to schools participating in the new scheme reflects very much Dept. of Education policy at the time. It begins:

> The collection of the oral traditions of the Irish people is a work of national importance. It is but fitting that in our Primary Schools the senior pupils should be invited to participate in the task of rescuing from oblivion the traditions which, in spite of the vicissitudes of the historic Irish nation, have, century in, century out, been preserved with loving care by their ancestors. The task is an urgent one for in

113 For more on the background to this scheme, see Briody 2006.
114 Ó Catháin and Ní Sheighin 1987, pp. xviii-xix (trans.).
115 Stith Thompson 1976 [1953], p. 11.

our time most of this important national oral heritage will have passed away for ever.[116]

If there was mistrust in the Civil Service, one would expect to find it in the Dept. of Finance. Surprisingly enough, there is little evidence of any real opposition to the scheme from that quarter. The reason for this probably lies in the fact that it was not a hugely expensive scheme, as neither the teachers nor the pupils received any financial reward for the work undertaken. The costs involved had to cover, for the most part, materials and postage. The fact that some 5,400 large memorandum books[117] had already been sent out as part of the 1934 Schools Folklore Scheme also helped to reduce costs. The Dept. of Finance was, however, determined to ensure that the state's money was not wasted on this occasion.

Although thousands of manuscript (memorandum) books had been sent out to schools in 1934, more of these large notebooks were needed, as it was estimated that 'the smaller schools will supply at least two complete note-books and that the larger schools will supply from three to five note-books – depending on the efforts of the pupils and the amount of folklore and tradition extant in the school districts.' The Dept. of Education therefore proposed purchasing '7,200 additional note-books – one copy to be sent to each school in September next and an additional copy or copies to be sent to individual schools on request during the remainder of the current school year.'[118] While these proposals got a reasonably smooth passage in the hands of Finance officials, the Dept. of Finance, in approving the scheme, informed Education that no new manuscript books would, for the time being, be purchased, except in cases where this was absolutely necessary. For the moment, schools would have to make do with the manuscript books sent them in March 1934. Forever cautious where state expenditure was involved, Finance also proposed that: 'At a later stage, when representative collections have been received from the schools, the Commission should be asked for their considered views as to the working of the scheme and the value of the material collected.' When such an assessment was complete, the Dept. of Finance would reconsider 'the question of supplying additional note books.' In the meantime, a sum 'not exceeding £50' was to be sanctioned 'for the printing of a Booklet and Circular, and to an expenditure not exceeding £10 on the supply of note books to those schools from which the books issued under the previous scheme have been returned.'[119] Despite a certain degree of caution, the Dept. of Finance's rather benign attitude towards this scheme, from beginning to end, is in stark contrast to the negative response requests for more funding by the Commission itself often elicited from that department. Nevertheless, Finance's failure to sanction the immediate purchase of new

---

116 Quoted in Ó Giolláin 2000, p. 134.
117 D/F S 046/0037/33: P. J. Coveney to Stationery Office. dated 13.12.1933.
118 D/F S 046/0037/33: Ó Néill to Sec. Dept. of Fin., dated 29.7.1937, pp. [2–3]. The cost of purchasing these manuscript books, of printing a booklet of instructions in Irish and English and a circular, as well as postage, would amount to £308. Ibid.
119 D/F S 046/0037/33: Doolin to Sec. Dept. of Educ., dated 5.8.1937.

manuscript books for all schools, as we will see below, was to have an effect on the workings of the scheme.

Persuading the teachers and their trade union would appear to have been more of a problem. Ó Catháin and Ní Sheighin speak above of the need to persuade 'busy teachers' and 'astute shrewd, hard-baked trade-unionists' to participate in the scheme. The problem with teachers was not just that this scheme might add to their workload, as was the case with the earlier scheme of 1934, they were once again worried that taking on work of this sort might have implications when it came to the assessment of their teaching. Seán Ó Súilleabháin says:

> Then we had to win over the teachers. They have an organisation, the Irish National Teachers Organisation in Dublin. We interviewed their executive council and they too were very helpful. They were slightly suspicious of the scheme, because, as you know, in Ireland and perhaps everywhere else the school inspector is the bane of the teacher's life. So what we had to do was to try to get this scheme of collecting going on in the schools so that the inspectors would not find fault with the teachers, that the teachers would not suffer in any way as a result of this scheme. [120]

The Dept. of Education in consultation with the Irish National Teachers Organisation (INTO) agreed that inspectors would take cognisance of the fact that teachers were not in a position to affect the standard of the collecting work being done by the senior pupils, unlike composition in Irish and English, which it was to replace. They also recognised that some areas were richer in tradition than others, and in certain areas, although abundant in folklore, pupils might have difficulties collecting material as a result of indifference among the population at large.[121]

The Schools Scheme in order to be successful required that teachers be instructed in the task they were being asked to perform. To this end, Seán Ó Súilleabháin prepared a booklet of instructions in English, entitled *Irish Folklore and Tradition*, and a corresponding one in Irish, *Béaloideas Éireann*. Both booklets contained hundreds of questions and suggestions for eliciting information on a wide range of folkloristic and ethnological topics, arranged under fifty five separate headings.

It was decided that only children in 'fifth and sixth standards', i.e. from eleven to fourteen years of age, would be involved. The principal teacher in each school was in charge of working the scheme, and instruction was given to them alone. Seán Ó Súilleabháin says:

---

120 Stith Thompson 1976 [1953], pp. 10–11. There was perhaps another reason why certain National School teachers and INTO officials may have needed to be persuaded to participate in this scheme and convinced that it would not result in a lowering of educational standards. By the mid-1930's many primary schoolteachers were dissatisfied with the demands being made on them as a consequence of the state's gaelicisation policies. Believing that these policies were having a detrimental effect on many schoolchildren, and frustrated by the failure of the Dept. of Education to take action, they commissioned their own report on the effects of gaelicisation in the classroom. See Kelly 2002, pp. 48–49.

121 Ó Baoill 1992, p. xvii.

...when the booklets were issued to the schools with an official letter by the department, Mr. Delargy and I went around the country nearly every Saturday and Sunday speaking to the various local branches of the teachers. In that way we gave lectures to every teacher that was involved in the scheme. This would take the form of a talk by one of us and then questions by the teachers for an hour.[122]

Nevertheless, it is unlikely that Ó Súilleabháin and Ó Duilearga managed to meet with and instruct all teachers involved in the scheme. Neither did the Commission directly instruct schoolchildren on the task before them. Given the great numbers of children and schools involved this would not have been possible. Instruction of the children had to be left to the principal teachers.[123]

Operation of scheme

The scheme was designed to operate in the following manner:

During the period from September to June in the school year 1937–38, the time allotted to English Composition for pupils in fifth and higher standards in Galltacht [English-speaking] areas, the time allotted to Irish Composition for these pupils in Gaeltacht areas, and the time allotted to Irish and English Composition for pupils in Breac-Ghaeltacht areas [areas with residual Irish], shall, as part of the ordinary school work, be devoted to Folklore composition and the recording of stories and traditions collected by the pupils in their homes and districts.[124]

Each week the teacher would chose a particular heading from Ó Súilleabháin's booklet, reading out the questions under that heading and transcribing them on the blackboard. The children would copy these questions 'and then when they went home they would question their people or the neighbours' about these matters, writing down in their jotters the traditions or information they could obtain. On 'composition day' in school, they would write down in their copybooks 'in the form of a composition the customs, beliefs, and tales which they had collected.' Subsequently, the teacher would get 'the best children in the school, the best at writing and spelling, to transfer this material into the standard notebook which the department issued to each school.'[125] However, not everything collected by the children and written into their composition

---

122 Stith Thompson 1976 [1953], p. 63.
123 Care was also taken to familiarise Schools Inspectors with the operation of the scheme, and during winter 1937 and spring 1938 Ó Duilearga and Ó Súilleabháin continued to address meetings of teachers around the country. UCD Lib., Spec. Coll., Morris Papers 15. 2.27 and ED [FL 9]: 'CBÉ. Miont 13ú Cruinniú, 10.6.1938', par. 111(g).
124 D/F S 046/0037/33: Dept. of Education Circular (9/37), dated September 1937, par. 1 (sent to Managers and Teachers of National Schools).
125 Stith Thompson 1976 [1953], pp. 11 and 64.

copybooks was transferred to the official manuscript books. The circular that the Dept. of Education sent out to all schools in September 1937 stated that the teacher should make a selection of material from the pupils composition copybooks to be transferred to the official manuscript books. One of the principles in making a selection of material was avoidance of repetition: 'Material collected by the pupils may be entered in their school jotters and the compositions written in their copybooks from that material. These compositions, or as much of them as is not unduly repeated, together with stories, songs, proverbs, and other material collected should be transcribed by selected pupils into the official Manuscript Books'.[126]

The scheme was to finish in June 1938, but because 'the school year was considerably well advanced before the Scheme was brought into operation generally, and as adequate supplies of Manuscript Books for recording the collections made by the pupils were not available in the early part of the year' the Minister for Education authorised the issuing of an additional circular to school managers and teachers informing them 'that the period of operation of this Scheme may be extended to the 31st December, 1938, in order to afford schools an opportunity of completing and recording the collections made under the various headings as set forth in the Booklet of the Folklore Commission.' Schools that completed 'the collection of all the material available in the school districts before the 31st December', 1938 were allowed to 'resume the normal programme of Irish and English Composition on the completion of the Folklore collection.'[127]

The reason why many schools were left without 'an adequate supply of Manuscript Books' in the early part of 1938 had to do with the initial decision of the Dept. of Finance that the manuscript books sent to schools in March 1934 must first be used up and their contents assessed by the competent authorities before any new manuscript books could be sent out. In January 1938, L. Ó Muirithe of the Dept. of Education wrote to the Secretary of the Dept. of Finance informing him that: 'Applications are being received daily in this Department for additional copies of manuscript books and it is anticipated that in the larger schools the majority of the books issued in 1934 will be completed in the course of a few weeks.' He also informed him that it would 'not be possible to obtain the considered views of the Folklore Commission on the value of material collected' at this juncture, as it would be necessary 'that the manuscript books be retained in the schools until the end of the school year at least, so that they may be available for examination by the Inspectors in assessing the rating of the teachers' general efficiency' as stipulated in the Dept. of Education's circular of September 1937. However, he added: 'many of the Department's Inspectors have an expert knowledge of the subject and all of them are acquainted with it.' The Director of the Commission had also informed the Dept. of Education 'that reports of a very favourable character as to the operation of the scheme have reached him from many areas throughout the country.' He then quoted a recent letter received

126 Dept. of Education Circular 9/37, op. cit., par. 3.
127 Dept. of Educ. Circular 10/38, op. cit. For some of the factors that delayed the scheme, see D/T S 15548A: 'Gearr-Thuar./1938-39', pp. [5].

from Ó Duilearga: 'This collecting scheme was a greater achievement than anything ever attempted in respect of folklore collecting anywhere in the world.' Finally, Ó Muirithe requested £130 to cover the cost of purchasing '[t]he additional 2,600 manuscript books required'.[128]

On this occasion the Dept. of Finance did not insist on any further assessment of the material collected before agreeing to sanction the purchase of additional books. The fact that the Dept. of Education was asking for only 2,600 additional memorandum books and not 7,200 as originally requested may have lessened any opposition in this quarter. Mindful of the failure of the earlier 1934 scheme, however, it informed the Dept. of Education that 'the Minister [for Finance] would be glad to receive, in due course, a report as to the value of the collection submitted to the Folklore Commission.[129] Despite the fact that the Dept. of Finance agreed promptly to this request, it would be well into spring 1938 before the Stationery Office would supply the Dept. of Education with the requested manuscript books; a delay caused, to a large extent, by bureaucratic procedures in respect of payment.[130]

At a meeting of the Commission in October 1938, some months after the Dept. of Education, in consultation with the INTO, had agreed to extend the scheme until the end of December, Pádraig Breathnach drew attention to the fact that 'not all the teachers understand that the small copybooks of the children were to be included with the large copybooks', and said that he would put 'a note in the Irish School Weekly informing teachers of this.' At the same meeting Éamonn Ó Donnchadha proposed that 'the scheme be kept in operation for longer'. In reply to this, Pádraig Breathnach said that 'he had no doubt that some of the teachers would go on with the scheme.' Ó Duilearga, however, felt that it would be best 'to leave the matter with the teachers themselves.' The meeting decided that the Director 'and two other members of the Commission should consult the Executive of the Teachers' Organisation about this matter.'[131] It is unlikely that Ó Duilearga wished the scheme to be extended any further, as there was much else to be done.[132]

Getting the manuscript books and the pupils copybooks safely to the Dept. of Education needed careful planning. To this end, in December 1938 the Dept. of Education issued a further circular to schools instructing teachers that 'the manuscript books and the copybooks for each school should be sent by parcel post to this Office not earlier than 1st January and not later than 12th January 1939.' Instructions were also given in respect of packaging, labelling, and posting the material. Teachers were also asked to make sure that 'the title label on the outside and inside of the cover of the Manuscript Books are filled in, and in respect of each entry in these books and also in the pupils' copy

---

128 D/F S 046/0037/33: L. Ó Muirithe to Sec. Dept. of Fin., dated 20.1.1938, pp. [3–4] (passage from Ó Duilearga's letter translated from Irish).

129 ED [FL 9]: Almond to Sec. Dept. of Educ., dated 22.1.1938.

130 See D/F S 046/0037/33: Pádraic Ó Dubhthaigh to Sec. Dept. of Fin., dated 11.3.1938.

131 ED [FL 9]: 'CBÉ. Miont. 14ú Cruinniú, 21.10.1938', par. 120(h) and par. 121 (trans.)

132 One project he wanted to see undertaken was arranging for Dr Albert Nilsson of the Nordic Museum to come to Ireland to conduct a sociological survey of some particular area. See ED [FL 9]: 'CBÉ. Miont. 14ú Cruinniú, 21.10.1938'., par. 124.

books, that the names and addresses of the pupils who collected the material and the name and address and age of the person (or persons) from whom the material was obtained, are also entered.' The circular added: 'Compliance with the foregoing instruction will greatly facilitate the folklore Commission in the cataloguing and editing of the material collected.'[133]

The harvest comes in

A very professional job was being brought to a close. In late January 1929, Ó Duilearga was able to inform a meeting of the Commission that 'more than twenty tons' weight of copybooks in all had come in, between full, half-full and blank books.' Given the cramped quarters of the Commission's Head Office it was not possible to store or 'sort properly' that amount of new material, 'even though special shelving had been put up in one of the rooms before Christmas to accommodate it.' They had been able to shelve only one third of the material; the other two thirds had to be put away in storage. Ó Duilearga informed the meeting that 'nothing could be done with it until more shelving was erected,' and in response to this the members present authorised him to request additional space for the collection from the President of UCD. Ó Duilearga also stated that the scheme could not be ' assessed until all the material collected would be put in proper order.' A cursory glance of a sample of the material was sufficient for him to state that 'there was now much information in the possession of the Commission that they would not otherwise have had for a long time, or ever, perhaps.'[134]

Given the bulk of the material that came in, it is not surprising that it took the Commission's small office staff the best part of three months to open the packages and put some sort of order on the material. In his Annual Report for 1938–1939 (dated June 1939), Ó Duilearga was able to inform the Government that the official manuscript books sent in from schools around the country amounted to 375,660 pages, and, in addition, the pupils' composition copybooks contained 650,000 pages of material, much of it duplicated in the official manuscript books. He assessed the scheme thus:

> It is clear from the material collected by way of this scheme that the partly Irish-speaking districts ('Breac-Ghaeltacht') and the English-speaking districts ('Galltacht') in general are full of lore ('seanchas') and anecdotes ('eachtraithe') that have never been recorded. It is only in the Gaeltacht, or almost so, that the full-time collectors of the Commission have been operating to date as it is there that certain aspects of oral literature were to be found in greatest abundance, and because it is there that the need to collect these [traditions] is most acute before they are lost along with the old people.

133 Dept. of Educ. Circular 12/38: 'Scheme for Collecting and Preservation of Folklore and Oral Traditions', December 1938.
134 ED [FL 9]: 'CBÉ. Miont. 16ú Cruinniú, 27.1.1939', par. 136 and par. 137 (trans.).

It is also necessary to send full-time collectors to the other districts outside the Gaeltacht, and verify and expand the material the schoolchildren have collected. This material from the schools will indicate what sort of lore is to be had in each area, and it will guide the adult collector in searching [for traditions].'

He also spoke of the need for more space for this collection.[135] However, the Government had other things on its mind as war loomed on the horizon. Neither had UCD any extra space to give the Commission. Soon the prospect of putting the Schools Collection in proper order would be out of the question, and more importantly the Commission's hope that the material collected by the nation's schoolchildren could be used to chart tradition and in this way assist further collecting could not be implemented immediately.

Without doubt the bulk of the credit for organising this scheme must go the Séamus Ó Duilearga and Seán Ó Suilleabháin.[136] However, it is well to note that both men in time were to see this collection somewhat differently than some folklorists see it today. Speaking at a conference in Paris in August 1937, before the scheme got under way properly, Ó Duilearga said: '...the great value of this scheme is that it will yield in a general way information about the folklore of the country, its distribution, variations, *etc.*, and will also point to further and detailed paths of investigation.'[137] Moreover, at the Indiana Midcentury Folklore Conference in 1950, Stith Thompson said:

> I understood from Mr. Delargy that the Irish Folklore Commission had received a great deal of leads towards good informants from the school children. He indicated to me that this seemed to be about the most valuable part of the work the school children had done in connection with the large program of collecting which we have already mentioned. Is that true Mr. O'Suilleabhain?

In reply Ó Súilleabháin said that the 'main value of the school collections for us was that they covered different parts of the country, to which we could never send our full-time collectors or even our part-time collectors.' The Schools Collection proved particularly valuable when opening up new parishes where the Commission had no contacts:

> What we do there is that we take part of the forty or fifty school volumes which we have received from that area and we go through [them] making a list, first of all of the men who were teachers of the children, and then looking through the folk tales and songs and so on, and making lists of

---

135 D/T S 15548A: 'Gearr-Thuar./1938-39', pp. [7–8] (trans.).

136 Nevertheless, Ó Duilearga signalled out two members of the Commission for playing a crucial role in getting the scheme under way, namely Prof. Éamonn Ó Donnchadha and Dr Pádraig Breathnach, as well as two Dept. of Education officials, Mr. Murray (L. Ó Muirithe) and Mr. Franklin. ED [FL 9]: 'CBÉ. Miont. 10ú Cruinniú, 15.10.1937', par. 86(e) and ED [FL 9]: 'IFC. Fin. Sub-Com./Min. 14th Meeting, 29.9.1937, par. 136.

137 Ó Duilearga 1937, p. 39.

the informants who gave them. We have been able to use these school books as [a] preliminary introduction.[138]

Ó Súilleabháin was speaking more of the Commission's intention than of the reality. In writing about the Schools Collection some six years after the Indiana conference (late 1956), Ó Duilearga said: 'It was the intention of the Commission to put the note-books at the disposal of the trained field workers, and to amplify the information when necessary, but the War made it impossible to carry this into effect.'[139] In the post-War period the Commission's collectors did make some use of the Schools Collection. For example, Jim Delaney before he began collecting for the Commission in July 1954 spent a month or so examining the material collected by schoolchildren in 1937–1938 in the area of Wexford to which he was being sent.[140] However, the Commission never managed to send collectors into many areas of the country that the Schools Scheme showed to be rich in tradition. (See Chapter VII/5 below).

Despite any reservations Ó Duilearga and Ó Súilleabháin had about the intrinsic value of the Schools Collection, in the euphoria that surrounded the successful completion of the scheme they were reported as saying 'that there has been nothing like it since the Four Masters' – referring to the great annalistic compilation of Mícheál Ó Cléirigh and his assistants in the seventeenth century, *Annála Ríoghachta Éireann*.[141]

Extent of the Schools Collection

The Commission initially received 4,271 completed or partially completed manuscript books. It estimated the material in these books to amount to approximately 2,087 completed manuscript books, approximately 375,660 pages in all. Later that year (1939) the Commission received a further 300 manuscript books or thereabouts via the Dept. of Education, bringing the total number of manuscript books, complete and partially complete, to 4,571.[142] How many pages of material these extra books contained is not clear. Seán Ó Súilleabháin in the late 1950's described the Schools Collection as containing 560,000 pages, while a decade later he lowered this figure to 500,000 pages.[143] Even if all the three hundred plus extra manuscript books that came to Head Office subsequent to the main bulk of the material were full, which is highly unlikely, that would only account for some 54,720 extra pages, giving a total

---

138 Stith Thompson 1976 [1953], pp. 28–29.
139 Ó Duilearga 1957, p. 184. In July 1940 the Commission's Main Collection was transferred to the west of Ireland and the Schools Collection to the suburbs of Dublin. Both collections were not to return to the Commission's Head Office until 1949. See Ó Catháin and Ní Sheighin 1987, p. xxiv.
140 RTÉSA B1203, interview with Jim Delaney (1983).
141 *The Irish Times*, Wednesday, February 1, 1939, p. 3.
142 D/T S 15548A: 'Gearr-Thuar./1938–39', p. [7] and ED [FL 9]: 'CBÉ. Miont. 17ú Cruinniú, 9.6.1039', par- 141(i).
143 See Ó Súilleabháin 1957, p. 453 and Ó Súilleabháin 1970a, p. 118.

of 430,320 pages. It would appear therefore that Ó Súilleabháin's figure of 560,000 pages (and his emended figure of 500,000) attempt to account not only for the amount of material in the manuscript books, subsequently bound into 1,124 volumes of approximately 500 pages each, but also for the extra material contained in the pupils' copybooks. In spring 1939 these copybooks were estimated to contain approximately 650,000 pages.[144]

These copybooks were never bound as such, but were in time arranged in filing boxes according to provenance. It would appear that Ó Súilleabháin, and other members of the Commission's staff, underestimated the amount of original material contained in these copybooks that was not copied into the official manuscript books. Speaking at the Mid-Century Conference in 1950, Seán Ó Súilleabháin said:

> I remember at the time when these notebooks came to us, the newspapers were making jokes that we were getting thirty tons of folklore. It certainly did weigh about thirty tons, but in any case we have those hundreds of thousands of twopenny copies. Who would ever go through them God only knows, but in any case they are there for preservation and for later use.

Ó Súilleabháin estimated that 'ninety per cent' of the material in the children's notebooks had been transferred to the large manuscript books.[145] This was an overestimate, but Ó Súilleabháin did not have the benefit of being able to examine these notebooks at his leisure to ascertain how the material in them correlated with the official manuscript book(s) each school sent in. We now know that a great deal of valuable material was left out of these official manuscript books for a variety of reasons. Dónall Ó Baoill, in his research into the Schools Scheme as operated in the Gaoth Dobhair area of Donegal, found that only a tenth of the material was transferred to the official books in some cases.[146] Today anybody doing research on the Schools Collection cannot ignore these copybooks. Not only do they contain much material not found in the official manuscript books, but these copybooks add an extra dimension to the Collection and, in time, may reveal a great deal about the operation of the scheme. Until these copybooks are catalogued and collated with the bound volumes of the Collection, we can only guess at the total amount of material brought in by the Schools Scheme, but it is certainly far in excess of Seán Ó Súilleabháin's emended figure of 500,000 pages.

---

144 D/T S 15548A: 'Gearr-Thuar./1938–39', p. [7].
145 Stith Thompson 1976 [1953], pp. 11–12. Ó Súilleabháin's mention of hundreds of thousands of such copybooks is inexact. A memorandum compiled in the mid 1940's puts the figure at 50,000 (D/T S 6916B: 'The Irish Folklore Commission', p. [4]; cov. letter dated 11.11.1946). Nowadays it is thought the collection contains around 40,000 such copybooks.
146 Ó Baoill 1992, pp.xxi-xxii.

3. The Collection of folk music and song

To collect or to wait

Although Ó Duilearga had referred to the need to collect folk song in his above-mentioned memorandum to de Valera in May 1933, the Terms of Reference of the Commission made no explicit mention of folk song nor folk music. This may have been an oversight, but it was to cause problems later on for the Commission, as we shall see below. Not surprisingly, given the fact that many members of the Irish Folklore Commission had an interest in folk song and music, soon after the Commission was established this matter was raised. At the second meeting of the Commission in late May 1935 Fr. Lorcán Ó Muireadhaigh asked whether 'it would be possible to collect traditional music ['sean-cheol'] under the Commission scheme.' The Director said that there were problems: 'a good collector of folklore was not always somebody who was capable of collecting music.' León Ó Broin was of the opinion that 'it was best to collect the words first and that the music could be collected later.' The meeting decided to defer the matter to a later date.[147] However, Ó Muireadhaigh was not satisfied with this arrangement and at the next meeting of the Commission he again raised the matter. He felt that 'some money could be set aside for the purpose of collecting music.' The Director expressed the opinion, however, that 'the type of machine being used by the collectors was not a suitable apparatus for that work.' Séamus [recording] Ó Casaide recommended that 'a sub-committee be appointed to investigate' the whole matter. This was agreed to and the following four members were appointed: Fr. Lorcán Ó Muireadhaigh, Fr. John G. O'Neill, Fionán Mac Coluim, and the Director. They were given power to consult outside experts, if necessary, and were requested to 'examine the question of collecting music and to furnish the Commission with a report.'[148]

---

147 ED [FL 9]: 'CBÉ. Miont. 2ú Cruinniú, 31.5.1935', par. 16 (trans.).
148 ED [FL 9]: 'CBÉ. Miont. 3ú Cruinniú, 11.10.1935', par. 25. As a result of recommendations of this sub-committee, Ó Duilearga put students, 'under the direction of Colm Ó Lochlainn, cataloguing 'tunes that had already been published', and also asked 'the collectors to furnish a list of the names of singers in their own areas.' ED [FL 9]:'CBÉ. Miont. 4ú Cruinniú, 17.1.1936', par. 30(g). See also ED [FL 9]: 'CBÉ. Miont.

The following April at a meeting of the Commission, Séamus Ó Casaide proposed that a proper recording apparatus be purchased for the collection of folk song and music. Although this motion was supported by Éamonn Ó Donnchadha, who said that 'a trained person should also be employed to work it', the Director did not agree to this proposal, saying 'that it was a very complex matter and one that needed to be investigated carefully.' It was consequently agreed to leave the matter to the music sub-committee.[149] One reason for his reluctance to support the above proposal was, no doubt, the cost involved in purchasing a suitable recording apparatus and employing somebody to work it. He was not against the purchase of such a machine, he told the next meeting of the Commission, as it 'would be suitable for taking down dialects, as well as music, and it would be very advantageous for the Commission to have such an apparatus.' This meeting on being informed by León Ó Broin that the Terms of Reference of the Commission did not specifically mention folk music, agreed to his suggestion that it seek the opinion of the Government on this matter.[150] However, although Ó Duilearga broached the matter in his first annual report to the Government and was able to inform the Finance Sub-Committee later that year that the Government had discussed the collecting of folk music and that the President, Éamon de Valera, had informed him 'verbally' of his interest, almost two years would elapse before the Commission received, in late August 1938, via the Dept. of Education, definite confirmation of the Government's support for extending the activity of the Commission to cover folk music and song.[151]

Otto Andersson and Nils Denker

Some ten days later Ó Duilearga wrote to von Sydow for advice on the matter. He informed him that: 'Nothing has been done to collect folk-music in Ireland since the foundation of our Commission, for the simple reason that I could not find anyone competent to undertake the work.' As von Sydow was shortly to visit Freiburg in Germany he asked him to discuss the matter with John Meier and ascertain if the latter 'knew of someone (*preferably* trained by him) who could collaborate with an Irish musician in both field and archive work — but mainly in the field.' He added:

> If we get an Irishman capable of doing the work I intend to send him to Meier for training. How great a shock it would be for such a one to see the immense work done in Freiburg! And so perhaps we might get another Seán [Ó Súilleabháin] this time for Irish music & for the establishment of an Irish folk-song archive under the Commission.

5ú Cruinniú, 17.4.1936, par. 41.

149 ED [FL 9]: 'CBÉ Miont. 5ú Cruinniú, 17.4.1936', par. 41 (trans.).
150 ED [FL 9]: 'CBÉ Miont. 6ú Cruinniú, 26.6.1936', par. 51 (trans.).
151 D/T S 15548A: 'Gearr-Thuar./1935–36', p. [3], ED [FL 9]: 'IFC. Fin. Sub-Com./Min. 8th Meeting, 15.10. 1936', par. 74, and ED [FL 9]: Ó Dubhthaigh to Ó Duilearga, dated 29.8.1938.

In the meantime, he asked von Sydow if he knew of anyone in Sweden who would be suitable for such work.[152]

Von Sydow recommended the services of Prof. Otto Andersson of Åbo (Turku) in Finland, who had already been to Ireland to attend the Feis Ceoil ('music festival'). While Ó Duilearga felt it 'would be of great value to have the assistance of a man of his experience and reputation,' in the event, the only time that would have suited Anderson to come to Ireland in the near future was March 1939, which did not suit Ó Duilearga as he would then be away in the United States.[153] Anderson suggested a female colleague of his, but this idea did not appeal to Ó Duilearga:

> You see our old country-people are so conservative that they would give songs more readily to a man than to a woman. Personally, I think that the Finnish lady seems to be excellent, and she knows English well and has wide experience. But I do not suppose that she could work a gramophone recording apparatus. Meier's people certainly can.

More was at stake than simply getting a suitable person to initiate collecting and give basic training to Irish musicians. Ó Duilearga had wider hopes for the project: 'You see, William, if this proposed experiment be a success it means that our Commission will be made permanent, and I think, under the circumstances, that we ought to try to get a first rate person to superintend the work.'[154] But getting 'a first rate person', at least a first rate male, was proving difficult. Von Sydow's trip to Freiburg had not resulted in anyone volunteering for the project and he now recommended the services of a young Swede, Dr Nils Denker, 'who had experience in recording folk-music by gramophone' and 'whose work was well thought of in Sweden.' Ó Duilearga proposed to bring Dr Denker to Ireland in August or September 1939, 'provide him with [a] gramophone recording apparatus, and make arrangements for a number of suitable young Irish musicians to work with him'.[155] To finance the project he requested a sum of £400 from the Dept. of Education. Although Education was favourable to this request it did not get an easy passage in the Dept. of Finance.

The fact that the Government has given its blessing in principle to the collecting of folk music, should have dispensed with any further discussion

---

152 LUB Saml. von Sydow: Ó Duilearga to von Sydow, letter dated 9.9.1938 (italics underlined in original). This letter is also revealing of Ó Duilearga's caution with respect to collecting folk music: 'I do not intend to undertake the task if I cannot get (as we say) the "makings" of a good investigator in Ireland. There is a chance, however, of someone turning up, and in that eventuality I want to be prepared.' John Meier was head of the *Deutsches Volksliedarchiv*, founded in Freiburg im Breisgau in 1914. For more on this institute, see Lixfield 1994, pp. 4–5.

153 ED [FL 9]: 'IFC. Fin. Sub-Com./Min. 21st Meeting, 21.1.1939', par. 194.

154 LUB Saml. von Sydow: Ó Duilearga to von Sydow, letter dated 17.12.1938, pp. 2–4. As Ó Duilearga intended accompanying the music collector to the field, this may partly explain his preference for a male collector. He would probably have felt uncomfortable travelling around the country with a foreign woman, and it might have given rise to gossip.

155 ED [FL 9]: 'IFC. Fin. Sub-Com./Min. 21st Meeting, 21.1.1939', par. 194.

of whether such work came within the Terms of Reference of the Commission or not. However, in the Dept. of Finance these Terms of Reference were nevertheless scrutinized to ascertain if they sanctioned collecting of this sort. One official was also worried that if the Commission were to extend its collecting to cover folk music, its other collecting might suffer as a result and it might be forced to seek an extension of its 'lease of life':

> Unless it could be shown that the added function of collecting folk music would not retard progress with their folklore task we should be slow to look with favour on the proposal. Obviously the provision of folklore materials for the public is of more practical value in the Irish revival movement than that of folk music and as such should take precedence.[156]

There was much deliberation between Finance officials on the matter, but in the event, despite the support of León Ó Broin, the Dept. of Finance's representative on the Commission, his superiors did not consider the matter urgent and refused to sanction a supplementary grant for the purpose in 'the current year'.[157]

The plan to bring Nils Denker to Ireland in August was never to materialise. The outbreak of war in autumn 1939 meant that the prospect of bringing an expert from Scandinavia was ruled out until peace would again reign in Europe. Moreover, soon the Commission would be asked by the Government to cut its expenditure rather than seek extra funding. Although Ó Duilearga had eventually, when pressed to do so, taken up the matter of collecting folk music with enthusiasm, it is perhaps right to say that it was never his top priority.[158] By autumn 1939, with the Commission's term of office drawing to a close, not to mention the advent of war, he had other preoccupations. There were those on the Commission, however, who felt that even in the changed circumstances of the time something should be done to expedite the collecting of folk music.

Liam de Noraidh

The Commission had been setting aside money for the purchase of a gramophone recording apparatus, but before it could purchase such a machine, Ó Duilearga, who had been in communication with the Thomas A. Edison Company in the United States, received an offer from the president of that company of a present of such a machine, 'free of charge'. It was operated

---

156 D/F S 101/0011/34: internal Fin. memo, L. S. F[urlong] to [T. S.] Kealy, dated 3.5.1938 [*recte* 1939].

157 D/F S 101/0011/34: internal Fin. memo L[eón] Ó B[roin] to Mr. Kealy, dated 11.5.1939, and Almond to Ó Dubhthaigh, letter dated 31.5.1939, p. [3].

158 For instance, at the folklore conference held in the Dept. of Education on October 16th, 1933 (see Chapter III/1), Ó Duilearga is recorded as saying that 'a good deal of unnecessary material such as Songs, etc. had to be taken down in order to humour the old people and this constituted a certain waste of time.' ED CO 3/15/9(495/I): 'Béal Oideas, 16th October, 1933', p. 2.

by electricity, but, Ó Duilearga informed a meeting of the Commission in January 1940, 'the Dept. of Physics in University College had promised to adapt it to work on batteries so that it could be transported in a car to be used in the countryside.' At the same meeting Fionán Mac Coluim mentioned that an acquaintance of his, Liam de Noraidh, would be willing to collect music for the Commission during the summer.[159] As the Commission had sufficient funds to employ de Noraidh for some months, it proposed that he 'be appointed collector of traditional music in the Déise country [also Decies, i.e. Co. Waterford and the extreme south of Co. Tipperary] for a probationary period of 3 months beginning either on the 1st or 15th May, 1940 at an inclusive salary of £20 per month.'[160] De Noraidh was fifty years of age at the time, and in poor health. Although the Dept. of Finance was worried that it might be asked to fund a much more extensive scheme 'if the preliminary survey being made in the Decies indicates that there still remains a substantial amount of folk music which is uncollected', it felt it could not reject the proposal to employ Liam de Noraidh for such a short period. Ominously, however, in an internal Finance memo T. S. Kealy had this to say:

> The collecting of unrecorded airs and music is of great importance, from the point of view of the development of musical education in this country. At the same time, I feel it would be unwise to let the Commission loose on the collection of Irish music on the scale on which they are collecting folklore. If we were to do that, the cost might easily run in to £20,000 or £30,000, and the expenditure would be out of all proportion to the results gained.'

He proposed sanctioning de Noraidh's appointment, but proposed an addendum 'that the Commission should be informed that the M[inister]/ Finance will not be prepared, in view of the present emergency, to increase the Commission's grant for 1941–42 for the purpose of the Folk Music Scheme.'[161]

Collecting with pen and paper

Liam de Noraidh began working for the Commission on May 27th, 1940. In a letter to Ó Duilearga he explained the method he planned to follow. He hoped to 'select a particular area and firstly to visit that area and to discover which people know the native airs, to listen to their renderings, to keep an active account of what music pieces I consider worth collecting, and then to arrange another visit with the machine (i.e. ediphone) in order to collect those pieces.' De Noraidh did not realise the problems of recording song and music by means of the Ediphone. It had to be explained to him that the needle of this apparatus 'was unsuitable to the high notes, and in such cases

---

159 ED [FL 9]: 'CBÉ. Miont. 19ú Cruinniú, 12.1.1940', par. 160.
160 D/F S 101/0011/34: Ó Duilearga to [Dept. of Educ.], dated 25.4.1940.
161 D/F S 101/0011/34: internal memo, T. S. K[ealy] to Almond, dated 16.5.1940.

the singers sounded as if they were screeching.'[162] Ó Duilearga's plan to use the gramophone recording apparatus presented to him by the Thomas A. Edison Company in the event came to nought. The apparatus arrived on May 25th, 1940 but, as Ó Duilearga explained in his annual report to the Government, 'despite the best efforts of the Commission this wonderful machine could not be adapted to the work of collecting dialects and music in the countryside because of difficulties in acquiring the parts needed from America or England.'[163] Given this situation, Ó Duilearga advised de Noraidh 'that it would be better to have recourse to the pen, to write down songs and to simultaneously attempt a transcription of their tunes.' The Director would as 'soon as the opportunity arose' accompany de Noraidh in the field and 'use the gramophone for sound-recording.' This was not to happen, however, and de Noraidh had to get used to working with pen and paper. In the beginning this was difficult for him. He complained:

> If I stop one of these singers while I am noting down the first phrase or two of the music ... he will be upset or even set astray, and very likely cannot resume without beginning again. He will thus have to make several beginnings, or at least have to sing the same song several times, for his music is elaborate and will require extreme care in getting all the ornament onto the paper.

He learned in time to do without a recording apparatus. In the field he employed 'a kind of music shorthand which is of no use to anybody but myself; in the office [of his shop] I reduce that to intelligible music script which everyone can read.' Using this method he was able to jot down 'both airs and words, which later he could 'arrange' and 'retranscribe'.[164]

In late August the Dept. of Finance agreed to the Commission's request that de Noraidh be granted another three months' employment and in December 1940 sanctioned his appointment as full-time collector.[165] Although the Commission's hope of recording folk song and music by means of a gramophone could not be realised at this juncture, de Noraidh's work in Co. Waterford and adjacent counties showed that there was a great deal of material yet uncollected. It also showed that those who felt there was no great urgency about collecting folk music were wrong. De Noraidh noted:

> It is heartbreaking to find how much is only partly remembered, how much is forgotten or completely lost. More than one singer has told me that he or she had not sung for forty years the songs I had written down from them. All tell you that they had many more songs long ago, but have forgotten them. One excellent singer of eighty years shook her head and said to me: 'Níl aon éileamh anois orthu!' ['There is no demand for

---

162 Quoted in Ó hÓgáin 1994, pp. 3 and 9.
163 D/T S 15548B: 'Gearr-Thuar./1940–41', p. 2. (trans.).
164 Ó hÓgáin 1994, pp. 7 and 9. De Noraidh owned a hardware shop.
165 D/F S 101/0011/34: Dept. of Fin. to Dept. of Educ., letters dated 26.8.1940 and 10.12.1940.

them now!'] You are always oppressed by the thought that what you are working on is the last remnant of a great art.'[166]

Although there is something formulaic about informants proclaiming the greater abundance of tradition in former times, such protestations can often be well founded. With modernisation and language change a great deal of tradition was lost in Ireland. There can be no disputing this fact.

In his report to the Government for 1940–1941, Ó Duilearga had great praise for de Noraidh: 'As for me, I am not knowledgeable on musical matters, and it is consequently difficult for me to assess the work of this collector, but I understand that his working methods and the collection he has assembled for us appeal greatly to those members of the Commission who have such knowledge.'[167] In his first year with the Commission, de Noraidh had done some collecting in west Cork as well as in east Munster, which was his main area of operation. In his second year as full-time collector he worked mainly in west Cork. As a result of ill health, however, he was forced to resign from his full-time post on March 31st, 1942, although he was to continue collecting in a part-time capacity for the Commission.[168]

Séamus Ennis

The Commission lost no time in appointing a successor to de Noraidh.[169] On June 1st, 1942 a young County Dublin man, Séamus Ennis was appointed full-time music collector after a trial period of six weeks. Unlike de Noraidh, Ennis was to work from Head Office, and as a result his duties differed in many respects from those of the former. In his first year with the Commission he transcribed a good deal of song material which the Commission had on Ediphone cylinders, some of which had been collected by full-time collectors. He also transcribed much of the [Fr. Luke] Donnellan collection of folk songs from southeast Ulster. This derived from the early part of the twentieth century and was acquired by the Commission in the summer of 1939. About 50% of the Ediphone cylinders of this collection were in perfect condition, the rest had mould on them.[170] Ennis's transcription of the Donnellan Collection was opportune as much of it would not have been possible to transcribe later due to deterioration of the wax cylinders. His transcriptions of this material constitute a valuable source for southeast Ulster song tradition.[171]

Although not a native speaker of Irish, Ennis knew the language very well and had a gift for acquiring the various dialects. Because of his linguistic

---

166 Quoted in Ó hÓgáin 1994, pp. 17 and 18.
167 D/T S 15548B: 'Gearr-Thuar./1940–41', p. 2.
168 D/T S 15548B: 'Gearr-Thuar/1941–42', p. 2.
169 The late Pádraig Mac Gréine told Ríonach uí Ógáin that Ó Duilearga, presumably around about this time, asked him to collect folk music full-time for the Commission, but he declined the offer. Information supplied me by uí Ógáin.
170 D/T S 15548B: 'Gearr-Thuar.1942–43', p. 6 and ED [FL 9]: 'IFC. Fin. Sub-Com./Min. 23rd Meeting, 9.9.1939', par. 216.
171 See Ní Uallacháin 2003, p. 369.

skills, and his youth, the Commission were able to send him to any Gaeltacht area. However, he collected mainly in Co. Galway, but also, to some extent, in Counties Donegal and Mayo, west Munster, and elsewhere.[172] Unlike de Noraidh, in time Ennis was to make use of the Ediphone as well as pen and paper on his field trips. However imperfect the Ediphone was for recording music, it definitely speeded up the collecting of song lyrics. Although Ennis used it extensively, he did not use it exclusively, and from a remark he made in a letter to Seán Ó Súilleabháin in early 1944, he would appear, initially at least, to have been somewhat reluctant to use it.[173]

Despite all the arguments against using the Ediphone to record folk music and song, the decision to use it for this purpose is clouded in a certain amount of mystery. When Ennis first began working with his main informant, Colm Ó Caodháin of Glinsce, Co. Galway in May 1943, he had recourse to pen and paper only to record the singer's repertoire of song and lore, but in June 1944 he began using the Ediphone to record from him. Ríonach uí Ógáin says that the use of the Ediphone made the work much easier for Ennis: '... for the collector did not any longer have to depend on pen and paper only, that he could do the transcription after he had completed the recording and could listen repeatedly to it.'[174]

During the five years Séamus Ennis spent with the Commission he collected proportionately far more songs than Liam de Noraidh had in his two years as full-time collector with the Commission. This he could not have done without the aid of the Ediphone. Perhaps Ennis was able to use his own ear and the Ediphone in combination to good effect. Kevin McCann has said of Ennis: 'Séamus was gifted with perfect pitch and could instantly recognise the key in which a song was being sung or a tune was being played. He could write down the notes of a song while it was being sung, and could write out a tune after hearing it played a few times.'[175] Be that as it may, it would appear Liam de Noraidh's method of collecting folksongs was certainly far more labourious and, for someone in frail health, certainly more arduous. Moreover, it may well have contributed to de Noraidh having to resign his position as full-time collector with the Commission after only two years.

Not only could the Commission send Ennis to any Gaeltacht area of Ireland, his linguistic abilities and versatility meant that he could be sent to, or work with material from, that other Gaeltacht, or rather Gàidhealtachd, beyond Ireland, Gaelic-speaking Scotland and Canada. In late 1946, Ennis was sent by the Irish Folklore Commission to assist John Lorne Campbell of the Isle of Canna in the Inner Hebrides to transcribe the music of songs collected by Campbell some years earlier among Scottish Gaelic speakers in Nova Scotia and Cape Breton on the eastern coast of Canada, as well as in Scotland itself. Ennis spent approximately five months in Scotland during which time he transcribed a substantial portion of Campbell's collection (168 pieces in all). He also learned Scottish Gaelic and travelled

---

172 For more on the extent and nature of Ennis's collecting, see uí Ógáin 2007.
173 See uí Ógáin 2001, pp. 325 and 327; letter translated by uí Ógáin.
174 Uí Ógáin 1996, p. 713. (trans.).
175 Quoted in Breathnach/Ní Mhurchú, *Beathaisnéis a Cúig*, p. 59.

throughout much of the Hebrides and parts of the Highlands collecting Gaelic folk music.[176]

Séamus Ennis was one of the major collectors of Irish folk music and song in the twentieth century, as well as being an acclaimed traditional musician himself. If he had continued with the Irish Folklore Commission, he would, no doubt, have added greatly to their collections of folk music, but as they were not able to pay him more than a meagre salary he resigned from the Commission in August 1947 to take up employment with Radio Éireann's (the Republic's national radio station) newly established outside broadcast unit. Writing over a year later in his annual report to the Government of Ennis's work and departure, Ó Duilearga spoke of the great work he had done during the years he spent with the Commission, and how he had managed to save ' a great deal of song and music that had not been previously collected.' Ending on a dramatic note, he stated: 'Since this person's departure no music has been collected in Ireland.'[177]

By this time the Commission was having difficulties recruiting full-time collectors due, to a large extent, to the fact that it could not pay them decent salaries or offer them any security of employment. Difficult as it was to recruit willing and suitable people for the job of full-time collector, recruiting a full-time music collector was far more difficult. The Commission had been extremely lucky to get music collectors of the calibre of de Noraidh and Ennis. It was not to be as lucky again. The vacancy left by Ennis's departure was never filled.

Mobile units record folk music

To some extent the urgency of filling Ennis's position was reduced by a number of developments. Shortly before Ennis left the employment of the Commission he went with Caoimhín Ó Danachair to south and west Kerry to record tales and songs on gramophone plates. This was the first time the Commission made permanent recordings of lore and song in the field, albeit with a somewhat makeshift recording apparatus.[178] The following year the Commission had a proper mobile recording unit at its disposal. Although it mainly concentrated on recording samples of tales and lore, it did collect a good deal of song and instrumental music.[179] Moreover, if the occasion arose, this unit could be sent to collect specifically the repertoires of folk singers and musicians. The fact that Radio Éireann now had a mobile broadcasting unit, and that Séamus Ennis was working for this unit, also meant that the collecting of folk song and music no longer solely depended on the Commission. Moreover, the BBC also became involved in recording Irish

---

176 D/T S 15548B: 'Gearr-Thuar./1946–47', p. 3.
177 D/T S 15548B: 'Gearr-Thuar./1947–48', p. 5.
178 ED Fl 6: 'CBÉ. Miont. 49ú Cruinniú, 27.6.1947', par. 379 (d).
179 By 1955 the Commission's mobile unit had recorded 550 folk songs and 340 independent tunes , as well as 220 'folk-poems, ballads, hymns'. ED FL 2: 'Irish Folklore Commission: Sound Recordings', dated 11.1.1955.

folk music around this time (August 1947) and sought the help of the Irish Folklore Commission in identifying storytellers, singers, and musicians.[180] When Séamus Ennis subsequently joined the staff of the BBC in 1951, it greatly expanded its collecting of folk music in Ireland, especially during the early 1950's.[181] As well as cooperating with the BBC in collecting folk music, the Commission also at times worked closely with Radio Éireann's mobile broadcast unit.[182]

Nevertheless, while the work of the Commission's mobile recording unit and the collecting of traditional music done by Radio Éireann and the BBC may have eased pressure on Ó Duilearga for a time, and possibly eased his conscience as well, the work being done by these bodies was in certain respects different from that which had been done by Liam de Noraidh and Séamus Ennis for the Commission, in respect of the documentation of the tradition at any rate. For instance, those who operated the Commission's mobile recording unit, although they might be termed collectors, did not employ the same methods as the full-time collectors. They were more like 'samplers' of the tradition. They did not delve deep into the tradition, nor did they stay long enough in any area to do so. They, for the most part, simply skimmed the surface: collecting sample tales, lore, and songs in order to have an acoustic record. The fact that they did not keep diaries of their work also distinguishes them from the full-time collectors. The same applies to those collecting folk song and music for Radio Éireann and the BBC. It was therefore only a question of time before pressure would come to bear on Ó Duilearga to appoint a full-time music collector. Space does not allow me to detail the efforts of various members of the Commission over the next two decades to have a full-time collector of folk music and song appointed. Suffice it to say here that Ó Duilearga resisted these attempts, feeling that the Commission, with its limited budget, had other priorities.[183] (For more on the Commission's mobile recording unit, see below.)

---

180 D/T S 15548B: 'Gearr-Thuar./1947-48', p. 7 and ED FL 6: 'CBÉ. Miont. 50ú Cruinniú, 28.11.1947', par. 393(f).
181 Vallely 1999, p. 26.
182 For an instance of this, see Ó Conluain in Ua Cnáimhsí 1988, p. ix-x.
183 I hope elsewhere to publish a fuller account of the Commission's activity in respect of folk music and song. See Munnelly 2004.

4. Collecting by means of questionnaire

Creating a pool of correspondents

Bairbre Ní Fhloinn in an article on the use of questionnaires by the Irish Folklore Commission, says: 'In his diary for 20 May 1928, Delargy makes reference to his first encounter with the Swedish questionnaire system, which obviously impressed him.' That was on his trip to Sweden and northern Europe in 1928. She also notes that the questionnaire system he then encountered had been used for some time in Sweden by various institutions to elucidate aspects of tradition.[184] Like much else he learned on his first trip to Sweden, Ó Duilearga was in time to put his newly acquired knowledge on the Swedish questionnaire system to use in Ireland. Nevertheless, it was not until the late 1930's that he was in a position to devise a systematic scheme for collecting tradition by means of questionnaires.

To have an effective questionnaire system, one needed a large number of correspondents spread evenly throughout the country. This was something that could not be achieved overnight. Although the numerous part-time collectors who contributed material to the Commission during the first few years of its operation could be utilised as questionnaire correspondents, such collectors were not to be found in every locality. However, the Schools Scheme of 1937–1938 gave the Commission the opportunity of creating an extensive network of questionnaire correspondents as 'between 300 and 500 teachers throughout the country' had shown 'great interest in the work of collecting folklore as was evidenced by the way they implemented the folklore scheme in the schools.'[185]

Despite the fact that the Commission had sent out a number of questionnaires in the first few years of its operations[186], Ó Duilearga himself felt that the Commission's questionnaire system proper got under way in November 1939 with the issuing of a short questionnaire on the Feast of St. Martin. In a letter he wrote to von Sydow in early 1940 he speaks of 'a new

---

184 Ní Fhloinn 2001a, p. 216.
185 ED [FL 9]: 'CBÉ. Miont. 17ú Cruinniú, 9.6.1939', par. 143 (trans.).
186 Its first questionnaire on *bataí scóir* ('tally sticks') was sent out in March 1936. Ní Fhloinn 2001a, pp. 218–219 and p. 226, n. 13.

departure' and in another letter to Stith Thompson says: 'We have started since the beginning of November last a Questionnaire system covering 26 of the 32 counties.' His reasons for thinking of this particular questionnaire as the first questionnaire proper may have been the number of copies sent out (727) and the number of replies received (419), as well as the amount of material that came in (approx. 2,000 pages) in a short period of time.[187]

As a majority of questionnaire correspondents were National School teachers recruited through the Schools Scheme, which did not cover Northern Ireland, there was a gap in the returns for the six north-eastern counties of Ulster. Ó Duilearga and members of the Commission realised that it was necessary to extend the Commission's network of questionnaire correspondents to the North.[188] However, although the Commission did manage in time to recruit a network of correspondents in Northern Ireland, Bairbre Ní Fhloinn notes that there were 'proportionately fewer correspondents from Northern Ireland than from' the South of Ireland, 'despite the greater density of population in the north.' She also notes that 'the comparative lack of involvement in the Schools' Scheme of schools in cities and major towns of the twenty-six counties also probably helps to explain the relative lack of correspondents in certain districts, especially in some of the eastern counties.'[189]

Maintaining a pool of correspondents

Although the questionnaire on the Feast of St. Martin had been sent to over 700 people and more than 400 replies had been received by late January 1939 (see above), this did not mean that the Commission could rely on the next questionnaire being necessarily answered by such large numbers. In time, slightly in excess of 500 replies came in for the questionnaire on the Feast of St. Martin. This appears not to have been exceeded. A questionnaire on 'The Last Sheaf' in 1940 brought in 336 replies, while another sent out in 1941 on 'The Blacksmith' resulted in 487 replies. It would appear that the only subsequent questionnaire, down until 1952, to produce anything like this number of replies was a questionnaire on 'Roofs and Thatching' sent out in 1945, which brought in 459 replies.[190]

During the early years of the Second World War, the Commission regularly sent out questionnaires.[191] In 1940–1941, some 5,286 pages of material were

---

187 LUB Saml. von Sydow: Ó Duilearga to von Sydow, dated 28, 29.1.1940, p. [2] and Lilly Lib. Stith Thompson Papers: Ó Duilearga to Thompson, dated 18.1.1940, p. 2.

188 ED [FL 9]: 'CBÉ. Miont. 18ú Cruinniú, 27.10.1939', par. 150(l).

189 Ní Fhloinn 2001a, p. 222.

190 ED FL 2: 'CBÉ. A List of the General Questionnaires issued by the Commission'. This document was drawn up by Caoimhín Ó Danachair and is dated 19.1.1955.

191 In order to stimulate the interest of questionnaire correspondents in folklore, and also as a means of rewarding them for their services, they were enrolled as members of the Folklore of Ireland Society, which entitled them to the latest copy of *Béaloideas*. Moreover, in the early years of the Commission's questionnaire system, at least, a letter of appreciation was sent to each correspondent at Christmas, along with a small festive booklet containing a miscellany of Irish tradition. Ó Duilearga in these letters used to avail of the opportunity to

acquired by means of questionnaire returns, approximately 18% of its total acquisition of material. The following year, 1941–42, this dropped to 4,787 pages (13.7% of total), and 1942–43 saw a further slight drop, 4,273 (13.2% of total).[192] The latter part of the War saw a sharp reduction in the overall acquisition of material by the Commission, partly due to the fact that full-time collectors were confined to their home areas because of the scarcity of petrol. This reduction in the overall intake of material is also reflected in the amount of material acquired by means of questionnaires. Although in his report to the Government for 1943–1944, Ó Duilearga claimed that '[t]here has been no reduction whatsoever, despite the War, in the enthusiasm of our correspondents around the country nor in the great interest they display in the work we are engaged in'[193], nevertheless, more than a thousand fewer pages were acquired in 1943–1944 compared to the previous year, and 1944–1945 saw a reduction of a further 1,000 pages (see Appendix 5). Writing to von Sydow in November 1945, Máire MacNeill says: 'The war interfered with the development of our questionnaire system – the making of contacts necessary to recruit correspondents was almost impossible owing to travel difficulties, many of our correspondents were busy with volunteer duties, and the suspense of the times turned people's thoughts from things like folklore. But we are hoping to make a big development now.'[194]

Máire MacNeill had received training in map-making in Uppsala in the late 1930's, and she appears to have had a lot to do with questionnaire scheme during the War: for example, in preparing questionnaires, communicating with correspondents, and processing questionnaire returns. MacNeill had, of course, many other duties, and there was a limit to what she could do. On rejoining the staff of the Commission in September 1945, Caoimhín Ó Danachair (see Chapter V/2) was given as one of his duties to 'improve and reorganise the Commission's Questionnaire Scheme'. He at once wrote to some of the old correspondents as well as to others requesting their help. As a result, he succeeded in augmenting the depleted ranks of correspondents and some 460 people were answering questionnaires by the end of March 1946.[195]

Types of questionnaires

The Commission sent out two types of questionnaires: general questionnaires and local questionnaires, the former being 'sent to correspondents all over Ireland, and which often varied considerably in their length and breadth of

thank correspondents for their services, inform them of the significance of the questionnaire system and of their work, and encourage them, if circumstances allowed, to widen the scope of their collecting for the Commission. For samples of these letters and booklets , see D/T S 6916A.

192 See Appendix 5.
193 D/T S 15548B: 'Gearr-Thuar./1943–44', p. 5 (trans.).
194 LUB Saml. von Sydow: letter dated 6.11.1945.
195 D/T S 15548B: 'Gearr-Thuar./1945–46', p. 5.

enquiry.' Local questionnaires, on the other hand, were 'more specific in nature' and were 'sent only to a limited number of respondents, or to people living in a particular area. This latter type of questionnaire could also be quite short.'[196] General questionnaires were of two kinds: a) those designed to record as much data as possible on a particular topic, and b) those seeking to elicit detailed replies on a narrower topic. For the purposes of making tradition maps the latter type of questionnaire was used. The reason for sending out local questionnaires was often because certain information was needed quickly about some topic or other, in many cases because of a query from some foreign or native scholar. The people from whom information was elicited for such questionnaires were not always regular correspondents. For example, in 1941–1942 a questionnaire on ball games in the old times was distributed for the Commission by Pádraig Ó Caoimh, Secretary of the Gaelic Athletic Association, to a hundred members of the Association.[197] The numbers receiving such questionnaires were often far less. For example, in summer/autumn 1956 the Commission distributed a lengthy questionnaire to thirty six persons on matchmaking to facilitate the scholar Kenneth Connell of the Queen's University, Belfast. By late January 1957 more than 1,300 pages of material had come in as a result of this questionnaire.[198] Sometimes a questionnaire would be sent only to the full-time and special collectors. For instance, in 1961 a questionnaire on the rosary was sent out to all the collectors to facilitate the research of a nun who was writing a thesis on this subject, special copybooks being provided for collectors in which to record the data in this case.[199] Similarly, in the mid-1960's a 'special questionnaire' on hurling and football, compiled by Br. Liam P. Ó Caithnia and Seán Ó Súilleabháin, was sent to all full-time and special collectors. This resulted in more than 600 pages of material being collected in a relatively short space of time.[200] Ó Caithnia was later to use this material in his monumental work on hurling, *Scéal na hIomána*, as well as on a work on football, *Báire Cos in Éirinn.*[201]

Although sending questionnaires to the Commission's collectors ensured that a large amount of material could be collected in a short space of time, usually to facilitate some scholar's research, the uneven geographic distribution of full-time and special collectors meant that large tracts of the country were left uncharted. The above questionnaire on hurling and football well illustrates this. While data was elicited in all the counties of the province of Connaught, only four of the nine counties of Ulster were covered. The Province of Leinster fared even worse, with data being elicited only from Counties Louth, Westmeath and Offaly, all in mid or north Leinster. No

---

196 Ní Fhloinn 2001a, p. 219.
197 D/T S 15548B: 'Gearr-Thuar./1941-42', p. 5.
198 ED FL 2: 'CBÉ. Miont. 86ú Cruinniú, 5.10.1956', p. 2, and 'CBÉ. Miont. 87ú Cruinniú. 29.1.1957', p. 2.
199 ED FL 4: 'CBÉ. Miont. 107ú Cruinniú, 26.6.1961', pp. 1–2.
200 ED FL 8: 'CBÉ. Miont. 128ú Cruinniú, 27.6.1966', attachment 'Tuar. an Stiúr. 3.3.1966–3.6.1966', p. 1.
201 See Ó Caithnia 1980 and 1984.

data from south Leinster nor from the whole of the Province of Munster, an area including many counties with a strong hurling tradition, was obtained. Of course, questionnaires of this sort, sent out to facilitate research in the hope of quick returns, should subsequently have been sent to a wider circle of correspondents. This did not happen in the case of this particular questionnaire, nor in the case of the questionnaire on the rosary, mentioned above. Neither would it appear to have happened in the case of most other local or restricted questionnaires sent out by the Commission.

However, in the case of one particular general questionnaire, the opposite did in fact happen: a general questionnaire gave rise to a more 'restricted questionnaire'. This involved the general questionnaire on the Great Famine of the 1840's, sent out in 1945 at the request of historians who were editing a centenary commemorative volume on the catastrophe. The questionnaire proper resulted in more than 900 pages of material being collected. However, it was decided to augment this material by sending a more detailed questionnaire along with special copybooks to the full-time collectors and certain other people. This resulted in approximately a further 3,750 pages of material being collected.[202]

The method

Each questionnaire was issued by the Commission in Irish and English. In order to ensure that 'the tradition is preserved exactly as heard', the Commission required of its correspondents that they record 'the information in the language in which it is preserved.' Filling in questionnaires in the vernacular also resulted in 'an interesting body of expressions and terms relating to a particular custom' being recorded.[203] However, as it turned out not all questionnaires were issued in bilingual form. At a meeting of the Commission in January 1959, the Chairman, Eric Mac Fhinn, asked why the recent questionnaire on the uses of furze was in English only. He was informed by the Director that it 'had been drawn up by the authorities of the National Museum of Ireland' and had been distributed by the Commission on behalf of the Museum.[204] Other questionnaires sent out by the Commission were also prepared by the staff of the National Museum. For example, in early 1962 the Commission distributed a questionnaire on the 'Uses of Straw, Hay, Rushes, Grass and Similar Materials'. Under an arrangement with the National Museum, although replies to questionnaires of this sort were first sent to the Museum, they were eventually deposited with the Commission.[205]

In order that questionnaires should produce optimal results, they had to be devised with care and were time-consuming to prepare. Many questionnaires were sent out by the Commission on the initiative of members of its staff, but in other cases, as already mentioned, questionnaires were sent out to

202 D/T S 15548B: 'Gearr-Thuar./1945–46', p. 4.
203 Ó Danachair 1945, p. 204.
204 ED FL 4: 'CBÉ. Miont. 97ú Cruinniú, 8.1.1959', p. 5 (trans.).
205 ED FL 4: 'CBÉ. Miont. 111ú Cruinniú, 16.3.1962', p. 2.

facilitate the research of outside scholars. One of the earliest questionnaires sent out for the Commission, in December 1938, was a questionnaire on 'Death Lore' on behalf of the German Celtic Scholar Hans Hartman. The staff of the Commission might have to assist outside scholars in drawing up the questions to be asked, but there was a dividend for the Commission in that every questionnaire on some particular subject or other sent to the field often resulted in a harvest of material for the archive and, of course, increased knowledge of rural folk culture. Unfortunately, the Commission was never able to send out as many separate questionnaires as they would have wished or needed to send. For example, despite the great emphasis placed on the quality and importance of Irish storytelling, no questionnaire on this subject was ever sent out. Ó Duilearga proposed drawing up such a questionnaire, but it would appear that due to pressures of work, and perhaps failing health, he had to abandon this project.[206] This is just one of many subjects for which a separate questionnaire would have greatly added to our knowledge of a particular subject.

The amount of material collected

In all the Commission collected in excess of 40,000 pages of material by questionnaire, bound in 166 volumes. Impressive as this figure appears, it has to be noted that the intake of material deriving from questionnaires is not evenly spread throughout the period from the late 1930's to the late 1960's. In the ten-year period 1939–1948, twenty five general questionnaires were sent out. However, for the periods 1949–1958 and 1959–1968 the figures are fifteen and five respectively. This does not give the complete picture, however, as almost a hundred questionnaires were sent out to a small number of people or to a restricted locality over the whole period. Some fifty of these were sent out before 1955. However, if we examine the number of pages (see Appendix 5) amassed via questionnaires, it is clear that there was a sharp fall-off from the late 1940's onwards. In the period 1939–1940 to 1947–1948, 31,530 pages of material were amassed by means of questionnaires; from 1948–1949 to 1957–1958, 6,064 pages were collected; and from 1958–1959 to 1967–1968, 2,819 pages were collected. Perhaps, it is more revealing to look at the percentage of material being collected by means of questionnaires vis-à-vis the total amount of material being acquired each year by the Commission. During the War years the Commission depended on questionnaire replies to augment its collections as it had to cut back on both full-time and part-time collecting. Consequently, in the post-War period we might expect to see a reduction in the amount of material being collected by means of questionnaires, but not of the size experienced in the late 1940's and early 1950's.[207]

---

206 See SKS Martti Haavio Papers 12:58:3: Ó Duilearga to Haavio, dated 19.11.1946.
207 Although the percentage of material being acquired by questionnaires picked up from the mid to the late 1950's, the figures for 1959 to 1966 (as shown in Appendix 5) are

The fall-off in the amount of material being acquired from the late 1940's onward is also reflected in Ó Duilearga's annual reports to the Government. During the War years and for a time in the post-War period the Commission's questionnaire scheme is given prominence in these reports. However, during the 1950's questionnaires sent out by the Commission come in for far less comment, and as the 1960's advance such commentary peters out. There is no doubt that the Commission's questionnaire system did not produce the results it was originally hoped it would produce. However one looks at the figures, it is obvious that the Commission's questionnaire system experienced a sharp decline from the late 1940's, both in terms of the number of country-wide questionnaires sent out and in respect of the amount of material amassed. There is no evidence to suggest that this decline was in any way influenced by misgivings about the method itself at this juncture, although the decline in the number of questionnaire correspondents may have made Caoimhín Ó Danachair reluctant to expend too much of his time on preparing and sending out general questionnaires. In an article in *Béaloideas* published in 1957, Ó Danachair stated that for the purpose of mapping tradition, a minimum of between three and four hundred correspondents, distributed evenly throughout the country, was required.[208] By this time the Commission's pool of questionnaire correspondents would appear to have fallen below that minimum.[209]

Bairbre Ní Fhloinn states that given the origins of the Commission's questionnaire scheme, in the Schools Scheme, which 'acted as a springboard for the recruitment of so many of the Commission's new correspondents', there was 'an almost inevitable falling-off in numbers' in later decades 'as many of the teachers grew older and retired.' [210] While this was certainly the case, to quite an extent, the reasons for the fall-off in the number of the Commission's questionnaire correspondents, which peaked around 1945, would appear to be more complex. In 1954 in a letter to Åke Campbell complaining about the direction of the Commission, Seán Ó Súilleabháin recommends: 'the regular issuing of questionnaires, following on a scheme which has been decided (as regards the subjects to be covered) well in advance'. He adds:

> You may not know that owing to the impossibility of getting Séamus [Ó Duilearga] to agree to the issue of questionnaires some years ago, we

somewhat misleading. It would appear, at first sight, that no material was acquired by means of questionnaire in this period. However, although the early 1960's was certainly not a very productive period in terms of questionnaires, what appears to have happened is that the questionnaires sent to correspondents during this period were sent out on behalf of the National Museum of Ireland or outside researchers, and while this material eventually came into the possession of the Commission, there was a delay of some years before this happened. Thus, the 1,400 or so pages of questionnaire returns acquired in 1966-67, most likely, represent the accumulated returns of a number of the previous years.

208 Ó Danachair 1957, p. 108.
209 e.g. a questionnaire on furze sent out by the Commission in 1958/59 received some 200 replies. D/T S 17378A: 'Gearr-Thuar./1958–59', p. 2.
210 Ní Fhloinn 2001a, p. 221.

lost the interest and goodwill of some hundreds of our correspondents. What Séamus should do is to delegate the power to issue questionnaires to Kevin [Caoimhín Ó Danachair] and myself – – keeping him informed of course, all the time. It has been impossible for years back to get him to make a decision himself, when urgently needed, or to get him to agree to the good suggestions from others. Any delay is deadly in this work.[211]

While there may be an element of exaggeration in what Ó Súilleabháin says above, his claim, for the most part, is corroborated by the figures. There was definitely a fall-off in the issuing of general questionnaires towards the end of the 1940's. Moreover, between 1939 and 1945 the average number of correspondents who replied to the Commission's questionnaires was around 300. However, for the period 1946 to 1952 the average is around 190 replies.[212]

Is it right to lay the blame for this at Ó Duilearga's door? The fall-off in the issuing of questionnaires towards the late 1940's can possibly be attributed to a number of factors. Ó Duilearga's deteriorating health around this time, which sapped him of energy and, perhaps, resolve, was certainly a contributory factor. But there were other factors that should be taken into account. The fact that Caoimhín Ó Danachair was from 1948 to 1952 occupied with the Commission's mobile recording unit, most likely reduced the amount of time he could devote to preparing questionnaires and maintaining and augmenting a pool of correspondents. Moreover, the person most suited to take over this task from Ó Danachair, Máire MacNeill, left the employment of the Commission in June 1949. With regard to the decline in the pool of correspondents in particular, a number of other factors may also have been involved. Some of the long general questionnaires sent out during the 1940's may also have contributed to a fall-off in the number of correspondents. It was naturally more difficult for correspondents, working on a voluntary basis, to research and complete questionnaires that sought a great deal of information, than it was to complete more specific questionnaires. Ideally, a long questionnaire should have been followed by a number of shorter questionnaires so as not to tire the correspondents. Moreover, delays in the issuing of *Béaloideas*, due to Ó Duilearga's many other pressing duties, meant that correspondents were very often left without this source of stimulation.

A final comment

Much further research needs to be done on the Commission's questionnaire system. It is only right that the bulk of such research should concentrate on the achievements of the system: i.e. on the great quantity of data collected, on the informants who supplied the data, and on the correspondents who gave of their free time to record much tradition that would otherwise have

---

211 ULMA Saml. Åke Campbell, subnr. 351: Ó Súilleabháin to Campbell, letter 12.7.1954.
212 Extrapolated from data found in ED FL 2: 'CBÉ. A List of the General Questionnaires issued by the Commission', dated 19.1.1955.

been lost. But the failings of the system also need to be addressed further. In a sense, one could say that the failure of the questionnaire system to live up to expectations is mirrored in the shortcomings of the Commission in other areas, e.g. its failure to expand part-time collecting significantly in the 1950's. Indeed the decline of the questionnaire system made the expansion of the Commission's network of part-time collectors all the more desirable. But instead of expanding, this 'network' atrophied to almost nothing (see Chapter VII/5 below).

Was the decline in the Commission's questionnaire system partly a victim of the souring of relations between Séamus Ó Duilearga, on the one hand, and Caoimhín Ó Danachair and Seán Ó Súilleabháin, on the other, from the early 1950's onward? (I will discuss these animosities in Chapter VI/2). If things had otherwise been right in the Commission, would problems that arose in connection with the questionnaire system have been put right in good time? In examining this whole question, it should also be kept in mind that the Commission's staff was always overstretched. Preparing questionnaires was a very time-consuming activity, and, moreover, the Commission had not the resources to process fully all questionnaire returns as they came in.

Writing of the Commission's questionnaire system in the mid-1940's, Caoimhín Ó Danachair said: 'In Ireland the system is comparatively new, but has already shown very good results, and will, with the cooperation of the correspondents, be continued until a large body of information is amassed.' More than three decades later, he ended a review of a volume of the *Österreichischer Volkskundeatlas* thus:

> The Austrian folk atlas is but one of many. Similar work is in progress in Germany, Sweden, Finland, Hungary, Poland, Russia, Greece and several other European countries. How soon will Ireland take its place among them?[213]

---

213 Ó Danachair 1977–1979, p. 277. To date no atlas of Irish folk tradition has been produced.

5. Extending the collecting to Northern Ireland

The situation in the North

It is unlikely that the Irish Folklore Commission would have extended its activities to Northern Ireland in the way that it did, if the systematic collecting of folklore was being organised by some body or other in the North at the time. There were people in Northern Ireland interested in having the oral traditions of the region collected and in such quarters the early success of the Irish Folklore Commission did not go unnoticed. Speaking many years later, Estyn Evans says:

> The success of the Irish Folklore Commission in Dublin, under the leadership of Dr. James Delargy (a product of the Glens of Antrim) was an argument which carried weight in some quarters, and even those who mistrusted the Commission's primary concern with things Gaelic felt that if folklore was to be collected in Northern Ireland the work should be done from Belfast rather than from Dublin.

Along with some others in the North, Evans appealed to the Vice-Chancellor of the Queen's University, Belfast to establish a similar commission for the North, but despite getting a sympathetic hearing, the outbreak of the Second World War meant that discussions on this matter had to be deferred.[214] Proposals around this time for a folk museum for Northern Ireland had also to be postponed because of the War. After the cessation of hostilities in 1945, efforts were again made to establish a folklore commission and folk museum for the North. Not surprisingly, there were other immediate priorities in the wake of a protracted war, but in time these efforts began to bear fruit.

However, it would appear that not all who were interested in initiating folklore collecting in the North believed collecting should be organised from Belfast, as Evans implies. Some, it appears, looked to Dublin for help as well as inspiration, or at least did so when no help was forthcoming from the North.

---

214 Evans 1988, pp. 91–92. The others involved were the historian T. W. Moody, the museum curator T.G.F. Paterson, Viscount Charlemount, and Dame Dehra Parker.

As early as autumn 1935 the question of collecting in the Six Counties was raised at a meeting of the Irish Folklore Commission. The Director said that 'he was not aware of any obstacle' to undertaking such work 'and that he had written to a couple of people in the north on the matter.'[215] Nothing, however, seems to have happened on this front for some time. Then in May 1938 at a meeting of the Finance Sub-Committee of the Commission, Ó Duilearga 'read a personal letter which he had received relative to the necessity of having folklore collected in the Six-County Area and the consideration of what steps might be taken towards bringing it about.' He was of the opinion 'that it might be possible to arrange' at the International Congress of Anthropological and Ethnological Sciences to be held in Copenhagen later that August for 'representations to be made' to expedite such collecting. This would suggest that at this stage, at any rate, he believed that the best way to proceed was to make representations to officials in the North. However, other possibilities open to the Commission were discussed at the above meeting. The minutes report: 'The whole question was discussed at some length, the suggestion being made that the Folklore of Ireland Society might properly devote some of its funds to collection in the Six-County area. It was decided, however, that the matter was one which required very careful consideration.'[216]

Whether Ó Duilearga succeeded in getting participants at the Copenhagen Congress to intercede with Northern Ireland officials or not on this matter, nothing seems to have happened as a result of this meeting. Moreover, later that year, aware of the sensitivities involved and of the need to tread with caution, he approached Joseph P. Walshe of the Dept. of External Affairs and told him of 'his desire to extend the operation of the Folk Lore Commission to the Six County area.' As a result of their discussions, Walshe spoke with de Valera on the matter, who 'whole-heartedly agreed' with the proposal. Walshe suggested that the Dept. of Education 'make semi-official enquiries from the Department of Education in Belfast', feeling certain 'that they can hardly have any objection – as Delargy is ready to meet them in every possible way so long as they will allow him or his colleagues to do the work or undertake to do it themselves.[217] Once again nothing appears to have happened. Almost a year later, at a meeting of the Finance Sub-Committee of the Commission, Ó Duilearga informed those present that over the previous two years 'influential people in Northern Ireland had been trying to get something done to collect the popular traditions of that part of the country.' Their efforts had failed and on October 10th, 1939 'a representative of these people had come to see him and told him that their view was that the country's folklore traditions should be in one central bureau, that they could not undertake collection work and that they felt that the Folklore Commission should extend its enquiries to the North-East.' Earlier that month Ó Duilearga had been summoned to a meeting with de Valera, who was doubling as Taoiseach and Minister for Education at the time, to discuss how to reduce the expenditure of the Commission 'in

215 ED [FL 9]: 'CBÉ. Miont. 3ú Cruinniú, 11.10.1935', par. 21(i) (trans.).
216 ED [FL 9]: 'IFC. Fin. Sub-Com./Min. 18th Meeting, 28.5.1938', par. 172 and 173.
217 D/F S 11281: 'Extract from letter...' J. P. Walshe to M. Moynihan [Dept. of the Taois.], dated 2.11.1938.

view of the nation's need for economy in the national emergency [i.e. outbreak of war in Europe]'. At their meeting De Valera asked Ó Duilearga 'to send him a memorandum setting forth whatever saving could be effected' in the remainder of that financial year and in the subsequent financial year. This Ó Duilearga promptly did on October 9th. However, he told the meeting of the Finance Sub-Committee that '[h]e wished that he had this information in his possession before his interview with Mr. de Valera' as 'it created a new situation and would demand more money than had been allowed for in his letter to the Minister.' Given de Valera's anti-partitionist sentiments, Ó Duilearga may have felt that he might welcome an opportunity to flout the border in this way. The rest of the Committee felt 'that all efforts possible should be made to initiate the collection of northern traditions', but that they would have to work within their reduced budget.[218] Finance had to take precedence over principle and politics.

At a meeting of the Commission proper some days later this matter was again discussed. Ó Duilearga spoke of the northern representative who had come to see him and said that it was the opinion of those in Northern Ireland interested in 'scientific work' ('obair ealadhanta') that the Commission should send a full-time collector to work in certain areas of the North, 'particular mention being made of the Fews in Co. Armagh'. He said he would consider seeking part-time collectors in the North.[219]

The identity of the 'representative' who came to see Ó Duilearga in early October 1939 is something of a mystery. Mention of the need to collect in the Fews area, a predominantly Catholic parish with a residual Gaelic tradition, might suggest that this representative was a Nationalist. However, at the next meeting of the Commission in January 1940, when this matter again came up for discussion, Ó Duilearga reminded the meeting 'that the matter had been discussed with different people in the Six Counties already'. He added:

> Those people had sought financial support from the government of the Six Counties in order to collect the folklore of those counties but they were told that it was not possible to grant it to them now. They would like two persons from the Six Counties to be adopted as members of the Commission. This request was not answered in writing but they were told by word of mouth that there would be difficulties attaching to it.[220]

Were the people who approached Ó Duilearga for help in collecting folklore in the North the same people whom Evans says appealed, in vain, to the Northern authorities in the pre-War period? Certainly the people who contacted the Irish Folklore Commission were not numbered among those in the North 'who mistrusted the Commission's primary concern with things Gaelic '. It may well be that although there may have been a certain degree of cooperation between Nationalists and Unionists in getting official support for

218 ED [FL 9]: 'IFC. Fin. Sub-Com./ Min. 23rd [recte 24th] Meeting, 23.10.1939', par. 208 and 213.
219 ED [FL 9]: 'CBÉ. Miont. 18ú Cruinniú, 27.10.1939', par. 150(1) (trans.).
220 ED [FL 9]: 'CBÉ. Miont. 19ú Cruinniú, 12.1.1940', par. 159 (trans.).

folklore collecting, certain Nationalists involved in the above representations to the Northern Ireland authorities, unknown to their Unionist colleagues or not, sought help from the South, at least when none was forthcoming from the North. If Estyn Evans had anything to do with representations made to the Irish Folklore Commission, or was aware of such representations, he subsequently chose to obscure the fact.

A full-time collector for the North

A few years later the Irish Government acted on the above request that two persons residing in Northern Ireland be appointed to the Commission, namely Pádraig Mac Con Midhe and Fr. Seán Ó Coinne.[221] Some two years later the Commission, even though still operating on a reduced War-time grant, employed Michael J. Murphy on a part-time basis to collect folklore traditions in Co. Down and in his native south Armagh.[222] The fact that he was requested to keep a diary of his collecting, unlike most other part-time collectors, may mean that Ó Duilearga had hopes of employing him full-time at a later stage.[223] In late 1949, Ó Duilearga was in a position to do just that. Michael J. Murphy was sent as a full-time collector to work in the Sperrin Mountains in the heart of Northern Ireland. Murphy tells us that Ó Duilearga in sending him to work in the Sperrins described his work as akin to that of 'a cultural intelligence officer'.[224]

Initially, it was with the financial assistance of Comhaltas Uladh, the Ulster sister-organisation to the Gaelic League, that Michael J. Murphy was employed full-time by the Commission. This organisation also helped the Commission employ Pádraig Ó Beirn as part-time cataloguer.[225] This was a case of cross-border cooperation by people who, for the most part, did not recognise the border. However, cooperation with those in the North who did recognise the border proved more problematic. In time the Commission was able to support Michael J. Murphy from its state grant-in-aid. Murphy was to remain with the Commission for the remainder of its operations, and to continue working for its successor, the Department of Irish Folklore.

The limits of cooperation

As I have stated above, in the post-War period efforts again began in the North to get state support for folklore collecting. By the early 1950's these efforts were beginning to show results. In 1953 the Committee on Ulster Folklife

221 D/T S 15548B: 'Gearr-Thuar./1942–43.', p. 7.
222 Murphy had previously sent material he collected to the Commission. D/T S 15548B: 'Gearr-Thuar./1944–1945', p. [6].
223 For some of his diary entries during this period, see Zimmerman 2001, pp. 407 ff.
224 Murphy 1974, p. 7.
225 D/T S 15548B: 'Gearr-Thuar./1949–50', p. [3], and 'Gearr-Thuar./1950–51', p. [5].

and Traditions was set up and received sufficient official funding from the Northern Ireland Tourist Board and the Ministry of Finance to appoint a full-time organiser to arrange for the voluntary collecting of folk traditions. The subsequent appointment of a full-time field-organiser made it possible to recruit around fifty competent voluntary collectors. From 1955 onwards the Committee on Ulster Folklife and Traditions published a journal, *Ulster Folklife*, Northern Ireland subscribers being encouraged to collect local traditions, just as subscribers of *Béaloideas* in the early days had been urged to do. In the mid-1950's this Committee also 'with the cooperation of the Ministry of Education and the church authorities responsible for denominational schools' organised a folklore scheme somewhat similar to the Schools Scheme organised in the South in 1937/1938. Although the idea of a folklore commission as such for Northern Ireland did not gain official acceptance, the Ulster Folk Museum Act of 1958 laid the ground for the establishment of a folk museum at Cultra Manor outside Belfast, opened some years later in 1964. In time the field-organiser of the Committee on Ulster Folklife and Traditions (which became the Ulster Folklife Society in 1961) along with its collections were transferred to the Ulster Folk Museum at Cultra.[226]

Although Evans and the Committee on Ulster Folklife and Traditions sought to imitate the Irish Folklore Commission in certain ways, the Commission does not appear to have played a very active role in establishing a body to collect folklore in the North. In any event, the Commission's annual reports to the Irish Government do not mention any such activity. This is in stark contrast to the role it played in the establishment of the School of Scottish Studies in the early 1950's (see below), and to the prominence given to that role in Ó Duilearga's official reports. This may have been partly tactical, as it may have been felt by those interested in folklore collecting on both sides of the border that for the Irish Folklore Commission to play too prominent a role in efforts to get systematic folklore collecting underway in the North of Ireland might have been counterproductive.[227] The fact that in 1951, Ó Duilearga recommended to the Belfast Museum that its employee George Thompson, Keeper of its recently established Department of Antiquities and Ethnography, should attend an international folk-life conference in Stockholm in order to acquaint himself with Scandinavian folk museums, would also indicate relatively harmonious relations at this time between the Commission and official bodies in the North interested in folk-life and folk tradition. Thompson travelled to this conference in the company of two members of the staff of the Irish Folklore Commission, Seán Ó Súilleabháin and Caoimhín Ó Danachair.[228]

Nevertheless, the level of cooperation one would have expected to develop between South and North in respect of folklore collecting and research did not develop. The reason for this may lie in the fact that there appears to

226 Evans 1988, pp. 92–94.
227 In a letter to the Dept. of Education , dated 15.11.1952, Ó Duilearga, referring to his efforts to encourage folklore collecting elsewhere, says, 'I have paid many a trip to the North of Ireland, and Scotland and to England, and recently to Wales, to encourage people to take action.' (trans.). D/F S 101/0011/34.
228 G. B. Thompson 1982, pp. 43.

have been, from the beginning, a certain antipathy between Ó Duilearga and Evans. At any rate, it is unlikely that these two men were ever very close, and events were to drive them further apart. The neutrality of the South of Ireland during the War is said to have soured Evans's attitude towards the South and its learned institutions in general. Nevertheless, it should be noted that some months after the end of the War, in September 1945, Evans went, at the request of Ó Duilearga, to do some fieldwork in southwest Co. Cavan, and subsequently forwarded a report on his findings to the Commission.[229] It should also be noted that during the course of the War, Evans in one of his publications paid tribute to the work of the Irish Folklore Commission.[230] Whatever about the War souring relations between Evans and Ó Duilearga, some years later something was to happen that most definitely left a sour taste in Evans's mouth.

Naturally, once organised efforts began in earnest in Northern Ireland to collect folklore, those involved were interested not only in finding out what material from the North the Irish Folklore Commission had in its collections, but, if possible, to acquire copies of such material. At a meeting of the Finance Sub-Committee of the Commission in November 1954, Ó Duilearga informed members that 'he had received a request from Dr. E Evans of the Department of Geography, Queen's University, Belfast, for microfilm copies of material relating to the six counties' and that the 'material was for the use of the Ulster Committee of Folklore, of which Dr. Evans was the Chairman.' Ó Duilearga 'felt that the request could be acceded to, provided the normal safeguards were observed.' It was decided, however 'to postpone the matter until the next meeting' as the Commission's 'microfilm apparatus was out of order'. At the next meeting, however, some four months later, Ó Duilearga stated 'that he had given the matter some thought and he felt it would not be desirable at this stage to accede to the request of the Ulster Committee.' The rest of the Finance Sub-Committee 'agreed with this decision and it was decided that the Director should communicate with Dr. E. Evans.'[231]

It is not clear what caused Ó Duilearga to change his mind. He had been on leave of absence between these two meetings and, as I suggest below in this study (Chapter VI/2), was in combative mood when he attended this meeting at the end of March 1955, believing that his colleagues, Caoimhín Ó Danachair and Seán Ó Súilleabháin, had been trying to wrest control of the Commission from him. He was determined to regain control, and rejecting the request of the Ulster Committee of Folklore may have been somewhat of a knee-jerk reaction. There may have been more involved, however, as it must be remembered that Ó Duilearga was very possessive of the Commission and its collections, and may well have, on reflection, feared that granting this request would diminish his overall control over these collections.

Despite this rebuff to the Ulster Committee of Folklore, cordial relations persisted, and developed, between Ulster ethnologists, all of them pupils of

---

229 Evans 1980, p. 1.
230 See Evans 1996, p. 258, n. 99.
231 ED FL 2: 'IFC Fin. Sub-Com./Min. 94th Meeting, 13.11.1954', par. 708 and 'IFC Fin. Sub-Com./Min. 95th Meeting, 28.3.1955', par. 714.

Evans, and some of the staff of the Irish Folklore Commission, particularly Caoimhín Ó Danachair. Evans in his *Irish Folk Ways*, published in the late 1950's acknowledges the assistance of both Caoimhín Ó Danachair and Seán Ó Súilleabháin, but it is interesting to note he makes no mention of Ó Duilearga.[232] Evans never again renewed his above request, but in 1961 the Director of the Ulster Folk Museum, George Thompson, sent a letter to Ó Duilearga requesting 'permission to make micro-film copies of the Ulster material in the archives of the Irish Folklore Commission.' The matter was discussed by the Finance Sub-Committee at its June meeting, and '[a]fter some discussion it was decided not to accede to this request.' In rejecting this request, the 'Sub-Committee stated that they would welcome any approved scholar who wished to consult the material in the Library or Archives of the Commission. If, however, permission were given for the making of such micro-film copies it would not be possible to regulate or control their use.'[233] The meeting the Commission itself held some days later was informed of this decision, but nobody present seems to have questioned it.[234]

One might have expected a more generous response to these requests, especially as the Commission had no qualms about providing the School of Scottish Studies with microfilm copies of material it had collected in Scotland, or Scottish material that it had otherwise acquired (see below). It also contrasts with the cordial relations the Commission had with the BBC, referred to above, and the willingness of both bodies to exchange material with each other. Moreover, the fact that the Commission's collector, Michael J. Murphy, was working much of the time in Northern Ireland, could be viewed as further justification for supplying copies of this material to a sister institution in the North. It is easy, of course, in hindsight to be critical of this refusal, but it should be stressed that in 1955, and again in 1961, Ó Duilearga was supported in his decision by members of the Finance Sub-Committee and the Commission proper. No voices, it seems, were raised on either of these bodies in support of extending a hand of cooperation across the border. It should also be remembered that, on a political level, relations between the South and the North were very cool during this period and it would be almost the mid-1960's before relations began to improve. The unwillingness of Ó Duilearga and the Commission to accede to these requests, whether influenced by political sentiment or not, most likely would not have met with the disapproval of the Southern political elite. To this day no copy of the collections of the Irish Folklore Commission (or part of them) has ever been deposited in any institution in Northern Ireland, although copies of the collection are available at various venues in the Republic. In a sense, one might say that although there has been much cooperation between folklorists and ethnologists on both sides of the Irish border in recent years, the political division of Ireland, dating from 1920/1921, still casts a shadow over folklore on the whole island.

232 Evans 1972 [1957], p. xv.
233 ED FL 4: 'IFC. Fin. Sub-Com./Min. 119th Meeting, 22.6.1961', par. 855.
234 See ED FL 4: 'CBÉ. Miont. 107 Cruinniú, 26.6.1961', p. 4.

6. Collecting in the Isle of Man and Gaelic Scotland

The Isle of Man

On July 23rd, 1947, de Valera paid an unofficial daylong visit to the Isle of Man. He was shown around the island by the Director of the Manx Museum, Basil Megaw, and the Attorney-General, Ramsey B. Moore. One of the places de Valera and his travelling companions visited was 'the open-air folk museum at Cregneash (in the very south of the Island), whose curator was Ned Maddrell, a native Manx Gaelic speaker.' When de Valera was told that 'no really adequate sound-recordings had been made of the few surviving native speakers of Manx Gaelic, he said that, if it would be helpful, he would be glad to ensure that the best technical facilities and "know-how" were made available for the purpose.' The Trustees of the Manx Museum took up his offer after first consulting with *Yn Cheshaght Ghailckagh* ('the Manx Language Society').[235]

It was not entirely true that no recordings had been made of Manx prior to this time. For example, the Norwegian linguistic and Celtic scholar, Carl Marstrander, had made recordings of Manx some seventeen years before, but these he had brought back with him to Norway and nobody in the Isle of Man was aware of their existence.[236] In any event, Manx was on death's door and there was an urgent need to record as much of the spoken language as possible before it became extinct. As things turned out, the native speaker of Manx de Valera met and spoke to that day in July 1947 was to be the last native speaker of the language, dying in December 1974.

De Valera's generous offer to the Manx Museum was easier made than realised. On his return to Ireland he contacted Ó Duilearga with a view to having the Commission record the last native speakers of Manx. Caoimhín Ó Danachair, in an interview with George Broderick more than thirty years later, says that de Valera learned from Ó Duilearga 'that the Commission had no sound-recording unit at all' and that de Valera 'ordered that one be obtained'.[237] Early the following month (August 1947) the Finance Sub-Committee sanctioned the

---

235 Broderick 1999, p. 62.
236 Ibid., p. 62, n. 14.
237 Ibid., pp. 62–63.

purchase of a new gramophone recording apparatus and later that year, after this equipment had arrived, the purchase of a van to transport it.[238] It was late April 1948, however, by the time this van was adapted for use as a mobile recording unit and other arrangements for the trip to the Isle of Man were finalised. The mobile unit was to be operated by Caoimhín Ó Danachair.

Ó Danachair's stay on the Isle of Man lasted from April 22nd to May 5th, during which time he recorded 'on twenty six 12- and 16-inch double-sided discs just over four hours of recorded material' from eight speakers, five men and three women. As Ó Danachair was twelve full days in the Isle of Man, one might imagine that his harvest might have been greater. George Broderick explains some of the reasons for this:

> The speakers would be brought together for the purpose of the recording, and some interesting material from this interaction was collected. However, the distance between the various speakers' homes was in most cases sufficiently far enough away to prevent ordinary day-to-day contact which would have produced a different sort of relationship between them (i.e. one of more familiarity), rather than one of formality on the occasions of the recordings. That is to say, that had the speakers been on more familiar terms with each other, more idiom and *Umgangsprache* might possibly have been elicited than at times the somewhat stilted and more reserved speech actually recorded.

Of course, it is not at all certain, as George Broderick points out, that these speakers even if they had been more familiar with each other would have conversed naturally in Manx. The material the Irish Folklore Commission collected in the Isle of Man ranged 'from long conversations to stories, recitations (from memory) of some song fragments, one or two hymns, to versions of the Lord's prayer.'[239]

The Commission's trip to the Isle of Man was considered by all a success. At the next meeting of the Commission, Ó Duilearga read out a letter of thanks from the Director of the Manx Museum. The meeting also expressed it gratitude at the good work done by Caoimhín Ó Danachair.[240] The Commission's work in the Isle of Man also helped increase interest in the island in doing further recordings with the last speakers of Manx and in collecting the folklore of the island more systematically. In early October 1948 a three-member delegation from the Isle of Man flew to Dublin to spend a day at the Commission – one of whose members was Basil Megaw of the Manx Museum. While at the Commission, they acquainted themselves with its work and methods. Some of the delegation expressed the wish of returning at a later stage to spend time at the Commission in order to learn how to initiate the collecting of Manx folklore.[241]

---

238 ED FL 6: 'IFC. Fin. Sub-Com./Min. 62nd Meeting, 9.8.1947', par. 504 and 'IFC. Sub-Com./Min. 63rd Meeting, 2.12.1947', par 509.
239 Broderick 1999, pp. 63 and 69.
240 ED FL 6: 'IFC. Fin. Sub-Com./Min. 65th Meeting, 19.6.1948', par. 522.
241 ED FL 6: 'CBÉ. Miont. 54ú Cruinniú, 29.10.1948', par. 416(i).

Ó Duilearga's interest in Gaelic Scotland

We have seen that as a young man Ó Duilearga went to the Isle of Barra in the Outer Hebrides to learn Scottish Gaelic. Unlike Ireland, the latter half of the nineteenth century had seen extensive collecting of folklore in Gaelic Scotland. In the years 1859-60, John Francis Campbell (Campbell of Islay), inspired by the work of Asbjørnsen and Moe in Norway, 'employed half a dozen collectors, including an Islay schoolmaster and gamekeepers on the Argyll estates, who went all over the West Highlands and Islands' collecting folktales for him. Campbell published part of this collection in his four-volume work *Popular Tales of the West Highlands* (1860-62), but much of the collection remained unpublished.[242]

Ó Duilearga was well aware that much folklore remained to be collected in Gaelic Scotland and he was anxious to see the riches of Scottish oral tradition recorded. In a letter he wrote to von Sydow in late 1936 he mentions the Folklore conference to be held in Edinburgh the following summer and says that he is reluctant to go because of his frustration with the inactivity of the Scots, or rather the Lowlanders, whom he accuses of being indifferent to Highlanders and Highland (i.e. Gaelic) tradition.[243] In the event, he did not attend the Edinburgh conference and his impatience with the Scots did not abate. If the Scots would not act, he would. The outbreak of the Second World War not only affected Ó Duilearga's plans for collecting folklore in Ireland, but would also appear to have postponed any plans he had for collecting in Scotland. However, in a short memorandum he prepared for the Dept. of Education in the summer of 1943 on the future work and organisation of the Commission, he mentions the desirability of extending the work of the Commission to western Scotland.[244]

Calum MacLean reconnoitres

With the War going on there was little Ó Duilearga could do to effect collecting in Scotland. However, from March 1945 the Commission had a native speaker of Scottish Gaelic on its staff, Calum MacLean (Calum Mac Gilleathain), employed as a temporary cataloguer of material in Scottish Gaelic in the Commission's possession. He also knew Irish and had done some part-time collecting for the Commission in Connemara in the early 1940's. It would appear that Ó Duilearga initially employed MacLean as a cataloguer with an eye to sending him to Scotland later as a collector. To this

---

242 Bruford and Macdonald 1994, pp. 23–24. In August 1934, Ó Duilearga, a friend of J. G. McKay's, addressed a letter to the Scottish Anthropological Society requesting that it publish two additional volumes of tales from the Campbell of Islay collection already prepared by McKay as well as a third volume that was in preparation. See Ó Duilearga 1934, pp. 457–459.

243 LUB Saml. von Sydow: Ó Duilearga to von Sydow, dated 4.12.1936, pp. 3–4.

244 ED CO 495 (8): 'Coimisiún Béaloideasa Éireann. Memorandum Gairid', dated 12.7.1943, p. [3].

end, MacLean was sent on a trial run to Scotland from December 6th, 1945 to February 18th, 1946 to assess the situation. A month of this time he spent on holidays, but the rest of the time he spent in consultation with various individuals and in undertaking some collecting.[245]

Everyone MacLean spoke to warmly welcomed the idea of the Irish Folklore Commission extending its collecting to Scotland, and nobody felt that the Commission was encroaching on territory that did not belong to it. Quite the opposite, in fact, appears to have been the case. MacLean reported that '[m]any people in Scotland expressed admiration of the work done by the Irish Folklore Commission and commended the Irish Government for financing and encouraging the work.' Moreover, the Rev. M. Maclean, 'a noted writer and figure in the Gaelic movement' not only supported the idea of the Irish Folklore Commission initiating collecting in Scotland, he felt that '[f]or the study of folklore Ireland and Gaelic Scotland would have to be treated as one', and that the Commission 'was the only body competent to deal with Scottish oral tradition.' Calum MacLean also spent several weeks collecting in his native island of Raasay where he discovered an abundance of tradition even among the young. As a result of this collecting, he realised that: 'In Scotland there is an immense field to be covered and much more than I, at least, ever expected still to be collected and committed to writing or recorded by the latest scientific devices.' He recommended:

> ...that the time is ripe to begin the systematic collection of Scottish and Gaelic folklore under the aegis of the Irish Folklore Commission. I have no doubt that the help of many people in Scotland will be forthcoming. Naturally a Scottish Folklore Institute would be the ideal aim, but, at the present juncture, Scottish Gaels would welcome the support of the Irish Folklore Commission.[246]

In his annual report to the Government for 1945–1946, Ó Duilearga began his account of MacLean's visit to Scotland and of the Commission's plans for collecting in Scotland thus: 'The Commission has long wished to collect and catalogue the folklore of Scotland, for the fruits of our work in Ireland will be wanting as long as the folklore of Gaelic Scotland will be left uncultivated ('gan saothrú').'[247] In putting the matter so, he knew that he would have the ear of at least one member of the Government, the Taoiseach, Éamon de Valera.

Difficulties with the Dept. of Education

Nevertheless, the Commission's proposals to extend its field of operations to western Scotland did not meet with such ready approval in the Dept. of Education. When Ó Duilearga in 1943 first broached the desirability of

---

245 D/T S 15548B: 'Gearr-Thuar./1945–1946', p. 7.
246 ED CO 495 (8): 'Report of Visit to Scotland. Dec. 7th 1945 – Feb. 17th 1946'.
247 D/T S 15548B: 'Gearr-Thuar./1945–1946', p. 7 (trans.).

extending the work of the Commission to Scotland in the not too distant future, Proinnsias Ó Dubhthaigh of the Dept. of Education dismissed the idea out of hand: 'I think this suggestion is so impractical that it need not be seriously considered.'[248] As this was written in an internal memo, Ó Duilearga probably did not realise that he would have an uphill battle with the Dept. of Education to convince them of the wisdom of such a venture. In any event, in order to extend its operations to Scotland, the Commission would need an increased grant, and this was not possible until the cessation of hostilities.

In May 1946, Ó Duilearga had an interview with the Minister for Finance, Frank Aiken, in which the latter 'assured' him 'of his interest' in the work of the Commission and 'encouraged' him 'to ask for an additional grant of £2,000, pending Government decision on the permanent establishment of the Commission.' Emboldened by his interview with Aiken, who was very sympathetic to the Irish language, Ó Duilearga wrote to the Dept. of Education. Among other things, he explained that this increased grant was to cover collecting in Scotland. He spoke of the 'most favourable opportunity' that there then existed for 'the extension of the work of collection to Scotland', and of Calum MacLean's discussions with 'several influential Scots who welcomed the project as there is no hope that such work will be undertaken by a Scottish institution.' MacLean, he informed them, was also 'confident that he will be able to enlist the help of several young Scots from various parts of the Highlands and Islands on a part-time basis.' The extension of the work to Scotland was also of international importance: 'I need hardly say that the undertaking of collection in Scotland, besides being a necessary complement to collection in Ireland and a most valuable addition to international scholarship, will redound to the credit of the Irish Government.'[249]

Some days after the Dept. of Education had received the above letter, Rita Ní Mhaolchatha of that department drew up a memorandum on this request of Ó Duilearga's for an increased grant to cover, among other things, collecting in Gaelic Scotland. She took a very critical stance in relation to the plan to extend collecting to Scotland:

> The situation is that the director has given no explanation of the need there is to initiate collecting in Scotland at present, and it is not clear, as far as I am aware, that such work comes within the terms of reference that pertain to the Commission that is there at present. The Director says that such collecting would advance international scholarship and that fame would accrue to the Irish Government as a result of the work. If international fame is to be associated with the work, surely Scottish scholars would like to keep control of the work themselves. It appears to me that Scottish scholars would have cause for complaint if the Irish Department of Education were to spend public money on such without getting permission from anybody beforehand. It would be better, in

---

248 ED CO 495(8): internal memo entitled 'Folklore Commission. Proposed Permanent Appointment etc.' signed FO'D (= Proinnsias Ó Dubhthaigh), 1.9.43.
249 ED CO 495 (8): Ó Duilearga to Sec. Dept. of Educ., dated 30.5.1946.

my opinion, if such a scheme were delayed until the Commission has independent status, so that they could discuss the matter directly with the authorities in Scotland. In the meantime, it appears to me that there is an urgent need to hasten the work in Ireland, in respect of collecting, cataloguing, and publishing. It would be better, in my opinion, to spend the extra money (£500) on making available some of the material collected in Ireland for students and the public without further delay.[250]

Ní Mhaolchatha was supported in her opposition by her superior, Proinnsias Ó Dubhthaigh, Assistant Secretary of the Department. Ó Dubhthaigh had from the outset opposed the Commission extending its operations to Scotland (see above), and was still wary of getting involved:

The proposal to send a Collector to Scotland is one which, in my opinion, requires careful consideration apart from the expense involved. If it is agreed to I think it would be very desirable to [seek?] an assurance from the responsible British Authorities (through the Department of External Affairs) that they have no objection. The Commission already has the largest collection of Folklore in the world, but no steps appear to have yet been taken for its scientific examination, or for publication of selections from it. Further additions to the collection will make this work more complicated and difficult. If collection is allowed to extend outside Ireland it is difficult to see where a limit is to be put. If the Gaelic speaking areas of Scotland were covered a case could easily be made for the inclusion of other areas. For these reasons I do not recommend approval of the proposal.

The Secretary of the Department, Mícheál Breathnach, was also critical of the proposal and requested Ó Dubhthaigh to enquire further about the matter from Prof. Ó Duilearga. Breathnach wished to know if the Scots were 'doing anything to collect their own folklore', and pondered: '[i]f it is so valuable it is amazing that it has not been collected already by them, and if it has, we need not collect it.'[251]

It would appear that Ó Duilearga had taken the Dept. of Education by surprise with this proposal to extend collecting to Scotland and that this explains, in part, the initial negative stance officials took towards it. Ó Duilearga had met with Minister for Education in the spring of the previous year and had gained his approval for extending collecting to Gaelic Scotland.[252] In the spring of 1945 he also broached this matter in a meeting with de Valera and gained his approval as well for the idea.[253] In a memorandum he sent the Taoiseach and the Minister for Education some

---

250 ED CO 495 (8): Educ. memo entitled 'CBÉ. Iarratas ar Dheontas Breise de £2,000', dated 3.6.1946 (trans.).
251 ED CO 495 (8): Educ. memo entitled '[I]FC. Application for Additional Grants, dated 8.6.1946'. Breathnach's reply, in Irish, appended (trans.).
252 ED CO 495 (8): Ó Duilearga to Sec. Dept. of Educ., 21.6.1946.
253 Ibid and D/T S 6916B: Ó Duilearga to de Valera, 7.3.1945.

months later, Ó Duilearga speaks of the importance of Gaelic Scotland for the investigation of Irish folklore:

> The oral traditions of Ireland and those of Gaelic Scotland form a natural unity; it is impossible fully to study or understand either without the other. For the student of Irish Gaelic tradition the oral literature and *seanchas* [lore] of Argyll and the Hebrides is as important as that of Cork and the Aran Islands.

He also says that the 'Department of Education has already indicated its approval of a suggestion by the Director that this work should be put in hands as soon as conditions permit.'[254] What he failed to realise, however, was that the Minister for Education appears not to have informed Education officials about his support for Ó Duilearga's proposal. Neither were they aware of the Taoiseach's support for collecting in Scotland.

Officials in the Dept. of Education were, no doubt, angry that they had not been kept informed by their political masters of developments, but there was little they could do to thwart this proposal once it had the support of their own Minister and the Taoiseach. On July 2nd, 1946, Mícheál Breathnach wrote to the Dept. of Finance requesting an additional grant of £2,000 for the Commission and enclosing a copy of a letter from Ó Duilearga, in which the latter explains that both the Taoiseach and the Minister for Education supported the plan to extend collecting to Scotland.[255] But for the fact that the Minister for Finance was also in favour of granting this increased grant to the Commission, most likely plans to collect in Scotland would have had to be abandoned, as strong opposition might have been expected from that quarter. Before agreeing to employing Calum MacLean as a part-time cataloguer of Scottish Gaelic material in the Commission's possession, the Dept. of Finance 'ascertained at the time that the Finance Sub-Committee was satisfied that this work fell within the terms of reference of the Commission.' They were also 'informed semi-officially that it was not proposed then to make any effort to add to the Scottish Gaelic material which the Commission already had and much of which had come from the Folklore Institute, who had employed a part-time Collector in the "old colonies" of Western Scotland.'[256] In different circumstances the Dept. of Finance might have sensed that they had been duped into sanctioning the employment of MacLean as a temporary cataloguer when Ó Duilearga's real intent was to employ him full-time in another capacity entirely. A different Minister for Finance might also have supported his officials in opposing the extension of collecting to Scotland, but Ó Duilearga had ensured both the support of their Minister as well as that of the Taoiseach and the Minister

254 D/T S 6916B: 'Memorandum on the IFC with Recommendations for its Development and Extension' p. 9. Italics underlined in original.
255 D/F S 101/0011/34: Breathnach to Sec. Dept. of Fin., dated 2.7.1946.
256 D/F S 101/0011/34: internal memo (untitled), addressed to Mr. Almond and Mr. Hanna, dated 15.7.1946. León Ó Broin, Finance's representative on the Commission, strongly supported the employment of MacLean.

for Education. In late July 1946 the Dept. of Finance sanctioned this grant of £2,000 for the Commission.[257]

MacLean begins collecting

Calum MacLean began collecting in Scotland in June 1946, even before official sanction for the payment of the funds to finance this extension of the work of the Commission came through. In his first year as full-time collector MacLean travelled all over the Hebrides and in his letters back to Head Office spoke of the 'great willingness of people to give him what native lore they possessed and of the warm welcome he received everywhere.' In his report to the Government for 1946–47, Ó Duilearga, in relating MacLean's activities for the previous year, states: 'I know of no better nor more suitable man for the job than he – it is work of ultra-importance not only for Scotland and for Ireland but for Europe and the world in general.' He could also report that MacLean's work had met not only with appreciation with all in Scotland who learned of his work, but that he had also received numerous promises from people willing to collect part-time for the Commission [258]

MacLean worked from his home in Raasay travelling throughout the Inner and Outer Hebrides collecting folklore with the Ediphone and transcribing it back in Raasay. During the years he collected for the Commission he worked with a number of spectacular storytellers, as well as collecting from numerous other informants. From one of his prime informants, Angus MacMillan of Benbecula, he recorded in February 1949 the longest folktale ever recorded in Scottish Gaelic, *Alasdair mac a' Cheird* ('Alasdair, son of the Tin Smith'). This ran to 58,000 words.[259] In the four and a half years he worked for the Commission in Scotland he collected material to fill some eighteen large volumes of folklore.[260] Although he was working further afield than the other full-time collectors, links with Head Office were maintained by means of correspondence and visits from the staff of Head Office.

MacLean's work was, however, initially hampered by lack of travel allowances for collectors. Part of the additional grant of £2,000 Ó Duilearga had requested was to cover travelling allowances for the collectors.[261] However, although the Minister for Finance had in his above interview (May 1946) with Ó Duilearga agreed in principle that the collectors should be paid travel allowances, nine months would elapse before the issue of expenses for the collectors was even partly resolved (see Chapter VI/1 below). Without travel allowances the plight of all the collectors was grave, but MacLean's situation was the worst of all. His basic salary was lower than that of the other collectors, although, given the territory he had to operate in, moving

257 Ibid.

258 D/T S 15548B: 'Gearr-Thuar./1946-47', pp. 5–6. (trans.)

259 W. F. H. Nicolaisen 1962, p. 162.

260 Megaw 1960, p. 122. In all, MacLean collected 10,000 pages of material for the Commission, the bulk of it in Scotland. D/T S 16378B/62: Gearr-Thuar./1960–61', p. 6.

261 ED CO 495 (8): Ó Duilearga to Sec. Dept. of Educ., dated 30.5.1946.

from island to island, his expenses were greater. He was still on a temporary cataloguer's salary, even though the nature of his work had changed totally. In November 1946, Ó Duilearga appealed to the Dept. of Education on MacLean's behalf. Comparing MacLean's work to that of the ethnological and antiquarian work of the Ordnance Survey of the 1830's and 1840's, he had this to say:

> It would be difficult to properly assess the importance of the work he is doing. It is almost a hundred years since any concerted effort was made to collect folklore in Scotland. I believe, without doubt, that in time the importance of the work now being done by MacLean will be appreciated more than the great work done by John O'Donovan and Eugene O'Curry a hundred years ago and Dr Douglas Hyde a half century ago. Not only is the benefit of that work not understood at the moment, but moreover the man carrying it out is receiving a pathetic salary.[262]

It would be early March 1947 before MacLean's salary would be raised to that of the other full-time collectors.[263]

School of Scottish Studies

The Commission's venture into Scotland was not destined to last for many years. Inspired by the Irish Folklore Commission, and encouraged and assisted by Ó Duilearga, pressure for official and institutional support for folklore collecting in Scotland began to grow. In May and June 1947, Ó Duilearga gave a number of lectures to various bodies in Scotland and conducted negotiations with certain interested parties. As a result of this encouragement, and of his publicising of the work of the Irish Folklore Commission, in December of that year he was able to inform the Finance Sub-Committee of the Commission that a 'Folklore Institute of Scotland' had been set up some months earlier. He added, however: 'It remained to be seen what work it would encompass, and what financial support it would be given.' He felt that until a viable folklore institute was in operation, 'it was essential to keep MacLean collecting for the Commission in the Hebrides and in Western Scotland.'[264] Ó Duilearga was right to be cautious. The new body was a hybrid between a society and an institute, reflected somewhat in its bilingual title, Cumann Beul-Aithris na h-Alba/Folklore Institute of Scotland – 'cumann' in the Gaelic title translating as society. The Institute's president was the Gaelic scholar and folklore collector, John Lorne Campbell, and its aim was to promote an interest in folklore amongst the population at large and to collect, preserve and research oral traditions, particularly

262 ED CO 495 (8): Ó Duilearga to Sec. Dept. of Educ., dated 6.11.1946, (trans.).
263 ED CO 495(8): J.E. Hanna to Sec. Dept. of Educ, dated 12.3.1947.
264 ED FL 6: 'CBÉ. Miont. 49ú Cruinniú, 27.6.1947', par. 379(j) and 'IFC. Fin. Sub-Com./ Min. 63rd Meeting, 2.12.1947', par. 311 [recte 511].

those of Gaelic Scotland.[265] Given the linguistic history of Scotland, and the fact that Gaelic Scotland had by this time come to occupy quite a marginal position in Scottish society, a body devoted primarily to collecting folklore in Scottish Gaelic was unlikely to get sufficient public funding. Although the foundations of the Folklore Institute of Scotland were shaky, the authorities were at last beginning to see the need for the folklore of Scotland to be collected. In May 1948 a delegation from the Scottish Advisory Council of Education came to Dublin to acquaint themselves at first hand with the work of the Commission, and later that year Ó Duilearga helped pave the way for a visit to Sweden by three members of the Council in order to investigate the organisation of folklore there.[266]

Also in 1948 the University of Edinburgh established the Linguistic Survey of Scotland 'in order to record and study Scots and Gaelic speech', and the following year, in conjunction with the survey, the idea took shape of founding 'a research centre for the study of, among other things, the oral and material folk traditions of Scotland' within the University. Prof. Angus McIntosh, head of the Survey, towards the end of the summer of 1949 wrote to Ó Duilearga on the matter. McIntosh recalls: 'This led, on 11 October, to a warm and positive letter of encouragement and at the very end of that year I found myself staying as a guest in his home and discussing in detail and at length the numerous problems that lay ahead.' The following summer (1950) McIntosh had further talks with Ó Duilearga at a Viking Congress in Shetland as well as with Dag Strömbäck of the University of Uppsala, who was also at this congress.[267]

These negotiations bore fruit and on January 1st, 1951 the School of Scottish Studies was set up in the University of Edinburgh. In late February 1951, Ó Duilearga, on the request of the Scottish authorities, spent five days in Edinburgh advising the Scots on how best to organise the collecting of folklore. In his report to the Government for 1950–1951, Ó Duilearga could announce with satisfaction.

> The Irish Folklore Commission, and especially the Honorary Director, have long been hoping that the Scots themselves would take responsibility for the collection of folklore in their own country. However excellent Calum MacLean was in doing that work for this Commission, the situation would be much better if the work was being done by the Scots. The Director was continually urging them to do that and promising every help from Ireland to any group that would undertake it. In the end this bore fruit when towards the end of the year it was decided to initiate the collecting of folklore under the auspices of the University of Edinburgh.

The new institute had asked the Commission to second Calum MacLean to them and this they agreed to do from January 1st, 1951. Ó Duilearga ended

---

265 Lysaght 1990, p. 42, n. 17.
266 ED FL 6: 'CBÉ. Miont. 53ú Cruinniú, 25.6.1948', par. 410(a) and 'CBÉ. Miont. 54ú Cruinniú, 29.10.1948', par. 416(j).
267 McIntosh 1980.

this account by expressing the wish, on behalf of the Commission, that the new institute would 'be successful and that the work done henceforth in Scotland would bear fruit, and be of benefit for the Gaelic population of both countries in addition to that of the cultured world.'[268]

Ó Duilearga's gamble/de Valera's Celtic Vision

There is no doubt that Ó Duilearga was taking a gamble in seeking to extend the Commission's collecting to Scotland. Given its limited resources, the Commission could ill afford to get involved in collecting in Scotland, and years might have elapsed before any body in Scotland would be in a position to take over from them. But for the foresight of Ó Duilearga much Scottish Gaelic tradition, and probably much else of Scottish oral tradition, would have been lost. For although the Scots would, most likely, eventually have got around to organising folklore collecting on their own, it probably would have taken much longer without the stimulus and input from Ó Duilearga and the Irish Folklore Commission. However, it is unlikely that Ó Duilearga would have succeeded in extending the Commission's work to Scotland but for the foresight of another individual.

Éamon de Valera was one of the few Irish politicians of his generation who could be said to have had a Celtic consciousness and vision. As President of the Executive Council of the Irish Free State he had addressed the Celtic Congress held in Dublin in July 1934. Speaking, in both Irish and English, at the opening meeting, he is reported as saying: 'I hope that your Congress will lead to new fervour in the pursuit of Celtic Studies and to organised cooperative effort to revive the Celtic languages amongst our peoples.' In addition, he offered financial support: 'the Government of Saorstát Éireann is ready to give substantial financial aid towards the carrying out of any practical plan of co-operative research which may be evolved at this gathering.' He also expressed the hope that the Congress would produce such a plan and that it would 'not dissolve until a permanent organisation has been formed to put it into effect.'[269]

Only snatches of de Valera's speech were reported in the newspapers. However, his notes for his opening speech in English give a fuller picture of his thinking on Celtic matters.

> There are other aspects of the life of the Celtic race in which you are interested. The time has come to make a serious study of the history of the race from the earliest times, and to arrive at some conclusions on early Celtic influences on Europe as a whole. Separate studies on various aspects of Celtic archaeology have been made. But the means have been lacking to give scholars in our different countries the opportunity of coming together and working in co-operation. The Irish Government

268 D/T S 15548B: 'Gearr-Thuar.1950–51', p. [2] & [6] (trans.).
269 *The Irish Independent* Tuesday July 10, 1934, p. 9.

are ready to give substantial financial aid for this purpose when definite proposals are put before them.

Conscious, most likely, that the concept of race was being used to create disharmony, inflame hatred, and justify discrimination in Europe and elsewhere at the time, he may have felt it necessary to justify his use of this term:

> I need hardly say that this Congress is being held in no spirit of race glorification. On the contrary, we desire and intend in all humility to make use of our common origin for the purpose of striving to increase the sum of human knowledge by studying in friendship and co-operation the sources of the civilisation of this section of the human race. And in doing so we invite most cordially the aid of scholars all over the world, to whatever branch of the human family they belong.[270]

De Valera's interest in developing cooperation between scholars in various Celtic countries, and elsewhere, in order to advance research into Celtic civilisation, explains his sudden decision when plans for the establishment for an Institute of Irish Studies in the spring of 1939 were being finalised by the Dept. of Education to broaden the duties of this institute to cover all the Celtic languages and cultures. This was his idea alone, and although it puzzled officials and scholars at the time and since, the seed of this idea had been sown five years before at the Celtic Congress held in Dublin in July 1934, if indeed not earlier. The projected Institute of Irish Studies was suddenly transformed into the School of Celtic Studies and instead of being an independent body was to constitute a school within the Dublin Institute for Advanced Studies (another 'sudden' idea of de Valera's, but possibly something that had been hatching in his mind for some time).[271]

Not every scholar of Irish at the time approved of de Valera burdening this new School with such a heavy responsibility in respect of Celtic Studies in general, and in hindsight we know that far more planning would have to have gone into this extension of its duties for it to function effectively in such a wide arena. Nevertheless, the Institute for Advanced Studies Act of 1940 proclaimed that independent Ireland had not only a duty to promote Celtic studies elsewhere, but also a right. The caution displayed by Dept. of Education officials when they first heard of Ó Duilearga's proposal to extend folklore collecting to Scotland would seem to indicate that they did not understand the full implications of this Act, nor the thinking of its chief architect that lay behind it. It was some time before they realised that Ó Duilearga had a trump card in his hand. For despite any other differences he might have had with de Valera over the future organisation of the Commission, and despite their different political allegiances, as noted above, in many respects both men thought along similar lines. Gaelic Scotland was

270 D/T S S 4476A: 'Notes for Opening Meeting of Celtic Congress. Dublin 9 July 1934'.
271 Ó Murchú 1990, pp. 24 ff.

certainly an area of agreement between them. When Ó Duilearga finally reported to the Government on the success of the Commission's venture into Scotland and of the establishment, as a result of its encouragement, of the School of Scottish Studies, de Valera would be out of power. It is unlikely that his successor, John A. Costello, fully realised what had been achieved, although his Minister for Education, Richard Mulcahy, definitely did.

Although de Valera deserves due credit for his role in this collecting expedition to the Hebrides, the bulk of the credit must go to Ó Duilearga and, of course, Calum MacLean, who worked at the coalface. Ó Duilearga's role in the founding of the School of Scottish Studies is rightly remembered as one of his great achievements. His obituary in *The Times* (London), in addition to describing his role in the creation of '[p]robably the most important and extensive national folklore collections in the world' in Dublin, rightly describes him as 'the chief catalyst in the creation of Edinburgh University's School of Scottish Studies', as well as noting that he 'played a leading role in the most significant developments of recent decades in folklore and folklife studies in the United Kingdom.'[272]

272 *The Times* July 4 1980, p. 19.

V The Work of Head Office

1. The Work of the Director

Organising programmes of work

Although drawing a salary from University College Dublin, Ó Duilearga's duties in that college, first as a statutory lecturer and later as professor, were minimal at most. Even though he is listed as giving lectures to students of Irish in the College Calendars up to the mid 1940's, it would appear that the lecturing he undertook in the College consisted mainly of 'pep talks' to encourage students to collect folklore in their free time. He was consequently free to devote all his energies to the Commission.

According to the terms of Reference of the Commission, the Director's duties involved the following:

> (1) To prepare programmes of work for consideration by the Commission and to organise and supervise the execution of such programmes as may be approved by the Commission and by the Minister for Education.
> (2) Subject to the approval of the Commission, to engage staff in such numbers and at such rates of remuneration and on such other conditions as may be approved by the Minister for Education with the sanction of the Minister for Finance.
> (3) To control and supervise the work of the staff of the Commission.[1]

Programmes of work sanctioned by the Commission needed not just the approval of the Minister for Education but indirectly also that of the Minister for Finance before they could be executed, and often involved a great deal of negotiation. This negotiation fell to Ó Duilearga, as did the task of negotiating with politicians and officials to get better funding and, in particular, better salaries for his staff, as well as a more permanent foundation for the Commission itself. As the Commission was initially expected only to run for five years, naturally its Terms of Reference did not deal with such matters as the future organisation of the Commission, and glossed over any problems that might arise in getting the approval of the Minister

1   UCDA Michael Tierney Papers LA30/436(10).

313

for Education and the sanction of the Minister for Finance for individual programmes of work the Director might propose. As things turned out, there were problems in profusion, and both the functioning and future organisation of the Commission were a constant worry for its Director. Negotiating with officials was a job in itself, but it was a job Ó Duilearga had to do on top of all his other duties. Moreover, in dealing with officials his personal charm may not always have sufficed. Meeting with top government officials, and politicians, when so much often depended on the outcome, would appear to have been stressful for him. In an interview, quoted above, in the 1970's, shortly after his retirement, he speaks of his first meeting with Éamon de Valera, and admits that he was no diplomat, and spoke from the heart.[2] On that particular occasion, speaking from the heart, and speaking his mind worked, but it did not always work. Moreover, not all his subsequent meetings with de Valera were to prove as harmonious and the resulting stress, along with endless negotiating with various officials, most likely contributed to the breakdown of his health in the late 1940's, and may have made him wary of dealing directly with officials during the last two decades or so of the Commission's operations.

Employing and supervising staff

As laid down in the Commission's Terms of Reference (see Appendix 1), Ó Duilearga chose the staff to be employed, and the Commission approved their appointment. Bríd Mahon says that he 'boasted that he had an unerring gift for picking the right man or woman for the job.'[3] Considering some of the exceptional people he employed, this is, for the most part, true. However, on a number of occasions a collector did not live up to his expectations and had to be dismissed. Not only did he choose his staff, he also tried to instill his own fervour in them. Bríd Mahon says: 'Delargy, who could sell sand to the Arabs or snow to men living in igloos, told us we were the custodians of the soul of Ireland, that it was our duty to help gather the fragments of a once great civilization before it was too late.'[4] As well as supervising his office staff, his work as Director took him around the country visiting the collectors in the field, not just when starting a new collector off, but throughout the period of operations of the Commission, although as his energies began to wane in the 1950's, his trips to meet up with collectors would appear to have become less frequent. These trips to the field had, naturally, to be fitted into an otherwise busy schedule. He also supervised the work of collecting from Head Office. For example, by checking the collectors' transcriptions against their recordings, as noted above, and by corresponding with them, as well as meeting with them from time to time at Head Office.

Sometimes he brought foreign visitors with him on his trips to meet up with collectors in order to show them the work of the Commission, killing

2   RTÉSA A5382, 'Here and Now' (1971).
3   Mahon 1998, p. 15.
4   Mahon 1998, p. 15.

two birds with the one stone, so to speak. The arrival of some foreign visitor or other might be the pretext for undertaking a particular trip to see one or more of his collectors, or could be fitted into his existing plans. It is obvious that these trips in the company of foreign visitors, some of them eminent folklorists, differed a good deal from his regular trips to the field and afforded him the opportunity to advertise the Commission's work as well as show hospitality to his visitors, either reciprocating hospitality already shown him on his trips abroad or anticipating hospitality to be shown him in times to come.[5] Ó Duilearga also did a certain amount of collecting on his trips to the field, and managed to get in some fishing (of which more below). However, the bulk of Ó Duilearga's personal collecting work was done prior to the setting up of the Commission. His later collecting was, to a large extent, incidental, undertaken either to initiate a new collector in the skills of the trade or to keep his own skills whetted. His visits to collectors not only allowed him to keep a watchful eye on their work and help them open up new areas, such trips also kept him in touch with the last bearers of the older tradition, whose lore he had vowed to save for posterity. Simply perusing manuscripts in Head Office, as they came in from the collectors, would not have been as satisfying as meeting with live narrators in the field. These trips no doubt caused him pain as well, as he could experience not only the death of individual custodians of the old lore of Gaelic Ireland, at first hand, but the rapid retreat of the Irish language itself in many areas, especially in those two areas in which he had first collected extensively, namely southwest Kerry, and northwest Clare.[6]

In order to facilitate his visits to collectors in the field, Ó Duilearga, since autumn 1937 had the use of a car, paid for by the Commission.[7] However, when he wished to become intimately acquainted with a new area, he was forced to abandon his car and take to walking. He has left us an account of how he used set about opening up a new area for collectors:

> ...I make my first acquaintance with the area by seeing as much of it as possible on foot, wandering with a fishing rod along the trout-streams or walking for the length of the day through hills or across the boglands which for me have a singular fascination. And in this pleasant way I meet farmers or herds, water-bailiffs and game-keepers, children returning from school, the postman on his rounds, or the local shopkeeper or teacher. From them I learn that so-and-so is a good storyteller or singer, that such an old woman has a large collection of ancient prayers and charms and is an expert in the lore of medicinal herbs. Or it may be that I meet the story-tellers themselves down by the river. I remember old Seán Ó Sé

---

5   For one such trip in the company of eminent foreigners, see Stith Thompson 1996, pp. 136 ff.

6   His annual reports to the Government rarely give details of his trips to the field to meet up with his collectors. But we know from the collectors' diaries and Ó Duilearga's correspondence that such trips were numerous, at least in the early years.

7   ED [FL 9]: 'IFC. Fin. Sub-Com. 2nd Meeting, 5.10.1935', par 19. Throughout his time as Director he was also paid expenses by the Commission.

coming along to help me land a salmon from the stream at the bottom of his land, and then we sat down on a grassy knoll, our faces to the sun and our backs to the wind, and smoked and chatted; and that was how I met one of the best Kerry story-tellers I have ever known.[8]

Lecturing at home and public relations work

Ó Duilearga's official duties, as laid down by the Terms of Reference of the Commission, did not involve public relations work as such, yet long before the Commission was set up he realised that cultivating good relations with the public at large, as well as with the academic community, was essential if the folklore of Ireland was to be saved. In a memorandum to Ernest Blythe regarding the setting up of the Irish Folklore Institute in early 1929, among the duties of the proposed institute, he stipulates the need for a) '[l]ectures on radio, in educational institutes and elsewhere', b) '[p]ropaganda in the public press', and c) [c]orrespondence with hundreds of persons in all parts of Ireland'.[9] During his time as Director of the Irish Folklore Institute, and later as Director of the Irish Folklore Commission, Ó Duilearga was to use all the above means to publicise the importance of saving Irish folklore and to seek the assistance of the public in this enterprise.

In his reports to the Government, especially during the Commission's early years of operation, Ó Duilearga on many occasion emphasises the importance of public support for its work. At the end of the Commission's first year of operations, he expressed, in particular, his gratitude to the hundreds of people around the country 'who gave generously the richness of the folk literature that they had inherited from their ancestors.'[10] Two years later he notes that the people of the countryside understand the 'national importance of the work, especially as the old Irish-way of life is daily fleeting ('éalú') from us at an incredible pace.'[11] There is no doubt that Ó Duilearga himself laid the foundations for much of the goodwill that collectors met with in the field. The diaries of the collectors abound with references to the high esteem he was held in by informants. However, public relations work was not just necessary to create goodwill among communities rich in folk traditions. It was also needed to encourage collecting.

Ever since the days of the Irish Folklore Institute, Ó Duilearga used from time to time lecture students in the teacher training colleges and at UCD in the hope of getting them interested in collecting folklore, and, of course, to impress on them the richness of Irish oral tradition. This work continued after the setting up of the Commission. We have seen above how, during the school year 1937–1938, both Ó Duilearga and Seán Ó Súilleabháin lectured to groups

---

8   Ó Duilearga 1963, p. 75.

9   D/F F 006/0002/29: memo entitled 'Irish Folklore Institute', cov. letter dated 17.1.1929.

10   D/T S 15548A: 'Gearr-Thuar./1935–36', p. [3] (trans.).

11   D/T S 15548A: 'Gearr-Thuar./1937–38', p. [1] (trans.).

316

of teachers all over the country in connection with the Schools Scheme then in operation (see Chapter IV/2). This type of intensive lecturing, entailing a lot of travel, must have taken its toll on both men, as indeed did less intensive public relations work, when it had to be fitted in to an otherwise very busy life. The success of the Schools Scheme and the subsequent recruitment of many National School teachers as questionnaire correspondents and part-time collectors probably reduced the need for intensive public relations work, for a time at least. Due to cutbacks during the Second World War, the Commission could only afford to retain a few part-time collectors but continued to utilise a network of questionnaire correspondents. However, by the late 1940's the ranks of questionnaire correspondents, deriving, in large part, from the Schools Scheme of 1937/1938, seem to have been thinned by natural attrition, as well as other factors (see above). This meant that once again there was a need to actively recruit people to work for the Commission. In the post-War period, by lecturing, and by other means, Ó Duilearga continued to seek people to collect part-time for the Commission. Over the next decade or more, his reports to the Government record him speaking from time to time to various vocational and student bodies. As the years went by, however, public relations work seems to have produced fewer and fewer returns.

With the passage of time, it would appear that it became more and more difficult to get people interested in collecting folklore, either in a full-time or part-time capacity. As part-time collectors of long standing died or, for whatever reason, stopped collecting, they were not being replaced in sufficient numbers to ensure a steady flow of material to the archives. Although his physical strength was waning, it does not appear that Ó Duilearga was any less effective as a public speaker or propagandist than formerly. Nevertheless, changes in society were probably making his audiences less receptive to his exhortations, and less willing to sacrifice their leisure time by contributing material to the Commission's archive. The writer Michael Coady as a young trainee teacher in St. Patrick's College Drumcondra in the late 1950's heard Ó Duilearga address the students on the subject of Irish Folklore. He says that when Ó Duilearga spoke in general terms of the work of the Commission, and of the importance of Irish folklore nationally and internationally, he was listened to attentively and his performance was superb, but when he went on to speak on the minutiae of the old traditional way of life itself, he lost the attention of his audience. This, he says, was the general consensus of his fellow students.[12] Society was shedding even traditions of more recent origin and turning its face towards the modern, and in so doing was becoming less and less sympathetic with the ideals that had led to the extensive collecting of folklore in the first place. By the mid-1960's the greater spending power of various sectors of the community, and the desire of the young in particular to spend their extra money on the pursuit of new modes of entertainment, new pastimes, and lifestyles (pleasures denied an earlier generation that had contributed greatly to the collecting of folklore) most likely resulted in a lessening of enthusiasm for collecting folklore among certain sections of

12   From conversations with Michael Coady as well as a written communication.

the population.[13] Be that as it may, the 1960's witnessed the Commission's core of part-time collectors continue to diminish.

Lecturing abroad and fostering international contacts

Receiving and accommodating foreign visitors in the first decade or so of the Commission was rather difficult, given the cramped quarters the staff had to work in. In a report he sent to the Taoiseach in late 1946, Ó Duilearga, under 'Disadvantages', complains of their cramped accommodation: 'three tiny rooms with a total floor space of less than 600 square feet.' He says: 'There are no facilities whatsoever for students or visitors, and interviews with important visitors have to be held under circumstances which reflect little credit on the Commission, due entirely to essential lack of ordinary facilities.'[14] When the Commission moved to new accommodation in 1949, it was easier for them to accommodate foreign scholars. In his report to the Government for the year 1950/1951, Ó Duilearga could relate that during the previous year hundreds of foreigners had visited the Commission seeking information on Irish traditional life. In addition, many learned foreign institutions had contacted the Commission. He added: 'It is certain that it is a long time since the Government of Ireland did something so important in respect of cultural matters to enhance the esteem of the country overseas as they did when they established this Commission.'[15]

As well as entertaining foreign visitors in Ireland, at the Commission's Head Office, in the field, and indeed in his home, as he often did, Ó Duilearga fostered foreign contacts by his travels abroad and by maintaining a lively correspondence with foreign scholars. Ever since his trip to northern Europe in 1928, Séamus Ó Duilearga deliberately cultivated the acquaintance of foreign folklore scholars. As a young man in Ireland, even before his 1928 trip, he had met two of the most important foreign scholars he would have close contact with later, namely Reidar Th. Christiansen and Carl Wilhelm von Sydow.

Fostering international relations was not something those who drew up the Terms of Reference of the Irish Folklore Commission thought worth including as one of the Director's responsibilities. At the time, the word 'international' was not the buzzword it is nowadays, and the Commission was expected to spend its state grant on work within Ireland. Nevertheless, there is little evidence that members of the Commission itself or government officials took a negative attitude towards requests by Ó Duilearga to travel abroad if some benefit or other would accrue to the Commission.[16] The Commission

---

13　It is interesting to note, in this connection, that although Ó Duilearga addressed the annual conference of the Irish National Teachers Organisation in 1965 in the hope of recruiting 400 to 500 teachers to collect local historical lore, his appeal, for the most part, fell on deaf ears. See ED FL 1: 'CBÉ. Miont. 124ú Cruinniú, 13.5.1965', par. 921.

14　D/T S 6916B: 'The Irish Folklore Commission', unpaginated, section 4 – sentence quoted above underlined in the original.

15　D/T S 15548B: 'Gearr-Thuar./1950–1951', pp. [7–8] (trans.).

16　It would appear, however, that the Chairman of the IFC, Eric Mac Fhinn, felt that Ó Duilearga catered too much for foreign visitors at the expense of potential Irish users of

in the early years could not afford to finance all of Ó Duilearga's foreign trips. However, in the post-War period, it was in a better position to give financial assistance towards his foreign travel. The development of air travel also meant that trips abroad need not be of such long duration, and so less disruptive of his duties as Director.

There is no doubt that benefits accrued to the Commission and to Ó Duilearga personally from his foreign travel, whether the purpose was lecturing, advising foreign governments or institutions on folklore collecting, or participating in conferences. Above all, his foreign travel allowed him to forge and maintain contact with foreign folklore scholars, to learn new things, to air his views on folkloristic matters, and to advertise the work of the Commission. It also allowed him to acquire books for the Commission's library and arrange for journal exchanges with *Béaloideas*. Finally, attendance at conferences also allowed him to participate in decision making on matters of mutual cooperation between folklorists in various countries.[17]

Conferences and foreign contacts also benefited him in more personal ways. In conjunction with the Lund folklore conference of 1935, Ó Duilearga, along with Stith Thompson, who was many years his senior, was made a member of the Gustavus Adolphus Academy. At this conference Ó Duilearga met the Finnish folklorist Martti Haavio for the first time. In the post-War period they renewed contacts at the Oslo conference of 1946, and two years later, on Haavio's suggestion, Ó Duilearga was appointed 'a member of the consultative editorial committee' of the Folklore Fellows Communications (FFC). This was indeed a great honour for him, and one he accepted with a degree of humility:

> I regard this appointment as a mark of your friendship. I have, indeed, been much touched by your offer, and while, I assure you, I am not really worthy of the honour conferred, I shall conscientiously do all that I can to forward the good work of this the most illustrious folklore publication series in the world.[18]

Many more honours were to follow for Ó Duilearga during the 1950's and 1960's, both international and national, but this must have been one of those that he cherished most. Having his name henceforth on the covers of FFC publications, in a sense, made him one of the 'Folklore Greats'. Now, more than ever, he trod an international stage, and honours came his way from all quarters. Not surprisingly, quite a number of his foreign trips made during the 1950's and 1960's were for the purpose of having an honorary doctorate conferred on him by some university or other (see Chapter VI/2).

Although Ó Duilearga was by the standards of the time a well-travelled man, it was mainly by means of a lively correspondence that he maintained

---

the Commission's collections. Ní Nia (MA thesis), p. 197.

17 For instance, at the Oslo conference of Scandinavian folklorists in 1946, Ó Duilearga was actively involved in negotiations to establish an International Folktale Institute to be based in Copenhagen. For more on this ill-fated Institute, see Bødker 1975, pp. 280–281.

18 Stith Thompson 1996, p. 125 and SKS Haavio Papers 12:58:7: letter dated 8.4.1948.

foreign contacts, and, of course, by encouraging foreigners to visit the Commission's Head Office and by entertaining them while in Ireland. With some, such as the Hungarian folklorist János Honti, who was to die tragically during the Second World War, he exchanged just a few letters,[19] with others, such as Stith Thompson and Åke Campbell, tens of dozens, and in the case of Carl Wilhelm von Sydow, in excess of a hundred and fifty letters and postcards. In those days, before English had become the universal, or near universal, lingua franca it was to become in time, maintaining foreign contacts meant knowing foreign languages. Some of Ó Duilearga's early letters to von Sydow are in Irish, but the vast majority are in English, with occasional postcards and extracts of letters in Swedish. Almost all von Sydow's letters to him are written in Swedish, with a few in Irish. This seems to have been the pattern with other scholars he communicated with: they wrote to him in their mother tongue or some recognised international language and he replied, for the most part, in English.

Maintaining this foreign correspondence, in an otherwise very busy life, certainly absorbed a lot of Ó Duilearga's time and energy, and came at a price. In his report to the Government for 1959–1960, he speaks of the need to attend 'to correspondence from the four distant corners of the globe' and adds: 'The burden of this correspondence falls for the most part on the Director, around 1,500 handwritten letters a year, and as the fame of the Commission spreads around the world, so too does his work.'[20] Three years later, in a similar report, he mentions the figure of '1500–2000 letters' that he had to write annually, and also complains of the burden of seeing to 'visitors from everywhere who come to us in order to do research or to study in the Commission's library, as its like is not to be found in Europe (including the United States) outside of Scandinavia.'[21] He might have delegated more of this correspondence to others, but even if he had wished to do so, with the deterioration in relations between him and some of his senior office staff, his freedom of action in this area was limited (see below Chapter VI/2). There is no doubt that writing such an amount of letters, some of them very long, was often a burden for him as his health failed and as he aged. At the same time, writing to old friends was also a source of solace for him, an escape from present troubles and tensions. Travel also took its toll on him as he got older. After the Kiel International Folklore Conference in autumn 1959 in a letter to Richard Dorson, he remarks that he is unlikely to attend another conference.[22]

What would appear to have been Ó Duilearga's last official trip abroad involved giving advice on folklore collecting. In August 1968, on the invitation of the Icelandic Minister for Education, Ó Duilearga and Dag Strömbäck spent two weeks in Reykjavík advising the Minister and the 'Institute of Manuscripts' ('Handrítastofnun') on how to set up an archive of

---

19 Dömöter 1978, pp. 40–41.
20 D/T S 15548B: 'Gearr-Thuar./1959–60', p. 5 (trans.)
21 ED FL 8: 'Gearr-Thuar./1962–63', p. 5.
22 Lilly Lib. Dorson Papers: Ó Duilearga to Dorson, dated 6.11.1959.

folk literature.[23] A year earlier he had visited the Faroe Islands on a similar advisory trip.[24] As a young man he had set out for northern Europe to seek advice on folklore collecting. Now he was a recognised expert, and his help in organising folklore collecting had been sought by various institutions and governments for more than twenty years. On one occasion, at least, he sought to give advice, without it being solicited. In the late 1950's while on a visit to Rome he met with the Secretary of Propaganda in the Vatican to discuss the possibility of getting the Catholic Church to record, using modern technology, the languages and oral traditions of the Third World, particularly those of Africa, that were, as Ó Duilearga describes, being 'bastardised by strange ideas and modernity'. He also proposed that an Archive of Linguistics and Folklore be established in Rome to house the material collected in this way. Initially, he appears to have been hopeful that something would come of his overture. In the end, however, nothing concrete came of it.[25] Apart from anything else, such a worldwide scheme would have taken someone with the energy and drive of the young Séamus Ó Duilearga to get it off the ground and to maintain it. As a young man, he once complained to von Sydow that English folklorists were too interested in the folklore of the colonies and had 'not yet discovered England.'[26] However, with the rapid changes sweeping the world in the post-War period, and with the demise of colonialism itself, these areas of the world now became a focus worthy of his attention.

23 ED FL 1: 'IFC. Fin. Sub-Com./Min. 142nd Meeting, 22.10.1968', p. 6. This 'Institute of Manuscripts' was later to be reconstituted as the Árni Magnússon Institute.
24 ED FL 8: 'CBÉ. Miont. 133ú Cruinniú, 13.10.1967', par. 984.
25 See Lilly Lib. Stith Thompson Papers: Ó Duilearga to Thompson, dated 30.5.1957, ED FL 4: 'Gearr-Thuar./1961–1962', p. 6, and ED Fl 4: 'CBÉ. Miont. 107ú Cruinniú, 26.6.1961', p. 7.
26 LUB Saml. von Sydow: Ó Duilearga to von Sydow, dated 30.8.1935.

2. The office staff of the Commission

Employing the first office staff

In the above-mentioned memorandum he sent to de Valera in May 1933, Ó Duilearga outlined the duties of the staff of the 'central office' (i.e. Head Office) for the scheme he proposed. They were 'to be employed in the cataloguing, filing and indexing of material collected by field-workers, following a definite plan.' However, they were not just to be employed arranging and processing the material sent in from the field. Apart from supplying collectors 'with paper, notebooks and other stationary' as well as other accessories, they were also to have an input into the work carried out by the collectors. For example, they would help the Director compile '[q]uestionnaires and other literature' to be 'circulated to field-workers as necessity arises'. In addition, Head Office would keep collectors informed of what had been collected already from particular people:

> It is vital that accurate information be placed at the disposal of the field-workers by using which they will avoid the danger of recording material from persons from whom such material has been obtained already. Slipshod and uncontrolled work means a waste of time, energy and public money. Thus a field-worker in Connemara must know what material has been obtained there already, the nature of such material, the names and addresses of those from whom it has been obtained, in order to avoid duplication.

Ó Duilearga saw this 'control work' as 'the main reason for the necessity for a small but competent staff who will supervise the work of the mobile field-worker, direct his attention to points on which information is required and to places where it is known certain desirable information exists.'[27]

Ó Duilearga, although mindful for the need to economise, insisted on 'having an adequate staff competent to deal effectively with the work of

---

27   D/T S 9244: 'Memorandum of Oral Tradition of Ireland', pp. 11–12. Later on the Commission would not be so worried about duplication, when they came to appreciate the folkloristic value of multiple recordings of the same material from the same informant.

supervising and checking the work of the collectors and of classifying and systematizing the results as they come in.' Without 'adequate staff and equipment in the central office' he could not 'advise that the survey be attempted, as a chaotic mass of material of overwhelming proportions and of no scientific value would be the only result, which would not justify the expenditure of a penny of public money.'[28] The minimum staff needed, apart from himself, who would act as Director, was: (a) an 'Assistant-Secretary '; (b) an Assistant 'to act as deputy for the Director during the latter's visits to the country in connection with the personal supervision of field-workers', and who would also help 'in the general organising work involved in' Head Office; (c) 'a trained and competent transcriber' of Ediphone recordings who would also 'check all the records made by field-workers (and transcribed by them) with the transcripts'; (d) a cataloguer to index, file, and catalogue the material forwarded by collectors; and (e) two typists.[29] This amounted to an office staff of six, but obviously he hoped in time to be granted a much larger office staff. Nevertheless, the conference held in the Dept. of Education in October 1933 (see Chapter III/1 above) on the reorganisation of folklore collecting, which Ó Duilearga attended, proposed an office staff of four only: an assistant secretary, a typist, a transcriber, and a cataloguer, whose combined salaries would come to £800, with an additional £100 expenses for the Director.[30] However, even this reduced indoor staff did not satisfy the Dept. of Finance. An internal Finance memo states:

> The estimates for Indoor Staff, both as to numbers and salary, are excessive especially if the number of field workers is restricted as seems essential. One person should be able to discharge the duties of Assistant and Typist and one other person could act both as Cataloguer and Transcriber.[31]

The Department of Finance had its way. Despite Ó Duilearga's reluctance to undertake the proposed folklore survey without adequate head-office staff, the Irish Folklore Commission started operations with a much smaller staff than had been demanded as a minimum by him. In fact, initially only two office staff, apart from the Director were appointed. Although, the number of full-time collectors was much smaller than originally hoped for by Ó Duilearga, this small office staff was to be a great handicap almost from the beginning, and was to seriously affect the work done at Head Office.

Máire MacNeill and Seán Ó Súilleabháin were the first office staff to be employed, the former as Office Manager and the latter as Archivist/Registrar. MacNeill, a Dubliner, was the daughter of Eoin Mac Néill, one of the founding

---

28 D/T S 9244: 'Memorandum of Oral Tradition of Ireland', p. 14.
29 Ibid., pp. 15–16. As collectors were expected to transcribe their own recordings, the transcriber referred to above, among other things, would, most likely, be employed transcribing the backlog of untranscribed recordings already made by Ó Duilearga (and others) in the field.
30 ED CO 3/15/9(495/I): 'Béal Oideas Conference, 16th October, 1933', pp. 3–4.
31 D/T S 9244; 'Observations of the Department of Finance on the Report of the Folklore Conference held on the 16th October, 1933', p. [3].

figures of the Gaelic League, Professor of Early Irish History at UCD, and former Minister for Education. Although employed in a secretarial capacity, Máire MacNeill was one of the most academically gifted of the staff of the Irish Folklore Commission and was to follow in her father's footsteps and become a fine scholar. Ó Súilleabháin was a native of Tuosist in southwest Kerry. He trained as a National School teacher, and had been working as a teacher for nine years or so prior to his employment by the Commission. In the late 1920's or early 1930's, Ó Súilleabháin and Ó Duilearga first made each other's acquaintance. Before their meeting Ó Súilleabháin had already begun collecting the traditions of his native parish, and had been a regular contributor to *Béaloideas* since 1931. In the early 1930's he did a correspondence degree in Celtic Studies with the University of London.[32] In the spring of 1935, on leave from his school, he attended lectures in University College, Dublin, and while there he was contacted by Séamus Ó Duilearga and offered the post of Archivist/Registrar in the Commission on the condition that he travel to Sweden for training. He accepted the offer and left shortly afterwards for Sweden, where he spent approximately three months (early March to early June). Ten weeks of this time he spent in Uppsala learning about the Swedish system of archiving and classifying folk material from Åke Campbell and his assistants, in particular Ella Odstedt.[33]

As the Dept. of Finance would not sanction more than two appointments to Head Office initially, the duties of both Seán Ó Súilleabháin and Máire MacNeill turned out to be far wider, and heavier, than originally envisaged for these posts by Ó Duilearga. Moreover, Finance had to be convinced as to the necessity for an Office Manager at all (for more on this matter, see Chapter VI/1). Ó Súilleabháin's actual job description when appointed was 'Archivist and Registrar', this post corresponding roughly to that of 'cataloguer' in Ó Duilearga's above memorandum. As we have seen above, the duties originally envisaged for this post involved the 'filing, indexing and cataloguing of manuscript material connected with the work of the survey,' However, in the absence of an 'Assistant' and 'transcriber' many of the duties envisaged for these positions fell to Ó Súilleabháin and, to a lesser extent, to Máire MacNeill.[34] Moreover, MacNeill had to function, for the first year at least, as both Office Manager and short-hand typist. However, as we will see below, her duties soon also began to involve cataloguing as well.

---

32 See E. Ó Súilleabháin 1994, pp. 89–91. Although not a native speaker of Irish as such, Seán Ó Súilleabháin acquired a near-native knowledge of Irish at an early age, both from his father, who was a native speaker of Irish and the headmaster of the primary school he attended, and in the locality from the older generation who still spoke Irish. Ibid., p. 89.
33 S. Ó Súilleabháin 1943, pp. 3 and 13.
34 Ó Duilearga also helped check the transcriptions the collectors sent in against their recordings. S. Ó Catháin 1989, p. 58 ff.

Cataloguing and archiving of material

One of the reasons for proceeding with the cataloguing of the material from the beginning of operations was to facilitate 'those interested in Irish and oral literature in Irish' who wished to examine and utilise the collections. The Commission had inherited approximately 50,000 pages of folklore from the Irish Folklore Institute. In its first year of operations it added 35,000 pages to this. During 1935/1936, some 13,675 pages of this amount were catalogued and 8,250 index cards completed. By May 1937 the Commission had added 60,123 pages of folklore to its collections. In all they now had 143,235 pages of folk tradition, had indexed 24,500 pages and had completed 18,600 index cards. Ó Duilearga in his annual report for 1936–1937 stressed that if the collection was to be utilised to the full, in time, the work of cataloguing needed to be executed slowly and painstakingly.[35]

By June 1937 he realised that the material was coming in at such a rate that extra help was needed to keep cataloguing apace with collecting. In a letter to the Dept. of Education he says:

> The experience of the first two years of work of the Commission has shown clearly how much the success of the enterprise is indebted to the selfless labours of Mr. Ó Súilleabháin who is the mainstay of our work. But it has also clearly shown that the task of cataloguing the mass of accumulated material is one which requires not only one cataloguer but several. The Commission has as a temporary measure called on the time of the Secretary, Miss MacNeill, to attempt to cope with the increasing arrears, and her services in this field show the same meticulous care so amply demonstrated in the daily routine of her own work. But the material is pouring in at such a rate that, to control it, and in controlling it to regulate the activities of the field-workers, we require immediately the services of at least one additional cataloguer at a salary of not less than £150 per annum.[36]

An internal Dept. of Finance memo, dated 16th July, 1937, thought the above request reasonable as well as the salary proposed. However, another Finance memo the following month suggested that the Commission could appoint an additional cataloguer from October 1st or postpone the appointment of a cataloguer and appoint the additional collector it sought.[37] In the event, the Commission decided 'that instead of appointing a new cataloguer it would be more desirable to transfer Miss MacNeill entirely to the cataloguing work and to appoint a shorthand typist to deal with correspondence and office routine.'[38]

Not only had Máire MacNeill been trained by Seán Ó Súilleabháin in the intricacies of cataloguing, she had also spent 10 weeks in Lund and Uppsala,

35   D/T S 15548A: 'Gearr-Thuar/1935–36', p. [2] and 'Gearr-Thuar/1936-37', pp. [3]–[4].
36   D/F S 101/0011/34: Ó Duilearga to Sec. Dept. of Educ., dated 24.6.1937, pp. [2]–[3].
37   D/F S 101/0011/34: E. Ní M[haolchatha] to Mr. Morris, dated 16.7.1937, p. [3], and internal Finance memo to Mr. Doolin, dated 10.8.1937.
38   D/F S 101/0011/34: Ó Duilearga to Sec. Dept. of Educ., letter dated 22.3.1938.

from December 1937 to February 1938, learning how to make tradition maps and also acquainting herself with the system of cataloguing.[39] Thus, appointing her instead of someone new, who would have to be initiated into cataloguing, had many short-term advantages, but in the long term it was probably a bad decision. For MacNeill was not being relieved of all her duties as Office Manager. For instance, she would continue to look after the accounts of the Commission.[40] As things turned out, she was never able to devote all her time to cataloguing, and an opportunity to appoint a full-time cataloguer was lost.

By June 1938 the Commission had 213, 603 pages of folklore, of which 45,000 pages were catalogued.[41] Even with Máire MacNeill's assistance, cataloguing the material progressed very slowly, and both Ó Súilleabháin and MacNeill were often of necessity occupied with other tasks. For example, from the beginning of January 1939 to the end of April 1939 neither of them was able to do any work on cataloguing as they had to arrange the material that had come in from the Schools Scheme (see Chapter IV/2 above). The Commission's Main Collection now amounted to 268,177 pages, and the Schools Collection to 1,025,000 pages (including official manuscript books and the pupils copybooks). The acquisition of such an additional amount of material not only added to the nightmare of cataloguing but greatly limited the space available to the Commission. Leaving aside the Schools Collection altogether, the task of cataloguing the ever-growing Main Collection was an uphill battle. By June 1940 the Commission's main collection comprised 305,884 pages of folklore, of which 80,600 pages were catalogued, some 122 volumes.

The War had an effect on cataloguing as indeed it did on every other aspect of the Commission's work. During the summer of 1940, 'as the war became more intense', the Commission's most important manuscripts. (i.e. the Main Collection) were removed to Altnabrocky, Erris, Co. Mayo, while the Schools Collection was housed in Rathfarnam, close to Dublin.[42] As a result, much of the cataloguing Ó Súilleabháin and MacNeill managed to do during the War years did not involve material sent in by the collectors, but rather the folklore found in printed sources or elsewhere.[43] In the middle of the War, Seán Ó Súilleabháin wrote to von Sydow: 'The cataloguing of the MSS. is very much in arrears owing to the smallness of our staff and the large amount of correspondence to be dealt with as a result of our questionnaire system.' Only 'about one-tenth' of the Main Collection had been 'excerpted' (i.e. catalogued for content) and none of the Schools Collection whatsoever. Ó Súilleabháin was, naturally, not happy with this state of affairs, but nevertheless hopeful

---

39 D/T S 15548A: 'Gearr-Thuar./1937–38', p. [4]. Six of the ten weeks she spent in Sweden were due her by way of annual leave. As she was only allowed 18 days annual leave, this would suggest that she had not taken annual leave since the inception of the Commission. Ibid., p. [4].

40 D/F S 101/0011/34: letter dated 22.3.1938.

41 D/T S 15548A: 'Gearr-Thuar./1937–38', p. [4].

42 D/T S 15548B: 'Gearr-Thuar./1940–41', p. 6 (trans.).

43 D/T S 15548B: 'Gearr-Thuar./1944–45', p. [5].

that in time things would improve: 'Something will have to be done to speed up the cataloguing. A larger staff will be needed, and may be provided when our present lease of life comes to an end in 1944.'[44]

As well as instructing questionnaire correspondents by letter (see Chapter IV/4), another time-consuming task of Ó Súilleabháin's, and one that restricted the time he could spend on cataloguing, was paginating and preparing the material that came in for binding. The time Máire MacNeill could devote to cataloguing was also limited by other duties. In particular, she had to take care of the financial accounts of the Commission, as well as look after the general needs of the office.

Towards the end of the War the cataloguing of Irish folklore sources was advanced by the appointment on the April 1st, 1944 of an additional cataloguer, Bréanainn Ó Ruanaighe. Ó Ruanaighe was holder of a BA degree from UCD and before being appointed was given a few months' training at Head Office. Unlike Ó Súilleabháin and MacNeill, who had to devote themselves to many tasks, Ó Ruanaighe was able to concentrate almost entirely on cataloguing. As most of the manuscript material was not readily accessible, having been transferred out of Dublin for safety, he also, initially at any rate, had to catalogue other sources. The first task set him was to catalogue the material in *Béaloideas*. The presence of a full-time cataloguer on the staff of the Commission naturally soon had an effect on the amount of cataloguing being done. In his annual report for 1945–1946, Ó Duilearga states that 'more material had been catalogued this year than in any year since the Commission was set up eleven years ago'. However, it would appear that most, if not all the material catalogued involved published sources, with the exception of Máire MacNeill's cataloguing of folklore material in the Ordnance Survey Letters housed in the library of the Royal Irish Academy.[45]

Although the War ended in early summer 1945, a year later the Commission's collections were still stored away outside Dublin for safekeeping. So even if the staff had been available to catalogue the material, their work would have been greatly hindered by these circumstances. As it was, the three members of staff trained in cataloguing continued to divide their time between different tasks. Many secretarial duties fell to Máire MacNeill with the departure of Íde Ní Eidhin, one of the Commission's two shorthand typists. Seán Ó Súilleabháin also continued to fit cataloguing into an otherwise busy schedule. Even Bréanainn Ó Ruanaighe could not devote all his time to cataloguing.[46] In his annual report for 1946–1947, Ó Duilearga complains about the lack of progress on cataloguing. More than three thirds of the Mss remained to be catalogued for want of staff:

> Cataloguing is slow, painstaking work, that would require three people, at least, to be engaged at it by day and night, if we are to catch up with what

---

44   LUB. Saml. von Sydow: letter dated 23.3.1943.
45   D/T S 15548B: 'Gearr-Thuar./1945–46', p. 6 (trans.).
46   Although Ó Ruanaighe could devote most of his time to cataloguing, he also had to answer queries from foreign scholars. His knowledge of both German and French may have been the reason why he was given this task.

has been collected – and being collected still by us. If the Commission were a permanent Institution, the cataloguers we badly need could be employed and trained to proceed with this urgent work.[47]

The departure of Ó Ruanaighe on August 31st, 1948 greatly affected the work of cataloguing. Ó Ruanaighe by this time had an MA in Celtic Studies. He was a talented young man, but had little prospect in the Commission. Not only did his departure from the Commission, in order to commence the study of medicine, have a negative effect on the Commission in the short term, it also had a long-term effect in depriving the Commission of a highly qualified member of staff, who if he had stayed and had been given a chance to develop as a folklorist, might have been a great asset later to the Commission. The problem in respect of cataloguing was compounded by the fact that the Main Collection was growing all the time. In 1943 in a letter to von Sydow (quoted above), Seán Ó Súilleabháin estimated that only about a tenth of the Main Collection had been excerpted. Five and a half years later, although the Main Collection had grown by many hundreds of volumes in the meantime, the percentage of material catalogued for content remained roughly the same.[48]

Given the problems encountered in advancing the cataloguing of the material in the Commission's possession, Ó Duilearga on the advice of Reidar Christiansen, who visited the Commission during December 1947, decided to initiate an 'interim-catalogue' as a stopgap solution until a proper team of cataloguers could be engaged to undertake a detailed catalogue of the material. Work began on this interim-catalogue immediately, but progress was slow as neither Seán Ó Súilleabháin nor Máire MacNeill could devote all their time to it.[49] However, the situation with regard to cataloguing improved greatly in late 1949. In the autumn of that year the Commission moved into new, spacious headquarters at 82 St. Stephen's Green. The Schools Collection was brought in from the suburbs at Rathfarnham, as the Commission now had room to house it along with the Main Collection, which had sometime previously been transferred back to Dublin from Co. Mayo. An increased grant also allowed the Commission to employ three Cataloguers. These were Ciarán Bairéad, Pádraig Ó Beirn and Janis Mezs (former Latvian diplomat, stranded in Ireland after the War). In addition, the newly appointed librarian, Dr Thomas Wall (Tomás de Bhál), was trained in cataloguing skills. In his annual report to the Government for 1949–1950, Ó Duilearga could again report progress: more material had been catalogued in the second half of the previous year 'than since the Commission was first established fifteen years ago.' Nevertheless, a great deal remained to be catalogued. The Commission's Main Collection now comprised 1,145 manuscripts. Of these, 145 had been fully catalogued; 129 interim-catalogued; and 871 remained uncatalogued. He proposed pressing ahead to compile an interim-catalogue of all the manuscripts before resuming the detailed cataloguing of the remaining material.[50]

47 D/T S 15548B: 'Gearr-Thuar./1946–47', pp. 7–8 (trans.).
48 Lilly Lib. Thompson Papers: Ó Súilleabháin to Thompson, dated 18.11.1948.
49 D/T S 15548B: 'Gearr-Thuar./1947–48', p. 5 and 'Gearr-Thuar./1948–49', p. 4.
50 D/T S 15548B: 'Gearr-Thuar./1949–50', pp. [4]–[5] (trans.). Ó Beirn was appointed

With more resources available to them the compilation of the interim-catalogue advanced relatively rapidly, although it was from time to time held up by the cataloguers having to attend to other duties. By this time the Commission had begun microfilming its collections, and this urgent task often had to take precedence over cataloguing. Ó Duilearga was ahead of his time in seeing the need for the custodians of folklore archives to microfilm their collections. In the early years of the Cold War, worried that Europe might once more be consumed in conflict and conflagration, and that Ireland this time around might not avoid being drawn into the arena of war, he wrote to Stith Thompson:

> Our worry at the moment is to get all our MSS microfilmed. For years – since the end of [World] War II – I have been urging people here & in Europe to consolidate their gains & to microfilm what they had. At long last, we have got a microfilm camera & reader & – no matter what other institutions are doing or, rather, not doing – we are taking no chances with dear Ivan Stalinovitch, & are getting all we can copied before all the sands run out. I wish to God the Swedes & Finns & the amazingly torpid DFS [Dansk Folkemindesamling (Danish Folklore Archive)] w[oul]d do something on the same lines. And when we have the cans of film finished out they go to a place of safety in the boglands.[51]

Another major task that delayed work on the cataloguing was the preparation of the official copybooks (manuscript books) in the Schools Collection for binding. This, along with many other tasks, occupied Seán Ó Súilleabháin for much of 1951–1952.[52] The transfer of Ciarán Bairéad from cataloguing to collecting that same year may have further delayed the completion of the interim-catalogue. Nevertheless, by spring 1954 all the manuscripts of the Main Collection had been interim-catalogued as well as a further 425 manuscripts of the Schools Collection. The interim-cataloguing of the Schools Collection was completed by spring of the following year.[53] Once the Interim-Catalogue of the Main Collection was complete, work commenced on transferring the information contained in its eleven bound volumes on to separate index cards for inclusion in the main subject index, which was

---

full-time cataloguer from 1.7.1950. Hitherto he had been employed part-time. Ibid.: 'Gearr-Thuar./1950–51', p. [5].

51   Lilly Lib. Thompson Papers: Ó Duilearga to Thompson, undated [Dec. 1950], pp. 3-4. The National Library of Ireland towards the end of the financial year 1946–47 began microfilming the Commission's collection for it, but as the Library had many other microfilming commitments progress was slow. In December 1950 the Commission purchased a microfilm camera and reader. D/T S 15548A: Gearr.Thuar./1946–47', p. 7 and Gearr-Thuar./1950–51', p. [5]. Microfilming of the manuscript holdings of the Folklore Archive of the Finnish Literature Society began in May 1955 and was first completed in 1959. Microfilming of new acquisitions continued in the following decades. Hirvonen et al 1981, p. 278 and Lehto 2004 (minor thesis) p. 7 ff. Only a small proportion of the Landsmålsarkiv in Uppsala was ever microfilmed, due to lack of resources. Information supplied by Marelene Hugoson.

52   D/T S 15548B: 'Gearr-Thuar./1950–51', p.[4].

53   D/T S 15548B: 'Gearr-Thuar./1953–34', p. 3 and ibid.: 'Gearr-Thuar./1954–55', p. 3.

reorganised by Ó Súilleabháin for the purpose with many new subheadings. By spring 1957 the reorganisation of the main index was complete.[54]

Much had been achieved by way of cataloguing since the late 1940's, but much remained to be done. By this time the Commission's team of cataloguers was also greatly diminished. Of the three cataloguers appointed in 1949, only Janis Mezs remained; Pádraig Ó Beirn having resigned in August 1955, and Ciarán Bairéad, as we have seen, was now working in the field as a full-time collector. Although Mezs knew a phenomenal number of languages, it would appear that his knowledge of Irish, such as it was, was not sufficient for him to catalogue manuscript material in Irish. Once the Interim-Catalogues were complete, he was employed cataloguing material in English.[55] The bulk of the Commission's Main Collection was, however, in Irish and by the late 1950's, Seán Ó Súilleabháin was again the only person on the Commission's staff competent, or at least available, to catalogue material in Irish. However, the time Ó Súilleabháin could devote to detailed cataloguing was again very limited.

Although a comprehensive subject catalogue of the Commission's collections was a desideratum, for the collections to be easily accessed and utilised by scholars and the public alike, a number of other catalogues were also needed. In pursuance of this goal, in January 1959 a young student, Liam Ó Searcaigh, was employed to compile a catalogue of the collectors (full-time, part-time, or other) who had collected material for the Commission since it was set up. When Ó Searcaigh left the employment of the Commission in October 1959, Anraí Ó Braonáin was taken on to continue this work. When the Index of Collectors was completed the following year, Ó Braonáin, with the assistance of Seán Ó Súilleabháin, went on to compile an Index of Informants. By 1965 this index was well on the way towards completion, with 1,551 manuscripts excerpted and only 120 left to be completed.[56] In early 1967, Ó Súilleabháin and Ó Braonáin began an Index of Localities from which material had been collected.[57] This task was to take them a year and a half or more. Ó Braonáin left the services of the Commission shortly before this index was finished. It was completed by Ó Súilleabháin in autumn 1968.[58]

Obviously with new material coming in all the time, these Indexes had to be kept up to date.

Shortly before the Irish Folklore Commission was disbanded and transferred to University College Dublin, Seán Ó Súilleabháin, in an international publication, outlined where the cataloguing of the Commission's collections then stood. While he could report that its Indexes of Collectors, Informants, and Localities had been kept up to date, in respect of cataloguing

---

54 D/T S 15548B: 'Gearr-Thuar./1955–56', p. 3 and ibid.: 'Gearr-Thuar./1956–57', p. 3.
55 D/T S 15548B: 'Gearr-Thuar./ 1955–56', p. 3.
56 D/T S 16378A: 'Gearr-Thuar./1958–59', p. 5; D/T S 16378A: 'Gearr-Thuar./1959–60', p. 4; D/T S 16378B/62: 'Gearr-Thuar./1960–61', p. 2; and ED FL1: 'CBÉ. Miont. 123ú Cruinniú, 4.3.1965', par. 910.
57 ED FL 8: 'CBÉ. Miont. 131ú Cruinniú, 16.3.1967', par. 971.
58 ED FL 8: 'CBÉ. Miont. 137ú Cruinniú, 25.10.1968', p. 2.

the content of the Main Collection, which then stood at 1,746 volumes (c. 720,000 pages), the situation was not at all satisfactory. He says: 'for lack of a large full-time cataloguing staff, only one-quarter of the main collections has been excerpted in a proper manner (according to the Irish adaptation of the Uppsala cataloguing system...)', while for the Schools Collection 'only a rough-and-ready catalogue has been compiled'. The Subject Index then comprised 250,000 index cards. Ó Súilleabháin estimated that in order to complete the Subject Index for the Main Collection and initiate and complete a subject index of the Schools Collection, 'a cataloguing staff of six persons' working 'for twenty years' would be required.[59]

Secretarial and Typing Staff

The Commission could not have functioned without shorthand typists as well as those with secretarial skills. Nevertheless, as we have seen above, for the first year or so of its operations, Máire MacNeill had to double as Office Manager and shorthand typist, as well as assist with supervising the work of the collectors.[60] However, in April 1936 the Commission was given permission to employ a shorthand typist, Eibhlín Ní Iarlaithe (Eileen O'Herlihy). In seeking permission from Finance to employ her, the Dept. of Education stressed that she would relieve Seán Ó Súilleabháin and Máire Mac Neill of some of their duties:

> It is essential that all available material should be catalogued as soon as possible so that the Commission may be in the position to supply each whole-time collector with information regarding the traditions known to have existed in the district in which he is working and so enable him to direct his enquiries to the best advantage.[61]

Eibhlín Ní Iarlaithe was not appointed by open competition as the Dept. of Finance agreed that 'in view of the specialised nature of the work and' of the applicant's 'proven suitability', there was no need to 'raise any question of competition.' She was already known to Ó Duilearga due to her typing work (through an agency) for the Folklore of Ireland Society.[62] The Dept. of Finance agreed to Ní Iarlaithe's appointment promptly.[63]

---

59 S. Ó Súilleabháin 1970, pp. 119–120. Ó Súilleabháin in this publication estimated the number of pages in the Commission's Main Collection to be c. 1,100,000 pages. This would appear to be somewhat of an overestimation, presumably derived at by him multiplying the number of volumes (1,746) by the maximum number of pages (in excess of 600) that some of them contained. However, many of these manuscripts contain far less than 600 pages. The figure of 720,000 pages I give above is based on Ó Duilearga's Annual Reports to the Government (see Appenix 5).

60 See D/F S 101/0011/34: Fin. memo, Ní Mhaolchatha to Morris, dated 25.3.1936.

61 D/T S 101/0011/34: Dept. of Educ. to Dept. of Fin., dated 13.3.1936.

62 See D/F S 101/0011/34: Fin. memo, Ní Mhaolchatha to Morris, dated 25.3.1936.

63 Ní Iarlaithe was twenty three years of age when she took up work with the Commission. She had studied Irish, French and German at UCD, but had not completed her degree.

She was to be the first of many shorthand typists to be employed by the Commission.

As in all institutions, a lot of the work fell on the typing staff, and as often happens their work got little recognition. Although Máire MacNeill's terms of employment as Office Manager and Secretary were not ideal, they were far better than the typists employed by the Commission (see Chapter VI/1). Just as Máire MacNeill ended up doing work that did not strictly belong to her post, the typists employed by the Commission often had to function more as secretaries than as typists as such. We have seen this already in the case of Eibhlín Ní Iarlaithe, who although employed as a typist, actually took over many of Máire MacNeill's duties as Office Manager.

As the work falling to Ní Iarlaithe was too great, another shorthand typist, Máire Ní Cheallacháin, was appointed as an extra shorthand typist on June 6th, 1938.[64] Ní Iarlaithe continued in her post until her marriage, resigning on September 9th, 1939. Her replacement, Bríd Mahon, was appointed on October 9th, 1939. This, like the two above appointments, was a temporary, non-pensionable post that could be terminated by a week's notice by either party. Mahon, unlike other young women taken on as shorthand typists by the Commission, was destined to stay with the Commission until it was disbanded in 1970, and was to be subsequently employed in the Department of Irish Folklore, University College Dublin. In 1949, on Máire MacNeill's departure, Mahon was promoted to Office Manager.[65] Her fate in being promoted was untypical of the Commission's office staff and was a result of a combination of circumstances (see below).

Not only were typists given various secretarial as well as sundry tasks to perform, sometimes they could be involved in very specialised work. Íde Ní Eidhin joined the staff of the Commission in the summer of 1943 as a shorthand typist on the resignation of Máire Ní Cheallacháin.[66] Ní Eidhin was a university graduate as well as having secretarial qualifications. She had, moreover, a very good knowledge of Irish. She had taught Irish as well as shorthand and typing in a Dublin secondary school before coming to the Commission.[67] During most of the time she was employed by the Commission she was engaged in typing material in Irish in the Commission's archives for publication in *Béaloideas,* as well as for a series of publications being planned by the Commission at the time. Among the materials she typed up from manuscript was over a thousand manuscript pages of tales and lore collected from Éamon 'a Búrc, the famous Galway storyteller. She continued this work until she resigned from the Commission. Although some officials in the Dept. of Finance thought that the ability to type material in Irish

She had, however, spent a year in a school in Czechoslovakia. She was an accomplished typist, had a good knowledge of Irish, having received her education through Irish and could type direct from manuscripts. See D/T S 101/0011/34: 'Eibhlín Ní Iarlaithe (Miss Eileen O'Herlihy)'. She was to marry the archaeologist Michael Duignan.

64   D/T S 15548B: 'Gearr-Thuar./1938–39', p. [5].
65   Mahon 1998, p. 57.
66   D/F S 101/0011/34: Dept. of Fin. to Dept. of Educ., dated 25.6.1943.
67   D/F S 101/0011/34: Ó Duilearga to Sec. Dept. of Educ., no date [May/June 1943].

from manuscripts was not so exceptional a skill for a shorthand typist,[68] the Commission were greatly affected by her departure on February 9th, 1946. Unlike many of the other shorthand typists before her and later, she did not resign in order to get married, but rather to take up more lucrative employment.[69] In his report to the Government for 1946–1947, Ó Duilearga under 'Typing of manuscripts for publication', says: 'Much less of this work was done this year than last year because there was no replacement for Íde Ní Eidhin on the Commission's staff'.[70] Not until Maureen McGeehan (Máirín Nic Ghaoithín) was appointed shorthand typist in spring 1950 was a replacement for Íde Ní Eidhin found.[71]

Maureen McGeehan was more than thirty when she joined the Commission. She had qualified as a primary teacher and was studying for an evening degree in University College Dublin. Her university studies were interrupted, however, when she was stricken in her mid-twenties with tuberculosis, and as a consequence was forced to spend a good deal of time convalescing abroad in Switzerland. It was during her convalescence that she became interested in research. Tom Dunne has said: 'her health had made further work as a primary teacher impossible, and she decided to try something less strenuous. She learned typing and with the help of Canon Boylan, her former school manager and a great support during her illness, she got a job in the Folklore Commission.'[72] Being a typist, or indeed filling any other position, in the Folklore Commission was no easy job, and it is doubtful if her health would have allowed her to continue at this post for long. If she had stayed, however, perhaps she might have turned her scholarly abilities towards folklore, and become another Máire MacNeill. As it was, however, history was to be her calling. Although exceptionally talented, it does not appear that she had the skills her predecessor had in respect of typing up material in Irish from the manuscripts, but she had other abilities above and beyond most of her colleagues. She continued in this post until December 21st, 1951 when she left to take up a post in the Department of History, University College Dublin. She was later to marry the Commission's librarian, Tom (Thomas) Wall, and is better know under her married name, Maureen Wall. She was to become one of the most eminent Irish historians of her day.

Máire MacNeill resigned her post as Office Manager on marriage in 1949. Even without the regulation that required women to resign on marriage, she would probably have left anyway, as her husband, Jack Sweeney, was an American and they went to live in Boston. Bríd Mahon was thirty one years of age when she became Office Manager, roughly the same age Máire MacNeill had been when joining the Commission. Mahon's elevation to the job of Office Manager was not just due to MacNeill's resignation on marriage. A number of other factors were involved. For example, as a result of the

68 See, e.g. D/F S 101/0011/34: internal Fin. memo to Mr. Feeny et al dated 14.8.1944.
69 D/T S 15548B: 'Gearr-Thuar./1945–46', and 'Gearr-Thuar./1946–47', pp. 5 and 8 respectively.
70 D/T S 15548B: 'Gearr-Thuar./1946–47', p. 8.
71 D/T S 15548B: 'Gear-Thuar./1949–50', p. [2].
72 Dunne 1989, unpaginated.

departure of the cataloguer Bréanainn Ó Ruanaighe from the Commission's employment in August 1947, Ó Duilearga in December of that year proposed to the Finance Sub-Committee that Bríd Mahon take over 'book keeping and business duties' from MacNeill so that the latter might be able to give more time to cataloguing.[73]

Máire MacNeill's marriage in her mid-forties was probably unforeseen by many of her colleagues. The Commission lost far more than an Office Manager when she left. They lost a versatile worker and scholar as well, who could turn her hand to any task required of her by Ó Duilearga. We have seen how she spent much of her time since her appointment in 1935 cataloguing and assisting Seán Ó Súilleabháin, as well as fulfilling her other duties. But already while working with the Commission she had commenced research into Irish folk tradition. In America she was to continue her research and produce a fine monograph, *The Festival of Lughnasa* (published in 1962). She was also in time to be given the opportunity to lecture in Harvard on Irish folklore. Leaving the Commission and Ireland behind her must have been a difficult decision, but there is no doubt that residence in America gave her opportunities denied to many of her former colleagues back home in Ireland. Her departure must also have been especially difficult for Ó Duilearga, for whom she was somewhat like a family member, as they had known each other since childhood.[74]

Bríd Mahon was not to marry, although in her autobiography she recounts how the Swedish Celtic scholar Nils Holmer proposed to her. She, with some hesitation, turned him down.[75] For her marriage to him would, most likely, have meant going to live abroad, as was the case with Máire MacNeill. In any event, it would certainly have meant her leaving the Commission. Bríd Mahon continued in her job as Office Manager until the disbandment of the Commission in 1970. When the Commission became a university department in 1971 she was given the job description 'folklorist (senior research)'.[76]

The 1950's saw a succession of shorthand typists. It also saw an increase in the workload of the Office Manager, especially with the increase in the Commission's staff. From 1938 right through the War until 1946 the Commission always managed to employ two typists. Since 1946, however, they had to make do with one.[77] When Maureen McGeehan left in December 1951, her post was filled by Cáit Nic an Ríogh (also spelled Nic Conraoi) from Ballinskelligs, where Ó Duilearga had begun his collecting in earnest in the mid-1920's.[78] Cáit Nic an Ríogh was replaced by Máire Ní Bhraonáin

---

73   ED FL 6: 'IFC. Fin. Sub-Com./Min. 63rd Meeting, 2.12.1947', par. 508 [*recte* 510].
74   For more on Máire MacNeill, see Almqvist 1988, Maureen Murphy 2004, and uí Ógáin 2005.
75   Mahon 1998, pp. 189–191.
76   For the purposes of equating her salary with those of the collectors, her job description in certain documents since the early 1960's was that of 'folklorist'. Moreover, in March 1966 the Finance Sub-Committee recommended that the title of 'Office Manager and Secretary' be changed to 'Secretary and Publications Officer'. ED FL 8: 'CBÉ. Miont. 127ú Cruinniú, 24.3.1966', par. 943.
77   ED FL 1: 'IFC. Fin. Sub-Com./Min. 126th Meeting, 6.7.1963', par. 898.
78   D/T S 15548B: 'Gearr-Thuar./1951–1952', p. 5.

on October 1st, 1953.[79] Ní Bhraonáin resigned her post as a shorthand typist on 30th April, 1956. She was replaced by Caitríona Ní Ruadháin who took up employment on May 1st, 1956.[80] Caitríona Ní Ruadháin in turn resigned her post as a shorthand typist on December 31st, 1959, due to her impending marriage.[81] Her successor, Máire Ní Mhaoláin, was to stay with the Commission until July 1963, once again resigning in order to get married. At the meeting of the Commission in July 1963 a special motion of thanks was proposed by the Chairman, Eric Mac Fhinn, for the 'good service she had rendered' in her four years with the Commission and it was agreed to give her a present of £50 as a mark of appreciation.[82]

When Máire Ní Mhaoláin resigned her post, Ó Duilearga at a meeting of the Finance Sub-Committee of the Commission took the opportunity to propose requesting a second typist. During the time the Commission had two typists, from 1938 to 1946, the annual grant-in-aid varied between £3,250 and £3,650. As the annual grant now stood at £19,318, he argued 'office work, general accounting has increased by more than six-fold.' Moreover, he added that the 'telephone switch alone with five extensions, plus a constant stream of callers takes up a large part of the duties of a single person.' In connection with plans to 'enlarge our scheme of publications', he suggested 'the services of a competent person capable of typing material in the Irish language are urgently needed.' Of Máire Ní Mhaoláin, he said that she had 'been outstanding in this respect', but that they had 'on occasions to resort to sending out manuscript material for typing.'[83]

Máire Ní Cheallacháin, or to give her married name, Mrs. Dillon (Máire Uí Dhiolúin), who resigned on marriage in 1943, is, along with Bríd Mahon, somewhat of an anomaly among the Commission's shorthand typists. She was destined to return to the Commission, first as a married woman, and later as a widow. She was initially brought back on a temporary basis in September 1963 when the Dept. of Education failed to find a suitable replacement for Máire Ní Mhaoláin. Although this was in breach of the marriage ban for women in the Civil Service, an exception in her case was made by the Dept. of Education.[84] Máire Dillon's husband died in January 1965, leaving her with four dependents and no pension. In spring 1965, Ó Duilearga asked the Dept. of Education to make her permanent, but instead that autumn the same Department informed the Commission that they intended reducing her salary, which then stood at the scale of £593 to £520 (i.e. just £10 per week). This meant a reduction of £73 in her annual pay. Given her circumstances, this was a serious setback to her. The Commission, however, came to her

---

79   D/T S 15548B: 'Gearr-Thuar./1953–54', p. 6.
80   D/T S 15548B: 'Gearr-Thuar./1956–57', p. 6.
81   D/T S 16378A: 'Gearr-Thuar./1959–60', p. 4 and Mahon 1998 p. 191.
82   D/T S 16378A: 'Gearr-Thuar./1959–60', p. 4, and ED FL 8: 'CBÉ. Miont. 116ú Cruinniú, 9.7.1963', par. 852 (trans.)
83   ED FL 1: 'IFC. Fin. Sub-Com./Min. 126th Meeting, 6.7.1963', par. 898. In this respect, it should be noted that during the 1950's the Commission had sometimes to do without a shorthand typist for some months, between the resignation of one typist and the appointment of a successor. See, e.g. D/T S 15548B: 'Gearr-Thuar./1951–52', p. 5.
84   ED FL 8: 'CBÉ. Miont. 117ú Cruinniú, 17.10.1963', par. 860.

aid, requesting the Dept. of Education to rescind this decision and to give her a permanent post as 'clerk-typist', which would involve a substantially higher salary for her.[85]

As well as informing the Commission of their intention to reduce Máire Dillon's salary, the Dept. of Education had also informed them that their request to employ an extra typist had been turned down, although the employment of two extra typists had earlier been recommended by the Dept. of Education. The Commission wrote to Education protesting this decision.[86] It would appear that the Dept. of Finance were responsible for both the above decisions. The Dept. of Education made representations on behalf of the Commission to Finance, but it took some time to get any satisfaction. By June 1966 the Director was able to tell the Commission that Máire Dillon's cut in salary had been restored, and that permission had been granted to employ another typist in the near future.[87] On September 1st, 1966 a shorthand typist, Gretta Dillon, was transferred from the Dept. of Education to work on the Commission's staff.[88] Henceforth the Commission would have two typists. Gretta Dillon was to be the last person to join the staff of the Commission in any capacity. She transferred with the Commission to UCD and worked for a number of years with its successor, the Dept. of Irish Folklore, before transferring to UCD's Department of Old Irish and Welsh.

Shorthand typists had little status in the society of the time and were viewed as easily replaceable. Nevertheless, the Commission was not insensitive to the working conditions of its typists and did its best to get better remuneration for them (for more on this, see Chapter VI/1). This is not to argue that the Commission's typists, and Office Manager, were always treated with the respect they deserved. Obviously, given the patriarchal world of the time, it would be surprising if this were the case.

Ethnologist/Caoimhín Ó Danachair

Of all the people employed by the Commission, Caoimhín Ó Danachair's position most approximates to that of full-time researcher. Ó Danachair, who was a graduate of UCD, after completing his primary degree, went to Germany in the late 1930's, where he was engaged in postgraduate research, but was forced to abandon his studies and return home as war loomed. Despite having to interrupt work on a doctoral dissertation, he was in many ways the most academically qualified of the Commission's staff, and was particularly well trained for work as an ethnologist.

Ó Danachair was originally employed in 1939 as a 'collector' but his duties also involved the investigation of the material culture of Ireland and the making of an archive of photographs of informants. He had been released

---

85 ED FL 2: 'CBÉ. Miont. 123ú Cruinniú, 4.3.1965', par. 911 and ED FL 8: 'CBÉ. Miont. 125ú Cruinniú, 21.10.1965', par. 928 (trans.).

86 ED FL 8: 'CBÉ. Miont. 125ú Cruinniú, 21.10.1965', pp. 928 (trans.).

87 ED FL 8: 'CBÉ. Miont. 128ú Cruinniú, 27.6.1966', par. 947.

88 ED FL 8: 'Gearr-Thuar./1966–67', p. 5.

to the Commission from the Irish Army, which he had joined on his return from Germany, but in May 1940 he had to return to the Army.[89] At the end of the War, Ó Duilearga asked him to take temporary leave from the Army and to commence working again with the Commission. He did so and in March 1946 he resigned altogether from the Irish Army.[90] In the early post-War period it was envisaged that he travel around the country investigating the material culture. However, initially his field work was hampered by the unwillingness of the Dept. of Finance to sanction travel allowances for him as well as for the other collectors (see Chapter VI/1 below).[91]

In autumn 1947 the Commission sent Ó Danachair for two months to Scandinavia to acquaint himself with various institutes involved in the study of folklife.[92] Then in 1948–1949 he was placed in charge of a mobile unit that went around the Irish speaking districts making gramophone records, in addition to taking photographs of informants (see below). In the early 1950's, however, he resumed full-time his ethnological work for the Commission, in particular his study of vernacular house-types. In 1952–1953 he had a chance to return to Sweden when the Commission seconded him to the University of Uppsala to lecture on Irish language and culture. This extended sojourn in Uppsala also gave him an opportunity to acquaint himself more thoroughly with the Dialect and Folklore Archive (Landsmålsarkivet) and Swedish ethnological institutions in general. He returned to the Commission in June 1953, where he again resumed his work on vernacular house-types.

Once the problem of travelling expenses was solved in the late 1940s, Ó Danachair's work took him a great deal into the countryside, first with the mobile recording unit and later on specific ethnological field trips. In respect of the latter, he divided his time between field work and research and the cataloguing of photographic material at Head Office. He was a skilled photographer, and much of the large collection of photographs in the Commission's archives was taken by him. Towards the late 1950's he began to give regular lectures in many parts of the country on folklife, but he was denied the chance to lecture at university level, apart from an occasional lecture to some college society or other. This was a great pity because he later proved to be an inspiring teacher. The 1960's saw him become more and more active in various international ethnographic societies. His national and international profile was on the rise throughout the 1960's, and his endless vigour was in sharp contrast to Ó Duilearga's waning energy.[93]

89   DE FL [9]: 'IFC. Fin. Sub-Com./Min. 23rd Meeting, 23.10.1939', par. 212 and D/T S 15548B: 'Gearr-Thuar./1940–41', p. 1.
90   D/T S 15548B: 'Gearr-Thuar./1945–46', p. 5.
91   D/T S 15548B: 'Gearr-Thuar./1946–47', pp. 4–5.
92   D/T S 15548B: 'Gearr-Thuar./1947–48', p. 6.
93   The above account of Ó Danachair's activities in the 1950's and 1960's is based mainly on Ó Duilearga's Annual Reports to the Government for the period.

3. Creating a sound archive

From gramophone recording apparatus to mobile recording unit

Writing in the *Irish Independent* in October 1938 about the fate of filled Ediphone cylinders forwarded by collectors to Head Office along with the accompanying manuscripts, Seán Ó Súilleabháin says:

> Here they are checked to ensure accuracy. Over four hundred which had a special linguistic or stylistic interest have up to the present been preserved. The others are shaved mechanically and sent out again to be refilled. These cylinders are not durable and cannot be used for making permanent records of dialects or traditions. They are not at all suitable for the proper recording of songs.[94]

However, even if Ediphone cylinders had been more durable and Ediphones capable of making higher quality recordings, the Commission would not have had the resources to keep most of its Ediphone recordings.

Ó Duilearga realised from the beginning that the Commission needed a different type of recording apparatus to make high quality and more permanent recordings. He broached the purchase of 'a portable gramophone recording machine', manufactured by the Fairchild Aircraft Corporation of America, in a special memorandum he sent to de Valera in May 1933:

> ...there is now on the market a portable machine, it will be possible to transfer from the wax Ediphone cylinder on to a permanent metal disc a selected number of records, and thus to preserve for all time, at a ridiculously small cost, a selection of tales, songs and other traditional material of the greatest importance from a national as well as an international standpoint.

The machine itself cost around $500, a substantial sum at the time, but as the record-discs cost only between fifteen and fifty cents a piece, and were

---

94   S. Ó Súilleabháin 1938.

of a 'permanent nature' it would be a good investment, and Ó Duilearga urged de Valera 'to consider favourably the suggestion that at least one of these machines be examined with a view to purchase and use as part of the equipment of the oral culture survey now contemplated.'[95] However, no special provision was made for the purchase of such an apparatus during the negotiations to set up the Irish Folklore Commission, and it would be a number of years before the Commission would be in a position to even consider the purchase of such a machine.

In time, as we have seen above (Chapter IV/ 3), the Commission began to set aside money for the purpose of purchasing a gramophone recording apparatus. In June 1939 at a meeting of the Commission, Ó Duilearga described a recording apparatus he had seen while visiting Harvard University and which was worked on 'gasolene'. A similar device, he informed the meeting, had been used to record music in Yugoslavia, Montenegro, and Albania. This apparatus could not only make original records but copies as well and was relatively cheap at $200. The extra turntable for making copies made it more difficult to transport in the field, but could always come in useful at Head Office. The Harvard people he was in contact with recommended that the Commission purchase the full apparatus, and the Commission agreed to do so immediately as there was 'surplus money left over from the previous year'.[96]

Instead of ordering this recording apparatus forthwith, Ó Duilearga seems to have followed up another lead, most likely in order to save money. While in America earlier that year, travelling by train from San Francisco to Oregon, he made the acquaintance of an employee of the Thomas Edison Company. This gentleman was intrigued to hear of the use the Commission was making of the Company's Ediphone machines and asked could he be of assistance.[97] As a result of this contact, and possible subsequent representations made to it by Ó Duilearga, the Thomas Edison Company decided to present him with a gramophone recording machine. This was electrically operated, but the Department of Physics in UCD had given assurances that it could be adapted to work on batteries, which would enable it to be transported throughout the country.[98] However, as we have seen above, when the apparatus did arrive from the United States in late June 1940, the Commission were unable to have it adapted for use in the field, and due to the intensification of the War the spare parts needed to adapt it could not be got from the United States or Britain. Nevertheless, during the War years the Commission managed to make some recordings of oral tradition at Head Office or elsewhere in Dublin until it eventually ran out of wax plates.[99]

---

95 D/T S 9244: 'Collection Of Oral Irish Tradition', pp. 18–19 and 21–22.
96 ED [FL 9]: 'CBÉ. Miont. an 17ú Cruinniú, 9.6.1939', par. 146 (trans.). The apparatus with two turntables Ó Duilearga saw was similar, it would appear, to the one especially commissioned by Milman Parry from the Sound Specialities Company of Waterbury, Connecticut, which was powered in the field from 'a motor-generator operated by a six volt automobile battery.' This may be what Ó Duilearga means by the apparatus he saw being worked by gasoline. For more on this apparatus, see Lord 2000 [1960], p. x.
97 RTÉSA A5382, 'Here and Now', Liam Nolan talking to Ó Duilearga (1971).
98 ED [FL 9]: 'CBÉ. Miont. 19ú Cruinniú, 12.1.1940', par. 160.
99 D/T S 15548B: 'Gearr-Thuar./1940–41', p. 2. The re-establishment of the Gaelic League's

In hindsight, Ó Duilearga's chance meeting with the above official of the Thomas Edison Company had unforeseen negative consequences, as it prevented the Commission from acquiring a machine more suitable to its needs and Irish conditions. Nevertheless, even if it had purchased such an apparatus, the progress of the War would most likely have prevented it from getting fresh supplies of gramophone plates as well as spare parts.

As the War drew to a close, Ó Duilearga had an interview with the Taoiseach, Éamon de Valera, in early March 1945. One of the matters discussed was the making of at least 20,000 gramophone plates of dialects in the Gaeltacht.[100] In a follow-up memorandum he prepared for de Valera he went into grater detail on this issue:

> The Commission has already made one hundred permanent gramophone records of folk-songs and tales. As soon as supplies become available again arrangements should be made for a systematic series of recordings in Ireland and Gaelic Scotland, of dialect material, both in Gaelic and Anglo-Irish [i.e. the English language as spoken in Ireland]. For this purpose portable recording equipment should be purchased which can be used in any part of the country by a trained collector to take down specimens of the speech, song, music, and traditions of the people, without any necessity for the costly expedient of bringing them to Dublin. The Commission has done pioneer work by its use of the Ediphone from the beginning, but recordings on wax such as those made by the Ediphone were never intended to be permanent, and it is not [recte now] possible to make permanent records by the use of the gramophone, magnetised wire and sound track.

He also proposed purchasing filming equipment, which 'could be transported anywhere in the country in its own van' and which 'would enable records of many varied kinds to be made.' Films of this sort, he said, would illustrate 'as nothing else could some features of rural life.' The recording and filming equipment together would require 'an initial expenditure of some £2,000', with running costs at around £1,000 per annum, although the exact cost would be difficult to calculate in advance. He also suggested that the 'services of a mechanic/motor-driver would probably be necessary.'[101]

The idea of a mobile recording unit was taking shape in Ó Duilearga's mind, but problems remained. In the above memorandum he had asked for far more than the establishment of a mobile recording unit to help create a sound archive, his overall plans required an almost fourfold increase in the Commission's budget. All he got, however, was the reinstatement of the Commission's annual grant-in-aid to its prewar level. This meant that plans

Oireachtas in 1939 facilitated this type of recording, as it meant that every autumn many bearers of tradition would congregate in the capital for a week to participate in various singing and storytelling competitions.

100 D/T S 6916B: Ó Duilearga to de Valera, dated 7.3.1945.

101 D/T S 6916B: 'Memorandum on the IFC with Recommendations for its Development and Extension.', pp. 26–27 and 37.

for a mobile unit had to be postponed. Nevertheless, with gramophone plates once more available, the Commission was again in a position to record a certain amount of tradition at Head Office in Dublin.

Caoimhín Ó Danachair and the mobile recording unit

With the resumption of regular postal communications in the wake of the War, the Commission in time managed to get its gramophone machine adapted for use in the countryside. In the summer of 1947, Caoimhín Ó Danachair and Séamus Ennis 'experimented with recording in the field' in west and south Kerry with, as Ó Danachair describes, 'apparatus partly borrowed and partly contrived from oddments of electrical apparatus.'[102] In reporting on this trip to the Commission, Ó Duilearga describes it as: 'the first time the Commission was able to operate the gramophone apparatus in rural houses', which in his opinion 'was a great advance'.[103]

We have seen above, how de Valera's desire that the Commission record the last speakers of Manx was to result in its deciding to purchase out of its meagre resources, without further procrastination, the equipment necessary for a proper mobile recording unit. There is a certain irony in this as de Valera shares some of the blame for the delay in establishing such a unit in the post-War period, as he failed to act on Ó Duilearga's numerous requests to him for an increase in the Commission's grant to allow it expand its activities on various fronts.[104]

By the time the Commission had its mobile recording unit up and running in March 1948, the days of gramophone field recordings were in many respects numbered. Indeed some six months earlier John Lorne Campbell lent the Commission, for the use of Calum MacLean in Scotland, a 'magnetic tape recorder' he had purchased in the United States.[105] This was the first use made by one of the Commission's collectors of a tape recorder. The following month Ó Danachair gave a demonstration to members of the Finance Sub-Committee 'of the use which might be made by the full-time collectors of magnetised wire-recording machines costing only $160 in the United States.'[106] Despite the relative low cost of these machines, it would be years before the Commission's collectors would be equipped with modern recording apparatus.

The maiden voyage of the Commission's mobile recording unit was not, as is sometimes claimed, to the Isle of Man, but rather to a small Gaeltacht 'colony'

---

102 Ó Danachair 1981, p. 312.
103 ED FL 6: 'CBÉ. Miont. 49ú Cruinniú, 27.6.1947', par. 379(d) (trans.).
104 By way of comparison, it should be noted that the Dialect and Folklore Archive (Landsmålsarkivet), Uppsala had a mobile recording unit in operation from 1946. Some field gramophone recordings were done by people associated with the Finnish Literature Society from the late 1930's, but the Society did not have its own mobile recording unit until 1951. Hedblom 1989, p. 16, Simonsuuri 1949, pp. 129 ff., and Laaksonen 2003, p. 222.
105 ED FL 6: 'CBÉ. Miont. 50ú Cruinniú, 28.11.1947', par. 393(c).
106 ED FL 6: 'IFC. Fin. Sub-Com./Min. 63rd, 2.12.1947', par. 509.

in Co. Meath where Caoimhín Ó Danachair in mid-March 1948 made recordings of Irish speakers who had been transferred there from the west of Ireland.[107] Moreover, some ten days before going to the Isle of Man, on April 12th, 1948, Ó Danachair, accompanied by Séamus Ó Duilearga, drove the Commission's van, containing its mobile recording equipment, to Co. Waterford to work with full-time collector Seosamh Ó Dálaigh. Ó Danachair and Ó Duilearga stayed in Co. Waterford and south Co. Tipperary until the evening of April 17th. Some weeks after his return from the Isle of Man, Ó Danachair returned to Co. Waterford to again work with Seosamh Ó Dálaigh.[108]

The Commission had been waiting for years to have its own mobile recording unit, and now that it had one, there was urgent work to be done. This Ó Danachair set about doing immediately. Periods in the field necessitated periods at Head Office processing and cataloguing the material, but the urgency of the task of recording meant he was on the road a great deal. This was to be the pattern of Ó Danachair's work for the next four years or so. He was to visit all Gaeltacht areas and many pockets of residual Irish elsewhere. Wherever he went, he worked with full-time and part-time collectors, whenever possible. If the Commission did not have a collector in the area, some person or other with a knowledge of local Irish speakers would be asked to assist. For instance, in June 1949, Ó Danachair was accompanied to east Cork by Brian Ó Cuív of the Dublin Institute for Advanced Studies to record residual Irish. Later that year Anthony Lucas of the National Museum of Ireland accompanied him to Counties Cork and Kerry to photograph 'old implements and other objects dealing with rural life.'[109]

Not only did the collectors assist him in making recordings, their working of a particular area would already have prepared the ground. As Ó Danachair explains:

> In most cases the storytellers and other contributors had already had all or part of their store of tradition recorded in written form, by the use of the Ediphone dictating machine. Thus they and their repertoires were already known to the Commission's field workers, and the making of sound recordings from them was greatly simplified, although such work is always trying, on the field worker as well as on the reciter of the material. As in the case of the Ediphone, the storytellers and others concerned were in all cases willing to record their voices, and usually were proud and happy to do so. And great was their delight when they heard part of the recording played back. The technicalities of the process caused no surprise, as they were quite familiar with gramophones and radios, but the experience of hearing their own and their friends' voices reciting the familiar material — this was a pleasure indeed.[110]

107 ED Fl 6: 'CBÉ. Miont. 53ú Cruinniú, 25.1.1948', par. 410(f). For more on the transfer of native Irish speakers to Meath and other eastern counties in order to relieve congestion in the West, see Dooley 2004, pp. 132–155 and Sammon 1997, pp. 157–160.

108 ED Fl 6: 'CBÉ. Miont. 53ú Cruinniú, 25.1.1948', par. 410(f). and Verling 2002.

109 D/T S 15548B: 'Gearr-Thuar./1949–50', p. [5].

110 Ó Danachair 1951, p. 184.

Ó Danachair was doubling as an ethnologist and sound recorder during this period. The Commission did not have the resources to employ someone specifically to operate the mobile recording unit, as Ó Duilearga earlier had hoped. Sometimes, as we have seen above in the case of his work with Anthony Lucas, Ó Danachair would concentrate on recording certain aspects of material culture rather than oral tradition as such, but in general he appears to have tried to kill two birds with the one stone while working in the field. In October 1950, however, a meeting of the Commission decided that Ó Danachair should be released temporarily from making gramophone plates of narrators to concentrate on research on Irish rural house-types, in libraries, archives, and in the field.[111]

Leo Corduff takes over

Ó Danachair's days with the mobile recording unit were numbered. He spent much of 1951–1952 working on his projected monograph on Irish rural house-types, although he did a certain amount of work with the mobile unit in the field, as well as assisting in the microfilming of manuscripts at Head Office. The Commission were contemplating removing Ó Danachair from this work to allow him to concentrate exclusively on ethnological work. In April 1952, Leo Corduff accompanied Ó Danachair with the mobile unit to west Mayo.[112] Henceforth Corduff was to work with the mobile unit without Ó Danachair. The latter spent the academic year 1952–1953 lecturing in Uppsala, and, other than sporadically, did not return to work with the mobile unit. Leo Corduff, a native of west Mayo, was the son of Michael Corduff, who had done part-time collecting for the Commission. A native speaker of Irish, although unable to write Irish, Michael Corduff recorded a good deal of the tradition of his native area in English for the Commission, much of it from his own recollection.[113]

Leo Corduff was initially taken on in early 1950 as a microfilm operator, on a very low salary. He was only twenty one years of age at the time. His promotion to the mobile recording unit involved a substantial increase in salary, which did not go unnoticed in the Dept. of Finance.[114] The rapid upgrading of his salary was necessary to allow him at least a tolerable salary for his new duties in the field, no matter how it appeared to Finance officials at the time. Moreover, the Commission desperately needed to keep him. He was good with machines, was interested in oral traditions, and was a native speaker of Irish. It would not have been easy to replace him if he had decided to leave for more lucrative employment in Ireland, or to emigrate to England, which was the lot of so many other young west-of-Ireland men and women

---

111 D/T S 15548B: 'Gearr-Thuar./1950–51', p. [5] (trans.).
112 D/T S 15548B: 'Gearr-Thuar./1951–52', p. 4 and 'Gearr-Thuar./1952–53', p. [3].
113 An elder brother of Leo's, Anraí Ó Corrduibh, a National School teacher, also did some part-time collecting for the Commission. Ó Duilearga had hoped to appoint him full-time collector. See ED [FL 9]: 'IFC. Fin. Sub-Com. Min. 4th Meeting, 9.4.1936', par. 43.
114 D/F S 101/0011/34: internal memo to Mr McGartoll, dated 24.1.1952, signed SÓL.

of his generation. Leo Corduff was to stay with the Commission until it was disbanded in 1970 and to transfer to UCD with the rest of the staff.

The last years of the Ediphone

By 1954 the Commission had made approximately 5,320 12-inch-disc sides, the bulk of the material being in Irish.[115] The day when the Commission would be in a position to preserve all field recordings was still far off, and neither at this stage was that the intention. A memorandum of Ó Danachair's describes precisely what the Commission's mobile unit sought to achieve: 'Since orally transmitted material loses much of its character when preserved in the written medium only, it is necessary, for a full record of tradition, to preserve certain examples of the material in sound records; this is especially true of songs, poems, music and folk tales.'[116]

As well as acquiring a new gramophone recording apparatus and a film camera in the late 1940's, the Commission also acquired a magnetised wire-recording machine. This was used for recording in remote areas, 'such as islands', inaccessible to the Commission's recording van.[117] However, due to lack of resources, Ó Duilearga's hope that it might be possible to equip all the collectors with wire recorders, or such like, could not be realised. In these circumstances, the Commission's collectors had to continue to use Ediphones. Moreover, in the early 1950's even maintaining its mobile recording unite was no easy task, given the Commission's limited resources. In May 1954 the Commission was able to buy a Vortexion tape recorder, which was more versatile for recording in the field than the cumbersome gramophone recording apparatus, but it was unable to replace the van which transported its mobile recording equipment, which by this time was in an acute state of disrepair.[118] By autumn 1954 of the nine Ediphone machines the Commission had for the use of its collectors 'not one was less than 16 years old and all were almost unfit for use.' Ó Duilearga felt that something needed to be done to alleviate this situation. He proposed that five 'light and easy to operate' tape recorders be purchased for the full-time collectors at £100 a piece. The Finance Sub-Committee trimmed down this proposal somewhat and suggested instead that the purchase of four such machines be included

---

115 Below is listed a) the content and b) the provenance of this Irish-language/Gaelic material. Content: Long folk-tales (610 items); anecdotes (380); poetic/song items (220); ethnographic descriptions (230); other traditional narratives (200); dialect material (80). Provenance: Donegal (1,300); Kerry (1,200); Waterford (320); Cork (260); Clare (180); Mayo (240); Galway (120); Tipperary (30); Louth (20); Gaelic Scotland (70); Isle of Man (90). ED FL 2: 'IFC – Sound Recordings', dated 11.1.1955.

116 Ibid.

117 See Ó Danachair 1951, p. 186, n. 7.

118 D/T S 15548B: 'Gearr-Thuar./1954–1955', p. 3, and ED FL 2: 'IFC. Fin. Sub-Com./Min. 93rd Meeting, 14 & 20.10.1954', par. 705. Recordings made with the Vortexion tape-recorder were subsequently transferred to gramophone discs at Head Office for more permanent storage. See ED FL 2: 'CBÉ. Miont.78 Cruinniú, 25.10.1954', p. [3].

in the Estimates for 1955–1956.[119] However, even though these Estimates, which were forwarded to the Dept. of Education, stated clearly that due to the 'decrepit condition' of its Ediphone machines the material being collected had 'fallen off sharply', the Commission's grant-in-aid was not increased to allow it to purchase any replacements. It had sought a grant-in-aid of £16,016 for 1955–1956, but only £14,000 was sanctioned.[120]

The following year the Commission lowered its sights and asked that a reduced sum of money be included in the Estimates that would, at least, have allowed some of its collectors to be equipped with new recording machines. Again this fell on deaf years, and its grant-in-aid was left at £14,000.[121] The situation did not improve the following year either, so that the idea of replacing the Ediphones had to be postponed indefinitely. An opportunity to purchase new recording machines for its collectors did occur in 1957 as the Commission had, due to unforeseen circumstances, a balance of £564 at its disposal. However, its van, now almost ten years old was no longer economic to keep on the road, and it was decided to use this money to replace it.[122]

It is easy to understand why the Commission had been unable to purchase tape recorders for its collectors, despite its aspirations in that direction, when we consider that its grant-in-aid had not been increased since 1954–1955 and was still in the late 1950's at £14,000 per annum, although in the intervening period 'the over-all running expenses of the Commission had increased' significantly. In fact, in the intervening years it had only been possible 'to keep within the grant because of the occurrence of vacancies on the staff which remained unfilled.[123] However, the Commission's grant-in-aid for 1960–1961 was increased to £16,900, and this allowed it once again to consider equipping all its collectors with portable tape recorders. Despite the increased grant, the Finance Sub-Committee moved with a degree of caution, partly because of all the other overheads it had to meet. The Commission could still not afford to rush headlong into purchasing tape recorders for its collectors. A number of models were first tested in the field to ascertain their suitability.[124] It also appears that priority was given to first equipping collectors working in Gaeltacht areas with tape recorders. The first collector to be provided with a tape recorder, in the summer of 1962, was Proinnsias de Búrca for use 'in the Mayo/Galway area.' De Búrca had been working for many years as a special collector, but he was soon to be reinstated as

119 ED FL 2: 'IFC. Fin. Sub-Com./Min. 93rd Meeting, 14 & 20.10.1954', par. 705

120 ED FL 2: 'For Estimates, 1955–56. Replacement of Ediphones' and D/F S 101/0011/34: Dept. of Fin. to Sec. Dept. of Educ., dated 15.1.1955.

121 ED FL 2: 'IFC. Fin. Sub-Com./Min. 97th Meeting, 20.10.1955', p. [3].

122 ED FL 2: 'IFC. Fin. Sub-Com./Min. 102nd Meeting, 11.3.1957', par. 756. In March 1957 the Finance Sub-Committee also sanctioned the purchase of a 'minifon recorder', which was 'light and easy to operate'. This was possibly intended for use by individual collectors, as the occasion arose. Ibid., par. 757.

123 ED FL 4: 'IFC. Fin. Sub-Com./Min. 117th Meeting, 6.1.1961', p. 2.

124 The first machine tested in the field was a Philips tape recorder lent to the Commission by one of its staff, Anraí Ó Braonáin. ED FL 4: 'IFC. Fin. Sub-Com./Min. 116th Meeting, 19.10.1960', par. 843.

a full-time collector.[125] Why he was chosen to be the first recipient of one of these new machines is not all that clear, but it may have been due to the fact that he was still collecting long folktales, for which he himself had a particular penchant. Ó Duilearga was in the habit of calling him the 'Quarry Man' because of this penchant. De Búrca liked to hew out, so to speak, large chunks of tales from the tradition in preference to shorter lore.[126] Later that year the three full-time collectors working in Gaeltacht areas (Seán Ó Cróinín, Séan Ó hEochaidh, and Ciarán Bairéad) were provided with Philips tape recorders, and in the spring of the following year it was decided to provide the remaining two full-time collectors, Michael J. Murphy and Jim Delaney, with battery-operated tape recorders.[127]

Advent of tape recorders and ensuing problems

The supplying of tape recorders to the collectors greatly facilitated their work, and increased the amount of material they could collect, but not necessarily the amount they transcribed, i.e. the number of manuscript pages they forwarded to Head Office. The fact that tapes were henceforth to be preserved rather than reused, as had been the case with Ediphone cylinders, meant that collectors were under less pressure, and as time went on a backlog of untranscribed tapes accumulated – many of these tapes were never to be transcribed.[128] Hitherto much, if not most, of the sound recordings done by the Commission's mobile recording unit and stored in its sound archive had involved the taking of samples of tradition in order to preserve an acoustic record of material, in many cases, already collected and transcribed from Ediphone cylinders that were subsequently shaved for reuse. In time, however, as a result of the acquisition of tape recorders by the collectors and sufficient resources to provide them with an abundant supply of tapes, the Commission's sound archive was to change from being an acoustic record of samples of tradition to being a large repository of tradition in itself, a counterpart to the Commission's Main Collection and not simply an addendum to it. This development may not have been foreseen. Initially, it would seem, it was hoped collectors, now that they had new recording equipment at their disposal, would continue to transcribe the bulk of what they collected. However, this was not to happen. Although the acquisition of tape recorders, must have been a godsend, transcribing with this new technology was not unproblematic. The collectors were human beings,

---

125 ED FL 4: 'IFC. Fin. Sub-Com./Min. 123rd Meeting, 26.6.1962', par. 876 and par. 877.

126 Recalled from conversations with Séamas Ó Catháin in the 1970's and 1980's.

127 ED FL 1: 'IFC. Fin. Sub-Com./Min. 124th, Meeting, 15.10.1962', par. 885 and 'IFC. Fin. Sub-Com./Min. 125th Meeting, 13.3.1963', par. 889. The battery-operated tape recorders supplied some of the collectors appear to have been Sony machines. The following March two more Sony tape recorders were purchased for the use of collectors as well as the Commission's first photocopying machine. ED FL 1: 'IFC. Fin. Sub-Com./Min. 128th Meeting, 12.3.1964', p. [2]. As some rural houses were still without electricity, battery -operated machines may have been found to be more convenient for collectors.

128 In some cases, this backlog could be quite substantial. See Bale 1993, pp. 64–65.

and not machines that could be reprogrammed overnight to adapt to this new medium. Moreover, none of them were young any longer, and a number of them were quite advanced in years. Neither were the Sony tape recorders supplied some of the collectors ideal for transcribing as it did not have 'a back-spacing device'. Although this model was effective for recording, the constant wear and tear for the dual purpose of recording and transcribing (the latter activity involving 'continual stopping, re-starting, rewinding and playing back') took its toll on the machines. In October 1967, and again in October 1968, Leo Corduff recommended that the best solution would be to provide each collector with a mains-operated tape recorder 'with a back-spacing device' to be 'used solely for transcription work' and a good-quality battery-operated machine for collecting.[129] It would be March 1969, however, before the Commission was able to equip all its full-time collectors with a Sony portable machine for field work and a Tandberg machine, with a foot control device, for transcription work.[130]

Legacy of sound recordings

It is hard to believe that a world-famous institute such as the Irish Folklore Commission was not in a position to equip its collectors with tape recorders until the early 1960's, and that the recording equipment they had to make do with for much of the 1950's was in such a poor state of repair that it affected the production of the collectors.[131] Not only did lack of proper funding delay the day when its collectors could be provided with modern recording equipment, but creating and maintaining the Commission's sound archive had to be done from start to finish on a shoestring budget. The acquisition of tape recorders by collectors in the last decade of the Commission added greatly to its sound recordings, but it also made the processing of this material at Head Office more difficult and added to the problems of future generations in utilising this material as there simply was not sufficient staff to process this material as it came in.

In October 1967, Leo Corduff in a memorandum to the Finance Sub-Committee outlined the problems he faced as the person responsible for the sound archive and microfilming:

> If the work of copying the sound and manuscript material is to be carried out at least two technicians are required. The danger is that all of the sound

---

129 ED FL 1: 'IFC. Fin. Sub-Com./Min. 139th Meeting, 12.10.1967', par. 1002 and ED FL 1: 'IFI. Fin. Sub-Com. Min. 142nd Meeting, 22.10.1968', par 1018.

130 ED FL 8: 'CBÉ. Miont. 138ú Cruinniú, 17.1.1969', p. 2 and ED FL 1: 'IFC. Fin. Sub-Com./Min. 143rd Meeting, 15.1.1969', par. 1028.

131 For instance, the Folklore Archive of the Finnish Literature Society acquired several tape recorders in the early 1950's for the use of its staff. By the end of the decade students, funded by the Society, were also making field recordings with tape recorders supplied to them. Hautala 1957, pp. 18–19 and Asplund 1992, p. 36. In Ireland at this time there were no student collecting expeditions as there were no students of folklore – the teaching of folklore having been neglected.

material will deteriorate with time. There is also the additional hazard that should a fire break out in the premises much of the manuscript material still remains to be microfilmed.

Corduff had initially been employed as a microfilm operator, and this continued to be one of his many duties. Although in 'the early years of micro-filming in the Commission, four members of the staff were engaged on the filming of the MSS.', due to lack of manpower, '[v]ery little microfilming [had] been done since 1962' and there was a huge backlog of manuscript material to be microfilmed. There was also a backlog of sound recordings to be copied, which Corduff estimated would take someone working full-time 'from one year to eighteen months to complete.' He also noted that the School of Scottish Studies had 'two technicians...engaged full-time on the copying of sound material.'[132] He might have added that his Scottish colleagues had also more up-to-date equipment to work with.

In the above memorandum, Corduff had also proposed the setting up a proper recording studio at Head Office, which would involve the updating of equipment. This was 'a matter of some urgency', in his opinion. The cost of updating the Commission's studio equipment would run to approximately £2,000. The Finance-Sub-Committee chose not to include such a large sum in the Commission's Estimates for 1968–1969. Instead, it forwarded Corduff's memorandum to the Dept. of Education.[133] The Commission was never in a position to employ two technicians to man its sound archive, nor, it would appear, did the Dept. of Education act on Corduff's proposal to provide the Commission with a proper recording studio. As the Government had already taken the decision to transfer the Commission to UCD, the Dept. of Education was unlikely to heed appeals from the Commission for large-scale developments. Such matters could be left to a later date.

Speaking of the early work of the Commission's mobile recording unit, Caoimhín Ó Danachair says that these recordings constitute 'some of the finest examples of folk narrative ever recorded in Europe'.[134] The sound archive of the Irish Folklore Commission stands as a monument to many: the collectors in the field and their informants, as well as Caoimhín Ó Danachair and Leo Corduff, particular the latter who spent most of his career assembling and maintaining this archive. The work Leo Corduff did for the Commission over the years was variously described in the official documentation. He has been classified as an assistant ethnologist, technical assistant, collector, and folklorist, and he was all those things. His work awaits a more detailed assessment than the present study can devote to it. Although he did a great deal of collecting in the field, it would be wrong, however, to assess this aspect of his work by the same yardstick as we measure the other full-time collectors. Ultimately, his collecting must be assessed on the quality of his recordings, as it involved, for the most part, the acoustic sampling of tradition rather than its investigation and documentation. This does not mean that

132 ED FL 1: 'IFC. Fin. Sub-Com./Min. 139th Meeting, 12.10.1967', par. 1,002.
133 Ibid.
134 Ó Danachair 1981, pp. 314–315.

he did not have potential to be a more conventional collector, nor that he did not have an interest in oral tradition. He was far more than a technician indifferent to the tradition he was sent to record, but he was a technician nevertheless, and it was his skills in this area that the Commission sought first and foremost to utilise.[135]

135 For an obituary of Leo Corduff, see Almqvist 1992–93. In August 1982, Anne O'Connor recorded Leo Corduff telling of his career with the Commission. This recording is now in the Department of Irish Folklore and should be of great interest to anyone seeking to assess his work.

Creating a research library

Not least of the Irish Folklore Commission's achievements was the assembling over three and a half decades of a large specialist library of books, journals, and pamphlets on folkloristic and related subjects. The basis for this library was already laid during the time of the Irish Folklore Institute. Although the Institute suffered from lack of funds, a special grant of £300 received in 1931 from the Carnegie United Kingdom Trust allowed it to purchase a certain amount books and it was able to bequeath some 300 books to the Commission.[1]

The Irish Folklore Commission was also to benefit from numerous book donations, both large and small from individuals, institutions, and governments, but as it was a better-funded body, it was also able to devote more of its resources to the purchase of books. The Commission, and the Institute before it, also managed to acquire many national and international journals by exchanging them for *Béaloideas*. Despite its reduced state grant during the Second World War, the Commission managed to continue to purchase books. However, if it were not for the acquisition of a number of important specialist libraries, the Commission's library would be wanting in many respects. It should also be noted that without extra state grants and help from other sources it would not have been able to purchase most of these libraries. In all, the Commission purchased four substantial private libraries. The first of these was the library of Ó Duilearga's mentor, Carl Wilhelm von Sydow, which reached the Commission in early summer 1950. It was von Sydow's wish that the Irish Folklore Commission should acquire his large collection of folkloristic works and the purchase of his library was negotiated, and it was transferred to the Commission, while he was still alive. The Dept. of External Affairs gave the Commission a grant of £500 towards purchasing this library, which cost in all £1,900.[2] Then in 1955 the Commission acquired the smaller, but nonetheless important, private library of Bartholomew Bowen of Sutton, Co. Dublin, which 'contained many valuable and rare items'. The Bowen library had originally belonged to Dublin balladeer and bibliophile Patrick Joseph McCall (1861–1919). It was especially good in respect of works on Irish music and song as well as placenames, local history, dictionaries and journals.[3] The following year the Commission purchased the library of the lexicographer and Icelandic scholar Sir William Craigie of Oxford. Like von Sydow, Craigie specifically wished the Commission to have his private library, and it was also purchased during his lifetime. However,

1   LUB Saml. von Sydow: Ó Duilearga to von Sydow, dated 20.12.1931, p. [1] and D/T S 15548A: 'Gearr-Thuar./1938–39', p. [5].
2   D/T S 15548B: 'Gearr-Thuar./1949–50', p. [4] and D/T S 15548B: 'Gearr-Thuar./1950–51', p. [7].
3   ED FL 2: 'IFC. Fin. Sub-Com./Min. 96th Meeting, 28.4.1955', par. 724 and D/T S 15548B: 'Gearr-Thuar. 1955–56', p. 5.

it took the Commission a number of years to finalise negotiations for the purchase of this library due to difficulties it had in getting sufficient funds for the purpose. In order to secure the support of the Dept. of Education for a state grant to purchase Craigie's library, Ó Duilearga was forced to appeal directly to the Taoiseach of the day, John A. Costello. With Costello's support the Dept. of Education agreed to the proposal and in time so too did the Dept. of Finance.[4] In his report to the Government for 1955–1956, Ó Duilearga thanks both the state and the UCD authorities for the financial assistance that made possible the purchase of this 'famous library' of some 3,500 books: 'It is greatly to Ireland's credit, in the opinion of the scholars of the world, that this fine, important library is now in the Commission's possession. Nothing comparable exists in these islands of Ireland and Great Britain.'[5] In purchasing this library Ó Duilearga was further strengthening those ties with northern Europe he had first set out to forge as a young man in the late 1920's. The final large private library acquired by the Commission was the library of Dr F. S. Bourke. This consisted of some 9,000 volumes and was described by Ó Duilearga to the Finance Sub-Committee as 'the finest single collection of Irish historical and topographical works outside of public libraries.' It was bought from Dr Bourke's widow with the help of businessman Joseph MacGrath, a grant from the National University of Ireland as well as a grant from the Irish Government.[6]

It was not simply Ó Duilearga's aim to assemble a large specialist library, when the Commission's resources allowed it, he saw to it that a librarian was also appointed. In 1949, after the Commission had moved to its more spacious headquarters in 82 St. Stephen's Green, Thomas Wall (Tomás de Bhál) was appointed librarian and assistant archivist. Dr Wall was a noted authority on books and had reorganised and catalogued a number of important libraries before coming to work at the Commission. Immediately prior to his taking up this post he had been employed in the Library of University College Dublin. Thomas Wall was a scholarly, reserved man, and although his academic interests had little to do with folklore as such, he was to serve the staff of the Commission well as librarian.[7] Some three years after Wall's appointment, in May 1952, a Hungarian refugee living in Ireland, Josef Szövérffy, joined the staff of the Commission as assistant librarian. Szövérffy, a Latinist, whose main area of expertise was medieval hymnology, also had a background in folkloristics. As the Commission had appointed a librarian only a few years previously, and as it had to function on a grant that was insufficient to meet its needs, his appointment

4   D/F S 101/0011/34: 'The Sir William Craigie Library', undated, D/F S 101/0011/34: Ó Raifeartaigh to Sec. Dept. of Fin., dated 19.12.1955, and ibid.: internal memo S.ÓL. to Mr. MacInerney, dated 23.12.1955.
5   D/T S 15548B: 'Gearr-Thuar./1955–56', p. 7 (trans.).
6   ED FL 4: 'IFC. Fin. Sub-Com./Min. 104th meeting, 5.2.1960', par. 834.
7   D/T S 15548B: 'Gearr-Thuar./1949–50', p. [2]. Wall was later to marry Maureen McGeehan, short-hand typist in the Commission from 1949–1951. See above.

at this juncture was certainly an extravagant move, especially as it seems Szövérffy had no training or experience in librarianship. To some extent, Ó Duilearga may initially have taken pity on this talented young refugee, who was teaching in a secondary school at the time, but employing him soon fitted in to his own greater plans for the Commission.[8] By this time the Commission's library contained publications 'in about twenty languages, including Finnish, Estonian, Russian, Polish, Lithuanian, Hungarian, Icelandic, the Scandinavian and Romance languages'[9] Although, the Commission's librarian, Thomas (Tom) Wall, could have catalogued works in languages he did not understand in respect of title and subject matter without too much difficulty, Ó Duilearga wished to make the Commission's library an indispensable Mecca for foreign scholars by the compilation of a detailed subject matter card-index of books and journals in the Commission's library. Szövérffy with his background and wide knowledge of European languages was, in many respects, ideal for the job. By autumn 1954 he had made around 100,000 reference cards 'of the books and their contents' in the Commission's library.[10] Szövérffy appears to have been favoured by Ó Duilearga and as relations deteriorated (see Chapter VI/2 below) between the Director and two of the senior members of his staff, Seán Ó Súilleabháin and Caoimhín Ó Danachair, he was someone Ó Duilearga could confide in. In any event, Ó Duilearga was very satisfied with Szövérffy's work. In an undated document deriving from the mid-1950's he has this to say of Szövérffy's card-index:

> This is the largest and only comprehensive card-index of printed folklore in the world. When the work is finished, it will contain 350,000 cards and we shall be able to give precise information concerning the smallest details of international and Irish folklore, particularly in oral literature and religious folklore. Apart from the great manuscript material, this fact will ensure the Commission a dominant part in world folklore studies.

In this document Ó Duilearga also claims that the Commission's library 'is the largest single collection of folklore books in Europe and presumably larger than the American collections.'[11] Whether this claim was true or not, there is no doubt that the Commission had a fine specialist library of books by this time, and was to continue to add to and improve its collection of books and journals. However, Szövérffy's card-index was never to be completed.

Szövérffy left the Commission in the summer of 1957 to take up an appointment as Professor of Medieval and Classical Latin in St. John's

---

8   D/T S 15548B: 'Gearr-Thuar./1952–53', p. [3] and SKS Haavio Papers, 12:58:30: Ó Duilearga to Haavio, dated 7.1.1952.
9   D/T S 6916D: 'Report about the Library and Folklore Catalogue', undated.,
10   D/T S 15548B: 'Gearr-Thuar./1953–54', p. 6 (trans.).
11   D/T S 6916D: 'Report about the Library and Folklore Collection', undated.

College, Montreal University.' It is unlikely that in the long run the Irish Folklore Commission could have managed to keep this talented and ambitious scholar, who was to have a distinguished career for himself as a Medievalist in Canada.[12] There is no doubt that he benefited from his years in Ireland and with the Commission, among other things adding a certain knowledge of Irish to the list of the languages he knew. Whether the Commission benefited from his presence on the staff is more difficult to ascertain. The year he left Ireland, Szövérffy published a book on Irish tradition and for some years after leaving Ireland was to continue to contribute articles on Irish folklore and literature to various journals,[13] but no more is heard of his card-index, for which Ó Duilearga had so many hopes. For such a card-index to be of any real value, it would not only have had to be completed but maintained and kept up to date. However, the Commission were never able to replace Szövérffy. The tens of thousands of cards his index comprised were transferred to UCD in 1971, along with the rest of the Commission's possessions, but had long before, it would appear, become an irrelevance if not indeed an embarrassment, for apart from the fact that it was never completed, it appears that there was some flaw in the referencing that made it virtually unusable.

Despite the fate of Josef Szövérffy's card-index, the creation from scratch of the Commission's research library was certainly a great achievement. Many individuals and institutions contributed to assembling this collection of books and periodicals over more than three and a half decades. Although not without *lacunae*, particularly in respect of certain related disciplines, the Commission was able to bequeath a unique, specialist library of national and international works to its successor in 1971, including many rare publications. This library enhances the collections of the Commission, serving as a companion or *bráthair taca* (literally 'supportive brother'), as Ó Duilearga put it[14], to them. Given the nature of the daunting task facing the Commission, to have assembled its extensive collections of oral tradition would have been achievement enough in itself, but to have succeeded in assembling such a fine library at the same time, makes the achievement of the Commission, and of Ó Duilearga, all the greater.

12   ED FL 2: 'IFC. Fin. Sub-Com. Min. 193rd Meeting, 13.6.1957', par. 768. In 1970 Szövérffy published a substantial work on medieval secular poetry, *Weltliche Dichtungen des lateinischen Mittelalters. Ein Handbuch. 1. Von den Anfängen bis zum Ende der Karolingerzeit*. For more on Szövérffy's latter career, see Vaslef and Buschhausen, 1986, 'Preface'.
13   Szövérffy 1957.
14   D/T S 15548A: 'Gearr-Thuar./1938–39', p. [5].

VI The Seeds of Discontent

1. Salaries and conditions of employment

Finance interference

The Terms of Reference of the Irish Folklore Commission stated that 'the Director is empowered, subject to the approval of the Commission to engage staff in such numbers and at such rates of remuneration and on such other conditions as may be approved by the Minister for Education with the sanction of the Minister for Finance.'[1] Naturally Séamus Ó Duilearga wished to provide adequate salaries for his collectors (and other staff) out of the budget allowed the Commission. The Dept. of Education was of like mind to him, appreciating the nature of the work to be undertaken by the collectors. The Dept. of Finance, on the other hand, was, to a large extent, more interested in keeping expenditure to a minimum than seeing to it that the staff of the Commission were duly compensated for their labours.

The degree to which the Dept. of Finance interfered in respect of salaries and related matters of the Commission's staff went against the spirit of the Terms of Reference of the Commission, which gave the Dept. of Education primary responsibility for the Commission, albeit with the sanction of Finance. Consequently, on July 2nd, 1935, Proinnsias Ó Dubhthaigh wrote to the Secretary of the Dept. of Finance:

> I am also to refer to previous inter-Ministerial correspondence relative to the Folklore Commission and in particular to the semi-official letter of the 24th November, 1934, addressed to the Minister for Education by the Minister for Finance, in which it was stated that it was not the intention that your Minister's Department should have every individual appointment submitted for scrutiny and that he was prepared to give a general authority for appointments on the understanding that the Minister for Education assumed responsibility for ensuring that the volume and quality of the work to be performed justified the appointments proposed by the Commission and that the remuneration, expenses and other

---

1   D/F S 101/0011/34: Proinnsias Ó Dubhthaigh to Sec. Dept. of Fin., dated 5.6.1935.

conditions (e.g. leave, etc.) are not more favourable than those that might be sanctioned for analogous work in the Public Service.[2]

The Dept. of Finance did not reply to this comment of Ó Dubhthaigh's.[3] Obviously, their interpretation of this matter was different to that of Education. Not until 1947 would they relax financial control of the Commission, and allow the Commission to decide what salaries it should pay its staff. An internal Finance memo of July 1935 reveals a somewhat cynical attitude towards the Commission in respect of Education's above proposals:

> Generally we approve the proposal of the D/Ed for the staffing of Folklore Commission. The Commission are financed by Grant-in-Aid & are really an outside body. Their officers will not be Civil Servants. In the light of the facts and the consideration that in the long run it will probably be in the interests of the Exchequer to keep the staffing costs as low as possible ... would you please advise on the conditions suggested for the several appointments.'[4]

To a very large extent, from the outset, the Dept. of Finance sought to keep the salaries of the Commission's staff as low as possible 'in the interests of the Exchequer'. Moreover, for more than two decades, Finance officials were to display little understanding of the nature of the work of the Commission's staff. This lack of understanding was particularly in evidence in respect of the appointment of the initial Head Office staff.

Salaries and conditions of the initial Head Office staff

The Dept. of Education originally proposed a salary of £250 per annum, rising to £350 by £10 annual increments, for Seán Ó Súilleabháin, the Commission's Archivist/Registrar, and a salary of £200 per annum, rising by £10 annual increments to £250, for Máire MacNeill, the Office Manager.[5] However, the salary proposed for MacNeill was objected to, and, indeed, the need for such a post questioned. An internal Finance memo of June 1935, while accepting that three collectors at least would be needed initially, states:

> I am by no means clear, however, that both an Archivist and Registrar and an Office Manager are required. On the information available it strikes me

2   D/F S 101/0011/34: Proinnsias Ó Dubhthaigh to Sec. Dept. of Fin., dated 2.7.1935.
3   However, an internal departmental memo notes: 'We must, I think, be careful not to appear to interfere with the Commission but in view of the exceptional freedom which it enjoys from detailed Finance Control, we would expect the D/Ed to further some kind of guiding comments on such items as are marked in pencil on the Accounts and to explain (e.g.) why their payment to the Irish Folklore Society is only £125 and not £250 as arranged when they were set up.' D/F S 101/0011/34: internal memo to Mr. Doolin, dated 9.9.36 - marginal note to above of same date.
4   D/F S 101/0011/34: internal memo, D.P. S[hanagher] to Estabs. Division, dated 9.7.35.
5   D/F S 101/0011/34: Proinnsias Ó Dubhthaigh to Sec. Dept. of Fin., dated 5.6.1935.

that the Registrar should be able to do all the office managing that will be necessary with the assistance perhaps of a Clerk or a Clerk-typist.

The writer, D. P. Shanagher, noted, however, that MacNeill had 'actually been serving on the staff of the Commission since the date of its establishment' some two months previously, so there was 'no option but to approve of her appointment'. As MacNeill's work could in this official's estimation, 'be carried out by a Clerk or Clerk-typist' he considered a salary scale of £150 per annum to be 'ample'.[6]

Education's proposed salary for Máire MacNeill met with even less sympathy from other Finance officials. W. F. Nally commented: 'On the scant information we have we incline to view that this is an over-glorified title for a very very [sic] simple clerical post and that whatever real work has to be done by the Commission will fall to be done by the Commission itself & by the Director.' He was obviously ignorant of the role of the Commission (i.e. the Advisory Board) if he thought it was going to contribute significantly to 'whatever real work has to be done'. He had even less understanding of the post of Archivist, and the qualities required for it: 'The Archivist may have a bit of searching and digging to do but we don't think he will have as hard a job as a teacher & it would probably be possible to find a man or a woman in the outside world to do the job well for £20 a month – or less'. He also stated that 'We definitely feel that the salaries shall be engaged on a monthly basis – not per annum.'[7] Reason prevailed and W. F. Nally did not have his way in respect of salaries: both the salaries of Seán Ó Súilleabháin and Máire MacNeill were to be calculated on an annual basis.

On June 19th, 1935, Finance informed the Dept. of Education of its refusal to appoint an Office Manager, and proposed instead 'to sanction the appointment of a Clerk with a salary scale of £150 – £7.10 – £200 per annum, inclusive.' The letter had a sting in its tail:

> As it would appear from the terms of the proposal submitted that the arrangements for these appointments, or some of them, had been made in advance of the Minister's sanction, I am to request that you will impress on the Director the necessity for a strict compliance in future with the terms of the approved scheme under which aid has been granted by the State to the Irish Folklore Commission.[8]

In the event, however, a meeting between representatives of the Departments of Finance and Education in late June 1935 cleared up some of the misunderstanding in respect of the duties of the Archivist/Registrar vis-à-vis the Office Manager. The latter post would involve 'the keeping of accounts,

---

6   D/F S 101/0011/34: D. P. S[hanagher] to Mr. Almond, dated 7.6.1935, pp. [1–2].
7   D/F S 101/0011/34: Gloss by W. F. N[ally] to Fin. memo T. S K[ealy] to Nally, dated 11.6.1935. Nally adds: 'We appear to have being brought into the picture very late in the day! Why have engagements been made (with salaries!) without the prior approval of our Department?'
8   D/F S 101/0011/34: W. Doolin to Sec. Dept. of Educ., dated 19.6.1935.

payment of salaries, supervision of the work of the collectors, etc.' As the person earmarked for this post, Máire MacNeill, had worked for the Irish Folklore Institute and had experience of similar work, Finance eventually agreed to her appointment but only on the stipulation 'that this scale would be sanctioned as an arrangement personal to the present occupant of the post and would be subject to review on the occurrence of a vacancy.'[9]

MacNeill was, somewhat vindictively, only allowed eighteen days' annual leave by Finance, although twenty four days had been requested for her. Seán Ó Súilleabháin was, however, after a degree of haggling, granted twenty four days' annual leave[10], as were the first three full-time collectors appointed (see below). In the case of these three collectors, it was only after the Dept. of Education stressed 'that the very nature of their duties under the Commission will compel the Collectors to work not only during the daylight hours but also at night' that Finance agreed to grant them twenty four days' annual leave.[11] Collectors subsequently appointed, however, had to make do with eighteen days' annual leave.

The terms of employment of the first staff employed by the Commission, be they indoor or outdoor staff, were roughly similar, and with slight adjustments were to continue in vogue until revised in the late 1950's and early 1960's in anticipation of the staff of the Commission becoming Civil Servants. In addition to matters concerning salaries and annual leave, referred to above, the following conditions of employment should be noted:

1) The posts were officially designated 'full-time, temporary, non-pensionable posts', and employees were not allowed to be engaged, or be associated, with in any other line of work.

2) Employees were expected to work at least forty-two hours per week, but their actual number of working hours was left to the discretion of the Director to determine 'from time to time'.

3) Each appointment was initially made for a one-year trial period and it could be terminated by either party at any time by giving a month's notice. In case of misconduct, however, the employee could be dismissed forthwith and no explanation as to the reason for dismissal need be given.

4) In addition to a designated period of paid annual leave, all employees were allowed paid sick leave in accordance with regulations in force in the Civil Service concerning unestablished officers.[12]

9   D/F S 101/0011/34: 'Note on Conference at Dept. of Fin. on the 28th June, 1935 in regard to the proposed appointments to the staff of the IFC', dated 3.7.1935.
10 D/F S 101/0011/34: C. S. Almond to Sec. Dept. of Educ., dated 18.7.1935.
11 D/F S 101/001/34: Ó Muirithe to Sec. Dept. of Fin., dated 16.7.1935 and D/F S 101/001/34: C.S. Almond to Sec. Dept. of Educ., dated 18.7.1935.
12 D/T S 6916D: extrapolated from 'CBÉ. Annálaidhe agus Cláradóir. Coiníollacha an Cheapacháin', 'CBÉ. Bainisteoir na hOifige. Coiníollacha an Cheapacháin, and 'CBÉ. Bailitheoir Lán-Aimsire. Coiníollacha an Cheapacháin' (trans.). Although full-time collectors were allowed a certain number of days sick leave, in the early years of the Commission those whose work was affected by illness, sometimes contracted by the nature of the work itself, were forced to resign as they were not able to collect the amount of

Differences in rates of pay of the initial collectors

The first three full-time collectors appointed were Liam Mac Coisdeala, Tadhg Ó Murchadha, and Nioclás Breatnach. The former two were given salaries of £250, rising to £300 by a £10 annual increment, and Breatnach a salary scale of £200 rising to £250, with an annual increment of £10. Their salaries it was understood would 'include travelling, subsistence, and incidental expenses', and as a result would be somewhat larger than their salaries as Vocational or National School teachers.[13] However, the next three full-time collectors, appointed shortly afterwards, Proinnsias de Búrca, Seán Ó hEochaidh, and Liam Mac Meanman, had to make do with the much lower salary of £150 per annum.[14] The reason for this discrepancy arising in the first place is bound up with the fact that the first three collectors appointed took leave of absence from pensionable jobs and in so doing had to, temporarily at least, forfeit pension rights. Nioclás Breatnach had less teaching experience, and most likely a lower salary as a teacher, than the other two: hence his somewhat lower salary. Moreover, the salary discrepancy between the higher- and the lower-paid collectors was in fact larger than the above figures indicate as it was also agreed, in the case of National School and Vocational School teachers with permanent positions, that they should be paid 15% extra in addition to their salary in lieu of forfeiting their pension rights.[15] Those subsequently employed as full-time collectors either did not have pensionable jobs, had only part-time employment, or were unemployed – hence their lower salary.

It should be noted that the lower salary of £150 per annum was not of the Dept. of Finance's making, but rather of the Commision's.[16] An internal Finance memo of July 1936, in respect of the lower salary scale, says: '£150 per annum to cover salary, travelling, sustenance and incidental expenses is absurdly low and as I say much less than we would have been prepared to agree to.' Be that as it may, although the writer of this memo, Leon Ó Broin, himself on the Board of the Commission, and also a member of its Finance Sub-Committee, states that Finance would not have objected to salaries of '£250 per annum, inclusive, plus something under £100 per annum for travelling etc.',[17] the previous July Finance in agreeing to the proposed salaries for the first three full-time collectors had made it clear that '[t]he salary scale

---

material required of them. This was the case with Seán Ó Flannagáin, although Ó Duilearga considered him an excellent collector otherwise. ED 11,309: 'IFC. Fin. Sub-Com./Min. 24th Meeting, 19.1.1940', par. 220. It should be noted, however, that in the 1950's and 1960's the Commission was much more tolerant of full-time collectors whose work was adversely affected by illness. In the early years, saving Irish folklore for posterity had to take precedence over feelings of compassion.

13 D/F S 101/001/34: Ó Dubhthaigh to Sec. Dept. of Fin., 5.6.1935.
14 D/F S 101/0011/34: Ó Duilearga to Dept. of Educ., dated 22.8.1935.
15 D/F S 101/0011/34: Almond to Sec. Dept. of Educ., dated 18.7.1935. In addition to Mac Coisdeala, Ó Murchadha, and Breatnach, Seán Ó Súilleabháin, the Commission's Archivist, was also awarded this extra 15%.
16 See D/F S 101/0011/34: Ó Duilearga to Sec. Dept. of Educ., dated 22.8.1935.
17 D/F S 101/0011/34: L. Ó B[roin] to Mr. Morris, dated 27.7.1936.

covers travelling and subsistence allowances and incidental expenses and no additional payments will be made under these heads.'[18]

In proposing this lower salary the Commission may have been endeavouring to employ as many collectors as its resources would allow in its first year of operations in order to get the collecting under way on as an extensive a scale as possible. However, it would also appear that the Commission considered this lower rate of pay as amounting somewhat to a trial salary, to be raised once the collector had proved his worth, or when circumstances allowed. To some extent there was also the idea that those on the lower salary would work closer to home, and those on a higher salary could be asked to travel outside their home areas. Nevertheless, the question of raising the salaries of the lower-paid collectors would sooner or later have to be tackled, for not only did the lower salaries give rise to dissatisfaction among those in receipt of such salaries, the work of these collectors was also adversely affected. In particular, those on the lower salary could not afford to buy and maintain a car. In June 1937, Ó Duilearga appealed to the Dept. of Education on the matter:

> Some of the collectors can no longer continue to fulfil their obligations to the Commission unless transport is provided for them. The Commission on several occasions has received a detailed account of the situation in which these men now find themselves, and both the Commission and the Financial [recte Finance] Sub-Committee are in complete agreement as to the urgency of the case, and the paramount necessity of having the matter settled once and for all.

The problem for the Commission was that it did not have the money to effect these increases, even if the Dept. of Finance would sanction them. Ó Duilearga informed the Dept. of Education: 'It would not be necessary to ask for the increased grant [£475] in the current financial year if it were not for the unexpectedly large submission of part-time contributions, which are paid for at a purely nominal rate, but which in the aggregate have made very considerable demands on our financial resources.'[19]

In the event, Finance did agree to raise the salary of those collectors on a salary of £150 per annum to £250 '[o]n the understanding that the three Collectors who now receive £150 a year will, in future, be required to perform duties and to cover areas comparable with those of the Collectors on the higher rate of pay'. They did not, however, accede to Ó Duilearga's request (in above letter) that these increases be made retroactive from April 1st, 1937, in order that each of the collectors could be paid 'a lump sum of £50 on the 1st October, 1937, towards the purchase of a motor car', as such an increase 'could not be justified on the grounds that these men have been performing the higher duties since the 1st April.'[20] Subsequent to autumn

---

18 D/F S 101/0011/34: W. Doolin to Sec. Dept. of Educ., dated 12.7.1935, p. [3].

19 D/F S 101/0011/34: Ó Duilearga to Dept. of Educ., dated 24.6.1937, pp. [1–2].

20 D/F S 101/0011/34: internal Fin. memo, Lynd to Doolin, dated 10.8.1937. Finance while sanctioning these salary increases, did not give the Commission the extra £475 it requested,

1937 full-time collectors employed by the Commission were paid at the rate of £250 per annum, inclusive of travelling expenses, etc. However, the lower salary of £150 continued to be paid to new full-time collectors during their trial period.[21]

Travelling and other Expenses for collectors

While henceforth there was less discrepancy between the salaries of the various full-time collectors than hitherto, the salaries of all the full-time collectors were by no means adequate, given that they were not paid any sort of expenses. If the Second World War had not intervened, collectors' salaries would, no doubt, have been increased in time, but the onset of war meant cutbacks in the state's expenditure. While the Commission's grant for 1938–1939 was increased by £1,000, it had to make do with £400 less for 1939–1940, and £600 less annually from April 1940 onwards.[22] The Commission tried to keep as many full-time collectors on its payroll for as long as possible during the War years. Inevitably, this meant that salaries could not be increased very much, if at all. Tomás de Búrca, taken on in September 1940, was to remain over a year on the lower trial salary of £150 and was only granted an increase by Finance on the stipulation that his work bring him outside his home locality.[23] Séamus Ennis, taken on as a collector of folk music in June 1942 at the lower rate, had to wait nine months for an increase in salary. From the summer of 1943 he was paid at the rate of £150 while resident in Dublin, and at the rate of £250 while doing fieldwork.[24] Due to lack of resources the Commission had to let two full-time collectors go in spring 1944, Seán Ó Cróinín and Proinnsias de Búrca.

The War ended with the full-time collectors still on pre-War salaries. However, in April 1946 the Dept. of Finance agreed that the full-time collectors should be paid an Emergency bonus of fifteen shillings per week for a married man and thirteen shillings for a single man, but refused to sanction travelling expenses, maintaining that these were already covered in their salaries.[25] The granting of this Emergency bonus did not go far enough towards providing adequate salaries for the full-time collectors. Moreover, during the latter years of the War when petrol was very scarce, many of those

in part, to effect these increases. Nonetheless, it did raise the Commission's annual grant for the following financial year, as requested, by the sum of £1,000. D/F S 101/0011/34: C. S. Almond to Sec. Dept. of Educ., dated 9.9.1937.

21   Such was the case with Seán Ó Cróinín, taken on full-time in April 1938 on a provisional salary of £150. See D/F S 101/0011/34: Ó Duilearga to Sec. Dept. of Educ., dated 28.3.1938.

22   See D/T S 15548A: 'Gearr-Thuar./1938–39', 'Gearr-Thuar./1939-40', and D/T S 15548B: 'Gearr-Thuar./1940–41'. In Ireland the financial year formally began at the beginning of April, a legacy from British times.

23   D/F S 101/0011/34: Dept. of Fin. to Dept. of Educ., dated 28.10.1941.

24   See D/F S 101/0011/34: Ó Duilearga to Sec. Dept. of Educ., dated 18.2.1943 and C. S. Almond to Sec. Dept. of Educ., dated 15.3.1943.

25   D/F S 101/0011/34: J.E. Hanna to Dept. of Educ., dated 30.4.1946.

who had cars, it would appear, were forced to dispose of them or take them off the road. In post-War Ireland they could no longer afford to run a car on their meagre salaries.

In May 1946, Ó Duilearga appealed to the Dept. of Education. While expressing thanks for the granting of the Emergency bonus, he went on to outline the unsatisfactory nature of the collectors' salaries. When the Commission had first been set up in 1935, living and maintenance costs were smaller than in post-war conditions. In addition, the Commission, lacking experience in such matters, had no way of estimating the costs involved in maintaining a collector in the field. Consequently, the rates suggested were 'provisional' estimates. He noted that even the rise granted to some of the collectors in 1937, was by no means adequate. However, as the Commission was to run for only five years, and as it was hoped a more permanent foundation would replace it, it was felt that in time better conditions would be granted to the full-time collectors. In the meantime, the term of office of the Commission had been extended on three separate occasions. Ó Duilearga commented that while such 'temporary measures' were unavoidable, '...the staff of the Commission lost out in a way that was not contemplated when the Conditions of Employment were first drawn up because neither the collectors nor the rest of the staff were made permanent, nor were their salaries raised beyond what they had been in the early years.'

He went on to say that £283 (the amount a collector's salary came to with the Emergency bonus) was not enough to allow a collector work away from home and maintain a car, as he would also have travel expenses, taxation and insurance to bear as well. He furthermore reminded the Dept. of Education that while country people had given the Commission's collectors their lore gratis, presents of tobacco, and such like, were expected as a matter of course, and that the collectors' salaries was supposed to cover such sundry expenses. It was not just a question of raising the salaries of collectors, but of putting them to work as was originally intended, to collect the folklore of Ireland before it was too late:

> The work day that we lose in our line of business ('gnó') can never again be retrieved. Folklore has to be written down this year, songs and music to be recorded on paper or wax, old houses and furniture and farm equipment and craft implements to be saved and documented - it is unlikely that some of these will be available next year unless seen to now.[26]

Ó Duilearga's appeal received a hearing in the Dept. of Finance, but, as was customary for Finance officials, ever in their sights was the possibility of ultimately lowering state expenditure. An internal Finance memo on Ó Duilearga's above request states:

> The sooner collecting is completed the sooner we can wind up the Commission and anything that tends to speed up collection is to be

---

26   D/F S 101/0011/34: Ó Duilearga to Sec. Dept. of Educ., dated 11.5.1946 (trans.).

commended. I agree with the Commission's view that £283 will not keep a collector full-time on the road and if the collection is speeded up thereby, I do not think that we will lose anything in the long run by giving travelling expenses. If the collectors have not enough money to travel and pay for lodgings they will not travel.[27]

Nevertheless, later that year Finance rejected the rates for travel allowances agreed upon by a joint meeting of Dept. of Education officials and a delegation from the Commission in September 1946, despite Proinnsias Ó Dubhthaigh's appeal to Finance that these rates be sanctioned. Ó Dubhthaigh argued that however bad the lot of the collectors was before the War, in the intervening years it had got far worse, and if forced to 'travel the country' as is necessary to fulfil the aims of the Commission, the collectors 'would be impoverished and it would break all the married men.' Instead, Finance proposed substantially lower rates, which Ó Duilearga was forced to reject, as such rates would not allow him send collectors to work outside their immediate home areas.[28] Despite appeals from Ó Duilearga, Finance refused to change its position on the question of expenses for the full-time collectors. However, in March 1947, it sanctioned salary increases for the collectors that could be backdated to November 1st, 1946 as long as the Commission kept within its budget for the current and coming financial year.[29] Although the Commission welcomed these increases in respect of the proposed subsistence allowances, it 'was unanimously of the opinion that they were inadequate', and requested the Director 'that representations to that effect should again be made to the Minister.' In his letter, Ó Duilearga complains that eight months have been lost in correspondence, and the objects for which the state set up the Commission largely frustrated.'[30] A few months later the Dept. of Finance decided to allow the Commission to itself decide on rates of remuneration for its staff, and in this way the impasse in respect of travelling expenses was finally resolved, but at a cost.

Dept. of Finance relaxes control

As a result of a meeting in late June 1947 between representatives of the Commission's Finance Sub-Committee and representatives of the Dept. of Finance and the Dept. of Education 'regarding the question of departmental control of the expenditure of the Folklore Commission, with particular references to the remuneration and expenses of the staff,' the Finance representatives promised to have the the the matter looked into to ascertain what

---

27 D/F S 101/0011/34: Bhreathnach to Almond, dated 22.5.1946.
28 D/F S 101/0011/34: Dept of Fin. to Dept. of Educ., dated 12.11.1946, and ED CO 495(8): Ó Duilearga to Ó Dubhthaigh, dated 24.11.1946.
29 ED CO 495(8): J.E. Hanna to Sec. Dept. of Educ, dated 12.3.1947 (trans.). Tadhg Ó Murchadha's salary was increased from £300 to £410, and the salaries of the other collectors from £250 to £350.
30 ED CO 495(8): Ó Duilearga to Sec. Dept. of Educ., dated 17.5.1947.

'the origin of the requirements of departmental sanctions' was, stating that 'subject to there being no fundamental difficulty arising out of the conditions on which the Commission was established', his Department would agree to have this requirement 'discontinued'. As it turned out, Finance discovered that the proposal for departmental sanction had originally come from the Dept.of Education. After considering the matter, officials decided 'that this control has operated to hamper the Commission and that it might be reasonably discontinued.'[31] Ó Duilearga was well pleased with this decision and in a letter of thanks says that this decision 'will henceforth make it possible to fulfil the aims of the Government in respect of the collection without loss of [any more] time.'[32] In time, as we saw above, Finance came to regret somewhat that it relaxed its grip on the Commission, and from time to time began to flex its muscle again.

Although salaries remained an issue right into the 1950's and beyond, at least after 1947 the Commission had much more freedom to increase the salaries of collectors, within the restraints of its grant-in-aid, of course. An increased grant from the late 1940's onward also gave the Commission more freedom to determine salaries. The Commission's grant in aid was raised from £3,650 in 1945/1946 to £6,250 in 1946/1947. Then in 1949/1950 it was almost doubled to £12,000. Without this extra funding it would not have been possible for the Commission to pay salary increases to its collectors as well as travel and subsistence allowances, nor would it have been possible for them to employ new collectors. However, the economic growth the South of Ireland experienced from 1945 to 1950 was followed by almost a decade of economic stagnation.[33] The substantial increase in the Commission's grant-in-aid for 1949/1950 was not to be repeated. The early 1950's saw a slight reduction in the Commission's grant, and numerous efforts by the Dept. of Finance to curtail its expenditure. In these circumstances it is not surprising to find that the salaries of the collectors and of the rest of the Commission's staff did not keep apace with salaries in other 'comparable' sectors. The Commission was not hamstrung to the same extent as it was prior to 1947, but its resources were never sufficient and the demands on them many.

One immediate result of the Dept. of Finance's easing of its control of the Commission in 1947 was the decision by its Finance Sub-Committee in June of the following year to raise the salaries of four members of the Head Office staff: Seán Ó Súilleabháin (£545 to £600), Máire MacNeill (£350 to £500), Caoimhín Ó Danachair (£350 to £600), and Bríd Mahon (£250 to £275). Although Ó Danachair's job had been variously described, as regards salary he had till then been treated as a collector. His salary was

---

31 D/F S 101/0011/34: untitled Fin. memo on meeting, signed J. E. H[anna] (dated 30.6.1947) and appended note, dated 3.7.1947. At this meeting, the Commission's representatives, Ó Duilearga and Michael Tierney, noted that, 'so far as they were aware' other bodies 'financed by way of a grant-in-aid' did not have to 'obtain specific departmental sanction for their expenditure.' Ibid.

32 ED CO 495(8): Ó Duilearga to Sec. Dept. of Educ., dated 11.8. 1947 (trans.).

33 For a brief description of the changing fortunes of the Irish economy from 1945–1959, see Ó Gráda 1997, pp. 21–29.

now being raised well above that of the collectors, as it was felt a man of his training and expertise should be rewarded. At this meeting Ó Duilearga also proposed raising the salaries of the other collectors, particularly that of Calm MacLean, but the other members of the Sub-Committee argued against doing so, as funds might be needed to fit out their new headquarters in 82 St. Stephen's Green.[34] In time, the salaries of the other collectors were raised, but the substantial gap that emerged in 1947 between Ó Danachair (and Ó Súilleabháin) and the full-time collectors in the field was not bridged significantly. By February 1951, Ó Súilleabháin with a salary of £750 per annum was the highest-paid member of staff, and was to keep this lead. He was followed closely by Ó Danachair with a salary of £700 per annum. As against this, the two longest-serving full-time collectors, Tadhg Ó Murchadha and Seán Ó hEochaidh had salaries of £510 and £450 respectively.[35] The substantial lead that Ó Súilleabháin and Ó Danachair, on the one hand, had in terms of salary was to remain over the next decade and beyond. By March 1962 all the full-time collectors, irrespective of years of service, were on an annual salary of £765 as against £1,234 for Ó Súilleabháin and £1,120 for Ó Danachair.[36] The full-time collectors had good reason to feel that some of their Head Office colleagues were coming out with much better salaries than they were, yet they do not appear to have ever sought redress on this matter, nor aired their grievances openly.[37] Ironically, as we will see below, when underlying tensions finally flared up in the Commission, it was not from the ranks of the full-time collectors but from the ranks of the two best-paid members of staff, but not well-paid it must be said.

Shorthand typists

Beyond any doubt the worst-paid members of staff of the Commission were its shorthand typists. Not only were they paid substantially less than the rest of the staff, they also had less paid annual leave than their colleagues, although they worked the same hours per week.[38] On the recommendation of the Dept. of Education, the first shorthand typist employed by the Commission in 1936, Eibhlín Ní Iarlaithe, was paid a salary 'appropriate to the post of typist in the General Service class of the Civil Service.'[39] The Commission

34   ED Fl 5: 'IFC Fin. Sub-Com./Min. 65th Meeting, 19.6.1948', par. 521.
35   D/F S 101/0011/34: memo 'Finance Sub-Committee Meeting of Folklore Commission on 14.3.51'.
36   EDFL 4: 'Salaries of the Full-time Staff of the Irish Folklore Commission, March 31, 1962'.
37   From various conversations I had with Seosamh Ó Dálaigh, I sensed that he was somewhat envious of the Head Office staff, believing them to have had better opportunities.
38   Eibhlín Ní Iarlaithe, the first shorthand typist to be employed by the Commission, was allowed only twelve days by the Dept. of Education, but when a second typist was appointed two years later the annual paid leave for the Commission's typists was raised to fifteen days. D/F S 101/0011/34: C. S. Almond to Sec. Dept. of Educ., dated 4.5.1938 (trans.).
39   D/F S 101/0011/34: Proinnsias Ó Dubhthaigh to Dept. of Fin., dated 13.3.1936.

needed shorthand typists skilled in typing Irish, at least, and preferably with wider skills in Irish, as much of its correspondence was conducted in Irish. Consequently, simply basing the salary scale for shorthand typists on the rates pertaining in the Civil Service worked to the disadvantage of both the Commission and its typists, as it failed to reward successful applicants for their special skills or ensure that shorthand typists with high skills in Irish would apply for posts in the Commission. As a result, when the Commission was recruiting its second shorthand typist in 1938, Ó Duilearga, sensing that it might be difficult to get a suitable person for the job, suggested that a somewhat higher salary of £2:10 per week should be offered.[40] The Dept. of Finance, however, rejected this proposal, insisting that Civil Service rates be adhered to. It would sanction a salary of no more than £2 per week with 'an annual increment of 2/6 per week up to 50/- per week.'[41] The successful applicant, Máire Ní Cheallacháin, by 1943, after five years' service, was earning only £2.10.0 per week (£130 per annum), the salary Ó Duilearga had originally asked for the post.[42] A more understanding attitude on the part of the Dept. of Finance, would certainly have facilitated the Commission's recruitment of shorthand typists. In the event, it was always difficult for the Commission to get shorthand typists with high skills in Irish, and, as we have seen above, as a result of the marriage ban, there was a high turnover in its shorthand typists.[43]

Pent-up frustration and agitation

During the 1950's the staff of the Commission received annual increments based on a salary scale set in autumn 1951. However, these increases were not substantial and Commission salaries fell behind those of people in similar employment, to the growing dissatisfaction of the staff. By the end of the decade most of the staff were near the top of their salary scale. The decision, in principle, by the Government in 1959 to make the staff of the Commission pensionable Civil Servants was not to have an immediate effect in improving the lot of the staff. It would take the Departments of Education and Finance almost six years to finally see that undertaking made a reality.

In October 1960 the office staff of the Commission sent a statement to Ó Duilearga, which they requested he place before the Finance Sub-Committee and the Commission to be forwarded 'to the proper authorities.'[44] In this statement they drew attention to the injustice suffered by the staff of the Irish Folklore Commission in respect of pay and conditions of employment, not just over the previous ten years, but indeed since 1935. The statement outlined

40   D/F S 101/0011/34: Ó Duilearga to Sec. Dept. of Educ., dated 22.3.1938.
41   D/F S 101/0011/34: C. S. Almond to Sec. Dept. of Educ., dated 4.5.1938 (trans.).
42   D/F S 101/0011/34: Ó Duilearga to Sec. Dept. of Fin., 18.2.1943.
43   As noted above in Chapter V/2, the Commission was to lose one of its most skilled shorthand typist, the university graduate Íde Ní Eidhin, not to marriage but to more lucrative employment, as the Dept. of Finance refused to raise her salary.
44   ED FL 4: 'IFC. Fin. Sub-Com./Min. 116th Meeting, 19.10.1960', par. 844.

the extent to which the staff of the Commission had been treated unfairly vis-à-vis Civil Servants and other public servants. It noted the following discrepancies between them and Civil Servants:

> 1. The present salary scales of the Commission's staff were last fixed in October, 1951.
> 2. In all that time, the only additional increment the staff had been granted was 'one of 10%, as from April 1, 1956.'
> 3. 'The married members of staff, who have children, have *not* been given the Marriage Children's Allowances, which are normally given to Civil Servants and others.'

In order to place this in perspective, the statement went out to contrast the fate of the Commission's staff with that of Civil Servants, teachers and Gardaí [Irish police] over the same period. After listing various salary increases these groups received in November 1952, November 1955, April 1958, and December 1959, the statement notes (underlined in original): 'This means that since October, 1951, Civil Servants, Teachers and Gardaí have received increments (against increased cost of living) amounting to 34% on first £250 and 19% on portion above.' The statement continued: 'The staff of the Commission, against this, have received only one increment of 10%.' They also noted that: 'These increases have been given to all professional Civil Servants, such as the staffs of the National Museum, [National] Library, Institute of Advanced Studies and similar bodies, while similar or even more generous increases have been given to other professional and academic bodies, such as University staffs.' Moreover, the statement notes that over the same period Trade Union workers had 'received no less than six separate increases to meet the increased cost of living.' The statement also drew attention to the fact that the staff of the Commission had no pension rights and that there were 'no opportunities for promotion and consequent increase in salary within the Commission's staff.'[45]

Although the Finance Sub-Committee decided to forward the above statement to the Dept. of Education and asked that its Estimates of Expenditure for 1961–62 be augmented to allow it to effect the increases asked for by the Commission's staff,[46] it was not a very opportune time for the Commission to propose that the discrepancies in pay between its staff and Civil and Public Servants be rectified. The Commission had been forced to live beyond its means for a long time, due to its inadequate state grant, and in November 1960 had to seek a supplementary grant of £1,000 from the Dept. of Education to cover its costs up to the end of the financial year, March 31st, 1961. The Dept. of Education, angry that the Commission was not keeping to its budget, refused outright to contemplate such an increase, forcing the Commission to take severe finance-saving measures for the rest of the financial year, including letting cataloguer Anraí Ó Braonáin go

---

45 ED FL 4: untitled and undated four-page document (italics underlined in original).
46 ED FL 4: 'IFC. Fin. Sub-Com./116th Meeting, 19.10.1960, par. 844.

for a couple of months, and confining collectors to their immediate home areas.[47]

The staff of the Commission were to get little satisfaction from the Dept. of Education, despite two further appeals made to it in June and November 1961.[48] What little was offered proved unacceptable to the staff and added to their sense of grievance. Their appeal of November 1961 had demanded an increase of 25% across the board for all staff, but this the Dept. of Education rejected outright some six months later.[49] A slight increase in its annual grant for 1962–1963, however, allowed the Commission at its June meeting, to sanction an increase of 16% for Seán Ó Súilleabháin and increases of 10% to the rest of the staff, backdated to April 1, 1962.[50]

Pensions for the staff

Meanwhile, despite this harsh treatment at the hands of the Dept. of Education, finally there was some movement on the question of pensions for the staff. In early January 1962 the Commission heard from the Dept. of Education that as a result of negotiations between Education and the Dept. of Finance, the Minister for Finance had agreed to propose to the Government that nine members of the Commission's staff, those with longest service, be appointed 'established Civil Servants'. It was further proposed to recommend to the Government that the short-hand typist, Máire Ní Mhaoláin, and the cataloguer, Anraí Ó Braonáin, who had each less than three years' service with the Commission be appointed 'unestablished Civil Servants'. However, in the case of one of the full-time Collectors, his status as a Civil Servant, 'established' or 'unestablished', would depend on whether he got a clean bill of health from the Chief Medical officer of the Civil Service. Omitted entirely from the list was the full-time collector Seán Ó Cróinín.[51] Ó Cróinín, who had resumed working with the Commission in 1959, did not have enough years of service to be considered for a pension, as his six years of service from 1938 to 1944 were not being taken into consideration. However, the Dept. of Education subsequently agreed to the Finance Sub-Committee's request that his name be included with the officers recommended for permanent appointment.'[52] It would be June of the following year before the Commission would receive draft proposals from Education in respect of pension rights and Civil Service status. Later that year a special meeting of the staff of the Commission elected Bríd Mahon to act as negotiator with the Departments of Education and Finance in order to finalise the details of the agreement.[53]

---

47   ED FL 4: 'IFC. Fin. Sub-Com./Min. 117th Meeting, 6.1.1961', par. 846.
48   See ED FL 4: 'IFC. Fin. Sub-Com./Min. 119th Meeting, 22.6.1961', par. 853 and par. 856, and 'Salaries of the Full-Time Staff of the IFC' as well as cov. letter, dated 17.11.1961.
49   ED FL 4: R. Ní Mh[aolchatha] to Ó Duilearga, dated 10.4.1962.
50   ED FL 4: 'CBÉ. Miont. 112ú Cruinniú, 28.6.1962', par. 817.
51   ED FL 4: 'CBÉ. Miont. 109ú Cruinniú, 8.1.1962', par. 797 (trans.).
52   ED FL 4: 'CBÉ. Miont. 110st Meeting, 6.2.1962', par. 804 (trans.).
53   ED FL 1: 'IFC. Fin. Sub-Com./Min. 126th Meeting, 6.7.1963', par. 897 and 'CBÉ. Miont./118ú Cruinniú, 4.1.1964', par.870.

Before an agreement could be finalised, however, Seán Ó Cróinín died suddenly in March 1965. Of his death, Bríd Mahon says: 'His dependants were given the two weeks' salary due and that was all. Within a year the widow was dead. It made the remainder of the staff, particularly the men with families, very unsettled.'[54] To be fair to the Commission, at their next meeting in May 1965 it proposed giving Ó Cróinín's widow, Siobhán, the equivalent of a year's salary.[55] However, this was easier said than done as the Commission's grant-in-aid was shortly to be reduced drastically on its staff gaining Civil Servant status. It would be late April 1968 before the Commission was able to pay the dependents of Seán Ó Cróinín a sum of £441 (less than half Ó Cróinín's annual salary at the time of his death).[56] As mentioned above, Ó Cróinín's wife, Siobhán, had died within a year of her husband in early 1966, leaving a young family with a double personal loss to bear and in poor circumstances.

There is no doubt that Ó Cróinín's sudden death must have cast gloom over the staff of the Commission, and brought them face to face with what must have long been a worry for many of them: namely what was to happen to their dependents if they should die in harness? However, seven months after Ó Cróinín's death the Commission was informed by the Dept. of Education that all its full-time staff were being made established Civil Servants, backdated to May 11th, 1965 (approximately two months short of Ó Cróinín's death in March of that year), with the exception of Proinnsias de Búrca, who was to be made an unestablished Civil Servant, and the typist Máire Dillon, whose salary Education now proposed lowering – leaving her much worse off, a widow with four dependent children.[57] We have seen above how the Commission got Máire Dillon's salary restored. She was to be made an established Civil Servant (Clerk-Typist), as requested by the Finance Sub-Committee, in November 1967.[58]

Proinnsias de Búrca was to remain an unestablished Civil Servant. Although he had nine years of service as a full-time collector from 1935-1944, and had worked both as a part-time and special collector for the Commission for twenty odd years, by the time Civil Servant status was being finalised for the Commission's staff, he had less than a year's service as full-time collector, after being reappointed in autumn 1964. Although he lost out compared to his colleagues, the Dept. of Education granted him an extension of service in 1969 when he reached 65 years of age[59], and this meant that he was still in the employment of the Commission when it was transferred to UCD in 1971. Along with the rest of the Commission's staff he was guaranteed a pension in the new arrangement. In the end, things worked out well for him, for if

---

54   Mahon 1998, pp. 188–189.
55   See ED FL 1: 'CBÉ. Miont. 124ú Cruinniú, 13.5.1965', par. 921.
56   See ED FL 1: 'CBÉ. Miont. 136ú Cruinniú, 28.6.1968', par. 998 and 'IFC. Fin. Sub-Com./Min. 142nd Meeting, 22.10.1968', par. 1020. From autumn 1965 the State would be directly responsible for paying the salaries of the Commission's staff – hence the reduced grant-in-aid.
57   ED FL 8: 'CBÉ. Miont. 125ú Cruinniú, 21.10.1965', par. 928.
58   ED FL 8: 'CBÉ. Miont. 134ú Cruinniú, 19.1.1968', p. 4.
59   ED FL 7: 'CBÉ. Miont. 140ú Cruinniú, 13.6.1969', par. 1029.

the Commission had continued under the Civil Service, as an unestablished officer he might not have received a pension.

Not included among the members of the full-time staff of the Commission who were made established or unestablished Civil Servants was Janis Mezs, then in his eighties. In his long life he had served two governments as a civil servant: first that of Imperial Russia and later that of independent Latvia. Special arrangements were made for him and he was henceforth the only person, apart from the cleaner, who was to remain on the payroll of the Commission. He was not entitled to a pension as such, but as he was already of pensionable age when he joined the Commission in 1949, in a way he already had a pension as well as a safe home. Thanks to Ó Duilearga, this refugee was given a surrogate pension after the two states he had worked for as a civil servant had effectively ceased to exist.

2. 'Cogadh na gCarad' ('The War of the Friends')

Setting the scene

In 1969, as we have seen above, shortly before the Irish Folklore Commission was disbanded, Seán Ó Súilleabháin made serious accusations against Séamus Ó Duilearga that were brought to the attention of the then Taoiseach, Jack Lynch. His criticisms of Ó Duilearga's direction of the Commission were not of recent origin, but, as we shall see below, extended over more than half the lifespan of the Commission. Some might argue that it would be best to leave these matters aside for the time being, until such time as all the participants in the dispute are long dead. There might be a case for doing so, if these tensions were only incidental to this study. This is not the case, however. The friction that arose between Ó Duilearga and some of his colleagues at Head Office, particularly in respect of matters of policy, not only poisoned the work atmosphere, but affected the day-to-day work of the Commission in fundamental ways.

At the outset it should be said that for the first decade or more of the Commission there seems to have been very harmonious relations between Ó Duilearga and his staff, particularly at Head Office.[60] Shortly before Seán Ó Súilleabháin arrived in Lund in March 1935, Ó Duilearga wrote to von Sydow, with whom the young Irishman was going to stay on his way to Uppsala: 'You will like Seán. He is my best friend here, & my wife & mother are as fond of him as if he were their own.'[61] Seán Ó Súilleabháin and Séamus Ó Duilearga were to remain on very friendly terms throughout the formative years of the Commission, up until the early 1950's or so. It is to be noted that Ó Súilleabháin in speaking of Ó Duilearga in his correspondence with others very often refers to the latter as 'Hamilton', the familiar name used by Ó Duilearga's family and close associates. Moreover, in the early years Ó Duilearga was often profuse in his praise not just of Ó Súilleabháin but other

---

60 The correspondence of Ó Duilearga and Ó Súilleabháin to various scholars abounds in evidence of harmonious relations at the Commission's Head Office: for example, the papers of Carl Wilhelm von Sydow, Åke Campbell, Stith Thompson, and Richard Dorson. See also uí Ógáin 2005, pp. 165–166.
61 LUB Saml. von Sydow: Ó Duilearga to von Sydow, dated 12.3.1935, p. 1.

members of his staff, both in official and private correspondence. In a letter to von Sydow in August 1947 he describes Caoimhín Ó Danachair as 'one of the very best workers I have ever met, and we rely upon him to do great things for Irish folklore.' Some months earlier, in a letter to Åke Campbell, he had also sung Ó Danachair's praises and expressed the hope that he be given an opportunity to spend some time at the Nordic Museum (Nordiska Museet) in Stockholm: 'He has proved himself to be a most intelligent and competent research- and field worker, and if he ever gets a chance he is the one man in a generation to make an Irish folk-museum.'[62]

Despite these harmonious relations, Ó Duilearga's style of leadership, even in the best of circumstances, might, in time, have contributed to a worsening of relations between himself and some of his staff. He liked to keep tabs on his staff, and being totally devoted to the task of saving the folklore of Ireland, he expected his staff to be equally dedicated.[63] He was also headstrong and liked getting his own way. However, circumstances in the Commission were not the best. One of the problems, as we have seen above, was that Ó Duilearga was paid a reasonably decent salary for his labours, and had security of tenure. His staff, on the other hand, were underpaid, for most of the time, and had no security of tenure and no pension rights. Given that this was the case, it is not surprising that as the years went by tension and differences of opinion arose between Ó Duilearga and members of his staff. Although various members of the Commission's staff may from time to time have nurtured a grievance against Ó Duilearga over some matter or other, this section will be concerned with friction that arose between the two most senior members of the Head Office staff, Seán Ó Súilleabháin and Caoimhín Ó Danachair, on the one hand, and Ó Duilearga, on the other, over the latter's direction of the Commission.

Ó Duilearga would appear to have enjoyed reasonably good relations with Ó Súilleabháin and Ó Danachair for the first few years of the 1950's. However, this should not be interpreted as implying complete approval, on their part, of his direction of the Commission for this period, for when these two senior members of staff eventually voiced criticisms of Ó Duilearga as Director, some of the issues they felt needed addressing appear to have been of long standing. But even if Ó Súilleabháin and Ó Danachair prior to this time had not differed with Ó Duilearga on any substantial matters of policy concerning the running of the Commission, there was one issue they would have felt needed to be addressed urgently, i.e. the semi-permanent status of the Commission and the lack of security and pension rights for staff. As we have seen above, after 1949, Ó Duilearga was reluctant to petition the authorities to rectify this situation, most likely because he feared that the stress of protracted negotiations might lead to a breakdown in his health. It would appear from what will be related below that Ó Duilearga never fully informed his staff of the difficulties which merging the Commission with UCD would entail. Many of the staff, it seems, at this time saw incorporation

---

62   LUB Saml. von Sydow: Ó Duilearga to von Sydow, dated 12.8.1947; and ULMA Saml. Åke Campbell, subnr. 247: Ó Duilearga to Campbell, dated 26.4.1947.

63   See, e.g. Mahon 1998, pp. 16, 44, 182, and 188.

into the College as the best way of securing pension rights, better salaries, and the level of recognition they felt their work deserved, and may not have understood Ó Duilearga's reluctance to actively seek once again to have the Commission made an integral part of UCD.

Åke Campbell's intervention

Ó Duilearga's health again broke down towards the end of 1953. In Caoimhín Ó Danachair's opinion, this breakdown was brought on 'when he tried to lecture in the University'. Moreover, although he was away from Head Office 'for three months', Ó Danachair says he would not agree to 'to appoint anyone to take charge of the business of the Commission.'[64] However, while it is quite likely that giving lectures in the University, especially if he was pressurised into doing so, may have caused a deterioration in Ó Duilearga's health, a letter he wrote to Åke Campbell a year after the event suggests that tensions in the Commission had a lot to do with it.[65] In another letter to the Estonian folklorist Oskar Loorits, Ó Duilearga says that he 'worked – and worried – too much in 1953' and that a combination of pressures of work, too much travel, as well as too much responsibility over the previous year led to him becoming 'seriously ill' by Christmas. So ill, in fact, that a specialist he consulted advised him to resign his post as Director of the Commission and 'take up less responsible work.'[66] Ó Duilearga's decision not to appoint a substitute while on leave of absence must partly be seen in the light of this advice. He may have feared that if he did appoint a substitute, he might be tempting fate, and that he might never return to his post.

Part of the time Ó Duilearga was away from Head Office he spent in France. In late February 1954, Seán Ó Súilleabháin wrote to Åke Campbell saying that he had 'had a card the other day from Séamus Delargy from Corsica' in which he said 'that he felt much better and hoped to be back here in early March'. Ó Súilleabháin adds: 'He was quite depressed and in low spirits before he left, but was all right physically, he said. We hope that his visit to France will give him new health and spirits.' Ó Súilleabháin had heard from Campbell of his intention to come to Ireland the following summer. He was overjoyed with this news, and knew that Ó Duilearga would also be delighted, and suggested that on the latter's return an official invitation might be sent to Campbell, and that his visit could be linked to 'the establishment of a Folk Museum or some such matter which will enable you to get a grant for travel expenses.'[67]

However, Campbell's trip was not destined to be linked to the establishment of a folk museum, but to another pressing matter.[68] Early in

---

64 ULMA Saml. Åke Campbell, subnr. 167: Ó Danachair to Campbell, dated 24.11.1954.
65 ULMA Saml. Åke Campbell, subnr. 165: Ó Duilearga to Campbell, dated 30.12.1954.
66 Kir. Muus. Loorits Papers: letter dated 3. 11.1954.
67 ULMA Saml. Åke Campbell, subnr. 159: Ó Súilleabháin to Campbell, dated 22.2.1954.
68 Despite the establishment of a number of regional folk museums, a national folk museum

1954 the issue of reorganising the work at Head Office was raised in the Finance Sub-Committee of the Commission, at the insistence of the staff, who presented proposals to the Director on the matter.[69] The dissatisfaction of the staff at the way the work of Head Office was being organised may well have been a factor causing Ó Duilearga's health to break down some months previously, but in the meantime he had recovered his spirits somewhat while away in France, and when he heard on his return that his old friend was planning to come to Ireland after an absence of many years, he sought to avail of Campbell's advice in reassessing the work of the Commission. In order to facilitate Campbell in seeking a travel grant from the Swedish authorities, Ó Duilearga sent him an official letter of invitation in March 1954, in which he outlined the purpose of the visit. In this letter he stresses that while the Commission's 'collections of Folk Narrative and of Belief and Custom are very large and comprehensive,' its 'collection of Ethnographic material is not equally developed'. The Commission, he informs him, were 'exploring ways and means of extending this side of our work, both in the field work and in preparation for publication' and would welcome Campbell's advice not only as 'a recognised authority on European ethnography' but as one with 'a first-hand knowledge of much of our Irish material'. In Ireland, Campbell would have an opportunity of discussing 'mutual problems and interests', of examining the Commission's collections, and of observing its collecting methods in the field. Ó Duilearga also asked Campbell to bring with him 'some demonstration or lecture material dealing with your work, and particularly with the Atlas of Swedish Folklore, as we are deeply interested in the possibility of developing such work in Ireland.'[70]

In seeking Campbell's help in these matters, Ó Duilearga was taking a chance, because Åke Campbell was not only an old friend of his, he was also an old friend of Ó Súilleabháin and Ó Danachair's. Both Ó Súilleabháin and Ó Danachair had worked with Campbell, in Sweden and in Ireland, and had in fact spent far more time in his company than Ó Duilearga ever had. Even before Ó Duilearga sent the above invitation, Ó Danachair was thinking along similar lines. In a letter to Campbell in early March he proposed getting the Commission to invite Campbell 'in order to hold a little conference with us on the question of initiating an Ethnographic Survey or Ethographic Atlas of Ireland'. As well as wanting Campbell to spend some time with him in the field, he said: 'We will want your advice, too, on many problems in our Archive here in Dublin, so you must be prepared to spend several weeks here.'[71]

Due to a combination of circumstances, Campbell almost had to cancel his trip to Ireland, but matters were eventually arranged so that he was able

would not be established in the Republic of Ireland until 2001. See Mac Philib 2005 and O'Dowd (2005).

69   ED FL 2: 'IFC. Fin. Sub-Com./Min. 92nd Meeting, 4.5.1954', par. 699.

70   ULMA Saml. Åke Campbell, subnr. 168: Ó Duilearga to Campbell, dated 12.3.1954 (incomplete letter).

71   ULMA Saml. Åke Campbell, subnr. 167: Ó Danachair to Campbell, dated 3.2.1954 [*recte* 3.3.1954].

to spend the month of June in Ireland.[72] During his time in Ireland both Ó Súilleabháin and Ó Danachair were to have ample opportunity to confide in him: to discuss their grievances about the organisation and direction of the Commission, and their hopes for the future. While in Dublin, Campbell stayed with Ó Danachair and his wife, Anne, but as Ó Súilleabháin lived next door, Campbell most likely also saw him a good deal after work as well as in Head Office.[73]

In Dublin, Campbell examined the Commission's work, and met members of staff. At a meeting he had with Ó Duilearga on June 14th he was asked by the latter to 'submit in writing' his 'impressions of various activities of the IFC – both in the Archive and in the field.'[74] Before leaving Ireland, Campbell wrote a rough draft of his report, most likely in Ó Danachair's house, and quite likely with his host to guide him. Moreover, shortly after his return to Sweden, he communicated with both Ó Súilleabháin and Ó Danachair on the matter of drafting this report. Consequently, these two senior members of the Commission's staff were to have a strong input into Campbell's report, in contrast to Ó Duilearga's input, which appears to have been minimal.

Towards mid July 1954, Séan Ó Súilleabháin, in response to a letter from Campbell, wrote to him with advice on what he should include in his report:

> Now, about the report which you will send to Séamus, Kevin [i.e. Caoimhín Ó Danachair] tells me that he has seen the draft of it which you wrote here and that he agrees with it fully. So do I, so far as Kevin has told me about it. I think that you should make it a very strong and candid statement, telling what you have found out about the Commission during your visit (a) by your own observations, and (b) by questions which you asked the staff. It is very necessary that you should speak your mind openly and fully in the report, as otherwise Séamus will not take any notice of what you say.

The complaints Ó Súilleabháin listed in this letter were not all of recent origin – some going back a number of years. Ó Súilleabháin listed four main grievances. Top of the list of points he wished Campbell to address he placed the need to instruct students in folkloristics:

> (a) the need for lectures to University students by either Séamus himself (I don't think he will ever give them himself), or by Kevin (ethnological matters) and myself (folklore). If lectures are not given regularly over a period of years, we will never be able to place the material in a proper

---

72 ULMA Saml. Åke Campbell, subnr. 165: Campbell to Ó Duilearga, letters dated 18.3.1954 and 22.3.1954.

73 Ó Súilleabháin lived in no. 21 Calderwood Avenue, Drumcondra and Ó Danachair in no. 22. While in Ireland, Campbell spent ten days on fieldwork along with Ó Danachair and the Northern Ireland ethnologist Ronald Buchanan. D/T S 15548B: 'Gearr-Thuar./1954–55', 5.

74 ULMA Saml. Åke Campbell, subnr. 165: Campbell to Ó Duilearga, 19.11.1954.

light, or be able to foster the interest of students and the public. I have no doubt that Dr. Michael Tierney [President of UCD] would be able to arrange for Kevin and myself to lecture in University College, but I doubt whether Séamus will ever encourage him to get this through.

Ó Súilleabháin also felt that not enough was being done to further cataloguing. Of course, these two questions were linked. If students could not be got to take an interest in folklore, where would a supply of future cataloguers come from? He advised Campbell to stress:

> (b) the need for getting ahead here at the Commission with the detailed catalogue. We have now completed almost (sic) the interim catalogue, which will serve until the proper catalogue can be finished. It will require many extra helpers, full-time as well as part-time.'

But it was not simply a case that there were problems with the organisation and direction of the work at Head Office. Ó Súilleabháin and Ó Danachair, it would appear, believed that Ó Duilearga was not devoting enough of his attention to the direction of fieldwork:

> (c) the promotion of the collection in the field by proper attention to the full-time and part-time collectors. Kevin could, perhaps, do this better than I, as his work will take him to the country in any case; he can drive a car (I can't).[75]

Ó Súilleabháin is not specific here in respect of how Ó Duilearga's direction of field work was wanting. It would appear, however, that he felt the latter was a) not devoting enough attention to the collectors, and b) as a result of his other duties (and possibly due to his declining energies), he was no longer able to do so properly. These problems were compounded, in Ó Súilleabháin's estimation, by the fact that Ó Duilearga was loath to take the advice of his staff. In a passage already quoted above, in connection with collecting by questionnaire (Chapter IV/4), but which would appear to refer to Ó Duilearga's general direction of collecting, he says: 'It has been impossible for years back to get him to make a decision himself, when urgently needed, or to get him to agree to the good suggestions from others.' Aware that this was an especially sensitive matter, Ó Súilleabháin advises Campbell to be careful in broaching it: 'Séamus is very touchy, and may take offence, so just stress the vital need for delegation of authority and responsibility.'[76]

In his letter to Campbell, Ó Súilleabháin also broached the question of publication. He stressed 'the need for encouraging members of staff (e.g. Kevin, Szövérffy, and myself) to write articles and make studies of certain problems.' He adds:

---

75   ULMA Saml. Åke Campbell, subnr. 351: Ó Súilleabháin to Campbell, dated 12.7.1954.
76   Ibid.

> Not only are we not encouraged but we are frowned on if we suggest such things. This attitude leads only to stagnation and frustration. (This again is *entre nous*). The fact is that Séamus himself will never write anything of a scholarly kind. He can never settle down to it. Two publishers have for years back been trying to get promised volumes of Irish folktales out of him – English publishers these – but they have no hope of getting anything from him. He uses all his energies in running around and on trivialities. There are many things that Kevin and Szövérffy and myself would like to undertake, but we get no encouragement, and every suggestion of the kind is shelved and never gets through.

As we will see below, what Ó Súilleabháin has to say here about Ó Duilearga's attitude to research and publication by members of the Commission's staff is somewhat of an over-simplification.

However, although Ó Súilleabháin and Ó Danachair had many criticisms of the direction of the Commission, at this stage there is little evidence of any personal animosity on their part towards Ó Duilearga. Ó Súilleabháin was, moreover, anxious that Ó Duilearga would find out about his writing to Campbell on these matters. He consequently requested Campbell to 'destroy this letter when you have used it for your purpose.' He adds:

> I have a very warm regard for Séamus, as you know, but he can make a person despair about the future of our work here. If he could only devote himself to his university duties and allow Kevin and myself to run the Commission, I think that things would go well with us. But – the Commission is his child and nobody else will be allowed to have any prime authority in it, while he is active.

Ó Súilleabháin also requested Campbell to 'send a strong report in – with a named copy for each member of the Finance Committee'. If this was done, he felt 'something may come of it.' He reminds him 'that Séamus loves praise, so let there be a good flavour of that in it.' He requested him not to mention that Ó Danachair or himself 'had any active part in your report apart from giving you information on points you raised.' He adds: 'If you let Kevin or myself have a copy of your report it would be fine, as we may not see it otherwise.' As a final precaution, in order to ensure that Ó Duilearga would not inadvertently find out, or suspect that members of his staff were communicating with Campbell in respect of his report, Ó Súilleabháin glossed the letter with a request that Campbell write to his home address 'about this whole matter or anything else at any time.'[77]

Even though Campbell sought and took the advice of both Ó Súilleabháin and Ó Danachair in compiling his report, it was not a case of them influencing him against his better judgement. Basically, all three men seem to have been in agreement as to what should go into the report. The same day as Ó Súilleabháin wrote the above letter to Campbell, Caoimhín Ó Danachair

---

77   Ibid., italics underlined in original.

wrote to him: 'Seán showed me your letter, and we discussed the points which you raised in it. We are in agreement with your views'. In this same letter Ó Danachair emphasised that it was 'absolutely necessary that the President of University College (Professor Tierney) and also Mr Price and other members of the Commission should see it.' He added: 'You know that it is quite possible that nobody but the Director will see it.'[78] Later in July, Ó Danachair again wrote to Campbell on receipt of a draft report on the Commission:

> Seán and I have both read over the draft report carefully, and we both think that it is very good. But we must remember that it will be read by a number of people who may not be fully sympathetic or even fully interested in it, and therefore we both think that it should be as short and as simple as possible. May I make a suggestion that you should put a title word at the beginning of each paragraph, and a conclusion or recommendation at the end of each paragraph? In this way, even those who are not sympathetic or interested must at least see what the report says and what it advises for the future. I have made a *precis* of your paragraph on the question of ethnography in the form which you suggest, following your ideas exactly but changing the form in order to influence those to whom the report will be sent.

Ó Danachair also broached another matter that had relevance to the report. There was talk of 'a union of the Commission with the University'. He informed Campbell: 'Our Director still hesitates, but is being pressed by several people to join the University.' Campbell's advice on this matter, Ó Danachair thought, 'will carry much weight.'

> As you know, the fault here is in the *organisation*, not in the scientific method or the general approach to the work. If a sound permanent organisation is achieved, the rest is a simple matter. As far as we can see, the best form of organisation would be a department of the University, as with the Landsmålsarkivet [Uppsala Dialect and Folklore Archive]. Therefore your advice in this question is very important.

In respect of when the best time would be to send the report, he suggested leaving it until September, as the Commission would be closed during August. In September 'everybody will be beginning work again after the holidays, and so will be *in rapport* with the spirit of the matter.'[79] Campbell's report was not, however, ready by September. One reason for the delay appears to have been his desire that Ó Danachair and Ó Súilleabháin look over his emended draft before he wrote the final draft. The fact that the staff of the Commission were on holidays in August delayed matters further. On his return from holiday in early September, Ó Danachair found a letter from

78 ULMA Saml. Åke Campbell, subnr. 167: Ó Danachair to Campbell, dated 12.7.1954.
79 ULMA Saml. Åke Campbell, subnr. 167: Ó Danachair to Campbell, undated [July 1954]. Italics underlined in original.

Campbell and 'the second part of the report' waiting for him. He returned it, obviously with comments: 'I hasten to return it to you. We find it excellent, and it should be very useful when it arrives in its final form.' Ó Danachair was very optimistic. Speaking of the 'discussion of attaching the Archive to the University' he says it is 'what we have always wanted', and adds: 'Your report will help this move very much, and, Deo volente, we shall at long last be established permanently.'[80]

In early October, Ó Súilleabháin reported to Campbell: 'Nothing new here. Work goes on as usual. Séamus is in better form since the summer, and we hope he will remain so.'[81] Later that month Liam Price raised the matter of the reorganisation of the work of Head Office at a meeting of the Finance Sub-Committee and 'asked the Director if he had considered further the reports submitted to him by the staff' on the matter. Ó Duilearga is reported as saying: 'that he had been very busy during the summer months but that as soon as possible he would deal with the matter.'[82]

Moreover, in a letter he wrote to Oskar Loorits some two weeks later he says that it was only since the 'end of September' that he had felt 'any great improvement' in his health, and that since his return from Corsica in the spring he had 'just carried on' from month to month, and though feeling better he 'must take precautions so as to avoid strain.'[83]

In any event, within less than a month of the above meeting his health had again deteriorated to such an extent that he was forced to go on leave of absence. A week later, Ó Danachair wrote to Campbell with the 'interesting news' that Ó Duilearga had 'taken half-a-year's leave of absence from the work of the Commission, in order to do some lecturing and other scientific work'. Ó Danachair had 'been appointed Deputy Director, to administer the work of the Commission' in his absence.[84] In a letter Seán Ó Súilleabháin wrote to Campbell some weeks later we learn more about what exactly Ó Duilearga intended to do during his absence from the Commission.

> Séamus has got six months free of office work, as Kevin has probably told you, so that he could give some lectures in the College and get ready two books of folk-tales which he promised years ago to two English publishers. He takes once a week a class from Prof. Michael Hayes and is reading to them the lectures he gave at the Sorbonne last Spring. It is not a class of students who are enrolled for their interest in folklore, but just an Irish language class – so it does not seem too promising for much good coming out if it. However, it does bring Séamus, even against his will, back to the College even once a week, and something more real from the folklore point of view may grow from it.[85]

80 ULMA Saml. Åke Campbell, subnr. 167: Ó Danachair to Campbell, dated 6.9.1954.
81 ULMA Saml. Åke Campbell subnr. 159: Ó Súilleabháin to Campbell, dated 9.10.1954.
82 ED FL 2: 'IFC. Fin. Sub-Com./Min. 93rd Meeting, 14&20.10.1954', par. 703.
83 Kir. Muus. Loorits Papers: letter dated 3.11.1954.
84 ULMA Saml. Åke Campbell, subnr. 167: Ó Danachair to Campbell, dated 22.11.1954.
85 ULMA Saml. Åke Campbell, subnr. 159: Ó Súilleabháin to Campbell, dated

Although ostensibly Ó Duilearga had taken leave to lecture and complete two books, it appears that his deteriorating health necessitated it. Ó Danachair in his above letter of November 22nd had informed Campbell that Ó Duilearga had been very agitated 'lately, but is much better since he went on leave.' However, in the circumstances, Ó Danachair felt that he should return the report on the Commission to Campbell, which the latter had sent him sometime prior to November 22nd, 'as I think it would do some harm at the moment.' He added 'I think you had better delay sending it to Séamus.' Nevertheless, he was satisfied with the report, stating that '[w]hen the new organisation of the Commission is being planned, the report will be most valuable.'[86] It seems friends and acquaintances of Ó Duilearga's were solicitous of his health. In another letter, Ó Danachair says: 'Meanwhile, I have been asked by the other Commissioners and other friends in the University to keep all matters connected with the running of the Commission away from him, so as to leave him no cause for worry.'[87]

Ó Danachair appears to have been unduly optimistic at this time for the Commission. Shortly after Ó Duilearga's departure on leave he informed Campbell that: 'a complete reorganisation of the Commission (probably in union with the University) [was] being discussed' and that he expected 'it will take place next March.'[88] In another letter he wrote to Campbell two days later he elaborates on this matter:

> As to the University, it is quite clear that the University wishes to have our Archive as part of itself. For a long time various people have been trying to persuade Séamus to agree to this, but his inability to make up his mind clearly on the question has postponed the union year after year. Now there is a good opportunity of doing something about it. Another aspect of the matter is this, that I am now in a position to discuss the matter with President Tierney and other authorities. Never before has any member of the staff of the Commission been given any degree of trust and authority, so as you can see, there are signs of a big change. And it is a good thing that it is happening now, as, frankly, the Commission's work was on the verge of breaking down completely.

Ó Danachair expected that 'soon after Christmas' he would 'have the opportunity of discussing' Campbell's report 'as part of the preparations for our proposed union with the University.' He ends his letter of November 24th to Campbell thus:

> You should know that one of the big reasons for this good development is your visit to Ireland last year [i.e. previous academic year], and your talks and discussions with Séamus and others. Also Dag Strömbäck and Reider Christiansen gave good advice. With God's help everything

---

13.12.1954.
86   ULMA Saml. Åke Campbell, subnr. 167: Ó Danachair to Campbell, dated 22.11.1954.
87   Ibid.
88   Ibid.

will turn out all right, and the work here in Ireland will be completely reorganised, and Séamus returned to his peace of mind. We owe a lot of this to you, Åke, my dear friend. And we really do hope to have you with us again next year.[89]

Little did Ó Danachair know that Åke Campbell would never visit Ireland again.

Ó Danachair's above letter seems to give the impression that the only thing that had hitherto prevented the Commission being fully incorporated into University College Dublin had been Ó Duilearga's indecision and inertia. As we have seen above in Chapter III, this was far from being the case. It may well be that Ó Duilearga did not keep his staff fully informed on negotiations with officials on re-establishing the Commission on a permanent footing. There is some basis, however, for Ó Danachair's assertion. As we have seen above, after 1949, Ó Duilearga seems to have been loath to broach the matter of the Commission's status with officials, partly because he may have feared that protracted negotiations might lead to his health breaking down again, and partly because he was a realist. There were huge problems to be surmounted if the Commission were ever to find a permanent home in UCD. Nevertheless, the fact that since the previous June, de Valera was out of office, and there was again an Inter-Party Government with General Richard Mulcahy as Minister for Education, did give some grounds for hope that the authorities might look more favourably on merging the Commission with UCD.

Not only was Ó Danachair unduly optimistic that the Commission before long would be placed on a permanent footing, he was also unduly optimistic that Ó Duilearga's leave of absence would lead to an improvement in his health as well as better relations with some of his staff. A week before Christmas 1954, Ó Danachair wrote to Campbell:

> Everything goes well here ... You will be glad to hear that Séamus is benefiting by his rest – we hope that he will be very much better soon. Indeed, it might be well if you sent him the report in a short time, say early in January.

Ominously, he added: 'Of course he does not believe that he is not in the best of health, and is often surprised if people suggest that he is not well. But we have been worried about him, and will all be very glad at his recovery.'[90]

Recovered or not, it would appear that Ó Duilearga was angry with his colleagues. It also appears that it was with some reluctance that he had agreed that Ó Danachair take charge in his absence.[91] The day before New Year's

---

89 ULMA Saml. Åke Campbell, subnr. 167: Ó Danachair to Campbell, letter dated 24.11.1954. Both Strömbäck and Christiansen had been in Dublin for UCD's jubilee celebrations the previous July. See ULMA Saml. Åke Campbell, subnr. 165: Campbell to Ó Duilearga, letters dated 18.3.1954 and 22.3.1954.

90 ULMA Saml. Åke Campbell, subnr. 167: Ó Danachair to Campbell, dated 19.12.1954.

91 ULMA Saml. Åke Campbell, subnr. 167: Ó Danachair to Campbell, dated 24.11.1954.

Eve 1954, Ó Duilearga wrote to Campbell telling him not to bother sending the report until he returned to the Commission, adding 'if I ever do'. He says how the 'unpleasant' attitude at Head Office before he left in mid-November had 'sickened' him, as it was totally unwarranted and incomprehensible to him. A similar attitude, he says, had been in evidence the previous year and had been the 'sole' reason why his health had broken down on that occasion. He had vowed that he would not allow a repeat of this behaviour to 'cause a relapse this year '[92]

By early January 1955, Ó Danachair was under no illusions about Ó Duilearga's health: 'Séamus has been away from the Commission for over two months now, but I am afraid the rest is not bringing any improvement in his health.' Nevertheless, Ó Danachair was not without hope: 'What the end of it all will be we do not know, but we are hoping for the best.' Whatever lay in store for the Commission on Ó Duilearga's return, in Ó Danachair's opinion, things were better in his absence. He told Campbell: 'Between ourselves, we are doing more work in the institute now than we have been doing for years, and there is a much better spirit among all the staff than there has been for a very long time.'[93] There may well be an element of exaggeration in this claim of Ó Danachair's. In reading the comments of the various protagonists in this dispute, it should be kept in mind that objectivity may sometimes have suffered at the expense of buttressing one's own case or inflicting a blow on the opposition.

Whether Ó Duilearga's health was improving or not, he was still a force to be reckoned with. In late January 1955 he wrote to Campbell, who was about to undergo an operation, asking him to forget altogether about the report, as '[u]nder the circumstances' it was best to let 'matters take their course.'[94] It would appear that by 'under the circumstances' he meant more than Campbell's approaching operation. As we will see, matters would be let 'take their course'.

By now his colleagues could have been under no illusion that Ó Duilearga would cooperate with them in respect of the reorganisation of the Commission. In late February, Ó Danachair informed Campbell: 'A curious symptom is that he agreed to my being made Deputy Director in his absence, but has never communicated with me since then – not even at Christmas. It makes me very sad to think of his present state, and of what he might have been.' Campbell had suggested to Ó Danachair that there should be a meeting of European folklore and folklife researchers in Dublin. Although Ó Danachair thought this a good idea, he saw difficulties even though Seán and himself would do their 'best to encourage the idea': 'It all comes from the same cause – Séamus is not well enough to arrange the matter himself, and he will not allow anyone else to do it. This affects every aspect of our work here.'[95]

Ó Duilearga had originally asked for leave of absence until the end of the financial year (i.e. March 31st, 1955) 'or until such time as the Committee

---

92   ALMA Saml. Åke Campbell, subnr. 165: Ó Duilearga to Campbell, dated 30.12.1954.
93   ULMA Saml. Åke Campbell, subnr. 167: Ó Danachair to Campbell, dated 1.2.1955.
94   ULMA Saml. Åke Campbell, subnr. 165: Ó Duilearga to Campbell, dated 29.1.1955.
95   ULMA Saml. Åke Campbell, subnr. 167: Ó Danachair to Campbell, dated 18.2.1955.

reconsidered the matter.' Under this arrangement, Ó Danachair would look after visitors, deal 'with correspondence and the day to day running of the office.' It was also agreed to that both Ó Danachair and Ó Duilearga 'attend meetings of the Commission and Finance Committee.'[96] This latter arrangement made no sense, if, as appears to have been the case, members of the Commission and friends of Ó Duilearga's in UCD felt he needed to get a total rest from the work of the Commission. This decision probably reflects Ó Duilearga's reluctance to agree to go on leave of absence in the first place, and more particularly to have somebody appointed deputy in his stead. As it happened, Ó Danachair presided, without Ó Duilearga, at two meetings of the Commission, on January 6th, 1955 and March 18th, 1955. However, it is interesting to note that Ó Danachair attended no meeting of the Finance Sub-Committee, the effective seat of power of the Commission. It was normal for such a meeting to be held in January, but in 1955 no such meeting was held. On March 28th, 1955 a meeting of the Finance Sub-Committee was held. Strictly speaking, Ó Danachair should have attended this meeting. However, only Ó Duilearga attended. The minutes of the meeting report:

> Referring to the leave of absence of the Director, and the assignment of certain duties to Mr. Danaher, it was decided to terminate these arrangements. It was decided that the Director would resume his duties as from Wednesday 13th April, and that Mr. Danaher revert to his normal position as from that date.[97]

The minutes record not a word of thanks to Ó Danachair, but they do record a particular decision which was to be the cause of much friction between Ó Duilearga and certain of his Head Office colleagues.

At the previous meeting of the Finance Sub-Committee, before Ó Duilearga went on leave of absence, he had proposed that 'with a view to safeguarding the use of the material in the archives of the' Commission, 'permission must formally be asked by anyone wishing to use material for the purpose of publications, lectures or radio talks.' People wishing to use material in any of the above ways, he proposed 'should request formal permission to do so.' The members agreed to Michael Tierney's suggestion that 'the granting of such permission should be regarded as part of the Director's official duties, and that the Director should be formally appointed by the Irish Folklore Commission to deal with this matter.'[98] However, the Commission never appointed him to act in this way. At the next meeting of the Commission in January 1955, at which Caoimhín Ó Danachair presided in the absence of the Director, this matter did not come up for discussion. Despite the fact that the Commission had not sanctioned this proposal, the Finance Sub-Committee on March 28th, 1955 saw fit to extend the scope of its earlier decision. On this occasion as well as proposing 'that a form should be drawn up for signature by anyone asking permission to use the

---

96   ED FL 2: 'IFC. Fin. Sub-Com./Min. 94th Meeting, 13.11.1954', par. 709.
97   ED FL 2: 'IFC. Fin. Sub-Com./Min. 95th Meeting, 28.3.1955', par. 715.
98   ED FL 2: 'IFC. Fin. Sub-Com./Min. 94th Meeting, 13.11.1954', par. 711.

material in the archives of the Irish Folklore Commission for the purpose of publications, lectures or radio talks, and that such permission should be in writing and should be given only by the Director', the meeting decided 'that this requirement should apply also to all members of the Commission's staff and should be brought to their notice.' Some of the above regulations would probably have been accepted by most people at the time as reasonable, but the fact that this meeting also decided that 'all articles or communications intended for publication in any form by members of the staff and relating to the work of the Commission are to be submitted to the Director, who may at his discretion bring them before the Committee for their approval', would appear to have been unduly restrictive.[99]

Some members of the Finance Sub-Committee were certainly aware of differences of opinion between Ó Duilearga and members of his staff on issues of policy. Given that this was the case, it is hard to understand how they could have acquiesced to such a restriction on members of staff. They may, of course, have been trying to placate an irate and possibly still convalescent Director, who was determined to resume control of the Commission. Again this decision, which had nothing to do with finance, was not brought before the Commission proper, and ten years would pass before the Commission would be officially informed of it. In acting this way, the Finance Sub-Committee would appear to have exceeded its powers. However, as noted in Chapter III/2, it must be said these powers were never clearly defined.

Ó Duilearga was back in command, and determined to keep control not only of what his staff did, but also of what they published. Yet it would appear that he was in no condition to resume all his duties as Director, nor was he in any great hurry to return to Head Office. By the end of April he had not yet come into work. The staff had, however, heard that he was going to Iceland. In late April, Seán Ó Súilleabháin informed Åke Campbell:

> He was at a meeting of our Finance Committee yesterday evening, but as it was after office hours, none of us met him; we do not attend these meetings at all, as you may know. I hope that he will be in good form when and if he returns, and that he will settle down to office work and lectures.[100]

Whatever about Ó Duilearga settling down to office work, he was never to give a series of lectures to Irish university students again.

Campbell's Report

Although Ó Duilearga had asked Campbell in late January 1955 to forget altogether about the report, he did in fact send a copy to Ó Duilearga.[101]

---

99 ED FL 2: 'IFC. Fin. Sub-Com./Min. 95th Meeting', 28th March 1955', par. 716.
100 ULMA Saml. Åke Campbell, subnr. 159: Ó Súilleabháin to Campbell, dated 29.4.1955.
101 Kir. Muus. Loorits Papers: Ó Duilearga to Loorits, dated 10.2.1955. Ó Duilearga in this

Although, as we will see below, no action was taken on this report and, it would appear, no member of the Commission ever saw it, it is worth looking at this report in some detail (as well as an earlier draft of it), for in these documents we see the Commission being measured not by a yardstick of a later time, but of its own time. As we will see shortly, Campbell appears to have revised the report he sent to Ó Danachair and Ó Súilleabháin in November 1954. At any rate, this 'November' version of his report is not found among Campbell's papers, nor have I come across a copy of it elsewhere. However, the earlier draft that survives, 'Report on Work of the Folklore Commission: notes and suggestions', would suggest that it was, in many respects, a hard-hitting document.

A covering letter to the 'lost' report of November 1954 survives among Campbell's papers, dated November 19th, 1954, and is addressed to Ó Duilearga. Even though he had discussed the work of the Commission with Ó Duilearga the previous June, and he had been asked by the latter to set down in writing his 'impressions of the different activities of your institute', he was very much aware that he was treading on sensitive ground. He stressed that he based his 'analysis of the situation in Ireland' and on his twenty five years' experience of working in the Landsmålsarkiv (Dialect and Folklore Archive) in Uppsala. He nevertheless felt the need to be frank:

> I have tried to be sincere above all – sincerity is the truest test of friendship. As I have so often said I have the greatest admiration for your pioneer work. I have a great love for Ireland, for you Séamus, and for all my Irish friends. And I have a great desire to do my part to assist Irish culture, and so I have done my best to make this report as good as I possibly can.[102]

However, in an earlier draft of this letter he is franker still. Speaking of his observations on the work of the Commission both in the field and in the archive, he says:

> But my admiration for what has been done does not make me blind to the truth that there are certain unsatisfactory features which must be removed. I am convinced that you are not asking for expressions of admiration and flattery, but for an honest criticism of what I have seen, and I ask you to believe that everything I say here is based upon my experience of similar work in Sweden.

It would also appear that he had been frank with Ó Duilearga when they had discussed the work of the Commission the previous June:

> You remember that I said to you that your staff in the Archive were afraid, and that this is not a good psychological basis for any successful work.

letter suggests that their 'letters crossed in the post'.
102 ULMA Saml. Åke Campbell, subnr. 165: Campbell to Ó Duilearga, dated 19.11.1954. It would appear that this letter was never sent to Ó Duilearga.

As a result of my examination of the work of the archive I am sure that this is true. And by the expression *afraid*, I mean that your colleagues live in an air of constant uncertainty, uneasiness, and doubt. This can easily be removed by the feeling of security which can only come from a good permanent organisation. It cannot come if the present system is continued.

This was a very blunt assessment indeed, and he caps it off by saying: 'I have now given you my frank opinion and measured judgement and I have not allowed insincere politeness to influence me.'[103]

He subsequently amended his covering letter to make it sound less harsh; whether he amended the report likewise is not clear, but seems probable. The draft of this report, mentioned above, which appears to have been written in the summer of 1954, took into account Ó Danachair's suggestion about having each paragraph clearly titled with a recommendation at the end. Even though Campbell seems to have emended and expanded this draft substantially before sending it to Ó Súilleabháin and Ó Danachair in November 1954, it is necessary to look at its contents, as it gives an honest assessment of many of the activities of the Commission, before circumstances may have forced Campbell to fudge matters.

Under 'Collecting and Field Work' it says:

Full-time paid collectors; these are not receiving sufficient direction. They should receive detailed instructions as to their work at regular intervals of one or two months. This should be done by the Archivist, Mr O Suilleabhain, in consultation with Mr. Danaher, so that both the spiritual and material aspects of the tradition may be suitably investigated by the full-time collectors.

Part-time paid collectors. This method of collecting is a most suitable and valuable one. The number of such collectors is, by Scandinavian standards, entirely too small. It should be increased several times, and detailed instructions should be given to them frequently, as to the full-time collectors, by the Archivist assisted by Mr. Danaher.

Ó Duilearga would have found much of the above difficult to accept, as the implication was that he had been neglecting to instruct the Commission's collectors. On the other hand, he would probably have agreed with what Campbell had to say on the need for an Ethnographic Survey, as this was an area of the Commission's work he himself thought needed developing. The report spoke of the need to supplement the accounts 'by peasants, craftsmen and such people, of their own life and activities.' He added:

This must be supplemented by a scientific examination, in the field, of all phases of folk life and folk culture. It may be noted that the establishment

---

103 ULMA Saml. Åke Campbell, subnr. 351: undated letter, begin. 'Dear S' (italics underlined in original).

of a folk-museum will not solve this problem, unless it is accompanied by an ethnographic survey. The possibility of such a museum in Ireland is still undecided, but the work of the ethnographic survey should be begun as soon as possible. Mr. Danaher is fully qualified to carry out such a survey; where the assistance of the paid and voluntary workers is required, he should be in constant consultation with the Archivist.[104]

There was no doubt, however, about the prominence being given to Seán Ó Súilleabháin and Caoimhín Ó Danachair in the above recommendations. On reading these recommendations, Ó Duilearga would have been justified in sensing that an attempt was being made to sideline him. Moreover, although the report does not say outright that Ó Duilearga should commence giving courses in the University, the implication was that he should:

> Every effort should be made to give Irish folk tradition a place in the University equal to that which it gets in Uppsala, Lund, Oslo and other Continental universities. [A s]eries of lectures should be given on folk belief and custom and on folk life and culture as well as on folk literature. The granting of Docent [i.e. (senior) lecturer] status to Mr. O Suilleabhain and Mr Danaher would ensure that the Professor would have two highly qualified helpers in planning and giving a course of lectures, and in conducting seminar exercises and guiding students. Dr. Szövérffy should be called upon for occasional special lectures on the European background to certain aspects of tradition in which he is particularly versed.[105]

This draft report is also critical of the organisation and direction of the Commission in its general recommendations and conclusion. Under 'In General' it said:

> The amount of material being collected does not seem to justify either the number of full-time collectors or the amount spent upon this part of the work. It would be better [by] far to reduce the number of paid full-time collectors and to increase the number of part-time collectors and of cataloguers.
>
> Much of the time and energy of the staff seems to be spent on matters of minor importance. A long-term policy of work, with each person's function clearly defined, and, most particularly, the assigning to the senior members of the staff of both the authority and the responsibility for carrying out their part of the work and taking complete control of the staff assigned to them, is absolutely necessary.

---

104 ULMA Saml. Åke Campbell, subnr. 168 'Report on Work of the Folklore Commission: notes and suggestions', pp. 1–2.
105 ULMA Saml. Åke Campbell subnr. 351:['Report on Work of the Folklore Commission: notes and suggestions'], p. 4. Pages 3 and 4 of this document are found in this file, pages 1and 2 in ULMA Saml. Åke Campbell, subnr. 168.

If this was not hard-hitting enough in respect of Ó Duilearga's direction of the Commission, the conclusion was more critical still:

> The whole matter is one of organisation. The setting up of the Institute on a sound, permanent, scientific basis, as outlined above, will be followed by increasing success in every aspect of the work. No improvement of any kind may be expected under the present system of organisation; more than that, it will probably end in chaos and the end of all useful work if it is continued. The Director of the Folklore Commission will perform a service of the greatest importance to Irish tradition, and earn the well-deserved gratitude of the European scientific world by bending his energies to overcoming the difficulties which may lie in the way of implementing the scheme.[106]

As I have said above, Campbell may well have softened the tone of the above as well as expanded it in the report he sent to Ó Súilleabháin and Ó Danachair in November 1954. Ó Súilleabháin in his letter of July 12th, 1954 had advised him to be fulsome in his praise of Ó Duilearga. This draft report contains little of this nature, so it most likely was added later. We know that the 'lost' report sent to Ó Danachair and Ó Súilleabháin in November 1954 did contain much praise of Ó Duilearga. Seán Ó Súilleabháin, in a letter to Campbell in which he refers to the contents of this report, says that, although he agreed with Ó Danachair that the report should not be shown to Ó Duilearga at this juncture, '[e]ven if it were shown to him, he would hardly object, I should say, to anything in it, as you praise him a good deal, and he likes praise (just as we all do, I suppose).' He congratulated Campbell on 'on the excellence of the memo in the present circumstances', and added: 'It could have been different in some ways, more critical in a practical way along certain lines, if Séamus were not as he is. It is just as well that you did not stress certain points, as such would not do any good at present.' This would imply that Campbell had softened the tone, and even the substance of the draft outlined above. Nevertheless it is interesting to note that Ó Súilleabháin says: 'You covered the whole ground very well, and I'm glad you referred to the crying need for lecturing on folklore topics.'[107] A report stressing 'the crying need for lecturing on folklore topics' might have been sufficient reason, in the eyes of some of his friends, for not showing it to Ó Duilearga given his state

---

106 ULMA Saml. Åke Campbell, subnr. 351: ['Report on Work of the Folklore Commission: notes and suggestions'], p. 4 (see previous footnote). It should be stressed that Campbell did not fully appreciate Ó Duilearga's preference for full-time collectors, as the concept of full-time collector was strange to him. The Uppsala archive was assembled by a combination of amateur collectors, academic folklorists, archive workers and students, as well as local part-time (paid) collectors and questionnaire correspondents. The folklore collections of the Finnish Literature Society were compiled in a similar fashion with the difference that folklore competitions greatly augmented its collections during the twentieth century, which was not the case with the Uppsala archive. My thanks to Marelene Hugoson and Jukka Saarinen respectively for verifying this matter.

107 ULMA Saml. Åke Campbell, subnr. 159: Ó Súilleabháin to Campbell, letter dated 13.12.1954.

of health at the time. However, it is most likely that it contained much else that would have been difficult for him to accept.[108]

As we have seen above, Ó Danachair returned the report Campbell sent him in November 1954, presumably with comments, saying: 'I think it would do some harm at the moment.' It would appear that Campbell revised, and possibly substantially doctored the report in December 1954, taking into account Ó Duilearga's poor state of health. At any rate, it is hard to believe that this 'revised' report, dated December 1954', is anything but a shadow of the document sent to Ó Danachair and Ó Súilleabháin the previous month. Above we have seen how Ó Danachair had the previous summer advised Campbell that the report 'should be as short and as simple as possible' and to 'put a title word at the beginning of each paragraph, and a conclusion or recommendation at the end of each paragraph', as it would 'be read by a number of people who may not be fully sympathetic or even interested in it'.[109] Campbell's report of December 1954 (i.e. final draft) conforms with none of these recommendations. It is long and wordy, and unclear as to its exact purpose. It is fulsome in its praise of the Commission and its Director, as Ó Súilleabháin advised, but it fudges many substantive issues. For example, under 'Collection', Campbell says nothing about there being too many full-time collectors, although he does say that, judging 'by Scandinavian standards', the number of the Commission's part-time collectors was 'too small'. Nor does he mention that the Commission's collectors were not, in his opinion, getting sufficient instruction. Instead he says, on the other hand, 'it has been my experience that the field-collector is encouraged and stimulated by visits from members of the archive staff. I have also found that he derives benefit from occasional visits to the archive for the purpose of assessing what has already been done and of planning future work.' On the question of the need for publication this 'revised' report is somewhat less evasive, but it fudges completely the question of teaching. The report seeks to explain why '[s]urprisingly few scientific papers on Irish folklore and folklife have been published by Irish scholars other than those connected with the IFC [Irish Folklore Commission] and the Folklore of Ireland Society' by the fact that 'folklore has only recently, and that in only one university, been recognised as a subject of Academic standing.' While that was, to a very large extent true, instead of advocating the teaching of folklore at UCD to begin with, the report simply says: 'The resources – personal and material – are at hand to accord Irish folk tradition its due place in more than one university.'[110]

Nowhere does this report appear so vague than in its summing up of the situation. One could read the conclusion (which is untitled) without thinking there was any outstanding problem with the organisation of the Irish Folklore Commission:

108 Ó Súilleabháin in the above letter says that it was 'on the advice of Dr. Michael Tierney' that Ó Danachair had decided 'not yet' to show the report to Ó Duilearga.

109 ULMA Saml. Åke Campbell, subnr. 167: Ó Danachair to Campbell, letter undated [July 1954].

110 ULMA saml. Åke Campbell, subnr. 51: ' Some Observations on the activities of the IFC as noticed during a recent visit to Ireland', pp. 3 and 10–12.

> Your institute has grown so much that *the organisation of your work* calls
> for great care and consideration. The activities of the archive have been
> divided into departments, each under its own specialist, who is responsible
> to the Director. This development was indeed foreseen and anticipated
> by Prof. Delargy at the very beginning (p. 3). The Director's function
> has been, first and foremost, to give direction and balance to this system
> of departments, to hold it together, to direct the work of departments by
> consultation with the specialist of the departments. If the Director wishes,
> he gives the specialist of a department full autonomy within the limits
> prescribed for the work in the same way as in our institutes in Sweden.
> The specialist prepares, in consultation with the Director, plans for the
> work. When this has been approved by the Director, the leader of the
> department in question gets the definite authority and responsibility to
> carry out this work, together with full control during the prescribed period
> of the staff assigned to the department, keeping the Director informed by
> reports of progress made and work planned.[111]

Campbell, while purporting to be describing what the situation was, is really
describing what he hoped might be the situation after a reorganisation and
redivision of duties in the Commission. But how was this to happen? Perhaps
he was hoping that members of the Commission would read between the lines,
and that Ó Duilearga himself might take the hint, without taking offence.

He then describes the division of work in the Commission, which is only
partly factual in that it gives responsibility for 'the direction of collectors
to' Ó Súilleabháin and Ó Danachair, which was far from being the case.
Commenting on this division, he says:

> This division of work has enabled the Director to pay particular attention
> to the relative importance of the various aspects of the scientific work,
> and to give priority to those of greatest importance while at the same time
> always remaining the heart and soul, the indispensable inspiration and
> driving force of the whole enterprise.

What were those for whom this report was intended to make of all this? After
all the work that went into compiling this report, it is hard not to believe that
Campbell in his final paragraph is passing on the responsibility to others:

> I believe I am not mistaken, if I say, that it is the desire of European and
> American folklorists to have the opportunity to visit IFC and its archive,
> the famous folklore centre, to enjoy the companionship of Professor
> Delargy and his collaborators and to benefit from the Director's ripe
> and generous scholarship. At the same time the visitors will have the
> possibility to see and hear the Irish storytellers and to study in the Irish
> milieu the typical exponents of Irish folk-culture. If the IFC would
> consider holding an international Congress for folklore in Dublin in the

111 Ibid., pp. 12–13, italics underlined in original.

near future, such a proposition, I feel sure, would be welcomed by the widest circle.[112]

This is a far cry from what he had written some months earlier in a draft, where he predicted that 'under the present system of organisation' no improvement could be expected, and the work of the Commission would 'probably end in chaos' (see above).

Nevertheless, Ó Duilearga found this 'revised' report, couched as it was in diplomatic language, offensive. He is very dismissive of Campbell's report in a letter to Oskar Loorits, stating that there was not a single recommendation in it of 'the slightest assistance' to him. He remarked to Loorits: 'I think Åke's health, and his anxiety not to offend anyone, are responsible for the curious review of the alleged activities of' the Irish Folklore Commission. In this letter, Ó Duilearga, interestingly, says that his health was restored and that he was 'busy for the first time for many years at [his] own affairs, writing, reading & putting in order [his] own papers which for a long space of time [he] had neglected in the interests of other people.'[113] Although 'disappointed' with Campbell, he appears not to have written to him on the matter. A letter he received in early March from Loorits seems to have been very supportive of him and he took great comfort in it. A further reply of his to Loorits reveals a defiant Director, who was biding his time before he took action against his colleagues, with whom he felt greatly aggrieved. The staff of the Commission owed everything to him, he said, and stated that he had had no 'communication' with any of them since going on leave of absence.

In the above letter to Loorits, Ó Duilearga again refers to Campbell's report and calls it an 'extraordinary document'[114], and in many respects it was: an extraordinary effort in obfuscation. The numerous copies of Campbell's revised report of December 1954 among his papers in Uppsala would suggest that he initially agreed to Ó Danachair's suggestion that each member of the Commission should get a copy, but that he subsequently changed his mind. As Ó Duilearga in January 1955 had requested him not to bother sending the report, and to let matters take their course, there was little that he could do but agree to his request, as it was Ó Duilearga in the first place who had asked him to compile such a report. As we have see above, however, he did send Ó Duilearga a copy of this report in early 1955.

Both Ó Súilleabháin and Ó Danachair probably realised by April 1955 that Campbell's intervention would come to nought and that an opportunity had been lost that might never come again. A tone of resignation is evident in Ó Súilleabháin's letters to Campbell in late spring and early summer 1955. At the end of April he informs Campbell that '[t]here is nothing new here'

---

112 Ibid., p. 13.
113 Kir. Muus. Loorits Papers: letter dated 10.2.1955. Ironically, this would suggest that perhaps the best course of action for Ó Duilearga, and one in the long run that might have been conducive to his health, and that would have allowed him concentrate on his scholarly work, would have been for him to give up his post as Director of the Commission.
114 Kir. Muus. Loorits Papers: letter dated 14.3.1955.

and that nobody at Head Office had yet seen Ó Duilearga although he was to return 'at the beginning of April'. Ó Súilleabháin had heard that he was to go to Iceland the following month and expressed the hope 'that he will be in good form when and if he returns and that he will settle down to office work and lectures.'[115] In early July, Ó Danachair wrote to Campbell '...things are exactly as they were before – there has been no change. We have heard nothing at all about your report, and I do not think that it has been shown to anyone.' Campbell had written to Ó Danachair informing him of his intention to travel to a folklore conference in Schleswig in northern Germany in early August. Ó Danachair had himself accepted an invitation to give a paper at this conference and says: 'There are many things we shall speak about when I see you. I am not without hope that we may be able to ask you to come to Ireland soon again.'[116]

Without the cooperation of Ó Duilearga, all the staff of the Commission could do was hope that things would turn out for the best. In December 1955, Ó Danachair told Campbell that Ó Duilearga seemed to be on the verge of another breakdown, but six months later he reported: 'Séamus is improved in general health, but there has been no change in the situation of the Commission.' Two months later Ó Duilearga himself informed Campbell of his restored health, which he says 'was much impaired in recent years'. He added: 'I am still in charge of the Commission. There is still much to do – in fact, we are only beginning!'[117]

The aftermath

Relations between Ó Duilearga and his two most senior colleagues at Head Office never returned to what they had been formerly. There is no doubt that an opportunity was lost in 1954 to overhaul the Commission.[118] The

---

115 ULMA Saml. Åke Campbell, subnr. 159: Ó Súilleabháin to Campbell, dated 29.4.1955. Some six weeks later, while Ó Duilearga was still away lecturing in Iceland, Ó Súilleabháin again wrote to Campbell about him: 'we expect him back about July 1. He is slow to settle down to work, and may never do it as we would wish.' Ibid: Ó Súilleabháin to Campbell, dated 14.6.1955.

116 ULMA Saml. Åke Campbell, subnr. 167: Ó Danachair to Campbell, dated 4.7.1955, and D/T S 15548B: 'Gearr-Thuar./1955–56', p. 6.

117 ULMA Saml. Åke Campbell, subnr. 167: Ó Danachair to Campbell, letters dated 17.12.1955 and 4.6.1956. ULMA Saml. Åke Campbell subnr. 165: Ó Duilearga to Campbell, letter dated 7.8.1956.

118 Another opportunity was lost in the early 1960's when Seán Ó Maonaigh of the Finance Sub-Committee requested that 'a complete reassessment' of the Commission's work until then be undertaken 'to see if any change in policy was required.' Although after some hesitation, Ó Duilearga agreed that Caoimhín Ó Danachair should draw up such a report, work on the report proved slow, and even though a draft was ready for circulation to members towards the end 1962, more than a year was to pass before every member of the Commission had had an opportunity to read and comment on it. The report was never forwarded to the Government as it was never finished, for reasons that are not clear. See ED FL 4: 'CBÉ. Miont. 106ú Cruinniú, 15.3.1961', p. 3, 'CBÉ. Miont. 108ú Cruinniú, 19.10.1961', p. 7, and ED FL 1: IFC. Fin. Sub-Com./Min. 128th Meeting', 12.3.1964, p. 2.

Commission continued on from year to year under Ó Duilearga's direction for another decade and a half or so. The substantive issues raised by the different drafts and versions of Campbell's report were, for the most part, never addressed, nor even discussed.[119] It did not end in 'chaos' as Campbell predicted it would if there were no restructuring of its work, but although much was done, and begun, in the years that followed, they were without doubt years of lost opportunity on many fronts. That the work of the Commission did not end in chaos is, to a large extent, due its staff, both at Head Office and in the field, not least to Seán Ó Súilleabháin and Caoimhín Ó Danachair. It would be unfair, however, to suggest that no credit attaches to Ó Duilearga for what was accomplished in this period. Together with members of the Finance Sub-Committee, down until 1965 when the staff became Civil Servants, he insured that the Commission had the resources to pay wages and its day-to-day running costs. There is no doubt that things might have been better if Ó Duilearga's style of leadership had been different, but they might possibly have been worse if he had gone under altogether, i.e. if his fragile health had forced him to step down as Director. There is no certainty that either Seán Ó Súilleabháin or Caoimhín Ó Danachair would have done a better job as Director, or been given the resources to do so.

In an article he published in *Ulster Folklife* in 1983, Caoimhín Ó Danachair says: 'as the nineteen-sixties progressed it became more and more apparent that the momentum of the Commission was running down under the burden of future uncertainty, wavering direction and diminishing returns.'[120] Whether he is correct in his description of Ó Duilearga's direction as 'wavering', there is no doubt that the Commision 'was running down', especially during the 1960's. The age structure of the staff in autumn 1969 is evidence enough of this. The youngest member of staff, the short-hand typist Gretta Dillon, was in her early twenties, almost twenty years younger than the next youngest member of staff. Of the rest of her colleagues, one was in her late forties, four in their fifties, five in their sixties, and one in his mid-eighties.[121] Given this age structure, as the 1960's advanced, with no teaching of folkloristics or ethnology in the Republic of Ireland, with no active policy of recruitment, with its Director approaching retirement age, and all of them getting older, the staff were right to be worried. Ó Duilearga was placing all his bets on the hope that the Government would eventually transfer the Commision to UCD. In the end, luck was on his side, but the Commission that was reconstituted in UCD in 1971 was only a shadow of its former self.

---

119 This is not to suggest that Campbell was invariably correct in his assessment of the Commission's work. For example, while the Commission certainly needed to utilise a wider network of part-time collectors, his contention that the amount of material being collected did not justify the number of full-time collectors employed is a complex question that cannot be adequately dealt with here.

120 Ó Danachair 1983, p. 11.

121 Their ages are here listed in descending order: Janis Mezs (85), Séamus Ó Duilearga (69), Seán Ó Súilleabháin (65), Proinnsias de Búrca (64), Ciarán Bairéad (63), Thomas Wall (62), Caoimhín Ó Danachair (55), Seán Ó hEochaidh (55), Micheal J. Murphy (55), Jim Delaney (53), Bríd Mahon (51), Máire Dillon (48), and Leo Corduff (39).

Although the failure of efforts to reorganise the organisation of the work of the Commission in 1954/1955 had a long-lasting effect on many aspects of its work, there is one area, however, where development somewhat along the lines proposed by Campbell, did occur, namely the expansion of the ethnological work of the Commission. This was something that Ó Duilearga himself thought needed urgent addressing, and although it would appear that relations between Ó Danachair and Ó Duilearga were not only never restored to what they had been formerly, but in time were to deteriorate even further, the evidence would suggest that Ó Duilearga did not impede Ó Danachair from making a systematic ethnological survey of the whole of the Republic. A great deal was achieved in this area in the late 1950's and 1960's. Such an undertaking was a mammoth task for one man, and there is no doubt that more might have been achieved if Ó Danachair had had the assistance of a body of students and postgraduates. He was, however, able to avail of the assistance of the collectors, especially the full-time collectors, a number of whom were particularly interested in material culture.[122] He was fortunate also that the Director of the National Museum since 1954, A. T. Lucas, had a special interest in ethnology and actively cooperated with the Commission to advance ethnological research; as the files of the Museum of Rural Life, Castlebar bear witness to. Ó Danachair could also draw on the assistance of ethnologists in Northern Ireland, with whom he enjoyed harmonious relations.

Research and publication

Nevertheless, it would be wrong to conclude that the deterioration of relations between Ó Duilearga and Ó Danachair did not have a profound effect on the latter's work. One area where this can be seen is in respect of research and publications. Seán Ó Súilleabháin in his above letter to Campbell in July 1954 claimed that not only were the staff of the Commission 'not encouraged' by Ó Duilearga 'to write articles and make studies of certain problems', but were 'frowned on if' they proposed doing so.[123] At the time, however, while Ó Duilearga might discourage, or frown on, certain research projects of members of his staff, there was little, in effect, he could do to thwart such projects. The decision of the Finance Sub-Committee in March of the following year (see above) to make it mandatory for the staff not only to seek permission 'in writing' from the Director 'to use the material in the archives of the Irish Folklore Commission for the purpose of publications, lectures or radio talks', but that 'all articles or communications intended for publication in any form by members of the staff and relating to the work of the Commission are to be submitted to the Director, who may at his discretion bring them before the Committee for their approval'[124] changed the situation

---

122 One such collector was Jim Delaney. See Delaney 1976, 1980, 1982, and 1990. See also Mac Philib 2000, pp. 1 ff.
123 ULMA Saml. Åke Campbell, subnr. 351: Ó Súilleabháin to Campbell, 12.7.1954.
124 ED FL 2: 'IFC. Fin. Sub-Com./Min. 95th Meeting', 28.3.1955', par. 716.

fundamentally. Some three decades later Caoimhín Ó Danachair claimed that '...research and publications by members of the Commission's staff was in the main discouraged, and access to the collected material made difficult by petty restrictions.'[125] Although he does not elaborate as to the nature of this restricted access, there is no doubt that the above decision by the Finance Sub-Committee is being referred to. Nor was this decision allowed to fall into abeyance in time, for on January 25th, 1966 the Finance Sub-Committee again discussed this matter and Ó Duilearga reported to the Commission two days later that the Sub-Committee considered this rule to be still in force and that the staff should be informed of this. However, there is no mention of the Commission sanctioning this 'rule' at this meeting; the absence of a quorum on this occasion is one possible reason for this.[126] The fact that it was found necessary to restate this ruling more than ten years after it was first set down, is evidence in itself of ongoing tensions in the Commission, but it also possibly points towards the ruling being flouted or ignored. Nevertheless, this ruling did have a very concrete effect on the published record of both Ó Súilleabháin and Ó Danachair.

In his work on wake amusements, *Caitheamh Aimsire ar Thórraimh* (1961), Seán Ó Súilleabháin gives approximately seven pages of written sources utilised in the research, but no references at all to the Commission's archive. That an archivist of a national folklore archive should not utilise sources in his own archive in such a work is remarkable, and indeed was commented upon by one reviewer – none other than Ó Duilearga'a fellow student and former colleague in UCD, Myles Dillon.[127] This is not to say that Ó Súilleabháin did not make use of sources in the Commission's Archive surreptitiously as he says in the introduction to the work: 'In addition to consulting published works, I questioned people whom I met from time to time about the wakes they themselves had experience of here and there throughout the country.'[128] There may well have been such personal informants, but we know from Ó Súilleabháin's correspondence with Åke Campbell that he was noting material on wake games in the Commission's collections as early as February 1955 and that he was thinking of doing, as he put it, 'a follow-up volume for FFC on Christiansen's The Dead and the Living.'[129] There is no doubt that he used sources from the Commission's collections in this work, although he implies otherwise. In this case Ó Súilleabháin chose subterfuge to get around the Finance Sub-Committee's ruling.

Similarly, in Caoimhín Ó Danachair's *The Year in Ireland* no archival sources are given, only printed ones. Nevertheless, in his introduction he says: 'The many people in the Irish countryside who, over the years, have helped with information are so numerous as to make their listing

125 Ó Danachair 1983, p. 11.
126 ED FL 8: 'CBÉ. Miont. 126ú Cruinniú, 27.1.1966', p. 3.
127 See Dillon's review of this work in *Celtica* vi (1963), pp. 289–290.
128 S. Ó Súilleabháin 1961, p. xiii (trans).
129 ULMA Saml. Åke Campbell, subnr. 159: Ó Súilleabháin to Campbell, dated 11.2.1955.
     'FFC' stands for the prestigious international Folklore Fellows Communications series, published by the Academy of Finland.

impossible; may I here express my thanks to them, for it is they who, in the final analysis, have made this book.'[130] Although *The Year in Ireland* is a popular work in which one would not expect to find extensive footnotes and a detailed listing of sources, one might expect that the collections of the Irish Folklore Commission would at least be mentioned, as there is no doubt that Ó Danachair drew heavily on these collections, particularly questionnaire replies, in compiling this work. Another popular work of Ó Danachair's, *Folktales of the Irish Countryside* (1967), offers further evidence of secret use of archival sources.[131]

We also find lack of references to the Commission's collections in much of Ó Danachair's academic work. For example, although the Commission sent out a questionnaire on 'Flails and Threshing' in the late 1950's, more than ten years later, in an article he published in a volume of *Ethnologia Europaea* dedicated to the memory of Sigurd Erixon, while he gives distribution maps that are obviously based, partly at least, on questionnaire replies, no reference is made to the collections of the Commission although in a footnote he thanks 'the numerous informants in many parts of Ireland without whose help this could not have been written.'[132] By not mentioning the Irish Folklore Commission, Ó Danachair could claim that this article did not come within the ruling of the Finance Sub-Committee of March 1954. Consequently, permission to use the Commission's collections did not have to be sought, nor had this article to be presented for scrutiny and approval. This subterfuge and evasion, however, came at a price for not only did it mean that many of Ó Danachair's academic articles lack a complete list of sources and notes, but as a result he was driven more and more towards writing for a popular audience.

Alan Gailey recalls that Ó Danachair told him 'that the reason he had done so much "popular" publishing was that it gave him an outlet denied him otherwise.'[133] Between 1955 and 1972, Ó Danachair published approximately seventy two articles and books for the popular market as against fifty five academic articles. Prior to 1955 he had only one popular publication to his name. The public gained, but one senses that scholarship suffered somewhat. He produced no substantial piece of research during this period. Speaking of the 'some two hundred and eighty two entries ' listed in Ó Danachair's festschrift, *Gold Under the Furze*, Alan Gaily and Chris Lynch in an obituary of him say: '[o]f these almost one hundred represent Caoimhín's scholarly writings.'[134] There is no doubt that, if circumstances had been different, the proportion of his scholarly writings vis-à-vis popular would be much greater. One might say that Ó Danachair dissipated his energies, to some extent at

---

130 Ó Danachair (Danaher) 1972, p. 12.
131 Ó Danachair says that the tales in this book, which derive from his home area of west Limerick, are recalled 'from my memory of the first telling of them to me'. However, as he subsequently collected many of these tales for the Commission and published some of them in *Béaloideas*, it is unlikely that he did not make, at least, some use of this source in compiling this work. See Ó Danachair (Danaher) 1988 [1967], p. 11.
132 Ó Danachair 1970, pp. 50–55.
133 Personal communication, letter dated 23.3.2005.
134 Gailey and Lynch 2002-2003, p. 121.

least, in writing for the popular market from the late 1950's onwards. This is not to diminish the value of these works, for they filled, and continue to fill, a very obvious niche, but he had much more to give by way of scholarship than he ever managed to give. It is, moreover, a tragedy that he never got around to giving us an overall view of Irish ethnology. While his popular works continue to be reissued for the market, many of his more scholarly writings remain hidden away in learned journals. A substantial core of these writings constitute a veritable mine of information on Irish material culture and Irish tradition in general, and a collection of the best of his academic production is a desideratum.

The Types of the Irish Folktale and *Folktales of Ireland*

Seán Ó Súilleabháin's record of publications from 1955 to 1970 also contains many items directed at a popular audience, and remarkably few academic articles that would have necessitated drawing on the Commission's collections. Nevertheless, he produced two substantial works during this period which not only involved utilising these collections but which also had Ó Duilearga's blessing. The first of these, *The Types of the Irish Folktale*, which he co-authored with Reidar Christiansen, was a major piece of research. It must be noted that the proposal to compile a catalogue of Irish *Märchen* for publication did not come from either Ó Súilleabháin or Christiansen, but from Stith Thompson. Thompson spent three weeks at the Commission's Head Office in November 1956, working on new editions of *The Types of the Folktale* and *Motif-Index of Folk-Literature*, and before leaving suggested that such a catalogue be prepared and that it might be published in the prestigious Folklore Fellows Communications series (FFC). The Commission had by this time classified more than 20,000 folktales in its collections.[135] Ó Duilearga, from the outset, had great hopes for this catalogue, believing that its publication would change the face of folktale scholarship worldwide.[136] The project also, it would appear, appealed to Seán Ó Súilleabháin, initially, perhaps, for no other reason than that it would advance the cataloguing of the material.

Thompson's visit to the Commission in November 1956 may also have contributed to a lessening of tensions between Ó Duilearga and certain of his staff. In any event, shortly after Ó Duilearga set Ó Súilleabháin working on this catalogue in January 1957 he informed Thompson that he had 'finally' taken the initiative to improve the 'strained relations' at Head Office and that things were 'much better'. He said that he himself was turning his back on the past and spoke of his hopes for 'a happier future.'[137] The 'happier future' Ó Duilearga hoped for was not to be, however. Relations remained tense between Ó Súilleabháin and him over much of the time it took to compile

---

135 D/T S 15548B: 'Gearr-Thuar./1956–57', p. 3.
136 See ED CO 495(1): 'An Coimisiún Béaloideasa. Agallamh (16/4/58) leis an Ollamh Ó Duilearga', signed T. Ó Raifeartaigh, 16.4.1958.
137 Lilly Lib. Stith Thompson Papers: Ó Duilearga to Thompson, letter 18.2.1957.

this catalogue, perhaps partly exacerbated by Ó Súilleabháin's feeling that Ó Duilearga had reneged on his part of the bargain. It had originally been agreed that both Ó Duilearga and Joseph Szövérffy would take care of classifying folktales in printed sources, leaving manuscript sources to Ó Súilleabháin. Speaking of this arrangement, Ó Súilleabháin in a letter to Stith Thompson in May 1957, says: 'I had no expectations at the time that either or both would do the job, and that is what has happened. Prof. Delargy now says he is too busy. Dr. Szövérffy is leaving us for a Professorship in Montreal – in any case, his Irish was not good enough to be able for the job.' This in effect, as Ó Súilleabháin explained, meant that 'after the huge task of doing the MSS lists has been finished by me, I will have to set about doing the printed [sources] cataloguing – you know that only a very small portion of the printed tales has been ever put on cards.' Ó Súilleabháin was aware that Ó Duilearga was contemplating getting the services of Reidar Christiansen to help with the work, but surmised that Christiansen would not be very interested in working with printed sources, as such work would take him away from the Commission's Head Office to the National Library of Ireland, as many of the works that needed to be consulted were not in the Commission's Library. Consequently, Ó Súilleabháin asked Thompson to write to Ó Duilearga and to stress 'the neccessity for getting somebody to start immediately on the cataloguing of the printed material.'[138]

Christiansen agreed to come and help with the compiling of a catalogue of Irish folktales, but nobody was specifically recruited to work with printed sources. Ó Duilearga looked forward to Christiansen's coming and shortly before he came, in a letter to Stith Thompson, expressed the hope that having Christiansen working at Head Office would 'make life more bearable for' himself. The same letter reveals a lonely, isolated Director in need of someone to talk to. Joseph Szövérffy before his departure to Canada was someone he could talk to; now he was gone and there was nobody 'to carry on his work.' Although Ó Duilearga 'was too busy' (see above) to help with compiling this catalogue, as agreed, he still felt he should have a say in the work, and this may have led to an incident of some sort between himself and Ó Súilleabháin over the layout of the catalogue. In the above letter to Thompson, Ó Duilearga complains that it was impossible to discuss anything with Ó Súilleabháin as he seemed to be 'a master of all masters' and unwilling to take advice. Apart from this difference of opinion with Ó Súilleabháin, he says, 'things are not too bad here'. His doctor had warned him that he must not have another breakdown, and he says he is determined that this should not happen.[139]

Christiansen joined the staff of the Commission in order to work on this project in September 1957 and remained until the end of June 1958. He was later to return to the Commission for six weeks or so in May/June 1960 to help finalise the text.[140] Although the publication bears both their names,

138 Lilly Lib. Stith Thompson Papers: Ó Súilleabháin to Thompson, dated 9.5.1957.
139 Lilly Lib. Stith Thompson Papers: Ó Duilearga to Thompson, dated 14.9.1957.
140 See D/T S 16378A and 16378B(62) 'Gearr-Thuarascálacha' [Annual Reports to Government] for 1957–58, 1958–59, and 1960–61.

there is no doubt that Ó Súilleabháin did the bulk of the work. Not only did he have to read through material in the Commission's archive and library, he also, as he feared, had to read through the extensive manuscript and book collections of the National Library of Ireland, the Royal Irish Academy, and Trinity College Dublin, as well as the archives of numerous publishing houses.[141]

Despite tensions between Ó Duilearga and Ó Súilleabháin, when the latter was doing his bidding he could be fulsome in his praise. A month before Christiansen left Ireland, after his first period working with the Commission, Ó Duilearga wrote to Thompson. He tells of progress on Ó Súilleabháin's 'huge address-book to our märchen, a truly gigantic task which only Seán could ever do, and in which he has been quietly aided and encouraged by Reidar Christiansen.' He describes an idyllic scene: Ó Súilleabháin lost among the 'book-stacks of our National Library where he has immured himself for many weeks' in search of 'elusive folktales' in 'obscure metropolitan & country newspapers & journals'. He spoke of his admiration for Ó Súilleabháin's 'industry' and of his 'admirable co-operation' with Christiansen, and of the 'peace' that all this had brought to 'a much harassed office.' He hoped that this 'state of affairs' would continue.[142]

It may well be that Ó Súilleabháin, although originally reluctant to undertake the cataloguing of printed sources in the National Library and elsewhere, may in time have come to view this task quite differently, as, among other things, it would have allowed him escape from the tensions of Head Office. It appears, however, that the better relations Ó Duilearga referred to above did not survive Christiansen's departure for long. In October 1959, Ó Duilearga again wrote to Thompson informing him that he had no idea of how things stood with the catalogue of folktales as Ó Súilleabháin had not been in communication with him for many months. However, he surmised that the catalogue was in 'an advanced state' and said that Christiansen was expected back in the spring 'to help in the final stage' of the work. Even though relations between them were once again strained, he had hopes that Ó Súilleabháin on completion of this catalogue would undertake a similar catalogue of Irish *Sagen* (legends), and was full of praise of Ó Súilleabháin's competency and willingness to do 'exacting cataloguing' of this sort, and says that he had 'no equal here in this field.'[143]

Despite the difficulties he had in preparing this catalogue, Ó Súilleabháin in a letter to Thompson, on its completion in September 1961, expresses satisfaction with the work and says: 'I expect that it will take a few years to see it through the press, but the main part of the work (long and tedious) is done'.[144] *The Types of the Irish Folktale* was eventually published in Helsinki in July 1963. The summer of 1963 also saw the reprinting, by an American publisher, of Ó Súilleabháin's monumental work *A Handbook of Irish Folklore*. The publication of both these works, as well as their international

141 D/T S 16378A: 'Gearr-Thuar./1958–59', pp. 2–3.
142 Lilly Lib. Stith Thompson Papers: Ó Duilearga to Thompson, dated 30.5.1958.
143 Lilly Lib. Stith Thompson Papers: Ó Duilearga to Thompson, dated 21.10.1959.
144 Lilly Lib. Stith Thompson Papers: Ó Súilleabháin to Thompson, letter dated 7.9.1961.

importance, is highlighted in Ó Duilearga's annual report to the Government for 1963–1964.[145] This is in marked contrast to the absence of any mention in the same reports of Ó Súilleabháin's much acclaimed work, *Caitheamh Aimsire ar Thórraimh*, published a few years earlier.

Ó Súilleabháin seems to have been willing to undertake a catalogue of *Sagen*, which was to be part of a European project. To this end, he attended a number of folk-narrative conferences at various venues in Europe and Reidar Christiansen, who had done a similar catalogue for Norway, also visited the Commission to advise him.[146] In the event, for whatever reason, Ó Súilleabháin was not to undertake such a catalogue, as Ó Duilearga hoped he would. He did, however, undertake another publication which had the full backing of Ó Duilearga, namely *Folktales of Ireland*. This work was published in 1966, but its genesis goes back to August 1960 when Richard Dorson wrote to Ó Súilleabháin about discussions he had been having with Chicago Press on producing an International Folktale Series in English 'intended for the reading public but presented according to modern principles of folk narrative scholarship.' He asked Ó Súilleabháin to edit an Irish volume for the series.[147] Ó Súilleabháin agreed to this proposal and discussed the matter with Ó Duilearga, who also liked the idea.[148]

It is not surprising that Ó Súilleabháin should have welcomed a chance to edit material from the Commission's archive. He believed strongly that the Commission should publish more of its collections, and felt that Ó Duilearga was not doing enough to facilitate such publication (See Chapter III/6 above). In summer 1963, Ó Duilearga agreed to Dorson's request that he write a preface for this work. Dorson left the length of this preface up to Ó Duilearga, suggesting that even 'a page or so' would suffice, but, for personal reasons, Ó Duilearga was not able to meet this commitment and later that year requested Dorson that he be relieved of the duty. He told Dorson that he had spoken to Ó Súilleabháin 'about the prefatory note and he has kindly allowed me to omit it.' He added 'I prefer to leave the introduction to his book to himself and to you. Any note of mine is unnecessary.'[149] As a result, Dorson spent a week in the Commission's library in March 1965 gathering material for a lengthy introduction to Ó Súilleabháin's work. The work itself was published the following spring. On receiving his copy of this book, Ó Súilleabháin wrote to Dorson: 'Your foreward is excellent, now that, once again, I read it in print. Even Delargy praised it! He himself should have written such a summary years ago.'[150] One can detect a note of criticism here, but also of resignation. It would appear that relations between Ó Súilleabháin and Ó Duilearga had improved somewhat by this time. Although differences on substantive issues of policy remained, and the

---

145 D/T S 98/6/455 S 16378B: 'Gearr-Thuar./1963–64', p. 2.
146 See, e.g. D/T S 98/6/455 S 16378B: 'Gearr-Thuar./1963–64', p. 2.
147 Lilly Lib. Dorson Papers: Dorson to Ó Súilleabháin, letter dated 30.8.1960.
148 Lilly Lib. Dorson Papers: Ó Súilleabháin to Dorson, dated 10.9.1960.
149 Lilly Lib. Dorson Papers: Dorson to Ó Duilearga and Ó Duilearga to Dorson, letters dated 27.2.1964 and 17.12.1964.
150 Lilly Lib. Dorson Papers: Ó Súilleabháin to Dorson, dated 11.5.1966.

whole question of publications and right of access to sources continued to be a running sore, the approach of old age, illness and bereavement within their respective families, as well as Christian charity may have mellowed both men (who were separated in age by only four and a half years), and brought about a certain accommodation, a degree of toleration. Not surprisingly, the publication of *Folktales of Ireland* is recorded in Ó Duilearga's report to the Government for 1966–1967.[151]

The heart of the problem

Ó Duilearga's support for the publication of *The Types of the Irish Folktale* and the *Folktales of Ireland* needs to be explained as it appears to contradict claims made by both Ó Súilleabháin and Ó Danachair that he restricted their access to and use of the Commission's collections. In this connection it should also be mentioned that Ó Duilearga in the early 1950's supported Ó Danachair's research into Irish house-types and his preparation of a monograph on the subject. However, while supporting Ó Danachair's research into this subject, the fate of this monograph, which although completed was never published, may have contributed to a souring of relations between author and Director, as Ó Danachair had been led to believe that the Commission would publish it. In January 1957, Ó Danachair wrote to Campbell.

> As you expect, the typescript of the book on the Irish House, which we worked over to-gether (sic) in Uppsala has been lying in the Commission since October 1953, and there seems to be less chance than ever that it will be published.[152]

It would appear that Ó Duilearga supported, at least, publishing projects that would enhance the international profile of the Commission. He may well have discouraged certain types of research that he considered of little import, believing, perhaps, that staff should not be distracted from more important work. But his attitude to publication was far more complex than this, and unfortunately space does not allow for it to be examined properly here. Suffice it to say, however, that although Seán Ó Súilleabháin in July 1954, as mentioned above, claimed that Ó Duilearga did not encourage, and indeed 'frowned' on his staff writing articles and researching 'certain problems', in the latter's reports to the Government for the mid-1950's the numerous publications of Joseph Szövérffy are highlighted.[153] Moreover, it is interesting to note that the publications, both academic and popular,

---

151 D/T S 97/6/516 S 18054: 'Gearr-Thuar./1966–67', p. 5.
152 ULMA Saml. Åke Campbell subnr. 167: Ó Danachair to Campbell, dated 18.1.1957. The reasons why this work was never published are not clear, but Josef Szövérffy claims that both Ó Duilearga and the Director of the National Museum of Ireland, A. T. Lucas, were not satisfied with it. Kir. Muus. Loorits Papers: Szövérffy to Loorits, 4.7.1954, p. 4. It must be said, however, that Szövérffy was not an impartial witness.
153 D/T S 15548B: 'Gearr-Thuar./1954–55', p. 5 and 'Gearr-Thuar./1955–56', p. 5.

of Caoimhín Ó Danachair from 1957 onwards are very often listed in Ó Duilearga's annual reports to the Government. In contrast, the publications of Seán Ó Súilleabháin for the same period, with the few exceptions noted above, do not come in for mention in these reports.

The question has to be asked whether Ó Duilearga actually refused permission to Ó Súilleabháin and Ó Danachair to utilise the Commission's collections in their research. In the early to mid-1960's, Ó Danachair told Alan Gailey 'quite categorically ... that he was not permitted by Delargy to publish any references to' the Commission's manuscripts, and Seán Ó Súilleabháin told him he 'was under similar restrictions.' Gailey also recalls that Ó Danachair once told him that Ó Duilearga 'believed that neither' of them, Ó Danachair or Ó Súilleabháin, 'was fit to publish academic material.'[154] That Ó Duilearga said something to this effect is corroborated by a letter of Joseph Szövérffy to Oskar Loorits. However, it would appear from Szövérffy's letter that, on this occasion at least, this may have been said in the heat of the moment and in the context of Ó Súilleabháin's and Ó Danachair's open personal criticism of him.[155]

It is very hard to get to the truth of the matter. Surely Ó Danachair and Ó Súilleabháin could have appealed to the Commission if they were being restricted in this way? There were people on the Commission whom they could have petitioned: people such as Eric Mac Fhinn, and Fionán Mac Coluim, who were critical of Ó Duilearga, not least on the question of publishing the Commission's collections. There is no evidence, however, that they ever did seek redress before the Commission, nor the Finance Sub-Committee. Why did they not do so? Did the failure of Åke Campbell's intervention in 1954/1955 convince them that the forces ranged against them were too great: that when it came to choosing between Ó Duilearga and his staff, those in authority would chose the Director of the Commission.

The evidence does not suggest that there was an actual ban as such on Ó Danachair and Ó Suilleabháin utilising the Commission's collections for the purpose of research and publication. This is not to say that Ó Duilearga may not on some particular occasion have sought to prevent one or both of these men from using the Commission's collections, either in a pique of anger or for a particular reason.[156] If, as I surmise, either Ó Súilleabháin or Ó Danachair, or both, were on some occasion or other refused permission to use the Commission's collections, this might have led to a situation where they refused to seek further permission. 'Once bitten, twice shy', the saying goes; but there seems to have been more than shyness involved. The word 'disdain' comes to mind. Neither Ó Súilleabháin nor Ó Danachair, it would appear, were going to give the Director the satisfaction of refusing them again, nor of seeing them ask, so they sought other ways to avoid having to ask permission. This could be done by utilising the Commission's collections, but by disguising this fact, or by writing articles and books for a popular audience where the detailed listing of sources would not be required. However, they

---

154 Personal communication from Alan Gailey, dated 23.3.2005.
155 Kir. Muus. Loorits Papers: letter dated 6.2.1955.
156 e.g. if he thought they would be better engaged working on something else.

did not always have to resort to such tactics, because for certain publications it was not necessary to ask permission, or else permission was a foregone conclusion. For instance, Ó Danachair published three articles in *Béaloideas* during the period 1955 to 1965 in which he utilised archival sources in an open manner.[157] These three articles deal with the results of questionnaire returns. It was in Ó Duilearga's interest, as much as it was in Ó Danachair's, that articles of this nature be published as it was hoped that by informing questionnaire correspondents of the rich body of information collected through their agency that they would be stimulated to continue their work, and that their numbers would be augmented. Ó Súilleabháin's contribution to Kurt Ranke's festschrift, which openly drew on the Commission's collections, also comes under this category.[158] Ó Duilearga could hardly have refused permission in this case, given the fact that Ó Súilleabháin at the time was part of a European project to catalogue *Sagen* in which Ranke had a leading role.

It would appear that when Ó Danachair and Ó Súilleabháin told Alan Gailey in the early 1960's that they were 'not permitted by Delargy to publish any references to' the Commission's manuscripts, they were somewhat simplifying the actual situation. Perhaps, because they resented the fact that the Finance Sub-Committee had given Ó Duilearga unduly restrictive powers over them in respect of access to sources and publication, it may, in time, have become a question of self-respect for both Ó Súilleabháin and Ó Danachair to defy him in whatever way they could on this issue. A bad situation may have been compounded by their belief that Ó Duilearga was abusing the powers given him by the Finance Sub-Committee, and that he had, in the circumstances, no moral right to restrict, in any way, what they published and what sources they used. If this approximates to the situation as experienced by Ó Súilleabháin and Ó Danachair, it, in effect, meant that, for all practical purposes, they were being refused permission to utilise the Commission's collections for research and publication purposes, for they would have had to humiliate themselves, in their eyes, if they were to fulfil the ruling of the Finance Sub-Committee that all publications utilising the Commission's collections should be presented to the Director for what in effect amounted to his imprimatur. They may on occasion have swallowed their pride; most of the time they would appear not to have.

Letting go the helm

There is no doubt that some of least of the grievances of Seán Ó Súilleabháin and Caoimhín Ó Danachair from the early to mid-1950's needed to be addressed, and that failure to do so at the time and later left a mark on the Commission, on both men, on the rest of the staff, and of course on Ó Duilearga. Things might have been different. There was a time when Ó Duilearga himself saw Ó Súilleabháin taking over from him. Writing

---

157 Ó Danachair 1957, 1963 and 1965.
158 Ó Súilleabháin 1968.

to von Sydow in late 1937 about Máire MacNeill's projected study trip to Sweden, he praised her abilities and said that she would make 'an excellent cataloguer', and along with Seán Ó Súilleabháin 'will be able to carry the Commission on without any assistance.' He added that he did not 'expect to be always with them' and that 'after a while', if he succeeded in making the Commission permanent, he would 'like to go back to [his] own work.'[159] The nature of the 'work' Ó Duilearga would like to have returned to is not so clear from this letter. I surmise that it involved, for the most part, field work and the editing of his own collections, rather than instructing students in folkloristics. Be that as it may, it shows that at an early stage in the life of the Commission, Ó Duilearga did not always envisage himself at the helm. When he wrote the above, he had no idea, of course, that the Commission was destined to remain in a state of semi-permanent limbo for more than three decades. It would be a long time before he could even consider stepping down. It is interesting to note, however, that almost two years before Åke Campbell's intervention in 1954, Ó Duilearga in a letter to Richard Dorson explained that his work as Director of the Commision had allowed him to give no more than 'an occasional lecture on folklore in University College', but added that he might yet 'retire from the rather distasteful administrative work of the Commission' and devote himself to research.[160] He was, however, never to do so, and he failed to complete a number of research projects he hoped to execute, particularly an edition of his extensive collections from County Clare. His efforts to publish his Clare collections over a period of some twenty years is a saga in itself, which cannot be told here, and was definitely hampered by his waning energies, by his life circumstances, and by an inability to unburden himself of certain duties by delegating them to others.

While Ó Duilearga's personality may have played a significant part in the dispute that arose with Seán Ó Súilleabháin and Caoimhín Ó Danachair over the direction of the Commission, his health was a crucial factor. In 1950, writing to Åke Campbell about an invitation he had received from Dag Strömbäck to give a series of lectures in Uppsala, he says that he had not 'got the old "drive"' and that he had not 'recovered fully' from his 'illness of two years' previously. He felt he would 'have to resign from many activities, and be careful about taking on extra responsibilities.'[161] As things turned out, not only did he go to lecture in Uppsala the following spring, he also lectured in Lund, Stockholm and Helsinki. In all, he spent three weeks away in Sweden and Finland and was quite exhausted on his return.[162] Moreover, a month or so prior to going to Scandinavia he had prepared and given five talks 'on the Third Programme of the BBC as well as prepared and given a public lecture'

---

159 LUB Saml. von Sydow: Ó Duilearga to von Sydow, dated 20.12.1937.
160 Lilly Lib. Dorson Papers: Ó Duilearga to Dorson, dated 9.6.1952. One notes the absence of any mention of teaching.
161 ULMA (TA) kapsel EIC: 53: Ó Duilearga to Campbell, dated 29.9.1950.
162 SKS Haavio Papers 12:58:15 and 12:58:20: Ó Duilearga to Haavio, letters dated 7.4.1951 and 17.5.1951.

at home.[163] One gets the impression that Ó Duilearga was taxing himself too much. Later that year he requested Seán Ó Súilleabháin to take over some of his duties. Ó Súilleabháin informed Campbell: 'Séamus has assigned me new work – looking after the field workers, etc., and I have far more to do than I had formerly.'[164] This would appear to have been a temporary arrangement, and was never formalised.

Although he undertook a good deal of foreign lecturing and travel in 1952 and again in 1953,[165] this may, in part, have been a type of escape rather than an indication of complete, or near complete, recovery. One could argue that Ó Duilearga probably never fully recovered his health after 1948. We have seen above how his health broke down in late 1953 and again in late 1954. Moreover, even though in August 1956 he reported to Åke Campbell that his health was fully restored (see above), he had a relapse again towards the end of the year and had to stay away from the office for some time. This relapse was partly brought on by difficulties he had with the printers of *Seanchas ón Oileán Tiar*, a collection of lore taken down by Robin Flower in the Great Blasket from Tomás Ó Criomhthain, which Ó Duilearga was editing. This particular relapse gave him a very bad fright, and although he recovered, he lived in dread of a recurrence.[166] In September 1957, he wrote to Stith Thompson of his resolve not to get another 'breakdown' as the doctor had warned him that the 'next time' would mean 'the end' for him.[167] As well as his own health, Ó Duilearga had his wife's health to contend with from the mid-1950's onward. A pillar of support for her husband as a younger woman, Maud Delargy as her health declined from the mid-1950's became a source of worry to him and in time sapped further his own diminishing reserves of energy.[168]

Whatever about Ó Duilearga's direction of the Commission being 'wavering' in the last decade or so of its operations, his energies were certainly waning, and this must have been a huge source of frustration for him. He really needed to delegate more responsibilities to his senior office staff, but even if he had wished to do so, given the tensions that existed at Head Office, that would have looked like capitulation. Releasing his grip on the Commission would in the long run have been in his own interests, but it was something which he found impossible to do. If he had confided more in his staff to begin with, some of them might have been more understanding of his situation, and differences of opinion as regards the direction of the Commission might have

163 SKS Haavio Papers 12:58:19: Ó Duilearga to Haavio, dated 25.3.1951.
164 ULMA Saml. Åke Campbell, subnr. 159: Ó Súilleabháin to Campbell, dated 17.12.1951.
165 D/T S 15548B: 'Gearr-Thuar./1952–53', p. [5], and 'Gearr-Thuar./1953–54', pp. 6–7.
166 Lilly Lib. Stith Thompson Papers: Ó Duilearga to Thompson, dated 18.2.1957.
167 Lilly Lib. Stith Thompson Papers: Ó Duilearga to Thompson, letter dated 14.9. 1957.
168 The scattered references in my sources tell little of Maud Delargy, who died on January 16th, 1965, but there is no doubt that she in various ways contributed to her husband's work and achievement: not just by keeping house and home for him, but by encouraging him to persist when he was often consumed with despair. The same could be said of Ó Duilearga's mother, Mary, who would appear from her son's correspondence to have been very supportive of his work.

been resolved amicably. Although Ó Súilleabháin and Ó Danachair were not lacking in sympathy for him initially, as Ó Duilearga was unwilling to deal with certain outstanding issues of policy they felt needed addressing, and, moreover, as he sought to keep control of the Commission by increasing his power over them, their sympathy naturally abated.

There is no doubt that Ó Duilearga felt extremely hurt by some of his staff 'turning against him', and that he failed to understand their seeming 'ingratitude' towards him. Without him there would have been no Commission, and now those he had brought on board in this great national and international enterprise were trying to sideline him, it appeared to him. When friends fall out, there is often little understanding of the other party, and this seems to have been the case in the Irish Folklore Commission. If Ó Duilearga's personality contributed to tensions in the Commission, the personalities of Seán Ó Súilleabháin and Caoimhín Ó Danachair, no doubt, also played a part in the eruption of tension to begin with and in its persistence. Both Ó Súilleabháin and Ó Danachair were exceptionally talented, in many respects more talented that Ó Duilearga. They were certainly more confident as scholars than he was. The fact that both men in the early 1950's had young families may also have made them more critical of Ó Duilearga's direction of the Commission than they might otherwise have been, as lack of job security and pension rights, as well as poor pay, would have been a constant worry for them. It is also possible that in the long term Máire MacNeill's departure from the Commission in 1949 had an adverse effect on relations in the Commission between Ó Duilearga and some of his staff. The Commission lost not only a very competent and versatile worker when she left its employment and went to America, Ó Duilearga lost a confidante, almost a family member. Her departure may have had the effect of further isolating Ó Duilearga from the Head Office staff. Although Ó Duilearga knew a great many people and had friends and acquaintances in very many countries as well as in Ireland, he was a lonely, isolated figure in very many ways. By the early 1950's four of his most important mentors and confidants were dead: Eoin Mac Néill died in 1945, Robin Flower in 1946, Osborn Bergin in 1950, and Carl Wilhelm von Sydow in 1952. In addition, his mother, whom he was strongly attached to, and who had lived with him under the same roof much of the time since the early 1920's, died in November 1951. Her death greatly affected him,[169] and along with his own weakening health most likely made him more aware that he himself was getting old, and added to his feelings of frustration, as so much yet remained undone. All the above factors may have contributed to the deterioration of relations with some of his staff.

In examining tensions in the Irish Folklore Commission between the Director and some of his staff, it should be remembered that although Ó Duilearga fell out with some members of his staff, he remained on harmonious terms with others, particularly with some (though not all) of his collectors. He may have been a difficult person, but he could also be a very pleasant person. For those who had to work with him, and under him, day in, day out

---

169 Lilly Lib. Stith Thompson Papers: Ó Duilearga to Thompson, dated 20.11.1951.

at Head Office, he may not have been an easy master, but there is no doubt he had a charm that reaped benefits for the Commission on trips to the field with informants, and with visitors he met in Ireland and on his foreign travels. This charm may, however, have worked against the interests of some of his staff, for combined with his style of leadership, and the patriarchal world of the time, it gave him a very high profile, both nationally and internationally, and took the attention away from his colleagues.

A lasting wound

In different circumstances, things might have turned out very differently. In his report to the Government for 1949–1950 Ó Duilearga says:

> Despite the advance that has been achieved during the course of the year, much else has to be done before it will be possible to say that the research and cultivation ('saothrú') and examination of the national tradition is being catered for satisfactorily. Large areas of the country remain unexplored and in respect of the Gaeltacht the extensive province of Connaught has been without a collector for many years. That has to be rectified without delay. The number of part-time collectors needs to be increased throughout the length and breadth of the country and to that end I need to find the opportunity and time and to reduce the office duties that I have had to look after for a long time. It is not possible to do everything. Whatever will be the outcome of it, I will have to pay special attention henceforth to the collection of folklore in the countryside.[170]

When he wrote the above, the Commission had been operating for over a year on a substantially increased grant, and was settling down in its new headquarters at 82 St. Stephen's Green. His own health was much improved, after the breakdown of the previous year. He was hopeful not just for the future of the Commission, but for his own future and health. Unfortunately, things did not turn out as he hoped, and as they might have.

This war between friends was a tragedy for all concerned, long affected the work of the Commission, and continues to have implications for Irish folkloristics even when all the protagonists are dead. While it is easy to apportion blame, and to point the finger at the person who wielded most power, in order to understand this dispute in all its complexities, it is necessary to realise that in disputes people are not always motivated, all of the time, by the loftiest of ideals. Space does not allow me to subject to scrutiny all the accusations Ó Súilleabháin made against Ó Duilearga in autumn 1969 (see Chapter III/6). Some of them stand without qualification, but some contain an element of exaggeration or generalisation. It must be remembered, however, that this outburst of Ó Súilleabháin's derived from years of pent-up frustration with his Director. He may have overstated his case somewhat,

---

170 D/T S 15548B: 'Gearr-Thuar./1949–50', p. [6].

but it should not have been necessary for him to do so. There were people on the Irish Folklore Commission who were aware that all was not right with the direction of the Commission, and that senior members of staff were not only not being consulted on policy but had serious grievances that were not being addressed. Åke Campbell's intervention failed in 1954/1955. Close associates of Ó Duilearga's such as Michael Tierney and Liam Price on the Finance Sub-Committee should have intervened, not on behalf of the staff of the Commission alone but also on behalf of Ó Duilearga. They did him no favour, in the long run, by deferring to his sensitivities, and protecting him. The Commission's staff as well as its Director all suffered from their failure, and they (i.e. Tierney and Price) also share the blame for what befell the Commission as a result of this dispute along with the blame, such as it may be, that accrues to the various protagonists.

Honorary doctorates

Given Ó Duilearga's high profile, and the great achievements of the Commission under his direction, it was natural that, in time, some university or other would award him an honorary degree. The first such degree did not come his way until September 1953 when St. Francis Xavier University, Antigonish, Nova Scotia awarded him a D. Litt. This honorary doctorate was only the first of many. Even if no differences of opinion had arisen between Ó Duilearga and members of his staff on other fronts, it is most likely that the awarding of so many honorary doctorates to him would in time have given rise to resentment. As it was, however, these honorary degrees seem to have exacerbated tensions between him and some of his staff. The Nova Scotia doctorate was followed in 1955 by ones from the University of Wales, the University of Dublin in 1957, and the Queen's University, Belfast in 1959. In July 1961, Ó Duilearga was awarded an honorary doctorate by the University of Edinburgh. This was followed in October of the same year by another honorary doctorate form the University of Iceland. He was to get yet another honorary doctorate from the University of Uppsala in 1964, and five years later, in July 1969, a D. Litt. from the National University of Ireland. That made eight honorary doctorates, in addition to numerous other honours awarded him by learned institutions and foreign Governments.

It is not surprising that all this recognition caused resentment among certain of his staff, especially as his colleagues were not to be recipients of similar honours. Letters Ó Duilearga wrote to Ciarán Bairéad in June and July 1961, before and after his trip to Edinburgh to receive an honorary D. Litt., reveal that the awarding of this degree would appear to have led to a display of undisguised displeasure at Head Office. Ó Duilearga insisted to Ciarán Bairéad that the honour was for the Commission and not for himself.[1] And so, in a sense, it was, but not all his colleagues saw it that way. No university in Ireland or abroad saw fit to award Seán Ó Súilleabháin or Caoimhín Ó Danachair an honorary doctorate during Ó Duilearga's time as Director of the Commission. In 1973, after Ó Duilearga's retirement, Caoimhín Ó Danachair submitted his publications to a panel of examiners convened for the purpose by the National University of Ireland and on the basis of this assessment was awarded a D. Litt. Máire MacNeill had been awarded a similar degree by the National University of Ireland under the same system in 1964 for her monumental work *The Festival of Lughnasa*. Some ten years later she was one of those who assessed Ó Danachair's publications for the National University of Ireland.[2] In 1976, Seán Ó Súilleabháin, at the age of seventy three, was awarded a D. Litt. (honoris causa) by the National University of Ireland after a lifetime of selfless devotion to Irish folklore and scholarship.

---

1   UCG Hard. Lib. Arch. Bairéad Collection, G/594 (1) and G3/590(2): Ó Duilearga
     to Bairéad, letters dated 22.3.1961 and 13.7.1961.
2   Maureen Murphy 2004, pp. 13 and 17.

It is remarkable that no Irish or foreign university honoured either Seán Ó Súilleabháin or Caoimhín Ó Danachair during the lifetime of the Commission. One might ask, however, even if they were being passed over for honorary degrees, why neither of them submitted their publications for assessment by the National University of Ireland before Ó Duilearga's retirement, say in the 1960's. The most likely reason is that their ongoing dispute with the Director of the Commission prevented them from doing so, as he most certainly would have been one of the examiners. This dispute, it would appear, also prevented both these scholars from undertaking a doctorate under Ó Duilearga. In the last year of his life Åke Campbell tried to arrange for Caoimhín Ó Danacahir to do a doctorate at the University of Uppsala, with his monograph on Irish House Types to be presented as a thesis. Ó Danachair was very enthusiastic about the idea, but Campbell's death in autumn 1957 deprived him of this opportunity. After his death Åsa Nyman wrote to Ó Danachair telling him that Campbell 'was not able to answer your last letter, but he talked about you the last days. He was very anxious for you but hoped that Dag Strömbäck could do something for you, if you still want to fulfil your plans of a doctor degree in Uppsala.'[3] For whatever reason, Ó Danachair does not appear to have pursued the matter further. As we have seen above, the fact that Ó Danachair did not have a doctorate greatly reduced his chances of succeeding Ó Duilearga in the Chair of Irish Folklore on the latter's retirement.

---

3   ULMA (TA) kapsel B1C: 44: Nyman to Ó Danachair, dated 18.10.1957.

VII
An Assessment of Aspects of the Commission's Work

1. Head Office and the field

Processing and cataloguing the material at Head Office

Given the sheer bulk of the material, both text and context, coming in to Head Office, and the lack of adequate staff to handle it, the processing of this material, of necessity, could not be dealt with as originally intended. It was initially envisaged that the material collected in the field would be catalogued reasonably soon after it was forwarded to Head Office. Lack of staff, however, often prevented this from happening. This not only delayed the cataloguing of the material as such, it also meant that various gaps in the material did not become apparent. Gaps occurred not only in respect of the content of tradition, but in respect of context as well. For instance, it seems unlikely that the diaries of the collectors were systematically scrutinised to see how well they supplied context.

We have seen above in Chapter IV/1 how Ó Duilearga had to accept far fewer office staff than originally, in May 1933, he had insisted to de Valera was required if the accumulation of 'a chaotic mass of material of overwhelming proportions and of no scientific value' was to be avoided.[1] Obviously, Ó Duilearga was overstating his case, but in accepting far fewer than the minimum office staff he initially sought, it is hard not to believe that he did not abandon his principles somewhat. In any event, collecting was never scaled down to keep pace with the processing and cataloguing of the material. Of course, the argument went: Collect today, catalogue tomorrow! Unfortunately, tomorrow was often too late. Collecting driven by a collecting priority, by the desire to amass, to harvest, to save for posterity as much as possible, rather than research-driven collecting, always runs this risk. Research-driven collecting could not have succeeded in assembling such a large archive in such a short space of time, but should the amassing of as large an archive as possible have been the priority, it would appear, to quite an extent, to have been?

As we have seen above, by the time the Irish Folklore Commission was disbanded in 1970, a very small office staff had succeeded in compiling a

---

1   D/T S 9244: 'Collection of Oral Tradition of Ireland', p. 14.

more or less complete index of informants, collectors, and localities, but the subject/content index was only about a quarter complete, although a rough catalogue (known as the 'interim-catalogue') existed for most of the material. This was no small achievement, but the lack of a complete index of the subject matter of the Commission's manuscripts (not to mention their sound recordings) was definitely a problem, and one the Commission bequeathed to its successor, the Department of Irish Folklore.[2]

Seán Ó Súilleabháin expressed the hope in the late 1960's that when the indexing of the subject matter of these manuscripts would be completed, 'there will not be too many lacunae exposed.' As he saw it, such lacunae would soon be difficult to fill: 'Ireland, like most other countries, is changing rapidly; the old life is dying away, the elderly informants are passing on, and information which would now be available, if sought, will not be on tap in years to come.'[3] This statement reads as if life in Ireland had stood still since the 1930's and 1940's. For surely if there were lacunae in the Commission's collections, many would date from an earlier period and those who could fill in these gaps were in many cases long dead. Ó Súilleabháin may have hoped that there would not be too many lacunae in the collections, but given the speed with which the material was collected and came in to Head Office, and the lack of staff to process it properly, there must, of course, have been many lacunae even from those areas most intensively covered by the Commission's full-time collectors, not to mention those other large lacunae, not only of a geographic nature (representing areas of the country not collected from or only very sparsely covered), but also lacunae in respect of gender, class, and subject matter.

Initially, Ó Duilearga did not envisage the Commission's full-time collectors transcribing material recorded by means of the Ediphone into copybooks as such. Rather, he proposed: 'Looseleaf pages will be used and when each dozen [Ediphone] records is transcribed the text corresponding will be sent, together with the records to the headquarters of the Commission, where the transcription will be checked with the records, and these filed, according to the nature of the material, in envelopes (the outside of which will show an adequate description of the contents) and will be filed away in steel, fire-resisting cabinets.[4] A similar system, of filing material in envelopes, was in use in the folklore archives in Uppsala and in Lund.[5] However, as things turned out, this plan was abandoned and collectors instead transcribed their material into copybooks which were on completion forwarded along with the corresponding Ediphone cylinders to Dublin, where transcriptions were checked and the copybooks paginated and bound together in volumes

2   More than thirty years after the Commission was transferred to UCD the subject index is nowhere near completion. The collections have, moreover, grown significantly since the early 1970's and this has made the task of cataloguing all the more difficult.
3   Ó Súilleabháin 1970, p. 120.
4   ED CO 3/15/9(495/II): 'Irish Folklore Commission. Memorandum 10.1.1935', p. [7].
5   When Ó Duilearga visited the Finnish Literature Society in the summer of 1928, much of their folklore collections would also have been filed away in envelopes. However, after 1935 or thereabouts it became the custom to bind the production of individual collectors. Laaksonen and Saarinen 2004, pp. 7–8.

of some 500 pages each. The original plan, if implemented, might have made subsequent retrieval of material easier, but it would most likely have made too great demands on the small staff at Head Office to process (and roughly catalogue) the material in this way.

The working methods of collectors

The type of systematised collecting the Irish Folklore Commission initiated in 1935 on a large scale was very streamlined. There is no doubt that the methods employed by the Commission's collectors, especially during the first decade or two of its operations, bear comparison with methods employed by collectors elsewhere; indeed in certain respects these methods were certainly in advance of methods employed in many other countries at the time. Although the collectors received a minimum of training, the choice of native speakers of Irish, many of them versed in oral tradition since childhood, greatly facilitated the work, and reduced the amount of training necessary to give them for the job in hand. The use of Ediphone recording machines, and the emphasis on verbatim transcriptions, as well as the initial checking of transcriptions at Head Office, greatly increased the quality of the collecting.[6] However, it should be remembered that not all transcriptions were verbatim. Collectors used the Ediphone to record folktales and certain other genres, but for the recording of lore they resorted to pen and paper, often only jotting down rough notes on the spot, and reconstructing a text later, on returning to their home or lodgings. Jim Delaney did not have the use of an Ediphone when he began collecting. Speaking of this method of note-taking and writing up later, Delaney says that he only managed to get 'the cream' of what the speaker said in this way. He adds that if he had a tape recorder he might have got two tapes from a session, but the most he ever got was some twelve to fourteen pages of 'closely written text.'[7] Michael J. Murphy, on the other hand, when collecting in Rathlin Island without the use of an Ediphone in the mid-1950's would write down what narrators told him 'on the spot' with the aid of 'a system of shorthand' he had learned. He would subsequently type up this material.[8] There is no doubt that a certain amount of data was lost when collectors were reconstructing interviews from rough field notes. In this respect it is worth noting Guy Beiner's astute observation:

> Even though the *Handbook* instructs collectors to "make no 'corrections' or changes" to oral accounts, the clear and confident handwriting in

---

6 Later on, however, when this kind of supervision ceased, there is no doubt that words and passages were sometimes inadvertently omitted (often leaving no semantic trace) during transcription from Ediphone cylinder or open-reel tapes, if the collector had not a chance to thoroughly check his transcription from start to finish. In some cases such omissions may be of little import, but in other cases they may change or distort the message of the text. My own experience of transcribing texts and checking the transcritions of others supports this observation.

7 RTÉSA B1204: 'Folkland', Séamas Ó Catháin talking to Jim Delaney (1983).

8 Murphy 1980, p. 16.

most IFC manuscripts (which in itself follows an instruction to "write as neatly and legibly as possible") suggests that the interviews were indeed carefully transcribed. There is the possibility that this process may have entailed subtle, perhaps unconscious, mechanisms of editing and even censorship, as the collectors, who were inevitably affected by the highly charged political and social climate of the newly independent Irish state, were aware that they were contributing to a national project.[9]

What Beiner has to say above, in my estimation, concerns mainly the writing of clean copies of interviews dictated in the field or the reconstruction of interviews from rough notes. I have come across little evidence that transcriptions from Ediphone or electronic recordings were rewritten in clean copy. Apart from any other considerations, collectors would normally not have had time to rewrite their transcriptions in this manner [10] It should be pointed out, however, with regard to the possible 'editing' and 'censorship' of interviews by collectors, that some informants were also aware they were participating in a great national project and that this may have had an effect on what they told collectors and even induced them to censor themselves at times. Moreover, in this regard, it is interesting to note Seosamh Ó Dálaigh's comments above on informants censoring material that had already been collected from them (see Chapter IV/1 above).

The keeping of a regular diary by the full-time collectors also meant that a great deal of contextual information was recorded about informants and in respect of the collecting itself. In addition, the copious correspondence between Head Office and the collectors, both full-time and part-time, which has been preserved, adds greatly to its value as a collection, and will be a mine of information for future researchers. In general, it would appear that there was less supervision of full-time collectors in respect of their diaries than was the case with their texts/transcriptions (which were systematically checked, initially at least). The great variety of style found in the collectors' diaries is, to some extent, only to be expected when one considers that each of them was, of course, an individual. However, some collectors were no doubt more appreciative of the value of this sort of contextual information. The fact that collectors were, it would appear, given more free rein in writing their diaries than in many other matters forces us to ask the question: why was this so? Was it, so some extent, a consequence of the lack of sufficient staff at Head Office to check the diaries the collectors were sending in? Was it partly due to far more emphasis being given to text than to context? Or

---

9   Beiner 2007, p. 42.
10   This does not mean that transcribing from Ediphone cylinders and open-reel tapes never involved editing. Despite instructions to write down verbatim what informants said, in the early decades of the Commission, collectors did not always include in transcriptions their own questions or interjections. Moreover, in an age before the development of discourse analysis and ethnopoetics, the importance of including in transcriptions all false starts, hesitations and other interruptions to the flow of speech was not generally understood. As a result many of the transcriptions produced by the Commission's full-time collectors may be somewhat conflated and appear more coherent and flowing than they were in actual delivery.

was there some question of principle behind it? Perhaps it was felt that diary keeping was an individual matter, requiring differences of style and method to be catered for. Many factors may have been involved. We might also ask what models, if any, collectors were given. How much detail was actually required of them? In time, collectors found their own style – the result being more satisfactory in some cases than in others. In assessing such diaries, it is well to keep in mind what Edward D. Ives says on this matter:

> Of all the tasks required of a good fieldworker, I find that keeping a journal is the toughest. I come home from an interview, and either I am tired or I must get immediately to other things or–most likely–both; consequently, the journal doesn't get written. I have good journals for less than half of my fieldwork over the past thirty five years, and I have had frequent occasion to regret that, because all too often the data I need when writing is just the sort of thing I would have put in my journal![11]

Less control over part-time collectors

While the Commission set in place a programme for the systematic recording of folklore by full-time collectors supervised from Head Office, it also depended, to quite an extent, on part-time collectors, over whom they had far less control. While part-time collectors might be advised by Head Office as to what sort of material they should collect, often being provided with lists of questions, the quality of their work could not be regulated to the same extent. Nevertheless, as they were paid piecemeal, if their work was found to be below the quality required by the Commission, they could be requested to effect certain changes in their working methods, or future collecting by them could be discouraged. In general, part-time collectors provided much less contextual information for the material they forwarded to the Commission than was the case with full-time collectors. Moreover, most part-time collectors did not keep a diary, and were not usually required or requested to do so. The fact that part-time collectors were not required to keep a regular diary, as a matter of course, was most likely done for practical considerations, as keeping a diary would have involved much extra work and would have been hard to justify unless the Commission were able to compensate them financially for this work. The Commission probably did not have the resources to do this, and even if it had, it might have been difficult to decide on a fair system of remunerating part-time collectors for such a task, as payment simply on the basis of the amount of pages completed would not have been all that satisfactory, given the fact that the quality of such work would, of necessity, have varied a good deal. Nevertheless, the fact that much less contextual information is available for material collected by part-time collectors (amounting to approximately 39% of the Commission's

11   Ives 1995, pp. 37–38.

Main Collection) has to be taken into account when assessing the quality of the Commission's collections as a whole.[12] It should be stressed, however, that the work of part-time collectors could be of very high quality, and that but for such collectors many areas of the country would not be represented in the Archive, apart from the Schools Collection. Indeed, some of the most fascinating gems to be found in the Commission's Archive were collected by part-time collectors.

In the main, however, there was much more likelihood of the work of part-time collectors falling below certain standards than was the case with the work of full-time collectors. This is not to say that the work of full-time collectors never leaves anything to be desired, nor that full-time collectors never took shortcuts. Given the pressures they at times worked under, it would be surprising if no shortcomings were to be found in their work. A thorough examination of each full-time collector would be necessary before final judgement can be passed on how effectively they carried out their work within the parameters set for them. Moreover, in any future assessment of the full-time collectors of the Commission, in particular, the justification for some of these parameters also needs to be examined.

Not only was it easier to keep tabs on full-time collectors than on part-time collectors, there was often less need to do so as their initial period of training and supervision gave the former an advantage over the latter. It has to be said, however, that the Commission's part-time collectors are not a homogenous group. Some collected a great deal of material and in so doing accumulated much experience and honed their collecting skills, while others collected very little. It should also be noted that some full-time collectors after leaving the employment of the Commission continued to collect part-time for it, their experience as full-time collectors standing them in good stead. In assessing the quality of the material collected by part-time collectors, it is also necessary to take into account when they collected for the Commission. In the first few years of the Commission a great deal of people collected part-time for it. For instance, in its first year of operation (1935–1936), 127 people collected part-time, contributing 17,819 pages of folklore. The following year (1936–1937) 242 people contributed part-time to the Commission's collections, adding 31,538 pages to its Main Collection. The following year again (1937–1938) the number of part-time collectors as such was only fractionally higher than the previous year, at approximately 250, but the number of pages collected by them had risen to 42,608. The quality of some of this material was, however, less than satisfactory, and the Commission decided to weed out the weakest collectors, so that in 1938–1939 part-time collectors contributed only 29,168 pages to the collection. This policy seems to have continued but the even greater drop in the amount produced by part-time collectors for 1939–1940, namely 13,697 pages, was also influenced by cutbacks due

---

12   In addition, the production of questionnaire correspondents and donors amount to approx. 6% and 1.5% of the Main Collection, respectively. It should also be remembered that the 50,000 pages (c. 7% of total) inherited from the Irish Folklore Institute was collected by part-time collectors and donors. See Appendix 5.

to the onset of war in Europe.[13] Never again would the amount collected by the Commission's part-time collectors exceed the figure of 13,697 pages for 1939–1940. In the early years the Commission was able to weed out part-time collectors whose work was below standard when the amount of material coming in from both full-time and part-time collectors was very great. This makes it all the more perplexing that at a later stage, approximately the mid-1950's to the mid-1960's, when the amount of material coming in to the Commission, of whatever provenance, had dwindled to a fraction of what it had been in the early days, that the shortcomings of certain part-time collectors went undetected or were ignored, so that they continued to collect material, and receive reward for it, long after the deficiencies of their work should have become apparent.[14] One explanation for this may be the fact that in the latter half of the 1950's there was a huge drop in the number of people collecting part-time for the Commission: twenty two in 1956–1957, and eight in 1957–1958. In the last decade or so of the Commission the numbers of part-time collectors were to dwindle even further, hovering between six and two. Given this situation, it is perhaps not surprising that material sent in by part-time collectors that fell below a certain standard was tolerated more than it would have been earlier. The Commission was no longer in a position to pick and choose.[15]

The exact measure of control the Commission exercised over part-time collectors during its heyday is not clear. When the correspondence maintained between part-time collectors and Head Office is made freely available, it should cast light on this matter.[16] Obviously, as I have already stated there was less control over them than there was over full-time collectors, but there may also have been less desire to control them. To have sought to control them more would have meant stretching the resources of the Commission and its Director to breaking point, as more control, of necessity, would have meant more supervision both in the field and at Head Office. Without an increase in office staff this could not have been achieved unless corners were cut elsewhere.

Suitability of full-time collectors for job

If not all part-time collectors were found satisfactory, what was the case with full-time collectors? In respect of the full-time collectors, Bríd Mahon tells us

13 See D/T S 15548A: Gearr-Thuarascálacha ('Annual Reports') for the years 1935–36, 1936–37, 1937–38, 1938-39' pp. [2], [3], [4], [4] and 5 respectively.

14 For more on one such rogue part-time collector, see Briody 1997. See also Almqvist 1990, pp. 103 ff.

15 The fact that Seán Ó Súilleabháin was busily engaged in compiling a catalogue of Märchen from January 1957 until the early 1960's, may also have contributed to the production of certain part-time collectors not been submitted to sufficient scrutiny.

16 In the late 1940's, Ó Duilearga stressed the need for extra assistance so that he himself could devote more of his time and energies to supervising part-time collectors, in particular, and to expanding the number of such collectors. D/T S 15548B: 'Gearr-Thuar./1945–50', p. [6].

that Ó Duilearga prided himself on his ability to chose the right man for the job. This is no doubt true, to a large extent, but this was not always the case. At times there was a real difficulty in getting suitable collectors, and maybe if in particular cases he had had more choice, Ó Duilearga might not have chosen certain individuals. During the first two decades of the Commission a number of the full-time collectors were dismissed when their work was found to be unsatisfactory.[17] Moreover, it took time for full-time collectors to learn their trade, and Ó Duilearga was a hard taskmaster. We have seen above how Tadhg Ó Murchadha's work was on one occasion found not to be satisfactory and that he was reprimanded. Other collectors also came in for adverse comment from Head Office and were cautioned. Keeping collectors on their toes seems to have been a feature of the early years of the Commission, rather than the later period.

In any event, it was not just a question of choosing the right man for the job. Conditions of work, at least in the first decade or so, were such that only the very dedicated or desperate, in some cases, would opt for such a job. But dedication, even desperation, was not enough. Without a doubt, Liam Mac Coisdeala was as good and dedicated a full-time collector as any employed by the Commission. He spent four years with the Commission, retiring in 1939 to resume his teaching post. The Commission probably never recovered from his departure, but what could they offer him to make him stay or come back? One has therefore to ask whether the job was right for the man? In Mac Coisdeala's case, it would appear not to have been. Yet despite, or perhaps because of, his short sojourn with the Commission, I think we are right to consider him one of the great collectors.

Many stayed longer than Liam Mac Coisdeala in the job, indeed some for all, or a large part, of their working lives. Admittedly, conditions got better for collectors in later years, but few of the young men who started out as full-time collectors with the Commission in the mid to late 1930s could have had any idea of what lay ahead. Moreover, a job that can suit one man at a particular stage of his life, might not suit him in changed circumstances. For some it was an opportunity of a job when jobs were scarce and hard to come by. For others, who had secure employment as teachers, or prospects of teaching posts, taking up employment with the Commission amounted to a sacrifice, as they had to make a decision to forfeit their pension rights, no mean decision to have to make at the time. Above all, the work of full-time collectors, in the early years, was best suited to young men, and it is no coincidence that most of those employed were in their twenties on commencing work, many in their early twenties.

Those who collected full-time for the Commission for many years obviously developed on the job in ways that those who spent only a short time with the Commission perhaps did not. This was not always the case, however, and as I have said above, in relation to Liam Mac Coisdeala, a short period of service with the Commission did not necessarily mean a less

17 It would not be appropriate to name those dismissed here until such time as an assessment of their work shows if dismissal was indeed justified or not.

proficient collector.[18] Indeed, it was as likely, given human nature, that some full-time collectors would go to seed as continue to develop over a long period of service. Moreover, it must be remembered that opportunities for full-time collectors to develop in certain ways in the Commission were few.

Limited opportunities for collectors to develop

The type of systematised collecting the Irish Folklore Commission initiated in 1935, outlined above, was in certain respects fine in theory and as a temporary measure, but in practice and in the long term, it limited the collectors' scope for development as folklorists. Once collectors forwarded material to Dublin, they, for the most part, never saw it again, unless they were called to Head Office with the specific purpose of filling in lacunae in their manuscripts or annotating them with contextual information of various kinds. Moreover, in respect of the diary notebooks the full-time collectors wrote, once they had sent off such a notebook, they most likely never saw it again. The collectors therefore produced texts and contextual documentation for others to use. It was not felt, however, that they would have had any further use for their transcriptions and diary notebooks in their roles as collectors. As Seán Ó Súilleabháin told the Midcentury International Folklore Conference in 1950: 'After the material once (sic) comes to Dublin, the collector has no particular control over or interest in the material.'[19] However, whether a collector was interested in the material or not subsequent to his collecting it, he had limited opportunities of accessing it. Of course, full-time collectors did keep other, rougher records, which remained in their possession for longer periods, perhaps even for ever in some cases. For example, they had notebooks in which they recorded the names of informants, as well as short descriptions of various items of their repertoires. These served as aides-memoire, but could not compensate for them not having ready assess to their diaries and transcriptions. One collector, however, Michael J. Murphy, was not affected by this. He typed up his transcriptions and diaries and kept a carbon copy for himself. Not surprisingly, perhaps, he is the only full-time collector to have written a book about his collecting, based on his diaries.[20]

I am not suggesting that full-time collectors should not have forwarded their transcriptions and diaries to Head Office in Dublin. Obviously, given the purpose of the work, they had to. But the fact that full-time collectors were severed from their collections and had few opportunities to consult them definitely stunted, or at least impeded, their development as folklorists. If they had been able to use Dublin as a home-base, or at least been given the opportunity of coming to Dublin for some months each year, or every alternate year, to work for a period at Head Office, they might have developed quite differently. In the early years of the Commission, when there was a pressing

18   As noted in Chapter IV/1, however, Mac Coisdeala had previous experience working part-time for the Irish Folklore Institute.
19   Stith Thompson 1976 [1953], p. 16.
20   M. J. Murphy 1974.

need to collect, this would not have been a practical policy, but as the years dragged on, some thought might have been given to utilising collectors differently.[21] As it was, the role and modus operandi of the collectors never seems to have been reviewed to any significant extent.

Moreover, when material from the Archives was published in *Béaloideas*, credit was naturally given to the collector involved, but rarely if ever was their work referred to as such, nor contextual information about their collecting given, such as extracts from their diaries. This in effect, though not intentional, gave collectors a lower profile than they deserved in making them appear mere 'hewers of wood and drawers of water'. Two collectors, Tadhg Ó Murchadha and Liam Mac Coisdeala were to contribute articles about their collecting work to *Béaloideas*, but far more could have been done in this respect. Other collectors may well have been asked to contribute accounts of this nature, but no other accounts of collecting by any collector appeared in *Béaloideas*. Seán Ó hEochaidh stands out among the full-time collectors, not just in respect of his quite extensive published production, but also because he would appear to have been encouraged by Ó Duilearga in his publication and research.[22]

'If you were appointed a collector, you remained a collector!'

It might happen that two collectors were working in the same area for a time, but in such cases one of them was most likely a part-time collector. Full-time collectors usually worked in isolation from each other. In the early years, at least, they had regular contact with Head Office through visits from Séamus Ó Duilearga, and occasionally from the Commission's Archivist, Seán Ó Súilleabháin, or when they were called to Dublin from time to time for consultation. However, they rarely, if ever, had opportunities to meet each other. Seosamh Ó Dálaigh feels that full-time collectors should have had an opportunity to meet in order to compare and contrast the various problems they encountered. He says of the collectors:

> We hardly ever met each other. We were strangers to each other. Perhaps we met two or three times together while I was collecting. The collectors

---

21 On one occasion in the late 1950's it was decided to transfer the full-time collector Jim Delaney for a period to work at Head Office as a temporary measure to help with cataloguing, but as things turned out it never materialised. ED FL 2: 'CBÉ. Miont. 89ú Cruinniú, 2.7.1957', par. 670 and 'CBÉ. Miont. 90ú Cruinniú, 4.10.1957', p. 2.

22 In late 1954, Ó hEochaidh gave a talk on Radio Éireann in the prestigious Thomas Davis series of lectures. See D/T S 15548B: 'Gearr-Thuars./1954–55', p. 5. Moreover, in early 1957, he recorded at Head Office an account of his collecting work, filling 30 gramophone discs. ED FL 2: 'CBÉ. Miont. 88ú Cruinniú, 19.3.1957', 4. I am not aware of any other collector who was recorded from in this manner. Between 1965 and 1969 Ó hEochaidh also gave occasional lectures in the Queen's University, Belfast (Ní Dhíoraí 1985, p. xxiii). This was done on the invitation of Prof. Heinrich Wagner, and certainly with the acquiesence of Ó Duilearga. Exceptionally good relations between Ó Duilearga and Ó hEochaidh, as well as the latter's innate talent for research, may have been contributory factors in his being favoured in this way.

should have had contact so that they would see and understand the problems that they all had in the various regions.[23]

Ó Dálaigh recalls meeting Proinnsias de Búrca for the first time at Ó Duilearga's funeral. This, in his opinion, was ridiculous.[24] Liam Mac Meanman, who worked for the Commission for only two years, also remembered that he had no contact with either full-time or part-time collectors, although he does not give any opinion, adverse or otherwise, on the matter.[25] Liam Mac Coisdeala also states, though not as a criticism, that full-time collectors never met each other, adding that they were in any event few in number and worked quite far from each other.

Not all collectors felt a need to meet other collectors. For example, not only did Mac Coisdeala not have contact with other collectors, he does not appear to have seen this as a disadvantage. He seems to have been quite satisfied with his regular contact with Séamus Ó Duilearga.[26] Such contact was, of course, important, but Seosamh Ó Dálaigh's criticism, in my view, is still valid. Collectors might, of course, meet each other by chance, especially part-time collectors who were working in the same general area. For instance, in the late 1930's two cousins, Aodh Ó Duibheannaigh and Aodh Ó Domhnaill were employed as part-time collectors in Rann na Feirste, Co. Donegal – sometimes even collecting from the same person.[27] Full-time collectors may also occasionally have met fortuitously at Head Office in Dublin.

Not only did full-time collectors rarely, if ever, meet each other, they had few prospects, and few, if any, possibilities of advancing in their careers. As the Commission was only meant to run for five years, initially this was not a problem as such, except perhaps for National School teachers who had forfeited their pensions in joining the Irish Folklore Commission. Even though Ó Duilearga from the very beginning had hopes of some sort of a more permanent organisation for the Commission within or outside of UCD, nobody in 1935 could have envisaged that the Commission as then constituted would continue for many decades. But as the years went by the question of career prospects for collectors became an issue. Seosamh Ó Dálaigh, who stayed fifteen years with the Commission says:

---

23   Tyers 1999, p. 90.
24   UCCRNG Tyers/Ó Dálaigh, tapescript 10, p. 3. Ó Dálaigh also says that if he had a say in how collecting should be done, he would send a number of collectors collecting together, as he feels they could learn from each other. Ibid. p. 3 (trans.). With regard to Ó Dálaigh's not meeting de Búrca during his time with the Commission, while remarkable, it can partly be explained by the fact that while de Búrca was in the employment of the Commission during the first eight years or so of Ó Dálaigh's term as full-time collector, for the rest of Ó Dálaigh's time with the Commission (1944–1951), de Búrca was not a full-time collector, having been laid off in 1944. The Second World War would also have greatly reduced the chances of both collectors meeting each other by chance or by design, at Head Office in Dublin, as travel was greatly restricted due to the scarcity of petrol.
25   UCCFA Liam Mac Meanman Questionnaire, questions 8 and 9.
26   UCCFA Liam Mac Coisdeala Questionnaire, questions 8 and 9.
27   MacLennan 1997, pp. 14–15.

Séamus Ó Duilearga, the Director, said that he did not know exactly how this work would end, and we were not permanent of course, we were just full-time, but it was not a permanent post, and there was no pension attached to it. But it seems to me, at any rate, if you were a collector, if you were appointed a collector, you remained a collector, and Seán Ó hEochaidh is proof of that, who is retired now a year or two. He spent forty seven years collecting.[28]

Is Ó Dálaigh correct in asserting that collectors were fated to remain collectors: that there was no possibility for them to advance/develop beyond their station? In this connection, it is necessary to say that it is unlikely that Ó Duilearga ever saw the collectors developing into anything other than collectors. In the late 1950's when suggestions were made to transfer some of the collectors to Head Office for the purpose of editing texts, he was not enamoured of the idea.[29] Ó Duilearga had recruited the collectors for a particular task. If collecting had stopped at a certain stage, or been brought to a halt, he might well have sought to employ some of the collectors in other capacities. But the collecting never stopped, nor did it radically change. Consequently, from his point of view, there was no need to envisage any other role for the collectors other than what he had originally prescribed for them. As regards giving the collectors opportunities to deepen their knowledge of folkloristics, it should also be remembered that Ó Duilearga began collecting before acquainting himself, to any significant extent, with the scientific study of folklore. Moreover, his eagerness to deepen his knowledge of the science of folkloristics marked him out, to quite an extent, from other active members of the Folklore of Ireland Society. He may therefore have felt that it was up to collectors to develop as folklorists as best they could within the constraints of their workload.

Although collectors learned a great deal about collecting and about oral tradition from work experience, if they were to advance beyond their station they would have required more education in folkloristics. It has to be remembered that while a number of the collectors had experience of collecting folklore before commencing work with the Commission, none of them had any grounding in folkloristics. The same pertained for Seán Ó Súilleabháin, who had no training in folkloristics before he went to Sweden for three months in spring 1935. However, while both Máire MacNeill and later Caoimhín Ó Danachair of the Head Office staff, in addition to Ó Súilleabháin, were given an opportunity to get further training in Sweden, similar opportunities were never afforded any of the collectors.[30] In this connection, it has to be noted that Calum MacLean, formerly a full-time collector with the Commission, after taking up employment with the School of Scottish Studies in the early 1950's was sent to study in Sweden for a year. One might ask why the Commission's collectors were never afforded a similar opportunity.

28   UCCRNG Tyers/Ó Dálaigh, tapescript 2, p. 5 (trans.).
29   See ED FL 4: 'CBÉ. Miont. 94ú Cruinniú, 26.6.1958', par. 698.
30   As noted in Chapter V/2, Máire MacNeill financed her own trip to Sweden.

However, the case of Caoimhín Ó Danachair might appear to belie Ó Dálaigh's above claim that once appointed a collector one remained a collector. Ó Danachair was originally appointed full-time collector in 1939, to work mainly in Co. Limerick, but spent most of the War years with the Irish Army. On his resumption of work with the Commission after the War his post came to be designated as that of ethnologist and he was based at Head Office – his remit being the study of material culture. It should be noted that his study of folklore and ethnology in Berlin and Leipzig before the outbreak of the Second World War gave him many skills and insights that facilitated his work later, and even his appointment as full-time collector in 1939 was somewhat anomalous in that although he was sent to the field to collect oral traditions, the understanding was that he would also be required to do ethnological investigation.[31] Moreover, as noted above, in the post-War period Ó Danachair's salary was much higher than that of any of the collectors. This may partly have been because of his academic qualifications, but the fact that he had skills and knowledge that none of his other colleagues had, made him indispensable if the Commission was to cater for material culture. It was consequently imperative to keep him at all costs.

But discrepancies between field and office staff were not simply a question of job designation. Séamus Ennis was employed as a full-time collector of music. Although he paid many trips to the field, he worked from Head Office, and had access to the Commission's library and archive, as well as other Dublin libraries. This afforded him opportunities which collectors confined to the field did not have. Ennis was also sent to work in Scotland for a time (see Chapter III/3). He did not stay long enough with the Commission for us to judge whether he would have developed his many talents to the full, as well as advance in his career. However, while working from Head Office did allow him to develop in ways not allowed to full-time collectors who were permanently based in the field, it has to be remembered that his terms of employment were never as good as those of Caoimhín Ó Danachair. Thus, while having collectors based at Head Office, or working partly from there, might have given them opportunities not enjoyed by those in the field, it would be wrong to conclude that being based at Head Office was in all cases an advantage for an employee of the Commission. For some it was also a place of limited opportunity. For instance, some jobs at Head Office were very poorly paid, such as that of cataloguer, and conseqnently the Commission found it difficult to keep the cataloguers it employed over the years.

While Seosamh Ó Dálaigh's above-mentioned claim that once appointed a collector, you remained a collector has to be qualified somewhat, it is nonetheless essentially true. The opportunities for collectors to advance in their careers were certainly few. Nevertheless, while no collector, apart from Caoimhín Ó Danachair, could be said to have been promoted, and while impediments were placed in the path of full-time collectors, they did, of course, develop as folklorists by dint of experience, especially those who spent many years with the Commission. Eibhlín Nic Craith says of Tadhg Ó

---

31   ED [FL 9]: 'CBÉ. Miont. 18ú Cruinniú, 27.10.1939', par. 153.

Murchadha: 'There is no doubt that Tadhg Ó Murchadha was a professional folklorist although he did not receive any academic training.'[32] In most cases, however, there was a limit to this development. While there is no denying the fact that many of the Commission's full-time collectors, as well as some of its part-time collectors, were exceptionally skilled as collectors, and had a vast knowledge of oral tradition, confined to the field they had few opportunities to acquaint themselves with folklore as an academic science, if they had wished to do so. They were, of course, familiar with such reference works as *A Handbook of Irish Folklore* and the *Types of the Folktale*. The library of the Commission might have offered ample opportunities for gaining a wider knowledge of the subject, but when collectors visited Head Office in Dublin they most likely had other things to occupy them than furthering their knowledge of folkloristics (see Chapter IV/1). Moreover, what books on folklore were available to them in 'local' or even Dublin bookshops would, for the most part, have consisted of anthologies of tales and lore in many respects similar to the material they were themselves collecting.

Collector-Folklorists

Given the workload of the full-time collectors, especially in the early years, it is hard to see where they could have found time for academic research. Their work would have had to be quite different to allow them to pursue, at their leisure, research interests of their own and publish extensively on them.[33] It should also be borne in mind that not all collectors would have wished to write about folklore matters, while others did not stay long enough to develop such an interest in the first place.[34] There is little doubt that Ó Duilearga saw his full-time collectors, for the most part, as 'hewers of wood and drawers of water'. However, while it is quite certain that he would not have approved of full-time collectors devoting an 'undue' amount of their time to independent research and publication, there is little evidence to suggest that he discouraged collectors, e.g., from contributing occasionally to *Béaloideas*. In different circumstances, he might have encouraged collectors to edit substantial parts of

32 Nic Craith (M.A. Thesis), p. 10 (trans.).
33 Nevertheless, some of the Commission's collectors, particularly Seán Ó hEochaidh and Michael J. Murphy, published extensively on folklore/folkloristic matters. Most of Calum MacLean's published production derives from the time after he was seconded to the School of Scottish Studies, while Ciarán Bairéad's publications and research interests, for the most part, lay outside folkloristics. Jim Delaney, like MacLean and Bairéad had a university education. In 1964 he published a substantial study of the nineteenth-century Irish folklorist Patrick Kennedy, based on research he had done more than ten years previously before he took up employment with the Commission. Most of his subsequent published work derives, significantly or not, from the post-Commission period. Finally, both Tadgh Ó Murchadha and Liam Mac Coisdeala published miscellaneous items of folklore in *Béaloideas* as well as a substantial article each, referred to above, recounting their experiences of collecting in the field.
34 Seosamh Ó Dálaigh, for example, would not appear to have had an inclination to write about folklore. I gathered this from conversations with him in the 1970's and early 1980's.

their collections, or undertake demanding, time-consuming research projects, but to the end collecting was to remain a priority for him.

Of course, if the Commission's full-time collectors had been allowed to develop more as collectors, into collector-folklorists in their own right, the type of salvage collecting undertaken by the Commission would not have been possible, but perhaps folkloristics would have developed earlier in the Republic of Ireland. Moreover, folklore collecting in the Republic of Ireland remained much the same in the 1960's as it had been in the 1930's, except that the acquisition of tape recorders by the collectors from late 1962 onwards facilitated collecting and made the workload of collectors, in some respects, lighter, as there was not the same urgency to transcribe what was recorded. Thus, in time the work of the full-time collectors became less arduous, but they remained, for the most part, what they started out as, namely collectors. And it is as collectors that each of them must be judged in time. Whatever their shortcomings, future generations hopefully will remember their achievements and the personal sacrifices that many of them made.

Both Seosamh Ó Dálaigh and Seán Ó hEochaidh were awarded Honorary Doctorates in the late 1980's by the National University of Ireland for their work for Irish folklore and the Irish language.[35] These were the only two full-time collectors to be honoured in this way. Moreover, Calum MacLean, who was seconded from the Commission to the School of Scottish Studies in 1951, 'a few weeks before his death' from cancer at the age of forty five in August 1960 'heard that the University of St. Francis Xavier, Antigonish, Nova Scotia, had decided to confer upon him the degree LL.D, *honoris causa*, in recognition of his work for the preservation of Gaelic oral tradition.'[36] More of the Commission's collectors should have been honoured in this way.

35   See Ó Ciardha 1989, pp. 165–166, and Ó Madagáin 1989, pp. 167–170.
36   Nicolaisen 1962, p. 163. For more on Calum MacLean's work, see also Megaw 1960.

2. The Commission's pioneering role

Text and context

Bo Almqvist has described Séamus Ó Duilearga 'as a pioneer in the field of contextual studies.' He clarifies this by saying: 'The interplay between an informant, his surroundings and his lore were explored in his work on Seán Ó Conaill and his repertoire.'[37] Almqvist is here referring to Ó Duilearga's magnum opus, *Leabhar Sheáin Í Chonaill*.[38] Although he does not say so specifically, in describing Ó Duilearga as a pioneer in contextual studies, he is, presumably, also referring to the systematic collecting undertaken by the Irish Folklore Commission's full-time collectors under his direction. This systematic collecting involved utilising mechanical recording machines on a large scale, placed great emphasis on verbatim transcriptions, and documented not only essential biographical details of narrators, such as name, age, and place of birth, but, in addition, a great deal of other contextual information such as the collecting situations, the personalities of the narrators, and details of their life histories.

It goes without saying that Ó Duilearga was not the first to have collectors seek out biographical particulars of narrators or record lore faithfully. Even within Ireland, as far back as 1873, John Molloy recommended that the basic biographical details of informants, such as name and address, should be noted and given when traditional material was being published.[39] Douglas Hyde and the Gaelic League later in the century gave would-be collectors similar advice and also stressed the need for recording texts with complete fidelity. In addition, Hyde and some of those who collected under the auspices of the League realised many of the problems of collecting by means of 'longhand transcription' without the aid of any mechanical recording apparatus, and in time succeeded in honing their collecting methods to improve the quality of their texts.[40] Indeed William Larminie, whose *West Irish Folktales and*

---

37   Almqvist 1981, p. 5.
38   See his introduction to Ó Duilearga 1977 [1948], passim.
39   Ó Macháin and Ní Shéaghdha 1996, p. 107.
40   Ó Conaire 1986, p. 125 and O'Leary 1994., pp. 97–98. In the first decade of the twentieth century the possibility of training League organisers in shorthand as well as the purchase

Romances was published the same year as the Gaelic League was founded (1893), in similar fashion to the Commission's collectors, went over his texts with narrators, and sometimes others in the locality, in order to elucidate 'difficult and doubtful parts'.[41] Thus, long before Séamus Ó Duilearga began collecting folk traditions systematically, collectors of folklore in Ireland had begun documenting contextual detail and laid down certain principals for recording traditions faithfully.

Nevertheless, there is no doubt that the Irish Folklore Commission, under Ó Duilearga's directorship, was, in many respects, a pioneering organisation for much of its period of operation. Moreover, the collectors of the Irish Folklore Commission displayed a degree of professionalism towards collecting that was far in advance of that found in many countries at the time. The Commission's collectors were not the first collectors to use mechanical recording machines to record tradition on a large scale, but they were among the first in Europe to do so.[42] Ó Duilearga was eclectic, taking ideas from many quarters. The collecting methods he had his collectors use were hardly original in any case, yet he was inventive in the ways he combined, applied and developed them. Moreover, Seán Ó Súilleabháin's *A Handbook of Irish Folklore* was not the first handbook of folklore to be produced, but it was the first based on the classification system of one folklore archive (the Landsmålsarkiv, Uppsala) and the contents of another (the Irish Folklore Commission). Nor should we think that all the credit for this innovativeness is due to Ó Duilearga himself. The collectors, as well as the Head Office staff of the Commission, were also inventive and as time went on adapted what they had learned from Ó Duilearga to the circumstances they found themselves in. A very concrete example of this is Tadhg Ó Murchadha's designing of a special carrier for his bicycle to transport the cumbrous Ediphone machine and cylinders over mountainous terrain (see Chapter IV/1 above).

Because the Archive of the Irish Folklore Commission was assembled at a late date, and because of the procedures adopted for recording contextual information by full-time collectors in particular, it contains far more contextual

---

of a number of recording machines to overcome the problems posed by the longhand transcription of folklore were also recommended by certain contributors to the League's newspaper, *An Claidheamh Soluis.* See Ibid., p. 98, n. 24.

41 See Zimmerman 2001, p. 315.
42 Some limited use had been made of the Ediphone to record Swedish dialects since the late 19th century, but the poor quality of the recordings produced discouraged folklorists from using this machine to record tradition. However, the Uppsala Landsmålsarkiv (Dialect and Folklore Archive) purchased a portable gramophone recording apparatus in 1935 for use in the field. Hedblom 1989, p. 15. Some Finnish collectors made use of the Phonograph (similar to the Ediphone), mainly to record music, in the early 20th century, but it was difficult to transport and its use never became common. The Phonograph recordings of the Finnish Literature Society's Sound Archive (a subsection of its Folklore Archive) date from 1905 down until the 1950's. In 1937 gramophone recordings began to be made in the archive. Virtanen 1988, p. 55, and Laaksonen and Saarinen 2004, p. 79. On one of the earliest uses of a Phonograph by a Finnish Folklorist, see Salminen, pp. 23 and 142 ff. On the use of the Ediphone/Phonograph in the United States to record oral tradition, see Erika Brady 1999.

information than many other archives that are older than it.[43] Apart from their copious correspondence with Head Office, the full-time collectors of the Irish Folklore Commission have left us two main sources of contextual information: the biographies of various narrators, and the collectors' field diaries.

The recording of biographical data

In the late 1930's, Carl Wilhelm von Sydow requested that the Commission 'publish some thoroughly well done biographies of tradition bearers.' He added that this was 'something which has been done in only a very limited way hitherto and a few volumes of this kind would therefore be of the greatest possible scientific interest and of greatest importance for ongoing folktale research.'[44] The Commission does not appear to have acted on this request immediately, but during the Second World War, when its collectors were confined to their localities due to a shortage of petrol, Ó Duilearga instructed Tomás de Búrca and Seán Ó hEochaidh to collect the life stories of two particular narrators. One of these life stories, that collected by Ó hEochaidh from Micí Mac Gabhann, was subsequently published.[45] In November 1945, von Sydow made a more ambitious proposal to the Commission: namely that it 'collect detailed information about every tradition bearer.' In a letter to Seán Ó Súilleabháin he stated:

> We must find out *how* they got their tradition, through inheritance at home or out in the community, on which occasions etc. And also when do these traditions come into play? When, in which company, on what occasions do they tell their tales? How do their listeners react? What sort of people do not react, do not bother to listen and to what extent do listeners take up and carry on the traditions? How does one progress from being a passive to an active tradition bearer? All these are extremely important questions for folklore research and there is no country in the world other than Ireland which can provide such valuable information about these matters. All in all the memoirs of tradition bearers are of the utmost value.[46]

---

43 For instance, the Folklore Archive of the Finnish Literature Society contains few collectors' diaries as such. Although some collectors furnished accounts of their collecting to the Society (e.g. in the form of reports or covering letters) this was not always done so systematically. Some Finnish folklorists did keep field diaries of their collecting expeditions, but these remained in their possession and are often found among their private papers rather than among the Society's folklore collections. However, the correspondence collectors maintained with the Society provides a great deal of context about the collecting and the material collected, as do notes appended by collectors to the collections themselves. Information, for the most part, supplied by Jukka Saarinen.

44 Quoted in uí Ógáin 2000b, p. 162, letter dated 15.9.1936 (trans. from Swedish).

45 D/T S 15548B: 'Gearr-Thuar./1942–43', p. 1, and 'Gearr-Thuar./1943–44', p. 2 . See also Ó Conluain 1959.

46 Quoted and translated from Swedish in uí Ógáin 2000b, p. 163, letter dated 'November 1945'.

Von Sydow emphasised to Ó Súilleabháin the importance of compiling such a 'memoir' for all narrators of tradition, not merely the 'best-known' or those with the 'most extensive repertoires', and implored him 'to see to it that this is carried out as comprehensively as possible.' This was asking a great deal, to say the least. I am not aware that the Commission ever set about elucidating questions of this sort in a systematic manner. One way it might have done so would have been to send out a questionnaire on storytelling and transmission. Ó Duilearga planned such a questionnaire, but like much else he planned to do, he never got around to doing it.[47]

Space does not allow me to treat in full of the Commission's efforts to record the biographies of its informants. A few comments will have to suffice. Given the extent of the Commission's operations, to have recorded extensive biographical accounts from its chief informants alone was beyond its capacity, as eliciting the main facts and events of anybody's life is slow, painstaking work at the best of times. Given the pressure the Commission's collectors worked under, concentrating more on collecting biographies would have meant collecting fewer texts as such. Moreover, it seems that it was often due to chance whether an informant's biography was recorded *in extenso* or not, and that it was something that was often left to last, after the rest of the narrator's stories and lore had been saved for posterity. There is no doubt that context played second fiddle to text with the Commission, and it would be surprising if it had been otherwise. It has also to be noted that biographical accounts were not recorded even from some spectacular informants the Commission worked with. Éamon 'a Búrc is a case in point. Although he was, perhaps, the most accomplished storyteller collected from by the Commission, in Ireland at any rate, it would appear that little or no biographical data was recorded from him.

The Commission certainly realised the importance of collecting biographical accounts from narrators. Even before von Sydow exhorted it to collect some sample biographies in the late 1930's, Ó Duilearga had himself collected details of the life histories of Seán Ó Conaill and Stiofán Ó hEalaoire, his two chief informants. However, in the case of both these narrators, it was only after he had collected much of their repertoires that he recorded details of their life stories from them.[48] However, the Commission was never able to collect as much biographical data from informants as it would have wished. This does, of course, affect the value of the collection overall, but, as I said above, given the large numbers of narrators involved and the small number of collectors who collected from them, it is not at all surprising that collecting data of this sort was often left aside for another day, and very often left too late. While the Commission's collections do contain some substantial biographies of certain narrators and numerous shorter biographical accounts, it should be remembered that even when no accounts of this sort were recorded from narrators, the collectors' diaries often record

---

47 Ibid., p. 163 and SKS Haavio Papers 12:58:3: Ó Duilearga to Haavio, dated 19.11.1946.
48 See Ó Duilearga 1977 [1948], p. xxvii-xxxii, and Ó Duilearga and Ó hÓgáin 1981, pp. 2–9, and 346.

personality traits and details of the life situations of informants. It is these diaries, rather than the biographical accounts which the Commission's full-time collectors compiled of certain key informants, that particularly enhance its Main Collection and give it a depth and dimension missing from many other folklore archives of that time and earlier. Nevertheless, in order to evaluate the contribution the Commission made to documenting the context of folklore collecting by means of collectors' diaries, one first needs to look at the genesis and purpose of these diaries

The genesis of the collector's diaries

The distinction between the keeping of a field diary and a personal or travel diary can often be quite blurred. In Ireland the keeping of a personal diary was mainly practised by middle- and upper-class Protestants until at least the beginning of the twentieth century, and was never to become all that general among educated Catholics.[49] For example, few of Ó Duilearga's contemporaries at UCD are known to have kept a personal diary, so his doing so from a relatively early age is remarkable in itself. As early as summer 1925, Ó Duilearga was keeping such a diary, that is three years before he undertook his study trip of northern Europe.[50] It may be of significance that Ó Duilearga's Professor of Modern Irish, Douglas Hyde, kept a personal diary from the age of fourteen. Hyde, among other matters, recorded details pertaining to his collecting in his diary, but he did not keep a field diary as such, nor, as far as I am aware, did he ever exhort collectors of folklore to keep this type of record of their collecting.[51]

Moreover, long before Hyde began collecting folklore, in Scotland, John Francis Campbell (Campbell of Islay) in the mid-nineteenth century recorded much about his collecting work in a personal diary.[52] It is not clear when Ó Duilearga became aware of the existence and nature of Campbell's diaries, but he may have learned something about their content from references in Reidar Th. Christiansen's magnum opus on Irish and Scottish Gaelic tradition, *The Vikings and Viking Wars In Irish and Gaelic Tradition*, published in1931.[53] As he had been a friend of Christiansen's for much of the previous ten years when this work was being researched, it is quite likely that he may also have been made aware of the content of Campbell's diaries earlier. In addition, it should also be noted that Ó Duilearga already by 1934, and possibly much earlier, was friendly with J. G. McKay, the foremost expert on the Campbell of Islay Collections.[54] However, it should be noted that while Campbell of

49 For more on Irish diary writing, see Lenox-Conyngham 1998, passim.
50 See Almqvist 1998, p. 115, n. 21.
51 See Daly 1974, pp. 26-29.
52 Dorson 1968, p. 402.
53 Christiansen 1931, pp. 61 and 66.
54 See Ó Duilearga 1934, p. 457. Certainly, as an older man, he was aware of these diaries. See Ó Duilearga 1960. Transcripts of Campbell's County Antrim diary are to be found among Ó Duilearga's papers in UCG Hard. Lib. Arch. G16, Box 4: unnumbered file.

Islay himself kept a diary containing, among other things, field notes, he does not appear to have requested his collectors to do so. They did, however, regularly furnish him with accounts of their collecting in their correspondence, and also added field notes to the tales and lore they transcribed.[55] In contrast to Hyde and Campbell, however, Ó Duilearga was not only to maintain a personal-cum-field diary throughout much of his adult life, he was, once the Irish Folklore Commission was set up in 1935, to have his collectors keep a field diary as a matter of course. So where did this idea come from?

It should be said at the outset that the idea of collectors of folklore keeping a field diary did not originate with Séamus Ó Duilearga. As far back as the 1830's and 1840's the Finnish folklorist Carl Axel Gottlund, a pioneer in developing fieldwork methods, kept extensive diaries of his many collecting trips, although it should be noted in his case that the distinction between what constitutes a personal diary and a field diary is also somewhat blurred.[56] Be that as it may, Gottlund did not inspire a tradition among Finnish folklore collectors of recording an account of their field trips in this manner. For instance, the folklorist Kaarle Krohn did not keep a diary of his extensive collecting trips in the 1880s, although he did send written reports of these trips to the Finnish Literature Society.[57] Other examples of European folklorists and ethnologists who recorded aspects of their fieldwork in diaries or field notes of various descriptions could be cited, but more pertinent to the matter in hand is to ascertain if folklorists in any country before 1935 exhorted others to keep (diary) accounts of their collecting or if they did so as a matter of course. It is interesting to note that in one of the lectures Ó Duilearga gave on his tour of German universities in early 1937, in speaking of the diaries of the Commission's collectors, he refers admiringly to the published field diaries (or memoirs based on field diaries) of two Continental folklorists, the Dane, Evald Tang Kristensen, and the German, Wilhelm Wissers, and pays special tribute to the latter's work, *Auf der Märchensuche*.[58]

The Estonian folklorist Oskar Kallas (and later diplomat) in the early twentieth century (1904) encouraged student collectors of folklore to furnish, along with their texts, accounts of their field work. Instructions on what to include in such reports were printed and distributed to collectors

---

55 For one such field note by Hector MacLean, see Ó Duilearga 1960, p. 128.
56 See Pulkkinen 2003, pp. 54 ff. Moreover, the Finnish linguist A. J. Sjögren kept a diary of his travels into remote parts of the Russian Empire in the first half of the nineteenth century. See Branch 1973 passim. Elsewhere (Briody 2005a, p. 30) I have stated that the Finnish folklore pioneer Elias Lönnrot, a contemporary of Gottlund's, kept accounts of at least part of his collecting trips in diary form. Although some of the reports he subsequently wrote up of his collecting trips, along with certain extant field notes of his, were reconstituted by a later editor as diary entries (Lönnrot 1981), I have since learned that no actual diary of any of his collecting trips has survived. Information supplied by Raija Majamaa.
57 See Evijärvi 1963, p. 28. Some Finnish folklorists contemporaneous with the Irish Folklore Commission did keep diaries, e.g. the Finnish folklorist Helmi Helminen kept extensive field diaries during her collecting in East Karelia between 1941–1944. See Järvinen 2004, p. 43.
58 Ó Duilearga 1943, p. 12.

and would-be collectors.[59] This gave rise to a tradition that has continued ever since among Estonian folklore collectors. Unlike the diaries of the Irish Folklore Commission that are bound in separate volumes, the diary accounts of Estonian collectors are kept in the archive alongside the material they provide a context for. However, many of these Estonian diary field notes are reminiscent of the descriptive accounts found in the diaries of the collectors of the Irish Folklore Commission.[60] When Ó Duilearga visited the Estonian Folklore Archives (Eesti Rahvaluule Arhiiv) in Tartu in July 1928, he would have had an opportunity to learn about this aspect of collecting in Estonia.

It should also be noted that before visiting Tartu he stayed in Tallinn with a daughter of Aino and Oskar Kallas,[61] Laine Poska. Oskar Kallas's wife, Aino, was a sister of Kaarle Krohn.[62] Thus, the likelihood that he learned something at least while in Estonia about these diary field notes is quite high. Moreover, from the 1920's onwards folklorists in Sweden were in the habit of writing *primäranteckningar* ('basic (field) notes'). Sometimes these were later worked up into fuller accounts, at other times they were not. Ó Duilearga's sojourn in Sweden from spring to autumn 1928 would also have provided him with ample opportunity to acquaint himself with this aspect of the work of Swedish folklorists. Assuming that on his trip to northern Europe in 1928 he learned about Estonian and Swedish practice in respect of the keeping of diary field notes by folklorists, it is to be noted that on his return to Ireland he did not set about encouraging Irish collectors to furnish similar accounts of their collecting. At any rate, no notice as to the desirability of such accounts was ever published in *Béaloideas* (although certain basic contextual information on informants continued to be asked for), nor am I aware that those who collected for the Irish Folklore Institute (with the exception of one particular group of collectors, for which, see below) were ever asked to supply such reports. It is also to be noted that neither Seán Ó Súilleabháin's guides for collectors, *Láimhleabhar Béaloideasa* (1937) nor his *A Handbook of Irish Folklore* (1942), mention the desirability of furnishing reports of field work. This is not to say that the content of Ó Duilearga's own field diaries, and his subsequent requesting of full-time collectors to keep a diary, may not have been influenced by what he learned of Estonian and Swedish field work practice on his trip to northern Europe, assuming, of course, that he did learn something about such matters. His diaries, in time, may elucidate more on this matter.

It is also to be observed that if it is the case that what Ó Duilearga learned of Estonian and Swedish practice in time influenced the decision to have the full-time collectors of the Irish Folklore Commission, on its establishment, keep a regular diary of their field work, nowhere in his published writings does he acknowledge this. For example, in the published version of the paper he read at the Paris Ethnology and Folklore Conference in August 1937, in which

---

59 Remmel 1997, p. 8.
60 For extracts of these Estonian field diary accounts, see ibid.
61 SKS Kaarle Krohn Papers: Ó Duilearga to Krohn, dated 3 July, 1928.
62 Laine Poska, later Laine Määr, almost the same age as Ó Duilearga, was to die tragically and violently during the Second World War. See Kallas 1989, p. 337.

he describes the work of the Commission, he simply says: 'Each collector records in detail in his official diary his experiences in the field : this aspect of collecting work has been much neglected in the past.'[63] One reason for his not acknowledging a possible debt to Estonian and Swedish folklorists, in respect of these diaries, was that even if he was indebted to them, it was only partly so. For it would appear that the genesis of the field diaries of the Commission's collectors is more complex, and possible owes as much, if not more, to Irish precursors as it does to Nordic or Baltic influence.

Speaking at the Midcentury Folklore Conference in Indiana in 1950, Seán Ó Súilleabháin states that the idea of the Commission's collectors keeping a field diary derived from a native source, namely the Irish Ordnance Survey of the 1830s–1840s:

> One of the greatest sources of information we have in Ireland is the ordnance survey books, which were made about a century ago by three men, John O'Donovan, Eugene O'Curry, and George Petry [*recte* Petrie]. They went around about a hundred years ago and took down all the place names of the country and recorded material of very great importance. But the greatest importance lies in the diaries kept by these men, because these diaries give the atmosphere in which the work was done. Now we are doing the same thing and are asking our collectors to keep a diary.[64]

Ó Súilleabháin's above account is somewhat misleading (it should be remembered, however, that he may have been speaking *ex tempore*). Although the officers of the Ordnance Survey (1820's to 1840's), or at least some of them, would appear to have been required to keep diaries of sorts ('journals'), none of these seem to have survived.[65] However, Ó Súilleabháin may partly have been confusing the 'memoirs' compiled by the staff of the Ordnance Survey (being general descriptive surveys of individual parishes [66]) with the correspondence sent to the Survey's head office of the Irish-language scholars John O'Donovan and Eugene O'Curry, in particular. These letters contain accounts of their fieldwork as well as copious notes on the antiquities, topography and traditions of the localities they visited.[67] It should be noted that the Ordnance Survey letters were being typed and bound in volumes in the Royal Irish Academy during the late 1920's and early 1930's, at a time when Ó Duilearga himself had close links with the Academy.[68] Bound as

---

63 Ó Duilearga 1937, p. 39.
64 Thompson 1976, p. 6.
65 See Andrews 2001, pp. 145–146.
66 For information on the ethnographic value of these memoirs, see Day 1984 and Ó Cadhla 2007. See also Doherty 2004.
67 For more information on these letters, see O'Donovan and O'Curry 1997, pp. iii-vi. Stiofán Ó Cadhla, comparing the medhodology of the Ordnance Survey of the 1830's and 1840's with that of the Irish Folklore Commission, equates the '"Memoir" or Letters' of the Survey's 'Civilian Assistants' with the 'field-diary' of the Commission's collectors. Ó Cadhla 1999, p. 90.
68 For more on the copying of these letters, see Ó Muraíle 1997, p. 72. See also Carroll 1993, p. 177.

they are, according to the county of provenance, these letters could be easily read as diaries, or be mistaken for such. In any event, the detailed accounts of some of the Commission's collectors are reminiscent of many of John O'Donovan's letters, by coincidence or otherwise.[69] Moreover, the fact that Ó Súilleabháin, a close associate of Ó Duilearga's, suggests such an origin for these diaries is most likely not without significance. In this context, it is worth mentioning that at the opening of the first meeting of the Commission on April 2nd, 1935, the Minister for Education, Tomás Ó Deirg, as mentioned above (Chapter III/2), drew attention to the work of the Ordnance Survey a hundred years before and described the task the Commission had before it as constituting a continuation of the interrupted work of the Survey in respect of Irish tradition.[70] There is a good deal of evidence to suggest that Ó Duilearga had an input into Ó Deirg's opening speech. Be that as it may, there is little doubt that Ó Duilearga himself was aware of the similarities between the survey of Irish oral tradition the Commission had been set up to carry out and aspects of the work of the Ordnance Survey of the previous century, and that he sought to emulate, and indeed surpass, that earlier survey in the thoroughness of its field work.

But the Ordnance Survey of a century or so before may not have been the only native precedent having a bearing on Ó Duilearga's decision to have his full-time collectors record the progress and context of their field work. Some decades before that Survey, another Northener, the collector of Irish folk music Edward Bunting, had set out to collect Irish tradition with a band of helpers. Of relevance to our discussion, in the early nineteenth century, Bunting employed the Gaelic scholar Pádraig Ó Loingsigh (Patrick Lynch) to write down the words of Irish songs in Ulster and north Connaught. A large collection of letters from Ó Loingsigh to Bunting from the field as well as a field diary survive. His letters (as well as his diary) resemble the descriptive letters of John O'Donovan and Eugene O'Curry a generation later in the detail they at times give of his collecting trips.[71] In the early twentieth century, Charlotte Milligan Fox published extensive extracts of these letters and diary, so that the working methods of Bunting and Ó Loingsigh would have been known to Séamus Ó Duilearga, who as a young man avidly scoured libraries in search of works dealing with Irish tradition.[72]

Nevertheless, I think the genesis of the Commission's diaries, in so far as it concerns Ireland, is still more complex. The full-time collectors employed by the Irish Folklore Commission were in many respects unique at the time, although they resemble, in certain respects, Campbell of Islay's paid helpers of the 1860's (see above). Nearer to home, however, and nearer to the Irish Folklore Commission in time, the full-time collectors of the Commission find an echo in the *timirí* (sing. *timire*) or travelling teachers/organisers of

---

69   See the many extracts from O'Donovan's letters in Boyne 1987, passim, and Ó Muráile 1997, passim.

70   *Irish Press* 3rd April, 1935, p. 7.

71   See Mac Giolla Fhinnéin 1993, pp. 116–119.

72   Fox 1911. For more on Bunting and his collections, see Vallely 1999, pp. 46–48 and C. Moloney 2000, passim.

the Gaelic League who roamed the Irish countryside in the early decades of the twentieth century. Although *timirí* were not required to keep a diary as such, they were required to send regular accounts of their activities to the League's head office in Dublin, and many of these accounts were subsequently published in *An Claidheamh Soluis*, as well as in other League publications. Moreover, the first *timire* employed by the League, Tómás Bán Ó Concheanainn, kept a diary of his activities as the accounts he forwarded to the League's head office often appear in diary format, i.e. a day-by-day account of events as they happened.[73] We know from the memoirs of another *timire*, Peadar Ó hAnnracháin, that he also kept diary notebooks of his work for the League.[74] Other *timirí* may also have kept a diary of their work but subsequently conflated diary entries into general reports when forwarding accounts of their activities to the League in Dublin.

Many of the League's *timirí* doubled as folklore collectors: people such as Fionán Mac Coluim and Peadar Ó hAnnracháin, who were later acquaintances of Séamus Ó Duilearga. In my opinion, given the circles he moved in, this activity of the League's *timirí* could not have gone unnoticed by Ó Duilearga, and there is a strong possibility that the accounts of their activities furnished regularly by these travelling teachers/organisers to the League's head office in Dublin also, in part, served as a model for the diary-keeping of the Commission's full time-collectors. Indeed, we learn from Peadar Ó hAnnracháin's *Fé Bhrat an Chonnartha* that he began writing his monumental memoirs, based on his *timire* diaries, sometime between the mid and late 1930's, but that certain people had been encouraging him to edit his diaries for many years before. Two of the people who encouraged him and advised him on how best to edit his diaries were Pádraig Ó Siochfhradha and Fionán Mac Coluim, both close associates of Séamus Ó Duilearga at the time.[75] If we think of the diaries of the Commission's collectors as not only providing contextual information on the collecting as well as aspects of the tradition for the benefit of future generations, but also as comprising a detailed log of the work of collectors for Head Office, a link with the work practice of the *timirí* of the Gaelic League seems all the more probable.

However, there is further evidence to trace the genesis of these diaries, in part, to the Gaelic League's *timirí*. After the establishment of the Irish Free State many of the League's *timirí* were employed as travelling Irish language teachers by Vocational Education Committees around the country. The Irish Folklore Institute in the early 1930's utilised the services of some of these Vocational Education teachers to collect folklore, among others those of Co. Cork. In the early summer of 1933, Irish teachers employed by the Cork Vocational Education Committee, who were released from some of their teaching duties to collect folklore, were required: to 'submit weekly

---

73 See Ó Ríordáin 2000, p. 45.
74 See Ó hAnnracháin 1944, pp. xv ff.
75 See ibid., pp. xvi and 730–731. Pádraig Ó Siochfhradha also kept a diary as a *timire* and continued keeping a diary for much of his life: Not all his diary notebooks have, it appears, survived. Telephone conversation with his grandnephew, Pádraig Ó Siochrú, Baile an Ghóilín, August 2005.

to the Chief Executive Officer, in the form of a journal, a report showing for each working day the districts which they have visited for the purpose of collecting material, names of persons interviewed, etc.'[76] These Vocational Education teachers were being paid to collect full-time, albeit for only part of the year, in contrast to other collectors who forwarded material to the Folklore of Ireland Society and the Irish Folklore Institute, some of whom were paid a set rate for the material they collected.

The purpose of the collectors' diaries

Although Ó Duilearga's decision to have his full-time collectors keep a regular diary was most likely influenced by both native and foreign precursors, there is no doubt that he had collectors do so in a much more systematic way than was previously done. Nevertheless, while the diaries which the full-time collectors of the Commission kept are a rich source of contextual information, and greatly increase the value of its Main Collection, it would appear that the decision to have full-time collectors keep a field diary was not made solely to document the context of the collecting. As I have implied above, the fact that the Vocational Education teachers of County Cork (and other counties), who were released from teaching for a few months of the year to collect folklore, were asked to furnish a journal-like account of their collecting activities, was definitely, in part at least, in order to supervise them. It is not clear if these accounts were to be forwarded to the Irish Folklore Institute via the Chief Executive Officer (or local equivalent) of the Technical Instruction Branch of the Dept. of Education or if they were simply for the use of the latter. Neither is it clear whose idea it was in the first place that these teachers should furnish accounts of this sort. Even if the idea did not derive from Ó Duilearga, it is fairly certain that he was aware that these collectors were furnishing such accounts. It is interesting to note that more or less around the time that these teachers were being released for this collecting work, negotiations were about to take place to reorganise the work of the Irish Folklore Institute. Ó Duilearga in his memorandum to de Valera of May 1933, in addition to having full-time collectors keep a field diary, proposed: 'Field workers to be in intimate touch with central office, to which they will furnish weekly statements on the work done, and accounts covering in detail personal charges, payments to informants, etc.'[77]

Once the question of employing collectors full-time became feasible, it became necessary to convince the authorities that these employees would be accountable. Diary notebooks would give Head Office a good idea of the day-to-day activity of the collectors, but they would only be forwarded when completed. On the other hand, furnishing weekly statements of work done to

76 Quoted in Ó Ríordáin 2000, p. 168.
77 D/T S 9244: 'Collecting of Oral Tradition of Ireland', p. 11, cov. let. dated 18.5.1933. By 'payments to informants' Ó Duilearga probably meant small presents of tobacco and such like, as it is certain that he never intended rewarding them financially for their tales and lore.

Head Office allowed for more regular scrutiny and control of the work being done by collectors – correspondence served the same purpose. In requesting full-time collectors to keep a diary, Ó Duilearga was also seeking to make available for future research a large body of vernacular Irish, at once distinct from the traditional material to be collected and yet intimately associated with it and with the communities that produced it. In a further memorandum he presented to the Minister for Education some months before the Commission began operations he says: 'Each collector will be expected to keep a diary in which he will record his experiences as a collector, details as to the area investigated, the results obtained, etc. It is felt that these diaries will be of very considerable value and interest both from a folkloristic, and (as they will be written in Irish) a linguistic point of view.'[78]

Further evidence that the keeping of diaries by collectors had a function above and beyond documenting the context of the collecting, is provided by the earliest field diaries produced for the Irish Folklore Commission. These earliest diaries are not to be found in the Commission's collections but in the recently renamed Institutet för Språk och Folkminnen (Swedish Institute for Language and Folklore) in Uppsala (formerly the Landsmålsarkiv). Åke Campbell's papers contain diaries kept by Caoimhín Ó Danachair and Liam Mac Meanman, who assisted him in fieldwork in June/July 1935 and received training from him for work they might later undertake for the Commission, recently established, but not yet functioning properly.[79] These diaries resemble those subsequently kept by the Commission's collectors in describing both the context of the field work as well as the ethnological data observed, although they are not as detailed. They differ, in this respect, from the field notebooks Campbell himself compiled in Ballinskelligs the previous year on his first trip to Ireland, which consist almost entirely of ethnological observations and illustrations.[80]

It would appear that Campbell asked his Irish assistants to keep these diaries instead of keeping them himself, but the initial idea came from Ó Duilearga. On June 17th, 1935, Ó Duilearga wrote to Campbell, who was then in the Maam districts of Co. Galway, telling him to keep a diary of his trip 'as it will be necessary for us to report to the Folklore Commission on the work done and the places visited.'[81] This diary was to contain more than an account of 'work done and the places visited', for three days later, Ó Duilearga in another communication reminded Campbell of the necessity of 'continuing to keep a detailed account of your expenses in a special notebook, and also, receipted bills, dockets, etc. All this information is required for the finance clerks.'[82] The fact that Campbell took these diaries back with him to Sweden

---

78 ED CO 3/15/9(495/II): 'Irish Folklore Commission. Memorandum 10.1.1935', p. [8].
79 ULMA Saml. Åke Campbell, subnr. 263(A), 266(B), and 257. Liam Mac Coisdeala and Proinnsias de Búrca also kept diaries when working with Campbell but they do not appear to be in the Uppsala Archive.
80 ULMA Saml. Åke Campbell, subnr. 260 and 261.
81 ULMA Saml. Åke Campbell, subnr. 203. For a description of this survey, see Lysaght 1993b.
82 ULMA Saml. Åke Campbell, subnr. 203, letter dated 20.6.1935.

caused a problem for the Commission. On July 19th, Séan Ó Súilleabháin wrote to him, on Ó Duilearga's behalf, asking him to send: 'the notebooks containing Danaher's [Ó Danachair's] and Costelloe's [Mac Coisdeala's] diaries by return post so that Miss McNeill can type out some copies and *return the notebooks to you within a few days*. The matter is urgent so please send them immediately.'[83]

Despite the above fuss over these early diaries, it did not become practice for the Finance Sub-Committee or the Commission itself to scrutinize these diaries to ascertain whether full-time collectors were doing sufficient work to justify the salaries being paid them. Most likely, once it was realised that the Dept. of Finance was not going to insist on being provided with a detailed breakdown of the work being done by each full-time collector, a more relaxed approach towards this matter was adopted.[84] It would be the mid-1940's before full-time collectors would be given expenses, so the question of their furnishing accounts of their expenses did not arise for the first decade of the Commission's operations.[85]

Nevertheless diaries could be used, and most likely were used, to keep an eye on collectors. In discussing the function(s) of these diaries it is interesting to note that in the case of one of the longest-serving collectors, Seán Ó hEochaidh, it would appear that after two decades or so of collecting he ceased writing a diary, although he continued collecting for almost three more decades. Why after twenty years of collecting was keeping a diary by him no longer required, if this was the case? Was he given a dispensation from this arduous task after years of devoted service because he was considered to have proven his worth, and possibly because of his close personal friendship with Ó Duilearga? Moreover, the special collector Mícheál Mac Énrí and the full-time collector Jim Delaney appear not to have kept field diaries, for whatever reason.

While there is no doubt that Ó Duilearga considered the keeping of a diary by collectors important, it has to be noted that these diaries feature very little in Ó Duilearga's own writings. This is not to say that he did not stress the importance of keeping a diary to collectors. For example, as Patricia Lysaght notes in a letter Ó Duilearga wrote to the Commission's collector in Scotland, Calum MacLean, in January 1949, 'he asked him to pay particular attention to the diary as the personal account of his work as a collector in Scotland would be especially interesting in time to come.'[86]

---

83 ULMA Saml. Åke Campbell, subnr. 203. Italics underlined in original.
84 It is interesting to note that a report of a conference held in the Dept. of Education in September 1946, attended by Ó Duilearga, to discuss the question of travel allowances and other expenses for the field staff of the Commission, states that 'No difficulty would arise in certifying claims for such an allowance, as each officer sends in a weekly statement of work ... and in addition, keeps a diary, giving all details of his activities'. ED CO 495(8): 'Coimisiún Béaloideasa Éireann', dated 16.9.1946.
85 It appears that collectors from the mid-1940's onwards furnished details of their expenses on a monthly rather than a weekly basis. Moreover, some collectors did not 'itemise their expenditure' and 'were dilatory in furnishing their monthly accounts.' See ED FL 3: Ó Catháin to Ó Maoláin, dated 9.7.1954, and 'CBÉ. Financial Year 1961–62'.
86 Lysaght 1990, p. 41, n. 8 (trans.).

Seán Ó Súilleabháin, at the Indiana Mid-Century Folklore Conference, said of the diaries of the Commission's full-time collectors: 'Now these diaries will, I think, be of great use later when our tales will be published.'[87] In time, Ó Súilleabháin himself was to make use of these diaries in editing material from the Commission's Archive for his *Folktales of Ireland*. In this work he gives a lot of contextual information from the collectors' diaries, as well as from other sources.[88] But this is rather an exceptional use of these diaries by a member of staff of the Commission. As noted above, Ó Duilearga's innumerable contributions to *Béaloideas* do not draw on these diaries as a source and contain very little else by way of context.[89] There is no doubt that he saw text as far more important than context.

Perhaps, in seeing these diaries simply through the prism of modern contextual studies we are distorting them somewhat. Although they appear to have had a dual (indeed a multi-) purpose, they were definitely intended as a record for future generations. As mentioned above in respect of the so-called 'diaries' of the Ordnance Survey workers of the second quarter of the nineteenth century, Seán Ó Súilleabháin has said: 'these diaries give the atmosphere in which the work was done.' Some seven years later, he wrote of the diaries kept by the Commission's collectors that they give 'a day-to-day (more correctly, a night-to-night) account of the activities of the collector in the field, and in bulk they give a good picture of how the work was carried out.'[90] Ó Súilleabháin's use of the word 'bulk' is most appropriate, for by the time the Commission wound up operations in 1970, the collectors' diaries amounted to approximately 59,000 pages. Of course, far more than bulk was involved. The diaries of the full-time collectors must be considered among the gems in the Commission's crown. Although some of the full-time collectors may have experienced the keeping of a diary as an extra burden to an already heavy workload, at least one collector realized the importance of these diaries. Writing in the early 1940's of his collecting until then, Tadhg Ó Murchadha expresses the hope that one day the diaries accompanying his texts will be published: 'it is my earnest hope that when that account will be available to the Irish-Minded ('Gaelach') people of Ireland that it will be as good as any heroic tale ('scéal fiannaíochta') ever composed, and of more interest!'[91].

---

87   Stith Thompson 1976, p. 7.
88   Ó Súilleabháin 1966.
89   However, in Ó Duilearga 1965 (p. 138) he does quote from a diary of Seán Mac Mathghamhna's.
90   S. Ó Súilleabháin 1957, p. 451.
91   Ó Murchadha 1941, pp 43–44 (trans.).

3. The neglect of more recent living tradition

'Dead clay' and 'living clay'

Gearóid Ó Crualaoich, commenting on the Commission's orientation towards collecting older traditions, notes that these were gathered 'more from the memories, than from the living behaviour of informants and culture bearers, who were themselves of course living in a society and a culture deeply transformed by the technology and social organisation of the contemporary modern world.'[92] In commenting thus, Ó Crualaoich has, of course, the benefit of hindsight and advances in recent scholarship. In concentrating on older traditions, the Commission was following approaches common in international folkloristic practice at the time. Nevertheless, it should be noted that the Commission's concentration on things old was criticised by at least one contemporary. The Irish language writer, language activist, and polemicist, Máirtín Ó Cadhain upbraided the Commission for being obsessed with everything old, and accused it of neglecting more recent tradition, particularly the living tradition of song composition in the Gaeltacht. In a controversial lecture on folklore delivered in 1950 he divided his arguments into two main sections: 'Cré Bheo' ('Living Clay') and 'Cré Mharbh'('Dead Clay'). In his opinion, the Irish Folklore Commission was interested only in 'dead clay' while it neglected the 'living clay' of the then Gaeltacht, and, by implication, the rest of the country as well.[93]

There is no doubt that Ó Duilearga and others engaged in the work of collection felt that the older, dying traditions had more intrinsic value, or needed more urgently to be collected than newer, more contemporary ones. This is not to imply that they would have seen no need to collect these newer traditions, nor that they would have been unaware of such traditions, but

---

92 Ó Crualaoich 2003, p. 160.
93 Ó Laighin 1919, pp. 129–169. It is difficult to say to what extent Ó Cadhain is right in his assertion that folklorists neglected this genre, as much of the collections of the Commission have not been catalogued. Ríonach uí Ógáin, who catalogued the songs collected by the Commission in one barony of Co. Galway, noted that many recent compositions (from the 1930's) were recorded, especially songs of praise. uí Ógáin (Ní Fhlathartaigh) 1976, p. x.

that their collection was not as urgent as that of the older tradition. In many respects this was a very practical decision: what to collect and what to leave for later. Moreover, the Commission's primary interest in collecting older tradition of necessity resulted in a tendency to collect from older informants. One result of this was that the collector was perhaps less in a position to observe the way older traditions were taking new shape, and new traditions being born, than might otherwise have been the case.[94]

Apart from international folkloristic practice, the nature of Irish tradition itself, particularly the rich seams of folklore to be found in the Irish language, would have oriented folklorists towards older tradition. Ó Duilearga is reported as describing some of the traditions that 'survived' the demise of the older traditional life and the change of language as 'thin gruel'.[95] There is little doubt that many of the Commission's collectors would have agreed with him that the older, dying traditions had more intrinsic value, or at any rate needed more urgently to be collected than newer, more contemporary ones. In time, however, the Commission would collect a good deal of 'thin gruel'. In many respects, given the exigencies of time and money, what to collect and what to leave for later was a very practical decision.

Although it is not specifically stated in its Terms of Reference, the Commission was established to save for posterity older traditions that were in danger of disappearing, especially those enshrined in the Irish language. For Ó Duilearga and his co-workers to have investigated the changing narrative conditions of the 1930's and 1940's would have demanded a lot more time and resources, and would have required quite a different approach to collecting and towards tradition in general. Neither is it certain that such an approach to collecting would have received official sanction. Nevertheless, however justified concentrating on collecting older material was in the short term, in the long term this approach, of course, ran the risk that the Commission might be left behind the times. Where Ó Duilearga and his colleagues can be faulted is not so much because they concentrated on collecting the older streams of tradition, but that in so doing they would appear, for the most part, to have failed to recognise the dynamism and continuity of the tradition. The fact that the Irish language was on the verge of extinction in many Breac-Ghaeltacht areas also militated against viewing the situation in the field as a continuum rather than as something final. Ó Duilearga himself took a rather fatalistic view of the decline of the Irish language, seeing little future for it beyond the last of the great storytellers. By the late 1940's he was particularly pessimistic about the situation in the province of Munster, as can be seen from his introduction to *Leabhar Sheáin Í Chonaill*.[96]

Given his views on the terminal decline of Irish, it is not surprising that he seems to have paid little attention to, or at least to have shown scant interest in, new traditions that might be forming in Gaeltacht areas, nor in old ones that were being transformed. In one respect, however, he did

---

94   The changing cultural milieu of the areas they worked is sometimes commented on in the collectors' diaries.
95   See S. Ó Catháin 1983, pp. 155–156.
96   Ó Duilearga 1977 [1948], p. xii.

recognise the continuity of tradition. In the early years of the Commission full-time collectors were sometimes sent to English-speaking districts where a modicum of residual Irish still remained or where Irish had been spoken within living memory. However, for the most part, their mission was to save the vestiges of Gaelic lore, not to collect new blossomings of tradition.[97]

97　E.g. in 1939–40, Seosamh Ó Dálaigh was sent to parts of north Kerry, west Limerick and mid-Tipperary. D/T S 15548A: 'Gearr-Thuar./1939–40', p. 4.

4. Neglect of urban tradition

Rural versus *urban, national* versus *international*

There is no doubt that the Irish Folklore Commission neglected to collect urban folklore. The reasons for it doing so can be explained both by Irish conditions and international folkloristic practice. Moreover, the fact that Irish for the most part had not survived as a community language in urban settings, to any significant extent, would in any event have precluded extensive collecting being undertaken in towns and cities, as the Commission for the first decade and a half or so concentrated its full-time collectors in rural west of Ireland, Irish-speaking districts.

In a public lecture Ó Duilearga gave in late 1929, he is quoted as saying: 'The culture of towns is international and that of the country is the only true national one.'[98] More than a decade later, in his introduction to Seán Ó Súilleabháin's *A Handbook of Irish Folklore*, speaking of the need to collect 'the traditions of the historic Irish nation' he wrote:

> Here as elsewhere the shoddy imported culture of the towns pushes back the frontiers of the indigenous homespun culture of the countryside, and the ancient courtesies and traditional ways of thought and behaviour tend to disappear before the destroying breath of 'the spirit of the age.'[99]

We might imply from this that he did not see the towns and cities of Ireland as belonging intrinsically to 'the historic Irish nation'. Whether this was the case or not, Ó Duilearga could when the occasion demanded pay at least lip service to the existence of folklore in towns and cities. In a lecture he gave to the Irish Book Fair in 1942 he stated: 'The main task of the Irish Folklore Commission is the recording of the oral traditions of Ireland wherever they are to be found, in the towns as well as the countryside, in English as well as

---

98 Ó Duilearga 1929, p. 8.
99 Ó Súilleabháin 1970 [1942], p. v. It would appear that Daniel Corkery's classic study of eighteenth-century Gaelic Ireland, *The Hidden Ireland*, first published in 1925 had a formative influence on the young Ó Duilearga, as it did on many of his generation. For more on Daniel Corkery and his ideas, see Maune 1993, passim.

in Irish.'[100] Of course, there may be a degree of rhetorical flourish in what he says here, but it is not simply that. He was not in principle against collecting the traditions of towns and cities, although his priorities lay elsewhere.[101] Moreover, Seán Ó Súilleabháin in his *Handbook* under 'Instructions to Collectors' does give some recognition to urban folklore. He says: 'There are very few people living in Ireland who are not tradition-bearers to some extent. Even city and town-born individuals possess traditional information concerning the ways and doings of those about them.' He goes on to say, however, that '[i]t is in country districts, however, that information is to be obtained in greatest abundance.'[102] Thus, while key figures in the Irish Folklore Commission recognised the existence of urban traditions, they initially, at least, did not place any great importance on such traditions, or at least placed less importance on them than on rural traditions.

Collectors and urban oral tradition

However, even if the Commission from the beginning had a more enlightened policy towards urban folklore, given the fact that for the first decade or so of its operations, it concentrated its full-time collectors in the Irish-speaking districts, situated mainly along, or adjacent to, the west coast, there was little likelihood of these collectors covering any of the main urban centres of the country outside those regions. We can therefore only speak of full-time collectors neglecting urban tradition insofar as they failed to collect the traditions of the urban centres within their regions of operation. When full-time collectors collected in an urban setting, it was very often to elicit traditions that were derivative, directly or indirectly, of the countryside. For example, Seán Ó Cróinín, who lived for many years in the small town of Macroom, collected a large amount of material from Pádraig Ó Crualaoi, who was a neighbour of his in the town. Although Ó Crualaoi had lived in Macroom for almost sixty years by the time Ó Cróinín began working with him, he was from the rural parish of Baile Bhuirne. The poetic traditions Ó Cróinín collected from him were not those of the town of Macroom as such but traditions pertaining to Cork poets of former times, when Irish was spoken throughout the county – in both rural and urban settings, it should be stressed.[103] This was not always the case, however. For instance, Jim Delaney collected a great deal of maritime lore from his father, a sea captain and a native of Wexford town. The Delaneys, like Ó Duilearga's paternal forebears had for generations ploughed the high seas,

100 Ó Duilearga 1942a, p. 22.
101 Mary Ó Drisceoil claims: 'Like the artists of the Romantic movement who painted out the squalor of the countryside, Séamus Ó Duilearga, the Director of the Irish Folklore Commission scrubbed out any reference to the urban life.'(M. Ó Drisceoil 2005, p. 187) While there may be a good deal of truth in this, she goes on to imply, it would appear, that Ó Duilearga held narrow exclusivist, perhaps even bigoted, views on what constituted Irishness. If that is indeed what she is implying, it is a simplification, to say the least.
102 Ó Súilleabháin 1970 [1942], p. xi.
103 See D. Ó Cróinín and S. Ó Cróinín 1982.

and Ó Duilearga may have had a personal reason for having these maritime traditions collected.[104]

While Jim Delaney seems to have been appreciative of the traditions of his native town[105], another full-time collector, Liam Mac Coisdeala, had a negative attitude towards the west of Ireland town he grew up in. Speaking of his native town, Kiltimagh, and its surrounds, he says:

> There were hardly ever anywhere on earth places more dull ('leimhe') and more lacking in native civilisation than the (large) towns of the English-speaking parts of Ireland ('Galltacht') for the past hundred years. Something of the learning and culture of the Gaeltacht remained in the countryside, even after the death of Irish. But that was not the case with large towns; instead of them being centres of inspiration and direction in cultural affairs for the areas surrounding them, they were in actual fact destroying and drowning whatever bit of cultural inheritance that reached the inhabitants of those areas.[106]

When we speak of urban versus rural in the context of Ireland from the 1930's to the 1960's, we should be careful. Many small towns, such as Macroom and Kiltimagh, were very rural in character, and hardly deserve to be designated 'urban'. Nevertheless, I will continue to use the term 'urban' to refer to the life and traditions of small towns, in addition to that of large towns and cities.

Given the fact that they were more numerous as well as their wider geographical spread, the likelihood of part-time collectors collecting urban traditions would have been greater than was the case with full-time collectors. However, anyone offering their services to the Commission as a part-time collector, could not but have been aware of the rural emphasis of the Commission. Consequently, it is no surprise to find that these collectors, even when residing in an urban area, very often contributed material that derived from the countryside. This is not to claim that the Commission would have discouraged any such persons from collecting urban traditions. The Commission welcomed material from whatever source, and received collections of urban folklore.

During the school year 1937–1938 schoolchildren also contributed material of urban provenance. However, as we have seen above, the number of schools in major urban areas that participated in this folklore scheme was limited by the fact that it was specifically stated that schools in the cities of Dublin, Cork, Limerick and Waterford could opt out of the scheme.[107] However, Galway city was not allowed to opt out of the scheme, for obvious reasons, as at least one area of the city was still partly Irish-speaking, and as the city was surrounded to the east and west by Irish-speaking areas.

Although the proposal to allow the urban schools of four of the state's five largest centres of population to opt out of the scheme did not originate

---

104 See Delaney 1973–74 and Delaney 1975–76.
105 In this regard, see especially Delaney 1997.
106 Liam Mac Coisdeala 1946, p.141 (trans.).
107 Ó Catháin and Ní Sheighin 1987, pp. xviii, n. 3.

with the Director of the Commission, he must take some of the blame for not opposing it. After all, he was the expert, and his opinion would have carried a lot of weight in some quarters. In this connection, it is interesting to note that Pádraig Ó Brolcháin of the Dept. of Education, an old Gaelic Leaguer, defended the proposal to include Dublin in the abortive 1934 Schools Folklore Scheme against Dept. of Finance objections. Among his reasons for including Dublin, was the fact that: 'The older areas of Dublin city such as The Coombe, The Pottle, Whitefriar Street &c are in reality comparatively rich in old tales and legends'. Ó Brolcháin died in July 1934, some months after stating the case for collecting Dublin folklore.[108] Perhaps, if he had lived, the 1937/1938 Schools Scheme would not have given Dublin schools (and those of the other cities listed above) the choice of opting out of the scheme. It must be said, however, that some schools in these cities did participate in the scheme.

Ó Brolcháin would appear to have been a lone voice in the Dept. of Education, and possibly elsewhere in the Civil Service. Long before Ó Súilleabháin's *Handbook* was published, and before the Dept. of Education gave the go-ahead for the 1937/1938 Schools Scheme, most educated Irish people interested in folklore and such matters would very likely have formed the opinion that the more genuine tradition was to be found in the countryside. Indeed, as discussed in Chapter 1 of this work, one could say that the basic ethos of the new state, and of the cultural movement that to a large extent brought it into being, gave primacy to the traditions of the countryside, and particular areas of it, believing that the soul of the nation was enshrined in the west of Ireland and in its Gaelic heritage. While the rural poor of the west of Ireland could be idealised by sections of the middle-classes and those in power, the slums in which many of the urban poor lived were seen by them as beds of immorality and vice.[109]

Wider context of neglect of urban tradition

Irish folklorists were not alone, however, in seeing the countryside as the main repository of tradition. Since folklore first developed as a field of study, the tendency was to study country folk and their traditions. There were lone voices, however, who sought to widen the concept of the term 'folk' to include the populations of towns and cities. One such voice was Joseph Jacobs. In the late nineteenth century, Jacobs argued that folklore could also exist in urban settings and that it did not simply consist of survivals. Jacobs, in rejecting 'the concept of a separate, historical, non-literate and anonymous folk' had this to say:

---

108 D/F S 046/0037/33: Ó Brolcháin to Sec. Dept. of Finance, dated 20.1.1934. It is, of course, quite likely that the Dept. of Fin. would have opposed the extension of the 1937/1938 Schools Scheme to all urban schools, given the poor showing of urban schools in the earlier 1934 scheme.

109 The rise of de Valera to power in 1932 saw a concerted effort to clear the slums of the large towns and cities and relocate their inhabitants in new housing estates.

> For, after all, we are the Folk as well as the rustic, though their lore may be other than ours, as ours will be different from that of those that follow us... Survivals are folk-lore, but folk-lore need not be all survivals. We ought to learn valuable hints as to the spread of folk-lore by studying the Folk of to-day. The music-hall, from this point of view, will have its charm for the folk-lorist, who will there find the *Volkslieder* of to-day.

As Georgina Boyes notes, Jacobs was far ahead of his time and 'accurately suggests the form Folkloristic theory eventually developed in the 1960s'.[110]

Even if Jacobs's ideas had fallen on more fertile soil elsewhere, given the roots of the Folklore of Ireland Society, and the independent Irish state, in the cultural ferment brought about by the Gaelic League (founded the same year Jacobs published the above), and given that the music-hall, and everything it represented, was anathema to the League and influential elements in the Irish Free State, it is unlikely that his ideas would have gained many adherents in Southern Ireland. Nevertheless, although it was not until the 1960's that folklorists began showing interest in urban lore, to any appreciable extent, in Sweden in the early 1940's, Carl Wilhelm von Sydow, Ó Duilearga's mentor, stressed the need to collect the traditions of manor houses and urban centres. Part of his interest in the traditions of manor houses and towns arose from his recognition of the fact that 'bourgeois culture' was important 'for a correct assessment of peasant traditions'. As a result of von Sydow's new interest, questionnaires on urban and manor culture were distributed and during 1940–41 the traditions of ten towns in southern Sweden were documented.[111] Von Sydow was twenty years or so ahead of his time. It is unlikely, given von Sydow's belief in the importance of Gaelic oral tradition, that he would have sought to distract Ó Duilearga from his chosen path and exhort him to collect the traditions of urban centres and those of manor houses in Ireland at this time or later. How aware Ó Duilearga was of this new direction in Swedish folkloristics is not clear. As the Second World War progressed, his contacts with Sweden were very infrequent.[112]

In the post-War period, however, a domestic critic of the Irish Folklore Commission drew attention to the fact that folklore was to be found in towns and cities as well as the countryside, and among all classes. Máirtín Ó Cadhain in early 1950, in a public lecture already referred to, remarked:

> Folklore is a permanent thing. It is being created before our eyes in Dublin, London, New York. The person who looks carefully will see a new version constantly [forming] on very ancient matters. The gods do not die. What they do is simply retreat to seclusion for a time.

Ó Cadhain believed folk traditions were not just to be found among citizens of Dublin with recent roots in the countryside but also amongst those whose

---

110 Quoted in Boyes 1993, pp. 16 and 21, n. 34.
111 Salomonsson 2000, p. 205.
112 His support for the teaching of urban local history and tradition, mentioned below, may partly derive from von Sydow.

rural roots stretched further back. Although raised in an almost monoglot Irish-speaking west of Ireland community, Ó Cadhain came to know Dublin and its people intimately, having, as a member of the outlawed IRA in the late 1930's gained, of necessity, a deep knowledge of underground Dublin: its pubs, its back streets, its tenements, its poor. However, in his opinion, folklore did not just belong to the poor: "I am not sure what folklore is, but I know this much that the 'educated classes' have as many 'myths and usages' and the same amount of 'illogical thinking' as any other class."[113] Speaking of the ideas expressed in this public lecture of Ó Cadhain's, Diarmuid Ó Giolláin says:

> In the critical literature on folklore, Máirtín Ó Cadhain was probably the intellectual who best understood the contradiction between the ideal of folklore and the social reality of traditional society. It is certain that nothing discursive on folklore was written during his time, and little has since been written, that is as powerful as what he wrote.'[114]

Ó Duilearga was never to answer Ó Cadhain in print, but it is interesting to note that later that year (1950), in an address to the congress of the Irish Vocational Education Association, he made an appeal 'that something be done to interest the students, not only of rural but also of urban [primary and vocational] schools, in the study of the local history (in the Scandinavian sense) not only of the countryside, but of the town and city as well.' He went on to say:

> By history I do not mean the compilation of dry disconnected facts culled from ponderous and often badly-edited works, masquerading under the title of 'local histories'–what I have in mind is the interpretation to the student of the local culture-landscape, a geographical, a cultural and a social–as well as political–historical interpretation. There is too much in our histories of the leaders, too little of the men who trailed the pike, or shouldered the gun from behind the 'Man on the White Horse,' too little of the meaning of the familiar commonplace which made no headlines in the annals of aristocratic Gaeldom, or in the biased chronicles of the superficial Anglo-Irish landlord historian.[115]

Ó Duilearga's appeal does not appear to have been acted upon; certainly the study of local history, in the sense he proposed, did not become an integral part of the school curriculum, although individual teachers may have managed to deal with aspects of local history (including folklore) in their classes.[116]

---

113 Ó Laighin 1990, p. 135 (trans.).
114 Ó Giolláin 2005, pp. 133–134 (trans.).
115 Ó Duilearga 1950, p. 48.
116 My understanding of the neglect of local studies at primary school level, at least, is informed by various conversations with the writer, and former National School teacher, Michael Coady.

An opportunity lost

Since the 1940's, in particular, the National Library of Ireland has accumulated a vast body of papers that derive from the 'big houses' of Ireland (equivalent to the manor houses of Sweden). These sources tell us much not only about the privileged lives of their owners, but also of their servants, who often lived under the same roof, and of the tenants who lived on their estates under roofs of varying quality: the well-to-do middlemen, comfortable and small farmers, and the landless poor.[117] The recent work by Gerard J. Lyne on the Lansdowne Estate in Kerry shows us how much estate papers, used in conjunction with other sources, can help to shed light on the lives of Irish people in former times, both great and small.[118] One result of the neglect of the traditions of Ireland's 'big houses' by folklorists and others is that we know little about many aspects of the lives of servants in these houses in the generation or two before their demise. As Terence Dooley, speaking of these servants, says: 'Unfortunately they themselves did not write their memoirs or leave any type of diaries behind that might provide an authentic insight into their daily lives, how they perceived their role in the big house or the relationship they had with their employees [*recte* employers].'[119] Not only folklorists were at fault here of course: one might also ask why no historians bothered to research the lore, and not just that of servants, of these houses when there were still people around who remembered them in their heyday.

One could also argue that historians as well as folklorists neglected Dublin, the greatest centre of population in the country. As a result of the rural orientation of the new state, C. Lincoln says of Dublin:

> The reality is that Dublin has rarely featured in recent history as a place meriting special attention. Its role as capital has seldom counted as a matter of any material consequence, still less as a locus of Irish 'culture' in which people should have pride. Dublin has enjoyed an ambiguous relationship with the country of which it is capital and the urban culture which it represents has seldom been viewed as something of value.[120]

Jacinta Prunty, in her study of Dublin slums during the nineteenth and early part of the twentieth century, notes:

> While weighed down by the voluminous information thus available, it must be noted that the voices least likely to appear in the records are those of the slum residents themselves. Little survives about local customs, music or dance or any type of amusement excepting tomes of disapproving scrutiny of the liquor and dram shops; references to the Irish language are scant, and separate subgroupings based on occupation or rural origin are difficult to distinguish in the written record.

117 For a guide to these sources, see Dooley 2007.
118 Lyne 2001.
119 Dooley 2001, p. 146.
120 Quoted in Tovey and Share 2000, p. 300.

She further notes that '[o]ral histories are the obvious means towards rectifying this imbalance' but laments that such oral histories of the Dublin slums as exist date 'largely from the early 1980's' and consequently can shed little light on the nineteenth century.[121] Without doubt, a great opportunity was lost to collect the oral traditions of Dublin of the post-Famine period. Things might have been different, as there appear to have been people on the Commission who were not opposed in principle to collecting Dublin traditions.[122]

Bríd Mahon, who worked in the Commission for more than thirty years, speaking of Ó Duilearga, says: 'One thing I shall always regret is his lack of interest in urban traditions, and more especially in those of Dublin. Our main task lay in gathering up the folk tradition of Gaelic Ireland before it was too late. Everything else must take second place.'[123] Unfortunately, she does not elaborate on this so it is difficult to know if he actually discouraged the collecting of urban/Dublin folklore on any particular occasion. However, I do not think we are right to conclude from what Mahon says that Ó Duilearga had any great antipathy towards the folklore of Dublin or that of other urban centres as such. In respect of urban folklore, Ó Duilearga was a man of his time, and as he got older he perhaps did not keep up with the times. In his submission to the Commission on Higher Education in the mid-1960's he did not list the collection of urban folklore as one of the tasks facing the Commission, although he did list continuing 'field-work as hitherto with special reference to English-speaking districts.'[124] 'English-speaking districts' could, of course, be meant to include the towns and cities of Ireland. Whether that was the case is difficult to determine.[125]

---

121 Prunty 1998, pp. 336–337.

122 e.g. in January 1957 Seán Ó Maonaigh proposed that the Commission should collect samples of the English speech of native Dubliners for the purpose of study. Nobody opposed his proposal although it does not appear to have been acted upon. Moreover, in 1964, Leo Corduff and Jim Delaney recorded lore from old Dublin city tailors relating to their traditional craft. ED FL 2: 'CBÉ Miont. 87ú Cruinniú, 29.1.1957', par. 648 and ED FL 8: 'CBÉ Miont. 120ú Cruinniú, 3ú 7.1964', p. 3.

123 Mahon 1998, p. 112.

124 *Commission on Higher Education II Report Volume* 1, p. 364.

125 Almost ten years after the Commission was disbanded the Irish Government gave its successor, the Department of Irish Folklore, a substantial sum of money to collect the oral traditions of Dublin. For more on this project, see Mac Philib 2006. In the 1990's a project was initiated to collect the working-class traditions of part of Cork city in cooperation with the Department of Folklore and Ethnology, University College Cork. See Desplanques 2000, pp. 183 ff.

5. Neglect of English-speaking rural areas

Initial prioritising of collecting in Irish

During the first ten years or more of its operations, the Commission concentrated its efforts, at least in respect of full-time collectors, on Irish-speaking districts. Given its meagre resources and the prevailing official ideology of the time that placed more value on the Gaelic past and traditions in the Irish language, it is not at all surprising that it should have done so. The very nature of Irish oral tradition also helped to tip the scales in favour of concentrating on collecting in Irish. However valuable the oral traditions of the English-speaking parts of Ireland were, nothing existed in these areas to equal the rich seams of tradition still extant in the Gaeltacht. Moreover, the fact that Irish was in rapid decline as a community language gave an added urgency to collecting in Irish as much of the folklore enshrined in that language was in danger of disappearing. Of course, certain traditions in English-speaking areas were also in danger of disappearing, and much lore was lost because of the concentration on Irish. Obviously, a choice had to be made, and Irish was given priority over English. If it had not been, a finger of accusation might well have been raised by a later generation against Ó Duilearga, the Folklore of Ireland Society, and the political authorities of the day for allowing a great deal of vernacular Irish to disappear without endeavouring to save it for posterity.

In the lecture Ó Duilearga gave at the Irish Book Fair in 1942, already quoted above, he stated:

> I am not content to know something of the fireside tales of Kerry or the folksongs of Conamara. I am interested in the folklore of Ireland, in the speech of Ireland, in the history of Ireland, in the geography of Ireland. Ulster planter and Leinster palesman, Norman and Saxon, they are all Irish, and in their traditions or what they have preserved of them I am equally interested.[126]

126 Ó Duilearga 1942a, p. 21.

Although given to rhetorical statements, I believe he was sincere in declaring his interest in the various strands of Irish tradition. Although the Commission, under Ó Duilearga's direction, saw the saving of traditions in the Irish language as a priority, its approach to Irish tradition, in theory at least, was not exclusive.[127] Moreover, it should also be stressed that with regard to documenting material culture, Ó Duilearga considered the whole of Ireland, north, south, east and west, to be of equal importance.

Cutbacks due to the advent of the Second World War probably delayed the spread of intensive collecting to non-Gaeltacht areas. It would be the late 1940's before a full-time collector would be appointed by the Commission to collect in English-speaking districts. Nevertheless, much material in English was contributed by part-time collectors during the early years of the Commission. The mid-1950's saw the appointment of a second full-time-collector to work in English-speaking districts (more of this collecting below). Moreover the network of questionnaire correspondents that the Commission built up covered, more or less, the whole country, but as mentioned above (Chapter IV/4), Bairbre Ní Fhloinn notes the relative lack of questionnaire correspondents in some of the eastern (Leinster) counties, in particular.

It has been estimated that approximately twenty per cent of the Commission's Main Collection is in English (amounting to c. 144,000 pp. from a total of c. 720,000 pp.). On the other hand, perhaps as much as ninety per cent of the Schools Collection is in English (c. 338,100 pp. from a total of c. 375,660 pp.).[128] Thus, as a result of collecting by full-time and part-time collectors, questionnaire correspondents, and primary school children, most rural English-speaking areas of the state are represented, to a lesser or greater degree, in the Commission's collections. However, it should be stressed, in respect of the Schools Collection, that the geographic spread of much of this material is uneven. Far more material was collected in the west, southwest and northwest of the state, i.e the provinces of Connaught, Munster and the part of Ulster within the state than in the province of Leinster (comprising roughly the east of the country). The combined population of Leinster, 1,219,501 (based on the 1936 census), contributed some 86,220 pages of material (i.e. material transcribed into the official manuscript books), while the part of Ulster within the southern state (Counties Donegal, Monaghan, and Cavan), with a population of 280,114 is represented by 65,340 pages of material. The returns for these Ulster counties are also proportionally higher, in respect of population, than the corresponding figures for the provinces of Connaught and Munster: 524,843(pop.)/104,580 pages and 941,392(pop.)/123,840 pages respectively.[129]

127 Nevertheless, in practice, as Guy Beiner notes, the Commission often neglected 'Ascendancy, Protestant and Loyalist traditions.' Beiner 2001, p. 225.

128 These figures refer to the official bound manuscripts, not to the children's copybooks, the bulk of which contain material in English.

129 The reasons for this uneven spread of material are complex. In general, counties with Gaeltacht populations or the presence of residual Irish or that had remained Irish-speaking until relatively recent times produced more material than counties that had experienced anglicisation earlier, such as many of the Leinster counties. I hope to publish a detailed study of this matter elsewhere.

Extending collecting in English

Despite the relatively poor returns for some eastern counties, in particular, the Commission, as a result of the Schools Scheme, realised that there was a wealth of folklore in the country that was waiting to be collected. Ó Duilearga, as mentioned above, in his report to the Government for 1938–1939 stated that full-time collectors should also be sent to other districts outside the Gaeltacht 'to verify and expand the material' collected by the schoolchildren.[130] The Commission never had the resources to do this. Nevertheless, full-time collectors in time began to work some English-speaking areas to a limited extent (see above). It was not until the late 1940s, however, that a collector, Michael J. Murphy, with no knowledge of Irish, was appointed full-time to collect exclusively in English. Ironically, the first area this collector was sent to, and where he was to stay collecting for a number of years, was the Sperrin Mountains of Co. Tyrone in Northern Ireland, where many of the older generation still knew Irish and spoke it among themselves. Later Michael J. Murphy was to extend his area of activity to cover most of the counties of Northern Ireland and the border counties of the Republic.

In the mid-1950's another collector, Jim Delaney, was appointed to collect in English-speaking areas. Unlike Michael J. Murphy, Delaney knew Irish, although, with only one or two exceptions, he collected material only in English.[131] Murphy and Delaney were the only full-time collectors to collect exclusively in English. It is noteworthy that apart from a year Delaney initially spent collecting in his native Co. Wexford, both these collectors spent their careers collecting in north Leinster, east Connaught, and Ulster. Delaney, who, as mentioned above, had written an MA thesis on the nineteenth-century Wexford folklorist, Patrick Kennedy, was initially sent to collect in Co. Wexford 'to follow in the footsteps' of Kennedy and to ascertain how much tradition survived in Kennedy's home area.[132] Ó Duilearga had a particular interest in Kennedy as he was one of the first collectors of Irish Folklore. Delaney might have been left in the southeast of the country but for the fact that during a visit to north Longford, where his wife was from, in the summer of 1955 he discovered that the area was rich in tradition. Although on holiday, he began collecting from one spectacular informant, Frank MacNaboe. The richness of MacNaboe's fund of lore and traditional knowledge made a deep impression on Delaney when he compared it to his 'experience on the south and east coast of Wexford.' Although Delaney had planned to continue his work in south Wexford, when he informed Ó Duilearga of his discovery in north Longford, he received the 'laconic note: "stay where you are."'[133] He was never to return to collect in the southeast.

---

130 D/T S 15548A: 'Gearr-Thuar./1938–39', p. [8] (trans).
131 RTÉSA B1203, 'Folkland', Séamas Ó Catháin speaking to Jim Delaney. For some of the formative influences on this collector, see Delaney 1997.
132 Delaney 1990, p. 15 and RTÉSA B1203. For an account of Delaney's collecting work in 'Kennedy Country', see Delaney 1988.
133 Delaney 1990, pp. 15–16.

The decision to transfer Jim Delaney to northwest Leinster was certainly taken because it was considered to be richer in tradition than Co. Wexford. Whatever Delaney felt about this transfer at the time, in retrospect, it seems, he did not regret it. In north Longford there was an abundance of informants with a lot of lore to collect from, while in the parts of Wexford where he had been collecting there were only a few such informants. It is interesting to note, however, that Delaney, who was later to develop a keen interest in material culture and folklife, says that while working in Wexford he was not interested in such matters: 'The way I was trained, folklife didn't come into it at all.' Moreover, in the case of one of his Wexford informants, who knew a great deal about thatching and material culture in general, he says: 'I didn't get what I should have got from John Quigley.' Presumably, by this he means that if he had developed a specific interest in folklife by the time he began working with this informant, he would have succeeded in eliciting more from him on such matters. Delaney believed that north Longford was richer in tradition because it 'was a place that had been cut off' and had been 'untouched by railways' and other harbingers of modernity. He felt Wexford was 'too far east' to be rich in folk tradition.[134]

However, there is no doubt that a great deal of tradition was to be had in Wexford and the southeast of the country generally, although it may not have been as near the surface, so to speak, as in north Leinster, and might have taken collectors longer to elicit and record. Delaney's transfer to north Longford was certainly Wexford's loss and the failure of the Commission to have a full-time collector work the southeast subsequently compounded this loss.[135]

Continued priority of Irish over English

Despite the appointment of Murphy and Delaney, collecting in Irish would seem to have remained a priority to the very end of the Commission. In this respect, it has to be noted that none of the special collectors employed by the Commission from the early 1950's onward collected (exclusively or even significantly) in English. By this time a great deal had been collected in Irish, and the arguments that had been made in respect of traditions in Irish in the 1930's could now be made in respect of many traditions in English, i.e. that they, and the way of life that sustained them, were on the verge of extinction. While Ó Duilearga had from the beginning a vision of what needed to be done in respect of the Gaeltacht and Breac-Ghaeltacht, it is not at all clear whether he had a vision in respect of the prerequisites of collecting in English-speaking districts. A more piecemeal policy seems to have been in operation in respect of the latter than the former.

---

134 RTÉSA B1203.
135 Ó Duilearga hoped in time to send a full-time collecter to Kilkenny in the southeast, but this was never realised. See ED [FL 10]: 'IFC. Fin. Sub-Com./Min. 76th Meeting, 29.1.1951', par. 691.

In this connection, it is interesting to note that in the memorandum he drew up for de Valera in May 1933, he lists the 'Areas of Investigation' of his proposed 'Folk Culture Survey' as follows:

A^1. Gaeltacht
A^2. Breac-Ghaeltacht
B. Certain areas which though at present English speaking could have been classed as A^2 within living memory.
C. English speaking areas.[136]

It would appear from this that, initially at least, areas of the country that had long been English-speaking were to be given less priority than areas where Irish had survived until relatively recent times. Although the above memorandum had to be hastily written, and was intended only for a five-year folklore survey of the country, the same collecting priorities, to quite an extent, seem to have governed the whole thirty five years of the Commission's lifespan.

Of the approximately one hundred and twenty five people who collected part-time for the Commission between the mid-1940's and the disbandment of the Commission in 1970 listed in Ó Duilearga's annual reports to the Government, 62%, at least (seventy eight collectors in all), collected in counties where there were Irish-speaking communities or else residual Irish: Galway had twenty three part-time collectors, Mayo had twenty, Kerry thirteen, Donegal and Cork seven each, and Waterford and Clare four each. Moreover, in these counties, a very large percentage of the material collected was collected in Irish-speaking districts or areas with residual Irish. While many western counties had numerous part-time collectors working them, this was not the case in the east of the country. Meath, Kildare, and Offaly had only one part-time collector each in this period; Laois, Louth and Kilkenny had two; while Wexford had four. Dublin had seven part-time collectors in this period, but some of these collected in western Irish-speaking districts while on holiday, rather than in their native county. Two eastern counties, Monaghan and Wicklow had no part-time collectors in this period.[137]

In the post-War period, up until the end of the 1950's and into the 1960's, collecting in Galway and Mayo amounted to 35% of all part-time collecting. This seems somewhat incongruous, given the fact that Galway had again a full-time collector from 1951 onwards, and Mayo was served by three special collectors during the 1950's and early 1960's, and from 1951–1954 had a full-time collector, Mícheál Ó Sírín, and again from 1964 onwards when Proinnsias de Búrca was reappointed full-time collector. Was it simply a case that the majority of part-time collectors who offered their services to the

---

136 D/T S 9244: 'Collection Of Oral Tradition Of Ireland' p. 13.
137 I have utilised Ó Duilearga's Annual Reports to the Government ('Gearr-Thuarascálacha') for 1944–45 to 1969–70 to compile the above statistics: The statistics as presented may not be entirely accurate as some part-time collectors may have been omited from these reports. Part-time collecting in the period 1935–1944 also heavily favoured Gaeltacht counties or counties with residual Irish.

Commission happened to be from western counties and lived in or adjacent to Irish-speaking districts, or was there a policy of preferring part-time collectors from western counties? We might also ask if sufficient efforts were made to recruit part-time collectors for English-speaking areas of the country not covered by full-time collectors during the last decade or so of the Commission, when a great deal had already been collected in Irish. More research needs to be done on this question, and also to elucidate why part-time collecting more or less dried up in the late 1950's and early 1960's.

Nevertheless, however much one may regret that the traditions of large parts of the English-speaking areas of the country went unrecorded (or under-recorded), the decision to concentrate, initially at any rate, on Irish-speaking districts was understandable in the context of the time, and given the prevailing ideology, not at all surprising. Taking into account the richness of the Irish language tradition, and the precarious position of the language itself, concentrating on collecting in Irish was, in my opinion, justifiable for the first decade or so of the Commission. However, from the 1950's onwards more efforts should have been made to collect the traditions of the English-speaking parts of the country more systematically and more evenly than was done. A younger Séamus Ó Duilearga might have tackled the problem in a more systematic way, but, as we have noted above, his energies were waning by the early 1950's. In this respect, it is interesting to note what the historian R. V. Comerford says of the work and achievement of the Irish Folklore Commission:

> The Commission's concentration on the Irish language and its native speakers was justified in objective terms, insofar as the concern was to capture the fragments of a disappearing way of life, but that scarcely justifies the Herderian notions about nationality that were involved. Whether the language on balance benefited from the identification with the rescue of the past is another matter. The chances are that in time to come, the collection of the Irish Folklore Commission will yield up things beyond the imagining of its compilers. Here surely is an outstanding example of a national treasure that in fact has but limited bearing on nationality, but would not exist but for the desire to edify the nation.[138]

138 Comerford 2003, p. 246.

6. Female collectors and female informants

Obstacles to employing women as full-time collectors

We have seen above that the Irish Folklore Commission employed no women as full-time collectors during the thirty five years of its existence, although many females contributed to the collection as part-time collectors, as questionnaire correspondents, or as schoolgirl-collectors, mainly via the Schools Scheme. There were, of course, problems to be surmounted in employing women as full-time collectors. In the first place, even if a woman had been appointed as a full-time collector by the Commission, given the marriage ban in respect of women in the Civil Service, she would have had to resign her position on marriage. As it took time for a full-time collector to learn the trade, and as there was no way of predicting when a woman employed in such a capacity by the Commission might opt for marriage, this would have acted as a disincentive to employing women as full-time collectors to begin with. On the other hand, men were usually employed for a trial period before being appointed full-time, and some full-time collectors spent only a couple of years with the Commission, and one, Seán Mac Craith, even less than a year.

I am not aware that Ó Duilearga or the Commission ever considered the pros and cons of employing a woman as a full-time collector.[139] Given the patriarchal world of that time, and the fact that all the members of the Commission were men, it is quite likely that the question never arose. Apart from the marriage ban on women in the Civil Service, which applied to the Commission, although its staff were not Civil Servants until 1965, there were other factors that would have worked against employing women as full-time collectors. The job of full-time collector was physically very exacting, especially in the early years of the Commission. Not only was a great deal demanded from collectors, the Ediphone each full-time collector was supplied with weighed between 19 and 25½ kg,[140] and would have been no mean feat for a woman to have carried over rough terrain, as the homes of some informants

---

139 See Chapter IV/3 above, however, on Ó Duilearga's reluctance to have a foreign woman come to give instruction on collecting folk music and song.

140 Tyers/Ó Dálaigh, tapescript 1, p. 2.

were not accessible by road. The work of a full-time collector also involved being out late at night, and often entailed travelling to remote homesteads, and in many cases meant working with men living on their own. Moreover, even if the Commission had been willing to employ a woman as a full-time collector, and a woman had been found to take on this arduous task, others in the community might have objected. It might have been seen as improper in certain quarters for a young, unattached woman to be 'traipsing' around the countryside at all hours of the day or night.

Nevertheless, even if there were practical difficulties to be overcome in employing women as full-time collectors and of making the position attractive to women, it might have been possible to think of employing a woman as a roving collector, based in Dublin as the music collector and ethnological collector were. Her job would have been to work with women, and in particular, to elicit from them traditions and knowledge pertaining to women that might not be divulged so easily to male collectors. That presumes, of course, an awareness of the importance of women's lore and folklore, that is probably somewhat anachronistic. It should, however, be noted in this connection that the Gaelic League employed a number of women as *timirí*, travelling teachers, in the period 1899–1923. The work of these teachers, as I have noted above, resembled that of folklore collectors in certain respects, and indeed *timirí* sometimes doubled as collectors of folklore.[141] Moreover, once the salary of full-time collectors was raised to allow them to purchase cars, one of the obstacles to employing women collectors should have been removed, as this would have given them greater security in moving about the countryside. One might also argue that a woman collector might not have had the same need to use the Ediphone recording apparatus if she was working mainly with women. Although many more women knew long folktales than were recorded from, it is generally accepted that women were better at shorter kinds of lore. For such lore the collectors usually used pen and paper rather than the Ediphone.

It this respect, it should also be noted that long before the Irish Folklore Commission was set up, in the United States women ethnographers had begun using the Ediphone/phonograph to effect. Erika Brady writes: 'Relatively few women had had access to even the limited formal academic training available in fieldwork-related disciplines at the turn of the century, and they were further burdened with the expectation that their work would display an inappropriate level of "feminine" subjectivity. Perhaps reacting to these critical stereotypes, a striking number of women collectors used the phonograph expertly and extensively...' However, of the numerous women ethnographers she lists who used the phonograph, one might ask how many of them were women of means, for she also tells us that although Franz Boas was 'exceptional in his encouragement of women as ethnographers', nevertheless, 'his sponsorship was not an entree into the almost exclusively male precinct of institutional

---

141 Eibhlín Ní Chróinín was the only woman *timire* employed by the Gaelic League in the early twentieth century, but a number of others were employed a decade or so later. For a list of the League's *timirí* employed from 1899–1223, see Ó Cearúil 1995, pp. 121–127.

employment.'[142] Thus, although there were problems in employing women collectors, these problems were not insurmountable. Even the marriage ban might have been overcome, if there had been a will to employ a woman collector.[143]

There is no doubt that the fact that the Commission employed no women as full-time collectors must have had a bearing on the nature of the material collected. Obviously certain matters would have been more difficult to collect from women by male collectors. On the other hand, the fact that these collectors were usually local (or when they moved outside their locality, from roughly the same cultural background as their informants) may have lessened the reticence of women in speaking on certain matters to male collectors.[144] Certainly, the impression one gets from reading Seosamh Ó Dálaigh's diaries concerning his work with Peig Sayers is that the rapport that existed between them would have allowed many feminine matters to be discussed fairly freely. Moreover, in the Gaeltacht, where puritanism had not penetrated to the same extent as in some other parts of the countryside, women might not have been so reticent on certain matters in mixed company. Nonetheless, there is no doubt that the lack of women full-time collectors must have had an effect on what was collected in the Gaeltacht as well as in the rest of the country, and, of course, on the amount of material collected from women.

The weighting of collecting in favour of male informants would appear to have been the result of a number of factors involving women's roles in the household and in the community as well as the esteem, or lack of it, they were held in. Clodagh Brennan Harvey in discussing 'the thorny problem of the inadequacy of the extant record of the participation of women in Irish traditional storytelling', in addition to dealing with the crucial role of male collectors, also draws attention to the fact that 'storytelling so often occurred in same-sex groups'.[145] Women often narrated lore in situations where no men were present. Such venues had been more common in the past, such as summer pasturage, but others survived down until the time of the Irish Folklore Commission. Men might occasionally intrude on, or participate in, such gatherings of women, but their presence would most likely affect the atmosphere of the gathering in some way. Consequently men although they might have had an idea that women narrated tales or lore, or entertained themselves verbally in other ways, might have had either a very unclear or distorted picture of what took place in such gatherings when no men were present. For example, Peadar Ó Concheanainn, a native of Inis Meáin,

142 Erika Brady 1999, p. 87. In this connection it should be mentioned that the Irish folk music collector Charlotte Milligan Fox, who around 1912 used the Ediphone to collect folk songs, almost twenty years before Ó Duilearga first began using this recording apparatus, was a woman of some means. See Ó Macháin 1995, pp. 29–31. For this almost forgotten collector, see Kit and Cyril Ó Céirín 1996), pp. 78–79.

143 For instance, in 1927 a married women, Máiréad Ní Ghráda, was appointed 'Woman Organiser' to the Irish state radio station, 2RN (precursor of Radio Éireann), an exception being made in this case. Two years later another married woman, Kathleen Roddy, was appointed to the same position. See Pine 2002, p. 142.

144 In this respect, see Yocom 1985, pp. 51–52.

145 Harvey 1989, p. 120.

talks of 'airneán ban' (women's nighttime gathering usually for some sort of communal work such as spinning) on his native island, but tells us next to nothing about the lore narrated at such gatherings, or how the women entertained themselves.[146]

Women's household work did not finish with the coming of evening. Although men may also have had tasks to perform after the onset of darkness in winter, they were less likely to be occupied with household tasks or the care of children. Apart from anything else, the fact that it was customary for men to go house visiting is evidence enough of this. In a society where there was a lot of segregation of men and women, male informants were also more likely to know of other male informants and to hold them in high esteem.[147] The fact that the Commission also placed a good deal of importance on collecting folktales, at least in the first decade or so of its operations, also has a bearing on this matter. Although women may have known folktales and narrated them on certain occasions, especially to children and young people, the fact that men narrated folktales in more public situations obviously had an effect on the way women were perceived as narrators of folktales by men in the community and consequently by collectors. As women were less likely to narrate folktales in public venues where the company was adult and mixed, this would have contributed to them having a lower profile in the eyes of male informants or other men who might be questioned about potential narrators in the area.

It should be remembered that much of men's lore, particularly the narration of Märchen and heroic tales, was associated with public performance. Women's narration of tales and lore, on the other hand, was often more low-key and more private. Moreover, women's narration was, as Clodagh Brennan Harvey notes above, often out of sight of men, and also because it was often associated with work of some sort, it may have been viewed differently by men, as of less importance than the lore of men. But it was not just a question of informants and other men the collectors encountered in the field holding set views about women as bearers of tradition. Collectors, as products of their own communities and time, may also have internalised certain views of women as narrators.

In the early 1940's, Seán Ó hEochaidh, in an account he wrote of storytelling in his native Teileann, said that he never heard of women relating long folktales, although many women were renowned for their knowledge of 'minor lore, song and prayers, at which they often excelled men.'[148] More than twenty years later, speaking of the whole of County Donegal, he noted that singers and those expert in religious lore tend to be women.[149] Obviously women had lots of other lore, apart from 'minor' and religious lore, and Seán Ó hEochaidh himself collected other sorts of lore from women, but it is nonetheless interesting that he makes this distinction. In a radio interview he gave in 1992, some ten years after retiring, in respect of women not

146 Ó Concheanainn 1993, pp. 41–42.
147 See also Lysaght 1998 on this matter, p. 271.
148 UCDIFC: 1118, pp. 62–63.
149 Ó hEochaidh 1966, p. 9.

knowing folktales, he commented: 'The poor women were busy raising their families.'[150] However, it should be said that women in 'raising their families' often did narrate folktales to children, both their own and those of their neighbours.

The ratio of female to male informants

Fionnuala Nic Suibhne has calculated that of an estimated 40,000 or so informants in the Commission's Main Collection only 6,000 are women.[151] If this were true, even allowing for mitigating circumstances, it would be quite a damning statistic. However, one has to question the accuracy of this ratio of 6:1 in favour of male informants, for the simple reason that whatever the number of informants in the Index of Informants is today, the microfilm copy of the Index that Nic Suibhne based her calculations on, which derives from the mid-1970's, contained nowhere near 40,000 informants. Nic Suibhne, it seems, presumed that this official figure of 40,000 was correct, but it would appear to be the result of a mistake, or rather a series of mistakes and miscalculations.

When indexing of the informants in the Commission's Main Collection was first completed in autumn 1965, it contained between 18,000 and 18,500 cards.[152] The number of informants was less as some of these cards would have been surplus cards, i.e. head-cards, cross-references, and cards listing material referring to the same informant. The Commission's Main Collection comprised 1,689 manuscript volumes at this time. From autumn 1965 to autumn 1969 the Main Collection grew by a further 57 volumes. However, if we are to believe figures supplied by Seán Ó Súilleabháin, the number of informants in this Index leaped in this four-year period by at least 12,500 informants, to 30,000.[153] I say 'at least' because, as stated already, the above figures for 1965 do not represent the number of informants as such, only the number of cards. The Commission was disbanded some months later in March 1970 and the following year reconstituted in UCD. The Main Collection continued to grow during this period. In 1972 the Index of Informants is reported as containing 40,000 informants, an increase of 10,000 on the figure of 30,000 for 1969, although only 44 manuscript volumes had been added

---

150 RTÉSA AA5318, 'No Word of a Lie', Cathal Portéir talking to Dr Seán Ó hEochaidh, 21/7/1992.

151 Nic Suibhne 1992, p 12. No index of informants has yet been compiled for the Schools Collection, but Patricia Lysaght says that 'the evidence of three publications drawing on that Collection is that the schoolchildren collected mainly from men—their fathers and neighbours'. Lysaght 1998, p. 271, n. 83. However, two other published anthologies of material from this Collection, would suggest a more even gender ratio in certain localities. See Ó Baoill 1992, pp. 341–401, and Mac a' Bhaird 2002, pp. 116–121.

152 See ED FL 1: 'CBÉ. Miont. 124ú Cruinniú, 13.5.1965', par. 920; ED FL 8 Box 759: 'CBÉ. Miont. 125ú Cruinniú, 21.10.1965', par. 929 and 'Miont. 126ú Cruinniú, 27.1.1966', attachment 'Tuar. an Stiúr. 29.9.1965–8.1.1966', p. 1.

153 Ó Súilleabháin 1970a, pp. 118–119.

to the collection in the meantime.[154] The Main Collection continued to grow after 1972, and down until the mid-1970's at least (when it was microfilmed) the Index of Informants was kept up to date. However, the figure 40,000 has become frozen in time it would appear.[155]

It is highly unlikely that Ó Súilleabháin counted all the cards in this Index in 1969 to determine the number of informants when preparing an article on the Commission for the *Journal of the Folklore Institute*. Most likely what he did was take a sample of cards, or a number of samples, from the Index, discounting the surplus cards, and in this way estimate how many actual informants it contained. However, given the nature of the Index, a representative sample would have been difficult to take. Down until autumn 1965 when the Index of Informants was first brought to completion, it was the custom to record numerous references to the same informant on the same card. In subsequent years, it would appear, it became customary to write separate cards for each new reference to a particular informant. This change of practice, which continued after 1971, greatly expanded the number of cards in the Index. Thus, the Index of Informants contains two strata of cards, intermingled. For example, the 5,000 or so pages of material from Peig Sayers are referenced on some 23 index cards, while informants from whom only a relatively small amount of material was collected might be recorded on numerous cards in the Index, often with only a single reference on each card.

A preliminary examination of the Index of Informants as frozen on microfilm circa 1976/1977 shows that there are somewhere in the region of 33,100 and 33,400 cards on the four spools of microfilm, substantially less than the quoted figure of 40,000.[156] This, it must be again stressed, refers to the number of cards, not the number of informants. Getting a representative sample of this particular Index in order to determine the number of informants is beset with difficulties, and perhaps the only way to determine for certain the number of informants it contains would be to subject each individual card to thorough scrutiny. This would be a mammoth task and to be executed properly would require a team of researchers. Nevertheless, numerous samples I took, ranging from 50 to 520 consecutive cards, from various parts of the Index, show that it contains a high percentage of surplus cards. The number of surplus cards in these samples varies from 20% to 50%. Even if the various samples I took are unrepresentative, there is no doubt that the Index contains a substantial number of 'surplus cards' and that the actual number of informants as recorded circa 1976/1977, when it was microfilmed, is far less than the number of cards, 33,100 to 33,400, I estimate it contained at that time. My findings, are, as I say, only preliminary, but they point to

---

154 *The Department of Irish Folklore (Roinn Bhéaloideas Éireann)* [1972–73] and Almqvist 1975, p. 16, n. 1.

155 *See The Department of Irish Folklore and its Archive* [1993], unpaginated.

156 I counted the cards on the two longest spools, spool 36 and spool 37. Spool 37 (containing c. 8696 cards) is fractionally longer than spool 36 (containing 8343 cards). The other two spools, 38 and 39, are fractionally shorter that spool 36. I calculated that each of these spools has somewhere in the region of 150 to 300 cards less than spool 36.

the need for a thorough examination of the Index of Informants as recorded in the mid-1970's. Until such a task is completed, estimates of the ratio of male to female informants that the Irish Folklore Commission collected from must remain tentative. What is certain is, that the ratio of male to female informants is substantially less than the 6:1 estimated by Nic Suibhne.[157] Nic Suibhne fell into an easy trap as there was no information available to her as to how and when the Index of Informants was compiled. Indeed, the only substantial publication on the Commission, available to her at the time, might have given her the impression that the Commission's indexes date from a period earlier than they actually do and that greater care was taken to keep track of 'informants and collectors' than was always the case.[158]

Full-time vs part-time collecting

In examining the question of gender and collecting by the Commission we also need to distinguish between full-time and part-time collectors, something Nic Suibhne does not do. We should remember that approximately 40% of the material in the Main Collection was collected by paid part-time collectors or donated to the Commission by various individuals. This was material over which the Commission had far less control, in some cases no control whatsoever. With regard to the Commission's part-time collectors as such, it has to be said that some of them were very part-time indeed, only skimming the surface of the areas they worked, if even that. Other part-time collectors collected a great deal and collected from a greater cross-section of their community. The more a part-time collector worked an area, the greater the chance their collecting would be cross-gender, and the greater the control the Commission could exert over them. Thus, while the Irish Folklore Commission may, in general, have collected from far more men than women, the degree to which its full-time collectors 'neglected' women informants needs to be assessed further. In the case of the Main Collection, ideally each collector, both full-time and part-time, should be assessed separately to ascertain to what extent certain collectors had more of a preference for male informants over female compared to other collectors. An examination

---

157 Eibhlís Ní Dhuibhne, says 'a cursory check of informants' names in the IFC Archive indicates that somewhere between a quarter and one-third of the names are those of women' and furthermore that studies 'of particular folktale types have suggested that about one-third of their narrators are women.' Ní Dhuibhne 2001, p. 1217. Although in no way conclusive, Ní Dhuibhne's calculations may ultimately be shown to be closer to the actual ratio of female to male informants in the Commission's Main Collection than Nic Suibhne's estimate. In this connection, it is interesting to note that Guy Beiner, speaking of the nineteenth-cenury oral historiography of the Rebellion of 1798, says: 'Revisiting the oral historiography of Ninety-Eight with a gender awareness in mind calls attention to the fact that throughout the nineteenth century the collectors of 1798 oral traditions in Ulster were all men. This reflects the wider pattern of scholarly historiography, which was clearly male dominated. However, closer examination of accounts of the Rebellion that were collected orally reveals that at least a third of the interviewed informants were women.' Beiner 2003, p. 90.

158 See Almqvist 1977–79, p. 16.

of certain notebooks in the Commission's archive belonging to full-time collectors Liam Mac Meanman (1936–37), Nioclás Breatnach (1937), Liam Mac Coisdeala (1936), and Seosamh Ó Dálaigh (1940) reveal male/female ratios of approximately 3:1, 11:1, 4.5:1, and 7:1 respectively.[159] It should also be stressed that the ratio of men to women informants collected from by a given full-time collector might vary over time. However, the simple ratio of men to women in some cases obscures as much as it reveals. For example, in respect of Seosamh Ó Dálaigh's above ratio of 7:1 for a period covering the early 1940's, his notebook records him collecting from forty seven male informants but from only seven female. It should be noted, however, that six of Ó Dálaigh's female informants together had only twenty five items of folklore recorded from them, while from the remaining informant, Peig Sayers, 432 items were recorded. This latter amount exceeded the number of items collected by Ó Dálaigh from male informants during this period with one exception, that of Séan Crithin of Cill Maolcéadair, west Kerry, from whom 563 items of tradition were recorded during this period. The 432 items recorded from Peig Sayers not only exceed the amount recorded from all other male informants, apart from Seán Crithin, but in the vast majority of cases dwarfs the number of items of lore recorded by Ó Dálaigh from male informants during this period. It is possible that the intensive work Ó Dálaigh did with Peig Sayers at this time limited the number of women informants, in particular, he worked with at this time.[160]

The geographical spread of major women informants

While further study of individual collectors should reveal more on male/ female ratios in respect of the Commission's informants, and as a result in time we may be able to arrive at a reliable approximation, at least for the Main Collection, of the numbers of male informants vis-à-vis female informants collected from by the Commission, there is no doubt that far more material was collected from men than from women. Fionnuala Nic Suibhne, in her MA thesis, lists one hundred and thirty women in the Commission's Main Collection from whom a hundred pages or more of material were collected. Only nine women had more than a thousand pages collected from them; eleven more had between five hundred and a thousand pages of material; seven between four hundred and five hundred; nine between three hundred and four hundred; thirty between two hundred and three hundred; and sixty five between one hundred and two hundred pages. In total, the number of pages of folklore collected from these one hundred and thirty three women amounts to approximately 47,700 pages, only a fraction of the 720,000 plus

159 Information extrapolated from UCDNFC: 1303, pp. 1–188 (Mac Meanman); 383 passim (Breatnach); 1303, pp. 189 ff. (Mac Coisdeala) and 1294 passim (Ó Dálaigh).
160 Whatever Ó Dálaigh's overall male/female ratio for all of his fifteen years with the Commission may yet be shown to be, as noted by Eibhlís Ní Dhuibhne, he was certainly comfortable working with women. Ní Dhuibhne 2001, p. 1217.

pages (Main Collection) collected by the Commission and its predecessors.[161] Nic Suibhne does not give the number of pages collected from the 5,865 or so remaining women informants listed in the Commission's (Department of Irish Folklore's) Main Collection, so we can only surmise what the aggregate of the material collected from them would be. It is unlikely to be all that extensive.

However, it is not enough to look at the amount of material recorded from women in contrast to men. For instance, as men, in general, were more proficient at narrating folktales, or at least seem to have had more of a preference for narrating long tales, it is not surprising that the amount, in terms of pages, collected from certain men, skilled in this genre, would loom large when set beside shorter lore collected from certain women. Consequently, it would be better to contrast the number of individual items of tradition collected from men and women. Bo Almqvist has said, in respect of the Commission's work: 'It is obvious, too, that certain genres—for instance folk narratives, and especially the longer and most spectacular hero tales and *Märchen*—have been more extensively collected than less conspicuous, but no less important, genres and items.'[162] Thus, much lore, both that of women as well as men, was not collected by the Commission, or not collected to the extent it should or could have been. As women were less likely to specialise in long genres, it would appear that they 'lost out' more than men because of the above preference of collectors, but only further research will tell the full truth.

The amount collected by women collectors

Speaking of the folklore collecting in Co. Cork, the largest county in Ireland, Gearóid Ó Crualaoich notes that although four male collectors collected more than a thousand pages, no female collectors did so. Thirty one males collected between one hundred and a thousand pages, but only seven females did so. The bulk of female collectors (forty one in number) collected less than a hundred pages, as against two hundred and fifteen males. In all, in Co. Cork, forty eight females collected folklore material in contrast to two hundred and fifty five males.[163] In another study, this time of County Clare, Ó Crualaoich notes that twenty nine female collectors 'between them collected 500 pages', but he adds that one hundred and forty of these pages were collected by one individual.[164] The remaining twenty eight collectors would have collected on

---

161 See Nic Suibhne (MA thesis), Appendix 1, pp. 157–160.
162 Almqvist 1977–79, p. 14.
163 Ó Crualaoich 1993, p. 927.
164 Ó Crualaoich 2000, p. iii. Ó Crualaoich's figures for Cork and Clare, it should be noted, cover not only the period of operations of the IFC, but also of its predecessors, as well as collecting done by/for the Department of Irish Folklore from 1971 to c. 1977. The same is true for the overall figure of 575 female collectors which Fionnuala Nic Suibhne lists in her MA thesis. Moreover, this group of collectors is also very heterogenous, consisting of paid part-time collectors, questionnaire correspondents, schoolchildren who contributed to the Commission's Main Collection via folklore competitions and other channels (many

average approximately thirteen pages each. While we have no comparable statistics for other counties, I estimate that of some two hundred and twelve persons who collected a significant amount of folklore (i.e. in excess of 170–200 pages) part-time for the Commission and its two predecessors, approximately 19% were women. However, it must be said that few women collected well in excess of 200 pages of folklore, while many men did.

A final word on gender matters

The fact that, as noted by Fionnuala Nic Suibhne, Seán Ó Súilleabháin's *A Handbook of Irish Folklore* does not contain much of the information that modern-day folklorists would expect to find in such a book also limited the amount of specific women's lore that was collected by the Commission. For example, in the *Handbook* there is 'only one reference to menstrual blood' under the heading 'Heart and Blood' in a section of the book dealing with the human body. Nic Suibhne also notes that there is only one reference to sexual intercourse in the work and that the questions dealing with human birth mainly concern customs about human birth rather than women's attitude to, and experience of, giving birth, and such like.[165] It should be noted, however, that Ó Súilleabháin based his *Handbook* on the system of classification used in the Uppsala Landsmålsarkiv, and while he may have censored certain subjects of a 'sensitive' nature found in that archive to suit Irish conditions,[166] at the time the Uppsala Dialect and Folklore Archive would have given scant recognition to women's culture as such (not to mention women's sexuality), and while possibly not as reticent on sexual matters in general as Ó Súilleabháin's *Handbook*, the archive would not have contained an abundance of material on such matters.[167]

In reviewing this whole question of gender and the Commission, it is necessary to keep it in perspective, for as Gearóid Ó Crualaoich, speaking of the preference of the Commission's collectors for male informants over female, says:

> Obviously this is a situation not confined to Irish folklore or to folklore only as a discipline. There is a wide appreciation today of how much of a male bias has pervaded all aspects of social and cultural studies heretofore, and of how necessary it is to take this factor into account when analysing and interpreting evidence produced under such conditions.[168]

of them in the post-Commission era), and female donors of material which may or may not have been collected by the donors themselves. Many of the women who collected for the Commission did so during the early years of its operations. Many others were occasional questionnaire correspondents.

165 Nic Suibhne M.A. thesis, pp-x-xi (trans.).

166 Ó Súilleabháin would have been aware that in dealing too openly with certain matters he ran the risk of getting into trouble with the Irish Censorship Board. For more on Irish censorship at the time, see Carlson 1990, pp. 3 ff.

167 Lilja 1996, p. 159, as well as a personal communication from Marlene Hugoson.

168 Ó Crualaoich 1993, p. 926.

470

Nevertheless, while it is only right to view Irish folklorists of previous generations as products of their time, it is interesting to note that the work of the one major woman collector of Irish folklore, Lady Augusta Gregory, which predated the Commission, has more or less been ignored by Irish male folklorists. Patricia Lysaght fails to find any mention of Lady Gregory in Ó Duilearga's writings and suggests that her gender may have been one of the reasons why her work was ignored by Irish male folklorists. Lysaght also demonstrates a marked preference for male informants in anthologies of folklore edited by Irish men.[169] This, of course, raises the question whether Irish male folklorists of the time were misogynists, or does this simply reflect the preponderance of the material collected from male informants. Space does not allow me to deal with this question here. In respect of Ó Duilearga, however, it should be said that his neglect of Lady Gregory is not as complete as Lysaght suggests. In a newspaper article he published in 1938 he does afford Lady Gregory a measure of recognition, however meagre.[170]

It is quite likely that the employment of full-time female collectors would have resulted in more material being recorded from women, as Patricia Lysaght in her above study of Lady Augusta Gregory suggests.[171] It should be noted, however, that Lady Gregory, who collected folklore in the west of Ireland in the early twentieth century, was not only a woman of independent means, she was also one of independent mind. If women had been employed as full-time collectors by the Commission, they would not have had a free rein, no more than male full-time collectors had, and in all likelihood they would have had less. They would also, like the Commission's male full-time collectors, have been products of their time. It is interesting to note that in her study *Child Murderess and Dead Child Traditions*, Anne O'Connor lists forty three versions of 'The Legend of the Unrepentant Child Murderess' from the Main Collections of the Irish Folklore Commission, where the name of both collector and informant is recorded. Of these, twenty seven versions were collected by men from men; five by women from men; nine by men from women; and two by women from women. Family relations, in some cases, may have influenced who was collected from across genders. For instance, one of the male collectors collected from his mother, another from his grandmother, whereas at least one of the female collectors collected from her father. In all, thirty two versions were collected from men, eleven from women. As this legend dealt with a subject of intimate concern to women, it is reasonable to assume that many more versions of it could have been elicited from women than was done. It is interesting to note, however, that of the seven women who collected versions of this legend only two collected from women.[172]

One cannot, of course, generalise on the basis of a single study, but, nevertheless, we should not assume that female collectors of that time would have had some sort of natural preference for women informants. Even if

169 Lysaght 1998, pp. 265 ff.
170 Ó Duilearga 1938.
171 Lysaght 1998, pp. 271–272.
172 Data extrapolated from O'Connor 1991, pp. 175–178.

they had not, they might, of course, have developed such a preference over time. But that would have necessitated that 'the time' itself would have been different. For women's lore to have been collected in abundance, as against simply more lore from women, far more than female full-time collectors would have been needed. There would also have had to be an understanding of the importance of women's lore to begin with. Folklorists of the period, in Ireland and elsewhere in Europe, tended to stress the harmony of rural life. Recognising the separateness of women's lore, or rather the existence of a body of lore possessed by women separate from that possessed by men, and partly in opposition to men, would have run the risk of highlighting disharmony and divisions between the sexes.

Conclusion

Some general comments

How does one sum up such an involved story as that of the setting up, the making permanent, and the functioning of a great institution like the Irish Folklore Commission? In my introduction I referred to the fact that this institution so well known in its heyday, both at home and abroad, is, relatively speaking, little known nowadays, and even among those who have some knowledge of its existence, not a great deal is known of its achievements – and achievements there were in great abundance. The Irish Folklore Commission must rank among the better success stories of the young, independent Irish state. Rarely was government money so well spent; rarely were the returns so great and impressive. In little over a decade a folklore archive to rank in size with archives in the Nordic and Baltic countries was created, from scratch almost. Not only in terms of size was it great, but in respect of quality also. Of course, being assembled at a relatively late stage, the collection benefited from developments in collecting methods and techniques elsewhere. But the Irish Folklore Commission was also innovative in adapting and developing these methods and techniques beyond what had hitherto been done. In this respect, particular mention must be made of the Commission's network of full-time collectors, native to the communities they worked, who as well as collecting folklore on an extensive scale also systematically documented their own work in field diaries.

In Section 8 of Chapter III, I comment on the alternatives to transferring the Commission to UCD, and in Chapter VII many aspects of the Commission's work and methodology are assessed. Consequently, it is not necessary to cover this ground again here. In respect of Chapter VII, it should be said that each of the areas I examine would require a far more comprehensive study than that which I have been able to devote to it. In this chapter, for the most part, it has not been my intention to reach definitive conclusions, but rather to point the way for those who would undertake further research, especially those who live in Ireland and who have access to a greater range of sources than has been available to me.

Deconstructing the work of any institution, or of individuals, is fraught with dangers and it is easy to fall into the trap of being too critical, and of

473

applying to the subject yardsticks not of the time. My somewhat critical approach to the Irish Folklore Commission, on the other hand, has, in part, been a reaction to a lack of criticism in respect of that institution and its activities, particular of its Director, evidenced in many writings over the past thirty years. I leave it to the reader to determine which is the better approach. I sincerely hope that my work will not be seen simply as a work of deconstruction, although it does, of necessity, involve a lot of deconstructing. I hope that it will also be seen to have constructed something as well, and that it will give to present and future researchers, as well as other readers, some idea of the great achievements of the Irish Folklore Commission, and of the complexities of its achievements.

The section of the above work which deals with the setting up and making permanent of the Irish Folklore Commission (Chapter III), while not claiming to be definitive, is, as presented above, as comprehensive as the available sources allowed. No other study to date has looked at the efforts to set up the Commission and to secure a future for its collections and staff within or outside of a university setting.[1] Although one sometimes reads and hears about the problems Séamus Ó Duilearga encountered with government officials, the nature of these problems, and his struggle to overcome them, is left to the imagination. The above study outlines in detail the nature of that struggle, and tells of the toils and tribulations of Ó Duilearga, in particular, in his efforts to achieve a secure future for the Commission. Whether he was right to seek to incorporate the Commission into UCD must remain an open question. Some of the problems involved in transferring a national institution from state ownership to private ownership only became apparent after he had achieved his lifelong ambition of seeing the Commission reconstituted as an integral part of his alma mater, University College Dublin, and some only became apparent after his death in 1980. Below I will briefly look at the fate of the collections of the Irish Folklore Commission after they were transferred to UCD in 1971. Not to do so would be to leave this study somewhat incomplete. However, before I do so, I will comment on some of the main actors in the above story.

The actors

Seán Ó Conaill and the Commission's informants

Of the thousands of informants the Irish Folklore Commission (and its precursors) collected from, pride of place must go to Seán Ó Conaill, or to give him his full pedigree, preserved in oral tradition, 'Seán Dhónail Mhuiris' 'ach Séartha, 'ach Séartha Í Chonaill' ('Seán son of Dónal, son of Muiris, son of Séartha, son of Séartha Ó Conaill'). The Commission certainly collected from more accomplished storytellers than he, although he must rank among

---

1   Apart from Gerard O'Brien's recent rather brief treatment of the IFC. See Gerard O'Brien 2004, pp. 109–120.

the best collected from in this period, but if it were not for his willingness to painstakingly dictate his repertoire of tales and lore to a young man from the Glens of Antrim, and for the friendship and hospitality he and his wife, Cáit Ní Chorráin, showed that sensitive and talented young man over a period of some eight years, Séamus Ó Duilearga might never have been inspired to save the lore of Ireland for posterity, nor might the Irish Folklore Commission have been set up. Theirs was a chance meeting, but it was a meeting waiting to happen, to some degree at least. There is no doubt that Ó Conaill was a creative artist, and long after the practice of storytelling had died out in his area he kept alive his art by narrating tales aloud to himself while tending his cattle on the mountainside. But for the arrival of Séamus Ó Duilearga in the small mountain hamlet of Cill Rialaigh in August 1923, Ó Conaill's voice, along with his tales, would have died on the mountainside with him, as well as a great deal besides.

Not all the storytellers the Irish Folklore Commission collected from were as gifted as Seán Ó Conaill, although many were, but all of the Commission's storytellers and other informants, like him, gave of their time, and often a great deal of their time, to its collectors without any financial reward. The arrival of the Commission's collector may at times have been an inconvenience to the household, but informants and their families accommodated the collectors, appreciative, to varying degrees, of the national importance of the work. The presence of the collector may, of course, have lightened the routine of everyday life and shortened the long winter nights in those times before radio, television, and motorised transport would change the nature of rural life. Nevertheless, there is no doubt that the collectors of the Commission were beholden to their informants and their families. Nobody was more aware of this than Ó Duilearga himself, and to the end of his life he expressed his gratitude to the people of rural Ireland who gave freely of their lore and facilitated the work of the Commission's collectors in numerous other ways.

Many of the descendants of the Commission's informants may be disappointed at not finding the names of their relatives mentioned in the above study. Naturally, in a study of this sort only a mere fraction of the total number of informants the Commission collected from could be named, in most cases simply to fill in detail on some point or other. Hopefully, in time more of the tales and lore of individual informants will be published as well as in-depth studies on particular tradition bearers, and in this way recognition given to these people who gave so generously of what they had to the Commission's collectors. Studies that would deal with the sacrifices of informants and their families generally also need to be written. Any such study must deal with the question of whether it was right or not to collect extensively from informants, many of whom were eking out a bare existence, without rewarding them financially, apart from giving them an occasional ounce of tobacco or small bottle of whiskey. This is a complex issue, but in researching the riches of the collections bequeathed by the Commission to posterity, we should never lose sight of the poor material conditions of so many of the informants, without whose cooperation this whole enterprise would have foundered.

The collectors

I have met a number of the full-time collectors of the Commission, and I have listened to others of them in the Sound Archive of RTÉ. Listening to someone like the full-time collector Seán Ó hEochaidh, whom I never met, tell about his work has been a sobering as well as a humbling experience, as has been meeting face to face those of the collectors I have met over the years. All the full-time collectors I met or heard interviewed on tape were men of dignity and depth. Many of them lived to a ripe old age, but none are now alive. Also dead are almost all the Head Office staff, some of whom I also knew.

The full-time and special collectors of the Commission have had to take a back-seat in the above study, because of the focus of this research. Most of them are encountered in the text, but all too fleetingly. Their names are listed in Appendix 3, as well as their period of service with the Commission. Despite the lack of space given to them in this work, these men, less than twenty five in all, are the real heroes of this story. They were the backbone of the Commission, who made tremendous personal sacrifices in amassing this great collection: working much of the time for pitiable wages, and being overworked much of the time also, while receiving no extra financial reward. Some of them damaged their health due to the strain of the work and the inclement weather they often had to brave to reach isolated homesteads. One of them, Seán Ó Cróinín, died tragically 'in harness'. Each of them has a story, which, by means of their diaries, correspondence, and other documentation, will, I hope, some day be told. The work of each needs to be assessed in detail to determine their strengths and weaknesses: to see how they developed as collectors, the range and scope of their work, and also to see if at times they took short cuts, and if they did, to understand why. The pace of their work, particularly in the early days of the Commission, was such that it is no wonder that sometimes short cuts were taken, and that at times the work of some collectors fell below certain desired standards. But such shortcomings, in the case of most collectors, pale in the face of their achievement. Even in the case of those few full-time collectors who were dismissed, a thorough assessment of their work needs to be undertaken to determine, among other matters, whether dismissal was justified.

Neither should the contribution of the hundreds of part-time collectors (including questionnaire correspondents) in assembling these great collections be forgotten: men and women who together collected some 39% of the Commission's Main Collection. Although the work of some of these collectors is deficient in certain respects, the best of it can rank with the work of the full-time and special collectors. The work of major individual part-time collectors, in particular, also needs to be assessed. Moreover, whatever the failings of some of these collectors, without the contribution of part-time collectors many areas of the country would only be represented by the Schools Collection. In accessing the work of these collectors, the amount of training and guidance each received must be taken into account (this also applies to full-time and special collectors). The Commission might have been able to keep more of its part-time collectors for longer if it had been able to devote more time to them. There is no doubt that much more material, and from more areas, could have been contributed by part-time collectors, especially during the last two decades of the Commission. Lack of manpower to oversee this type of collecting, the waning energies of the Commission's Director, as well as lack of resources, all contributed to the underutilisation of part-time collecting. Changing times and declining interest in folklore among certain sections of the public, such as schoolteachers, also played a part in the fall-off in the Commission's team of part-time collectors. Nevertheless, one of the finest collections made by a part-time collector for the Commission, that of Patrick C. Power of Ballyneill National School in south Tipperary, dates from the late 1950's and early 1960's. He was one of only a handful of part-time collectors the Commission had working for it at the time. In different circumstances, more people might have been recruited to work for the Commission on a part-time basis, but the decline of the network of part-time collectors in the final decade or so of the Commission could be said to have been symptomatic of a more general decline in the Commission's operations.

The thousands of schoolchildren who collected for the Commission, mainly in the school year 1937–1938, were also part-time collectors of a type. Some of them may have been rather unwilling contributors to this great national enterprise, and a certain amount of them copied material collected by their school companions, or from printed sources, and passed it off as genuine. However, most of these schoolchildren, it would appear, diligently went about the task given them. The quality, and indeed quantity, of the material collected by these children was influenced by such factors as the amount of instruction given them by their teachers, by the level of cooperation they received from their immediate families and the community at large, and by the richness, or apparent lack of richness, of the local oral tradition. The Schools Collection is poor on contextual data, with little more than the barest minimum information on informants being given, but nevertheless it contains a great deal of lore that would otherwise have perished. More needs to be learned about the children who collected for the Commission: their memories of the School Scheme, their teachers, their family and communal background, and the lives they lived after leaving school.[2] Most of them, who are still alive, are now in their eighties, so augmenting the contextual data of the Schools Collection is a race against time.

The Head Office staff

If the full-time and special collectors were the backbone of the Commission, their work would have been impossible without the backup of the Head Office staff. Those who worked at Head Office did not have to brave the elements and work such unsocial hours as the men in the field, but their lot was only

---

2   Many of the senior pupils who participated in the Schools Scheme came to adulthood from the mid to the late 1940's, and were to be part of the huge exodus from Ireland in the 1950's in particular. It has been estimated that '[o]ne in three of those aged 30 or under in 1946 had left the country by 1971.' E. Delaney 2004, p. 81.

somewhat less harsh. Poor salaries, few, if any, prospects of promotion, and lack of any pension rights were a reality for them for most of the three and a half decades of the Commission's operations. If the story of each of the Commission's full-time collectors needs to be told, full biographies of some of the Head Office staff are also required, particularly of the two who have figured most in this study, Seán Ó Súilleabháin and Caoimhín Ó Danachair, as well as an assessment of the work of both men, published and archival/field.

Two more different people one could hardly imagine than Seán Ó Súilleabháin and Caoimhín Ó Danachair: the former small in stature, self-effacing, and with a distinctive, quivering voice; the latter large in build, outgoing and exuberant. Without the devotion of Ó Súilleabháin to his work, and without the help given him over the years by assistants such as Máire MacNeill, Brian Ó Ruanaighe, Janis Mezs, and Anraí Ó Braonáin, all of whom have left their mark on the various catalogues, the Archive would to this day be little more than a collection of manuscripts; valuable, of course, but difficult to use. It is easy to gain the impression that Seán Ó Súilleabháin assembled these catalogues single-handed, but that was not the case. Nevertheless, to him, I think, goes the lion's share of the credit for overseeing the work of cataloguing over three and a half decades.

Caoimhín Ó Danachair's ethnological work involved frequent trips to the field where he investigated and surveyed various aspects of folklife and material culture. Unlike the Commission's full-time collectors, he had the opportunity to process the results of his field work at Head Office, and could thus develop in ways not allowed them. He was a skilled photographer and also an accomplished ethnographic map maker. The extensive photographic collection of the Commission was compiled and catalogued by him, very many of the photographs being his own. Ó Danachair was the member of the staff of the Commission whose academic training most equipped him for the work he was engaged in for much of his career. Being almost fourteen years younger than Ó Duilearga, he was, probably, the obvious successor to lead the Commission on the Director's retirement, but, as we have seen above, circumstances were to deprive him of this opportunity. If he had been appointed Professor in 1971, the orientation of the new Department of Irish Folklore might have been more towards folklife studies. We have seen how the falling-out between Ó Duilearga and certain members of his staff in the last two decades of the Commission greatly affected Ó Danachair's chances of getting the Chair of Irish Folklore and leading the new department in UCD. Tensions in workplaces were not unique to the Irish Folklore Commission, but in this case, at any rate, they were to have long-term consequences for one of its employees at least, and possibly for the direction the Commission's successor was to take.

No assessment of the work of the office staff of the Commission should fail to mention Máire MacNeill. For the first fifteen, crucial, years of the Commission she was one of its mainstays. Although employed initially as its Office Manager and Secretary, the Commission, from the beginning, also availed of her many other talents both as cataloguer and researcher. She was of a scholarly bent, following in the footsteps of her famous father,

Eoin Mac Néill, and after resigning from the Commission on her marriage in 1949 was to blossom as a scholar. Her magnum opus, *The Festival of Lughnasa* (1962), is without doubt the greatest single scholarly achievement of any member of the Commission's staff. In mentioning her we must not forget all the female shorthand typists who served the Commission down through the years, without whose dedication the Commission could not have functioned. Their names do not figure in *Béaloideas*, although they typed most of the material in that journal, and rarely in other publications of the Commission and the Folklore of Ireland Society, which they had a part, and usually a large part, in producing. How many of them are still alive would be difficult to determine. Most of them left the Commission on marriage, took their husband's name, and passed into anonymity. The role they played in the story of the Irish Folklore Commission should not be forgotten. One of them, Bríd Mahon, who was later to become the Commission's Office Manager and Secretary, has written a memoire.[3]

The Commission's Board

The contributions of members of the Commission also need to be remembered, i.e. those who sat on the Board of the Commission itself, as well as on its Finance Sub-Committee, year in year out, supporting and advising the Director, and at times, when able, keeping a check on him. Men such as Fionán Mac Coluim, Seán Mac Giollarnáth, and Liam Price, who diligently attending meetings over three decades until old age and failing health finally forced them to step down. Many members, who were old or not blessed with robust health when the Commission was set up, died along the way: men such as Peadar Mac Fhionnlaoich, the Commission's first Chairman, Séamus Ó Casaide, and Énrí Ó Muirgheasa. The contributions of government representatives such as Léon Ó Broin, Seán Ó Maonaigh, and Feardorcha Ó Dúill also need to be recalled. Although at times they had to spell out the harsh financial realities to the Director and other members of the Commission, their role, in the main, was a constructive one, and their presence on the Commission made relations between Ó Duilearga and government departments, particularly the powerful Dept. of Finance, less tense than they might otherwise have been.

As much of the focus in this study has been on efforts to have the Commission made permanent, something must also be said of the other main players, apart from Ó Duilearga, involved in this long saga: Éamon de Valera, Michael Tierney, Pádraig Ó Siochfhradha, and Eric Mac Fhinn.

Éamon de Valera

Éamon de Valera certainly deserves our gratitude for agreeing to set up the Irish Folklore Commission in the first place. Without his insight and

---

3   Although this book gives interesting insights into the workings of the Commission, it could be more informative on the actual work of shorthand typists and the Office Manager.

support, however limited and coloured by other designs it may have been, it is unlikely that the Commission would ever have been established. However, while he fought tooth and nail in 1940 for the establishment of his own brainchild, the Dublin Institute for Advanced Studies, against the opposition of the universities and many in his own party, he prevaricated on making the Commission permanent, never formulated precise plans for re-establishing it[4], and for a time appears to have played a game of cat and mouse with Ó Duilearga, to the latter's detriment, for it most likely contributed to breaking his health. Nevertheless, while never spelling out in any detail his plans for a reconstituted Commission, he remained adamant that it should not be reconstituted in UCD, or in any university college for that matter. Long before de Valera lost power in February 1948 he could have pushed for the acceptance of one or other of his proposals for making the Commission permanent, but he preferred not to press the issue, possibly in order to exhaust the opposition, and to avoid a struggle. If he had wished, he could, most likely, have established the Commission as an independent body or within the Institute for Advanced Studies. Perhaps if he had retained power in 1948, he might have done so. Neither solution might have been the best solution, but either solution would have been better than to allow the Commission to go on existing in a kind of semi-permanent limbo into the 1950's and 1960's, as was allowed to happen.

There is no doubt that de Valera saw the intrinsic value of the Commission's collections, not just as comprising a part of Ireland's cultural inheritance but also as a source and inspiration for both native and international scholarship. He was, however, despite his interest in native culture and despite his scholarly leanings, above all a politician, and politics very often got in the way of other interests with him. No one can doubt his great love of the Irish language and ardent desire that it be revived, but he can be faulted for not doing enough to save the Gaeltacht or spreading a real knowledge of Irish throughout the country. Politics got in the way of reviving Irish, and to some extent one can also say that is what happened with regard to his approach to the Irish Folklore Commission, its Director, and its collections. Moreover, despite his support for the collecting of folklore, de Valera may well have seen Irish folklore as somewhat of a 'poor relation' when viewed against the rich material treasures of Ireland's 'Golden Age', its extensive medieval and early-modern literary remains, and Ireland's contribution to European civilisation in general. Neither was he alone among Irish nationalists in viewing folklore so. Despite official Government support (both actual and as voiced) and despite the high profile the work of the Irish Folklore Commission enjoyed among elements of the public, especially during the first two decades or so of its operations, it should be noted that folklore in Ireland, in contrast to certain other emerging European nation states, such as Finland, did not feature significantly in the formative period

---

4   De Valera was reluctant to put anything on paper. He told his biographer, T. P. O'Neill: 'If you write something down people know what you're going to do ... are warned and may be in a position to stop you. So always keep your policy under your hat.' Quoted in Bowman 1982, p. 341.

of Irish Nationalism, in the nineteenth and early twentieth centuries, nor later in the independent Irish state.

Moreover, while there is no doubt a connection between de Valera's support for the intensive collecting of Irish folklore and his idealisation of a harmonious peasant society (best expounded in his oft-quoted St. Patrick's Day speech of 1943[5]), and while he most likely hoped that the collections being amassed by the Irish Folklore Commission might contribute to maintaining and buttressing a separate Irish national identity in the face of anglicisation, it must be noted that neither he, nor his Fianna Fáil party, ever seriously attempted to put any mechanism in place that would have imparted to coming generations, via the primary schools, even a modicum of the traditional lore bequeathed by past generations that the Commission managed to save for posterity. Despite support for folklore studies among elements in the Dept. of Education in the late 1920's and early 1930's, and despite the Schools Folklore Scheme of 1937–1938, which was a once-off venture, the study of oral tradition was not to become an integral part of primary education. Thus, the claim that is sometimes made[6] that de Valera and Fianna Fáil's support for collecting folklore in the 1930's was part of a greater plan for society needs to be questioned, or at least qualified.[7]

Michael Tierney

Michael Tierney has got a bad press in certain quarters over the past decade or so. He is seen as an authoritarian figure by many, a bigot by some, and by others as some sort of proto-fascist, at least in the 1930's. There is no doubt that he was an authoritarian, but as regards the other two characterisations of him, this is not the place to comment on them, except to say that they are simplifications that do the man an injustice. Tierney was a complex man and only a full-length biography can do justice to him.[8] Although there were others on the staff of UCD who were sympathetic to the collecting of Irish folklore, it was Tierney who was the mainstay of that support. Without his interest in the work of the Folklore of Ireland Society, the Irish Folklore Institute, and the Irish Folklore Commission, particularly the last-mentioned body, Ó Duilearga's task would have been much more difficult. Tierney was without doubt a useful friend for Ó Duilearga to have, and was able to come to the

---

5   See Moynihan 1980, pp. 466–469.
6   For instance, in Ó Drisceoil 2005, p. 187.
7   At secondary school level, attended by only a minority of the school-going population up until the late 1960's, books such as the dictated autobiography of the famous storyteller Peig Sayers, *Peig*, were on the syllabus, but their purpose was to impart to students a knowledge of vernacular Irish, not to inform them about traditional society as such or make them aware of the exceptionally rich cultural inheritance of the Gaeltacht. Traditional texts of this sort were, for the most part, taught out of context and had little appeal for most students. The failure by Fianna Fáil, and other administrations, to establish a national folk museum during the lifespan of the Commission, despite numerous promises, is further evidence that imparting a knowledge of traditional folklife was not viewed as a priority by either de Valera or his political opponents.
8   For a short biography of Tierney, see Martin Tierney 2002, pp. 1–36.

latter's aid on numerous occasions. However, there was a price to be paid for too close an association with Tierney, as we have seen above. While Tierney, and colleagues of his both in UCD and in the other constituent colleges of the National University of Ireland, were within their rights to oppose gaelicisation policies they did not agree with, Tierney's unbending stance to even allowing a modicum of Irish-medium teaching in UCD set him on a collision course with the Irish-language movement and elements in the Fianna Fáil party, and further tarnished that college's reputation, and national credentials, in their eyes. Tierney was not against the Irish language, but for many in the Irish language movement for all practical purposes he was, as was his college. For Tierney maintaining his opposition to teaching through Irish, even on a limited scale, became a principle in itself. Not an inch would he give on this issue, when even a symbolic gesture towards Irish-medium teaching might have gone a long way to ameliorating opposition to him and his college in certain official and Irish language quarters. The failure of UCD, the largest university college in the country, to initiate Irish-medium instruction, even on a modest scale, contributed to weakening the state's revivalist policies, and most likely played a part in their eventual abandonment, but it also, as I argue above, greatly affected the fortunes of the Irish Folklore Commission and played a crucial role in keeping it in a semi-permanent limbo for decades.

While there is no question of the sincerity of Tierney's interest in Irish folklore, he could not but have been aware that helping the Irish Folklore Commission would also serve the interest of UCD. Tierney was forever solicitous of the welfare of his college, and he was also a very patriotic man. By helping the Irish Folklore Commission, UCD was able to raise its national credentials which were so much in question at the time; credentials that had been robbed from it as a result of many prominent members of its staff taking the pro-Treaty side (and by implication, the pro-British side) in the Civil War, and subsequently by the rise of the Fianna Fáil party, heirs to the vanquished in that war, as the dominant force in Irish political life. Nevertheless, despite the perceived advantages that would accrue to UCD if it should get custody of the Commission and its collections, I believe that Tierney always had the welfare of the Commission at heart. If UCD had got custody of the Commission during Tierney's presidency, he would have done his utmost to see to it that it was treated with the respect and care that a great national institution deserved. Unfortunately, he was long retired by the time the Commission was transferred to UCD, and had only a few years to live.

Pádraig Ó Siochfhradha and Eric Mac Fhinn

We have seen above how Pádraig Ó Siochfhradha played a pivotal role in the setting up of both the Folklore of Ireland Society and the Irish Folklore Institute. Although he remained President of the Society down until his death in 1964 and sat on the board of the Institute for the five years of its existence, he declined an offer to be on the Board of the Commission. Initially he was someone whom Ó Duilearga could turn to for advice and depend on, but in time divergences emerged between them on the future organisation of folklore collecting. Despite his declining a place on the Board of the Commission, Ó Siochfhradha worked behind the scenes in 1934 to restrict the control of the UCD authorities over any folklore collections amassed under its auspices in the event that the Government might decide to reconstitute the Irish Folklore Institute in the College. Later he was to be vehemently opposed to incorporating the Irish Folklore Commission into UCD and played a significant, behind-the-scenes role in thwarting renewed efforts to have the Commission transferred to the College in the late 1950's. His opposition to UCD was relentless, and his opinion held weight not just in Irish-language circles but also in the upper echelons of Fianna Fáil. If he had been alive in 1968 he would certainly have fought to keep the Commission out of UCD, and if his old friend Éamon de Valera had not retired in 1959, and were still Taoiseach a decade later, it is fairly certain that the Commission would not have been transferred to that college.

Depending on one's point of view, one can view Ó Siochfhradha's behind-the-scenes actions in respect of the Commission in purely negative terms, seeing him as motivated by narrow linguistic designs only, but this would be unfair to him. He was genuinely motivated by the need to protect the interests of the Folklore of Ireland Society and the public's access to the collections that were in the process of being assembled. He also feared that the Folklore of Ireland Society might lose its identity if the work of folklore collecting were to be taken over by UCD, and be subsumed in that academic body. As long as he was alive there was an independent voice in the Society. Although he never attended a university, nor had his horizons broadened by study abroad, he was a scholar of no mean ability.

Pádraig Eric Mac Fhinn's credentials for being Chairman of the Irish Folklore Commission were no more than those of many other Irish-language scholars with an interest in folklore who had been appointed by the Government to the Commission. Indeed, his ecclesiastical credentials may have decided his appointment as Chairman in 1942. Like Pádraig Ó Siochfhradha, Mac Fhinn's opposition to incorporating the Commission into UCD was determined, to a very large extent, by the College's attitude towards the revival of Irish. Unlike Ó Siochfhradha, however, who moved on a far wider stage, he did not have the same political influence. While Mac Fhinn's opposition to incorporating the Commission into UCD was taken into account by officials of the Dept. of Education in 1958, their decision not to transfer the Commission to UCD at this juncture was based only in part on his opposition. Moreover, his proposal to the Commission on Higher Education in 1965 for incorporating the Commission into University College Galway rather than into UCD, while not without its merits, would not appear to have been all that well argued. After all, given that the bulk of the Commission's Main Collection was in the Irish language, there was a strong case to be made for transferring it to UCG. It is easy to characterise Mac Fhinn's opposition to UCD as the unreasoned opposition of someone who had a one-track mind when it came to the revival of Irish, but something he said at the special meeting of the Commission in June 1958 displayed a lot of perspicacity. The Minutes of the meeting report:

> The Chairman said [referring to Ó Duilearga's stance] that he understood
> well and respected the loyalty of people to their own college, but he would
> be loath to take personal circumstances into account, especially as it was
> intended to recommend a permanent settlement that *will be there when
> we are all gone.*[9]

All those who attended that special meeting of the Commission in late June
1958 are dead; most of them long dead. Many of the members present did
not live to see 'a permanent settlement' for the Commission agreed on by
officials. Some, if they had lived, would have vigorously opposed the transfer
to UCD. Mac Fhinn survived the Commission by many years and, most
likely, lived long enough for him to feel that he was justified in opposing
transferring the Commission to UCD, and Ó Duilearga lived long enough for
him, possibly, to wonder if his preference for a permanent home in UCD for
the Commission was indeed the best solution. Be that as it may, as we will
see below, UCD was not to prove the safe haven for the Commission that
proponents of incorporation into that college had often argued it would be.

The Civil Servants

The names of many Civil Servants have figured in this study. Little is known
of most of these men and women. We know in most cases what they were,
i.e. their rank within their department, but rarely who they were, where they
came from, what their educational background was, what their interests were.
A number of them such as León Ó Broin and Tarlach Ó Rafartaigh were
scholars of distinction, but few of them it would appear had a university
education.[10] Many of the men were products of schools run by the Christian
Brothers, where some of them had imbibed the philosophy of Gaelic Ireland
characteristic of those schools in the early decades of the independent Irish
state. Although the Civil Service never became gaelicised to any real extent,
as was originally intended by Ernest Blythe, in time some of the lower ranks
did. A good deal of the correspondence dealing with the Irish Folklore
Commission is in Irish and we can at times see evidence of Irish-language
loyalties in the internal memoranda of certain Civil Servants.

Irish Civil Servants of the early decades of native government have
sometimes been accused of being narrow. We have seen examples of
narrowness in the above study, but to be fair to these men and women,
one would have to say that much of this narrowness was the result of the
economic policies pursued by the state at the time. Governments in those days
balanced their budgets and the Dept. of Finance kept a tight rein on Ministers
and their Departments. Narrowness and narrow-mindedness there was, of

---

9   D/T S 6916D: 'CBÉ. Miont. an Chruinnithe Speisialta, 27.6.1958', p. 7 (trans. – italics
    mine).
10 Among those who had a university training were Seosamh Ó Néill, who under 'Joseph
    O'Neill' was to become a successful novelist; Micheál Breathnach, author of a fine
    autobiography, *Cuimhne an tSeanpháiste* (1966); and Máire Bhreathnach, who was later
    to become a well-known spokesperson for Catholic family values.

course, but Irish Civil Servants did not have a monopoly on such qualities. One could also mention the narrowness of university administrators who sought the least difficult way to incorporate the Irish Folklore Commission into UCD without contemplating all the implications of such a move. Or the narrow-mindedness of those politicians (legislators) as well as members of the Irish-language movement who sought to keep the Commission out of UCD, for ideological reasons, without considering the damage which leaving the Commission in a semi-permanent limbo inflicted on it and its staff. Nevertheless, of the Civil Servants who dealt with the Commission, few it has to be said had any real appreciation of the international importance of the collections of the Irish Folklore Commission, and many of those who saw its national importance failed to see that a substantial state investment was necessary if these collections were to be treated properly. Ó Duilearga was wont to resort to rhetoric when making the case for more funding or permanent status for the Commission, or when pressed for details would produce elaborate memoranda containing more and more costly requests. A different approach might have been more productive of results.

After years of being allowed to exist in a sort of limbo, Irish legislators finally decided to find a permanent home for the Irish Folklore Commission. The Civil Servants, acting for their political masters, who negotiated the transfer of state property to a private educational institution either did not sufficiently consider the national implications of this move, or chose not to heed them. Most of those involved in these negotiations probably felt that justice was finally being done.

Séamus Ó Duilearga

Finally, we come to Ó Duilearga himself. While the Irish Folklore Commission had on its staff, both in the field and at Head Office, many talented individuals, there is no doubt that Séamus Ó Duilearga was the pivotal figure. Without him there would have been no Commission. He may have been less talented, in certain respects, than some of his colleagues, but he was driven by a determination of steel that none of them possessed. Some of the shortcomings of the full-time collectors can be laid at his door. He could be a hard taskmaster, driving his collectors, particularly in the early years, sometimes beyond what they should have had to endure. His stipulation that full-time collectors produce so much folklore per week at times may have had an unintentional negative effect on the nature and quality of what was collected. Although his constant emphasis on the quantity of folklore being amassed by the Commission, and on the size of its collections in world terms, may have been meant, in part, to impress officials at home, there was the danger that quantity would at times take precedence over quality and that the achievement of the world's biggest folklore archive might become, to some extent, an aim in itself.

Ó Duilearga can also be accused of shortsightedness in his neglect of teaching, and perhaps also, to a lesser degree, of naivety in his efforts to incorporate the Commission into UCD. His style of leadership can also be questioned. Such criticisms, as do other criticisms of him made above, have, of course, to be set against his many achievements, not just in directing the work of the Commission and in assembling a great archive, but also in persisting in his endeavours to have the Commission adequately financed and placed on a more permanent footing. In hindsight, however, one might argue that perhaps he should have settled for less; that he should have agreed to de Valera's various proposals for re-establishment without UCD, particularly the proposal to establish the Commission as a School of the Dublin Institute for Advanced Studies, which would have provided an academic and prestigious milieu for the collections and staff of the Commission.

Shortly before the collections of the Commission were transferred to UCD, Séamus Ó Duilearga in a radio interview on his life and life's work, for the programme 'Here and Now' (see above), was asked by the interviewer whether he had any regrets. He said that he regretted that he was not older 'because if we had started the work and if I was associated with the work twenty to twenty five years before we did start....Belfield wouldn't be big enough to hold the material we would have got.' One should note that the Belfield campus he was referring to was a much smaller campus than that which now houses the collections which he had amassed. Obviously, he was exaggerating, but no doubt a great deal was lost that might have been saved if collecting had started earlier. But folklore is always being lost. Ó Duilearga to the very end saw folklore, for the most part, in terms of collecting. If he had been able to bequeath to future generations an even larger archive than the one he did, would that be a good thing in itself? It would certainly have made the work of the small staff who have to administer UCD's Archive of Irish Folklore much more difficult.

It is unlikely that the systematic collecting of Irish folklore could have been begun earlier, e.g. in 1910 or 1915, even if a young, enthusiastic Séamus Ó Duilearga had been on the scene, as the political climate of the time would not have been conducive to such work. Fortunately, Ó Duilearga was on the scene when he was, for that was the right time, although only just, for the job, or one of the jobs, that needed to be done. Of course, it was only by chance that a person of his calibre came on the scene, and that he travelled the road he chose. In different circumstances he might have gone to sea like his paternal forebears or, if his priestly vocation had held, on the Missions to Africa or the Far East as a Vincentian Father. Moreover, if he had been awarded a travelling studentship in 1922, something he eagerly sought, he might have returned from Europe to devote his life to mainstream Celtic Studies rather than to folklore. We owe the collections of the Irish Folklore Commission to a chance series of events, and above all to the determination of this ambitious young man from the Glens of Antrim.

Séamus Ó Duilearga turned his back on the seafaring tradition that the Delargys had pursued for generations, sailing to the four corners of the globe. Yet he travelled many seas in his long lifetime, both physically and metaphorically, and always retained something of the air of a ship's captain, in his devotion to duty, in his stern demeanour with his crew, and in his steely determination to see his ship through, come fair or foul weather. He led an adventurous life whether in the field, at his desk, on lecture trips at home and abroad, or pursuing what after the Irish language and oral tradition was his life's passion, fly-fishing. Although he lived in an age when academics had far fewer opportunities to travel than today, he was a well-travelled man by any standards. His wide knowledge of languages, which few academics could nowadays emulate, also allowed him to roam far and wide in his reading. He aged before his time, which was partly due to broken health, and partly, I believe, due to an attitude of mind, oriented as he was since early manhood towards old people, the custodians of the old traditions he cherished so much and devoted his life to preserving. Failing health certainly affected his direction of the Irish Folklore Commission, and perhaps his judgement, during the last decade or so of the Commission's operations. Like many an aging sea-captain he found it difficult to let go the helm. By the time he steered his ship into the 'safe haven' of Belfield, i.e. the new campus of University College Dublin, in 1971, he was an old and weary man. That supposedly safe haven has proven a rather turbulent mooring for his beloved collections. Perhaps a younger Ó Duilearga might have noticed that the coast had changed greatly, that the UCD he had known most of his working life, was passing, if not already altered beyond recognition.

The Aftermath

A safe haven?

If the Commission escaped from Limbo, the Gates of Heaven were not exactly thrown open to it. For a time, however, it seemed as if its long years of suffering and perseverance were over. There was definitely hope in the air, and there were good reasons for the staff of the Commission to be hopeful. They were in new, if not ideal, headquarters; they were at last an integral part of an academic institution; the economic climate of the country was, despite certain fluctuations, relatively good; the life's blood of the nation was no longer being drained by emigration, emigrants in fact were coming home; free secondary education was swelling the numbers enrolled in Irish universities; and among the many young students graduating from Irish universities there would soon, for the first time, be graduates in Irish Folklore, from UCD's newest department, the Department of Irish Folklore.

Neither were such hopes mere illusion. There is no doubt that in the early 1970's there was a lot of goodwill towards the new Department of Irish Folklore in UCD, both on the part of the College authorities and the academic staff. The very fact that it was headed by an exotic Irish-speaking Scandinavian, Bo Almqvist, for a time would have caused some to view the new department in a positive light, if for no other reason. There were early signs, however, that troubled waters lay ahead. A little over a month after the Commission was transferred to UCD, President J. J. Hogan wrote to the Secretary of the Dept. of Education, Seán Mac Gearailt, about the state's grant to the College for the year 1971–1972, which fell 'far short' of projected expenditure. In respect of the newly created Department of Irish Folklore, he had this to say:

> Our understanding is that the College will be responsible for such charges as we have previously met [in respect of the Irish Folklore Commission]. The grant must therefore be increased by the amount provided by the state for the Folklore Commission up to now, increased in accordance with the rise in costs. We cannot accept that Folklore should be starved on entry to the College, nor that existing activities of the College should be starved for its maintenance.[11]

Even with the best will on the part of the College authorities, without sufficient state grants UCD simply could not afford the Irish Folklore Commission. This had always been the case, but it would appear that the negotiations between the Dept. of Education and the College authorities on transferring the Commission to the College made little or no provision for the expansion of its operations, at least nothing substantial of this nature seems to have been put in writing. Folklore was not 'starved' on entry into UCD, but it has never been properly funded.

J. J. Hogan retired a year or so after penning the above passage. His departure signalled the changing of the old guard in UCD. The older generation of academics and College administrators that had witnessed the foundation of the state, many of whom had been imbued with varying degrees of nationalistic fervour, was passing, as well as the world they knew. This was also the generation that had presided over the setting-up of the Irish Folklore Commission and taken pride in the close cooperation that existed between the Commission and the College as its collections grew and became world-famous. Many factors were to contribute to the young Department of Irish Folklore and its collections having a rough passage in UCD over the next three and a half decades. The first decade that lay ahead was to prove a turbulent one for the college and the state. On the wider economic and political front, the 1970's were to witness an international oil crisis and world recession, and reckless government spending at home, which would see the Republic of Ireland brought to the verge of bankruptcy within ten years of the Commission's transfer to UCD. This decade also saw traditional universities come under threat and have to compete for limited funding with new institutes of technology. Moreover, within Irish universities, faculties of arts were forced more and more to justify their existence in the eyes of officialdom. The 1970's also saw the state distance itself further from the Irish language. We have seen that the previous decade had already witnessed a weakening of some of the nationalistic principles upon which the state had been founded. The re-emergence of armed struggle by the IRA in 1969, mainly in Northern Ireland, and the intensification of politically motivated violence throughout the 1970's saw a further jettisoning of nationalistic fundamentals in the Republic, particularly by elements of the middle classes and intelligentsia. The very notion of a United Ireland as a justifiable or desirable aspiration came to be questioned by many. Moreover, the Irish language began to be seen by some as sectarian and divisive in respect of

---

11   UCD. Report of the President (1972), p. 31, in UCDA: Min. of the Gov. Body Vol. 31.

Northern Ireland. The very legitimacy of the Gaelic/Celtic inheritance as the dominant element in the island's past also began to be questioned. Ireland was now seen to be a rich cultural mosaic: a home of various different ethnic groups; the Gaelic/Celtic inheritance being just one of several. Gaelic Ireland was not only dead, its historical importance, its relevance for present and future generations of Irish people, North and South, was more and more coming under scrutiny in certain influential quarters. Being, to a very large extent, the repository of traditions in the Irish language and dealing with Gaelic Ireland, the Department of Irish Folklore could not, indirectly at least, but have been affected by these changes in attitudes, especially among intellectuals, academics and officials.

The coalition government of Fine Gael and the Labour Party that came to power in February 1973, in accordance with their joint election manifesto, promptly abolished 'compulsory' Irish for the Leaving Certificate Examination and as a requirement for entry to the Civil Service. Fianna Fáil, now in opposition, protested, but they themselves shortly before, while in Government, had delivered a severe blow to the Irish language when in negotiating the Republic's terms of entry to the European Economic Community they had rejected Brussels' offer to make the Irish language one of the Community's official and working languages. In the event, Irish was given a certain limited status as a Treaty language, but for almost twenty years the public were kept in the dark as to who was responsible for the failure to secure official status for Irish at this time. No other action by Irish politicians and officials symbolises the drawing of a curtain on a past they wished to leave behind as much as this episode.

This was not a climate conducive to the expansion of the staff and activities of UCD's new Department of Irish Folklore. In the above circumstances, it is not surprising that the requests of the Department for more resources fell on deaf ears, to a large extent, in its first decade of operations, and indeed in later decades. Nor was inadequate staffing the sole problem facing the Department. I have mentioned above that the space provided the Commission on its transfer to UCD was not adequate to accommodate its collections; neither was the room designated as an archive purpose-built. Not only was it not fireproof and secure, within a few years it was shown to be a fire hazard in itself, as part of one of its walls was made of flammable material. It must be remembered, however, that the Commission had to be accommodated in the Arts/Commerce Block of the Belfield Campus at short notice, and to be fair to the College the space provided to house the Commission's collections and staff was probably initially considered as a temporary solution, until better accommodation could be provided. However, temporary solutions have often a tendency to take on an air of permanence, and this is what happened in this case.

The Irish Folklore Commission was in existence for thirty five years; another thirty five years have passed since the Commission was transferred to UCD. More than thirty five years ago the collections of the Irish Folklore Commission were, in effect, disposed of by the state with evidently few real safeguards being given to their treatment and care in the long term. This is not to question the integrity and motives of the officials involved. Nevertheless, the state continues to provide for the collections through a grant to the College via the Higher Education Authority, but this grant has not been sufficient over the years to build up an adequate team of researchers, cataloguers, and collectors. In the intervening years a number of efforts have been made by the College to give the Department of Irish Folklore more space and accommodate its collections more securely. What has been offered by the College to date has either proved unsatisfactory to the Department or has been withdrawn or postponed. Today the Department of Irish Folklore, and more specifically its collections, occupies the same 'temporary' accommodation hurriedly designed for it more than thirty five years ago. In September 2005 the Department of Irish Folklore as such ceased to exist, along with all other departments (and faculties) in UCD. Folklore, as a degree subject, now forms part of the School of Irish, Celtic Studies, Irish Folklore and Linguistics in the College of Arts and Celtic Studies. Moreover, in September 2005 the research and archival/collecting functions of Department of Irish Folklore were reconstituted (or at least renamed) as 'The Delargy Centre for Irish Folklore and the National Folklore Collection'.

Need for statutory protection

Speaking of UCD's campus at Belfield, Donal McCartney says: 'Belfield stands today as a monument to Michael Tierney's vision.'[12] In the same way, one can say that the collections of the Irish Folklore Commission stand as a monument to Séamus Ó Duilearga. But the monuments of both men no longer seem to suit each other. They did when the Commission was an underfunded, semi-permanent body that UCD kindly took under its wing, but now that the College has grown beyond what anyone could have imagined thirty years ago, the heir to the Commission has been left, to a large extent, unprotected – a fledgling that no one really wants. One wonders what either man would think of what has befallen these collections since they were transferred to UCD, and what they would think of the seeming lack of interest in Ireland's Gaelic and medieval heritage evidenced over the past decade and more in the College both men devoted their lives to serving. Given the history of the Commission's collections in UCD over the past thirty years, the question of the ownership of these collections is something that requires urgent public debate. From the outset, the failure to re-establish the Commission with some sort of semi-independent status within the College by establishing a governing board to oversee its work, with representatives of other university colleges and various vested interests, as recommended by the Commission on Higher Education, greatly added to the problems of the Commission's successor, and raises the question whether its collections need some sort of statutory protection within the College. The body set up in 1972 to regulate such matters as access to the collections as well as cataloguing and publishing, Comhairle Bhéaloideas Éireann/The Folklore of Ireland Council (see Chapter III/6 above), was

---

12   McCartney 1999, p. 279.

more representative of UCD than of wider national and academic interests and, in any event, had no powers to insist that the College and the State live up to their commitments to care for these great collections. The fact that Comhairle Bhéaloideas Éireann has only recently been reappointed after being left moribund for almost twelve years (between 1994 and 2006) is evidence enough of how little real power or influence it had.

The future of the collections

Securing the collections is essential, but what of their future utilisation? As the bulk of the Main Collection of the Irish Folklore Commission is in the Irish language, its utilisation is, to a great extent, tied up with the fate of the Irish language itself; certainly its widespread utilisation is. Despite the hopes of Irish Revivalists, politicians, and government officials, the collections of the Irish Folklore Institute and its successor, the Irish Folklore Commission, even if they had been published *in extenso* would not have turned the tide in respect of restoring Irish. For the publication of these collections to have had any effect in that regard, it would have had to form part of a much wider, comprehensive plan to reinforce what the Irish was being taught in the schools in society at large, and to ensure the economic viability of the Gaeltacht. No such plan was ever formulated. The attempt to regaelicise the country was piecemeal, at once too ambitious and not ambitious enough. The burden of restoration was placed on the shoulders of schoolchildren and their teachers, with few opportunities provided for pupils to use Irish after leaving school.

It is anybody's guess whether the Irish language will survive as a spoken vernacular. This generation will probably decide whether it will or not. Despite the precarious position of the language in the Gaeltacht, there have been signs of a resurgence of interest in Irish elsewhere, particularly with the rapid growth of Irish-medium primary education in recent decades. Moreover, in early summer 2005 the EU Council of Ministers decided to agree to a belated request by the Irish Government that Irish be made an official working language of the EU. This came into force on January 1st, 2007. The above decision may augur well for the future of Irish or it may not. Be that as it may, the collections amassed by Séamus Ó Duilearga and his fellow-workers will continue to attract the interest of folklorists, particularly those who know Irish. Of course, these collections were never intended to be the preserve of folklorists (and/or ethnologists) alone, but to be drawn on by scholars of various disciplines and the general public. As well as comprising a great body of tradition to occupy researchers for generations to come, these collections constitute a huge repository of vernacular Irish to be drawn on by future Irish-language scholars and enthusiasts alike as a source of knowledge, enrichment, and regeneration as spoken Irish thins further on the ground and is assailed from all sides by a global culture not dreamed of in the late 1920's when state support was first sought by Séamus Ó Duilearga and others in the Folklore of Ireland Society to help save for posterity the richness of Irish oral tradition, and such state support was given in the hope that it would help in efforts to restore the Irish language.

Over the past thirty years the academic study of folklore/ethnology in the Republic of Ireland has put down roots in Dublin and Cork, and to a lesser extent in Galway. However, with the present restructuring of Irish universities, there is no guarantee that these two subjects will survive as independent disciplines in the future. This has also a bearing not only on the utilisation of the Commission's collections in times to come, but indeed on their preservation in the long term. It is my earnest hope that this study in addition to making a contribution to the history of Irish and European folkloristics, may also contribute, in some way, towards securing a better future for these great collections, as well as advance research into Irish oral tradition and material culture.

Glossary of Terms

Anglo-Irish Treaty
This treaty, which established of the Irish Free State, was signed on December 6th, 1921. Exactly a year later, on December 6th, 1922, the Irish Free State officially came into being. Although the Anglo-Irish Treaty did not create a completely sovereign state, the general perception nowadays is that Irish independence dates from this time, rather than from 1949 when the Republic of Ireland was declared. In any event, in this work, for convenience' sake, the post-1921 period is referred to as 'independent Ireland'.

An tOireachtas
See Oireachtas (2).

An Claidheamh Soluis
Weekly newspaper of the Gaelic League, 1899–1932.

Army Comrades Association
See Blueshirts.

Ascendancy
The (Protestant) land-owning class.

Army Mutiny
This refers to an aborted attempt at mutiny by certain officers of the Free State Army over fears of demobilisation and other grievances that came to a head in March 1924.

Black and Tans
A paramilitary force employed by the British during the Irish War of Independence to pacify parts of the country. Feared and hated for their ruthlessness.

Blueshirts
Popular name for the Army Comrades Association: a body of ex-service men of the Irish Free State Army, founded in 1932. This association was initially established to defend free speech against the heavy-handed tactics of IRA supporters of Fianna Fáil in the 1932 General Election, but it was, under the leadership of General Eoin O'Duffy, to develop strong proto-fascist tendencies and, for a number of years, constituted a threat to the stability of the state.

Boundary Commission
The name given the Commission set up under the terms of the Anglo-Irish Treaty (1921) to consider the redrawing of the border between the South and the North of Ireland. It sat from late 1924 to late 1925.

Bunreacht na hÉireann
The official name for the new Irish Constitution of 1937, which replaced the Constitution of the Irish Free State of 1922.

Bataí scóir ('tally sticks')	As a means of inducing language change during the 19th century, in particular, it was customary to hang a stick around the necks of children. Each time a parent heard a child speak Irish they put a notch on the stick, and physical punishment would subsequently be administered by the teacher at school in accordance with the number of notches on it (sing. bata scóir)
Civil Service/Civil Servants	The non-military (non-naval) paid service (servants) of the state
Coiste Gnótha	Executive committee of Gaelic League
Cumann na nGaedheal	This political party was set up by supporters of the Anglo-Irish Treaty in April 1923. The Irish title means 'Society or Organisation of the Native Irish (Gaels)'.
Dáil [Éireann]:	The Lower House of the Irish Parliament. It means 'Assembly of Ireland'.
Dublin Castle	Centre of British administration in pre-1921 Ireland and symbol of British rule
Dublin Institute for Advanced Studies:	World-renowned research institute established mainly on the initiative of Éamon de Valera in 1940. Initially it comprised two schools: the School of Celtic Studies and the School of Theoretical Physics. In 1947 a School of Cosmic Physics was added to the Institute. These three schools reflect de Valera's own cultural and scholarly interests.
Executive Council	This was the official name for the government of the Irish Free State. The 1937 Constitution replaced this term by the term 'the Government of Ireland ('Rialtas na hÉireann' in Irish).
Éire	The main historical name in Irish for the island of Ireland. The semantics of modern usage in English are, however, problematic. The 1937 Irish Constitution declared that the official name of the state was Éire, but another article of the Constitution stated that the territory of the state comprised the whole island of Ireland, not simply the area then recognised by international law. Although sometimes used in English to refer to the southern Irish state, in this sense, it can be pejorative. The genitive of Éire is Éireann.
Economic War	This term refers to the economic dispute between Britain and the Irish Free State resulting from de Valera's abolition on entry into office in 1932 of the Oath of Allegiance to the British Monarch and his refusal to pay 'land annuities' to compensate Britain for financing the transfer of land from landlords to farmers a generation or so earlier. The dispute lasted from 1932 to 1938. The duties imposed by Britain in retaliation on Irish farm produce, in particular,

494

greatly affected larger farmers. Although this 'War' was highly controversial domestically at the time, and for a time badly damaged Anglo-Irish relations, it ended amicably and secured for Southern Ireland the return of a number of ports which Britain had continued to hold in accordance with the terms of the Anglo-Irish Treaty. The return of these navy bases left Britain's defences weakened on the eve of the Second World War, but made it possible for the South of Ireland to adopt a position of neutrality during the War.

Emergency

In neutral South of Ireland, the period of the Second World War was at the time and later referred to as 'the Emergency'. The name derives from the state of emergency declared by the Irish Government at the outbreak of the War in 1939.

Easter Rebellion

Rebellion staged during Easter week 1916 against British rule in Ireland. Although ostensibly a failure and confined, for the most part, to Dublin, its suppression, and the execution of most of the leaders, was ultimately to prove the undoing of British rule in the South of Ireland.

Feis

Name given to a type of cultural gathering organised regularly by the Gaelic League or under its auspices (pl. feiseanna). It usually involved singing, dancing and very often, in Irish speaking districts, story-telling competitions.

Feis Cheoil

An offshoot of the Gaelic League devoted to the promotion of music in Ireland. Feis Cheoil (also spelled Feis Ceoil) literally means 'music festival'.

Free State, Irish

The autonomous Irish state established by the Anglo-Irish Treaty was officially known as the Irish Free State (in Irish as Saorstát Éireann). In theory the Irish Free State continued to exist until 1949 when the South of Ireland left the Commonwealth and a fully-sovereign republic was declared; in practice the new Constitution of 1937 abolished the Irish Free State and instituted a republic in all but name.

Gael

Irishman or -woman (also Scottish Highlanders) of native stock whose ancestors spoke Irish – often used in an exclusivist sense.

Gaelic

In this work Gaelic used as an adjective refers to the Irish language or Irish-language tradition. In this usage it may also refer to the Scottish Gaelic language and culture or to the joint Gaelic culture of both countries. Although Gaelic is sometimes found in 'quotations' in this work to refer to the Irish language, for the past number of decades the exclusive use of Gaelic in writing or speech to describe the Irish language has tended to be pejorative and thus is avoided in this work.

Gaelic League	An organisation established in 1893 to preserve Irish as a spoken language in Ireland. In time it was to propose reviving Irish as the main spoken vernacular of the country. In the early twentieth century it became a major force in Ireland and although it was non-political until 1915, in accordance with its constitution, it played a formative role in moulding the generation of nationalists who were to wrest power from the British in the early 1920's. Known in Irish as Conradh naGaeilge.
Galltacht/An Ghalltacht:	The term formerly used in Irish-language and official government circles for the English-speaking districts of Ireland. The term literally means 'foreign part', i.e anglicised part, in contrast to Gaeltacht. The term is rarely used nowadays.
Gaeltacht/An Ghaeltacht:	Irish-speaking district or collectively all the Irish-speaking districts of Ireland (older spelling, Gaedhealtacht).
Gàidhealtacht:	Scottish Gaelic equivalent of Gaeltacht, referring not just to areas where Gaelic is still spoken but also to the Highlands in general.
Government of Ireland Act	Enacted by the British Government in 1920 during the height of the Irish War of Independence. This Act established two jurisdictions for the island of Ireland, one with a government in Dublin and another with a government in Belfast. It was accepted by Ulster Unionists but rejected by most Irish Nationalists.
Gúm, An	An Gúm is the state-owned Irish-language publishing house.
Fianna Fáil	Political party founded by Éamon de Valera in 1926 when he and his followers broke from anti-Treaty Sinn Féin and decided to enter Dáil Éireann. Since 1932 it has been the main political party in the South of Ireland. Fianna Fáil means 'Soldiers of Destiny'.
Fine Gael	Political party formed in 1933 when Cumann na nGaedheal merged with the National Centre Party and the National Guard (i.e. Blueshirts). Fine Gael means 'Kindred or Tribe of the Native Irish (Gael)'.
Governor General	The British monarch's official representative in the Irish Free State.
Home Rule	The term used for the aim of Irish constitutional Nationalists from 1870 to 1918 to achieve an element of political and fiscal autonomy for Ireland within the United Kingdom.
Irish Parliamentary Party	This is a collective name for those Irish Nationalist representatives who attended the British Parliament from 1874 to 1922 and whose aim was to achieve Home Rule (see above) for Ireland. They were not always a united

496

party, often comprising disparate groupings. The Party was virtually obliterated by Sinn Féin in the 1918 General Election.

Irish Civil War

The outbreak of civil war in Ireland in the Summer of 1922 resulted from a split in Sinn Féin and its military wing, the IRA, over the terms of the Anglo-Irish Treaty. Hostilities lasted from June 1922 to Spring 1923 with the pro-Treaty forces being victorious. Although the Civil War resulted in a relatively small number of casualties, there was much destruction of property (including cultural property) and it left a legacy of bitterness that cast a shadow over the following decades.

Irish War of Independence

The name is usually used to describe the violence of the years 1919–1921 perpetrated by the military wing of Sinn Féin (the Irish Republican Army/IRA) and British forces in Ireland which culminated in the signing of the Anglo-Irish Treaty in December 1921. See Black and Tans.

Irish Volunteers

Paramilitary army established by Irish Nationalists in 1913 to defend the promise of Home Rule by Britain's Liberal Government against Unionist (see below) opposition.

Loyalist

Somewhat similar in meaning to Unionist (see below) in the context of Northern Ireland. For the most part, it refers to more working-class Unionists, rather than to middle- or upper-class ones. It also has connotations of support for political violence, or at least support for the threat of violence, in order to maintain the union with Britain.

North

Colloquial way of referring to Northern Ireland used by Nationalists– used in this work to avoid too much repetition.

NUI

National University of Ireland established in 1908 and consisting of four constituent colleges at Dublin, Cork, Galway and Maynooth.

Oireachtas (1)

The Irish Legislature, comprising Dáil Éireann and Seanad Éireann.

Oireachtas (2)

Annual cultural festival of the Gaelic League established in 1897 and modelled on the Welsh Eisteddfod.

Partition

The division of the island of Ireland into two jurisdictions enacted by the Government of Ireland Act of 1920 and solidified by the Anglo-Irish Treaty of 1921.

President of Executive Council

This was the official name for the head of the government of the Irish Free State, superceded by Taoiseach after the 1937 Constitution was approved.

Republic of Ireland

The official name for the South of Ireland since 1949. In this work it may sometimes also refer to the period from 1937 to 1949 when the South was a republic in all but name.

Revival (Gaelic)	This term refers to both the efforts of the Gaelic League and later the independent Irish state to revive the Irish language as the spoken vernacular of Ireland.
Rising	See the Easter Rebelling
RTÉ	Radio Telefís Éireann (formerly Radio Éireann) – the Republic of Ireland's state broadcasting corporation
Saorstát Éireann	The title of the Irish Free State in Irish
Seanad [Éireann]	The Upper House or Senate of the Irish Parliament
Sinn Féin	Political party founded in 1905. Initially it sought a dual-monarchy solution to the Irish problem based on the Austrian-Hungarian model but in the post-1916 period it espoused complete separation from Britain. The name Sinn Féin means 'Ourselves' and this name is reflected in the party's self-sufficient economic philosophy. This philosophy was to dominate most of the period of the Irish Folklore Commission, and in time was to retard the state's economic growth. Most modern political parties in the Republic of Ireland, including modern Sinn Féin, the political wing of the Provisional IRA, trace their origin directly or indirectly to this party.
Six Counties, the	Colloquial way of referring to Northern Ireland by Nationalists.
South, the	Colloquial way of referring to the Irish Free State or Republic of Ireland.
Taoiseach	Official title for the Prime Minister of the Republic of Ireland, and of the Irish Free State from 1937 to 1949. It literally means 'chief', 'chieftain' or 'one in charge' and derives from medieval Ireland.
Townland	A land division. Ireland is divided into over 60,000 townlands.
T.D.	Abbreviation for Teachta Dála – official name for Deputies (i.e. elected representatives) of the Lower House of the Irish Parliament, namely Dáil Éireann.
Twenty Six Counties, the	Colloquial way of referring to the Irish Free State and later the Republic of Ireland.
Ulster Volunteer Force	Paramilitary force founded by Ulster Unionists in 1913 to oppose Home Rule for Ireland and, in particular, to defend the interests of Ulster's Protestant majority against domination by a government in Dublin.
Unionist	A term originally used to describe Irish people who wished to maintain the status quo with Britain and who were opposed to even a measure of autonomy for Ireland. Most Unionists were Protestants. In the post-1920 period

the term is used to describe those in Northern Ireland who wish to maintain the political link to Britain.

Vice-Regal Lodge

Official residence of the Viceroys of Ireland in the pre-1922 period and of the Governors General of the Irish Free State from 1922 to 1932. It is now known as Áras an Uachtaráin and is the official residence of the President of Ireland (Uachtarán na hÉireann).

List of Abbreviations of Locations of Primary Sources

Col. Íde = Coláiste Íde, An Daingean
D/F = files of the Dept. of Finance, National Archives, Dublin
D/T = files of the Dept. of the Taoiseach, National Archives, Dublin
ED = files of the Dept. of Education, National Archives, Dublin
Kir. Muus. = Eesti Kirjandusmuuseum/Estonian Literary Museum, Tartu
Lilly Lib. = Lilly Library, University of Indiana
LUB = Lund University Library
NLI = National Library of Ireland
RTÉSA = Sound Archives of Radio Telefís Éireann
SKS = Suomalaisen Kirjallisuuden Seura/Finnish Literature Society, Helsinki
UCCFA = University College Cork: Folklore Archive
UCCRNG University College Cork: Dept. of Modern Irish
UCDA = University College Dublin: School of History and Archives
UCD Lib. Spec. Col. = University College, Dublin: James Joyce Library, Special Collections
UCDNFC = University College Dublin, Delargy Centre for Irish Folklore and the National Folklore Collection
UCG Hard. Lib. Arch. University College, Galway. Hardiman Library, Special Archives
ULMA = Institutet för språk och folkminnen/Swedish Institute for Language and Folklore, Uppsala
ULMA (TA) = Tjänstearkivet (a Civil Servants' Archive attached to Institutet för språk och folkminnen, Uppsala)

A note to footnotes referring to Primary Sources

In the case of primary sources, as far as possible, to facilitate those who will follow in my wake, I give the page numbers when the document is several pages in length. If there is no pagination, I supply page numbers in square brackets. In the case of certain documents, (a, and b below) I usually give the paragraph (par.) rather than the page number. In order to reduce the length of the title of certain official documents, I abbreviate 'Irish Folklore Commission' to 'IFC' and its Irish-language equivalent, Coimisiún Béaloideasa Éireann' to 'CBÉ'. I also further abbreviate the Dept. of the Taoiseach, Dept. of Finance, and the Dept. of Education to Dept. of Taois., Dept. of Fin., and Dept. of Educ. respectively. Four particular sets of oft-quoted documents have been abbreviated in the following manner:

> a) e.g. 'Coimisiún Béaloideasa Éireann. Miontuairisc an 49ú Chruinnithe, 27 Meitheamh 1947 (Irish Folklore Commission. Minutes of the 49th Meeting, 27 June 1947) abbreviated to 'CBÉ. Miont. 49ú Cruinniú, 27.6.1947',
> b) e.g. 'Irish Folklore Commission. Finance Sub-Committee. Minutes of the Sixty-Second Meeting, 9 August, 1947' abbreviated to 'IFC. Fin. Sub-Com./Min. 62nd Meeting, 9.8.1947',
> c) e.g. 'Gearr-Thuarasgabháil ar Obair Coimisiún Béaloideasa Éireann i gCóir na

Bliana 1935-36' (Report of the Irish Folklore Commission for the year 1935–36) abbreviated to 'Gearr-Thuar./1935–36',

d) e.g. 'Tuarascáil an Stiúrthóra ar Obair an Choimisiúin i Rith na Tréimhse 3 Márta – 3 Meitheamh 1966' (The Report of the Director on the Work of the Commission from 3 March to 3 June 1966) contracted to 'Tuar. an Stiúr. 3.3.1966–3.6.1966'[11]

In referring to primary sources in the College Archives of University College Dublin, 'Min. of Gov. Body' stands for 'Minutes of Governing Body', and 'Min. of Acad. Coun.' for 'Minutes of Academic Council'. In referring to primary sources in the possession of the Library of the University of Lund and the recently renamed Swedish Institute for Language and Folklore (Institutet för språk och folkminen) in Uppsala , I use the abbreviation 'Saml.' (< samling 'collection') to refer to a private collection of papers, and, in the case of the latter institution, 'subnr.' (< subnummer) to refer to a particular file among the Åke Campbell papers. Some of Campbell's correspondence with Irish folklorists derive from a separate state archive (Tjänstearkivet, abbreviated TA) housed in the same building as the Swedish Institute for Language and Folklore. Files from this collection are referred to with the term 'kapsel'.

Education Files

Many of the Education files utilised in this work were consulted in the Dept. of Education. Other Education files, ten in all, that I consulted in the National Archives of Ireland were subsequently found to have been given reference numbers that bore no relation with their nature and contents, and it was decided to rename them. These files are currently being renamed. The ten files that were originally given inappropriate reference numbers are referred to in my footnotes with the designations (somewhat abbreviated from their original designations) FL 1, FL 2, FL 3, FL 4, FL 5, FL 6, FL 7, FL 8, CO 495(1), and CO 495 (8) respectively. When they are renamed, their new designations will retain the above letters and numbers but will be longer. They should consequently be easily identifiable.

The files that I consulted in the Dept. of Education have recently been sent to the National Archives and their designations are also in the process of being altered somewhat in accordance with normal procedure. I refer to two of these files with the following designations:

CO 3/15/9(495/I) and CO 3/15/9(495/II)

Two other unnamed files have been utilised in this work, one of them extensively, the other to a very limited extent. The first of these is referred to as [FL 9] and it contains minutes of the Commission and Finance Sub-Committee from 1935 to 1945 as well as miscellaneous correspondence. The other file, which contains Minutes of the Commission and Finance Sub-Committee from 1950–1954, is referred to as [FL 10].

1   [1]This particular type of report is usually included in the body of the Minutes of the quarterly meetings of the Commission itself ('a' above), although they are sometimes appended. They are rarely referred to directly in this work.

Primary Sources and Bibliography

1a. Primary Sources/Ireland:

Coláiste Íde, An Daingean
(Col. Íde)
Pádraig Ó Siochfhradha Papers

Franciscan Archive, Killiney
Éamon de Valera Papers (now housed in UCDA)

National Archives of Ireland
Files of the Dept. of the Taoiseach (D/T)
Files of the Dept. of Finance (D/F)
Files of the Dept. of Education (ED)

National Library of Ireland
(NLI)
Gaelic League Minutes
Eoin MacNeill Papers
Séamus Ó Casaide Papers

National Museum of Ireland/Museum of Rural Life, Castlebar
Various files

Radio Telefís Éireann: Sound Archive
(RTÉSA)
Various interviews and programmes

University College Cork: Folklore Archive
(UCCFA)
Questionnaire returns on work of Irish Folklore Commission (late 1980's)

University College Cork: Dept. of Modern Irish
(UCCRNG)
Transcripts of Pádraig Tyers' interviews with Seosamh Ó Dálaigh

University College Dublin: School of History and Archives
(UCDA)
Ernest Blythe Papers
R. Dudley Edwards Papers
Michael Hayes Papers
Eoin MacNeill Papers
Cearbhall Ó Dálaigh Papers
Michael Tierney Papers
Governing Body Minutes (Min. of Gov. Body.)
Academic Council Minutes (Min. of Acad. Counc.)

University College, Dublin: James Joyce Library, Special Collections

(UCD Lib. Spec. Col.)
Henry Morris/Énrí Ó Muirgheasa Papers

University College Dublin, Delargy Centre for Irish Folklore and the National Folklore
Collection
(UCDNFC)
Diaries and notebooks of the Irish Folklore Commission's full-time collectors as well as the
Indexes of the Main Collection (consulted on microfilm at the Boole Library, University
College, Cork and the John Paul II Library, St. Patrick's College, Maynooth)

University College, Galway. Hardiman Library Special Archives
(UCG Hard. Lib. Arch.)
Bairéad Collection
Séamus Ó Duilearga Collection

1b. Primary Sources/Nordic and Baltic:

Helsinki
Finnish Literature Society/Suomalaisen Kirjallisuuden Seura
(SKS)
Martti Haavio Papers
Kaarle Krohn Papers

Lund
Lund University Library/Universitetsbiblioteket, Lund
(LUB)
Carl Wilhelm von Sydow Papers

Tartu
Estonian Literary Museum/Eesti Kirjandusmuuseum
(Kir. muus.)
Oskar Loorits Papers

Uppsala
Swedish Institute for Language and Folklore/Institutet för Språk och Folkminnen
(ULMA)
Åke Campbell Papers

1c. Primary Sources/North America:

Indiana
University of Indiana, Lilly Library
(Lilly Lib.)
Stith Thompson Papers
Richard Dorson Papers

2. Unpublished Theses

Ní Nia, Gearóidín, 'An tAthair Eric Mac Fhinn agus Ar Aghaidh' [Fr. Eric Mac Fhinn
    and the monthly *Ar Aghaidh*] (MA thesis, Dept. of Modern Irish, University College,
    Galway, 1994)
Nic Craith, Eibhlín, 'Tadhg Ó Murchadha agus Béaloideas Uíbh Ráthaigh' [Tadhg Ó
    Murchadha and the Folklore of Uíbh Ráthach] (MA thesis, Dept. of Irish, University

College Cork, 1991)

Nic Suibhne, Fionnuala, 'Cuntas ar ghnéithe de shaol an Bhaineannaigh as insint bhéilfhaisnéiseoirí mná Ó Chúige Uladh' [Aspects of female life from the oral accounts of Ulster women narrators] (MA thesis, Dept. of Folklore and Ethnology, University College Cork, 1990)

Lehto, Leena, 'Aineistoja pienoiskoossa. Suomalaisen Kirjallisuuden Seuran kansanrunousarkiston mikrofilmauksesta' [Microfilming the Folklore Archive of the Finnish Literature Society] (National Archives of Finland, minor thesis in archiving, 2004)

3. Unascribed Brochures and Leaflets

Comóradh Céad Bliain Bhreith Shéamuis Uí Dhuilearga. Centenary of the Birth of James Hamilton Delargy (University Industry Centre, University College Dublin; 1999)

The Department of Irish Folklore (Roinn Bhéaloideas Éireann) - dated internally 1972–73.

The Department of Irish Folklore and its Archive, dated internally, 1993.

Óráidí ag Oscailt Roinn Bhéaloideas Éireann i gColáiste Ollscoile Bhaile Átha Cliath Dé Máirt, 28 Meán Fómhair 1971/ Speeches made at the opening of the Department of Irish Folklore at University College, Dublin, on Tuesday, 28th September 1971.

4. Irish Government Publications

An Coimisiún um Athbheochan na Gaeilge. An Tuarascáil Dheiridh [Commission on the Revival of Irish. Final Report] (Oifig an tSoláthair; Baile Átha Cliath n.d),

Bunreacht na hÉireann. Constitution of Ireland

Commission on Higher Education 1960–67 II. Report Volume I (Government Publications; Dublin 1967)

Commission on Higher Education 1960–67 II. Report Volume 2 (Government Publications; Dublin 1967)

Ireland. Census of Population 1936. Preliminary Report (Stationery Office; Dublin 1936)

Public and General Acts Passed by the Oireachtas of Saorstát Éireann during the year 1934 (Dublin 1935)

Seanad Éireann. Díospóireachtaí Párlaiminte/Parliamentary Debates

Seanad Éireann. Tuarasgabháil Dheiridh ón gCoiste ar Láimhscríbhinnibh Gaedhilge. Final Report of Committee on Irish Manuscripts (Stationery Office; Dublin 1924)

University College Dublin Act, 1934

Works of reference

Breathnach, Diarmuid/Máire Ní Mhurchú,

Beathaisnéis 1882–1982 [National Biography] 5 vols. *(*An Clóchomhar Tta; Baile Átha Cliath 1986-1997)

Chubb, Basil, *The Government and Politics of Ireland* (Oxford University Press; 1974)

Coakley, John, and Michael Gallagher, Politics in the Republic of Ireland (Routledge; London 1999)

Newspapers and and Popular Periodicals

An tUltach
Comhar
Elias

Feasta
Irish Independent
Irish Schools Weekly
The Capuchin Annual
The Dublin Magazine
The Irish Book Lover
The Irish Press
The Irish Stateman
The Irish Times
The Star
The Times (London)

Local Irish Journals

An Linn Bhuí
Journal of Cork Historical and Archaeological Society
Journal of the Kerry Archaeological and History Society
Journal of the Tipperary Historical Society
The Glynns. Journal of Antrim Historical Society
The Past. The Organ of the Uí Cinsealaigh Historical Society
Seanchas Ardmhacha

Academic Journals

Analecta Hibernica
Béaloideas
Béascna. Journal of Folklore and Ethnology
Celtica
Éire-Ireland
Ethnologia Europaea
Fabula
Folklore
History Ireland
History Workshop
Irish Journal of Anthropology
Irish Review
Journal of American Folklore
Journal of the Folklore Institute
Journal of the Royal Society of Antiquaries of Ireland
Journal of Folklore Research
Laos
Lochlann
Lore and language
NIF Newsletter
Proceedings of the Royal Irish Academy
Sinsear. The Folklore Journal
Studies
Scottish Studies
Studia Fennica
Svenska landsmål och svenskt folkliv
Ulster Folklife
Virittäjä
Western Folklore
Zeitschrift für celtische Philologie
Zeitschrift für celtische Philologie und Volksforschung

Books and articles

Aarne, Antti, *Verzeichnis der Märchentypen* (Academia Scientarium Fennica; Helsinki 1910).

Adams, G. B. 'Aspects of Monoglottism in Ulster' *Ulster Folklife* 22 (1976), pp. 76–87.

Allen, Trevor, *The Storm Passed By. Ireland and the Battle of the Atlantic 1940–41* (Irish Academic Press; Dublin 1996).

Almqvist, Bo, *The Uglier Foot (AT 1559B*)* (Comhairle Bhéaloideas Éireann; Baile Átha Cliath 1975).

Almqvist, Bo, 'Irish Folklore Commission: Achievement and Legacy', *Béaloideas* 45–47 (1977–79), pp.6–26.

Almqvist, Bo, 'In Memoriam: Séamus Ó Duilearga', *Sinsear* 3 (1981), pp. 1–6.

Almqvist, Bo, 'Dr. Máire MacNeill-Sweeney (1904–87). In memorium', *Béaloideas* 56 (1988), pp. 220–223.

Almqvist, Bo, 'The Mysterious Mícheál Ó Gaoithín, Boccaccio and the Blasket Tradition', in *Béaloideas* 58 (1990), pp. 75–140.

Almqvist, Bo, 'Seán Ó Dubhda, Bailitheoir Béaloidis: A Shaothar agus a Thréithe'[The Folklore Collector Seán Ó Dubhda], in Pádraig Ó Fiannachta (ed.), *Ár bhFilí* [Our Poets] (Oidhreacht Chorca Dhuibhne; Baile an Fhirtéaraigh 1991), pp. 89–116.

Almqvist, Bo, 'Leo Corduff.1929–1992', *Béaloideas* 60-61 (1992–1993), pp. 287–290.

Almqvist, Bo, 'Bláithín agus an Béaloideas'[Robin Flower and Folklore], in Mícheál de Mórdha (ed.), *Bláithín: Flower* (An Sagart; An Daingean 1998), pp. 97–116.

Almqvist, Bo, 'James J. Delaney 1916–2000', *Béaloideas* 69 (2001), pp. 183–189.

Almqvist, Bo, 'C. W. von Sydow agus Éire: Scoláire Sualannach agus an Léann Ceilteach' [C. W. Von Sydow and Ireland. A Swedish Scholar and Celtic Studies], in *Béaloideas* 70 (2002), pp. 3–49.

Andrews, J. H., *A Paper Landscape. The Ordnance Survey in Nineteenth-Century Ireland* (Four Courts Press; Dublin 2001[1975]).

Anttonen, Pertti, *Tradition Through Modernity. Postmodernism and the Nation-State in Folklore Scholarship* (Finnish Literature Society; Helsinki 2005).

Arensberg, Conrad M., *The Irish Countryman. An anthropological study* (Waveland Press; Prospect Heights, Illinois 1988 [1937, 1968]).

Arensberg, Conrad M. and Solon T. Kimball, *Family and Community in Ireland* (Clasp Press; Ennis 2001 [1940] Third Edition; ed. Anne Byrne, Ricca Edmondson and Tony Varley).

Asplund, Anneli, 'Äänitearkiston vaiheita', *Elias* 3 (1992), pp. 34–39.

Atkinson, John A., Iain Banks and Jerry O'Sullivan (eds) *Nationalism and Archaeology* (Cruithne Press; Edinburgh 1996).

Austin, Valerie A., 'The Céilí and the Public Dance Halls Act, 1935', *Éire-Ireland* (Fomhar-Fall 1993), pp. 7–16.

Bale, Anna, 'Seanchas "ad finem"; sracfhéachaint ar shaothar Chiaráin Bairéad. Bailitheoir Béaloidis, 1951–1975' [The folklore collector Ciarán Bairéad], *Sinsear* 7 (1993), pp. 62–70.

Barrington, Dónal, 'The North and the Constitution', in Brian Farrell (ed.) *De Valera's Constitution and Ours* (Gill & Macmillan; Dublin 1988), pp. 61–74.

Beiner, Guy, 'Orality lost: the archives of the Irish Folklore Commission and folk historiography of *Bliain na bhFrancach*', in Hiram Morgan (ed.) *Information Media & Power Through the Ages* (University College Dublin Press; 2001), pp. 222–244.

Beiner, Guy, 'Oral Herstoriography', in Edna Longley, Eamonn Hughes and Des O'Rawe, *Ireland (Ulster) Scotland: Concepts, Contexts, Comparisons* (Cló Ollscoil na Banríona; Belfast 2003), pp. 86–93.

Beiner, Guy, *Remembering the Year of the French. Irish Folk History and Social Memory* (University of Wisconsin Press; Madison 2007).

Belanger, Jacqueline, 'The Desire of the West: The Aran Islands and Irish Identity in Grania', in Leon Litvack and Glenn Hooper, *Ireland in the Nineteenth Century.*

Regional Identity (Four Courts Press: Dublin 2000), pp. 95–107.

Bergin, Osborn and Carl Marstrander (eds), *Miscellany presented to Kuno Meyer* (Max Niemeyer; Halle 1912).

Bhreathnach-Lynch, Síghle, 'Commemorating the hero in newly independent Ireland: expressions of nationhood in bronze and stone', in Lawrence W. McBride (ed.) *Images, Icons and the Irish Nationalist Imagination* (Four Courts Press; Dublin 1999) pp. 148–165.

Binchy, Daniel, 'Heinrich Bruning', *Studies*, 21 (September 1932) pp. 385–403.

Binchy, Daniel, 'Adolf Hitler', *Studies*, 22 (March 1933), pp. 29–47.

Binchy, Daniel, *Osborn Bergin* (University College Dublin; 1970).

Bødker, Laurits, *Talt og Skrevet 1940–1974* (Institut for Folkemindevidenskab, Københavns Universitet; København 1975).

Borchgrevink, Anne-Berit Østereng, 'Séamus Ó Duilearga Retires', *Lochlann* (1974), pp. 169–170.

Bowman, John, *De Valera and the Ulster Question 1917–1973* (Clarendon Press; Oxford 1982).

Boyce, George D., *Nationalism in Ireland* (Routledge; London 1991 [1982]).

Boyne, Patricia, *John O'Donovan (1806–1861)* (Boethius; Kilkenny 1987).

Boyes, Georgina, *The Imagined Village. Culture, ideology and the English Folk Revival* (Manchester University Press; 1993).

Brady, Erika, *A Spiral Way. How the Phonograph Changed Ethnography* (University Press of Mississippi; Jackson 1999).

Bramsbäck, Birgit (ed.), *Societas Celtologica Nordica. Proceedings of Inaugural Meeting and First Symposium 26 May 1990 at Uppsala University* (Acta Universitatis Upsaliensis. Studia Anglistica Upsaliensia 76; Uppsala 1991), pp. 53–73.

Branch, Michael, *A.J. Sjögren – Studies of The North* (Suomalais-Ugrilainen Seura; Helsinki 1973).

Breatnach, Caoilte, *Memories in Time. Folklore of Beithe 1800-2000* (Beagh Integrated Rural Development Association; Tubber 2003).

Breatnach, Nioclás, *Ar Bóthar Dom* [On my Travels] (Coláiste na Rinne; Rinn Ó gCuanach 1998a).

Breatnach, Nioclás, 'Seanriadóirí' [Old Stagers], *An Linn Bhuí* 2 (1998b), pp. 71–85.

Brennan, Helen, *The Story of Irish Dance* (Brandon; Dingle 1999).

Bringéus, Nils-Arvid, 'Folkkulturen och Folklivsarkivet', in Nils-Arvid Bringéus (ed), *Folklivsarkivet i Lund 1913–1988* (Lund 1988 = *Skrifter från Folklivsarkivet i Lund* 26).

Briody, Mícheál, 'Mícheál Ó Gaoithín – Storyteller', in Folke Josephson (ed.), *Celts and Vikings. Proceedings of the Fourth Symposium of Societas Celtologica Nordica;* Göteborg 1997 = *Meijerbergs Arkiv för Svensk Ordforskning* 20), pp. 153–185.

Briody, Mícheál, 'The collectors' diaries of the Irish Folklore Commission: a complex genesis', *Sinsear* 9 (2005a), pp. 27–45.

Briody, Mícheál, '"Publish or Perish!". The Vicissitudes of the Irish Folklore Institute', *Ulster Folklife* 51 (2005b), pp. 10–33.

Briody, Mícheál, 'Énrí Ó Muirgheasa agus Scéim na Scol 1934' [Énrí Ó Muirgheasa and the 1934 Schools Scheme], *Béascna* 3 (2006), pp. 1–22.

Broderick, George, *Language Death in the Isle of Man* (Niemeyer; Tübingen 1999 = Linguistiche Arbeiten 395), p. 62.

Brown, Terence, *Irelend. A Social History 1922–1985* (Fontana Press; London 1985).

Browne, Noël, *Against the Tide* (Gill and Macmillan; Dublin 1986).

Bruford, Alan and Donald A. Macdonald (eds), *Scottish Traditional Tales* (Polygon; Edinburgh 1994).

Carlson, Julia, *Banned in Ireland. Censorship and the Irish Writer* (Routledge; London 1990).

Carney, James, 'Literature in Irish, 1169–1534', in Cosgrove 1987, pp. 688–707.

Carroll, Denis, *They Have Fooled You Again. Micheál Ó Flannagáin (1876–1942) Priest, Republican, Social Critic* (The Columba Press; Dublin 1993).

Cheape, Hugh (ed.), *Tools and Traditions. Studies in European Ethnology Presented to Alexander Fenton* (National Museums of Scotland; Edinburgh 1993b).

Chestnutt, Michael, 'The Demise of Historicism in Nordic Folktale Research', in Michael Chestnut (ed.), *Telling Reality. Folklore Studies in Memory of Bengt Holbek* (Copenhagen & Turku; 1993), pp. 235–253.

Christiansen, Reidar Th., *The Vikings and Viking Wars in Irish and Gaelic Tradition* (Norske Videnskaps Akademi; Oslo 1931).

Clear, Caitriona, 'Women in de Valera's Ireland 1932–1948: a reappraisal', in Doherty and Keogh 2003, pp. 104–114.

Comerford, R. V., *Inventing the Nation. Ireland* (Arnold; London 2003).

Connolly, Philomena, *Medieval Record Sources* (Four Courts Press; Dublin 2002).

Corish, Patrick J., *Maynooth College 1795–1995* (Gill & Macmillan; Dublin 1995).

Corkery, Daniel, *The Hidden Ireland* (Dublin 1924).

Cosgrove, Art, 'Hiberniores Ipsis Hibernis', in Art Cosgrove and Donal McCartney (eds) *Studies in Irish History. Presented to R. Dudley Edwards* (University College Dublin; 1979), pp. 1–14.

Cosgrove, Art (ed.), *A New History of Ireland II. Medieval Ireland 1169–1534* (Clarendon Press; Oxford 1987).

Cronin, Mike, *The Blueshirts and Irish Politics* (Four Courts Press; Dublin 1997).

Crooke, Elizabeth, *Politics, Archaeology and the Creation of a National Museum of Ireland* (Irish Academic Press; Dublin 2000).

Crowley, Tony, *The Politics of Language in Ireland 1366–1922* (Routledge; London 2000).

Daly, Mary E., *Industrial Development and Irish National Identity*, (Syracuse University Press; New York 1992).

Day, Angélique, '"Habits of the People": Traditional Life in Ireland 1830–1840, as recorded in the Ordnance Survey Memoirs', *Ulster Folklife* 30 (1984), pp. 22–36.

de Brún, Monsignor [Pádraig], 'Saothar Ollúna agus Léachtaithe i nGaillimh' [The Work of the Teaching Staff of University College Galway], *Comhar* Márta 1950. p. 11.

Delaney, Enda, 'The Vanishing Irish? The Exodus from Ireland in the 1950's', in Keogh et al 2004, pp. 80-86.

Delaney, James G., 'Patrick Kennedy', *The Past* 7 (1964), pp. 9–88.

Delaney, James G. (Séamas S. Ó Dúshláine), 'Wexford Sea Traditions', in *The Past* 10 (1973–74), pp. 58–72.

Delaney, Séamas G. [James G.], 'Going Deepwater', *The Past* 11 (1975–76), pp. 21–36.

Delaney, J.G., 'Fieldwork in South Roscommon', in Ó Danachair (ed.) 1976, pp. 15–29.

Delaney, J. G., 'The harvest in north Offaly', in Harman Murtagh (ed.), *Irish Midland Studies. Essays in Commemoration of N.W. English* (The Old Athlone Society; Athlone 1980), pp. 239–249.

Delaney, James G., 'Three Midland Storytellers', *Béaloideas* 50 (1982), p. 44–53.

Delaney, James G., 'At the Foot of Mount Leinster. Collecting Folklore in the Kennedy Country in 1954', *The Past* 16 (1988), pp. 3–27.

Delaney, James G., 'Collecting Folklore in Ireland', *Lore & Language* June 1990, pp. 15–37.

Delaney, James G., 'Wexford Memories', *The Past* 20 (1997), pp. 53–79.

Dillon, Myles, review [Seán Ó Súilleabháin's *Caitheamh Aimsire ar Thórraimh*] *Celtica* vi (1963), pp. 289–290.

Doherty, Gabriel and Dermot Keogh, *De Valera's Irelands* (Mercier Press; Cork 2003).

Doherty, Gillian M., *The Irish Ordnance Survey. History. Culture and Memory* (Four Courts Press; Dublin 2004).

Dömötör, Tekla, *János Honti – Leben und Werk* (Academia Scientarium Fennica; Helsinki 1978 = FFC No. 221).

Donovan, Brian C. and David Edwards, *British Sources for Irish History 1485–1641. A*

Guide to manuscripts in Local, Regional and Specialised Repositories in England, Scotland and Wales (Irish Manuscripts Commission; Dublin 1997).

Dooley, Terence, *The Decline of the Big House in Ireland. A Study of Landed Families 1860–1960* (Wolfhound Press; Dublin 2001).

Dooley, Terence, *'The Land for the People'. The Land Question in Independent Ireland* (University College Dublin Press; 2004).

Dooley, Terence, *The Big Houses and Landed Estates of Ireland* (Four Courts Press; Dublin 2007).

Dorson, Richard M., 'Collecting in County Kerry', *Journal of American Folklore* 66 (1953), pp. 19–42.

Dorson, Richard M., *The British Folklorists. A History* (The University of Chicago Press; 1968).

Dowling, Michelle, '"The Ireland that I would have". De Valera and the creation of an Irish national image', in *History Ireland* (Summer 1997) pp. 37-41.

Dunne, Tom, 'Maureen Wall (née McGehin) 1918–1972: a memoir', in Gerard O'Brien (ed.), *Catholic Ireland In the Eighteenth Century. Collected Essays of Maureen Wall* (Geography Publications; Dublin 1989), unpaginated.

Edwards, David, 'Salvaging History: Hogan and the Irish Manuscripts Commission', in Donnchadh Ó Corráin (ed.), *James Hogan. Revolutionary, Historian and Political Scientist* (Four Courts Press; Dublin 2001), pp.116–132.

Edwards, R. Dudley, 'Professor MacNeill', in Martin and Byrne (eds.) 1973, 279–297.

Ellis, Steven G., *Ireland in the Age of the Tudors 1447–1603. English Expansion and the End of Gaelic Rule* (Longman; London 1998).

Erixon, Sigurd, 'The Position of Regional Ethnology and Folklore at the European Universities', *Laos* (1955), pp. 108–159.

Evans, E. Estyn, *Irish Folk Ways* (Routledge & Kegan Paul; 1972 [1957]).

Evans, E. Estyn, 'Gleanings from County Cavan', *Ulster Folklife* 26 (1980), pp. 1–7.

Evans, E. Estyn, 'The early development of folklife studies in Northern Ireland', in Gailey 1988, pp. 91–96.

Evans, E. Estyn, *Ireland and the Atlantic Heritage. Selected Writings* (The Lilliput Press; Dublin 1996).

Evans, Timothy H., 'Folklore as Utopia. English Medievalists and the Ideology of Revivalism', *Western Folklore* 47 (1988), pp. 245–268.

Evijärvi, Irja-Leena, *Kaarle Krohn. Elämä ja Toiminta* [Kaarle Krohn. Life and Work] (Suomalaisen Kirjallisuuden Seura; Helsinki 1963).

Fallon, Brian, *An Age of Innocence. Irish Culture 1930–1960* (Gill & Macmillan; Dublin 1998).

Farren, Margaret and Mary Harkin (eds), *It's Us They're Talking About. Proceedings from the McGlinchey Summer School 1998* (Donegal n.d. [1999]).

Farren, Sean, *The Politics of Irish Education 1920–1965* (The Queen's University of Belfast, Institute of Irish Studies; 1995).

Fischer, Joachim and John Dillon, *The Correspondence of Myles Dillon 1922–1925* (Four Courts Press; Dublin 1999).

FitzGerald, Garret, 'Estimates for baronies of minimum level of Irish speaking amongst decennial cohorts, 1771–1781 to 1861–1871', *Proceedings of the Royal Irish Academy* 84C (1984), pp. 117–155.

FitzGerald, Garret, *Reflections on The Irish State* (Irish Academic Press; Dublin 2003a).

FitzGerald, Garret (2003b), 'Eamon de Valera: the price of his achievement', in Doherty and Keogh 2003b, pp. 185–204.

FitzGerald, Garret, 'Irish-Speaking in the pre-Famine Period: A Study Based on the 1911 Census Data for People Born before 1851 and Still Alive in 1911', *Proceedings of the Royal Irish Academy* 103C (2003c), pp. 191–283.

Fox, C. M., *Annals of the Irish Harpers* (London 1911).

Gailey, Alan (ed.), *The Use of Tradition. Essays Presented to G.B. Thompson* (Ulster Folk and Transport Museum; Holywood 1988).

509

Gailey, Alan and Chris Lynch, 'Caoimhín Ó Danachair, 1913–2003', *Folk Life* 42 (2002–2003), pp.121–124.

Garvin, Tom, *Nationalist Revolutionaries in Ireland* (Clarendon Press; Oxford 1987).

Garvin, Tom, *1922. The Birth of Irish Democracy* (Gill & Macmillan; Dublin 1996).

Garvin, Tom, 'The Aftermath of the Irish Civil War, in Doherty and Keogh 2003, pp.74–83.

Hanly, Joseph, *The National Ideal. A Practical Exposition of True Nationality appertaining to Ireland* (Dollard Printinghouse; Dublin 1931).

Harkort, Fritz, Karel C. Peeters, Robert Wildhaber (eds.), *Volksüberlieferung. Festschrift für Kurt Ranke zur Vollendung des 60 Lebensjahres* (Verlag Otto Schwartz & Co; Göttingen 1968).

Harvey, Clodagh Brennan, 'Some Irish Women Storytellers and reflections on the Role of Women in the Storytelling Tradition', *Western Folklore* 48 (1989), pp. 109–128.

Hautala, Jouko, 'The Folklore Archives of the Finnish Literature Society', in *Studia Fennica* 7 (1957), pp. 2–36.

Hayes-McCoy, G. A., 'Museums and our National Heritage', *The Capuchin Annual* (1971), pp. 128–135.

Hedblom, Folke, 'Sex årtionden med ULMA. Högtidsföreläsning vid ULMA:s 75-årsjubileum den 9 April 1989' [Six Decades of the Dialect and Folklore Archive, Uppsala], *Svenska landsmål och svenskt folkliv* 1989, pp. 7–24.

Hepburn, A. C., *The Conflict of Nationality in Modern Ireland* (Edward Arnold; London 1980).

Herranen, Gun and Lassi Saressalo, *A Guide to Nordic Tradition Archives* (Nordic Institute of Folklore; Turku 1978).

Herzfeld, Michael, *Ours Once More. Folklore, Ideology, and the making of Modern Greece* (University of Texas Press; Austin 1982).

Hirvonen, Maija, Anna Makkonen and Anna Nybondas, *15 vuosikymmentä. kirjallisia dokumentteja erään seuran historiasta* [Documents from fifteen decades of the history of the Finnish Literature Society] (Suomalaisen Kirjallisuuden Seura; Helsinki 1981).

Holbek, Bengt, *Interpretation of Fairy Tales* (Academia Scientiarum Fennica; Helsinki 1987 = FF Communications No. 239.

Honko, Lauri, 'Types of Comparison and Forms of Variation', *Journal of Folklore Research* 23 (1986), pp.105–124.

Honko, Lauri, 'Recommendation on the Safeguarding of Traditional Culture and Folklore Adopted by UNESCO', NIF Newsletter 1/1990, pp. 3–7.

Honko, Lauri (ed.), *Thick Corpus, Organic Variation and Textuality in Oral Tradition* (Finnish Literature Society; Helsinki 2000 = Studia Fennica Folkloristica 7).

Hull, Eleanor, 'Folklore Collecting in Ireland', *Journal of the Cork Historical and Archaeological Society* 17 (1911a), pp. 27–33.

Hull, Eleanor, 'Folklore Collecting in Ireland', *Journal of the Royal Society of Antiquaries of Ireland* Vol. 41 (1911b), pp. 188–190.

Hutchinson, John, *The Dynamics of Cultural Nationalism. The Gaelic Revival and the Creation of the Irish Nation State* (Allen & Unwin; London 1987).

Ives, Edward D., *The Tape-Recorded Interview* (The University of Tennessee Press; Knoxville 1995).

Järvinen, Irma-Riitta, 'Kylä ja erämää. Helmi Helmisen perinteentallennusmatkat Itä-Karjalaan 1941–1944' [The Village and the wilderness. Helmi Helminen's collecting trips to East Karelia] in Pekka Laaksonen, Seppo Knuuttila and Ulla Piela (eds) *Kentäkysymyksiä* [Field Issues] (Suomalaisen Kirjallisuuden Seura; Helsinki 2004), pp. 43–60.

Kallas, Riitta (ed.), *Kolme Naista, Kolme Kohtaloa. Aino Kallaksen kirjeenvaihtoa Ilona Jalavan ja Helmi Krohnin kanssa vuosina 1914–1955* [The Correspondence of Aino Kallas] (Suomalaisen Kirjallisuuden Seura; Helsinki 1989).

Kelly, Adrian, *Compulsory Irish. Language and Education in Ireland 1870s – 1970s* (Irish Academic Press; Dublin 2002).

Keogh, Dermot, *Twentieth-Century Ireland* (Gill & Macmillan; Dublin 1994).

Keogh, Dermot, *Ireland and The Vatican* (Cork University Press; 1995).

Keogh, Dermot, *Jews in Twentieth-Century Ireland* (Cork University Press; Cork 1998).

Keogh, Dermot, Finbarr O'Shea and Carmel Quinlan (eds), *Ireland in the 1950's. The Lost Decade* (Mercier Press; Cork 2004).

Korb, Anu, Janika Oras, and Ülo Tedre, *The Estonian Folklore Archive* (Estonian Academy of Sciences; Tallinn 1990).

Krohn, Kaarle, *Die folkloristiche Arbeitsmethode* (Oslo 1926).

Kuhn, Hugo and Kurt Schier (eds), *Märchen, Mythos, Dichtung. Festschrift zum 90 Geburtstag Freidrich von der Leyens am 19 August 1963* (Verlag C. H. Beck; München 1963).

Laaksonen, Pekka, and Jukka Saarinen, *Arkiston Avain. Kansanrunousarkiston kortistot hakemistot luettelot lyhenteet* [A Key of the Finnish Literature Society's Folklore Archive] (Suomalaisen Kirjallisuuden Seura; Helsinki 2004).

Laaksonen, Pekka, 'Lapin ja Ruijan retket 1963–1964 [Trips to Lapland and Finnmark] in Pekka Laaksonen, Seppo Knuuttila and Ulla Piela (eds) *Tutkijat Kentällä* [Researchers in the Field] (Suomalaisen Kirjallisuuden Seura; Helsinki 2003), pp. 219–236.

Lee, J. J., *Ireland 1912–1985. Politics and Society* (Cambridge University Press; 1995 [1989]).

Leerson, Joep, *Mere Irish and Fíor-Ghael* (Cork University Press; 1996).

Lenox-Conyngham, Melosina (ed.), *Diaries in Ireland. An Anthology 1590–1987* (The Lilliput Press; Dublin 1998).

Lilja, Agneta, *Föreställningen om den ideala uppteckningen* [The Notion of the Ideal Record] (Dialekt- och folkminnesarkivet; Uppsala 1996).

Lixfield, Hannjost, *Folklore and Fascism. The Reich Institute for German Volkskunde* (Indiana University Press; Bloomington 1994).

Lydon, James, *The Lordship of Ireland in the Middle Ages* (Four Courts Press; Dublin 2003 [1972]).

Lyne, Gerard J., *The Lansdowne Estate in Kerry under the Agency of W. S. Trench 1847-72* (Geography Publications; Dublin 2001).

Lysaght, Patricia, 'Cuairteanna Eitneolaíochta Sualannacha in Albain. Åke Campbell in Innse Ghall sna blianta 1939 agus 1948–Tuairiscí in Éirinn' [Irish accounts of Åke Campbell's ethnological trips to Scotland], *Sinsear* 6 (1990), pp. 24–49.

Lysaght, Patricia, 'Don't go without your Beaver Hat! Seán Ó Súilleabháin in Sweden in 1935', *Sinsear* 7 (1993a), pp. 49–59.

Lysaght, Patricia (1993b), 'Swedish Ethnological Surveys in Ireland 1934–35 and their Aftermath', in Cheape 1993, pp. 22–31.

Lysaght, Patricia, 'Perspectives on Narrative Communication and Gender: Lady Augusta Gregory's Visions and Beliefs in the West of Ireland (1920)', *Fabula* 39 (1998), pp. 256–276.

Lönnrot, Elias, *Matkat 1828–1844* [Journeys 1828–1844] (Weilin+Göös; Espoo 1981).

Mac a' Bhaird, Proinnsias, *Cogar San Fharraige. Scéim na Scol in Árainn Mhór 1937–1938* [The Schools Scheme in Aranmore] (Coiscéim; Baile Átha Cliath 2002).

Megaw, Basil (B. R. S. M.), 'The Late Calum I. Maclean', *Scottish Studies* 4/2 (1960), pp.121–123.

McCann, Jack, 'James Hamilton Delargy', in *The Glynns* 9 (1981), pp. 62–63.

McCartney, Donal, 'MacNeill and Irish-Ireland', in Martin and Byrne 1973, pp. 77–97.

McCartney, Donal, *The National University of Ireland and Eamon de Valera* (The University Press of Ireland; Dublin 1983).

McCartney, Donal, *UCD. A National Idea* (Gill & Macmillan; Dublin 1999).

Mackechnie, J., *Catalogue of Gaelic manuscripts in selected libraries in Great Britain and Ireland* 1–2 (Boston 1973).

Mac Coisdeala (Mac Coisdealbha), Liam, 'Im' Bhailitheoir Béaloideasa' [My Work as a Folklore Collector], *Béaloideas* 16 (1946) 141–171.

Mac Coisdeala, Liam, 'Fear Inste an Scéil/The Storyteller' in Kevin O'Nolan (ed.),

Eochair Mac Rí in Éirinn/Eochair, a King's Son in Ireland (Comhairle Bhéaloideas Éireann; Baile Átha Cliath 1982) pp. 26–39.

McCullagh, David, *A Makeshift Majority. The First Inter-Party Government, 1948–51* (Institute of Public Administration; Dublin 1998).

MacDonagh, Oliver, *States of Mind. A Study of Anglo-Irish Conflict 1780–1980* (George Allen & Unwin; London 1983).

Mac Giolla Fhinnéin, Brian, 'Pádraig Ó Loinsigh: Saol agus Saothar' [Pádraig Ó Loinsigh. Life and Work], *Seanchas Ardmhacha* 15/2 (1993), pp. 98–124.

McIntosh, Angus, 'Professor Séamus Delargy', *Scottish Studies* 24 (1980).

Mac Laughlin, Jim, *Reimagining the Nation State. The Contested Terrains of Nation-Building* (Pluto Press; London 2001).

MacLennan, Gordon W., *Seanchas Annie Bhán. The Lore of Annie Bhán* (The Seanchas Annie Bhán Publication Committee; Dublin 1997).

Mac Philib, Séamas, 'Rush Rafts in Ireland' *Ulster Folklife* 46 (2000), pp. 1–7.

Mac Philib, Séamas, 'A Folk Museum for Ireland. The National Museum of Ireland, Ard-Mhusaem na hÉireann – Country Life, Castlebar, Co Mayo', *Sinsear* 10 (2005), pp. 124–131.

Mac Philip, Séamas, 'Dublin South County to North Inner City: An Urban Folklore Project', *Béaloideas* 74 (2006), pp. 103–121.

Mahon, Bríd, *While Green Grass Grows. Memoirs of a Folklorist* (Mercier Press; Cork 1998).

Marstrander, Carl, 'Deux Contes Irlandais.' in Bergin and Marstrander 1912, pp. 371–486.

Martin, F. X. and F. J. Byrne (eds), *The Scholar Revolutionary. Eoin MacNeill, 1867–1945, and the making of modern Ireland* (Irish University Press; Shannon 1973).

Maume, Patrick, *Life That is Exile. Daniel Corkery and the Search for Irish Ireland* (The Institute of Irish Studies, The Queen's University of Belfast; 1993).

Moloney, Colette, *The Irish Music Manuscripts of Edward Bunting (1773–1843. An Introduction and Catalogue* (Irish Traditional Music Archive; Dublin 2000).

Molony, John Neylon, *A Soul came into Ireland. Thomas Davis 1814–1845* (Geography Publications; Dublin 1995).

Moran, Gerard and Raymond Gillespie (eds), *Galway. History & Society* (Geography Publications; Dublin 1996).

Moynihan, Maurice (ed.), *Speeches and Statements by Eamon de Valera 1917–1973* (Gill and Macmillan; Dublin 1980).

Mulcahy, Risteárd (ed.), *Richard Mulcahy (1886–1971). A Family Memoir* (Aurelian Press; Dublin 1999).

Mullins, Gerry, *Dublin Nazi No.1. The Life of Adolf Mahr* (Liberties; Dublin 2007).

Munnelly, Tom, 'Collectors of English-language songs for the Irish Folklore Commission, 1935–1970', in Ian Russell and David Atkinson (eds), *Folk Song. Tradition, Revival and Re-creation* (The Elphinstone Institute, University of Aberdeen; 2004), pp. 210–217.

Murphy, Maureen, 'Máire MacNeill (1904–1987)', *Béaloideas* 72 (2004), pp. 1–30.

Murphy, Michael J., *Tyrone Folk Quest* (Blackstaff Press; Belfast 1974 [1973]).

Murphy, Michael J., 'Folklore Collector on Rathlin', *Sinsear* 2 (1980), pp. 16–20.

Murray, Damien, *Romanticism, Nationalism and Irish Antiquarian Societies, 1840–80* (Maynooth Monographs Series Minor III; Maynooth 2000).

Nash, Catherine, '"Embodying the Nation' – The West of Ireland Landscape and Irish Identity", in Barbara O'Connor and Michael Cronin (eds), *Tourism in Ireland: A Critical Analysis* (Cork University Press: 1993), pp. 86–87.

Ní Dhíoraí, Áine, *Na Cruacha. Scéalta agus Seanchas* [The Bluestack Mountains. Stories and Lore] (An Clóchomhar Tta; Baile Átha Cliath 1985).

Ní Dhuibhne, Eibhlís, 'International Folktales' in Angela Bourke et al (eds), *The Field Day Anthology of Irish Writing. Volume IV. Irish Women's Writing and Traditions* (Cork University Press; 2001), pp.1214–1218.

Ní Fhloinn, Bairbre (2001a), 'In Correspondence with Tradition: The Role of the Postal

Questionnaire in the Collection of Irish Folklore', in Ó Catháin et al 2001, pp. 215–228.

Ní Fhloinn, Bairbre (B.NíF.), 'James G. Delaney', *The Irish Times* Monday, April 23rd, 2001b.

Ní Uallacháin, Pádraigín, *A Hidden Ulster. People, songs and traditions of Oriel* (Four Courts Press; Dublin 2003).

Nic Suibhne, Fionnuala, '"On the straw" and Other Aspects of Pregnancy and Childbirth from the Oral Tradition of Women in Ulster', *Ulster Folklife* 38 (1992), 12–24.

Nicolaisen, W. F. H., 'Calum MacLean. (1915–1960)', *Fabula* 5 (1962), pp. 162–164.

Ó Baoill, Dónall P., *Amach as Ucht na Sliabh* Iml. 1 [From Under the Mountain vol. 1] (Cumann Staire agus Seanchais Ghaoth Dobhair; 1992).

Ó Baoill, Pádraig and Feargal Ó Béarra, *Glórtha Ár Sinsear. Béaloideas Oirdheisceart na Gaillimhe* [The Folklore of South East Galway] (Loughrea History Society; 2005).

O'Brien, Gerard, *Irish Governments and the Guardianship of Historical Records, 1922–1972* (Four Courts Press; Dublin 2004).

O'Brien, Máire Cruise, *The Same Age as the State* (The O'Brien Press; Dublin 2003).

Ó Broin, León, *Just Like Yesterday. An Autobiography* (Gill and MacMillan; Dublin n.d.).

Ó Buachalla, Breandán, *I mBéal Feirste cois Cuain* [The Irish language in Belfast] (An Clóchomhar Tta; Baile Átha Cliath 1969 [1968]).

Ó Buachalla, Breandán, 'Art Mac Bionaid Scríobhaí' [Art Mac Bionaid, Scribe], *Seanchas Ard Mhacha* 9 (1979), pp. 338–349.

Ó Caithnia, Liam P., *Scéal na hIomána* [The Story of Hurling] (An Clóchomhar Tta; Baile Átha Cliath 1980).

Ó Caithnia, Liam P., *Báire Cos in Éirinn* [Football in Ireland] (An Clóchomhar Tta; Baile Átha Cliath 1984).

Ó Cadhla, Stiofán, 'Mapping a Discourse: Irish Gnosis and the Ordnance Survey 1824–1841' in *Culture, Space and Representation. A Special Issue of the Irish Journal of Anthropology*, Vol. 4 (1999), pp. 84–109.

Ó Cadhla, Stiofán, *Civilizing Ireland. Ordnance Survey 1824–1842: Ethnography, Cartography, Translation* (Irish Academic Press; Dublin 2007).

O'Carroll, J.P., and John A. Murphy (eds) *De Valera and His Times* (Cork University Press; 1986), pp. 47–61.

Ó Catháin, Brian (ed.), *Scoláirí Léinn* [Scholars] (An Sagart; Maigh Nuad 2005 = *Léachtaí Cholm Cille* 35)

Ó Catháin, Séamas, 'Passing the Time' (review), *Béaloideas* 51 (1983), pp. 155–156.

Ó Catháin, Séamas, and Caitlín Ní Sheighin, *A Mhuintir Dhú Chaocháin, Labhraigí Feasta!* [People of Dú Chaocháin, Henceforth Speak Out!] (Cló Chonamara; Indreabhán 1987).

Ó Catháin, Séamas, 'Printíseacht Sheáin Uí Eochaidh Lúnasa 1935–Eanáir 1936' [Seán Ó hEochaidh's Apprenticeship], in Seosamh Watson (ed.) *Oidhreacht Ghleann Cholm Cille* [Glencolmkill Heritage] (An Clóchomhar Tta; Baile Átha Cliath 1989), pp. 49–85.

Ó Catháin, Séamas, 'Nordiska forskare inom keltisk folklore och filologi', in Bramsbäck 1991a, pp. 53–73.

Ó Catháin, Séamas, 'The Irish Folklore Archive', *History Workshop* 31 (1991b), pp. 145–148.

Ó Catháin, Séamas, 'Liam Mac Meanman 1913–1991', *Béaloideas* 60–61 (1992–1993), pp. 290–295.

Ó Catháin, Séamas, 'Scéim na Scol' [The Schools Scheme], in Farren and Harkin [1999], no pagination.

Ó Catháin, Séamas et al (eds), *Northern Lights. Essays in honour of Bo Almqvist* (University College Dublin Press; 2001).

Ó Catháin, Séamas, 'Institiúid Bhéaloideas Éireann (1930–1935)' [The Irish Folklore Institute], *Béaloideas* 73 (2005), pp. 85–110.

Ó Cearúil, Colm, *Aspail ar Son na Gaeilge* [Apostles for Irish] (Conradh na Gaeilge;

Baile Átha Cliath 1995).

Ó Céirín, Kit & Cyril, *Women of Ireland. A Biographical Dictionary* (Tíreolas; Kinvara 1996), pp. 78–79.

Ó Ciardha, Tadhg, 'Óráid ar Bhronnadh Chéim Oinigh ar Sheosamh Ó Dálaigh' [Oration at the Conferral of an Honarary Doctorate on Seosamh Ó Dálaigh], *Béaloideas* 57 (1989), pp. 165–166.

Ó Conaire, Breandán (ed.), *Douglas Hyde. Language Lore and Lyrics* (Irish Academic Press; Dublin 1986).

Ó Concheanainn, Peadar, *Inis Meáin: Seanchas agus Scéalta* [The Tales and Lore of Inishmaan] (An Gúm; Baile Átha Cliath 1993 [1931]).

Ó Conluain, Proinnsias (ed.), *Rotha Mór an tSaoil* [The Great Wheel of Life] (Oifig an tSoláthair; Baile Átha Cliath 1959).

O'Connor, Anne, *Child Murderess and Dead Child Traditions* (Academia Scientiarum Fennica; Helsinki 1991 = FFC No. 249).

O'Connor, Anne, *The Blessed and the Damned. Sinful Women and Unbaptised Children in Irish Folklore* (Peter Lang; Bern 2005).

Ó Cróinín, Donncha, 'Seán Ó Cróinín 1915–1965. Bailitheoir Béaloideasa' [The Folklore Collector Seán Ó Cróinín], *Béaloideas* 32 (1964 [1966]), pp. 1–42.

Ó Cróinín, Donncha/Seán Ó Cróinín, *Seanchas Phádraig Í Chrualaoi* [The Lore of Pádraig Ó Crualaoi (Comhairle Bhéaloideas Éireann; Baile Átha Cliath 1982).

Ó Crualaoich, Gearóid, 'The Primacy of Form: A "Folk Ideology" in de Valera's Politics', in O'Carroll and Murphy 1986, pp. 47–61.

Ó Crualaoich, Gearóid, 'County Cork folklore and its Collection', in O'Flanagan and Buttimer 1993, pp. 919–940.

Ó Crualaoich, Gearóid, 'Introduction', in Westropp 2000, pp. i-iv.

Ó Crualaoich, Gearóid, 'De Valera's other Ireland', in Doherty and Keogh 2003, pp. 155–165.

Ó Cuív, Brian, *Irish Dialects and Irish-Speaking Districts* (Dublin Institute for Advanced Studies; Dublin 1971 [1951]).

Ó Cuív, Brian, 'The Irish Language in the Early Modern Period', in T. W. Moody, F. X. Martin and F. J. Byrne (eds), *A New History of Ireland III. Early Modern Ireland* (Clarendon Press; Oxford 1976), pp 509–545.

Ó Cuív, Brian, 'Irish language and literature, 1845–1921', in W.E. Vaughan (ed.), *A New History of Ireland VI. Ireland Under the Union, II, 1870–1921* (Clarendon Press; Oxford 1996), pp. 432–432.

Ó Danachair, Caoimhín, 'The Questionnaire System', *Béaloideas* 15 (1945 [1946]), pp. 203–217.

Ó Danachair, Caoimhín, 'Irish Folk Narrative on Sound Records', *Laos* 1 (1951), pp. 180–186.

Ó Danachair, Caoimhín, 'Some Distribution Patterns in Irish Folk Life', *Béaloideas* 25 (1957), pp. 108–123.

Ó Danachair, Caoimhín, 'The Spade in Ireland', *Béaloideas* 31 (1963), pp. 98–113.

Ó Danachair, Caoimhín, 'Distribution Patterns in Irish Folklore', *Béaloideas* 33 (1965), pp. 97–113.

Ó Danachair, Caoimhín (Kevin Danaher), *Folktales of the Irish Countryside* (The Mercier Press; Cork 1988 [1967]).

Ó Danachair, Caoimhín, 'The Flail in Ireland', *Ethnologia Europaea* 4 (1970), pp. 50–55.

Ó Danachair, Caoimhín (Kevin Danaher), *The Year in Ireland. Irish Calendar Customs* (The Mercier Press; Cork 1972).

Ó Danachair, Caoimhín (ed.), *Folk and Farm. Essays in Honour of A.T. Lucas* (Royal Society of Antiquaries of Ireland; Dublin 1976).

Ó Danachair, Caoimhín, *A Bibliography of Irish Ethnology and Folk Tradition* (The Mercier Press; Cork 1978).

Ó Danachair, Caoimhín, review of *Österreichischer Volkskundeatlas, sechste Lieferung, erster Teil, Béaloideas* 45–47 (1977–79), pp. 276–277.

Ó Danachair, Caoimhín, 'Sound Recording of Folk Narrative in Ireland in the Late Nineteen Forties', *Fabula* 22 (1981), pp. 312–215.

Ó Danachair, Caoimhín, 'The Progress of Irish Ethnology, 1783–1982', *Ulster Folklife* 29 (1983), pp.3–17.

Ó Dochartaigh, Pól, *Julius Pokorny 1887–1970. Germans, Celts and Nationalism* (Four Courts Press; Dublin 2004).

O'Donoghue, David, *Hitler's Irish Voices. The Story of German Radio's Wartime Irish Service* (Beyond the Pale Publications; Dublin 1998), pp. 25–26.

O'Donovan, John and Eugene O'Curry, *The Antiquities of County Clare. Ordnance Survey Letters 1939* (Clasp Press; Ennis 1997).

O'Dowd, Anne, '"There's a Time for all Things"', *Sinsear* 10 (2005), pp. 132–146.

Ó Drisceoil, Mary, 'The Excluded Voice? Thurles Folklore', *Journal of the Tipperary Historical Society* 2005, pp.187–193.

O'Driscoll, Mervyn, *Ireland, Germany and the Nazis. Politics and Diplomacy, 1919–1939* (Four Courts Press; Dublin 2004).

Ó Dúbhshláine, Mícheál, *An Baol Dom Tú? Muintir Chorca Dhuibhne agus an Ghaeilge 1860–1940* [West Kerry and the Irish language] (Conradh na Gaeilge; Baile Átha Cliath 2000).

Ó Duilearga, Séamus, Tóruidheacht Duibhe Lacha Láimh-ghile' [The Pursuit of Bright-Handed Dubh Lacha], in *Zeitschrift für celtische Philologie* 17 (1928), pp. 347–370.

Ó Duilearga, Séamus, 'A Venerable Heritage', *The Star* November 23, 1929, pp. 1 & 8.

Ó Duilearga, Séamus (J.H. Delargy) and Kathleen Mulchrone, *Catalogue of Irish Manuscripts in the Royal Irish Academy* 'Fasciculus V' (Royal Irish Academy; Dublin 1930).

Ó Duilearga, Séamus, 'The Ms. Collections of Campbell of Islay', *Béaloideas* 4 (1934), pp. 457–459.

Ó Duilearga, Séamus, 'An Untapped Source of Irish History', *Studies* 25 (September 1936), pp. 399–412.

Ó Duilearga, Séamus, 'The Irish Folklore Commission and its Work', in *Conférences* (Paris 1937), pp. 37–40.

Ó Duilearga, Séamus, 'Recording Tradition. We Work in Haste with Death at Our Elbow', *The Irish Independent* September 27, 1938.

Ó Duilearga, Séamus [J. H. Delargy], 'The Study of Irish Folklore', *The Dublin Magazine* July–September 1942a, pp.19–26.

Ó Duilearga, Séamus, 'Irish Stories and Storytellers. Some Reflections and Memories', *Studies* (March 1942b), pp. 31–45.

Ó Duilearga, Séamus, 'Volkskundliche Arbeit in Irland von 1850 bis zur Gegenwart mit besonderer Berücksichtigung der "Irischen Volkskunde-Kommission"', *in Zeitschrift für keltiche Philologie und Volksforschung,* 23 (1943), pp. 1–38.

Ó Duilearga, Séamus, *Leabhar Sheáin Í Chonaill* [The Book of Seán Ó Conaill] (Comhairle Bhéaloideas Éireann; Baile Átha Cliath 1977 [1948]).

Ó Duilearga, Séamus, 'The Folklore of Ireland', in *Irish Vocational Education Association Dublin* (1950) *Congress*, pp. 38–50.

Ó Duilearga, Séamus (ed.), *Seanchas ón Oileán Tiar* [Lore from the Great Blasket] (An Cumann le Béaloideas Éireann; Baile Átha Cliath 1956).

Ó Duilearga, Séamus (J. H. Delargy), 'Local Traditions. Folklore', in James Meehan and David A. Webb (eds), *A View of Ireland* (British Association for the Advancement of Science; Dublin 1957) pp. 178–187.

Ó Duilearga, Séamus, 'Eoin Mac Néill', *Feasta* Lúnasa 1959, pp. 16–18.

Ó Duilearga, Séamus (J. H. Delargy), 'Three Men of Islay', in *Scottish Studies* 4 (1960), pp. 126–133.

Ó Duilearga, Séamus, *Cnuasach Andeas* [Collection of Lore from the South] = *Béaloideas* 29 (1961).

Ó Duilearga, Séamus, 'Irish Tales and Story-Tellers', in Kuhn and Schier 1963, pp.

63–82.

Ó Duilearga, Séamus, 'Notes on the Oral Tradition of Thomond', *Journal of the Royal Society of Antiquaries of Ireland* 95 (1965), pp. 133–147.

Ó Duilearga, Séamus, 'A Personal Tribute. Reidar Thorolf Christiansen (1886–1971)', *Béaloideas* 27–28 (1969–1970), pp. 345–351.

Ó Duilearga, Séamus and Dáithí Ó hÓgáin, *Leabhar Stiofáin Uí Ealaoire* [The Book of Stiofán Ó hEalaoire] (Comhairle Bhéaloideas Éireann; Baile Átha Cliath 1981).

Ó Duilearga, Séamus, *Seán Ó Conaill's Book* (The Folklore of Ireland Council; Dublin 1981b).

Ó hEochaidh, Seán, *Sean-Chaint Theilinn* [The Old Language of Teelin] (Institiúid Árd Léighinn; Bhaile Átha Cliath 1955).

Ó hEochaidh, Seán, 'In Memoriam: Niall Ó Dubhthaigh', *Béaloideas* 28 (1960), pp. 134–137.

Ó hEochaidh, Seán, 'Sean-chainnt na gCruach, Co. Dhún na nGall' [The Old Language of the Croaghs] in *Zeitschrift für celtische Philologie* 29 (1962–64), pp. 1–90.

Ó hEochaidh, Seán, 'An Seanchas Beo', *Feasta* Meitheamh 1966, pp. 7–12.

O'Flanagan, Patrick and Cornelius G. Buttimer (eds), *Cork. History & Society* (Geography Publications; Dublin 1993), pp. 919–940.

Ó Giolláin, Diarmuid, *Locating Irish Folklore. Tradition, Modernity, Identity* (Cork University Press; 2000).

Ó Giolláin, Diarmuid, *An Dúchas agus an Domhan* [The Vernacular and the World] (Cork University Press; 2005).

Ó Glaisne, Risteárd, *De Bhunadh Protastúnach* [Of Protestant Extraction] (Carbad; Baile Átha Cliath 2000).

Ó Gráda, Cormac, *A rocky road. The Irish Economy since the 1920s* (Manchester University Press; 1997).

O'Halloran, Clare, *Golden Ages and Barbarous Nations. Antiquarian Debate and Cultural Politics in Ireland, c. 1780–1800* (Cork University Press; 2004).

Ó hAnnracháin, Peadar, *Fé Bhrat an Chonnartha* [Under the Mantle of the Gaelic League] (Oifig an tSoláthair; Baile Átha Cliath 1944).

Ó Héalaí, Pádraig, 'Seán Mac Mathúna–Fear an Chín Lae', *Béaloideas* 68 (2000), pp. 99–126.

O'Hegarty, P. S., *The Victory of Sinn Féin* (Talbot Press; Dublin 1924).

Ó hUallacháin, Colmán, *The Irish and Irish - a sociolinguistic analysis of the relationship between a people and their language* (Assisi Press; Baile Átha Cliath 1994).

Ó hUiginn, Ruairí (ed.) *Scoláirí Gaeilge* [Irish-language Scholars] (An Sagart; Maigh Nuad 1997 = *Léachtaí Cholm Cille* 27).

Ó Laighin, Seán, *Ó Cadhain i bhFeasta* [Ó Cadhain's writings in *Feasta*] (Clódhanna Teoranta: Baile Átha Cliath 1990).

O'Leary, Philip, *The Prose Literature of the Gaelic Revival 1881–1921* (The Pennsylvania State University Press; 1994).

O'Leary, Philip, *Gaelic Prose in the Irish Free State 1922–1939* (University College Dublin Press; 2004).

Ó Loingsigh, Pádraig, *Bordóinín. A History of the Parish of Caherdaniel* (Oidhreacht na Stéige; Cathair Dónall 1999).

Ó Macháin, Pádraig (ed.), *Riobard Weldon. Amhráin agus Dánta* (The Poddle Press; Baile Atha Cliath 1995).

Ó Macháin, Pádraig and Nessa Ní Shéaghdha, *Catalogue of Irish Manuscripts in the National Library of Ireland* Fasciculus XIII (Dublin Institute for Advanced Studies; 1996).

Ó Madagáin, Breandán, 'Óráid ar Bhronnadh Chéim Oinigh ar Sheán Ó hEochaidh' [Oration at the Conferral of an Honorary Doctorate on Seán Ó hEochaidh], *Béaloideas* 57 (1989), pp. 167–170.

O'Meara, John J., 'William Larminie 1849–1900', *Studies* 36 (1947), pp. 90–96.

Ó Muimhneacháin, Aindrias, *Dóchas agus Duainéis. Scéal Chonradh na Gaeilge 1922–1932* [The Gaelic League from 1922–32] (Cló Mercier; Corcaigh [c.1975]).

Ó Muimhneacháin, Aindrias, 'An Cumann le Béaloideas Éireann' [The Folklore of Ireland Society], *Béaloideas* 45–47, (1977–1979), pp. 1–5.

Ó Muirgheasa, Énrí [Henry Morris], 'National Tradition', *The Irish School Weekly*, April 5, 1930, pp. 437–438 and April 12, 1930, p. 454.

Ó Muraíle, Nollaig, 'Seán Ó Donnabháin', in Ó hUiginn 1997, pp. 11–82.

Ó Murchadha, Tadhg, 'Scéalaithe Dob Aithnid Dom' [Storytellers I Knew], in *Béaloideas* 11 (1941), pp. 3–44.

Ó Murchú, Máirtín, *Scoil an Léinn Cheiltigh.Tuarascáil Leathchéad Blian/School of Celtic Studies. Fiftieth Anniversary Report 1940-1990* (Dublin Institute for Advanced Studies; Dublin 1990).

Ó Murchú, Máirtín, *Cumann Buan-Choimeádta na Gaeilge. Tús an Athréimnithe* [The Society for the Preservation of the Irish Language] (Cois Life Teoranta; Baile Átha Cliath 2001).

Ó Murchú, Máirtín, *Ag Dul ó Chion. Cás na Gaeilge 1952–2002* [Loss of Affection. The Case of Irish 1952–2002] (An Aimsir Óg; Baile Átha Cliath 2002).

Ó hÓgáin, Dáithí, *Binneas Thar Meon . A Collection of Songs and Airs made by Liam de Noraidh in east Munster* Vol. 1 (Comhairle Bhéaloideas Éireann; Baile Átha Cliath 1994).

Ó Riagáin, Pádraig, *Language Policy and Social Reproduction: Ireland 1893–1993* (Clarendon Press: Oxford 1997).

Ó Riain, Seán, *Pleanáil Teanga in Éirinn 1919–1985* [Language Planning in Ireland] (Carbad/Bord na Gaeilge; Baile Átha Cliath 1994).

Ó Ríordáin, Traolach, *Conradh na Gaeilge i gCorcaigh 1894–1910* [The Gaelic League in Cork] (Cois Life Teoranta; Baile Átha Cliath 2000).

Ó Súilleabháin, Eoghan, 'Seán Ó Súilleabháin (1903–96) Múinteoir agus Cartlannaí Béaloidis' [Seán Ó Súilleabháin. Teacher and Folklore Archivist] *Journal of the Kerry Archaeological and Historical Society* 27 (1994), pp. 89–106.

Ó Súilleabháin, Seán, 'Folklore Collector at Work' *Irish Independent* Monday, October 3, 1938.

Ó Súilleabháin, Seán, 'Trí Mhí sa tSualainn', *Comhar*, Mí na Nodlag, 1943, pp. 3, 13, &14.

Ó Súilleabháin, Seán, 'The Collecting and Classification of Folklore in Ireland and the Isle of Man' *Folk-Lore* 68 (December 1957), pp. 449–457.

Ó Súilleabháin, Seán and Reidar Th. Christainsen, *The Types of the Irish Folktale* (Academia Scientiarum Fennica Helsinki 1967 [1963] = FFC No. 188).

Ó Súilleabháin, Seán, *Folktales of Ireland* (University of Chicago Press; 1966).

Ó Súilleabháin, Seán, 'The Devil in Irish Folk Narrative', in Harkort et al 1968, pp. 275–286.

Ó Súilleabháin, Seán, 'Research Opportunities in the Irish Folklore Commission', *Journal of the Folklore Institute* 7/2–3 (1970a), pp. 116–125.

Ó Súilleabháin, Seán, *A Handbook of Irish Folklore* (Singing Tree Press; Detroit 1970b [1942]).

Ó Súilleabháin, Seán, *Caitheamh Aimsire ar Thórraimh* [Irish Wake Amusements] (An Clóchomhar Tta; Baile Átha Cliath 1980 [1961]).

Otway-Ruthven, Jocelyn, 'Medieval Ireland, 1169–1485', in T. W Moody (ed.), *Irish Historiography 1936–70* (Irish Committee of Historical Studies; Dublin 1971), pp. 16–22.

Palmer, Patricia, *Language and Conquest in Early Modern Ireland* (Cambridge University Press; 2001), p. 1.

Peer, Shanny, *France on Display. Peasants, Provincials and Folklore in the 1937 Paris World's Fair* (State University of New York Press; 1998).

Peltonen, Ulla-Maija, 'Kalevalan riemuvuoden kilpakeruu ja hyvän kerääjän käsite' [The Kalevala Centenary Folklore Competition and the Concept of a Good Collector], in Tuulikki Kurki (ed) *Kansanrunousarkisto, lukijat ja tulkinnat* [The Folklore Archive, readers and interpretations] (Suomalaisen Kirjallisuuden Seura; Helsinki 2004), pp. 199–217.

Pine, Richard, *2RN and the origins of Irish Radio* (Four Courts Press; Dublin 2002).

Prunty, Jacinta, *Dublin Slums, 1800–1925. A Study in Urban Geography* (Irish Academic Press; Dublin 1998).

Pulkkinen, Risto, *Vastavirtaan. C.A. Gottlund 1800-luvun suomalaisena toisinajattelijana: psykobiografinen tutkimus* [C.A. Gottlund. A Finnish 19th-century dissident] (Yliopistopaino; Helsinki 2003).

Quinlan, Carmel, "'A Punishment from God": The famine in the Centenary Folklore Questionnaire', *Irish Review* 19 (Spring/Summer 1996), pp. 68–86.

Regan, John M, *The Irish Counter-Revolution 1921–1936. Treatyite Politics and Settlement in Independent Ireland* (Gill & Macmillan; Dublin 2001 [1999]).

Remmel, Mari-Ann (ed.), *Rahva ja luule vahel: kogumispäevikuid aastaist 1878–1996* [A Selection of collectors' diary entries from the years 1878–1996] (Eesti Kirjandusmuuseum; Tartu 1997.

Riordan, Susannah, 'The Unpopular Front: Catholic Revival and Irish Cultural Identity 1932–48', in Cronin and Regan 2000, pp. 98–120.

Riggs, Pádraigín, 'Eleanor Hull (1860–1935)', in Brian Ó Catháin 2005, pp. 7–39.

Robinson, Philip, *The Plantation of Ulster* (Ulster Historical Foundation; Belfast 2000 [1984]).

Ruane, Joseph and Jennifer Todd, *The dynamics of conflict in Northern Ireland. Power, conflict and emancipation* (Cambridge University Press; 1996).

Salminen, Väinö, *Vallattomilta vaellusvuosilta* [Wild Wandering Years] (Otava; Helsinki. 1946).

Salomonsson, Anders, 'Documentation and Research', in Honko 2000, pp. 197–213.

Sammon, Patrick J., *In the Land Commission. A Memoir 1933–1978* (Ashfield Press; Dublin 1997).

Shaw, Francis, 'The Irish Folklore Commission', *Studies* 33 (1944), pp. 30–36.

Simonsuuri, Lauri, 'Huomioita kansanperinteen tallentamisesta äänilevyihin' [On Making Sound Recordings of Tradition] *Virittäjä* (1949), pp. 125–131.

Simms, Katherine, *From Kings to Warlords* (The Boydell Press; Woodbridge 2000 [1987]).

Skeealyn Vannin - Stories from Mann (Manx National Heritage; Douglas 2003).

Skjelbred, Anne Helene Bolstad, 'Possibilities and Limitations: A Critical Look at a Norwegian Tradition Archive', in Honko 2000, pp. 595–611.

Stephens, Shane, 'The Society of Irish Tradition 1917–1919', *Béaloideas* 67 (1999), pp.139–169.

Stout, Matthew, 'Emyr Estyn Evans and Northern Ireland: the archaeology and geography of a new state', in Atkinson et al 1996, pp. 111–127.

Strömbäck, Dag, 'The Institute for Dialect and Folklore Research in Uppsala', in Geraint Jenkins (ed.), *Studies in Folklife. Essays in Honour of Iorwerth C. Peate* (London 1969), pp. 16–27.

Szövérffy, Joseph, *Irisches Erzählgut im Abendland. Studien zur vergleichenden Volkskunde und Mittelalterforchung* (Berlin 1957).

Thompson, G. B., 'Applied Folk-Life Study – a Personal View', in Alan Gailey and Dáithí Ó hÓgáin (eds), *Gold Under The Furze. Studies in Folk Tradition presented to Caoimhín Ó Danachair* (Dublin 1982), pp. 43-49.

Thompson, Stith, *The Types of the Folktale* (Academia Scientiarum Fennica; Helsinki 1928).

Thompson, Stith, *The Folktale* (University of California Press; Berkeley 1977 [1946]).

Thompson, Stith (ed), *Four Symposia on Folklore* (Greenwood Press; Westport, Connecticut 1976 [1953]).

Thompson, Stith, *A Folklorist's Progress. Reflections of a Scholar's Life* (Special Publications of the Folklore Institute No. 5; Bloomington 1996).

Tierney, Martin (ed.), *A Classicist's Outlook. Michael Tierney KSG, MA, D.Litt. 1894–1975* (Martin Tierney; Dublin 2002).

Tierney, Michael, 'What did the Gaelic League Accomplish? 1893–1963', *Studies* 52 (Winter 1963), pp. 337–345.

Tierney, Michael, 'Foreward', in Bo Almqvist, Breandán Mac Aodha, and Gearóid Mac Eoin (eds), *Hereditas. Essays and Studies presented to Professor Séamus Ó Duilearga* (The Folklore of Ireland Society; Dublin 1975), pp. ix-xv.

Titley, E. Brian *Church, State, and the Control of Schooling in Ireland 1900–1944* (McGill-Queen's University Press; Montreal 1983).

Tovey, Hilary and Perry Share, *A Sociology of Ireland* (Gill & Macmillan; Dublin 2000).

Tyers, Pádraig, *Abair Leat. Seosamh Ó Dálaigh ag caint le Pádraig Tyers* [Seosamh Ó Dálaigh speaking with Pádraig Tyers] (An Sagart; An Daingean 1999).

Tynni, Aale, *Vieraana Vihreällä Saarella* [A Guest in the Emerald Isle] (Werner Söderström Osakeyhtiö; Porvoo 1954).

Ua Cnáimhsí, Pádraig, *Róise Rua* [Red Róise] (Sáirséal Ó Marcaigh; Baile Átha Cliath 1988).

Ua Súilleaháin, Seán, 'Osborn Bergin', in Ó hUiginn 1997, pp. 150–176.

uí Ógáin, Ríonach (ní Fhlathartaigh), *Clár Amhrán Bhaile na hInse* [Catalogue of Songs from Ballinahinch Barony] (An Clóchomhar Tta; Baile Átha Cliath 1976).

uí Ógáin, Ríonach, 'Fear Ceoil Ghlinsce: Colm Ó Caodháin' [The Folk Singer Colm Ó Caodháin], in Moran and Gillespie 1996, pp. 703–748.

uí Ógáin, Ríonach, 'Seán Mac Mathúna (1876–1949): Bailitheoir Béaloidis', *Béaloideas* 68 (2000a), pp. 139–159.

uí Ógáin, Ríonach, 'Some Comments on Context, Text and Subtext in Irish Folklore', in Honko 2000b, pp. 159–179.

uí Ógaín, Ríonach, 'Scéala aduaidh' [News from the north] in Ó Catháin et al 2001, pp. 316–329.

uí Ógáin, Ríonach, 'Máire Mac Néill (1904–1987): Scoláire Béaloidis' [The Folklore Scholar Máire Mac Néill], in Brian Ó Catháin 2005, pp. 159–185.

uí Ógáin, Ríonach, *Mise an Fear Ceoil. Séamus Ennis. Dialann Taistil 1942–1946* [Séamus Ennis's Field Diaries] (Cló Iar-Chonnachta; Indreabhán 2007).

Vallely, Fintan (ed.), *The Companion to Irish Traditional Music* (Cork University Press 1999).

Valiulis, Maryann G., *Portrait of a Revolutionary. General Richard Mulcahy and the Founding of the Irish Free State* (Irish Academic Press; Dublin 1992).

Valiulis, Maryann G., '"Free Women in a Free Nation": Nationalist Feminist Expectations for Independence", in Brian Farrell (ed.), *The Creation of the Dáil* (Blackwater Press; Dublin 1994), pp. 75–90.

Vaslef, Irene and Helmut Buschhausen (eds), *Classica et Mediaevalia: Studies in Honor of Joseph Szövérffy* (Classical Folia Editons; Leyden 1986).

Verling, Máirtín, 'Seosamh Ó Dálaigh sa Rinn' [Seosamh Ó Dálaigh in Ring], *An Linn Bhuí* 3 (1999), pp. 6–18.

Verling, Máirtín, 'Camchuairt na nDéise' [A Tour of the Déise], *An Linn Bhuí* 6 (2002), pp. 1–15.

Verling, Máirtín, *Leabhar Mhaidhc Dháith. Scéalta agus Seanchas ón Rinn* [Stories and Lore of Mícheál Turraoin] (An Sagart; An Daingean 2007).

Virtanen, Lea, *Suomalainen Kansanperinne* [Finnish Folk Tradition] (Suomalaisen Kirjallisuuden Seura; Helsinki 1988)

Ward, Margaret, *Unmanageable Revolutionaries. Women and Irish Nationalism* (Pluto Press; London 1983).

Watson, Seosamh, 'Séamus Ó Duilearga's Antrim Notebooks - I Texts' *Zeitschrift für celtische Philologie* 40 (1984), pp. 74, 78–80.

Welch, Robert (ed.), *The Oxford Companion to Irish Literature* (Clarendon Press; Oxford 1996)

Westropp, Thomas J., *Folklore of Clare. A Folklore Survey of County Clare and County Clare Folk-Tales and Myth* (Clasp Press; Ennis 2000).

Wills, Claire, *That Neutral Island. A Cultural History of Ireland During the Second World War* (Faber and Faber; London 2007).

Whitaker, T.K., 'James Hamilton Delargy, 1890-1980' *Folk Life* 20 (1981–82), pp.

101–106.

Whitaker, T.K., 'James Hamilton Delargy', *The Glynns. Journal of Antrim Historical Society* 10 (1982), pp. 23–30.

Whyte, J. H., *Church and State in Modern Ireland 1923–1979* (second edition) (Gill and Macmillan Dublin, 1980)

Yocom, Margaret R., 'Woman to Woman: Fieldwork and the Private Sphere', in Rosan A. Jordan and Susan J. Kalčik (eds) *Women's Folklore, Women's Culture* (University of Pennsylvania Press; 1985) 45–53.

Zimmerman, Georges Denis, *The Irish Storyteller* (Four Courts Press; Dublin 2001).

Appendices

APPENDIX 1

Irish Folklore Commission. Terms of Reference

I (1) A Commission entitled "The Irish Folklore Commission" to be appointed by the Executive Council.
(2) The Commission to consist of 21 persons including the Director.

II The following to be the Terms of Reference of the Commission:

(1) To consider, after such consultation with University and other Authorities as the Commission may deem desirable, and to submit from time to time for the approval of the Minister for Education, programmes of work connected with Irish Folklore research prepared by the Director and, subject to such approval, to arrange for
(a) the collection, collation, and cataloguing of oral and written folklore materials; and
(b) the editing and publication of such materials when thought desirable.

(2) Subject to necessary safeguards, the Commission to arrange to give access, at reasonable times, to its collected materials to students and scholars desiring to avail thereof for the purpose of study and / or publication.

(3) The Commission from its Grant-in-Aid to contribute to the Folklore of Ireland Society the sum of £250 per annum to be expended by the Society on extended publication of Irish Folklore material in a form suitable for the general public, e.g., the more frequent publication of the Journal "Béaloideas", and / or the reduction of its price to the public.

(4) The Commission to meet not less frequently than once every quarter.

(5) The Commission to present an annual Report and Statement of Accounts to the Minister for Education for submission to the Executive Council.

(6) The Commission to be responsible for the safe custody of its collected materials, such materials to be deemed always to be the property of the State.

III The Director to be appointed by the Executive Council and his powers and duties to include the following:

(1) To prepare programmes of work for consideration by the Commission and to organise and supervise the execution of such programmes as may be approved by the Commission and by the Minister for Education.

(2) Subject to the approval of the Commission, to engage staff in such numbers and at such rates of remuneration and on such other conditions as may be approved by the Minister for Education with the sanction of the Minister for Finance.

(3) To control and supervise the work of the staff of the Commission

IV (1) Subject to the approval of Dáil Éireann, a sum not exceeding £3,250 per annum to be made available for the work of the Commission for five years, this sum to cover all expenditure in connection with the work of the Commission, including cost of staff, office accommodation, equipment, collection, publication, contribution to Folklore of Ireland Society, etc.

(2) The sum mentioned in the preceding clause to be provided as a Grant-in-Aid and expenditure therefrom not to be submitted for examination by the Comptroller and Auditor General; in matters involving expenditure, however, the Commission will work under the general supervision of the Minister for Education.

(3) The Commission to make its own arrangements as regards accommodation, the assistance of the Office of Public Works to be available if required.

(4) Arrangements to be made, if the Commission so desires, for seconding a Civil Servant, for work in the office of the Commission subject to the usual arrangements regarding recoupment.[1]

1   D/F S 101/0011/34: 'Irish Folklore Commission [Terms of Reference]'.

APPENDIX 2

(a) Membership of the Irish Folklore Commission 1935–1970

		1930's	1940's	1950's	1960's
		mid/late	early/mid/late	early/mid/late	early/mid/late
Daniel Binchy	1935	x/o			
Adolf Mahr	1935	x/x			
Fr. Lorcán Ó Muireadhaigh	1935	x/x			
Peadar Mac Fhionnlaoich	1935	x/x	x/d. 1942		
Séamus Ó Casaide	1935	x/x	x/d. 1943		
Énrí Ó Muirgheasa	1935	x/x	x/xd. 1945		
Fr. John G. O'Neill	1935	x/x	x/o/o		
Prof. Osborn J. Bergin,	1935	x/x	x/x/xd. 1950		
Dr. Pádraig Breathnach	1935	x/x	x/x/x	x/d. 1951	
Prof. Éamonn Ó Donnchadha	1935	x/x	x/x/x	x/d. 1953	
Fr. Seán Ó Coinne	1943		o/x/x	x/r. 1953	
Prof. Éamonn Ó Tuathail	1935	x/x	x/x/x	x/x/d.1956	
Prof. Cormac Ó Cuilleanáin	1953			o/x/x	x/r. 1963
Seán Mac Giollarnáth D.J.	1935	x/x	x/x/x	x/x/x	x/r. 1964
Fionán Mac Coluim	1935	x/x	x/x/x	x/x/x	x/x/d. 1966
Liam Price D.J.	1935	x/x	x/x/x	x/x/x	x/x/d. 1967
Séamus Ó Duilearga	1935	x/x	x/x/x	x/x/x	x/x/x
Mon. Eric Mac Fhinn	1935	x/x	x/x/x	x/x/x	x/x/x
Prof. Michael Tierney	1935	x/x	x/x/x	x/x/x	x/x/x
Pádraig Mac Con Midhe	1943		o/x/x	x/x/x	x/x/x
Dept. of Finance and Education representatives					
Finance					
León Ó Broin	1935	x/x	x/x/r. 1947		
Seán Ó Maonaigh	1947		o/o/x	x/x/x	x/x/x
Education					
Lughaidh Maguidhir	1935	x/o	o/o/x	x/x/r. 1954	
Pádraig de Breit	1937	o/x	x/r. 1940		
Peadar Ó Muircheartaigh	1940		x/x/r. 1947		
Pádraig Ó Maoláin	1953			o/x/x	x/x/r. 1965
Liam Ó Laidhin	1965				o/x/or. 1965
Feardorcha Ó Dúill	1966				o/x/x

In chart d. = died; r. = retired; x = being present for roughly a third of a decade; o = being absent over a similar period of time.

Some notes on certain members:
It would appear Fr. John G. O'Neill ceased attending meetings of the Commission during the course of the Second World War. He retired from his post in Maynooth College in 1941 (Corish 1995, p. 479) and went to minister to a parish in Co. Limerick. Pádraig Mac Con Midhe was head of the Gaelic Athletic Association at the time of his appointment to the Commission while Fr. Seán Ó Coinne was a parish priest in the diocese of Armagh when appointed to the same body. A scholarly man, Ó Coinne was later to have a distinguished ecclesiastical career. For more on him, see An tUltach Márta 1963, p. 9. Uinnsean Déis was appointed Dept. of the Gaeltacht representative on the Commission in July 1957 but appears not to have attended any meetings.

(b) Finance Sub-Committee

		1935's	1940's	1950's	1960's
		mid/late	early/mid/late	early/mid/late	early/mid/late
Séamus Ó Duilearga	1935	x/x	x/x/x	x/x/x	x/x/x
Liam Price (Chairman)	1935	x/x	x/x/x	x/x/x	x/x/x
Séamus Ó Casaide	1935	x/x	x		
Michael Tierney	1943		o/x/x	x/x/x	x/x/x
Fin. reps.					
León Ó Broin	1935	x/x	x/x		
Seán Ó Maonaigh	1947		o/o/x	x/x/x	x/x/x
Educ. reps.					
Lughaidh Maguidhir	1935	x/o	o/o/x	x/x/1954	
Pádraig de Breit	1937	o/x	x/r. 1940		
Peadar Ó Muircheartaigh	1940		x/r. 1947		
Pádraig Ó Maoláin	1953			o/x/x	x/x/r. 1965
Liam Ó Laidhin	1965				o/x/o r. 1965
Feardorcha Ó Dúill	1966				o/x/x

To interpret above chart, see explanations in Appendix 2(a).

(c) Initial nominations to Irish Folklore Commission

Affiliation	Name and Title
Folklore of Ireland Society	District Justice Seán Mac Giollarnáth
	Prof. Éamonn Ó Tuathail,
	Fionán Mac Coluim
Royal Irish Academy	Prof. Osborn J. Bergin
	Prof. Daniel A. Binchy
	Prof. Michael Tierney,
University College Cork	Éamonn Ó Donnchadha
University College Galway	Fr. Eric Mac Fhinn
St. Patrick's College Maynooth	Rev. Prof. John G. O'Neill,
National Museum of Ireland	Dr Adolf. Mahr
Royal Society of Antiquaries of Ireland	District Justice Liam Price
Dept. of Finance	León Ó Broin
Dept. of Education	Lughaidh Maguidhir
Gaelic League	Peadar Mac Fhionnlaoich
Comhaltas Uladh	Fr. Lorcán Ó Muireadhaigh
Teacher Representative	Dr. Pádraig Breathnach
Gaelic Scholars	Mr Séamus Ó Casaide
	Énrí Ó Muirgheasa
	Dr Douglas Hyde
	Séamus Ó Duilearga
	Pádraig Ó Siochfhradha

[1]D/T S 6916A: 'Cabinet Minutes', dated 8.2.35. Affiliations and ages, where known, of proposed mei added.

APPENDIX 3 *Full-time and special collectors*[1]

Began	Name	Born	Period of Service	Counties	Died
1935–36	Liam Mac Coisdeala	1906	1.8.1935–31.8.1939	Ga, (Ma, Cl)	1996
1935–36	Proinnsias de Búrca.	1904	1.9.1935–31.03.1944 (1953 –1964 spec.) 1.10.1964–31.3.1970 (+1975)	Ga, (Ma)	1976
1935–36	Seán Ó hEochaidh	1913	1.9.1935–31.3.1970(+ 1983)	Do, (Ma, Sl)	2002
1935–36	Tadhg Ó Murchadha	1896	1.9.1935–31.3.1958	Ke, (Co, Cl)	1961
1935–36	Liam Mac Meanman	1913	9.9.1935–30.8.1937	Do	1991
1935–39	Nioclás Breatnach	1912	1.11.1935–30.6.1937	Wa, (Ti)	2002
1936–37	Brian Mac Lochlainn		1.8.1936–30.9.1939	Ga	-
1936–37	Proinnsias Ó Ceallaigh	1893	1.9.1936–30.11.1936	Co	1971
1936–37	Seosamh Ó Dálaigh	1909	1.8.1936–31.10.1951	Ke, (Co, Li, Ti, Wa)	1992
1936–37	Seán Ó Flannagáin	1909	1.10.1937–31.1.1940	Ga, Cl	1995
1938–39	Seán Ó Cróinín	1915	1.4.1938–31.3.1944 16.1.1959–14.3.1965	Co	1965
1939–40	Caoimhín Ó Danachair	1913	15.1.1940–31.5.1940	Lm	2002
1940–41	Liam de Noraidh	1888	27.5.1940–31.3.1942	Wa, (Co, Ti)	1972
1940–41	Tomás de Búrca	1917	1.9.1940–31.5.1944	Ma	1957
1942–43	Séamus Ennis	1919	1.6.1942–15.8.1947	Ga, Ma, Do, Cl, Ke, Co, Ln, Lm, Ca, Wa, We	1982
1946–47	Calum MacLean	1915	1.6.1946–31.1.1950	Scotland (Ga)	1960
1949–50	Michael J. Murphy	1913	1.11.1949–31.3.1970 (+1983)	An, Ar, Dn, Lo, Ty (Ca De, Fe, Me MoSl)	1996
1951–52	Ciarán Bairéad	1905	1.6.1951–31.3.1970 (+ 1975)	Ga, (Cl, Ma)	1976
1951–52	Pádraig Ó Móghráin	1888	1.7.1951–31..3.1956	Ma	1966
1951–52	Mícheál Ó Sirín	c. 1925	1.10.1951–30.6.1954	Ma	1993
1952–53	Seán Ó Dubhda	1878	1.9.1952–31.1.1962	Ke	1962
1954–55	Mícheál Mac Énrí	1888	1.4.1954– Autumn 1964	Ma	1991
1954–55	Jim Delaney	1916	1.7.1954–31.3.1970 (+ 1986)	Le, Ln, Of, Ro, We (Ca, Du/ci,Ga, Kk, La, Ti, Wm)	2000
1955–56	Seán Mac Craith		5.6.1955–30.11.1955	Cl	-

[1] Counties abbreviated as follows: An(Antrim); Ar(Armagh); Ca(Cavan); Cl (Clare); Co(Cork); Cw(Carlow);De(Derry); Dn(Down); Do(Donegal); Du(Dublin County); Du/ci(Dublin City);Fe(Fermanagh); Ga(Galway); Ke(Kerry); Kd(Kildare); Kk(Kilkenny); La(Laois); Le(Leitrim); Li(Limerick); Lo(Louth); Ln(Longford); Ma(Mayo); Me(Meath); Mo(Monaghan); Of(Offaly); Ro(Roscommon); Sl (Sligo); Ti (Tipperary); Ty(Tyrone);Wa(Waterford); We(Wexford); Wi(Wicklow); Wm (Westmeath).

APPENDIX 4

A selection of part-time collectors[1]

Connaught
Galway
Bairbre Ní Chonaire
Liam Ó Coincheanainn
Tadhg Ó Coincheanainn

Leitrim
Liam Ó Briain
Tomás Ó Máirtín
Séamas Ó Piotáin

Mayo
Pádraig Bairéad
Michael Corduff

Roscommon
James J. O'Donnell

Sligo
Brigid Ní Ghamhain

Munster
Clare
Seán Mac Mathghamhna

Cork
Áine Ní Chróinín
Diarmuid Ó Cruadhlaoich
Conchubhar Ó Ruairc
Ciarán Ó Síocháin

Kerry
Máire Breathnach
Muiris Mac Gearailt
Eibhlín Ní Sheaghdha
Seán Óg Ó Dubhda
Br. P. T. Ó Riain
Eoghan Ó Súilleabháin

Limerick
Peadar Mac Domhnall
Colm Ó Danachair
Pilib Ó Conaill

Tipperary
Peadar Mac Domhnaill
Patrick C. Power

Waterford
Seán Ó Dúnaidhe
Pádraig Ó Fionnúsa
Pádraig Ó Milleadha

Leinster
Carlow
Patrick O'Toole
Edward O'Toole

Kildare
Br. P. T. Ó Riain

Kilkenny
Tobias Kavanagh
Eoghan Ó Ceallaigh

Laois
Áine Uí Chiarmhaic

Longford
Philip Ledwith
Pádraig Mac Gréine

Louth
P. J. Gaynor
Tomás Mac Cuilleanáin

Meath
P. J. Gaynor
Mathew O'Reilly

Offaly
Pádraig Ó Conchubhair

Westmeath
Philip Ledwith
Joseph Wade
Nora Wheeler

Wicklow
Tomás Ó Síoda

Wexford
Seán de Buitléir
Domhnall de Buitléir
Mary Dunphy
Tomás Ó Ciardha

Ulster
Antrim
Jeane Cooper-Foster
Liam Mac Reachtain

Armagh
Tomás Ó Cuilleanáin

Cavan
P. J. Gaynor

Derry
Jeane Cooper-Foster
Seán Mac Diarmada

Donegal
Proinnsias Mac Grianna
Aodh Ó Domhnaill
Aodh Ó Duibheannaigh
Áine Nic an Leagha

Down
P. J. Gaynor
Liam Mac Reachtain

Fermanagh
Alex Mac Connell

Monaghan
Tomás Ó Cuilleanáin

Tyrone
Eoghan Ó Ceallaigh

1   This list contains only a fraction of all those who collected part-time for the Commission. All thirty two counties, apart from Co. Dublin are represented. Some of the collectors listed collected in more than one county, and some on the list collected far more than others. I hope elsewhere in time to publish a fuller list of those part-time collectors who collected a significant amount for the Commission.

APPENDIX 5.

Growth of the Main Manuscript Collection

	Full-time collectors		Part-time collectors		Quest. returns	Donations	Annual total
year	no. of pages	no. of coll.	no. of pages	no. of coll.	no. of pages	no. of pages	no. of pages
1935–36	16,577	6	17,819	127			34,396
1936–37	28,585	9	31,538	242			60,123
1937–38	25,872	9	42,608	250			68,480
1938–39	25,406	9	29,168				54,574
1939–40	20,560	9	13,697		3,450 9.1%		37,707
1940–41	18,640	8	5,332		5,286 18.1%		29,258
1941–42	18,039	7	12,013		4,787 13.7		34,839
1942–43	14,784	7	12,096		4,273 13.2%	1,290	32,443
1943–44	13,392	7	5,958	3	3,005 13.0%	764	23,119
1944–45	7,646	5	5,683		1,974 12.1%	956	16,259
1945–46	7,875	4	4,901		5,507 29.1%	600	18.883
1946–47	9,348	5	4,106	17	1,874 11.8%	576	15,904
1947–48	7,626	5	7,233	16	1,374 7.8%	1,370	17,603
1948–49	6,577	4	6,776	15	39 0.3%	45	13,437
1949–50	7,892	5	5,464	22	0%	932	14,288
1950–51	6,501	5	7,605	25	462 3.0%	950	15,518
1951–52	7,524	7	4,792	17	732 5.6%	54	13,102
1952–53	7,907	6	4.963	23	469 3.4%	294	13,633
1953–54	8,294	5(3)	3,523	15	0%		11,817
1954–55	6,350 (3,233)	5 (4)	6,136	24	1,116 6.5%	450	17,285
1955–56	7,677 (3,460)	6 (4)	5,505	19	1,352 7.5%	37	18,031
1956–57	4,464 (3,281)	5 (3)	4,495	22	1,330 9.6%	327	13,897
1957–58	3,999 (3,241)	5 (3)	2,904	8	600 5.6%		10,744
1958–59	3,070 (2,518)	5 (3)	2,641	5	800 8.9%		9,029
1959–60	5,476 (2,852)	5 (3)	2,882	4	0%		11,210
1960–61	5,136 (2,754)	5 (3)	3,600	6	0%		11,490
1961–62	5,265 (2,200)	5 (3)	1,440	2	0%		8,905
1962–63	4,710 (2,104)	5 (2)	1,273	3	0%		8,087
1963–64	4,763 (2,300)	5 (2)	750	5	0%		7,813
1964–65	4,700	6	1,771	6	0%		6,471
1965–66	3,772	5	580	4	0%		4,352
1966–67	3,818	5	200	2	1,407 25.9%		5,425
1967–68	3,613	5	500	4	612 12.0%	328	5,053

1968–69	3,805	5	200	2	87 2.20%		4,092
1969–70	2,800	5	237	3			3,037

Total   360,406 53.5%   260,389 39%   40,536 6%   8,973 1.5%   670,304

Inherited from the Irish Folklore Institute +50,000

Overall total   720,304

The above chart is based on Ó Duilearga's Annual Reports to the Government ('Gearr-Thuarascálacha') covering each financial year (April 1st to March 31st) of the Commission's operations. The figures presented in these Reports are approximations.[1] The official figure of 50,000 pages of material inherited from the Irish Folklore Institute is also an approximation, and may well be somewhat of an overestimate.

Full-time collectors: In these two columns I give the number of pages collected by special collectors, where specified, in brackets and the number of such collectors also in brackets.

Part-time collectors: Ó Duilearga's Annual Report for 1938-39 does not give the number of part-time collectors but it does state that the number of such collectors was deliberately reduced from the previous year in order to weed out the weakest. Neither does his Annual Report for the following year, 1939-40, specify the number of part-time collectors, but from the reduced number of pages collected by them we can surmise that the number of such collectors was further reduced. During the period of the Second World War the Commission could only afford to employ a handful of part-time collectors and their number is usually not stated. In the post-War period the names of part-time collectors are listed in these Reports.

Questionnaire returns: The annual acquisition of material by means of questionnaire is also given as a percentage of the total annual acquisition of material. Duilearga's Annual Reports do not give the number of questionnaire correspondents, only the number of pages acquired.

Donations: Many individuals gave donations of folklore material to the Commission, much of it collected by themselves, but in other cases consisting of collections of folklore that came into their possession. In the early ears of the Commission the distinction between donors of material and part-time collectors is somewhat blurred in Ó Duilearga's Annual Reports. For this reason the above total number of pages received from donors is probably an underestimate.

1   The fact that Ó Duilearga's quarterly reports to the Commission usually overlapped the financial year may have necessitated rounding off figures for his Reports to the Government.

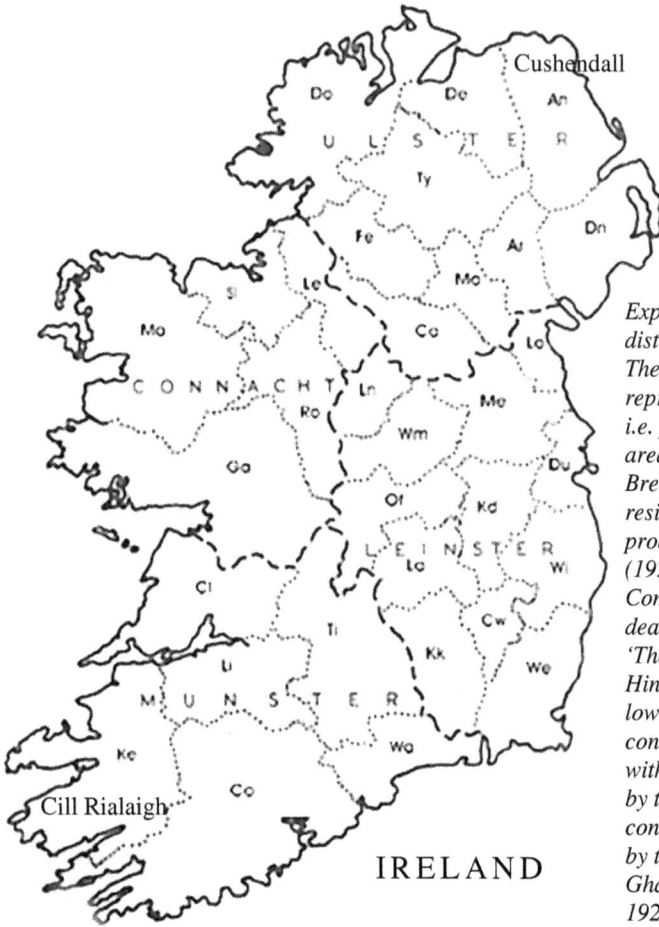

Cushendall

Cill Rialaigh

IRELAND

Explanatory note on Irish-speaking districts as represented on map: The blackened areas in the above map represent Gaeltacht (or Fíor-Ghaeltacht, i.e. predominantly Irish-speaking areas) areas, while the shaded areas represent Breac-Ghaeltacht areas or areas with residual Irish. These are based on the maps produced by the Gaeltacht Commission (1926). However, the findings of this Commission need to be treated with a great deal of caution. As Pádraig Ó Riagáin says: 'There appears to be substance in [Reg] Hindley's claim (1991: 68) that areas with low percentages of Irish-speakers were consistently underestimated and areas with higher percentages overestimated by the Commission's enumerators. As a consequence the Fíor-Ghaeltacht as defined by the Commission is larger, and the Breac-Ghaeltacht smaller, than the findings of the 1926 Census appear to justify.' Ó Riagáin 1997, p. 51.

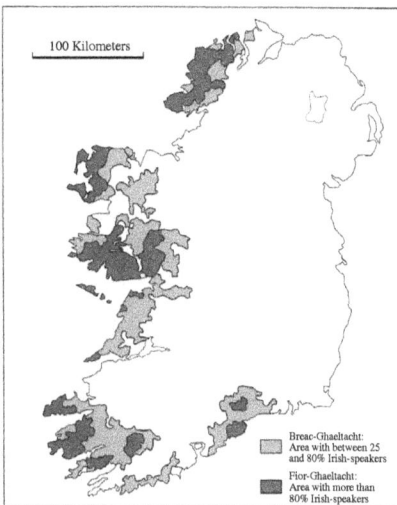

100 Kilometers

Breac-Ghaeltacht:
Area with between 25
and 80% Irish-speakers

Fíor-Ghaeltacht:
Area with more than
80% Irish-speakers

Irish-speaking and partly Irish-speaking areas c. 1926.

Index of Names

Only persons mentioned in body of text (pp. 19–492) are listed below. In the case of Séamus Ó Duilearga, whose name occurs throughout this work, the man and his activities can be traced by making use of the detailed Contents of this work. Irish-language place names mentioned in the text are appended below along with their equivalent English-language form. A subject index can be had by contacting the author.

Irish-language placenames:

Studia Fennica Ethnologica

Making and Breaking of Borders
Ethnological Interpretations, Presentations, Representations
Edited by Teppo Korhonen, Helena Ruotsala & Eeva Uusitalo
Studia Fennica Ethnologica 7
2003

Memories of My Town
The Identities of Town Dwellers and Their Places in Three Finnish Towns
Edited by Anna-Maria Åström, Pirjo Korkiakangas & Pia Olsson
Studia Fennica Ethnologica 8
2004

Passages Westward
Edited by Maria Lähteenmäki & Hanna Snellman
Studia Fennica Ethnologica 9
2006

Studia Fennica Folkloristica

Creating Diversities
Folklore, Religion and the Politics of Heritage
Edited by Anna-Leena Siikala, Barbro Klein & Stein R. Mathisen
Studia Fennica Folkloristica 14
2004

Pertti J. Anttonen
Tradition through Modernity
Postmodernism and the Nation-State in Folklore Scholarship
Studia Fennica Folkloristica 15
2005

Narrating, Doing, Experiencing
Nordic Folkloristic Perspectives
Edited by Annikki Kaivola-Bregenhøj, Barbro Klein & Ulf Palmenfelt
Studia Fennica Folkloristica 16
2006

Studia Fennica Historica

Medieval History Writing and Crusading Ideology
Edited by Tuomas M. S. Lehtonen & Kurt Villads Jensen with Janne Malkki and
Katja Ritari
Studia Fennica Historica 9
2005

Moving in the USSR
Western anomalies and Northern wilderness
Edited by Pekka Hakamies
Studia Fennica Historica 10
2005

Derek Fewster
Visions of Past Glory
Nationalism and the Construction of Early Finnish History
Studia Fennica Historica 11
2006

Modernisation in Russia since 1900
Edited by Markku Kangaspuro & Jeremy Smith
Studia Fennica Historica 12
2006

Seija-Riitta Laakso
Across the Oceans
Development of Overseas Business Information Transmission 1815–1875
Studia Gennica Historica 13
2007

Industry and Modernism
Companies, Architecture and Identity in the Nordic and Baltic Countries during
the High-Industrial Period
Edited by Anja Kervanto Nevanlinna
Studia Fennica Historica 14
2007

Studia Fennica Linguistica

Minna Saarelma-Maunumaa
Edhina Ekogidho – Names as Links
The Encounter between African and European Anthroponymic Systems among the
Ambo People in Namibia
Studia Fennica Linguistica 11
2003

Minimal reference
The use of pronouns in Finnish and Estonian discourse
Edited by Ritva Laury
Studia Fennica Linguistica 12
2005

Antti Leino
On Toponymic Constructions
as an Alternative to Naming Patterns in Describing Finnish Lake Names
Studia Fennica Linguistica 13
2007

Studia Fennica Litteraria

Changing Scenes
Encounters between European and Finnish Fin de Siècle
Edited by Pirjo Lyytikäinen
Studia Fennica Litteraria 1
2003

Women's Voices
Female Authors and Feminist Criticism in the Finnish Literary Tradition
Edited by Lea Rojola & Päivi Lappalainen
Studia Fennica Litteraria 2
2007

Studia Fennica Anthropologica

On Foreign Ground
Moving between Countries and Categories
Edited by Minna Ruckenstein & Marie-Louise Karttunen
Studia Fennica Anthropologica 1
2007

www.ingramcontent.com/pod-product-compliance
Lightning Source LLC
Chambersburg PA
CBHW051427290326
41932CB00049B/3261